Short Stories
for Students

National Advisory Board

Dale Allender: Teacher, West High School, Iowa City, Iowa.

Dana Gioia: Poet and critic. His books include *The Gods of Winter* and *Can Poetry Matter?* He currently resides in Santa Rosa, CA.

Carol Jago: Teacher, Santa Monica High School, Santa Monica, CA. Member of the California Reading and Literature Project at University of California, Los Angeles.

Bonnie J. Newcomer: English Teacher, Beloit Junior-Senior High School, Beloit, Kansas. Editor of KATE UpDate, for the Kansas Association of Teachers of English. Ph.D. candidate in information science, Emporia State University, Kansas.

Katherine Nyberg: English teacher. Director of the language arts program of Farmington Public Schools, Farmington, Michigan.

Nancy Rosenberger: Former English teacher and chair of English department at Conestoga High School, Berwyn, Pennsylvania.

Dorothea M. Susag: English teacher, Simms High School, Simms, Montana. Former president of the Montana Association of Teachers of English Language Arts. Member of the National Council of Teachers of English.

Short Stories for Students

Presenting Analysis, Context, and Criticism on
Commonly Studied Short Stories

Volume 7

Ira Mark Milne, Editor

GALE GROUP

Detroit
San Francisco
London
Boston
Woodbridge, CT

Short Stories for Students

Staff

Editorial: Ira Mark Milne, *Editor.* Tim Akers, Dave Galens, Jeffrey W. Hunter, Maria Job, Angela Yvonne Jones, Daniel Jones, Deborah A. Stanley, Polly Vedder, Timothy J. White, Kathleen Wilson, *Contributing Editors.* James P. Draper, *Managing Editor.*

Research: Victoria B. Cariappa, *Research Team Manager.* Cheryl Warnock, *Research Specialist.* Patricia T. Ballard, Corrine A. Boland, Wendy Festerling, Tamara Nott, Tracie A. Richardson, *Research Associates.* Timothy Lehnerer, Patricia Love, *Research Assistants.*

Permissions: Maria Franklin, *Permissions Manager.* Kimberly Smilay, *Permissions Specialist.* Kelly Quin, *Permissions Associate.* Sandra K. Gore, *Permissions Assistant.*

Production: Mary Beth Trimper, *Production Director.* Evi Seoud, *Assistant Production Manager.* Cindy Range, *Production Assistant.*

Graphic Services: Randy Bassett, *Imaging Database Supervisor.* Robert Duncan, Michael Logusz, *Imaging Specialists.* Gary Leach, *Graphic Artist.* Pamela A. Reed, *Imaging Coordinator.*

Copyright Notice

Table of Contents

Why Study Literature At All?

Short Stories for Students is designed to provide readers with information and discussion about a wide range of important contemporary and historical works of short fiction, and it does that job very well. However, I want to use this guest foreword to address a question that it does *not* take up. It is a fundamental question that is often ignored in high school and college English classes as well as research texts, and one that causes frustration among students at all levels, namely—why study literature at all? Isn't it enough to read a story, enjoy it, and go about one's business? My answer (to be expected from a literary professional, I suppose) is no. It is not enough. It is a start; but it is not enough. Here's why.

First, literature is the only part of the educational curriculum that deals directly with the actual world of lived experience. The philosopher Edmund Husserl used the apt German term *die Lebenswelt*, "the living world," to denote this realm. All the other content areas of the modern American educational system avoid the subjective, present reality of everyday life. Science (both the natural and the social varieties) objectifies, the fine arts create and/or perform, history reconstructs. Only literary study persists in posing those questions we all asked before our schooling taught us to give up on them. Only literature gives credibility to personal perceptions, feelings, dreams, and the "stream of consciousness" that is our inner voice. Literature wonders about infinity, wonders why God permits evil, wonders what will happen to us after we die. Literature admits that we get our hearts broken, that people sometimes cheat and get away with it, that the world is a strange and probably incomprehensible place. Literature, in other words, takes on all the big and small issues of what it means to be human. So my first answer is that of the humanist—we should read literature and study it and take it seriously because it enriches us as human beings. We develop our moral imagination, our capacity to sympathize with other people, and our ability to understand our existence through the experience of fiction.

My second answer is more practical. By studying literature we can learn how to explore and analyze texts. Fiction may be about *die Lebenswelt*, but it is a construct of words put together in a certain order by an artist using the medium of language. By examining and studying those constructions, we can learn about language as a medium. We can become more sophisticated about word associations and connotations, about the manipulation of symbols, and about style and atmosphere. We can grasp how ambiguous language is and how important context and texture is to meaning. In our first encounter with a work of literature, of course, we are not supposed to catch all of these things. We are spellbound, just as the writer wanted us to be. It is as serious students of the writer's art that we begin to see how the tricks are done.

Seeing the tricks, which is another way of saying "developing analytical and close reading skills," is important above and beyond its intrinsic literary educational value. These skills transfer to other fields and enhance critical thinking of any kind. Understanding how language is used to construct texts is powerful knowledge. It makes engineers better problem solvers, lawyers better advocates and courtroom practitioners, politicians better rhetoricians, marketing and advertising agents better sellers, and citizens more aware consumers as well as better participants in democracy. This last point is especially important, because rhetorical skill works both ways—when we learn how language is manipulated in the making of texts the result is that we become less susceptible when language is used to manipulate us.

My third reason is related to the second. When we begin to see literature as created artifacts of language, we become more sensitive to good writing in general. We get a stronger sense of the importance of individual words, even the sounds of words and word combinations. We begin to understand Mark Twain's delicious proverb—"The difference between the right word and the almost right word is the difference between lightning and a lightning bug." Getting beyond the "enjoyment only" stage of literature gets us closer to becoming makers of word art ourselves. I am not saying that studying fiction will turn every student into a Faulkner or a Shakespeare. But it will make us more adaptable and effective writers, even if our art form ends up being the office memo or the corporate annual report.

Studying short stories, then, can help students become better readers, better writers, and even better human beings. But I want to close with a warning. If your study and exploration of the craft, history, context, symbolism, or anything else about a story starts to rob it of the magic you felt when you first read it, it is time to stop. Take a break, study another subject, shoot some hoops, or go for a run. Love of reading is too important to be ruined by school. The early twentieth century writer Willa Cather, in her novel *My Antonia*, has her narrator Jack Burden tell a story that he and Antonia heard from two old Russian immigrants when they were teenagers. These immigrants, Pavel and Peter, told about an incident from their youth back in Russia that the narrator could recall in vivid detail thirty years later. It was a harrowing story of a wedding party starting home in sleds and being chased by starving wolves. Hundreds of wolves attacked the group's sleds one by one as they sped across the snow trying to reach their village. In a horrible revelation, the old Russians revealed that the groom eventually threw his own bride to the wolves to save himself. There was even a hint that one of the old immigrants might have been the groom mentioned in the story. Cather has her narrator conclude with his feelings about the story. "We did not tell Pavel's secret to anyone, but guarded it jealously—as if the wolves of the Ukraine had gathered that night long ago, and the wedding party had been sacrificed, just to give us a painful and peculiar pleasure." That feeling, that painful and peculiar pleasure, is the most important thing about literature. Study and research should enhance that feeling and never be allowed to overwhelm it.

Thomas E. Barden
Professor of English and
Director of Graduate English Studies
The University of Toledo

Introduction

Purpose of the Book

The purpose of *Short Stories for Students* (*SSfS*) is to provide readers with a guide to understanding, enjoying, and studying short stories by giving them easy access to information about the work. Part of Gale's "For Students" Literature line, *SSfS* is specifically designed to meet the curricular needs of high school and undergraduate college students and their teachers, as well as the interests of general readers and researchers considering specific short fiction. While each volume contains entries on classic stories frequently studied in classrooms, there are also entries containing hard-to-find information on contemporary stories, including works by multicultural, international, and women writers.

The information covered in each entry includes an introduction to the story and the story's author; a plot summary, to help readers unravel and understand the events in the work; descriptions of important characters, including explanation of a given character's role in the narrative as well as discussion about that character's relationship to other characters in the story; analysis of important themes in the story; and an explanation of important literary techniques and movements as they are demonstrated in the work.

In addition to this material, which helps the readers analyze the story itself, students are also provided with important information on the literary and historical background informing each work.

This includes a historical context essay, a box comparing the time or place the story was written to modern Western culture, a critical overview essay, and excerpts from critical essays on the story or author. A unique feature of *SSfS* is a specially commissioned overview essay on each story by an academic expert, targeted toward the student reader.

To further aid the student in studying and enjoying each story, information on media adaptations is provided, as well as reading suggestions for works of fiction and nonfiction on similar themes and topics. Classroom aids include ideas for research papers and lists of critical sources that provide additional material on the work.

Selection Criteria

The titles for each volume of *SSfS* were selected by surveying numerous sources on teaching literature and analyzing course curricula for various school districts. Some of the sources surveyed include: literature anthologies, *Reading Lists for College-Bound Students: The Books Most Recommended by America's Top Colleges; Teaching the Short Story: A Guide to Using Stories from Around the World,* by the National Council of Teachers of English (NTCE); and "A Study of High School Literature Anthologies," conducted by Arthur Applebee at the Center for the Learning and Teaching of Literature and sponsored by the National Endowment for the Arts and the Office of Educational Research and Improvement.

Input was also solicited from our expert advisory board, as well as educators from various areas. From these discussions, it was determined that each volume should have a mix of ''classic'' stories (those works commonly taught in literature classes) and contemporary stories for which information is often hard to find. Because of the interest in expanding the canon of literature, an emphasis was also placed on including works by international, multicultural, and women authors. Our advisory board members—current high-school teachers— helped pare down the list for each volume. Works not selected for the present volume were noted as possibilities for future volumes. As always, the editor welcomes suggestions for titles to be included in future volumes.

How Each Entry Is Organized

Each entry, or chapter, in *SSfS* focuses on one story. Each entry heading lists the title of the story, the author's name, and the date of the story's publication. The following elements are contained in each entry:

- **Introduction:** a brief overview of the story which provides information about its first appearance, its literary standing, any controversies surrounding the work, and major conflicts or themes within the work.

- **Author Biography:** this section includes basic facts about the author's life, and focuses on events and times in the author's life that may have inspired the story in question.

- **Plot Summary:** a description of the events in the story, with interpretation of how these events help articulate the story's themes.

- **Characters:** an alphabetical listing of the characters who appear in the story. Each character name is followed by a brief to an extensive description of the character's role in the story, as well as discussion of the character's actions, relationships, and possible motivation.

  Characters are listed alphabetically by last name. If a character is unnamed—for instance, the narrator in ''The Eatonville Anthology''—the character is listed as ''The Narrator'' and alphabetized as ''Narrator.'' If a character's first name is the only one given, the name will appear alphabetically by that name.

- **Themes:** a thorough overview of how the topics, themes, and issues are addressed within the story. Each theme discussed appears in a separate subhead, and is easily accessed through the boldface entries in the Subject/Theme Index.

- **Style:** this section addresses important style elements of the story, such as setting, point of view, and narration; important literary devices used, such as imagery, foreshadowing, symbolism; and, if applicable, genres to which the work might have belonged, such as Gothicism or Romanticism. Literary terms are explained within the entry, but can also be found in the Glossary of Literary Terms.

- **Historical and Cultural Context:** This section outlines the social, political, and cultural climate *in which the author lived and the work was created.* This section may include descriptions of related historical events, pertinent aspects of daily life in the culture, and the artistic and literary sensibilities of the time in which the work was written. If the story is historical in nature, information regarding the time in which the story is set is also included. Long sections are broken down with helpful subheads.

- **Critical Overview:** this section provides background on the critical reputation of the author and the story, including bannings or any other public controversies surrounding the work. For older works, this section may include a history of how story was first received and how perceptions of it may have changed over the years; for more recent works, direct quotes from early reviews may also be included.

- **Sources:** an alphabetical list of critical material quoted in the entry, with bibliographical information.

- **For Further Study:** an alphabetical list of other critical sources which may prove useful for the student. Includes full bibliographical information and a brief annotation.

- **Criticism:** an essay commissioned by *SSfS* which specifically deals with the story and is written specifically for the student audience, as well as excerpts from previously published criticism on the work.

In addition, each entry contains the following highlighted sections, if applicable, set separate from the main text:

- **Media Adaptations:** where applicable, a list of film and television adaptations of the story, including source information. The list also includes stage adaptations, audio recordings, musical adaptations, etc.

- **Compare and Contrast Box:** an "at-a-glance" comparison of the cultural and historical differences between the author's time and culture and late twentieth-century Western culture. This box includes pertinent parallels between the major scientific, political, and cultural movements of the time or place the story was written, the time or place the story was set (if a historical work), and modern Western culture. Works written after the mid-1970s may not have this box.

- **What Do I Read Next?:** a list of works that might complement the featured story or serve as a contrast to it. This includes works by the same author and others, works of fiction and nonfiction, and works from various genres, cultures, and eras.

- **Study Questions:** a list of potential study questions or research topics dealing with the story. This section includes questions related to other disciplines the student may be studying, such as American history, world history, science, math, government, business, geography, economics, psychology, etc.

Other Features

SSfS includes "Why Study Literature At All?," a guest foreword by Thomas E. Barden, Professor of English and Director of Graduate English Studies at the University of Toledo. This essay provides a number of very fundamental reasons for studying literature and, therefore, reasons why a book such as *SSfS,* designed to facilitate the study of literature, is useful.

A Cumulative Author/Title Index lists the authors and titles covered in each volume of the *SSfS* series.

A Cumulative Nationality/Ethnicity Index breaks down the authors and titles covered in each volume of the *SSfS* series by nationality and ethnicity.

A Subject/Theme Index, specific to each volume, provides easy reference for users who may be studying a particular subject or theme rather than a single work. Significant subjects from events to broad themes are included, and the entries pointing to the specific theme discussions in each entry are indicated in **boldface.**

Entries may include illustrations, including an author portrait, stills from film adaptations (when available), maps, and/or photos of key historical events.

Citing Short Stories for Students

When writing papers, students who quote directly from any volume of *SSfS* may use the following general forms to document their source. These examples are based on MLA style; teachers may request that students adhere to a different style, thus, the following examples may be adapted as needed.

When citing text from *SSfS* that is not attributed to a particular author (for example, the Themes, Style, Historical Context sections, etc.) the following format may be used:

> "The Celebrated Jumping Frog of Calaveras County." *Short Stories for Students.* Ed. Kathleen Wilson. Vol. 1. Detroit: Gale, 1997. 19-20.

When quoting the specially commissioned essay from *SSfS* (usually the first essay under the Criticism subhead), the following format may be used:

> Korb, Rena. Essay on "Children of the Sea." *Short Stories for Students.* Ed. Kathleen Wilson. Vol. 1. Detroit: Gale, 1997. 42.

When quoting a journal essay that is reprinted in a volume of *Short Stories for Students,* the following form may be used:

> Schmidt, Paul. "The Deadpan on Simon Wheeler." *The Southwest Review* XLI, No. 3 (Summer, 1956), 270-77; excerpted and reprinted in *Short Stories for Students,* Vol. 1, ed. Kathleen Wilson (Detroit: Gale, 1997), pp. 29-31.

When quoting material from a book that is reprinted in a volume of *SSfS,* the following form may be used:

> Bell-Villada, Gene H. "The Master of Short Forms," in *Garcia Marquez: The Man and His Work* (University of North Carolina Press, 1990); excerpted and reprinted in *Short Stories for Students,* Vol. 1, ed. Kathleen Wilson (Detroit: Gale, 1997), pp. 90-1.

We Welcome Your Suggestions

The editor of *Short Stories for Students* welcomes your comments and ideas. Readers who wish to suggest short stories to appear in future volumes, or who have other suggestions, are cordially invited to contact the editor. You may write to the editor at:

Editor, *Short Stories for Students*
The Gale Group
27500 Drake Rd.
Farmington Hills, MI 48331-3535

Literary Chronology

1821: Gustave Flaubert is born in France on December 12.

1843: Henry James is born in New York, New York, on April 15.

1861: The U.S. Civil War begins when Confederate forces capture Fort Sumter in South Carolina.

1862: Edith Wharton is born in New York, New York, on January 24.

1865: The U.S. Civil War ends; Abraham Lincoln is assassinated.

1877: ''A Simple Heart'' by Gustave Flaubert is published in his *Three Tales.*

1880: Gustave Flaubert dies on May 5.

1882: James Joyce is born in Dublin, Ireland, on February 2.

1885: Isak Dinesen is born in Rungsted, Denmark, on April 17.

1885: D. H. Lawrence is born in Eastwood, Nottinghamshire, England, on September 11.

1891: Zora Neale Hurston is born in Eatonville, Florida, on January 7.

1897: William Faulkner is born in New Albany, Mississippi on September 25.

1899: Vladimir Nabokov is born in St. Petersburg, Russia, on April 23.

1899: Ernest Hemingway is born in Oak Park, Illinois, on July 21.

1902: John Steinbeck is born in Salinas, California, on February 27.

1903: ''The Beast in the Jungle'' by Henry James is published in his short story collection, *The Better Sort.*

1911: ''The Odour of Chrysanthemums'' by D. H. Lawrence is published in the *English Review.*

1912: The *U.S.S. Titanic* sinks on her maiden voyage.

1914: With the assassination of Archduke Ferdinand of Austria, long-festering tensions in Europe erupt into what becomes known as the Great War.

1914: ''The Dead'' by James Joyce is published in his short story collection *Dubliners.*

1916: Henry James dies in London, England, on February 28.

1916: ''The Easter Rising,'' in which Irish nationalists take control of the Dublin post office and declare a provisional government apart from British rule, takes place on April 24.

1917: Russian Revolution takes place. Czar Nicholas II abdicates the throne and a provisional government is established.

1918: World War I, the most deadly war in history, ends with the signing of the Treaty of Versailles.

1920: The 18th Amendment, outlawing the sale, manufacture, and transportation of alcohol-- known as Prohibition--goes into effect. This law led to the creation of ''speakeasies''--illegal bars--and an increase in organized crime. The law is repealed in 1933.

1920: The efforts of the Women's Suffrage movement, directed by women such as Susan B. Anthony and Elizabeth Cady Stanton, finally succeeds. The 19th Amendment, which granted the right to vote to women, is adopted.

1921: Edith Wharton wins the Pulitzer Prize for fiction for her novel *The Age of Innocence.*

1925: ''Spunk'' by Zora Neale Hurston is published in *Opportunity: A Journal of Negro Life.*

1925: ''A Guide to Berlin'' by Vladimir Nabokov is published.

1927: ''Hills Like White Elephants'' by Ernest Hemingway is published in the magazine *transition.*

1928: Gabriel Garcia Marquez is born in Aracataca, Columbia, on March 6.

1929: The stock market crash in October signals the beginning of a worldwide economic depression.

1929: *The Sound and the Fury* by William Faulkner is published.

1930: D. H. Lawrence dies of tuberculosis in Vence, France, on March 2.

1930: John Barth is born in Cambridge, Maryland, on May 27.

1930: ''A Rose for Emily'' by William Faulkner is published in *Forum.*

1931: ''Pomegranate Seed'' by Edith Wharton is published in *Ladies' Home Journal.*

1937: ''The Chrysanthemums'' by John Steinbeck is published in *Harper's* magazine.

1937: Edith Wharton dies in St. Brice-sous-Foret, France, on August 11.

1938: Raymond Carver is born in Clatskanie, Oregon, on May 25.

1939: World War II begins when Nazi Germany, led by Adolf Hitler, invades Poland; England and France declare war in response.

1940: John Steinbeck is awarded the Pulitzer Prize for Fiction for *The Grapes of Wrath.*

1941: James Joyce dies in Zurich, Switzerland, on January 13.

1941: John Edgar Wideman is born in Washington, D.C., on June 14.

1945: World War II ends in August with the atomic bombing of Hiroshima and Nagasaki, Japan.

1947: Octavia Butler is born in Pasadena, California, on June 22.

1949: William Faulkner wins Nobel Prize for literature.

1950: Senator Joseph McCarthy of Wisconsin sets off the ''Red Scare'' that leads to government hearings and blacklisting of suspected communists.

1952: Rohinton Mistry is born in Bombay, India.

1953: Ernest Hemingway is awarded the Nobel Prize for Literature.

1954: United States Supreme Court, in *Brown vs. Board of Education of Topeka,* rules unanimously that public school segregation is unconstitutional under the 14th amendment.

1958: ''The Ring'' by Isak Dinesen is published her short story collection *Anecdotes of Destiny.*

1960: Zora Neale Hurston dies in Fort Pierce, Florida, on January 28.

1961: Ernest Hemingway commits suicide in Ketchum, Idaho, on July 2.

1962: John Steinbeck is awarded the Nobel Prize for Literature.

1962: William Faulkner dies in Byhalia, Mississippi, on July 6.

1962: Isak Dinesen dies in Rungsted, Denmark, on September 7.

1963: President John F. Kennedy is assassinated in Dallas, Texas, on November 22.

1967: ''Lost in the Funhouse'' by John Barth is published in the *Atlantic Monthly.*

1968: ''A Very Old Man with Enormous Wings'' by Gabriel Garcia Marquez is published.

1968: John Steinbeck dies of heart disease in New York, New York, on December 20.

1972: President Richard Nixon resigns following the Watergate scandal.

1973: John Barth is awarded the National Book Award for his novel *Chimera.*

1975: Saigon, the South Vietnamese capital, falls to the North Vietnamese army, bringing an end to the Vietnam War.

1977: Vladimir Nabokov dies in Monteux, Switzerland, on July 2.

1981: ''Cathedral'' by Raymond Carver is published in *Atlantic Monthly.*

1982: Gabriel Garcia Marquez wins the Nobel Prize for Literature.

1984: John Edgar Wideman wins the PEN/Faulkner award for fiction for *Sent for You Yesterday.*

1984: ''Bloodchild'' by Octavia Butler is published in *Isaac Asimov's Science Fiction Magazine.*

1985: Octavia Butler is awarded both the Hugo and Nebula Awards for best novellette for ''Bloodchild.''

1987: ''Swimming Lessons'' by Rohinton Mistry is published in his short story collection *Tales from Firozsha Baag.*

1988: Raymond Carver dies of lung cancer in Port Angeles, Washington, on August 2.

1989: The Berlin Wall, a symbol of the 28 years of division between East and West Germany, is torn down.

1989: ''Fever'' by John Edgar Wideman is published in his short story collection *Fever.*

1990: Soviet leader Mikhail Gorbachev's policy of *glasnost* results in the fracturing of the Iron Curtain. By December the Soviet flag is lowered from the Kremlin.

Acknowledgments

The editors wish to thank the copyright holders of the excerpted criticism included in this volume and the permissions managers of many book and magazine publishing companies for assisting us in securing reproduction rights. We are also grateful to the staffs of the Detroit Public Library, the Library of Congress, the University of Detroit Mercy Library, Wayne State University Purdy/Kresge Library Complex, and the University of Michigan Libraries for making their resources available to us. Following is a list of the copyright holders who have granted us permission to reproduce material in this volume of *SSFS*. Every effort has been made to trace copyright, but if omissions have been made, please let us know.

COPYRIGHTED EXCERPTS IN *SSFS*, VOLUME 7, WERE REPRODUCED FROM THE FOLLOWING PERIODICALS:

American Imago, v. 27, Summer, 1970. Copyright 1970 by The Association for Applied Psychoanalysis, Inc. Reproduced by permission of The Johns Hopkins University Press.—*American Literature,* v. XXXIV, May, 1962. Copyright © 1962, renewed 1990 Duke University Press, Durham, NC. Reproduced with permission.—*Ariel: A Review of International English Literature,* v. 28, July, 1997 for ''Spaces of Translation: Bharati Mukherjee's 'The Management of Grief''' by Deborah Bowen. Copyright © 1997 The Board of Governors, The University of Calgary. Reproduced by permission of the publisher and the author.—*The CEA Critic,* v. 56, Winter, 1994. Copyright © 1994 by the College English Association, Inc. Reproduced by permission.—*English Language Notes,* v. XXVIII, September 1990. Reproduced by permission.—*Interpretations: A Journal of Idea, Analysis, and Criticism,* v. 15, Fall, 1983. Reproduced by permission.—*Journal of Modern Literature,* v. 13, March, 1986. © Temple University, 1986. Reproduced by permission.—*The Langston Hughes Review,* v. XII, 1993. Copyright, 1993 by The Langston Hughes Society. Reproduced by permission.—*The Markham Review,* v. 8, Spring, 1979. © Wagner College 1979. Reproduced by permission.—*Mark Twain Journal,* v. XVI, Summer, 1972. Reproduced by permission.—*Modern Fiction Studies,* v. 34, Spring, 1988. Copyright © 1988 Helen Dwight Reid Educational Foundation. Reproduced with permission of the Helen Dwight Reid Educational Foundation, published by Heldref Publications, 1319 18th Street NW, Washington, DC 20036-1802.—*Nineteenth-Century Fiction,* v. 24, September, 1969 for ''The Minister's Black Veil'' by W. B. Carnochan. Copyright © 1969 by The Regents of the University of California. Reproduced by permission of the publisher and the author.—*Papers on Language & Literature,* v. 23, Winter, 1987. Copyright © 1987 by The Board of Trustees, Southern Illinois University at Edwardsville. Reproduced by permission.—*Studies in American Fiction,* v. 16, Autumn, 1988. Copyright © 1988 Northeastern University. Repro-

COPYRIGHTED EXCERPTS IN *SSFS,* VOLUME 7, WERE REPRODUCED FROM THE FOLLOWING BOOKS:

PHOTOGRAPHS AND ILLUSTRATIONS APPEARING IN *SSFS,* VOLUME 7, WERE RECEIVED FROM THE FOLLOWING SOURCES:

King Oliver's Creole Jazz Band, Chicago, 1923, photograph. Archive Photos/Frank Driggs Collection. Reproduced by permission.—Kincaid, Jamaica, photograph by Jerry Bauer. © Jerry Bauer. Reproduced by permission.—London, Jack, photograph. The Library of Congress.—Mukherjee, Bharati, photograph. AP/Wide World Photos. Reproduced by permission.—O'Connor, Flannery, photograph. AP/Wide World Photos. Reproduced by permission.—Old church, c. 1900, photograph. Archive Photos, Inc. Reproduced by permission.—Poe, Virginia, wife of Edgar Allen Poe, only known portrait, Enoch Pratt Free Library, photograph. AP/Wide World Photos. Reproduced by permission.—Robot submersible SCARAB retrieved Air India flight 182's cockpit voice recorder from 6,700 feet of water under the Atlantic, Cork, Ireland, July 10, 1985, photograph. AP/Wide World Photos. Reproduced by permission.—The Apollo Theater on 125th Street in the Harlem section of New York City, March, 1971, photograph. AP/Wide World Photos. Reproduced by permission.—"The Overcoat," movie still. The Kobal Collection. Reproduced by permission.—Twain, Mark, photograph. The Library of Congress.—Two customers entering "Tops" Diner, 1952, photograph. AP/Wide World Photos, Inc. Reproduced by permission.—Two young boys sitting on a wooden fence, boy on the right is holding a rifle while the other boy points, photograph. Lambert/Archive Photos, Inc. Reproduced by permission.—View of aging wine in underground cellar, Archive Photos, Inc. Reproduced by permission.—View of Antigua, photograph by Max Hunn. Archive Photos, Inc. Reproduced by permission.—Wharton, Edith, 1905, photograph. The Library of Congress.—Wilde, Oscar, photograph. The Library of Congress.—Yukon Trail, photograph. UPI/Corbis-Bettmann. Reproduced by permission.

Contributors

BILY, Cynthia. Instructor of English at Adrian College in Michigan. Contributor to reference publications including *Feminist Writers, Gay and Lesbian Biography,* and *Chronology of Women Worldwide.* Entries: "The Cask of Amontillado," "Girl," and "The Stone Boy."

BRENT, Liz. Ph.D. in American Culture, specializing in cinema studies, from the University of Michigan. Teacher of courses in American cinema, freelance writer and editor. Entries: "The Blues I'm Playing," "Girl," "A Hunger Artist," and "The Stone Boy."

BURNS, Bonnie. A writing specialist at Emmanuel College with special studies in film studies, nineteenth-century British literature, and gay and lesbian studies. Entry: "Neighbour Rosicky."

CHANG, Yoonmee. Ph.D. candidate in the English Department at the University of Pennsylvania. Entries: "The Man That Corrupted Hadleyburg" and "The Management of Grief."

DEIGNAN, Tom. Teaching Assistant in American Cultural Studies at Bowling Green State University. Entry: "The Life You Save May Be Your Own."

EGGLESTON, Robert. Ph.D. and instructor of English at Okanagan University College, in Kelowna, British Columbia. Entry: "The Daffodil Sky."

GIRARD, Theresa M. Ph.D. candidate at Wayne State University, instructor of introduction-to-fiction classes. Entry: "The Daffodil Sky."

GRAUER, Lalage. Professor of Canadian Literature at Okanagan University College, in Kelowna, British Columbia. Entry: "Raymond's Run."

HENNINGFELD, Diane Andrews. Associate professor of English at Adrian College in Michigan and contributor to reference works for Salem Press. Entry: "The Management of Grief."

KORB, Rena. Freelance writer and editor with a master's degree in English literature and creative writing. Entries: "Roman Fever" and "The Stone Boy."

LE BLANC, Ondine. Has been instructor at the University of Michigan, editor, and free-lance writer. Entry: "The Blues I'm Playing."

LUTZ, Kimberly. Instructor of writing at the New York University School of Continuing Education. Entry: "The Canterville Ghost."

MACRORIE, Robin. Has been instructor of literature and composition at the University of Notre Dame. Entry: "Waldo."

MADSEN HARDY, Sarah. Ph.D. in English literature at the University of Michigan, freelance writer and editor. Entry: "The Stone Boy."

MONTBRIAND, Timothy. Instructor of writing and literature at Oakland University and St. Mary's College in Michigan. Entry: "The Minister's Black Veil."

SONKOWSKY, Michael. Has been instructor of English at the University of Pennsylvania. Entry: "The Overcoat."

WIDDICOMBE, Jill. Freelance editor of college textbooks, resident of Alaska. Entry: "To Build a Fire."

The Blues I'm Playing

Langston Hughes

1934

In many ways, ''The Blues I'm Playing'' exemplifies the qualities that dominate the prose and poetry of Langston Hughes. The author is a major figure on the landscape of American poetry and may be the best-known on the landscape of African-American poetry. First published in *Scribner's Magazine* in May, 1934, and in the collection *The Ways of White Folks* that same year, ''The Blues I'm Playing'' combines Hughes's irony, his directness, and his use of dialect. It also conveys powerful messages about race relations, the beauty of blues and jazz, and the black artist's experiences in the white-dominated world of modern art. The story of a young black pianist, Oceola Jones, and her conflict with her self-appointed white patron, Dora Ellsworth, ''The Blues I'm Playing'' embodies Hughes's belief in the fortitude and dignity of black Americans.

Author Biography

James Langston Hughes was born on February 1, 1902, in Joplin, Missouri. Hughes was the only child of James Nathaniel Hughes and Carrie Mercer Hughes nee Langston. The elder Hughes left soon after his son's birth, eventually settling in Mexico, where he prospered in a variety of business ventures. Young James and his mother, however, struggled to make ends meet. He spent many years living with various relatives and family friends as his

mother traveled in search of work. When his mother was remarried and settled in 1914, he joined her in Cleveland, Ohio. At Central High School, he proved himself as a student and as an athlete, and began writing poetry and short fiction for the school's literary magazine.

After graduating from high school, Hughes taught English in Mexico for a year. He also became a regular contributor to the *Crisis*, a magazine published by the NAACP and one of the cornerstones of the early fight for civil rights. In 1921, Hughes spent a year at Columbia University in New York City. There he studied English literature and explored the city's rich social and intellectual life. He also became a regular at events sponsored by the American Socialist Society. After leaving Columbia University, Hughes supported himself and his mother—who now lived in Harlem—with a variety of menial jobs. In 1923, he signed on as a cabin boy with a freighter bound for West Africa. He travelled across Europe for the next two years, living hand-to-mouth at different times in Holland, France, and Italy. When he returned to the United States in 1925, he and his mother and a half-brother settled in Washington, D.C.

During this time of education and travel, Hughes had continued to send poetry regularly to the *Crisis* and other journals. He was already experimenting with sound and rhythm, looking for a way to incorporate jazz and other aspects of black culture into the genre. In 1925, his efforts were recognized with prizes from both the *Crisis* and *Opportunity* magazines. At the end of that year Hughes had his first taste of real celebrity when the poet Vachel Lindsay read some of Hughes's poems to his own audience. The morning after the reading, when Hughes came to the hotel where he worked, he was greeted by a number of photographers and reporters curious about the "Negro busboy poet." Hughes's first book, *The Weary Blues,* followed in 1926, aided by the first of his white patrons, critic Carl Van Vechten. The collection showcased both his experiments with style and his determination to focus on African-American life and race relations. Although the book met with considerable praise, some critics—including prominent black artists—responded harshly to Hughes's form and content. That response set a pattern for the rest of his career.

Throughout this period, Hughes published frequently in a variety of publications, both black and mainstream. He had also returned to college at Lincoln University in Pennsylvania just before the publication of *The Weary Blues,*. In 1927, Hughes published his second book—*Fine Clothes to the Jew*—and co-founded a literary journal, *Fire*, specifically for African-American writers. In 1929, Hughes earned his Bachelors degree from Lincoln University. At the end of the decade, Hughes began a significant patron-protegee relationship with the wealthy Charlotte (Mrs. Rufus Osgood) Mason, an elderly widow who often sponsored black artists. Mason supported Hughes through the composition of his first novel, *Not Without Laughter,* published in 1930. However, a rift developed between Mason and Hughes soon after. The relationship ultimately provided Hughes with the material for "The Blues I'm Playing."

While traveling in the Soviet Union in 1932, Hughes happened onto the book that would inspire his development as a short fiction writer—*The Lovely Lady,* a collection of short stories by English author D. H. Lawrence. Lawrence's directness, his irony, and his willingness to make fiction carry a social message prompted Hughes to rethink the potential of short fiction. He began composing stories right away, publishing several in magazines. More importantly, he built up the collection that would become *The Ways of White Folks* in 1934. The power of these stories set a standard that Hughes would continue to uphold in many subsequent volumes. One of his most popular pieces, the first of what became known as his "Simple" stories, appeared in the 1940s. This piece was significant not only for its artistic strength but also because the story was printed in the *Chicago-Defender,* a black-owned newspaper with a black audience. Whereas Hughes had written his earlier works primarily for a white audience, from the late 1930s onward he became known as one of the first authors to write for and enjoy a wide popularity among black readers.

As Hughes's career matured, he became more and more explicitly political both as an artist and as an individual. As a correspondent for the *Baltimore Afro-American* in 1937, he lived in Madrid during the Spanish Civil War. During the rise of the Civil Rights struggle, his publications in the 1950s and 1960s addressed the political upheaval and the conditions of black life. Probably one of his most significant works, the verse collection *Montage of a Dream Deferred,* published in 1951, articulated the hardship and disillusionment that called for social and political change. Hughes continued to be active and prolific until his death from congestive heart failure on May 22, 1967. In the year of his death,

Hughes published *The Panther and the Lash: Poems of Our Times.*

Plot Summary

I: *Introduction*

"The Blues I'm Playing" opens in the middle of the story that will follow. Oceola Jones, the young black pianist, is in Paris studying music at the expense of her white Manhattan patron, Dora Ellsworth. An exposition of Mrs. Ellsworth's character and background ensues: her deceased husband's wealth and their childlessness allow her to pursue life as a patron of the arts, supporting young artists. The narrator also informs us that some confusion underlines Mrs. Ellsworth's motivation as a patron: her choices in protegees seem to be as much driven by the beauty of the protegee as by the extent of his or her talent. By implication, then, we know that Oceola possesses beauty as well as talent, since about her "there had been no doubt." The young pianist supports herself before meeting Mrs. Ellsworth by teaching piano, directing a church choir, and playing at house parties in Harlem. She comes to the attention of Mrs. Ellsworth via Ormand Hunter, a white music critic. He persuades the reluctant Oceola to play for Mrs. Ellsworth at her home. Even before Oceola has played, Mrs. Ellsworth begins "treating her as a protegee: that is, she began asking her a great many questions she would not dare ask anyone else at first meeting." When Oceola plays for Mrs. Ellsworth, she includes, among classical selections, a rendition of *St. Louis Blues*. Through these two actions, the inquisitiveness and the musical selection, the author prepares the ground for the conflict that follows.

II: *"The Period of Oceola"*

Mrs. Ellsworth devotes herself to her new protegee, beginning what the narrator calls "the period of Oceola." Oceola, however, keeps a certain emotional distance from the older woman, suspicious of Mrs. Ellsworth's desire to give her things *"for art's sake."* Her mistrust is exacerbated when Mrs. Ellsworth pries for information not just about Oceola's musical background, but about her personal life as well. Most significantly, Mrs. Ellsworth learns that Oceola lives with Pete Williams, a man who works as a train porter but plans to go to medical school. Pete will become central to the conflict between the women. Mrs. Ellsworth finishes the interview by overcoming Oceola's reluc-

Langston Hughes

tance: she will give up her present work to devote herself to developing her talent, all at Mrs. Ellsworth's expense.

True to her word, Mrs. Ellsworth sends Oceola a check that same evening. Mrs. Ellsworth also begins occupying herself with the details of the young woman's private life. Concerned about Pete's presence, Mrs. Ellsworth asks Ormand Hunter to ask his maid, who attends church with Oceola, to glean information from the rumor mill. Deciding that she does not know enough about Oceola's environment, Mrs. Ellsworth orders a book by Carl Van Vechten, *Nigger Heaven*, generally considered the white curiosity seeker's tour of Harlem. Finally, after she has gone to bed, Mrs. Ellsworth's entertains herself by imagining Oceola in different dresses, with Hughes revealing the first hint of a repressed sexual fascination.

III: *The Conflict Begins*

Determined to remove Pete from Oceola's life and to remove Oceola from Harlem, Mrs. Ellsworth sets about a plan to take charge of her protegee. After another meeting at her home, Mrs. Ellsworth offers to drive Oceola to her apartment in order "to see the inside of this girl's life." She invites herself up to Oceola's apartment, which she deems unacceptable, announcing that Oceola must move out of Harlem altogether and relocate to Greenwich Village—the current locus of the arts in New York City. Oceola, however, resists, stalling the move until that fall, when Pete will go away to a medical school for African-American students. Mrs. Ellsworth accepts the compromise and leaves for her summer season in Bar Harbor, Maine, a resort town favored by New England's elite.

IV: Training in Paris

After several years, Oceola's life has changed considerably under Mrs. Ellsworth's sponsorship. She lives in Greenwich Village and devotes her days to practice and study. The only element Oceola retains from her old life is Harlem house parties, at which she now plays for free. Mrs. Ellsworth begins taking Oceola away from the city on weekends to her resort home in upstate New York. On occasion the two women find it necessary, because of limited space, to share a bed, revealing Mrs. Ellsworth's repressed desire: "Then she would read aloud Tennyson or Browning before turning out the light, aware all the time of the electric strength of that brown-black body beside her." In close conjunction to this feeling is Mrs. Ellsworth's persistent worry that Oceola lives too much in the concrete world, especially in her relationship with Pete, now at medical school in Atlanta. Determined that Oceola will learn to "sublimate" all physical desires to her art, Mrs. Ellsworth arranges for her to study in Paris.

There, as in Greenwich Village, Oceola lives in the city's artistic ghetto, the Left Bank, and spends her days studying with a teacher, Philippe. She also explores the world of Paris' African-French population, mostly immigrants from Algeria and the French West Indies. Oceola listens in on their aesthetic and political debates, most of which strike her as too removed from the practicalities of real life. We also learn that Oceola has little faith in the belief that art could heal relations between blacks and whites. Oceola does, however, discover one aspect of Paris that she loves—dance halls:

> In Paris, Oceola especially loved the West Indian ball rooms where the black colonials danced the beguine. And she liked the entertainers at Bricktop's. Sometimes late at night there, Oceola would take the piano and beat out blues for Brick and the assembled guests. In her playing of Negro folk music, Oceola never doctored it up, or filled it full of classical runs, or fancy falsities. In the blues she made the bass notes throb like tom-toms, the trebles cry like little flutes, so deep in the earth and so high in the sky that they

understood everything. And when the night club crowd would get up and dance to her blues, and Bricktop would yell, "Hey! Hey!" Oceola felt as happy as if she were performing a Chopin etude for the nicely gloved Oh's and Ah-ers in a Crillon salon. (Excerpt from "The Blues I'm Playing")

At times, Mrs. Ellsworth visits her protegee in Paris. They attend classical music recitals, at which Mrs. Ellsworth persists in her belief that Oceola experiences music in the same disembodied trance that she does. In her wishful thinking, she fails to recognize Oceola's love for music that is sensual and dynamic. Oceola does, however, enjoy aspects of Mrs. Ellsworth's company, especially when the two travel outside of the city. For example, at Versailles, the palace of eighteenth-century Queen Marie Antoinette, Mrs. Ellsworth reveals her girlhood love for France's culture and "romantic history." We discover that she once had her own musical facility—a talent for singing French songs—that apparently died when her husband failed to appreciate it. Around this, the two women almost approach an emotional connection.

The period of Oceola's formal training closes as her "development at the piano blossomed into perfection." She gives several performances in Europe, all meeting with rave reviews and considerable publicity. She returns to New York in 1930, planning a concert for the coming fall. Her return is also timed so that she can attend Pete's spring graduation. After the visit with Pete, Oceola writes to Mrs. Ellsworth—again in Bar Harbor for the summer—that they have decided to be married at Christmas. The tension that has been building beneath the surface of the relationship between the women emerges in Mrs. Ellsworth's reply: she reprimands Oceola for sacrificing her career to marriage and a family. Oceola insists that she need not choose between the two things that she loves. But a concert at Town Hall in the fall convinces Mrs. Ellsworth otherwise: since the critics don't "go wild," it must be the fault of Pete, a "monster" who has—or so she thinks—destroyed Oceola's genius.

Disappointed at Oceola's determination to marry, and perhaps at her own inability to gain control over Oceola's life, Mrs. Ellsworth distances herself from the young woman. The conflict comes to a head in another meeting in Mrs. Ellsworth's drawing room. When Mrs. Ellsworth criticizes Oceola's choices, Oceola responds with an assertion of personal and cultural pride, insisting that she has been away from the black community for too long and that she needs to immerse herself in it again. The argument finally turns to Pete and his impending visit on Thanksgiving, for which Oceola makes no apology or defense, leaving Mrs. Ellsworth powerless to influence her.

V: Conclusion

Oceola's final performance for Mrs. Ellsworth takes place in the drawing room that has been the setting for many of their encounters. Their conflicts, wholly undiminished, come to the surface as Oceola ends her musical program with a powerful blues variation. Mrs. Ellsworth protests that this music is not worthy of the money she has spent on Oceola; Oceola responds by asserting her freedom, saying "This is mine." Mrs. Ellsworth, in the end, is unchanged, still rejecting Oceola's life-affirming jazz in order to "stand looking at the stars."

Characters

Antonio Bas

Another artist in Mrs. Ellsworth's patronage, Antonio Bas never actually appears in the story; his name appears at the beginning and toward the end. Mrs. Ellsworth mentions him at the conclusion, possibly in an effort to chide Oceola for rejecting the conditions of her money.

Dora Ellsworth

The narrator introduces Mrs. Ellsworth as a wealthy, middle-aged, white widow with no children. These qualities become central to the progress of the story as they influence Mrs. Ellsworth's artistic patronage. Mrs. Ellsworth's motivation for artistic patronage—helping a constant retinue of young artists–is not a pure love of art, but rather is mixed with a desire both for intimacy and for power. As Oceola Jones's patron, Mrs. Ellsworth attempts to shape the young woman's sensibility and, ultimately, her life. Hughes depicts Mrs. Ellsworth as the embodiment of a traditional demand that art be "transcendental." Accordingly, art should be above life, and, for Mrs. Ellsworth, above sensuality. She attempts to live her life in a wholly "sublimated" state. This means that she directs all of her passions toward non-sensual endeavors and admirations, especially toward the arts. However,

traces of a physical passion in her do betray themselves. For example, Mrs. Ellsworth's sexuality reveals itself in the description of those weekends that she and Oceola share a bed in the mountains. Similar feelings are suggested in a glimpse of Mrs. Ellsworth's past, before and during her marriage, when she was actively involved in the romantic aspects of French history and culture. The narrator implies that her husband's failure to appreciate her love for "simple French songs" may have squelched her passion. But now Mrs. Ellsworth is the one who fails to appreciate someone else's passion. As much as Mrs. Ellsworth admires Oceola's talent, she never understands Oceola's love of jazz, and she does not respect Oceola's love for the black community in Harlem. Consequently, Mrs. Ellsworth becomes Oceola's nemesis, her opposite in all values, and the obstacle that Oceola must overcome on her way to her own fulfillment.

Mrs. Ellsworth

See Dora Ellsworth

Mr. Hunter

See Ormand Hunter

Ormand Hunter

Ormand Hunter's character is the critic who first brings Oceola Jones to Mrs. Ellsworth's attention. This character may have been based on Carl Van Vechten, a white critic who made a special project of championing black artists. Hunter's own lack of sensitivity is suggested by his willingness to collude in Mrs. Ellsworth's attempts to pry into Oceola's private life.

Oceola Jones

A talented young pianist who works hard to earn a living, Oceola Jones becomes the protegee of a wealthy white woman, Mrs. Dora Ellsworth. A very practical woman, Oceola mistrusts Mrs. Ellsworth, and she maintains a determined degree of independence from Mrs. Ellsworth throughout their relationship. This independence proves vital to Oceola as it becomes evident that she and Mrs. Ellsworth have different, even hostile, views of art and music. Mrs. Ellsworth demands that Oceola's music be detached, bodiless, and restricted to the classical tradition. Oceola, however, is drawn to music that expresses life and sensuality, and she embraces a repertoire ranging from classical selections to traditional black spirituals and contemporary innovations in blues and jazz. This approach to art reflects Oceola's approach to life in general—she refuses to give up her physical and emotional life, represented by Pete Williams, despite Mrs. Ellsworth's urging. Similarly, even as Oceola appears to be headed for a brilliant musical career and financial security otherwise unavailable to a black woman, she remains dedicated to the black community in Harlem. In the final confrontation between Mrs. Ellsworth and Oceola, Oceola appears to dismiss her growing career—though not her love of music—for the sake of racial pride and a better life. Oceola's experiences with her patron largely derive from Hughes's experiences with his own patron; consequently, the reader can, to some degree, see Oceola as a mouthpiece for the author's own opinions.

Pete Williams

Pete Williams is a train porter who lives with Oceola Jones in Harlem and who later attends a medical school in Atlanta. Pete Williams gradually becomes the focus of all of Mrs. Ellsworth's hostilities. When her plan for Oceola to become properly ''sublimated'' to a bodiless art fails, Mrs. Ellsworth blames that failure on Pete and, by suggestion, on Oceola's love and desire for him. Although Pete appears only briefly in the story, the moment is striking because it also provides the one mention of segregation.

Themes

In ''The Blues I'm Playing'' Langston Hughes depicts the conflict between a young black pianist, Oceola Jones, and her wealthy white patron, Dora Ellsworth. In the course of their relationship, the two women clash in their views on music, beauty, and sexuality.

Race and Racism

''The Blues I'm Playing,'' like all of the stories in *The Ways of White Folks*, reveals to the reader, through form and content, one of the many ways in which racism can operate. While some stories portray the most obvious acts of racism, ''The Blues I'm Playing'' makes explicit a subtle, racist pater-

nalism. Mrs. Ellsworth embodies the way that paternalism can hide racism, both from herself and others, because it is apparently so well-intentioned: Mrs. Ellsworth wants to help Oceola, so how could she be racist? Hughes's narrative illustrates how.

Mrs. Ellsworth's racism begins, in a sense, with her ignorance: she believes that she has never known a black person before. This belief betrays her narrowness of vision, since we can assume that she has certainly interacted with many black people, mostly as servants of some sort or another; at the very least, we know that Ormand Hunter's maid is black. Implicitly, then, her thought suggests that she has never quite seen any African American as a person—as an individual one might get to know.

The paternalism with which Mrs. Ellsworth approaches all of her protegees, although it has something to do with an admiration for raw talent, also assumes a certain inferiority on the part of these young artists, Hughes suggests. She believes that they require not just money, but also refinement and her insight and guidance. In this association between the lack of money and the supposed lack of refinement and insight, Mrs. Ellsworth's patronage tends to be classicist. This classicism enters into her relationship with Oceola, but it is secondary to the function of racism. The financial and social limitations on Oceola's life, because they are embodied in her Harlem apartment, become in Mrs. Ellsworth's mind a function of black life. Mrs. Ellsworth is determined to remove Oceola from Harlem and ultimately from New York. Perceiving Oceola as held back by her connection with her black community, Mrs. Ellsworth fails to notice that Oceola does not ask for or even particularly want her help.

In finding so much of black culture distasteful, Mrs. Ellsworth assumes that the values and traditions of European and white American culture are inherently superior. While Oceola is capable of finding power in many different musical traditions—she is not a racial chauvinist about music—Mrs. Ellsworth rejects jazz and blues out of hand because they are not classical. Finally, Mrs. Ellsworth also makes the logical error of ''universality'': she sees the products of European culture as ''universal,'' transcending their cultural and economic origins; conversely, she sees the products of African-American culture as necessarily tied to that culture and, therefore, not universal. Coupled with Mrs. Ellsworth's distaste for black culture is, paradoxically, a fascination and desire that some critics refer to as "exoticism." That is, she tends to look at Oceola as an intriguing, exotic object. She finds Oceola "the blackest—and most interesting of all" her protegees. Wondering about why, she speculates that "it was that Oceola really was talented, terribly alive, and that she looked like nothing Mrs. Ellsworth had ever been near before. Such a rich velvet black, and such a hard young body!"

The presence of this kind of subtle, often "well-intentioned" racism becomes especially clear when one looks at "The Blues I'm Playing" in context: many other stories in *The Ways of White Folks* treat these same dynamics even more directly. Articulating his insights, Hughes confronts his readers with subject matter that had rarely, if ever, appeared in fiction before. Furthermore, he used narrative strategy to challenge racism. For example, Hughes incorporates dialect and blues rhythms for their beauty, rather than for caricature; the narrator frequently identifies Mrs. Ellsworth as " white," making her race as immediate and marked as Oceola's, if not more so.

Sex

At the conclusion of "The Blues I'm Playing" Oceola gives one last private recital for her patron. As Oceola incorporates a powerful blues variation into her program, the two women's attitudes about music come to the fore. Explicitly at this moment, as elsewhere in the story, the music represents their contrasting views of passion and sexuality. A fully sensual life is fundamental to Oceola's character: she ultimately cannot accept success without it. By making Oceola his protagonist and presenting her relationship with Pete in a sympathetic light, Hughes chooses to portray sexual intimacy in positive terms. Mrs. Ellsworth, on the other hand, represents the most repressive aspects of nineteenth-century Western culture. In her demand that the artist become disembodied—a pure soul gazing up at the stars and denying its body on earth—Mrs. Ellsworth denies the presence of passion in her own life. She believes that she has "sublimated" her sexual desires—that she has directed all sexual energy into non-physical admirations. Her responses to Oceola, however, betray the sexuality that still resides, repressed, beneath her veneer of artistic purity: "Oceola really was talented, terribly alive, and . . . she looked like nothing Mrs. Ellsworth had ever been near before. Such a rich velvet black, and such a hard young body!" In this way, Hughes suggests that desire cannot be overcome or removed from one's life; it

Topics for Further Study

- House parties initially provide Oceola with income and later with an important link to Harlem. Using books and other sources about the history of black life in New York City, write a description of a Harlem house party or rent party.

- Oceola takes a rather unconventional approach to planning her wedding. Find the description and speculate about the significance of this in relation to her character and the story's meanings.

- Did you find that your feelings about any of the characters changed significantly as you read the story? If yes, try to locate and explain the passages that influenced you.

- Oceola's stepfather played in a minstrel show, which was a very popular form of entertainment at the turn of the century. Do a short research paper on minstrel shows, looking especially at the images of African Americans they presented.

- If Oceola has triumphed at the end of the story—as most critics agree—why does Mrs. Ellsworth have the last line?

---

will make itself evident, one way or another. Through his description of Oceola, he questions why one would even try to remove this part of human life.

Art

The conflict that Oceola and Mrs. Ellsworth have over music is, more broadly, a debate about art and beauty. According to Mrs. Ellsworth, true art must follow certain very traditional conventions: she "still believed in art of the old school, portraits that really and truly looked like people, poems about nature, music that had soul in it, not syncopation." She believes, furthermore, that these conventions are not simply conventions, but in and of themselves constitute artistic quality. It is this assumption that limits her ability to find most unfamiliar forms beautiful, as we see in her response to the jazz that Oceola loves. For her part,

Oceola remains open to the possibility of finding beauty anywhere. Open to all kinds of music, she is not limited by the conventions of her own background. She can, for example, be "crazy" about the music of Rachmaninoff. Nor does she glorify, as did some black artists of the period, the conventions valued by white patrons like Mrs. Ellsworth. When Oceola encounters this kind of fellow artist in Paris, her experiences reflect Hughes's own struggle in the Harlem Renaissance, which promoted the idea of "the New Negro." According to Hughes, the aspiration to produce works of art that satisfied only European tradition denied the beauty and value of African tradition, African-American culture, and people of African descent.

Style

Narrator

In many ways, the narrative voice of "The Blues I'm Playing" is not likely to strike the contemporary reader as radical. This third-person voice uses simple and clear prose, providing very direct exposition-explanation about the characters' backgrounds and feelings. Nonetheless, when Hughes was writing in the 1920s and 1930s, both his short fiction and his poetry challenged many readers' expectations. First, the language was too direct, in explicit opposition to the prevailing standards of the era. These had been greatly influenced by turn-of-the-century writers like Henry James, who held to the practice of "show, don't tell." Hughes, however, often tells. Second, this voice borrows from black dialect, more at some times than at others. This use of colloquialism is not exaggerated to the point of caricature; Hughes presents the phonic beauty of oral language, rather than making a joke of it. Third, as the narrative voice allies itself with Oceola and black characters in general, it places the reader in a position that was quite novel for the time: looking at the white world from a black perspective. This would have been a new experience to both black and white readers, in different ways.

Irony

The gaze that Hughes's narrator directs at the white world is marked by a powerful irony. It is in this sense that Hughes achieves a "deceptive and *profound* simplicity," in the words of Hoyt W.

Fuller. The simplicity or seeming naivete of the voice veils what are actually harsh and sometimes painful realizations. So, for example, when the narrator informs us in all sincerity that Oceola's "apartment was just as [Mrs. Ellsworth] thought it would be. After all, she had read Thomas Burke on Limehouse," we are expected to see the sharp criticism beneath the surface. Limehouse and Harlem are not interchangeable, and a white writer characterizing an ethnic ghetto usually resorted to stereotypes.

Setting

Because of the subject matter and the largely unprecedented viewpoint that Hughes uses, settings in "The Blues I'm Playing" carry a great deal of meaning. The narrative primarily moves between Mrs. Ellsworth's house and the apartments that Oceola lives in, with a particular stress on her life in Harlem. Each of these places is presented from an unusual perspective. A Madison Avenue house belonging to someone of Mrs. Ellsworth's resources would have been stately and impressive, but we see it only as "grey stone" with "a butler who actually wore brass buttons." We first see Oceola's apartment in Mrs. Ellsworth's negative assessment, framed by her ignorant reliance on inappropriate sources ("The apartment was just as she thought it would be. After all, she had read Thomas Burke on Limehouse.") Consequently, the ensuing description, which tells us simply how small the apartment is, points to Mrs. Ellsworth's privileged narrowmindedness. Oceola's insistence that she is happy in Harlem suggests her ability to see value Mrs. Ellsworth cannot. By contrast, Mrs. Ellsworth's drawing room—full of monetarily valuable objects—becomes a sterile and hateful place. By presenting the mansion in a negative light and the small apartment in a positive light, Hughes challenges readers' assumptions.

Historical Context

Harlem

At the beginning of the twentieth century, African-Americans were still fighting an uphill battle against the prejudices and social forces that had kept slavery alive until the 1860s. Most African Americans still lived in the rural south, trying to earn a

Compare & Contrast

- **1933:** Lynch mobs kill forty-two blacks as lynchings increase in the southern U.S. states.

  1991 and 1992: Los Angeles police officers beat unarmed Rodney King, and the following year the officers charged in connection with the beating are acquitted. The worst riot for violence and looting in U.S. history follows the verdict.

- **1948:** Nationalist Afrikaner bloc wins the election in South Africa on an apartheid platform that favors the separation of the white and black races with the whites in power.

  1992: South African whites vote 2 to 1 to give a mandate to the president of the country to end white-minority rule.

- **1939:** The Daughters of the American Revolution refuse to rent Constitution Hall to Marian Anderson because of her race, although Anderson had been proclaimed as the world's greatest contralto by European critics. An audience of 75,000 gathered at the Lincoln Memorial to hear Anderson on Easter Sunday.

  1987: Popular black soul and Rhythm and Blues singer Anita Baker makes a music video of her performance "One Night of Rapture" at Constitution Hall.

living from agricultural labor. Now technically free to go where they wished, however, they began moving to the cities of the northeast, where black neighborhoods like Harlem took root. Although discrimination and hardship still limited their opportunities and economic well-being, the 1920s brought with it a spirit of optimism that blossomed with the Harlem Renaissance. The black intellectuals and artists who comprised this movement believed that their works, which displayed traditional erudition and talent, would compel white Americans to see African Americans in a new—and equal—light. For a time, it seemed to work: white critics and patrons directed their attention and money to black artists, making possible once unimaginable exhibits and integrated social gatherings. Furthermore, Harlem itself was in vogue among white New Yorkers: a Saturday night on the town might consist of bar-hopping from one Harlem nightclub to another, taking in shows that featured jazz musicians and black dancers. The vogue was not, however, necessarily anti-racist: many of the clubs that catered to white patrons and featured black entertainers refused to allow entrance to black patrons.

There was, however, a Harlem that was by and for black New Yorkers, a Harlem glimpsed in the

house parties at which Oceola loves to play and in the church that is also central to her social life; both institutions were vital to the black community in Harlem, although at times for separate social groups. While Harlem provided relative safety and a strong sense of community for black New Yorkers, it also reflected the poverty that plagued African Americans in general. With few exceptions, the people of Harlem struggled to make ends meet. Hughes stresses this when he describes Oceola waiting in Mrs. Ellsworth's drawing room, "afraid to move for fear she might knock something over—that would take ten years of a Harlemite's wages to replace, if broken." When the stock market crashed in 1929, the U.S. economy went with it, devastating the job market for all people. Only a few, as Oceola notes about Mrs. Ellsworth, were wealthy enough to coast through the Great Depression.

Segregation

When Harlem was celebrating the hope of the new century in the northeast, segregation still ruled the daily lives of African Americans in the south. Although Hughes makes it clear to his readers that racism dominated race relations in New York, its presence is much more pronounced in the Atlanta that Pete speaks of. There, Oceola could not enter a hotel through the front door; if Mrs. Ellsworth stayed in their home, they would run the risk of ''a lynching.'' Although not mentioned in Hughes's story, we know that segregation also meant separate bathrooms and water fountains, as well as exclusion from many business establishments. On a broader scale, although African Americans had the nominal right to vote, to own property, to receive an education, and to hold a job, many of these rights were undermined by racist practices, some of which were even carried out within town and state governments. Not until the advent of Civil Rights in the 1950s would these conditions begin to change.

Critical Overview

The Ways of White Folks and ''The Blues I'm Playing'' established Hughes's reputation as a short story writer on its publication. He was already known as a poet, having gained celebrity with several publications in the 1920s, during the height of the Harlem Renaissance, a movement fostered by black artists and intellectuals. His short fiction, like the poems that preceded it, were—in context—daring and controversial. While many readers acclaimed his work for its beauty and directness, others—many of them leading black intellectuals of the day—complained that he put on display the ''lowest'' and most stereotypical aspects of black life. Some of these readers, like Mrs. Ellsworth in ''The Blues I'm Playing'', considered art something that should rise above race and everyday life—a view that Hughes attacks in his story. But Hughes saw himself as presenting the beauty inherent in the lives of black Americans.

When Langston Hughes published *The Ways of White Folks* in 1934, he was already known for the poetry he had published in the 1920s. While most readers had praised his verse, many leaders of the black community criticized the young author, drawing him into a heated debate about art and race relations. Hughes's poetry, because it drew its language from black dialect and drew its rhythms from jazz and blues, failed to adhere to the conventions of Western art. To many black intellectuals, proving their facility with these conventions was central to the project of the Harlem Renaissance; dialect was a caricature, an insult to the black community. De-

spite many positive reviews, the 1934 volume of short stories revived this criticism because most of the stories explicitly took as their subject matter the ordinary people who lived in neighborhoods like Harlem. Rather than setting up a new black hero for white Americans to see, these critics charged, Hughes was putting the community's worst and most stereotypical elements on display. ''The Blues I'm Playing'' captures Hughes's response to these critics. In the face of Mrs. Ellsworth's distaste, Oceola embraces her community in its everyday life. Like Hughes, she insists on its value and beauty, and she will not cooperate with the effort to erase African-American history and culture.

As these concerns about Hughes's work in general drew less attention, critics began to focus interpretation on particular elements in ''The Blues I'm Playing'': the function of music, the function of sexuality, and the function of racism and racial identity. For the most part, critics have agreed in their assessments. Studies of the presence of jazz and blues in the story note not just its centrality, but also the meaning that music takes on—its evocation of the earth and the body and, consequently, of life. It is, through these same associations, also fundamental to the element of sexuality in the story. Critics agree that ''The Blues I'm Playing'' charts a conflict between sexual repression and affirmation. While Oceola and Pete obviously stand for the latter, Mrs. Ellsworth sometimes appears to champion the former and at other times to be its victim. Most critics take for granted Mrs. Ellsworth's repressed sexual desire for Oceola, but some disagreement appears in analyses of her character. While Peter Bruck and Hans Ostrum, for example, portray her as essentially fearful and almost pathetic, Robert Bone and Steven Tracey stress her desire for power over Oceola, comparing her to a slave owner. All in all, however, most critics today concur in Peter Bruck's determination that this story ''marks one of Hughes's outstanding achievements in this genre and established him as a serious writer of satirical short fiction.''

Criticism

Liz Brent

Brent has a Ph.D. in American Culture, specializing in cinema studies, from the University of

King Oliver's Jazz Band in Chicago in the early 1920s. Lil Hardin is on piano. Her husband, Louis Armstrong (behind her, on trumpet), would become one of the best-known jazz musicians of his era.

Michigan. She is a freelance writer and editor and teaches courses in American cinema. In the following essay, she discusses the conflicting perspectives on "art" represented by the two main characters in the story.

Langston Hughes's short story "The Blues I'm Playing" portrays the relationship between a young, working class African American pianist, Oceola Jones, and her elderly, wealthy, white patron, Mrs. Dora Ellsworth. Hughes juxtaposes Oceola's and

Mrs. Ellsworth's perspectives on their relationship through contrasting the meaning and significance of music to each woman. For Mrs. Ellsworth, music or "art" is an abstraction which, if "pure," rises above the banalities of everyday life. For Oceola, on the other hand, music is a living, breathing practice which is fully integrated with her personal, everyday experiences. These two different perspectives on music, or "art," are portrayed as an issue of both race and class which ultimately divides the two women. Through this juxtaposition, Hughes's story

What Do I Read Next?

- An early and central argument for racial equality in the United States, W. E. B. DuBois's *The Souls of Black Folk* was also fundamental to the Harlem Renaissance and its vision of African-Americans raised up through intellectual and artistic achievements.

- An influential book of short stories by British author D. H. Lawrence, *The Lovely Lady* confronts the reader with undisguised social critiques. The volume had a considerable impact on Hughes, convincing him that short fiction could be a valuable genre.

- Hughes's autobiography, *The Big Sea*, describes in detail his relationship with his patron, Charlotte Mason; that dynamic was, he acknowledged, the model for "The Blues I'm Playing."

is a social commentary on Black/White relations in the U.S., and a critique of the high/low distinction between "pure" art and "folk" art.

Art for art's sake

The central conflict which develops between the African American musician and her white patron in this story revolves around how each conceptualizes the role of "art," in this case music, in the artist's life. The rich, white Mrs. Ellsworth can, quite literally, "afford" to conceptualize "art" as separate from everyday necessities, such as earning a living. To Oceola, on the other hand, Mrs. Ellsworth's concern with "pure art" as an end in itself, separate from everyday life, is absurd, at best, "for she had never met anybody interested in pure art before. Just to be given thing's for *art's sake* seemed suspicious to Oceola."

The nature of this difference in perception is based in broader assumptions throughout White Western culture about the distinction between "pure" art and "folk" art, or "high" art and "low" art. "Pure" or "high" art has generally been considered distinct from any particular use-value, and set apart from the activities of daily life. "Folk" or "low" art has been used to designate art which grows out of non-white, non-Western or impoverished cultures, and which often serves a practical function within that culture. For instance, a patchwork quilt made by someone's grandmother in her home for the purpose of staying warm would generally be considered a "folk" art, while an abstract fabric sculpture hanging in an art museum would be considered "pure" art. Art which serves no other purpose than to be art is referred to as "art for art's sake." In Hughes's story, the differences between the white woman's and the black woman's understanding of the role of art in the life and culture of the artist hinges on this distinction. More specifically, white Western classical music is pitted against the African-American musical traditions of jazz and blues.

For Mrs. Ellsworth, "art" becomes a substitute for life, as she lives only vicariously through the young artists whom she supports: "she had no interest in life now save art, and the young people who created art." Her "generosity" toward the struggling young artists she patronizes comes in the form of taking care of their financial needs so that they may devote themselves fully to "art" without the distractions and corruption of daily struggle. Among her "protegees," Oceola, for Mrs. Ellsworth, is merely a means of diversion, as the older woman has no genuine interest in music itself. Her interest in "aiding the arts" is really an excuse for treating other human beings as hobbies, rather than as individuals. Oceola is described as if she were merely a phase in the old woman's life, rather than as a real individual with whom she develops a personal relationship. "Then began one of the most interesting periods in Mrs. Ellsworth's whole experience in aiding the art. The period of Oceola."

Furthermore, Mrs. Ellsworth perceives Oceola almost as an object of art in herself, similar to one of the expensive Persian vases which adorn her home. Oceola's blackness, for Mrs. Ellsworth, is not an ethnic or community identity, with personal relationships and real economic and social struggles, but a characteristic that makes her "interesting," as if she were an artifact from a foreign country. Her interest in "art" and "beauty" is actually an expression of her view of the artists themselves as objects of beauty, rather than as real individual people, for "she was sometimes confused as to where beauty lay in the youngsters or in what they made, in the creators or the creation." Mrs. Ellsworth regards Oceola herself as a novelty object, to be added to her collection of protegee's, "She was tremendously intrigued at meeting Oceola, never having had before amongst all her artists a black one." At one point, she thinks of Oceola almost as a toy doll for her to play at dressing up, for "Mrs. Ellsworth began to think in bed about what gowns would look best on Oceola. Her protegee would have to be well-dressed." And, when she goes to a dressmaker to have an outfit custom made for Oceola, she refers to the young woman as if she were merely a piece of fabric which needed a matching color. When she asks the dressmaker, "what kind of colors looked well with black," the dressmaker does not realize she is talking about a person, and she must clarify, "not black fabrics, but black skin."

The darkness of Oceola's skin becomes almost a fetish for Mrs. Ellsworth, for whom she is a curiosity, because of their racial differences and her lack of familiarity with black people. "Mrs. Ellsworth couldn't recall ever having known a single Negro before in her whole life, so she found Oceola fascinating. And just as black as she herself was white." Mrs. Ellsworth's obsessive "interest" in Oceola focuses on the novelty of her blackness. Of all her protegees, Oceola is described as "the blackest and most interesting of all." Mrs. Ellsworth even becomes fascinated with the very body of the young musician, for "she looked like nothing Mrs. Ellsworth had ever been near before. Such a rich velvet black, and such a hard young body!"

Mrs. Ellsworth further regards Oceola as an object of study, as if she were a specimen from a foreign culture.

> Before going to bed, Mrs. Ellsworth told her house-keeper to order a book called *Nigger Heaven* on the morrow, and also anything else Brentano's had about Harlem. She made a mental note that she must go up there sometime, for she had never yet seen that dark section of New York; and now that she had a Negro protegee, she really ought to know something about it.

Even Oceola's modest living conditions are a point of interest for Mrs. Ellsworth, who is unable to see poverty or financial struggle as a real problem experienced by real people, but as simply a backdrop for this "interesting" musician, whom she coddles like a prized possession. Mrs. Ellsworth's knowledge of how poorer people live is derived solely from books, and her assessment of Oceola's apartment is almost clinical, as if she were reading a page out of a book, rather than visiting a friend in her home.

> In this final confrontation, Oceola makes the blues triumph over the very idea of 'pure art.'"

> The apartment was just as she thought it would be. After all, she had read Thomas Burke on Limehouse. And here was just one more of those holes in the wall, even if it was five stories high. The windows looked down on slums. There were only four rooms, small as maid's rooms, all of them.

Mrs. Ellsworth regards Oceola as a valuable object, an artifact from a foreign culture, to add to her collection of "protegees," just as she displays a collection of "jade vases and amber cups worth thousands of dollars" in her music room.

Living the Blues

In taking her on as a protegee, Mrs. Ellsworth wishes to remove Oceola from her African American community in order to give her the opportunity to devote herself to the purity of "art for art's sake." For Oceola, by contrast, music is not a pure abstraction called "art," which rises above everyday life, but both grows out of and expresses her life as a whole, and is an integral part of her relationships, financial concerns and community. When Mrs. Ellsworth first meets Oceola, the young woman's music is part of her role in her community as a teacher and member of the church, is central to her social life, and is her sole means of livelihood. Her life is socially, culturally and spiritually rich, and financially stable. When Mrs. Ellsworth wishes to meet her, "She had said she was busy every day. It seemed that she had pupils, rehearsed a church choir, and played almost nightly for colored house parties or dances. She made quite a good deal of money."

For Mrs. Ellsworth, classical music is a form of "pure art," distinct from what she regards as lower art forms emanating from African-American culture. To Oceola, however, classical music in the white European tradition, and jazz or blues in the African-American tradition, are all part of her repertoire, between which she makes no hierarchical distinctions. When she first plays for Mrs. Ellsworth at her home, Oceola unceremoniously plays a blues tune, mixed in with several classical pieces. ''She played the Rachmaninoff Prelude in C-sharp Minor. She played from the Liszt Etudes. She played the 'St. Louis Blues.' She played Ravel's 'Pavanne pour une Engante Defunte.'" But for Oceola, playing in the drawing room of a rich white woman she hardly knows is second to playing at an event within her own community which is both a social occasion and a benefit concert to support the cause of African Americans. Her time playing for Mrs. Ellsworth is limited because ''she was playing that night for a dance in Brooklyn for the benefit of the Urban League.''

The role of music in Oceola's life is also integral to her personal relationships with her parents, as well as her family history, their role in their church and community, and their financial circumstances. As she explains to Mrs. Ellsworth:

> Papa had a band, that is, her stepfather. Used to play for all the lodge turnouts, picnics, dances, barbecues. You could get the best roast pig in the world in Mobile. Her mother used to play the organ in church, and when the deacons bought a piano after the big revival, her mama played that, too. Oceola played an organ, also, and a cornet.

In Oceola's description of her upbringing, playing music remains integral to her family and community life, throughout their changing circumstances.

> Mama got a job playing for the movies in a Market Street theater, and I played for a church choir, and saved some money and went to Wilberforce. Studied piano there, too. Played for all the college dances. Graduated. Came to New York and heard Rachmaninoff and was crazy about him.

Nevertheless, Mrs. Ellsworth insistently attempts to remove Oceola from her African-American community, relationships and cultural influences, as well as from economic necessity, in order to make it possible for her to pursue ''pure'' art, in the form of classical music performance for white, European audiences. For Mrs. Ellsworth, getting and keeping Oceola out of Harlem is a central priority to her project to ''increase the rapprochement between art and Oceola.'' Mrs. Ellsworth regards art as an abstract beauty from which life is only a distraction. When Oceola decides to wait until Pete leaves for medical school before moving out of Harlem, Mrs. Ellsworth reproaches her with a high-minded aphorism about making ''art'' a priority over personal relationships: '''Art is long,' reminded Mrs. Ellsworth, 'and time is fleeting, my dear.'''

In distinguishing ''pure'' art from everyday life, Mrs. Ellsworth repeatedly pits ''art'' against

''love.'' She thus attempts to separate Oceola from love by keeping her from her boyfriend, Pete Williams, who later becomes her fiance. Mrs. Ellsworth hopes that, once out of Harlem and on the road to a successful career as a piano performer, '''She won't need him,''' because '''She will have her art.''' When Oceola informs Mrs. Ellsworth of her engagement to Pete, the white woman feels that ''love had triumphed over art.'' On their last meeting, she criticizes Oceola for choosing love over art, as ''she began to reproach the girl aloud for running away from art and music, for burying herself in Atlanta and love '' Mrs. Ellsworth's high-minded, abstract ideas about art as transcendent are expressed through imagery of the stars in the sky, which rise above the earth. ''You could shake the stars with your music,'' she tells the young woman. The elderly woman goes on to describe Oceola's marriage through imagery which descends to the level of dirt and death. She describes Oceola's decision to marry Pete as ''digging a grave for yourself.''

While Oceola makes her relationship with her boyfriend and her participation in her community a priority, Mrs. Ellsworth values Oceola only in isolation from her community and relationships. The story suggests that Mrs. Ellsworth's attempts to make Oceola a ''successful'' pianist only serve to distance the young woman from her full, emotionally and culturally rich life within her African-American community. Mrs. Ellsworth ''wondered why anyone insisted on living in Harlem.'' But to Oceola, Harlem is her lifeblood. '''I've been away from my people for so long. I want to live right in the middle of them again.''' And, in talking with her fiancee, Oceola again expresses her wish to live among fellow African Americans, rather than in the upper class white world in which Mrs. Ellsworth wishes to place her. '''Let's live in Atlanta, where there are lots of colored people, like us.'''

Hughes further implies that for Oceola, a young black woman in the 1930s, Mrs. Ellsworth's dreams for her success as a classic pianist are unrealistic. Unlike Mrs. Ellsworth, Oceola is fully aware of her social and financial status, reasoning that ''Anyway, during the present depression, it was pretty hard for a beginning artist like herself to book a concert tour so she might just as well be married awhile.'' Mrs. Ellsworth, on the other hand, is rich enough to float above the concerns of everyday people as indicated by the fact that not even the Great Depression affects her financial status. ''And [Oceola] came home to New York a year after the stock market crash and nobody had any money except folks like Mrs. Ellsworth who had so much it would be hard to ever lose it all.''

The sheer love of jazz

Mrs. Ellsworth's desire to groom Oceola for the pursuit of the ''pure art'' of classical music is met with conflict most specifically by Oceola's ''sheer love of jazz.'' As Oceola continues to play at Harlem house parties, for free, Mrs. Ellsworth objects to the mixture of dance and alcohol with a musical form which she regards as primitive, describing it as ''the most tom-tom music she had ever heard.'' She prefers music which she associates with abstract concepts, such as the ''soul'' and the ''eternal,'' which, both literally and figuratively, rise above human concerns.

> So in the spring, Mrs. Ellsworth organized weekends in the up-state mountains where she had a little lodge and where Oceola could look from the high places at the stars, and fill her soul with the vastness of the eternal, and forget about jazz. Mrs. Ellsworth began to hate jazz especially on grand piano.

Oceola, on the other hand, makes no such distinctions between art and life. She ''merely lived and loved it.'' She even finds the high-minded conversation among her fellow black artists in France to be absurd. ''Why did they or anybody argue so much about life or art?'' she wonders. Oceola, in fact, never forgets the most basic human concerns, such as the need for food, in relation to her art. ''Only the Marxian students seemed sound to her, for they, at least, wanted people to have enough to eat. That was important, Oceola thought, remembering, as she did, her own sometimes hungry years. But the rest of the controversies, as far as she could fathom, were based on air.'' Oceola is particularly baffled by Mrs. Ellsworth's obliviousness to the basic economic necessities of people such as herself. ''Why did white folks think you could live on nothing but art? Strange! Too strange! Too strange!''

While Mrs. Ellsworth continually pits art and music against life and love, Oceola sees her music as fully enmeshed with life and love. ''Music, to Oceola, demanded movement and expression, dancing and living to go with it.'' In contrast to Mrs. Ellsworth's lofty ideas about ''pure art,'' Oceola is happiest playing blues and jazz for free at a club. Hughes describes her music in terms rich with imagery and feeling and rooted in African culture. ''In the blues she made the bass notes throb like tom-toms, the trebles cry like little flutes, so deep in the earth and so high in the sky that they understood

everything.'' To Oceola, her music belongs as much in the church as it does in the dance club, as much in the realm of the body as in the realm of the spirit. ''She liked to teach, when she had the choir, the singing of those rhythmical Negro spirituals that possessed the power to pull colored folks out of their seats in the amen corner and make them prance and shout in the aisles for Jesus.''

In the final meeting between Oceola and Mrs. Ellsworth, the ongoing conflict between each woman's perception of the role of art in the life of the artist comes to a head. While Mrs. Ellsworth had tried her best to make ''art'' triumph over ''love,'' Oceola demonstrates through playing that blues and jazz music encompasses love and the spirit, the earth and the sky, within the realm of music and art. She plays ''a Negro blues, a blues that deepened and grew into rollicking jazz '' In this final confrontation, Oceola makes the blues triumph over the very idea of ''pure art.'' Her playing flows into ''an earth-throbbing rhythm that shook the lilies in the Persian vases of Mrs. Ellsworth's music room.'' The lilies in the expensive imported vases symbolize the white woman's efforts to remove the black woman from her community and display her like an object of art in the cold atmosphere of her music room.

The final exchange between Oceola and Mrs. Ellsworth sums up the nature of their different views on art and different social statuses. Oceola expresses herself through singing a blues song while playing piano. The words to the blues song begin, ''Oh if I could holler / like a mountain jack,'' and continue, ''I'd go up on de mountain / And call my baby back.'' The desire to ''call my baby back'' suggests a strong impulse to use the ''hollering'' of music for expressing feelings of love. Mrs. Ellsworth's response to this sentiment, which she coldly states, rather than singing, underscore's her continued desire to hold ''art'' high above human emotion and experience. Picking up from the song lyrics, the elderly white woman asserts that, were she to ''go up on de mountain,'' she would abandon ''love'' in favor of an abstract notion of art as something which remains above the world of human emotion. Rather than ''call my baby back,'' she would choose to ''stand looking at the stars.''

Conclusion

''The Blues I'm Playing'' is a celebration of the role of Blues and Jazz music in African American life and culture. The story is an argument against assimilationism suggesting that making it in the white world comes at the expense of the richness and beauty of black culture and community. It is simultaneously a critique of the high/low distinction between ''pure'' art and ''folk'' art, a distinction based on racist and classist social hierarchies.

In his own writing career, Hughes seems to exemplify these ideals in choosing to write about ordinary, everyday, working class black folks. And while he was criticized by black writers and intellectuals for perpetuating negative images of blacks, this was the very category of people among whom he gained enormous popularity, and he became the first black writer ever to earn his living solely from his writing. In writing for and about his fellow African Americans, Hughes succeeded in achieving his own black American Dream, suited to his own aesthetic and social values. Years before the Black Power Movement which arose in the 1960s, Hughes's message in this story could be summed up, as critic Linda Patterson has pointed out, by the slogan, ''Black is beautiful.''

Source: Liz Brent, for *Short Stories for Students*, The Gale Group, 2000.

Ondine Le Blanc

Le Blanc has taught at the University of Michigan and is currently an editor and free-lance writer. In the following essay, she discusses the subtle ways in which Hughes conveys his social message in the story.

When in 1932 Langston Hughes first found himself interested in writing short fiction again, he was visiting the Soviet Union on a filmmaking project with some other artists. Like many other Americans at the time, Hughes believed that socialism could help in the search for social justice. He personally had been involved with left-wing organizations at least since his first year of college. However, the trend in fiction of the period was not to convey a social message but rather to emphasize aesthetic technique and experimentation, a concentration on the art itself or on psychological detail. Critics generally agree that it wasn't until Hughes read in the Soviet Union a book of short stories by English writer D. H. Lawrence, whose sharp irony and unabashed critiques filled *The Lovely Lady*, that Hughes decided he could express his political concerns about race relations through fiction. So began

the stories, including ''The Blues I'm Playing,'' that would constitute *The Ways of White Folks.*

While other prominent fiction writers of the period—James Joyce, for example—focused on challenging readers' expectations with a disruption of the prose itself, Hughes subtly inverted the world with the techniques he used in ''The Blues I'm Playing.'' That is, he showed his readers the world from a black woman's perspective, an experience that most likely would have been entirely new to both black and white readers. Many of the elements that are fundamental to any work of fiction—characterization, setting, narrative voice—take on an extra function in ''The Blues I'm Playing'' since they show us the white world from a critical distance.

''The Blues I'm Playing'' is, like all of the other stories in *The Ways of White Folks,* a study in race relations. Consequently, every aspect of how Mrs. Ellsworth treats Oceola is not simply the portrayal of a personal dynamic, of two psychologies interacting, but rather the portrayal of how white treats black. Mrs. Ellsworth's paternalism, her ignorance, her rejection of Pete, and her desire for Oceola, all appear in relation to that type of interaction. The ignorance that Hughes depicts would have been typical of such a segregated world, although segregated more subtly in New York than in a southern city like Atlanta, as Pete points out. Mrs. Ellsworth firmly believes that she has never known an African American before only because it has never been necessary for her to interact with an African American before. Economic and social inequality not only kept blacks and whites apart, but relegated blacks to service roles; Mrs. Ellsworth would never have encountered an African American as her equal before. In her effort to educate herself, she turns to Carl Van Vechten's *Nigger Heaven,* a shallow study full of stereotypes. It was considered progressive by many white readers but insulting by black readers.

Of course, in her paternalism, Mrs. Ellsworth does not quite view Oceola as her equal. Despite the young woman's superior talent, Mrs. Ellsworth persistently believes that Oceola lacks not just money, but certain cultural and emotional advantages. The older woman looks down upon her protegee's attachment to the physical and sensual world. This sensual world is manifested in jazz, Harlem, and Pete, and all these represent her connection to her black community and culture. In her determination to remove Oceola from all these things for the sake of "pure art," Mrs. Ellsworth fails to see them as beautiful or at all valuable. Throughout the story, she remains disdainful of black culture.

While Hughes makes Mrs. Ellsworth an embodiment of this kind of racism, he also makes her guilty of "exoticism." The desires that Mrs. Ellsworth so doggedly represses are directed toward Oceola because of, not in spite of, Oceala's race. Mrs. Ellsworth is specifically intrigued by Oceola's blackness: "Oceola really was talented, terribly alive, and . . . she looked like nothing Mrs. Ellsworth had ever been near before. Such a rich velvet black, and such a hard young body!" Mrs. Ellsworth resolves the contradiction by rejecting Oceola's culture but embracing her "essence"—some essential "blackness" supposedly not rooted in Harlem but in some fundamental racial quality. This myth, not uncommon even today, casts African Americans as innately—for example—more sensual and more rhythmic than European Americans. But this idea, although often meant to be complimentary, is still steeped in prejudice.

The subject matter, given emphasis by Hughes in spite of the unfashionableness of conveying an overt message, demanded that the reader acknowledge certain forms of racism perhaps not visible before to many readers. The subject matter had less to do with the impact of the story than did Hughes's use of perspective: he put his reader at Oceola's side. Most European and American writers of the time and their predecessors were white, wrote about white characters, and wrote for white readers. While non-white readers developed double vision, becoming familiar with a white point of view, as well as their own point of view, white readers could remain comfortable with their single view of life. In "The Blues I'm Playing," the narrator, through perspective and irony offers the reader a seat that shows not just Oceola's point of view, but specifically Oceola's view of white and black cultures. For the white reader, then, to be reading about a white character—Mrs. Ellsworth—as a person marked by her race would, most likely, have been an unprecedented experience. And Hughes has very explicitly marked Mrs. Ellsworth with her race. References to Mrs. Ellsworth as "white" are more frequent than references to Oceola as "black." Mrs. Ellsworth's actions are identified specifically as the actions of a white person. Her assumptions, thrown onto unfamiliar ground when contrasted with Oceola's, become "white" assumptions. Mrs. Ellsworth assumes that Oceola must be uncomfortable in her

> " Mrs. Ellsworth's actions are identified specifically as the actions of a white person. Her assumptions, thrown onto unfamiliar ground when contrasted with Oceola's, become 'white' assumptions."

small Harlem apartment. But, in fact, Oceola is most uncomfortable in Mrs. Ellsworth's drawing room, where the expensive objects strike her not as inherently beautiful but as oppressive and dead—even the lilies are symbolic of death.

In the 1920s and 1930s, the first two decades of Hughes's prolific career, many black artists and intellectuals sought equality for African Americans. Many of these same people, however, criticized Hughes' work, believing that his bold depictions of everyday black life would only reinforce for white readers their negative stereotypes of blacks. Only more recently have critics seen the subtler techniques with which Hughes approached his readers. Now, however, it is recognized that the critique of race relations in "The Blues I'm Playing" also embraces black community and culture. When we see the richest of white American culture through Oceola's eyes, we see its supposedly inherent beauty undermined. Hughes does not suggest that black Americans achieve equality with whites by adopting white values alone, but rather suggests that everyone love beauty wherever it is found, as Oceola loves classical music without sacrificing jazz.

Source: Ondine Le Blanc, "Overview of 'The Blues I'm Playing,'" for *Short Stories for Students*, The Gale Group, 2000.

Steven C. Tracy

Tracy leads a blues band and has published books on the blues and on Langston Hughes. In the following essay, he offers his interpretation of the conflict between Dora Ellsworth and Oceola Jones, focusing on the significance of the blues in the story and on the meaning of Oceola's name.

In his short story "The Blues I'm Playing," from *The Ways of White Folks* (1934), Langston Hughes presents us with a compelling portrait of two women whose approaches to life and art cause them to sever a relationship that could have continued to be advantageous to each of them. In elderly white patron Mrs. Dora Ellsworth, who was based partially on Hughes's ex-patron Charlotte Mason, Hughes portrays a widow whose lack of fecundity, both physiologically and creatively, abetted by beliefs in Platonic and Manichaean dualism, leads her to exercise a Nietzschean "master morality" and to adopt an artistic aesthetic, art for art's sake, that divorces art from the living of life. In Oceola Jones, Hughes shows a quietly rebellious woman who subverts a number of sexual and racial stereotypes and in the process succeeds in defining herself and challenging Mrs. Ellsworth's aesthetic. Through Oceola, Hughes demonstrates how a positive self- and racial image brings about self-confidence, success, and a unified vision of life. Oceola declares her independence from the strictures of Mrs. Ellsworth, but just as surely declares her dependence on Pete and her community for the support she needs to help make her what she can be; and the community recognizes the need it has for Oceola—a need she sets about fulfilling. She has, then, not only the freedom but the courage to choose her direction. And it is in the blues that Oceola finds the artistic freedom, range of emotion, and intellectual and spiritual energy equal to expressing her feelings about the nature of existence.

Hughes makes it clear that Mrs. Ellsworth is, in a sense, trying to be a mother to her young charges, Oceola and Antonio Bas, because of her own emotional aridity and loneliness. Because her wealthy husband is dead and she has no children of her own, Mrs. Ellsworth, feeling deserted, unfulfilled, and bitter, allows her own personal barrenness to direct her young charges away from personal relationships and life-directed thoughts that would interfere with her domination and away from their movement *toward* their own art, so that they can give birth to things out of their minds and not their bodies. She has adopted, clearly, the Platonic mind/body dualism and, perhaps, a Manichaean dualism as well, given the regular contrast and opposition between black and white in the story.

In Mrs. Ellsworth's view, the mind is associated with right, whiteness, and goodness, the body with wrong, blackness, and evil. Ellsworth views the "intrusion" of Pete, Oceola's African-American boyfriend, as the intrusion equivalent to that of a psychic and economic vampire whom she hopes to drive away by exposure to the "sunlight" of her ideas. James Emanuel [in *Langston Hughes*, 1967] speculates that "unappreciated sensitivity" has led Mrs. Ellsworth to her mindset, and indeed she does seem to fear male domination in a way that suggests that she had been in some way limited personally, perhaps artistically, by her relationship with her husband. However, Mrs. Ellsworth seems to have absorbed the power relationships established by society enough to be unaware of the fact that her attitudes and actions do the same thing to her charges that (we assume) her husband did to her. She assumes, in other words, that her money, her power, gives her the right to place limits on "her" artists, as her husband's maleness, and thus dominance, had given him the right to do to her. Her "unappreciated sensitivity," if indeed she had it, did not teach her to appreciate sensitivity that she did not understand, or care to understand, in others.

Mrs. Ellsworth obviously feels it is her right and duty—indeed her place—to exercise control over artistic concerns and endeavors, not only because she has the money to do so, but because the money offers her the status of authority and intellectual superior[ity] as well. Mrs. Ellsworth is someone whose knowledge of the inherited values of Western culture in the world of art is sufficiently developed to value the accomplishments of the past masters recognized by the guardians of *her* culture, but insufficiently sympathetic to "foreign" developments that would represent real advances in art. She guards the Western past and tradition because *that* is where she is master, where she is in control. Actually, the control she has is economic, bequeathed to her by a male, her late husband; and it is this economic independence granted to her that she wishes to pass on to Oceola—but with artistic and aesthetic strings attached, a strong sexual attraction, and a desire to run Oceola's life that indicates that Mrs. Ellsworth has learned from her husband, and male authority, well. Plato asserts in *The Republic* that because art is an imitation of an imitation and thus removed from reality and eternal beauty, the person most capable of appreciating true beauty is the intellectual, not the artist. Therefore art should be subject to the control of the intellectual. And this is, in fact, what Mrs. Ellsworth wants for herself—in direct contrast to Oceola's desire to please herself, her audience, and her "people" with the variety of music they all want. To one who doesn't worry about paying the rent, playing for rent parties is uncommonly vulgar; but to one who has those worries, it is commonly voluntary.

Friedrich Nietzsche describes, in *Beyond Good and Evil*, what he believed to be the root of the problem that Hughes has torture Mrs. Ellsworth (or does she use it to torture Oceola?) and makes her what she is. She possesses what Nietzsche terms a perverted "master morality." Because she is unable to actuate her own will creatively—perhaps as a result of her husband's inability or lack of desire to understand her own forays into singing—she seeks to substitute power over others, in Oceola's case someone she views as both an exotic and a child, for her own inability to create. This is her "sublimation" (Nietzsche's term), and it explains her "master morality," her desire to direct or control the lives of others, in terms of her own weaknesses. When she encourages Oceola to sublimate her soul, Mrs. Ellsworth does so with the weight of Plato and Nietzsche behind her, and with the desire to control Oceola's life, to have her own "period," the period of Oceola, as she calls it. Ironically, her ability to control Oceola represents for her a fecundity she lacks, and it is not difficult to see her controlling of Oceola's life as being analogous to Mrs. Ellsworth's getting her menstrual period, proving herself still capable of giving birth and thus creating something of her own. The joke here, of course, is that if she has her period she is most likely not with child, so her imagined state is an illusory one at best. When Mrs. Ellsworth first meets Oceola, she is intrigued at the thought of having a Black among *her* artists. She is an owner, or at least deludes herself that she can own people like Oceola. However, at the very point at which she deludes herself into believing that she is freeing Oceola, she is making a subtle and insidious attempt to enslave her.

Part of that attempt at enslavement draws philosophically on the ideas of Walter Pater and the Aesthetic Movement in championing the phrase and concept of art for art's sake. Separating art from some kind of useful purpose places art in a realm where the wealthy Mrs. Ellsworth, retreating from the mundane reality of life with the help of her money, can deal with it as the exclusive property of someone of her class and background who has the time to cloister herself in delicate parlors and lose herself in some imaginary artistic realm. "But you must have time," Mrs. Ellsworth tells Oceola when Oceola says that she is too busy with work to study formally. Later, when Hughes introduces the carpe diem theme as Mrs. Ellsworth cautions Oceola that "Art is long. . . and time is fleeting. . . ," Oceola

> **She is self-assured, comfortable and happy with her culture and her abilities, and is thus not defensive about Ellsworth's intrusions into her private life or attitudes about her people."**

replies, "Yes, ma'am . . . but I get nervous if I start worrying about time." Whereas Mrs. Ellsworth worries about time—in this case Oceola's—as if it were her own, Oceola prefers not to do so, electing to concentrate on doing things as they can be done, on living more immediately, and on flowing with her life rather than flooding it nervously or frantically toward some destination that would be destroyed by the deluge. Art, then, takes its place in a continuum rather than existing outside of or over it, and takes its character from a continuum as well. The concept of pure art is totally alien to Oceola's aesthetic system. Like the idea of a "pure" race, which is very likely at least partially behind Mrs. Ellsworth's retreat from contemporary life, pure art in Mrs. Ellsworth's case is the creation of a master mentality that is in many ways afraid of both Oceola's reality and itself.

And pure art has nothing to do, Mrs. Ellsworth believes, with syncopation, blues, jazz, or spirituals. She is decidedly not a modernist where music is concerned. For her, art must have a certain dignity and propriety of her own definition, and clearly African-American music didn't have them. The selections that Oceola played for Mrs. Ellsworth at their first audience reflected Oceola's interests: the Rakhmaninov *Prelude in C Sharp Minor*, with its melancholy and nostalgia, possesses at times a blues-like sadness; the Liszt *Etudes*, from the pen of the greatest piano virtuoso of his time, reflect his imaginative and technical advances; Ravel's *Pavanne Pour Une Enfante Defunte* demonstrates one of Ravel's lifelong sympathies with the ancient, exotic worlds and experiences of children and animals; and Handy's "St. Louis Blues," which Ellsworth would have grudgingly granted as a concession to

Oceola's background and inexperience, demonstrates the popular possibilities for folk material of African Americans. Oceola demonstrates through her selections not only her virtuosity but also her respect for imagination and innovation. Ravel himself, in fact, produced a jazz-like syncopation in *Concerto for the Left Hand*, and a G-Major piano concerto that was touched by jazz as well. It is certainly ironic that Mrs. Ellsworth is impressed by the works of classical composers like Ravel, who flirted with jazz, and with their innovations and independence, but is herself unable to break through and accept the achievements and possibilities of jazz the way Milhaud, Gershwin, Ives, and Stravinsky could. But then, she needs the cloak of respectability wrapped around what she likes, and that cloak is for her necessarily made of a heavy European fiber.

Of course, it is significant that Oceola is a pianist, since the piano is one of the few instruments that women were encouraged or allowed to play at the time. Linda Dahl [in *Stormy Weather: The Music and Lives of a Century of Jazz Women*, 1984] discussed its importance as an artistic, but not an economic, outlet for women:

> The piano is one of the few instruments that seem more or less free of sex stereotypes to the extent that it does carry unconscious gender associations. Those associations deliver an ambiguous message. On the one hand, for example, Jelly Roll Morton recalled hesitating to take up piano for fear of being thought a ''sissy''; on the other hand, though playing the piano has been approved as a desirable feminine refinement, making a professional career of it was considered decidedly unladylike and was an option reserved largely for men.

Rosetta Reitz points out [in *Piano Singer's Blues: Women Accompany Themselves*, 1982] that women ''profoundly influenced many of our most distinguished male jazz pianists,'' citing the influence of Mamie Desdoumes on Jelly Roll Morton, the mothers of James P. Johnson and Willie ''the Lion'' Smith on their sons, Mazie Mullins on Fats Waller, a grade school teacher on Fletcher Henderson, and two Washington, D.C., pianists on Duke Ellington (*Piano Singer's Blues*). Indeed, during the pre-World War II period, such outstanding women pianists as Bernice Edwards, Victoria Spivey, Myrtle Jenkins, Louise Johnson, Georgia White, Gladys Bentley, and Hociel Thomas recorded as featured artists or accompanists, demonstrating that there were women who plied their talents as pianists either as a career or an avocation; and a pianist in the sacred field, the great Arizona Dranes of the Church of God in Christ, was just one of many women

whose pianistic skill graced the church services and recordings of multitudes of African-American churches. Hughes's choice, then, of the piano as an instrument for Oceola is entirely within the reality of the acceptability of the piano as an option available to women in both non-professional and sometimes professional areas. Playing the piano allowed Oceola to express a part of her personality that might otherwise have been repressed or gone unexplored.

From the very first words of the story, Hughes emphasizes the importance of possessing an identity, opening with the name of the woman who is the primary force of the story. Her name is important in that through it Hughes is able to provide some subtle characterization. Linda Dahl reports in *Stormy Weather* that Mary Lou Williams remembered a pianist named Oceola playing in Kansas City, and Hughes may have been familiar with that performer, though he mentions her nowhere else in his autobiographical writings. It is likely that the use of that name stems from Hughes's familiarity with the historical figure for whom nineteen towns, plus various counties, streets, a Navy destroyer, and a mountain have been named: Osceola, the famous chief of the Seminole tribe in the Second Seminole War. [According to John K. Mahon in *Dictionary of Afro-American Slavery*, 1988], the Seminoles counted among their tribe, friends, and allies a rather large element of African American ex-slaves who had fled largely from the abuses of the South Carolinians and felt a kinship with the Seminoles, who also not only had suffered similar abuses, but also possessed ''religious, ceremonial, governmental, and mythical similarities'' that had parallels to the African heritage of the slaves. Those African Americans who were slaves to the Native Americans were in fact more like feudal vassals than chattel slaves, and the combination of the runaway slave problem and the relatively better treatment at the hands of the Native American masters was enough to provoke the U.S. government into declaring war on the Seminoles twice, once in 1817–18 and again in 1835–42. It was during the second war that Osceola rose to prominence because of his success in battle.

Osceola's name lends a number of associations to Hughes's character in the story. It strengthens, on one hand, the autobiographical elements of the story, given that in real life the first love of Hughes's patron Charlotte Mason was Indians, suggesting that in her interest in Oceola Mrs. Ellsworth has a parallel to the lover of primitives in Hughes's life. More important are a number of pertinent facts related to the historical figure. Although most sources report that the name ''Asi-Yahola'' means ''black drink singer,'' referring to a ceremonial drink, Charles B. Cory reported in 1896 that the name signified ''rising sun,'' and Oceola is certainly that. Not only is she, for Mrs. Ellsworth, at the beginning of a great career, ready to be polished and finished, as Ormond Hunter notes, like new furniture, she is also a youthful choir director and rent party pianist who loves her neighbors and neighborhood and seeks to warm her community with the heart of its own technique and passion. The Seminole chief, though, was noted for his fighting, his bravery in battle, and his war whoop—especially remarked [upon] by several commentators—which is in stark contrast to the much more subtle, calm rebellion of the female Oceola Jones.

Oceola Jones *wonders* at Mrs. Ellsworth's generosity; merely sidesteps Mrs. Ellsworth's question about the location of her biological father (on the heels of a discussion of how big Billy Kersands's mouth was, it is hard not to think about how big Ellsworth's mouth is here); politely refuses Ellsworth's first attempt to extricate her from Harlem, though she ultimately does move; puzzles over the arguments that fellow students have at the Left Bank concerning art; and patiently resists Mrs. Ellsworth's attempts to separate her and Pete. Oceola is, indeed, constantly under siege, captured for a time under the white flag of truce, like the chief was, but ultimately escaping by simply walking away— unlike the chief, who died in captivity. What is admirable about Oceola in this story is that she has the strength *not* to whoop, not to insult, not to say ''none of your nasty business, white woman,'' not to strike out; but to state calmly her objectives and desires, to try various opportunities, to resist gently those directives with which she disagrees, and to walk away richer and with dignity without having compromised her integrity. She is self-assured, comfortable and happy with her culture and her abilities, and is thus not defensive about Ellsworth's intrusions into her private life or attitudes about her people. Her war, then, has been won in her own mind, and her confrontation with the enemy, Ellsworth (who had been informed of Oceola's presence by the great white hunter, Ormond), is a victory without bloodshed, but a victory nonetheless. The Seminole chief's victory was only a partial and posthumous one; later much romanticized and mythologized, buried with military honors, the subject of poems, plays and novels, he took on an heroic stature in American popular culture that living

Native Americans might not enjoy. Most of Osceola's people were removed from their land, and Osceola died in captivity, though not without taking 1500 of the enemy and twenty million dollars in U.S. war expenses with him. Oceola Jones winds up on the verge of being married, and to return to live among ''her people,'' with two years of professional training to her credit, and a feeling of calm with herself.

Oceola Jones's victory comes about because she refuses to let Mrs. Ellsworth define her. The opening lines of the story, with their clipped cadence and bloodless tones, reflect Ellsworth's aesthetic:

> Oceola Jones, pianist, studied under Philippe in Paris.
> Mrs. Dora Ellsworth paid her bills. The bills included
> a little apartment on the Left Bank and a grand piano.

The sentences are very neat, economical, and passionless. Oceola is a pianist, nothing more—that is enough. She studies in the ''correct'' location with the ''correct'' person, and is significantly described as being ''under'' him, subjugated to his aesthetic values; she has an economic arrangement that removes her from the mundane worries of daily life; and she is allowed for that life only a ''little'' apartment, while for her art she is supplied with something ''grand.'' At this time Oceola is not the sole beneficiary of Mrs. Ellsworth's attention. Mrs. Ellsworth is also seeking to be the patron of the significantly-named Antonio Bas, whose surname evokes associations with bas-relief, sculpture carved in a flat surface so that the figures are only slightly three dimensional. As in Shaw's *Pygmalion*, Ellsworth seeks to take the rough base and mold it in her image of what it could or ought to be; and Ellsworth wants the figure to be only slightly three dimensional, always compliant with her wishes. Bas, in fact, ends up with Mrs. Ellsworth at the conclusion of the story when the Oceola-Ellsworth relationship deteriorates, most likely because of his acquiescence rather than any special genius he might have. Mrs. Ellsworth had, after all, once dismissed a soprano because she smelled like garlic, living ''to regret bitterly her lack of musical acumen in the face of garlic'' when the soprano later became a great success.

But Oceola avoids the Ellsworth ambush and maintains her own identity independent of Ellsworth's vision of what Oceola is or ought to be. Oceola tells Mrs. Ellsworth what she needs to know about her past and family—no more—calmly reports her devotion and aid to Pete, sacrifices at one point her technical progress for Pete's benefit, and laments at one point ''I've been away from my people so long . . . I want to live right in the middle of them again.'' She prefers, we might say, being in bed with Pete to being in bed with Mrs. Ellsworth. Mrs. Ellsworth would characterize the preference as being for the pleasures of the body over the pleasures of the mind, an avoidance, perhaps, of her own sublimated sexual attraction to ''the electric strength of that brown-black body beside her.''

Oceola would not employ that characterization. At their parting audience, just as Mrs. Ellsworth begins to express her fears about men, Oceola plays the blues, described by Hughes in blatantly sexual terms. It starts as a sensuous slow blues of seductively wandering fingers and ''soft and lazy syncopation,'' building to a more rollicking and driving passion, climaxing with an ''earth-throbbing rhythm that shook the lilies in the Persian vases of Mrs. Ellsworth's music room,'' returning to the slow and sensuous denouement of the blues with which she began. In Oceola's microcosmic and artistic drama, which drowns out the voice, the imperatives, of Mrs. Ellsworth and her aesthetic, we see the playing out of Oceola's own aesthetic. While Mrs. Ellsworth continues to try to define Oceola's artistry in economic terms—''Is this what I spent thousands of dollars to teach you?''— Oceola emphasizes the blues as a marriage of intellectual, technical, and personal emotional impulses, a unified approach that does not compartmentalize or deny anything about her life, but builds from it, moves to its feel, swells to its height, and always returns to what is most elemental and honest about it. It is a protean force, not fixed or static in Persian vases removed from Nature to adorn in an artificial environment, but emotionally complex and broadranging. ''These are the blues . . . I'm playing,'' Oceola announces, and she means that statement two ways: she is playing the blues, and now *she* is playing, from herself.

Interestingly, Hughes makes it clear that the music has a voice of its own, a message it delivers. After the first and before the last line of the message, Hughes includes the words ''sang the blues'' to indicate that indeed it communicates by virtue of what it is, from what tradition it comes. Rather than letting the blues act as a means of separation and unproductivity, as Mrs. Ellsworth does, Oceola fuses her sadness and hope into a work of art that affirms humanity and self pride. After all, the bass notes are said to throb like ''tom-toms,'' suggesting that the blues recall what Hughes saw as the ancient and earthy power of her African ancestors. Thus, historically, geographically, intellectually, emotional-

ly, sexually, and artistically, the blues is represented as being both unifying and useful. Mrs. Ellsworth's response to the song doesn't make much sense practically. ''If I could holler,'' the song begins; Mrs. Ellsworth responds that she would stand looking. In her hands (or rather mouth), the lyric's emotional construction is undercut by an unfulfilling delivery: if one can holler, why does one merely *look*? Why mention the ability to holler if in fact one has no intention of doing so? It is because she is an observer, not a creator, and someone unused to being enough in touch with herself and the meaning of her life to consider it worthy of individual, personal artistic expression. Quite appropriately, the line she supplies, ''And I . . . would stand looking at the stars,'' violates the true words lyric not only in spirit, but in form. Mrs. Ellsworth's line doesn't rhyme, as do the lines of the song, probably taken from Leroy Carr's version of ''How Long How Long Blues'' as performed by Carr or someone like Jimmy Rushing. Her line is clearly decontextualized, underscoring how foreign the tradition and the spirit are to Mrs. Ellsworth.

Mrs. Ellsworth has the last word in Hughes's story, but one has to wonder, as the song asks: how long she'll have it, or how long blacks will have to suffer it.

Her speech seems little more than broken wind as she delivers her final words. The ''stars in her eyes'' prevent her from realizing that she is doomed to remoteness from the object of her admiration: her sense of what she and others ought to be. ''How long has that evening train been gone?'' the song asks. Mrs. Ellsworth didn't even know that darkness had fallen long before Oceola, having bought a railroad of her own, rode off on her own track.

Source: Steven C. Tracy, ''Blues to Live by: Langston Hughes's 'The Blues I'm Playing,''' in *The Langston Hughes Review*, Vol. XII, No. 1, 1993, pp. 12–18.

Robert Bone

In the following excerpt, Bone discusses the conflict between Oceola Jones and Dora Ellsworth and the significance of the blues to the story.

[T]he complex vision of the blues, even as it balances the claims of hope and disillusionment, absorbs both attitudes in a higher synthesis. The blues, as Richard Kostelanetz has remarked, is a ''tightly organized lyric form in which the singer narrates the reasons for his sadness, usually attributed to his failure to attain the ideal role he conceives for himself.'' The blues are born, in short, out of the inexorable tension of dream and actuality. By mediating poetically between the two, the form itself makes possible a bittersweet and retrospective triumph over pain.

The centerpiece of *The Ways of White Folk* is ''The Blues I'm Playing.'' This story is a fictional account of Hughes's relationship with [his former patron], Mrs. Mason. The black heroine, Oceola Jones, is a gifted young pianist equally at home in the jazz or classical tradition. Her white antagonist, Mrs. Dora Ellsworth, is a rich and aging patron of the arts. The plot traces the successive stages of their relationship: discovery and sponsorship; increasing efforts to dominate not only the musical career, but the private life of her protegee; a crisis following the girl's announcement of her impending marriage; and eventual estrangement, after a painful, parting interview.

The dramatic conflict centers on the girl's stubborn effort to preserve her black identity in the face of her patron's determined onslaught. Mrs. Ellsworth looks on Oceola as a kind of refractory material that resists cultivation or refinement. She is in short a missionary. Mrs. Ellsworth embodies that Faustian urge toward total possession of another human being which informs so much of the short fiction of Edgar Allan Poe. This is the urge responsible for slavery and other forms of European empire. Oceola fights with all her strength to fend it off, and to establish her life on an independent footing.

''The Blues I'm Playing'' is at once an arraignment of Western culture and an affirmation of Negro folk forms. The classical and jazz idioms, which compete for Oceola's loyalty, give dramatic substance to the theme of cultural dualism which is basic to the Harlem Renaissance. In the sexual sphere, conflicting codes divide the two women. Oceola has a lover she is helping through medical school, and whom she ultimately marries. Mrs. Ellsworth hopes that she will learn to sublimate her sexual desires through art. An irreconcilable conflict thus unfolds between the Platonist and transcendental values of the patron (symbolized by her aspiration toward the stars) and the earthy, down-home folk morality of her protegee.

A sublimated sexuality implies a disembodied art. Through Mrs. Ellsworth, Hughes is satirizing the otherworldly strain in Western art. He decries the separation of art from life, and the transcendental impulse to resolve all human contradictions in the vastness of eternity. Through Oceola's music,

on the other hand, Hughes defines his own esthetic. Hers is an art grounded in folk sources, steeped in sensuality, and based on the life-affirming rhythms of the blues. It is a music close to dance, full of movement and expression, vibrant with the joy and pain of living. The blues is an art of paradox and ambiguity, and it is through this form that Langston Hughes has chosen to express his complex sense of life.

In the end, Hughes resorts to a satiric image. The final scene takes place in Mrs. Ellsworth's music room, whose decor is dominated by a row of Persian vases filled with white lilies. As Oceola entertains her patron for the last time, she breaks into a jazz rhythm that shakes the long-stemmed flowers in their rootlessness and artificial isolation: ''Mrs. Ellsworth sat very still in her chair looking at the lilies trembling delicately in the priceless Persian vases, while Oceola made the bass notes throb like tomtoms deep in the earth.''

Source: Robert Bone, ''The Ways of White Folks,'' in his *Down Home: A History of Afro-American Short Fiction from Its Beginnings to the End of the Harlem Renaissance*, G. P. Putnam's Sons, 1975, pp. 254–60.

Sources

Bruck, Peter. ''Langston Hughes: 'The Blues I'm Playing,''' in *The Black American Short Story in the 20th Century*, B. R. Gruener Publishing, 1977, pp. 71-84.

Patterson, Linda. Quoted in ''(James) Langston Hughes,'' in *Contemporary Authors Online*, The Gale Group, 1999.

Ostrom, Hans. ''The Ways of White Folks,'' in his *Langston Hughes: A Study of the Short Fiction*, New York: Twayne Publishers, 1993.

Further Reading

Emanuel, James A. *Langston Hughes*, New York: Twayne Publishers, 1967.
    An authoritative, early study of ''The Blues I'm Playing'' that analyzes the story in terms of thematics.

Gates, Henry Louis, Jr. *The Signifying Monkey*, Oxford University Press, 1988.
    A landmark study of African-American fiction that demonstrates the influence of African tradition and folklore on ''The Blues I'm Playing.''

The Canterville Ghost

Oscar Wilde

1887

"The Canterville Ghost" was first published serially in 1887 in *Court and Society Review*, a magazine for the leisured upper classes. The story did not immediately receive much critical attention, and indeed Wilde was not viewed as an important author until the publication, during the 1890s, of his novel *The Picture of Dorian Gray* (1891) and of several well-received plays, including *The Importance of Being Earnest* (1895). In 1891, "The Canterville Ghost" was republished in *Lord Arthur Savile's Crime, and Other Stories.*

The collected stories were severely criticized by contemporary reviewers; early critics found Wilde's work unoriginal and derivative. More recently critics have celebrated Wilde's ability to play with the conventions of many genres. In "The Canterville Ghost," Wilde draws upon fairy tales, Gothic novels, and stories of Americans abroad to shape his comic ghost story. Though Wilde offers a comic treatment, he finds inspiration for Sir Simon's character in Alfred Tennyson's serious poem "Maud," as well as in the Romantic poet Samuel Taylor Coleridge's "Christabel." Critics also point to the possible influence of Henry James's *Portrait of a Lady* (1881) on "The Canterville Ghost."

Wilde used a myriad of comic sources to shape his story. Thomas De Quincey's "Murder Considered as One of the Fine Arts," a satirical essay, is one apparent source. Wilde would also have been aware of Jane Austen's *Northanger Abbey* (1818), a

parody of the Gothic novel so popular in the early nineteenth century. Finally, Wilde's own experience on the lecture circuit in the United States undoubtedly helped him ridicule stereotypical American behavior. Indeed, one of the major themes in the story is the culture clash between a sixteenth-century English ghost and a late nineteenth-century American family. But the story also examines the disparity between the public self and the private self, a theme to which Wilde would return again in his later writings.

Author Biography

An important figure in the literary Decadence movement, a literary movement that challenged Victorian standards at the end of the nineteenth century, Oscar Wilde lived a life that shocked conventional standards and eventually led to the dismissal of much of his work. Born in Dublin, Ireland, in 1854, he was the son of William Wilde (later knighted), a surgeon, and Jane Francesca Elgee, a writer who used the pseudonym Speranza. Wilde attended both Trinity College in Dublin and Oxford University, and later settled in London. Influenced by the English writer, Walter Pater, Wilde embarked on a literary career and published *Poems* in 1881.

He married Constance Lloyd, a wealthy Dubliner, in 1884, and they had two children, Cyril and Vyvyan Holland. As the editor of *Woman's World*, Wilde espoused the values of aestheticism and his belief in "life for art's sake." His wardrobe included green carnation buttonholes and velvet knee breeches; not surprisingly, his attire attracted both followers and parody. Most notably, in 1881 Gilbert and Sullivan wrote *Patience*, a comic opera that ridiculed both the aesthetic movement and Wilde.

Wilde's work enjoyed a great deal of critical success from 1888 to 1895, when he published his only novel *The Picture of Dorian Gray* (1891) and his popular plays: *Lady Windermere's Fan* (1892), *A Woman of No Importance* (1893), *An Ideal Husband* (1895), and *The Importance of Being Earnest* (1895). These plays satired contemporary high society and treated potentially serious issues with wit and humor.

Wilde's world exploded at the height of his popularity. Beginning in 1886, Wilde was involved in homosexual relationships, first with Robert Ross, and later (and more disastrously) with Lord Alfred

Douglas, a poet. When the Marquis of Queensberry, Lord Alfred's father, accused Wilde of homosexuality in 1895, Wilde denied the charge and sued for libel. Not only did Wilde lose the libel suit, he was arrested and sentenced to two years hard labor for "gross indecency between male persons." The scandal destroyed Wilde's reputation and health. Though he produced serious poems, collected in *The Ballad of Reading Gaol* (1898) as well as an essay confession *De Profundis* (1905) while in prison, Wilde did not write after his release. Divorced and bankrupt, Wilde wandered through Europe under the assumed name Sebastian Melmoth until his death in Paris in 1900.

Plot Summary

Purchasing Canterville Chase

As the story opens, Horace B. Otis, the brusque American minister, ignores the warnings of several English friends and buys the haunted Canterville Chase. Lord Canterville desires to sell the home but feels honor-bound to tell Otis stories of skeleton hands and mysterious noises. However, Otis refuses to believe in the existence of ghosts.

The Persistent Blood Stain

The Otis family moves into the Chase, a Tudor mansion. Mrs. Lucretia Otis, disturbed by a blood stain in the sitting-room, orders that it be removed at once. But the housekeeper, Mrs. Umney, explains that the blood stain dates back to 1575, the day Lady Eleanore de Canterville was murdered by her husband, Sir Simon, and cannot be removed. Washington Otis, the oldest son, quickly declares that Pinkerton's Champion Stain Remover and Paragon Detergent will prove a match for even so historic a stain. Before the housekeeper can stop him, Washington drops to his knees and scrubs out the blood. Thunder and lightening greet his success, and Mrs. Umney faints in fear. The stain, however, reappears the following morning, and again Pinkerton's is applied. But each successive morning brings a new stain, and the Otises begin to believe that the Chase really is haunted.

The Ghost Appears

Several nights later, Mr. Otis awakes to the sound of clanking metal. In the hallway, he encoun-

Oscar Wilde

and begins to use Mr. Otis's Rising Sun Lubricator. The twins continue to torment the Ghost, setting traps along the corridor to trip him. The Ghost, in one final effort, prepares an elaborate costume, "Reckless Rupert, or the headless Earl," to revenge himself on the twins. When he tries to enter the twins' bedroom, a jug of water crashes down on him, leaving Sir Simon with a severe cold and no hope of scaring the Otises.

Virginia Otis and the Canterville Ghost

As the Ghost dreams of his past glory, the Otis family carries on with their normal pursuits. The young Duke of Cheshire, madly in love with Virginia, arrives as a guest. One day after riding with the Duke, Virginia stumbles upon the Ghost's hiding place. Pitying him, Virginia entreats Sir Simon to behave himself. But, in a well-known passage, the Ghost replies:

> "It is absurd asking me to behave myself," he answered, looking around in astonishment at the pretty little girl who had ventured to address him, "quite absurd. I must rattle my chains, and groan through keyholes, and walk about at night. . . . It is my only reason for existing."
>
> "It is no reason at all for existing, and you know you have been very wicked. Mrs. Umney told us, the first day we arrived here, that you had killed your wife."
>
> "Well, I quite admit it," said the Ghost petulantly, "but it was a purely family matter, and concerned no one else."
>
> "It is very wrong to kill any one," said Virginia, who at times had a sweet Puritan gravity, caught from some old New England ancestor.
>
> "Oh, I hate the cheap severity of abstract ethics! My wife was very plain, never had my ruffs properly starched, and knew nothing about cookery. Why, there was a buck I had shot in Hogley Woods, a magnificent pricket, and do you know how she had it sent up to table? However, it is no matter now, for it is all over, and I don't think it was very nice of her brothers to starve me to death, though I did kill her."
> (Excerpt from "The Canterville Ghost")

Though she berates him for stealing her paints to refurbish the blood stain, this exchange marks the beginning of Virginia's sympathy for the Ghost. Virginia offers to help the Ghost emigrate to America. He declines claiming that all he wants is to sleep in the Garden of Death. Sir Simon asks Virginia to pray for his soul, so that he can finally rest. Despite the pleas of the huntsmen embroidered on the tapestry and the gargoyles carved on the chimney-piece, Virginia takes the Ghost's hand and follows him into another dimension.

ters a ghost with burning-red eyes, matted hair, and heavy chains. As a practical American, Mr. Otis suggests to the Ghost that Tammany Rising Sun Lubricator will quiet his chains. The Ghost, stunned by this effrontery, is further insulted as the young Otis twin boys throw pillows at his head. The Ghost retires to his chamber and ponders his past glories of terrifying housemaids and driving members of the aristocracy to madness and suicide. Refusing to be intimidated by upstart Americans, the Ghost plans his revenge. Meanwhile, the Otises discuss the Ghost and note the changing hues of the sitting-room bloodstain. Only the beautiful fifteen-year-old Virginia Otis cannot laugh as the stain mutates from red, to purple, to bright emerald green. When the Ghost next appears, the twins shoot pellets at it. But more insulting is that after the Ghost tries to scare the family with a hideous laugh, Mrs. Otis offers him Dr. Dobell's tincture to cure his indigestion.

Sickened by the experience, Sir Simon retreats for a few days before making another attempt to horrify the Otises. However, when the Ghost next appears, it is he who is frightened. The twins create a fake ghost out of a hollow turnip, bed curtain, kitchen cleaver, and broom. Their trick succeeds, and Sir Simon, humiliated, gives up on his bloodstain

Virginia Lost and Found

Virginia's family and the Duke search for her. At the last stroke of midnight, the house shakes, and Virginia appears at the top of the stairs. She explains that she has been with the Ghost and has brought him eternal rest. Sir Simon, in turn, has given her a box of jewels. Virginia leads her family into a secret room where they find the skeletal remains of Sir Simon. Four days later, Sir Simon, with much ceremony, is buried. A few years later, Virginia marries the young Duke, who was struck by her kindness to the Ghost. Even after marriage, however, Virginia resists her husband's entreaties and refuses to reveal what happened when she disappeared into the wall with Sir Simon. But she states simply that the Ghost taught her the meaning of Life, Death, and Love.

Characters

Sir Simon Canterville

See Ghost

Cecil

See Duke of Cheshire

Duke of Cheshire

Desperately in love with the fifteen-year old Virginia Otis, the boyish Duke of Cheshire proposes after watching her win a pony race. However, his guardians pack him off to Eton, and he must wait to marry. But his impetuousness cannot be quelled. When Virginia vanishes, he insists on being part of the search party. As soon as she reappears, he smothers her with kisses. His devotion is rewarded, and Virginia consents to become the Duchess of Cheshire.

Ghost

The Ghost, or Sir Simon Canterville, has haunted Canterville Chase since he was starved to death in 1584 by his dead wife's brothers. They murdered him because he had murdered his wife for the trivial reasons that she was plain and a bad housekeeper. For three hundred years, Sir Simon has frightened the inhabitants of Canterville Chase and has relished his role as resident ghost. He has appeared as "The Headless Earl," "The Corpse-Snatcher of Chertsey Barn," and "The Blood-sucker of Bexley

Media Adaptations

- "The Canterville Ghost" was loosely adapted into a film by the same name in 1944. In this version, set in World War II, Charles Laughton plays a cowardly ghost who meets a cowardly descendent played by Robert Young. Directed by Jules Dassin, released by MGM, the film is available from MGM/United Artists Home Entertainment.

- A 1991 production of "The Canterville Ghost" from "Wonderworks" features a ghost who must haunt an old manor house until he learns to conquer his fears. Produced by Helios Productions, the film is available through Public Media Video.

- An animated version was produced in 1986 by Orkin-Flaum Productions.

- NBC broadcast *The Canterville Ghost*, adapted for television by Bell System Family Theatre, in 1975.

- Patrick Stewart stars as Sir Simon, and Neve Campbell as Virginia in the 1996 Hallmark production of *The Canterville Ghost*, directed by Syd Macartney.

- *The Saturday Evening Ghost* was the title of a 1936 stage adaptation by Samuel French.

- Darwin R. Payne wrote a 1963 stage version of "The Canterville Ghost."

Moor" as well as other incarnations. However, when the rational American Otises arrive, the Ghost realizes that his audience does not appreciate his performance. No matter what he tries, he cannot frighten the Otis family. Weary and despairing, Sir Simon begs Virginia Otis to pray for him so that he can finally achieve eternal rest. Initially the butt of the twins's pranks and an annoyance to the practical Otises, the Ghost becomes an object of sympathy. Before he goes quietly to his grave, he gives Virginia a box of priceless jewels.

Mr. Horace B. Otis

The boisterous head of the Otis family, Mr. Otis first dismisses tales of a ghost in his newly purchased English house, arguing that the modern country of America has already bought up anything of value from the Old World. Sir Simon is stunned when Mr. Otis demands that the ghost use Tammany Rising Sun Lubricator to quiet his haunting chains so that the family may get some sleep. Mr. Otis is a calm man who scolds the twin Otis boys for throwing pillows at the ghost, and then reasons that if the ghost will not use the lubricator, the family will take away his chains. Mr. Otis leads the search for the missing Virginia and eventually consents to letting her marry into the aristocracy.

Mrs. Lucretia Tappan Otis

The spirited matriarch of the Otis clan, Mrs. Lucretia Tappan Otis, a former New York beauty, is renowned for her "superb profile." Sir Simon views her as a gross materialist because she offers him Dr. Dobell's tincture for indigestion; she has misunderstood his ghostly laugh as a sign of a medical disorder. Generally undisturbed by the Ghost's performances, Mrs. Otis introduces her neighbors to such American pleasures as clambakes. Except for understandable anxiety at Virginia's disappearance, Mrs. Otis possesses a "really wonderful amount of animal spirits."

Virginia Otis

Virginia Otis, the somewhat puritanical, beautiful fifteen-year old daughter of the American Minister, has already inspired the love of the young Duke of Cheshire as the story begins. In the first part of the story, the reader does not learn much about Virginia's personality. She hangs back as the rest of her family either plots against the Ghost or attempts to cure him of his clanking chains and scratchy voice. When Virginia encounters Sir Simon, she pities him and tries to help the weary spirit. Sir Simon tells her that if she prays for him, he will finally gain eternal rest. She bravely takes his hand and, ignoring warning voices, follows him into another dimension. Later, Virginia marries the young Duke. Her husband entreats her to tell him what happened the fateful night with the Ghost, but she refuses. Virginia asserts, though, that she is grateful to Sir Simon, for he taught her that Love is stronger than both Death and Life.

Stars and Stripes

See Twins

Twins

The youngest children of the Otis family, the twins are wild hooligans. They throw pillows at the ghostly Sir Simon's head, hit him with their peashooters, and throw nuts along the corridor in an effort to trip the Ghost. Irrepressible, the twins achieve their greatest triumph when they create their own ghost from a hollowed-out turnip, a bed curtain, and a kitchen cleaver. Their constant pranks leave Sir Simon shaken, as his every plan for revenge is thwarted by the twins's efforts.

Themes

Culture Clash

From the beginning of "The Canterville Ghost," Wilde compares the behavior of the American Otises with that of the British upper classes. Lord Canterville warns Mr. Horace B. Otis that the presence of a ghost has made Canterville Chase uninhabitable. Mr. Otis, however, remains a skeptic. If there were any ghosts in Europe, he reasons, Americans would have bought them along with all that is old and venerable in Europe. Europe is for sale, and Americans are buying, which is why the Otises can purchase Canterville Chase in the first place.

Even the Otises, who espouse American superiority, cannot deny the Ghost's existence after he appears to them in chains. But the Ghost, who has been scaring the wits out of the English aristocracy for three hundred years, cannot produce a scream from a single Otis. They counter his chains with lubricant, his bloodstains with Pinkerton's detergent, and his ghostly laugh with cough syrup. As Americans, they refuse to accept the dismal English weather, much less a noisy ghost.

In many ways, the Ghost represents all that is rotten and decaying in Europe. A murderer, he relishes choosing identities that will provoke particular horror in his victims. His many costume changes, from "The Headless Earl" to "The Bloodsucker of Bexley Moor," reveal his underlying shallowness. The Ghost plays a part, but there is no substance to him, or for that matter to the class he represents. Pitting the New World against the old, the Otises and their can-do attitude shake up tradition.

Aesthetics

The Otises do not understand the aesthetics of the Ghost. Mr. Otis believes that bad English weather is due to overcrowding, that there is not enough

Topics for Further Study

- Investigate the Society for Psychical Research, founded in 1882. You may want to consult the *Journal of the Society for Psychical Research*; the *Journal of the American Society for Psychical Research*; *The Founders of Psychical Research*, by A. Gauld (1968); or *Psychical Research: A Guide to its History, Principles and Practices*, edited by I. Grattan-Guinness (1982). Who were the "ghostbusters" of the Victorian era? How widespread was the belief in ghosts? Compare real life attitudes to ghosts to the attitudes held by the characters in "The Canterville Ghost."

- Research the Aesthetic Movement, also known as the Decadent Movement. You may want to consult literary anthologies as well as the following books: Elizabeth Aslin's *The Aesthetic Movement: Prelude to Art Nouveau* (Frederick A. Praeger, 1969); *Aesthetes and Decadents of the 1890s: An Anthology of British Poetry and Prose* (Vintage Books: 1966), edited by Karl Beckson; and *The "Yellow Book": Quintessence of the Nineties* (Anchor Books, 1964), edited by Stan-

ley Weintraub. What were the goals of this movement? What did the artists and authors involved believe? How does "The Canterville Ghost" fit into this movement?

- The Otis family uses "Pinkerton's Champion Stain Remover and Paragon Detergent" to remove the Ghost's blood stains, and offers "Tammany Rising Sun Lubricator" and "Dr. Dobell's Tincture" for the ghost's various ailments. How were such products marketed in the late nineteenth century? Consult sources such as newspapers from the 1890s, Sear's catalogs from that time, or books such as *Selling Culture: Magazines, Markets, and Class at the Turn of the Century*, by Richard Ohmann (1996); *Soap, Sex, and Cigarettes: A Cultural History of American Advertising*, by Juliann Sivulka (1997); or *Early American Advertising* by Bob Perlongo (1985). Compare advertisements for other nineteenth-century miracle medicines and cleansers to the Otis family's claims for their products' effectiveness.

---

good weather to go around. But he fails to make the connection between crashing thunder and lightening and a haunted, Gothic mansion. Likewise, when Mr. Otis offers Sir Simon (the Ghost) Tammany Rising Sun Lubricator to oil his chains, Mr. Otis fails to appreciate the ghostliness of clanking metal. Sir Simon's artistry, be it his laugh or his chains, is overlooked by the Otises, who see the Ghost's attributes as problems to be solved.

But Sir Simon is a careful artist who longs for an understanding audience. Virginia Otis, the fifteen-year old daughter of the Minister, is also an artist. However, she longs to paint sunsets, and, as the Ghost has stolen her bright colors to refurbish his bloodstain, she is compelled to paint gloomy midnight scenes. Thus she enters into the Ghost's aesthetics and eventually follows him (tem-

porarily) into his world. Decadence lies behind the Ghost's artistry; he seeks no moral objective other than perfecting his art. Wilde, one of the English Decadents, believed in "art for art's sake," much like Sir Simon.

Atonement and Forgiveness

While the Ghost's aesthetics and the culture clash between Americans and the British are treated comically in the story, the theme of atonement and forgiveness takes on a more serious tone. When Sir Simon first begins to speak with Virginia, he feels more victim than victimizer. After all, he has only murdered his wife, an ugly woman and a bad cook, while the Otis clan humiliates him at every turn. Virginia will not accept his version of events, but eventually pities him.

Sir Simon has not been able to sleep since his wife's brothers starved him to death three hundred years before. He seeks peace, but cannot find it on his own. Virginia must pray for him if he is ever truly to rest. By forgiving the Ghost, Virginia can fulfill the prophecy: "When a golden girl can win / Prayer from out the lips of sin, / When the barren almond bears, / And a little child gives away its tears, / Then shall all the house be still / And Peace come to Canterville." Pure of heart and unafraid in her innocence, Virginia consents to help the Ghost.

In doing so, Virginia also reconciles American and British values. She has accepted the tradition of the Ghost and melds it with her American sense of hope for a better future. She is rewarded with a casket of valuable jewels and, eventually, marriage to the young Duke of Cheshire. In Virginia, Wilde creates a fairy-tale princess who, open to both past and present, can atone for ancient sins and represent a hopeful future.

Style

Setting

"The Canterville Ghost" is set in the English countryside in the late nineteenth century. Canterville Chase, where most of the story takes place, is described in Gothic terms. It is an old mansion with secret rooms and passageways, long corridors, carved gargoyles, stained glass windows, and oak paneling. Portraits of long-dead Canterville ancestors, ancient tapestries, and a suit of armor add to the medieval-like setting. Frequent thunder and lightning storms also contribute to the gloomy atmosphere. In short, Canterville Chase seems to fit the stereotype of a haunted house.

Stereotypes

Oscar Wilde explores several stereotypes in the story. Canterville Chase boasts the comic book attributes of a haunted house and would be immediately recognized as such by its contemporary audience. Similarly Mr. Horace B. Otis, as an outspoken republican who rejects European ascendancy and believes in the power of the American dollar, represents another stereotype. He and his family discuss the superiority of all things American, from accents to actresses. The Otises also embrace scientific rationalism and believe in the solutions promised by "Pinkerton's Champion Stain Remover and Paragon Detergent" and "Tammany Rising Sun Lubricator."

Young Virginia Otis is described as a Puritan believing in the simple differences between right and wrong. American forthrightness is contrasted to the decadence and decrepitude of an outdated English aristocracy, embodied in the Ghost, Sir Simon. Sir Simon has no morals; he murdered his wife because she was a bad cook and plain. British aristocrats are seen as stuck in familiar patterns. For three hundred years, generations of Cantervilles accepted the presence of a ghost and did nothing to stop the cycle of hauntings. By contrast, the Otises scrub out blood stains and offer to oil the Ghost's creaky chains, proving that American common sense can outmatch tradition.

Fairy Tale

Oscar Wilde explored fairy tale conventions in several of his works. In "The Canterville Ghost," he introduces Virginia Otis, a fairy-tale type heroine. Critics have likened her to the princess in "The Frog Prince." In that fairy tale, the princess has to put aside her ingrained dislike of amphibians, and, in a leap of faith, kiss the frog. Similarly, Virginia must believe that there is a soul worth saving in the murderous and grisly Sir Simon. Her actions lead to a happy ending: she marries a Duke and receives a casket of valuable jewels from the Ghost.

Aestheticism and Decadence

Oscar Wilde was part of a late nineteenth-century movement known as aestheticism or decadence. Proponents of this movement believed in "art for art's sake," and sometimes in "life for art's sake." In other words, the moral purpose of both art and life is to produce beauty. Beauty is the ultimate goal. In many ways, Sir Simon, the Canterville Ghost, practices such a credo. He painstakingly assembles costumes to represent true ghostliness more perfectly. He spends all his time studying and preparing the art of horror. The Otises, however, fail to appreciate his numerous incarnations and do not see the art behind his performances. Crass materialists, the Otises destroy the Ghost's art. They scrub out his carefully maintained bloodstain and finally convince him to oil his clanking chains. As a misunderstood artist, the Ghost gains the reader's sympathy. But in many ways, Sir Simon is a parody of the very movement to which his creator belonged.

Compare & Contrast

- **1880s:** Homosexuality is considered a moral outrage and perversion punishable by jail. Homosexual relationships are hidden from societal view.

  1990s: Although homosexuality is more accepted, many states still have laws against homosexual acts. Many people consider the homosexual lifestyle as opposed to religious doctrine. Legislation to sanction gay marriages and gays in the military has failed. Many states have passed anti-discrimination laws in response to vicious hate crimes that target homosexuals.

- **1880s:** Nineteenth-century Europe and America

are enamored with such practices as phrenology, the belief that a person's character traits are apparent in the shape of his or her skull. Some Victorians also believed in Mesmerism, developed earlier in the century by Franz Anton Mesmer. He suggested the possibility of mind control through hypnosis.

1990s: The practice of alternative medicine is on the rise, as many people turn away from technological advances and the complicated health care system. Instead, they use massage techniques, yoga, acupuncture, and other techniques to address serious health issues.

Historical Context

Oscar Wilde wrote at the end of the Victorian period, named for Queen Victoria. This period marked the rise of a growing middle class in Great Britain. This middle class had gained wealth through the technological advances of the Industrial Revolution, as well as a result of Britain's expanding empire. The values of this class stood in marked contrast to the values of an older aristocracy. Members of the aristocracy had traditionally depended on land for income and were used to inheriting wealth rather than earning it. The middle class idealized the importance of the family, thrift, and hard work. However, many working-class Victorians lived in poverty and squalor. Government commissions microscopically examined the living conditions of the poor in an attempt to improve everything from sewage systems to education. Mid-Victorian novelists used their art to bring attention to the social problems of the day.

Aesthetic Backlash

Oscar Wilde was a follower of the Aesthetic—also known as the Decadent Movement—which had

developed in France and had been introduced into England in the late 1800s. The Decadents believed that beauty should be valued above all else. Believing in "art for art's sake," the Decadents shunned the social problem novels that flourished earlier in the Victorian period. As Oscar Wilde wrote in his famous preface to *The Picture of Dorian Gray*, "No artist has ethical sympathies. An ethical sympathy in an artist is an unpardonable mannerism of style." In other words, Wilde thought that moral judgments devalued the artistry of paintings and literature. Most Decadents also deviated from the moral values of their time period, experimenting with sex and drugs. Critics have noted that in "The Canterville Ghost" Sir Simon exhibits Decadent sensibilities.

Science

In "The Canterville Ghost," Mr. Horace B. Otis declares that "the laws of Nature are not going to be suspended for the British aristocracy." The nineteenth century saw many advances in science. Charles Darwin had presented his theory of evolution in *The Origin of Species* in 1859. The opening of the Natural History Museum in London in 1881 allowed for the greater spread of recent scientific knowledge. Advances were made in medicine, as vaccines were found for such diseases as rabies and anthrax. Scientists were better able to interpret the natural world as they discovered the size of atoms and the physical makeup of the sun. Also, in 1882, Viennese physician Joseph Breuer began using hypnosis to cure hysteria, marking the early beginnings of modern psychoanalysis.

Many nineteenth-century Europeans and Americans also sought answers in the more questionable sciences that flourished in their day. Phrenology, the belief that a person's character traits are apparent in the shape of his or her skull, is one example of a Victorian pseudo-science. Some Victorians also believed in Mesmerism, developed earlier in the century by Franz Anton Mesmer. He suggested the possibility of mind control through hypnosis. The Society for Psychical Research was established in 1882 to prove the existence of ghosts. Oscar Wilde refers to this society in "The Canterville Ghost." Mrs. Otis, a rational American, announces her intention of joining the society. The Otises' inability to distinguish between science and pseudo-science parodies Victorian faith in science.

Critical Overview

Even before the scandal of Wilde's trial for homosexuality and subsequent imprisonment (1895–1897), critics had a difficult time separating Wilde's life from his works. Indeed, Wilde's credo of "life for art's sake," or sometimes "art for art's sake," encouraged the comparison. Proponents of this school of thought believed that the creation of beauty is the moral purpose for both life and art. The French author Andre Gide believed that Wilde achieved artistic greatness through his life rather than his literary achievements. James Joyce, the renowned Irish novelist, saw little to appreciate in Wilde's literature, but nonetheless saw him as a martyr to art.

More recently, critics have come to appreciate the merits of Wilde's stories. Many suggest that Wilde reinvented and interpreted his life through his works. Philip Cohen, in his book *The Moral Vision of Oscar Wilde*, views Wilde's life in the 1880s reflected in "The Canterville Ghost." First, Cohen notes the coincidence of dates: "The Canterville Ghost" is set in 1884, the year Wilde married, and three hundred years after Sir Simon murdered his wife. This "correspondence of dates" marks the story as "the transformation of life into confessional art."

Cohen argues that here, as in many of his stories, Wilde "depicts a radical discrepancy between the self—or, more accurately, selves—he paraded before the public, on the one hand, and his private self, on the other." Like the Ghost, Cohen argues, Wilde suffers beneath a mask-like exterior. Wilde was hiding a homosexual relationship from public view. The Ghost, allowed to rest at the end of the story, finds forgiveness where Wilde cannot. Cohen views the trencher and ewer placed just outside the skeleton's reach as evocative of the Eucharist. Christian salvation for sin was denied Sir Simon for many years, and Wilde is likewise denied as long as he wears a mask.

Lydia Reineck Wilburn has more recently argued that the stories collected in *Lord Arthur Savile's Crime and Other Stories*, and in particular "The Canterville Ghost," should be read for more than just their moral dimensions. She shows how Wilde grapples with the idea and role of the audience in these stories—ideas he also explored in his essays. Wilde, Wilburn notes, "presents at least three contradictory stances about performance: that the audience should be ignored by the artist during the creation of his artwork, that the audience's participation in the aesthetic experience is limited to being receptive to and molded by the artist's work, and that the audience plays a major role in bringing about the aesthetic experience."

Thus, Wilburn asserts, "The Canterville Ghost" is primarily about the nature of performance. The reader should recognize the Ghost as an actor struggling, for the first time, against an unresponsive audience. The Otis family, Wilburn suggests, performs more successfully. The twins, after all, easily frighten Sir Simon with their fabricated ghost. Also, Wilburn sees more sophistication in what earlier critics may have called derivative. As Rodney Shewan argues, Wilde plays with the conventions of other genres: ghost stories, fairy tales, Gothic novels. He expects his readers to understand these references. The housekeeper, for instance, should be readily identifiable as a figure pulled from a Gothic novel. This, Wilburn argues, foregrounds the "fiction-making" of the story. However, Wilde's reliance on these references also makes him rely on his reading audience, much as the Ghost relied on

Scene from MGM's 1944 film adaptation of "The Canterville Ghost," starring Charles Laughton, Robert Young and Margaret O'Brien.

the Otises. Without an appreciative audience, the performance will fail.

A century after Wilde's trial for homosexuality, critics no longer judge his works on the basis of the morality of his personal life. However, the critics do take into account the events of his life and their influence on his work. Therefore, much is made of masks and performance in all of his literature, and "The Canterville Ghost" is no exception. Where once critics wrote it off as too frivolous and light for serious consideration, they now focus on the dark side of Wilde's comedy.

Criticism

Kimberly Lutz

Lutz is currently teaching writing at the New York University School of Continuing Education. In the following essay, she examines the importance of masks and performances in "The Canterville Ghost."

Many critics of Oscar Wilde's "The Canterville Ghost" find dark and profound meanings beneath what Philip K. Cohen calls in *The Moral Vision of Oscar Wilde* "the camouflage of hilarity." Cohen

What Do I Read Next?

- *The Turn of the Screw*, expatriate American writer Henry James's 1898 short novel, is a densely symbolic ghost story. A young governess tries to save her charges from the ghosts of Miss Jessel and Peter Quint. But do the ghosts exist only in her mind?

- An earlier Henry James novel, *The Portrait of a Lady* (1881), tells the story of Isabel Archer, an independent American woman. Her adventures in Europe demonstrate the differences between American and European society. Isabel must navigate these differences at her own risk.

- Oscar Wilde's only novel, *The Picture of Dorian Gray* (1891), examines in detail the moral problems of living a double life. The title character, despite his depravity, remains ever youthful while his portrait grotesquely ages and shows outward signs of Dorian's grave sins.

- *Northanger Abbey* (1818) is English novelist Jane Austen's parody of the Gothic genre so popular in the early eighteenth century.

- Praised by Oscar Wilde, Walter Pater's essay on William Morris's poetry, ''Aesthetic Poetry'' (1868), helped influence the Decadence movement of the late Victorian period.

- James Walvin, a contemporary historian, presents a compelling overview of the Victorians in *Victorian Values* (1987). Walvin offers a view of nineteenth-century England that cuts through recent stereotypes of this era.

---

argues that this seemingly light ghost story ''faithfully renders Wilde's life during the mid 1880s,'' a time when Wilde, by necessity was leading a double life. By 1886, he was involved in a homosexual relationship with Robert Ross and had also been married for two years. Both his marriage and the social mores of late Victorian England demanded that Wilde hide his affair.

In ''The Canterville Ghost,'' Cohen finds Wilde almost confessional, condemning the wearing of masks and the ''radical discrepancy between the self—or, more accurately, selves—he paraded before the public . . . and his private self.'' Lydia Reinbeck Wilburn in ''Oscar Wilde's 'The Canterville Ghost': The Power of an Audience,'' reads the story as a reflection of Wilde's aesthetic vision, if not his moral vision. Wilburn sees Wilde grappling with questions about the function of audience. How important is the audience to an artist? How important should an audience be? Wilburn notes that Wilde addressed similar issues in his essays and criticism. However, in ''The Canterville Ghost,'' she finds Wilde more receptive than he was in his critical works to the idea that an artist needs an appreciative audience to successfully perform. Though Wilburn and Cohen reach different conclusions in their studies, both fundamentally see ''The Canterville Ghost'' as an essay on performance and mask-wearing, and both extract a serious interpretation from the work.

That ''The Canterville Ghost'' is about masks and performance is easy to concede. The Ghost, Sir Simon, studies the art of haunting. He constantly prepares for his role as a ghost. The narrator shows him reflecting upon his past successes when first rebuffed by the Otis family: ''With the enthusiastic egotism of the true artist he went over his most celebrated performances, and smiled bitterly to himself as he recalled to mind his last appearance as the 'Red Reuben, or the Strangled Babe,' his *debut* as 'Gaunt Gideon, the Blood-sucker of Bexley Moor,' and the *furore* he had excited one lovely June evening by merely playing ninepins with his own bones upon the lawn-tennis ground.''

Sir Simon uses a theatrical vocabulary to describe his past roles. ''Debut'' and ''furore'' indicate both his performance and the audience for whom he plays. Actors debut new roles to audiences, and a furore is caused when a play is a smash hit. Even when not performing, the Ghost exhibits the stereotypical affectations of actors and dandies—men who gave exaggerated attention to their appearance. Sir Simon has created a dandyism for ghosts. This is not unlike Oscar Wilde who, adorned in velvet breeches and with a green carnation in his buttonhole presented himself as a brilliant dandy to London society. Similarly, the narrative emphasizes Sir Simon's attention to clothes: "He was simply but neatly clad in a long shroud, spotted with churchyard mould." Sir Simon pays as much attention to his gruesome attire as any dandy. Indeed, it can take the Ghost up to three hours to don an appropriate costume.

Despite the Ghost's dedication to his role, the American Otis family proves a most unreceptive audience. When the Ghost rattles his chains, Mr. Horace B. Otis suggests that Tammany Rising Sun Lubricator would stop the clanking. When the Ghost effects "his celebrated peal of demoniac laughter," Mrs. Otis offers Dr. Dobell's tincture as a cure for indigestion. Disgusted by the "gross materialism" of the Otises, Sir Simon eventually abandons his art and holes himself up in a secret room. The Ghost views his failure to scare the Otises as tragedy, and Wilburn and Cohen use his failure as a jumping off point in their criticism.

However, the comic tone of the story belies any attempt to read pathos into the Ghost's self-pity. "The Canterville Ghost" parodies actors, dandies, American materialism, aristocratic excess, ghost stories, and Gothic conventions. From the outset, the story is comic, and it disarms readers by its apparent lightness. Dialogue in "The Canterville Ghost" foreshadows the witty nonsense spoken in Wilde's later plays. Each member of the Otis family is summed up in a witty characterization that marks him or her as the subject of comedy rather than tragedy. Of Mrs. Otis, formerly Miss Lucretia R. Tappen of New York, we learn "in many respects, she was quite English, and was an excellent example of the fact that we have really everything in common with America nowadays, except, of course, language." Of the eldest son, Washington, we are told, "Gardenias and the peerage were his only weaknesses. Otherwise he was extremely sensible."

Both descriptions point to a comic theme thoroughly exploited in "The Canterville Ghost": the farcical result of the American/British culture clash. Americans in England were ridiculed for their atro-

> " The nature of performance is an important theme in Oscar Wilde's works, but the theme does not necessarily lead to serious reflection."

cious slang and peculiar accents, a point noted in the story when the Otises, with stereotypical American assumed superiority, expound on "the sweetness of the New York accent as compared to the London drawl." Likewise, despite their protestations in favor of democracy, Americans were perceived to be envious of the English aristocracy. Therefore, at the end of the tale, Virginia Otis "received the coronet," or married the Duke, which as the narrator explains, "is the reward for all good little American girls."

The story begins and ends by parodying stock characters. Comic moment succeeds comic moment throughout the narrative. Given this, how is the reader to treat a ghost story seriously when the Ghost is not taken seriously by the characters he attempts to haunt, and the characters are merely sketched stereotypes?

Perhaps, as Wilburn argues, the reader needs to accept that each character in "The Canterville Ghost" acts a part. The Ghost may be the only character who meditates upon performance, but surely Mrs. Otis who once played a "celebrated New York belle" and now trades on "her superb profile," also stays in costume throughout the story. Mrs. Otis, however, has realized that one cannot play the same role forever, and like an accomplished actress moves gracefully from girlish ingenue to mature character parts. Sir Simon's failure springs from a point that Wilde would later return to in his only novel, *The Picture of Dorian Gray*. First, Sir Simon is jolted into reality when the Otises fail to respond correctly to his haunting. Up until this point there has been no difference between the Ghost's public and private selves. Sir Simon, before the Otises arrived, truly lived by Oscar Wilde's motto: "Life for art's sake." Sir Simon, in other words, had no identity other than that of evil ghost.

Like the Ghost, Sybil Vane, the beautiful actress in *The Picture of Dorian Gray* realizes that she has no identity beyond her nightly performances. In this dark and disturbing novel, this realization causes Sybil to commit suicide. Initially, the title character, Dorian Gray, falls in love with Sybil because she is a wonderful actress. Each night she plays a different heroine in a Shakespeare play. Dorian can believe that she is actually Juliet or Desdemona even though she acts in a filthy theater with bad actors. When Sybil realizes, however, that she is not a Shakespearean heroine, but an actress in a cheap playhouse, she loses her ability to act. Dorian cannot love the real Sybil, only the ideal she represented in her roles. Similarly the Ghost can exist solely as a performer of a part. Once his public refuses to believe in his part, the Ghost loses his identity.

The nature of performance is an important theme in Oscar Wilde's works, but the theme does not necessarily lead to serious reflection. While Sybil Vane's suicide must be read as a tragedy, that Sir Simon gives up haunting to seek a final resting place can be interpreted differently. First, the Ghost's performance has had a good run. A Broadway play that lasted three hundred years would be considered a success indeed. Also, the other characters in "The Canterville Ghost" show every indication of keeping up their own performances. The Otis family embrace their character roles, and play out the American stereotypes to their fullest. If they inhabit a world where everyone performs a role, at least Wilde has created a rich variety of parts. Death, in the story, is a picturesque garden that awaits the exhausted actor. The specter of Oscar Wilde and his real life tragedy haunts much interpretation of "The Canterville Ghost," but here, Wilde created a comedy.

Source: Kimberly Lutz, "Serious Comedy? Finding Meaning in 'The Canterville Ghost,'" for *Short Stories for Students*, The Gale Group, 2000.

Lydia Reineck Wilburn

Wilburn is a professor of English at Pepperdine University. In the following essay, she examines Wilde's exploration of the role of the audience in "The Canterville Ghost," focusing on Virginia as an audience for the ghost.

Although Wilde's short story collection *Lord Arthur Savile's Crime and Other Stories* has enjoyed some critical attention, most of the discussion has focused on the comic and moral content of the stories, especially the relationship between the crimi-

nal and the artist. But a closer examination of the stories suggests that Wilde was also exploring various concepts of a theory of performance—specifically the artist's and audience's roles in the artistic performance. Wilde was using the texts, particularly "The Canterville Ghost," to work through problems involving the audience's power over different phases of the artist's performance.

In his works Wilde presents at least three contradictory stances about performance: that the audience should be ignored by the artist during creation of the artwork, that the audience's participation in the aesthetic experience is limited to being receptive to and molded by the artist's work, and that the audience plays a major role in bringing about the aesthetic experience. These contradictions are either stated outright in his essays and letters, or they are implied or presented in his stories. In *Intentions* and numerous other reviews and letters to editors, Wilde strenuously resisted the notion that the audience could have an active role in what Wolfgang Iser [in *The Implied Reader*, 1975] calls the aesthetic experience, that moment brought about by the "convergence of text and reader." Wilde, with his classical education and Paterian tastes, thought that the artist should stand aloof from the audience's preconceptions about art; as artist, his role was to perform, thereby delivering aesthetic dictates to his audience and shaping their notions and tastes. But running counter to his stated directives was the fact that by nature he was very much a public performer, one who depended on the interaction between artist, audience, and artwork. Wilde needed his audience if he were to create, a lesson he learned late but well when, imprisoned, he was deprived of the audience he sought. And his early stories (although minor works) show the public to be crucial to the making of illusion and even to the artist's well-being. This [essay] will focus on "The Canterville Ghost," not only because it has always been one of Wilde's most popular early stories (so popular that it has been produced recently as a television movie), but, more importantly, because it is one whose subtext undercuts Wilde's stated critical positions.

The conflicting notions of the audience's role preoccupied Wilde throughout his career, and they have preoccupied his critics, who continue to search for a resolution to these contradictions. Recent studies of Wilde's work, however, have begun to point out ways in which some of his fictional and dramatic works embody and advance the various tenets of his critical thought. But as yet critics have not accounted adequately for the diversity of his critical stances, nor have they established a connection between his early concern with performance on the one hand and his continuing distrust of the audience's role in the aesthetic experience on the other. Richard Poirier's *The Performing Self* presents a conception of literature which accounts for these complexities. Poirier here puts forward a theory of performance focusing on the local energy of the writing effort and effect rather than on a coherent canon of works. Poirier describes literature as a performance of the self, a playful activity, a solitary "self-discovering, self-watching response" to the chaos of existence. For the artist, the self-discovery in creation produces a feeling of "narcissistic power" as he momentarily gains control of his environment. During this first aspect of the creating act the most exciting considerations for the artist are himself and the rarefied, self-absorbed atmosphere of the performance. Poirier adds, however, that after this phase, another self emerges from the completed performance, a public self that looks outward to audiences for publicity, for confirmation of the creative act, or even for "historical dimension." The artist's creative energies, now in the public sphere, strive for "love" from the public and "compet[e] with reality itself for control of the minds exposed" to the artwork.

Poirier's two-phase analysis of creative acts allows us to see that through his contradictions Wilde was trying to talk about different aspects of performance. Thus, when Wilde states in "The Soul of Man Under Socialism" that an artist takes no notice of the public, he means this to describe the self-consulting, self-discovering phase of the creative act. And the contradictory statement in the same essay that the artist is to shape the public's taste and temperament refers to the second phase of the performance: thus the artist now wants to affect what T. S. Eliot would call the literary tradition.

Later, when Wilde pushes these notions further, examining the audience as co-shapers of the aesthetic experience, we recognize that Wilde foreshadows Iser's concerns as well as other modern theories. In his fiction Wilde anticipates Victor Shklovsky's notions of laying bare the devices of fiction by pointing to the audience's and artist's roles as makers [in *Russian Formalism*, translated by Lee T. Lemon and Marion J. Reis, 1965]. In many of these stories Wilde self-consciously displays the human attempt to use form so as to structure fiction and reality, suggesting Donald Woods Winnicott's concepts of creativity and play in his collection *Playing and Reality*. Winnicott

> " Wilde needed his audience if he were to create, a lesson he learned late but well when, imprisoned, he was deprived of the audience he sought."

demonstrates that the healthy individual, from infancy, engages in continual interplay in the "potential space" between himself and the outside world, both to separate himself from it and to establish an interrelationship with it. Wilde's story "The Canterville Ghost" presents an example of such ongoing creativity as the characters create other fictional characters or objects: the twins recreate the Canterville Ghost out of advertising slogans, they create their own "Otis Ghoste," and Virginia "comes to life" for readers because Wilde encourages us to help create her from the plethora of previously written fictions and myths inhabiting the text. Thus writer, audience, and text all join in the creation of the story.

When readers first encounter Wilde's short stories, their frivolous and somewhat risque content seems to show Wilde as minimally concerned about the reader's power in the aesthetic experience. Nor does he seem interested in shaping the reader's tastes, aesthetic judgment, or world view. Yet a closer examination of the underlying concerns of the works points to a different understanding of these stories. Each of the stories in the collection *Lord Arthur Savile's Crime and Other Stories* depicts an artist-figure grappling with his or her role in relation to the audience. In two of the stories, *"Lord Arthur Savile's Crime"* and "The Model Millionaire," Wilde portrays the artist blithely creating or enacting roles without the necessity of the audience's complicity. But in the other two stories, "The Canterville Ghost" and "The Sphinx Without a Secret," the audience is shown to be crucial to the making of the illusions and to the artist's self-satisfaction. Although all four stories focus on the creating self, only "The Canterville Ghost" concerns us here, for this story alone explores Wilde's multiple interests in the artist and the audience as creators.

In this story, a *nouveau-riche* American family, the Otises, moves to England and searches for an old English mansion to buy. But they choose a home that is haunted by a murderer's ghost—the original tenant, Sir Simon de Canterville. Unlike their English neighbors, the upstart Americans refuse to take the Ghost seriously; instead, they satirize and parody his stunts and horrors. This response eventually depresses the Canterville Ghost. He tries to find other ways to affect them, even to the point of compromising his art. Yet, he is unwilling to quit his occupation altogether, for he is a responsible being. We soon discover, however, that he cannot leave even if he wants to until someone comes to release his soul from the earthly plane into the final resting place. Virginia, the only daughter of the Otises, takes on that role, befriending and thereby releasing him. In gratitude, the Ghost presents her with the Canterville jewels. Thereafter she marries a young neighboring Duke, and they settle into happy domesticity.

Wilde published "The Canterville Ghost" along with three other stories, in book form in July 1891, but they had each been published in sophisticated society journals four years earlier. "The Canterville Ghost—A Hylo-Idealistic Romance: The Redemptive Heroine" was the first to appear, published in the 3 February and 2 March 1887 issues of *Court and Society Review* (a short-lived journal catering to the sophisticated tastes and leisured interests of the upper classes). Ghost stories were very much in demand throughout the nineteenth century, in part because of the influence of the Gothic novel and because of the resurgence of interest in paranormal occurrences (as evidenced by the establishment of the Society for Psychical Research in 1882). In *Blackwood's Edinburgh Magazine*, for example, where Wilde was to publish "The Portrait of Mr. W. H." (July 1889), ghost stories were part of the monthly fare, whether written as real attempts at horror, investigations into the supernatural, or comedies about ghosts. Similarly, ghosts are of concern to characters in major fiction of the nineteenth century such as *Northanger Abbey, Wuthering Heights* and "The Turn of the Screw." Thus, Wilde could count on seasoned audiences for "The Canterville Ghost." Given a receptive audience, he tries through the subtext to enlarge their awareness about fiction-making and about the arbitrary reality created by language.

In the beginning of "The Canterville Ghost" Wilde focuses on performance by pointing both to the first (narcissistic) and second (public) phases of the Ghost's creations. The Canterville Ghost glories in his artistry, taking every opportunity to provoke fresh terror in the new residents in the mansion, and he recalls his most celebrated performances with "the enthusiastic egotism of the true artist." His performances are elaborate, theatricalized with costumes and alliterative titles such as "Red Ruben, or the Strangled Babe," "Gaunt Gibeon, or the Blood-Sucker of Bexley Moor," and "Martin the Maniac, or the Masked Mystery." The humorous alliteration draws attention to the artificiality of ghost stories as well as to the Ghost as conscious fiction-maker.

But almost immediately Wilde introduces the problem most artists must contend with when performing: an unreceptive audience that prevents the performance from reaching completion. Such is the American family—a pragmatic, mundane group who simply refuse to be terrorized, rendering the Ghost's artistic efforts ineffectual. Confronted with the Ghosts's various attempts to horrify, the boys treat the performer like a mere schoolboy opponent, hurling pillows and water balloons at him, and even spitting pellets from peashooters at him. His performances having failed with the twins, the Ghost hopes to gain proper publicity from the adults, by perhaps precipitating screaming fits, fainting spells, or possibly heart attacks from them, but they give him only what they would an ordinary mortal displaying such behavior—Tammany Rising Sun Lubricator for his noisy chains and Dr. Dobell's tincture for his "indigestion." And despite the Ghost's laudable attempts to provide them a terrifying bloodstain every night, Washington prosaically scrubs it away with Pinkerton's Champion Stain Remover and Paragon Detergent. Such pragmatic responses to the Ghost's horrific performances convince him that his audience does not deserve the bloodstain: they are, he sniffs, clearly incapable of appreciating the "symbolic value of sensuous phenomena."

The Ghost refuses to admit to himself that his audience will never engage in his performances, and he gives them one more chance. He prepares his most terrible deed to date: to gibber and moan horrifically while stabbing himself repeatedly through the neck. On his way to do this he pauses at the corner, only to receive a terrible shock. The twins have upstaged his performance, creating an apparition of their own, seemingly a parody of a ghost. The poor Canterville Ghost is "frightened witless," and "never having seen a ghost before" he retreats hastily. Naturally, the humor of this passage comes from seeing a ghost being frightened by a ghost. But

Wilde also seems to be wrestling here with the role of the audience in the creating process. We see in this scene that the artistic ghost, unlike the twins when they were the audience, responds receptively to their performance, as an audience should; he suspends his disbelief and follows their aesthetic suggestions. For example, when he cannot actually make out what the scroll proclaims, the Ghost creates the statement himself: it must, he assumes, present "some scroll of shame," "some record of wild sins," "some awful calendar of crime." Not until the dawn will he be able to see that he owes his fright more to his own imagination than to the concrete details—the turnips and cloth— of the twins's artifact. His previous response was thus an aesthetic experience resulting from his collusion with the artistry of the twins, whereas their creative intention seemed to be mainly mockery. When the Ghost can read the scroll's actual message, he realizes the twins' satiric and insulting intent:

YE OTIS GHOSTE
Ye Onlie True and Originale Spook.
Beware of Ye Imitations
All others are Counterfeite.

Thus has his audience (now the artists) transformed his centuries of horrific productions to the ephemeral palaver of American advertisements. Worst of all, the scroll pronounces the Canterville Ghost's artistry counterfeit and imitative. Demoralized, he now inhabits their fiction—that he simply was not capable of terrorizing his audience as the "Onlie True and Originale Spook" could do so well.

It is certainly true that he was not able to involve them in his artistry as they were able to involve him. But we see that the Canterville Ghost is a more receptive audience than were the twins: unlike them, he is open to many different kinds of artistic experience. We also see that the twins are not as philistine as the Ghost would have us think, for they are themselves capable of creating, even if only slapstick, buffoonery, or satire. Unfortunately though, their narrow artistic interests do not include the Ghost's particular creations; they simply refuse to take them seriously. Wilde, in his career, would struggle with this same plight: how to get audiences to hear his works, how to keep them from ridiculing or dismissing him.

In despair, the Canterville Ghost draws on his last reservoir of discourse to conjure up a revenge. Desperately, he tries his most deadly invocation and awaits the second crowing of the cock: "When Chanticleer had sounded twice his merry horn, deeds of blood would be wrought, and Murder [would] walk abroad with silent feet." But again, his art—the ability to evoke the power residing within words—fails him: apparently for the first time in the history of conjuring, Chanticleer crows only once. Frustrated, humiliated, and at last cowed, the Canterville Ghost sinks into a dark depression.

His expectations undermined by the audience's lack of interest, the Ghost realizes (as Wilde himself eventually would) that he must reconsider his roles, search for new masks, and renovate his performances. Through the manipulation of objects and language, the young Americans have evoked a potential space where the Ghost must define himself anew, but the only role left him is that of Victorian duty or convention. Even though the Americans have hurt his feelings, he dutifully and politely "traverse[s] the corridor" every Saturday between midnight and three o'clock, now having oiled his chains and removed his noisy boots, "to take every possible precaution against being either heard or seen." In other words, by wrongly trying to please his audience, by giving in to their expectations, the Ghost has let the audience take over his future performances: they have told him he can perform, but only without demanding their attention. The Americans thus not only refuse to participate in his public performance but now they also dictate to him how to structure his private first phase of creation: so long as he eliminates everything from his performance which might attract their attention, he can dress up as "Black Isaac, or the Huntsman of Hogley Woods" or however he desires. If they are not asked to respond to his performances, they will not have to grapple with their preconceptions about his performances—or about reality. Rather, they can continue with their own philistine assumptions, namely that ghosts (or artists) are to be ignored or harassed, but not to be taken seriously (thus the twins tie strings across the corridors to trip him and make a butter-slide from the top of the oak staircase to the opening of the Tapestry Chamber, the last of which causes the Ghost a severe fall). Clearly they are exactly the kind of audience any artist of Wilde's cast fears.

But even if Wilde's ghostly alter-ego has surrendered control of his art to his audience, Wilde has not. His wit, inverted cliches and paradox draw attention to himself and the audience as performers in life and art. His rhetorical devices show us how to lay bare the arbitrary acceptance of the reality created by language, categories, and assumptions of the age. As in "Critic as Artist" Wilde shows us how we are "slaves of words." Through the humorous paradox that the ghost of a murderer would remain polite and dutiful in other areas of his existence, Wilde places the notions of duty, sincerity, and sin into the realm of play. Further, Wilde succeeds in upending conventional notions of good and evil when he elicits from the reader some sympathy for the Ghost who had committed a crime but who now is responsible, concerned for others, and polite. Delighting in paradox, Wilde playfully manipulates our point of view until the attentive reader can question the stability of words such as "evil," "earnest," "sin," or "responsibility." By thus pointing to the artificiality of language, Wilde again makes his audience aware of themselves as performers of the reality around them.

In addition, Wilde playfully calls our attention to our assumptions about language and moral categories in the scenes with Virginia and the Canterville ghost. When Virginia, a "sweet Puritan," scolds him for murdering his wife, the Ghost, a complex "personality" like the murderer Thomas Griffiths Wainewright (treated in Wilde's "Pen, Pencil, and Poison"), responds aptly and wittily, transforming ethical concerns into aesthetic concerns. In a display of panache, the Ghost tells Virginia that he murdered his wife primarily in aesthetic defense against her ordinary face, her negligent housekeeping habits, and her unimaginative cookery:

> "It is very wrong to kill anyone," said Virginia, who at times had a sweet Puritan gravity, caught from some Old New England ancestor.
>
> "Oh, I hate the cheap severity of abstract ethics! My wife was very plain, never had my ruffs properly starched, and knew nothing about cookery. Why, there was a buck I had shot in Hogley Woods, a magnificent pricket, and do you know how she had it sent up to table? However, it is no matter now, for it is all over, and I don't think it was very nice of her brothers to starve me to death, though I did kill her".

Wilde orchestrates this scene with such whimsical irony that any indignation or outrage the reader might feel at such monstrous behavior is absolutely undercut. Only for a moment at the end of the story does Virginia, the Ghost's new audience (and now his new biographer), succeed in evoking for us any sense of real pain, sin, or remorse felt by the Ghost, when she points out Sir Simon's manacled skeleton, showing that he died in agony, vainly reaching towards food and drink placed just out of his reach. Of course Wilde's reader soon recognizes this description as a Gothic cliche, after which he or she rescinds any emotional investment in the Ghost's predicament. The fluid stances Wilde uses to describe Sir Simon's life allows him to call our attention to other arbitrary structures upon which we base our judgments. And if the modern reader knows (just as a limited number knew then) that when this story was published Wilde himself had begun to violate society's sexual codes, then the reader can bring Wilde's own "crime" to the story's appeal for flexible judgments about morality.

Of course, Wilde's main concern with any character's sins or indiscretions is whether the behavior results in an enlarged, multiplied (Paterian) self. Those personalities who explore new arenas of experience, and thus perform new facets of the self, are seen as artists, whether of life or artifact. In this story Wilde celebrates characters who have tried on other masks in life (or in death). The ghost of course is one such character, as is Mrs. Lucretia Tappan Otis, who has played the roles of "celebrated New York belle" in the past and is currently playing a handsome matron with a "superb profile." But whereas Mrs. Otis has only dabbled in the artistry of the self, her daughter Virginia will wholeheartedly engage in such artistry. By risking her chaste reputation in order to embark on a secret, romantic escapade (an activity which, when camouflaged with the excuse that one is visiting a sick relative, Wilde later would term "bunburying" in *The Importance of Being Earnest*), Virginia recreates the self, paralleling Wilde's other artist/criminal figures. After this romantic rite of passage, Virginia becomes an artist of the self. But unlike the ghost, she successfully dictates artistic terms to her audiences within the story, whether to her husband and family or to the ghost himself. They receive or contribute to her performances as she desires: her family accepts her version of reality while she was with the ghost, and because of her love the ghost allows her to remake his gothic drama of revenge and depression into a tragicomedy of forgiveness and peace. Possibly, her dominant position in relation to her audience is meant to suggest Wilde's desires regarding his own role with his audiences.

We watch Virginia's character take on more masks and become an aggregate of performances as the story progresses. Originally we see her as a fifteen-year-old "amazon," "lithe and lovely as a fawn," whose freshness provides a contrast to the aesthetic, amoral ghost. Her essential naivete is suggested when she sweetly offers the ghost a sandwich and has the imaginative capacity to believe in him before the others do: as the story's subtitle indicates, she is the "hylo-idealist" of this "romance." Soon, however, the reader realizes that Wilde's text provides potential space for the reader to negotiate Virginia's characterization through the echoes of previous texts inhabiting this text. Virginia's name, for example, emphasizes that she will be a conciliator between the English families and her own; ''Virginia'' recalls both the English Queen and the American state named for that queen. Nor is it an accident that the only other woman besides Virginia that the ghost admires is the Virgin Queen (he mentions that she had complimented his performance at the Kenilworth tournament). In addition, the description of Virginia as an amazon suggests a tie to the mythic world, just as the second part of the subtitle (''The Redemptive Heroine'') opens up possibilities for ties to other literary heroines and even to the Virgin Mary. When we consider Virginia's role in the story—she leads the Ghost through the darkness so that his soul may find final rest—there is also a clear echo of Dante's Beatrice. And, just as Beatrice rebuked Dante when he reached the top of Purgatory, so Virginia sternly reminds the Ghost that it is ''very wrong to kill anyone,'' and later she chastises him for being rude, dishonest, ''horrid, and vulgar.'' Virginia/Beatrice even usurps Dante's role when she returns to the others with her new vision. Thus we see Wilde using familiar literary models to encourage his audience to respond creatively to the story; his text calls attention to our own roles as receptive readers (and therefore creators) who can fill the gaps in the text, a possibility which Wilde in ''Critic as Artist'' seems to support for the critic or for any sensitive, educated reader: ''The critic occupies the same relation to the work of art that he criticizes as the artist does to the visible world of form and colour, or the unseen world of passion and of thought . . . . Indeed, I would call criticism a creation.'' Yet Wilde seems ambivalent about a reader's being too free with a text. His confident statement about the creative critic or reader contrasts markedly with Wilde's anxious Canterville Ghost, whose audiences ignore his artistic guidance and eventually force him to relinquish control of his art. Wilde in this story wants to shape the audiences's responses more than he implied in ''Critic as Artist.''

One area, however, where Wilde's shaping hand is perhaps too subtle for many readers is that of Virginia's bunburying. Wilde handles the sexual goings-on between the ghost and Virginia so discreetly that they have remained hidden from the audiences within the story as well as from most readers of the story. The energy of the story focuses on the performance of concealment, yet Wilde also enjoys the game of implying that there is something

to reveal. First, we recall that Virginia is seduced by the Canterville Ghost's ''dreamy voice'' and his poetically persuasive rhetoric. But beneath this artist's smooth words of poesy is found another familiar line, used by countless men to seduce countless virgins—that a good woman's love can redeem a man's crooked soul. The ghost points to the inscription on the library window (quoted below) and promises Virginia that he wants her only to pray and weep for him and thereby release his soul. But even a cursory glance at the prophecy on the library window shows that the ghost is withholding something in his interpretation of these lines. Readers who know Wilde's works remember his later statement in *The Picture of Dorian Gray* that the soul can be cured by means of the senses, and there are certainly numerous sensuous details in this scene.

In the context of what follows between Virginia and the ghost, the inscription can suggest that the ghost looks forward to sexual fulfillment and consequent gratitude (''When a golden girl can win Prayer from out of the lips of sin''), and there is the hint of a rite of passage for the golden girl (''And a little child gives away its tears''). Virginia is fifteen, and possibly Wilde is suggesting the familiar relationship between an older artist and a younger lover. Several other details in the text also suggest a sexual seduction. When the ghost gratefully kisses Virginia's hand, his hands are ''cold as ice,'' but his lips are burning ''like fire,'' a description which underlines his sensual nature. Further, the ghost clutches her hand tightly, and Virginia goes with him into the darkness, despite the warnings from the gargoyles (symbols of human lusts) and from the huntsmen on the tapestry (an image suggesting that Virginia is the prey). As they reach the threshold of the ''great black cavern'' he ''pull[s] at her dress'' to hasten her in.

And there is other evidence to suggest that Virginia has indeed been bunburying. When Virginia returns after being alone with the ghost for eight hours she brings with her a casket of jewels (a gift usually presented to a lover). Later, she is given the widow's place in Sir Simon's funeral procession. Such precedence reinforces the idea that probably she was not just praying and weeping during that entire eight hours. Years later, when queried by Cecil (who is by that time her husband) she will not give details about her visit with the ghost, saying only that she owes Sir Simon ''a great deal'' because he taught her to see ''what Life is, and what Death signifies, and why Love is stronger than both.'' The Duke seems satisfied enough with this answer as long as her heart is his, though her explanation sounds suspiciously like an excuse used by a bunburyist. This interpretation finds further support when Virginia, by then a respectable matron, blushes at the thought of telling her children about her activities. Rodney Shewan calls this conclusion "the feminist's answer to '*Lord Arthur Savile's Crime*,'" for in this case the wife, not the husband, has "sacrificed" herself and kept the secret from her spouse. Such poetic justice no doubt would be much appreciated by the fashionable (and perhaps jaded) readers of *Court and Society Review*. But taking Shewan's observation further, we can also see that the importance of this scene for Wilde is that Virginia has added to the aggregate of her self. She has transformed herself from a one-dimensional cliche to a multi-faceted romance. She has become an artist of the self.

By the end of the story we begin to synthesize Wilde's contrapuntal concerns about performance. Not only do the characters, plot, and language explore the nature of performance, but the story's structures play with it as well when they elude easy categorization. The spoof of a ghost story slides into erotic intrigue, and the young Duke's idyllic love story with Virginia plays with elements of Old Comedy as she bunburies with an older man. The marriage of the Duke and Virginia reconciles the old world with the new, and Virginia, now a Duchess, proudly wears the Canterville jewels. Further, the Duke is able to live with his wife's unwillingness to share her secret, trusting her to love him in spite of the unexplained event in her past. Even though the story ends on a question (whether she will tell her children her secret), readers feel the ending provides closure: Virginia has been so successful in her life's artistry thus far that we are confident she will create an appropriate fiction about her secret for her children when the time comes.

Wilde further reminds readers of his notions about creativity when the ghost of Sir Simon, because of the intercession of Virginia (his artistic audience), receives forgiveness and love from her, which, as Poirier points out, is at bottom what every personality and artist strives to achieve when presenting a performance to the public. Sadly, though, he now desires that Virginia's love serve only to grant him deliverance to his final death. Perhaps the ghost's achievement of final rest suggests that last aspect of the creative process which every artist experiences—the depletion and emptiness following the completion of any artwork. Or perhaps the ghost's desire to attain final rest suggests his recog-

nition that the mode of performance he loved so much (horrifying the inhabitants of the mansion) no longer has a receptive audience, and thus there is no point in going on with it. This possibility would be a dark one for Wilde since, like the ghost, he too devotes much of his creative energy to shocking (and sometimes horrifying) his audiences.

This last observation leads us back to one of Wilde's anxieties about performance which is not fully resolved in the story—namely the role of the artist in relation to the audience and the work. For beneath the comic tone and paradoxical style of the story, we sense the Ghost's earnestness about his artistry and his genuine despair over his failure to reach his audience on his own terms. Perhaps comedy and paradox are Wilde's defenses against the real pathos an artist feels when his performance is not given even polite consideration by the audience. The Canterville Ghost tries several roles in his increasingly desperate attempt to achieve—at the least—confirmation from his audience so that he can know that public aspect of the performing self. But he is able to do so only when he becomes respectable, dutiful, and self-effacing—a grim alternative for any artist, but especially one of Wilde's cast. Perhaps the ghost's last fling with Virginia was Wilde's way of retrieving for his alter-ego some bit of liveliness, complexity, and personality to compensate for his necessary surrender to the audience.

Such was the way Wilde handled rejection from his audience in his own works and life (until his imprisonment): he simply became more flamboyant and more subversive as he put off confronting the significant power of his audience. A main problem, then, that the reader must negotiate in Wilde's work is the same contradiction that threatened to undo his life: Wilde wants to prevent his audience from controlling his creative territory, but he also wants to encourage the audience in its responsibility to create its reality and fiction. Thus, Wilde always kept one eye on his audience, seeking out their recognition, and, like the ghost, he tried several means to persuade them to consider his vision. Just as the ghost needed to tell someone his artistic woes, so Wilde expended much energy writing letters to journals such as the *Pall Mall Gazette*, the *St. James Gazette*, the *Daily Chronicle*, the *Speaker*, and the *Daily Telegraph*, earnestly justifying the ways of his art to his public. Even his paradoxical style—although appreciated by persons such as the readers of *Court and Society Review*—was not only a means to shock his audience, but ultimately an attempt to persuade unbelievers to inhabit his world view, a view that language, values, and beliefs are arbitrary structures and that the artist's role is to guide the audience in its creations and structurings. Wilde wanted the success with his audiences that Virginia achieved with hers. So, in addition to writing letters to editors, he continued to explore and expose what he saw as the misguided power of audiences in his fiction and essays. The underlying text beneath the humor of the Ghost's defeat reveals to the readers that even though Wilde seemed in control of the witty and complex performance of ''The Canterville Ghost,'' on some level he knew (but chose not to believe, as his later life would show) that the audience had the power to control or to ruin a performance—or even an artist. It is perhaps significant that when Wilde published these stories in book form for the general public, the collection received mostly bad reviews. Like the Canterville Ghost, Wilde would have to try yet another mask.

Source: Lydia Reineck Wilburn, ''Oscar Wilde's 'The Canterville Ghost': The Power of an Audience,'' in *Papers on Language & Literature*, Vol. 23, No. 1, Winter, 1987, pp. 41–55.

Philip K. Cohen

In the following excerpt, Cohen examines numerous moral and religious dualities in ''The Canterville Ghost.''

The main action of ''The Canterville Ghost'' takes place in 1884, three hundred years after Sir Simon murdered his wife—and in the same year that Wilde married his. Whereas Wilde suggests his personal guilt, augmented by the betrayal of marriage, within *Lord Arthur Savile's Crime*, here they are present only through the correspondence of dates. Yet the transformation of life into confessional art is no less certainly his intention. He constructs this story, like so many of his other works, around the confrontation of saint and sinner. The distinguishing characteristic of ''The Canterville Ghost'' is its negative portrayal of the double life. Although Wilde might praise artificiality and the wearing of masks elsewhere, the ghost's experience reveals that this mode of existence is the lonely refuge of an anguished sinner, who gladly forsakes it to gain the peace that forgiveness brings. Finally, as he promises in the subtitle, ''A Hylo-Idealistic Romance,'' Wilde presents the conflict between materialism and idealism, an opposition he develops using the literary labels *realism* and *romance* in ''The Decay of Lying.'' ''The Canterville Ghost'' constitutes also

> He constructs this story, like so many of his other works, around the confrontation of saint and sinner."

Wilde's tentative testing of the fairy-tale genre, in which he casts the next major portion of his writings.

''The Canterville Ghost'' faithfully renders Wilde's life during the mid-1880s. Beneath the camouflage of hilarity, he depicts a radical discrepancy between the self—or, more accurately, selves—he paraded before the public, on the one hand, and his private self, on the other. The Canterville ghost, representing the first of these, has long practiced an art that Wilde himself mastered: ''insincerity . . . by which we can multiply our personalities'' through the wearing of masks. In a state of despair, the ghost looks back on past triumphs:

> With the enthusiastic egotism of the true artist he went over his most celebrated performances, and smiled bitterly to himself as he recalled to mind his last appearance as ''Red Ruben, or the Strangled Babe,'' his *debut* as ''Gaunt Gibeon, the Blood-sucker of Bexley Moor,'' and the *furore* he had excited one lovely June evening by merely playing ninepins with his own bones upon the lawn-tennis ground.

Sir Simon's antics not only yield the desired self-multiplication, but also they afford the additional pleasure of shocking the public. Wilde reiterates the relationship of haunting to art as he conducts his reader behind the scenes:

> It [i.e., the role of ''Reckless Rupert''] was, however, an extremely difficult ''make-up,'' if I may use such a theatrical expression in connection with one of the greatest mysteries of the supernatural, or, to employ a more scientific term, the higher-natural world, and it took him fully three hours to make his preparations.

The veteran thespian can boast a long list of hauntees gone mad as a result of his artistry. Although for most of his career he has been restricted to victimizing aristocrats and their servants, the installation of the Otis family at Canterville Chase presents him with the opportunity *epater le bourgeois*. However, their materialistic mentality proves more than a match for even his best performances.

Like the other arts, Sir Simon's languishes in an age dominated by science and common sense.

Wilde seems to be suggesting that creative energies might be directed toward more fruitful enterprises than the lost war against Philistinism. And certainly the story indicates that Sir Simon's efforts to transform his life, such as it is, into art yield no greater success than Dorian Gray's. Even had the age been more propitious, the poseur's existence could not have fulfilled the ghost—or Oscar Wilde. For, while the public figure has chosen society as victim, the private self has fallen prey to society. Sir Simon's defeat by an unappreciative audience is hilarious indeed when contrasted with the anguish of his inner being. As he tells Virginia, his wife's brothers murdered him nine years after he took her life. They committed that grim, vindictive act of revenge associated in *The Duchess of Padua* with Old Testament morality. Sir Simon's skeleton commemorates their vengeance and represents the man behind his and Wilde's masks:

> Imbedded in the wall [of a secret compartment] was a huge iron ring, and chained to it was a gaunt skeleton, that was stretched out at full length on the stone floor, and seemed to be trying to grasp with its long fleshless fingers an old-fashioned trencher and ewer, that were placed just out of his reach. The jug had evidently been once filled with water, as it was covered inside with green mould. There was nothing on the trencher but a pile of dust.

In this symbolic tableau, the Old Testament judgment that irrevocably damns sexual inversion has punished Sir Simon for his crime and shackled Wilde with mind-forged manacles that place salvation beyond his reach. The trencher and ewer suggest the Eucharist and the Christian dispensation of forgiveness for sin. Wilde sought New Testament mercy, but his socially instilled belief in Old Testament judgment, combined with imperfect faith in Christ's law of love, rendered it inaccessible to him at this time. The manacled skeleton might serve as emblem to *The Duchess of Padua*, which figures forth the same paralyzing entrapment between two moralities.

It has been observed that most of Wilde's works end with a ceremonial unmasking. "The Canterville Ghost" is no exception. But, whereas in the comedies a past crime or indiscretion is exposed, Sir Simon's evil deed has long been a matter of public record. In this story, Wilde lifts the poseur's successful mask to reveal the sufferer beneath. Sir Simon has actually been destroyed by the public he seems to have terrorized so ably. Masks, then, are a way to hide the scars of guilt and to taunt society for its lacerating morality. Certainly multiplication of personalities does not result in the fulfillment Wilde claims for it in other writings. In "The Canterville Ghost" he focuses on the shortcomings of this mode of existence, which he will unequivocally reject in *De Profundis*.

In his review of Yeats's *Fairy and Folk Tales of the Irish Peasantry*, Wilde offers a definition of ghosts that thoroughly applies to Sir Simon:

> The ghosts live in a state intermediary between this world and the next. They are held there by some earthly longing or affection, or some duty unfulfilled, or anger against the living; they are those who are too good for hell, and too bad for heaven.

The Canterville ghost longs for release from his protean series of roles; they are to him a form of purgatory rather than a means of self-realization. As did Guido and Beatrice, he longs for death: "Death must be so beautiful. To lie in the soft brown earth, with the grasses waving above one's head, and listen to silence. To have no yesterday, and no tomorrow. To forget time, to forgive life, to be at peace." But he cannot gain deliverance through his own efforts because he lacks faith; this he sacrificed by killing his wife. Stripped of his masks, his stage glory brought to an end, he tells Virginia of his spiritual despair: "You must weep for me for my sins, because I have no tears, and pray with me for my soul, because I have no faith, and then, if you have always been sweet, and good, and gentle, the Angel of Death will have mercy on me. . . . against the purity of a little child the powers of Hell cannot prevail." These lines provide the interpretative context for the chained skeleton. Sir Simon's lack of faith cannot be readily overcome like the transitory doubts of Guido, Beatrice, and Lord Arthur Savile, though he wants to believe as badly as they.

In *The Duchess of Padua* Wilde presents his characteristic saint-sinner confrontation and preaches the efficacy of forgiveness; but the play's deep-structure undercuts his sermonizing. *Lord Arthur Savile's Crime* depicts mock salvation through conversion to Philistinism. "The Canterville Ghost" incorporates the central confrontation of *The Duchess* and brings it to more optimistic issue. Although Sir Simon, like Guido and Beatrice, seeks salvation in death, Wilde expresses in the story an unqualified belief in the transformative powers of Christian love.

He casts the puritanical Virginia Otis as successor to Guido and predecessor of Lady Windermere, Hester Worsley, and Lady Chiltern. Initially, she categorically condemns Sir Simon's deed: "'It is very wrong to kill any one,' said Virginia, who at times had a sweet Puritan gravity, caught from some old New England ancestor.'' The ghost counters with a rejection of her moral standards: ''Oh, I hate the cheap severity of abstract ethics! My wife was very plain, never had my ruffs properly starched, and knew nothing about cookery.'' His first sentence deserves further consideration. But, rather than developing the argument, Wilde sounds a comic retreat. The debate soon gives way to Sir Simon's confession of despair and plea for Virginia's help.

She can overcome her puritanism, forgive the ghost, and lead him to salvation because she possesses the faculty of imagination. She, too, is an artist, specifically, a landscape painter. Prior to her conversion, she reviles the ghost for stealing her paints: ''as for dishonesty, you know you stole the paints out of my box to try and furbish up that ridiculous blood-stain in the library. . . . I never told on you, though I was very much annoyed, and it was most ridiculous, the whole thing.'' Ridiculous indeed, but his refurbishing efforts constitute more than the criminal's compulsive return to the scene of his crime. He is also asserting the claims of imagination against the sway of materialistic common sense, of the artist's craft against Pinkerton's Champion Stain Remover and Paragon Detergent. But he concedes victory to Pinkerton's: ''If the Otis family did not want it [i.e., the blood-stain], they clearly did not deserve it. They were evidently people on a low, material plane of existence, and quite incapable of apprehending the symbolic value of sensuous phenomena.''

Virginia's silent sacrifice of her paints separates her from the rest of her family and, in a sense, makes her, too, suffer art's defeat by Philistinism. But in such materialistic times, this defeat is inevitable. Creative energy, Wilde suggests, should be used to transcend, rather than hopelessly to battle, the hostile cultural environment. Virginia's powers of imagination enable her to rise above the family's mentality and the ''cheap severity of abstract ethics'' and to embrace the New Testament law of love. Thus she can lead Sir Simon into a transcendent realm of peace. Her ultimate artistry facilitates his salvation, which Wilde places beyond question: '''God has forgiven him,' said Virginia gravely . . . and a beautiful light seemed to illuminate her face.'' She has fulfilled the prophecy on the library window:

> When a golden girl can win
> Prayer from out the lips of sin,
> When the barren almond bears,
> And a little child gives way its tears,

> Then shall all the house be still
> And peace come to Canterville.

The barren almond blooms, suggesting the Tannhauser legend and the remission of sexual sins. And, as the opening lines indicate, Virginia has restored Sir Simon's faith.

According to its subtitle, ''The Canterville Ghost,'' is ''A Hylo-Idealistic Romance.'' *Hylo-Idealism* denotes the doctrine espoused by a small group of English free-thinkers during the 1870s and 1880s. From the murky morass of their journal articles, only one characteristic emerges clearly: militant atheism. It is highly unlikely that Wilde would preface his distinctly Christian story with an allusion to their philosophy. But *hylo-idealistic* does have relevance when one interprets its hyphen as an indicator of opposition; Wilde continually stresses the conflict between materialism, represented by the combining form *hylo-*, and Christian idealism. In this philosophical romance, the idealists overcome obstacles set up by the *hylists*.

The story actually encompasses three realms of experience. The Otis family, which subsists on a ''low, material plane of existence,'' views life through the scientist's microscope. Their treatment of the bloodstain and the twins' irreverent attacks on the ghost clearly indicate their attitude toward the supernatural. The ghost lives in a sort of limbo, occupying a purgatorial realm where, though he can defy reason and the laws of physical science, he cannot completely escape their authority. Finally, Wilde presents the transcendent realm of imagination and spirit. He associates the mundane world of reason and materialistic monism with Old Testament morality. Here Sir Simon has committed a crime and been punished; here he exists as a skeleton. The ghost's purgatory is suspended midway between matter and spirit; he can pass through walls, but must suffer the physical pain of barked shins; he has risen to taunt his murderers' descendants, yet he must live under the damning pronouncement of their moral code. The higher realm of spirit and peace is inseparable from the higher morality of the New Testament. Virginia, because she has both innocence and imagination, can depart from her family's materialistic plane of existence, enter empathetically into the ghost's purgatory, and finally conduct him into the spiritual realm.

The conflict between hylists and idealists clearly anticipates the central opposition in ''The Decay of Lying'' between the literary modes of realism and romance. In fact, ''The Canterville Ghost'' embodies precisely what Wilde bemoans in "Decay": "Facts are not merely finding a footing-place in history, but they are usurping the domain of Fancy, and have invaded the kingdom of Romance." These lines call to mind the Otis family's analogous invasion of Canterville Chase. Not surprisingly, as Wilde continues his lament, he finds in America the epitome of the destructive materialistic mentality:

> The crude commercialism of America, its materialising spirit, its indifference to the poetical side of things, and its lack of imagination and of high unattainable ideals, are entirely due to that country having adopted for its national hero a man [i.e., George Washington], who according to his own confession, was incapable of telling a lie.

The Reverend Otis, obviously the possessor of these characteristics, fittingly named his firstborn Washington. Just as Wilde engineers the triumph of imagination over fact in his story, so he asserts at the end of "Decay" that "Romance, with her temper of wonder, will return to the land." Both triumph and prophecy reflect Wilde's yearning for forgiveness and peace.

Source: Philip K. Cohen, "Marriages and Murders: 'Lord Arthur Savile's Crime' and 'The Canterville Ghost,'" in *The Moral Vision of Oscar Wilde*, Fairleigh Dickinson University Press, 1978, pp. 53–71.

Sources

Shewan, Rodney. "Fiction as Ingratiation—First Attempts at a Social Pastoral: 'Lord Arthur Savile's Crime,' 'The Canterville Ghost,' 'Lady Alroy,' 'The Model Millionaire,'" in his *Oscar Wilde: Art and Egotism*, Macmillan, 1977, pp. 32–5.

Wilde, Oscar. *The Picture of Dorian Gray*, 1891. Reprint. New York: Penguin Books, 1985.

Further Reading

Ellmann, Richard. "Introduction," in Oscar Wilde's *The Picture of Dorian Gray and Other Writings*, Bantam Books, 1982, pp. ix–xix.
    Ellmann gives an overview of the themes found in Wilde's major works.

Raby, Peter. *Oscar Wilde*, Cambridge University Press, 1988, pp. 1–11, 54–6.
    Raby offers a brief analysis of the significance of Wilde's life to his works, and explores the various influences on "The Canterville Ghost."

The Cask of Amontillado

Edgar Allan Poe

1846

"The Cask of Amontillado" was first published in the November 1846 issue of *Godey's Lady's Book*, a monthly magazine from Philadelphia that published poems and stories by some of the best American writers of the nineteenth century, including Nathaniel Hawthorne, Henry Wadsworth Longfellow, and Harriet Beecher Stowe. The story next appeared in the collection *Poe's Works*, edited by Rufus W. Griswold, Poe's literary executor, in 1850. By the time Poe wrote this story, he was already nationally known as the author of the poem "The Raven" (1844) and of several short stories collected in a book called, simply, *Tales* (1845). These earlier stories were widely reviewed and argued over by critics who found them brilliant and disturbing, and their author perplexing and immoral. Although "The Cask of Amontillado" was not singled out for critical attention when it appeared, it did nothing to change the opinions of Poe's contemporary admirers and detractors. Like Poe's other stories, it has remained in print continuously since 1850.

The story is narrated by Montresor, who carries a grudge against Fortunato for an offense that is never explained. Montresor leads a drunken Fortunato through a series of chambers beneath his palazzo with the promise of a taste of Amontillado, a wine that Montresor has just purchased. When the two men reach the last underground chamber, Montresor chains Fortunato to the wall, builds a new wall to seal him in, and leaves him to die. Several sources

for the story have been suggested in the last century and a half: Edward Bulwer-Lytton's historical novel *The Last Days of Pompeii* (1843); a local Boston legend; a collection of *Letters from Italy*; and a real quarrel Poe had with two other poets. Wherever Poe got the idea and the impetus for "The Cask of Amontillado," this story and Poe's other short fiction had an undisputed influence on later fiction writers. In the nineteenth century, Poe influenced Ambrose Bierce and Robert Louis Stevenson, among others. Twentieth-century writers who have looked to Poe include science fiction writer H. P. Lovecraft and horror author Stephen King.

According to Vincent Buranelli, Poe's short stories also influenced the music of Claude Debussy, who was "haunted" by the atmosphere of Poe's tales, and the art of Aubrey Beardsley, as well as the work of other composers and artists in the United States, Great Britain, and in Europe. Poe was criticized in his own time for daring to examine a crime with no apparent motive, and a murderer with no apparent remorse. For one hundred and fifty years, these themes have continued to challenge readers, who are attracted and repulsed by Poe's creation.

Author Biography

Edgar Allan Poe's early life was as strange and unhappy as some of his most famous fiction. When he born in Boston in 1809, his parents were actors in traveling companies; his father died in 1810 and his mother in 1811. Edgar and his sister and brother were left penniless, and Edgar was taken in by a Virginia merchant, John Allan, whose last name Edgar took as his middle name. Poe lived with the Allans in England from 1815 to 1820 and attended school there. His relationship with Allan was strained, because Allan was rather heartless and unsympathetic to his wife and foster son. When Poe began studies at the University of Virginia, the wealthy Allan refused to help support him, and Poe turned to gambling, with little success.

After a short time at the University, Poe moved to Boston and began his career as a writer. In 1827 he published his first volume of poetry, *Tamerlane and Other Poems*, at his own expense, but found few readers. These early poems were heavily influenced by the Romantic poets. His first paid publication was the short story "MS. Found in a Bottle" (1833), which drew the attention of a publisher who admired his work and who got him an editorial job.

He soon lost the job because of his drinking. Shortly afterwards, in 1836, he married his cousin Virginia Clemm, who was thirteen years old.

During the eleven years of his marriage to Virginia, Poe had a series of publishing successes and personal failures. He moved his family to New York and Philadelphia and back again, editing and contributing to various magazines. He published several short horror stories and narrative poems, including "The Murders in the Rue Morgue" (1841), one of the earliest detective stories ever written, the psychological horror story "The Tell-Tale Heart" (1843), and the melancholy poem "The Raven" (1845), which brought him national fame. His brilliance as a writer was now firmly established. Still, he could not escape his addiction to alcohol.

In 1846, after losing a series of editorships, Poe retreated with his wife to a cottage in Fordham, outside New York City, where they nearly starved. There Poe wrote "The Cask of Amontillado," its gloomy and cynical tone echoing Poe's own feelings. The Poe biographer William Bittner claims that the two characters in the story "are two sides of the same man Edgar Poe as he saw himself while drinking." A few months later Virginia died of tuberculosis, and Poe became despondent. He wrote several important pieces during this time, but though he tried again to give up drinking, he never succeeded. He died in Baltimore on October 7, 1849, at the age of forty, after an alcoholic episode.

Plot Summary

As the story opens, an unnamed narrator explains, "The thousand injuries of Fortunato I had borne as best I could; but when he ventured upon insult, I vowed revenge." There is no hint as to whom the narrator is speaking or writing, and the "thousand injuries" and the "insult" committed by Fortunato are never described. Nevertheless, the narrator contemplates his desire for revenge and his plan to "not only punish, but punish with impunity"; that is, to punish Fortunato without being caught or punished himself. Furthermore, he is determined not to act in secrecy, for Fortunato must know that his pain is handed to him by Montresor.

Fortunato has no idea that Montresor is angry with him—Montresor has given no hint of it. When

Montresor encounters his "friend" on the street one evening during the carnival season, Fortunato has no reason to be suspicious. Montresor asks Fortunato to come with him and sample a large cask of Amontillado, a type of wine, which Montresor has just purchased. Fortunato is justifiably proud of his ability to recognize good wines, and he is already drunk. He is easily persuaded to follow his friend, especially when Montresor assures him that if Fortunato cannot sample the wine for him, another man, Luchesi, will surely do it.

Montresor and Fortunato, who is dressed in his carnival costume of striped clothing and a conical jester's cap with bells, go to Montresor's palazzo. Conveniently, the servants are away enjoying the carnival, and no one sees them enter. They descend a long, winding staircase to the wine cellar and catacombs, the dark and damp tunnels and caverns beneath the palazzo where generations of Montresors have been laid to rest. As they walk on, they pass piles of bones and piles of wine casks, intermingled in the passageways. Montresor fusses over Fortunato's health and his schedule, knowing that the more he suggests Fortunato give up the quest, the more his companion will be determined to see it through.

As they walk along, the men converse in an idle way, about the potentially hazardous nitre forming on the walls, and the coat of arms of the Montresor family. To protect Fortunato from the damp, Montresor gives him drinks of two wines that are stored in the catacombs. When Fortunato reveals himself to be a member of the Masons, Montresor pulls a trowel from beneath his cape and declares that he, too, is a mason. Always Fortunato is pulled forward by the promise of the Amontillado.

Eventually they reach the last chamber, a crypt nearly full of piled bones with only a small alcove of empty space within. When Fortunato steps to the back to look for the Amontillado, Montresor quickly chains him to two iron staples fastened to the wall. He uncovers a pile of building stones concealed beneath some of the bones and begins to build a wall, sealing Fortunato in. As Fortunato recovers from his drunkenness and becomes aware of what is happening to him, he cries out for mercy, but Montresor pays no attention. He still refuses to speak of the offenses that have brought him to the point of murder, and Fortunato does not ask why Montresor is ready to kill him. Montresor finishes his wall and piles bones up against it, leaving Fortunato to die.

Edgar Allan Poe

In the last lines, Montresor the actor is replaced again by Montresor the narrator, who began the story. Now he reveals that the murder happened fifty years before. In Latin he speaks over Fortunato's body: "Rest in Peace."

Characters

Fortunato

Fortunato is an Italian friend of Montresor's, and his sworn enemy, whom Montresor has planned to "punish with impunity." Although Montresor's explains that Fortunato has committed a "thousand injuries" and a final "insult," no details of these offenses are given. Fortunato displays no uneasiness in Montresor's company, and is unaware that his friend is plotting against him. Fortunato, a respected and feared man, is a proud connoisseur of fine wine, and, at least on the night of the story, he clouds his senses and judgment by drinking too much of it. He allows himself to be led further and further into the catacombs by Montresor, stepping past piles of bones with no suspicion. He is urged on by the chance of sampling some rare Amontillado, and by his unwillingness to let a rival, Luchesi, have the pleasure of sampling it first. His single-

Media Adaptations

- The audio cassette collection *The Best of Edgar Allan Poe* (1987), read by Edward Blake, includes "The Cask of Amontillado" and thirteen other stories and poems. The set is published by Listening Library. A radio play version of the story, originally broadcast on the NBC University Theater, is available on the audiocassette *Nosology; The Cask of Amontillado; The Fall of the House of Usher* (1991), part of the Golden Age of Radio Thrillers series issued by Metacom. Other audio presentations include "The Cask of Amontillado" (1987) in the Edgar Allan Poe collection by Westlake House; *An Hour with Edgar Allan Poe* (1979), from Times Cassettes; and *Basil Rathbone Reads Edgar Allan Poe, a record album issued in 1960 by Caedmon.*

- The story has also been captured many times on film and videotape. Videotapes include *The Cask of Amontillado* (1991) from Films for the Humanities; *The Cask of Amontillado* (1982) from AIMS Media; *Tales of Edgar Allan Poe* (1987) from Troll; and a three-tape set that includes six stories by six authors, *Classic Literary Stories* (1987) from Hollywood Select Video. Film versions include a 16mm film from BFA Educational Media that is accompanied by a teacher's guide; another 16mm film from Films Incorporated, 1975; and a 35mm film from Brunswick Productions (1967) that analyzes and presents excerpts from the story.

---

mindedness, combined with his drunkenness, leads him to a horrible death.

Luchesi

Luchesi is an acquaintance of Montresor's and Fortunato's, and another wine expert. He never appears in the story, but Montresor keeps Fortunato on the trail of the Amontillado by threatening to allow Luchesi to sample it first if Fortunato is not interested.

Montresor

Montresor is the "I" who narrates the story, telling an unseen listener or reader about his killing of Fortunato fifty years before. Montresor is a wealthy man from an established family, who lives in a large "palazzo" with a staff of servants. He speaks eloquently and easily drops Latin and French phrases into his speech. He has been nursing a grudge against his friend Fortunato, who has committed several unnamed offenses against him, and has been coldly planning his revenge. Meeting Fortunato in the street one evening, Montresor takes this opportunity to lure his friend into the deepest catacombs beneath his palazzo, and there he chains Fortunato to the wall of a small alcove, seals him in behind a new brick wall which he builds even as Fortunato begs for mercy, and leaves him to die. Montresor's coldness sets him apart from many murderous characters and many Poe protagonists. Even as he tells the story fifty years later, he reveals no regret for his actions, and no real pleasure in them. This lack of feeling made Poe's early readers uncomfortable, and led some to accuse Poe of immorality in creating such a character.

Themes

Revenge

The force that drives Montresor to commit the horrible murder of Fortunato is his powerful desire for revenge. His first words in the story speak of it: "The thousand injuries of Fortunato I had borne as best I could; but when he ventured upon insult, I vowed revenge." The idea of revenge is repeated several times in the opening paragraph. Montresor will not rush to act, he says, but "at length I would be avenged"; he is determined to "not only punish, but punish with impunity." The terms of the revenge are quite clear in Montresor's mind. He will not feel fully revenged unless Fortunato realizes that his punishment comes at Montresor's hand; a wrong is not redressed "when the avenger fails to make himself felt as such to him who has done the wrong." In seeking revenge, Montresor is acting out the motto of his people, as it appears on the family coat of arms, *Nemo me impune lacessit* ("No one wounds me with impunity").

As countless critics have pointed out, the nature of the injuries and offenses is never revealed. Montresor appears to be telling or writing his story to someone who has more knowledge than Poe's reader ("You, who so well know the nature of my soul"), and who may be assumed to know something of Fortunato's conduct before the fateful night. Unlike Montresor's audience, however, Poe's audience/reader has no basis for judging the extent to which Montresor's actions are reasonable. The focus, therefore, is not on the reason for revenge, but on the revenge itself, not on why Montresor behaves as he does but only on what he does.

Just as Montresor does not reveal his motive for the crime, other than to identify it as a crime of revenge, neither does he share with his audience his response when the deed is done. Does Montresor feel better once Fortunato has paid for his insult? Does he feel vindicated? Does he go back to his rooms and celebrate the death of his enemy, or smile inwardly years later when he remembers how he was able to "punish with impunity"? He does not say. Nineteenth-century audiences scanned the story for hints of negative feelings. Is Montresor sorry for committing murder? Does he regret his actions? As he nears the end of his life does he look to God for forgiveness? Again, there is no hint or perhaps only the barest of hints. Poe's intention is to focus his story tightly. He does not explore the events leading up to the crime, nor the results of the crime, but focuses the story narrowly on the act of revenge itself.

Atonement and Forgiveness

Although the action of the story revolves almost entirely around the deception and killing of Fortunato, the questions in readers' minds have revolved around Fortunato's thoughts and deeds before the crime, and Montresor's thoughts and deeds afterward. While the time between their chance meeting and the laying of the last stone would have taken only five or six hours, the fifty years following are perhaps more intriguing. Is Montresor deceiving himself or his audience when he attributes his momentary sickness to "the dampness of the catacombs"? What has happened to Montresor over the intervening years, and why is he telling the story now? Is he hoping for forgiveness?

For forgiveness to occur, there must first be guilt and then atonement or remorse. Of course, there is no question of Montresor asking forgiveness of Fortunato, or reconciling with him, and no mention is given of Montresor's paying any reparations to Lady Fortunato. Atonement, if there is to be any, must be with God alone. At the time of the murder, however, Montresor hears and rejects Fortunato's appeal that he stop "For the love of

Topics for Further Study

- Investigate the history of the Free and Accepted Masons, a group to which Fortunato apparently belongs. How were Masons perceived in the United States during the nineteenth century? Why might Poe have chosen to make Fortunato a member?

- What is nitre (also known as potassium nitrate or saltpeter)? How would it form on the walls of the catacombs? Why might it be harmful?

- Research the field of heraldry, the medieval system of assigning and describing symbols displayed on a shield to identify families. Learn enough of heraldry's special vocabulary to explain the conversation between Montresor and Fortunato on the subject of Montresor's "arms."

- Learn what you can about European gentlemen's attire in the late eighteenth and early nineteenth centuries. Fortunato has been enjoying the carnival, and is dressed in motley. Montresor wears a silk mask and a *roquelaire*. What does the men's clothing reveal about their station in life, or about their character?

God, Montresor!" The murderer replies, "Yes, for the love of God!" but he does not stop building his wall. Surely he does not mean that he is acting for the love of God; instead, he is blatantly and defiantly rejecting it.

In other ways Poe keeps the idea of the Christian God in the foreground. Fortunato is chained to the wall in a standing position that some critics have compared to the posture of the crucified Jesus. His narrow space behind the wall echoes Jesus's placement in a tomb. The story's last words, *In pace requiescat* (Rest in peace), are taken from the Roman Catholic funeral ritual spoken in Latin. Critic John Gruesser believes that Montresor tells the story of his crime "as he presumably lies on his deathbed, confessing his crime to an old friend, the 'You' of the story's first paragraph who is perhaps his priest.'' Clearly Montresor's guilt is established as not just an earthly legal guilt, but guilt in the eyes of a God that both victim and murderer recognize. The question remains: Was Montresor ever sorry for what he did? Poe does not appear interested in answering the question, although he surely knew that he was raising it, and knew that he had placed the answer tantalizingly out of reach.

Style

Point of View and Narrator

''The Cask of Amontillado'' is told in the first person by Montresor, who reveals in the first sentence that he intends to have revenge from Fortunato. He tells the story to an unidentified ''you, who so well know the nature of my soul,'' but this ''you'' does not appear to respond in any way as Montresor delivers a long monologue. The most striking thing about Montresor's voice, in fact, is its uninterrupted calm and confidence. He tells the story from beginning to end with no diversion, no explanation, and no emotion. If he is gleeful at gaining his revenge, or if he feels guilty about his crime, he does not speak of it directly, and his language does not reveal it. Even at the most terrifying moment in the story, when Fortunato realizes that Montresor intends to seal him up behind a wall, the narrator is calm and detached: ''I had scarcely laid the first tier of the masonry when I discovered that the intoxication of Fortunato had in a great measure worn off. The earliest indication I had of this was a low mourning cry from the depth of the recess. It was *not* the cry of a drunken man. There was then a long and obstinate silence. I laid the second tier, and the third, and the fourth.''

By presenting the story in the first person, Poe avoids hinting at any interpretation of the action. Montresor is in control, deciding what to tell and what to leave out. A third-person narrator, even a limited narrator who could not see into the minds and hearts of the characters, would have presented a more balanced story. An objective narrator telling a terrible story objectively might be frightening, but even more frightening is a man telling without emotion the story of his own terrible crime.

Setting

The setting of ''The Cask of Amontillado'' has attracted a great deal of critical attention, because both the location and the time of the story are only vaguely hinted at. To bring touches of the exotic to his murky atmosphere, Poe freely combines elements of different nations and cultures. Fortunato and Luchesi are Italians, knowledgeable about Italian wines. Montresor, as argued convincingly by Richard Benton and others, is a Frenchman. Amontillado is a Spanish wine. Montresor's family motto, *Nemo me impune lacessit*, is the motto of the royal arms of Scotland. Sprinkled among the Latin motto and other Latin phrases are references to Montresor's palazzo, his *roquelaire*, his rapier, and his flambeaux. If Poe's readers could not be expected to identify the nationality of each element, so much the better for creating the impression that the story happens ''in another place and time.''

The time of the story may be guessed at. Montresor's short cape and rapier, the slightly formal vocabulary, and the torches used to light the men's way seem to indicate that the story takes place in the eighteenth or nineteenth century. Scholars tracing the family name of Montresor and the history of laws governing the Mardi Gras carnivals in France have placed the date of the murder more precisely; John Randall III and others believe the murder occurs in 1796, while Benton argues for 1787-88.

Gothicism

Poe is often considered a master of the Gothic tale, and ''The Cask of Amontillado'' contains many of the standard elements of Gothicism. Gothic stories are typically set in medieval castles and feature mystery, horror, violence, ghosts, clanking chains, long underground passages, and dark chambers. The term ''Gothic'' originally referred to the Goths, an ancient and medieval Germanic tribe, but over time the word came to apply to anything medieval. The first Gothic novel, Horace Walpole's *Castle of Otranto* (1764), was set in a medieval castle, and later works that attempted to capture the same setting or atmosphere were labeled ''Gothic.''

Poe was fascinated with the materials and devices of the Gothic novel, although he preferred to work in the short story form. He was a great admirer of Walpole, and of the American Gothic writer Charles Brockden Brown. ''The Cask of Amontillado'' takes many details from the Gothic tradition: the palazzo of the Montresors with its many rooms, the archway that leads to the ''long and winding staircase'' down to the catacombs, the damp and dark passageway hanging with moss and dripping moisture, the piles of bones, the flaming torches that flicker and fade, and the ''clanking'' and ''furious vibrations of the chain'' that Montresor uses to bind Fortunato to the wall. The overall atmosphere of brooding and horror also come from this tradition.

Some elements of the Gothic, however, Poe intentionally avoided: there is no hint in ''The Cask of Amontillado'', or in most of his horror stories, of the supernatural. Poe was quite clear on this point, explaining that the plot of a short story ''may be involved, but it must not transcend probability. The agencies introduced must belong to real life.'' Montresor's crime is terrible, but it is believable, and it is committed without magic or superhuman power. Although there may be a hint of the supernatural in his remark that ''for the half of a century no mortal has disturbed'' the pile of bones outside Fortunato's tomb, those beings that might not be mortal are not described, and indeed Fortunato does not reappear as a ghost or a vampire or a zombie. Poe uses Gothic conventions to create an atmosphere of terror, but then subverts the convention by using only human agents for terrible deeds. For Poe, it is not supernatural beings that people should fear; the real horror lies in what human beings themselves are capable of.

Historical Context

The Short Story

Although there have been stories as long as there have been people to tell them, many critics trace the beginnings of the short story as a genre of written prose literature consciously developed as an art form to the nineteenth century. Previously in the West there had been great ages of epics memorized or extemporized orally, narrative poetry, drama, and the novel, but it was not until the early 1800s that critics began to describe the short story as a specific art form with its own rules and structures. In Europe, Honore de Balzac and others were already writing and theorizing about the new form. An early American voice in the discussion was Poe's. In 1842 he wrote a review of Nathaniel Hawthorne's *Twice-Told Tales* (1842), a collection of thirty-nine brief stories and sketches, many dealing with the supernatural. In his influential review, Poe delineated the differences, as he saw them, between poetry, the novel and the ''short prose narrative.''

Rhymed poetry, according to Poe, was the highest of the genres. But the ''tale proper,'' he claimed, ''affords unquestionably the fairest field for the exercise of the loftiest talent, which can be afforded by the wide domains of mere prose.'' The novel was inferior because it could not be read in one sitting, therefore making it impossible to preserve a ''unity of effect or impression.'' The ideal short story, one that could be read in thirty minutes to two hours, was created to produce one single effect. If a writer's ''very initial sentence tend not to the outbringing of this effect, then he has failed in his first step. In the whole composition there should be no word written, of which the tendency, direct or indirect, is not to the one pre-established design.'' Poe praised Hawthorne and Washington Irving for their skill with the new form, and kept firmly to the goal of the ''single effect'' in his own fiction. For this reason, his prose is almost exclusively in the short story form, and he limited each story to a small number of characters, simple plots, small geographical areas, and short time frames, as demonstrated in ''The Cask of Amontillado.''

National Literature

In the first half of the nineteenth century, there was a great call for Americans to develop a national literature, by which was meant a body of works written by Americans, published by Americans, and dealing with particularly American characters, locales, and themes. The United States was still a young country, and most American readers and writers looked to Europe for great books and great authors, as well as for literary forms and themes. In 1837, Ralph Waldo Emerson gave an influential address titled ''The American Scholar,'' in which he called upon Americans to combine the best of European ideas with a determined self-knowledge, to create the new American intellectual who would best be able to lead the nation. Writers and publishers hoped that a national call for a national literature would create a stronger market for their products, which were being outsold by European imports.

Poe, although he had the same difficulty supporting himself through writing as his contemporaries, did not whole-heartedly embrace the movement. On the one hand, his published criticism and reviews railed against writers who wrote mere imitations of popular European writers. But neither did he approve of writing that was too patriotic, that offered cliched praise of the United States with little artistic merit. He was also critical of those who praised inferior work simply because it was American. Like Emerson, Poe believed in using elements from Europe if they were useful artistically, and he believed that international settings helped establish

Compare & Contrast

- **1830s:** An Anti-Masonic political party is formed in the United States, intended to counterbalance the supposed political influence of the Free and Accepted Masons. It is the first important third party in United States history.

  1990s: With six million members but no central authority, the Free and Accepted Masons are found in nearly every English-speaking nation, including a large membership in the United States. They are more widely known for social activities and for community service than for political activity.

- **1840s:** Poe, who did not graduate from college, is able to read Latin, French, German, Italian and Spanish, and expects his readers to have basic competence in Latin and French.

  1990s: Most American college graduates have taken two years or less of foreign language study.

- **1840s:** Writers are concerned that Americans do not have the attention span required to read long works of fiction. Poe writes, "We now demand the light artillery of the intellect; we need the curt, the condensed, the pointed, the readily diffused in place of the verbose, the detailed, the voluminous, the inaccessible."

  1990s: Educators and parents complain that young people, raised with televisions and computers, do not like to read for long periods, but prefer to get their information in short, visual forms. Politicians complain that voters will not listen to complex arguments and ideas, but are interested only in "sound bites."

---

universality. Still, he called upon American writers to use their imaginations to produce original and vital works. In "The Cask of Amontillado," therefore, he used a European setting to create his exotic and murky atmosphere, but within the structure of the new and distinctly American short story form.

Critical Overview

When it appeared in the monthly magazine *Godey's Lady's Book* in 1846, "The Cask of Amontillado," like most short stories published in locally distributed magazines, attracted no special critical attention. A year earlier, Poe had published a collection of *Tales*, which had been widely reviewed. Most of these reviews were favorable, praising Poe's powers of imagination and control of language. George Colton's review in the *American Whig Review* was typical in heralding the volume's "most undisputable marks of intellectual power and keenness; and an individuality of mind and disposition, of peculiar intensity." A few were not only negative but scathing, including Charles Dana's review in the *Brook Farm Harbinger* in which he describes Poe's stories as "clumsily contrived, unnatural, and every way in bad taste." Significantly, the collection of tales was read and reviewed in all parts of the country, and helped bring Poe to a much larger audience than he had previously enjoyed.

After Poe's death in 1849, his literary executor Rufus W. Griswold wrote an obituary in the *New York Tribune*, in which he slanderously exaggerated Poe's weaknesses. He described Poe as a "shrewd and naturally unamiable character" who "walked the streets, in madness or melancholy, with lips moving in indistinct curses." The following year, Griswold published an edition of *Poe's Works*. In response to the two Griswold projects came a flurry of writing about Poe, much of it praising the writing but condemning the writer. Typical was an unsigned 1858 review in the *Edinburgh Review*: "Edgar Allan Poe was incontestably one of the most worthless persons of whom we have any record in the world of letters." Over the next fifty years, negative writing about Poe focused on his moral character, as presented by Griswold, more than it focused on his work. Critics seemed unable to move beyond the general observation that Poe led a troubled life and wrote troubling stories. Although critics and scholars continued to read and examine Poe's short stories, and although French and German writers continued to admire Poe, his reputation and importance declined throughout the remainder of the nineteenth century.

By the beginning of the twentieth century, much of the public's distaste had worn off, and critics were able to write more objectively about Poe's achievements. In the early third of the century, Poe was widely praised for his poetry, but Gothicism had fallen out of favor and his stories were dismissed by such writers as T.S. Eliot and W.H. Auden. Though the poem ''The Raven'' had been examined individually from its first publication, ''The Cask of Amontillado'' had to wait until the 1930s to have critical articles devoted to it. In the 1930s and 1940s, critics focused on tracing Poe's sources, arguing that Poe borrowed his plot from other nineteenth-century writers, a murder case in Boston, a literary quarrel from his own life, or other sources. Writers in the 1990s returned to the question of sources as a way of revealing Poe's intentions. Richard Benton is among those who suggest that the story can be read as historical fiction, based on real historical figures and addressing social class issues of interest to nineteenth-century Americans.

Other critics at mid-century were concerned with exploring the significance of details in the story that readers might not be expected to understand without explanation. Kathryn Montgomery Harris in *Studies in Short Fiction* (1969) and James E. Rocks in the *Poe Newsletter* (1972) analyzed the conflict in the story between the Roman Catholic Montresor and Fortunato, a Mason. Rocks concluded that Montresor kills Fortunato because ''he must protect God's word and His Church against His enemies.'' Other writers in the same period explored the significance of the names ''Montresor,'' ''Fortunato,'' and ''Amontillado.''

The largest body of criticism of the story has examined Montresor's remorse or lack or remorse for his crime. Daniel Hoffman, in his *Poe Poe Poe Poe Poe Poe Poe* agrees with many others that Montresor is consumed by guilt. ''Has not Montresor walled up himself in this revenge? Of what else can he think, can he have thought for the past half-

Virginia Poe, wife of Edgar Allan Poe.

century, but of that night's vengeance upon his enemy?'' Others find no hint of guilt in Montresor, leading some early readers to reject the story as immoral. Bettina Knapp places ''The Cask of Amontillado'' among Poe's ''shadow tales,'' which do not ''offer values. No judgmental forces are at work. Crime is neither a negative nor a positive act. Poe's psychopaths do not distinguish between good and evil, nor do they usually feel remorse or guilt.'' This issue has become the central critical question for ''The Cask of Amontillado.''

Criticism

Cynthia Bily

Bily teaches English at Adrian College in Adrian, Michigan. In the following essay, she discusses the concepts of duplicity and doubling in ''The Cask of Amontillado.''

When Montresor decides that it is time to seek revenge for the ''thousand injuries of Fortunato,'' he does not make his feelings known. Although the honor code of the day might have called for a public challenge and a duel to the death, Montresor decides that he will not give ''utterance to a threat.'' Instead,

What Do I Read Next?

- *Bodies of the Dead and Other Great American Ghost Stories* (1997) is a collection of thirteen classic stories by Ambrose Bierce, Edith Wharton, Nathaniel Hawthorne and others.

- Bram Stoker's *Best Ghost and Horror Stories* (1997) is a collection of fourteen spine-tingling stories by the author of *Dracula*.

- *Restless Spirits: Ghost Stories by American Women, 1872-1926* (1997) collects twenty-two stories by well-known and long-forgotten writers including Zora Neale Hurston and Charlotte Perkins Gilman.

- *Behind a Mask: The Unknown Thrillers of Louisa May Alcott* (1995) demonstrates that the author of *Little Women* had a darker and more humorous side.

- "The Premature Burial" (1844), another one of

Poe's tales of horror, is a catalog of anecdotes examining the horrors of being buried alive.

- "The Tell-Tale Heart" (1843) is Poe's tale of a murderer who, unlike Montresor, is driven mad by guilt.

- In "The Imp of the Perverse" (1845), Poe explores a man's uncontrollable impulses to do things that he knows will harm him—a recurring theme in Poe's fiction.

- There are literally hundreds of anthologies of Poe's work to choose from. *The Fall of the House of Usher and Other Tales* (1998) is widely available, and includes several of Poe's influential horror and detective stories.

- Among the many Poe biographies, William Bittner's *Poe: A Biography* (1962) strikes the best balance between the scholarly and the popular.

---

while he waits for his opportunity, he behaves as though nothing is wrong: "It must be understood, that neither by word not deed had I given Fortunato cause to doubt my good-will. I continued, as was my wont, to smile in his face, and he did not perceive that my smile *now was at the thought of his immolation.*"

The word for Montresor's behavior is "duplicitous." It means that he is concealing his true motives and feelings beneath a deceptive exterior, that he is being two-faced. The word, of course, is related to "duplicate" and "duplex" and "double." Montresor is behaving as his own opposite in his dealings with Fortunato. As the story progresses, however, it will become clearer that the other side of Montresor's personality is not the smiling face he offers to Fortunato.

The story is filled with twins and opposites. The characters' names, for example, bounce off each other, two echoes of the same idea. The name "Montresor" carries the idea of "treasure," and

"Fortunato" implies "fortune." Two sides of the same coin, as it were. As the two men walk along the damp passageway, Montresor offers Fortunato two bottles of wine: Medoc, thought to have medicinal powers and promising to "defend us from the damps," and De Grave, a wine whose name means "of the grave." Just afterward, Fortunato makes a "gesticulation," a secret gesture that demonstrates that he is a member of the Free and Accepted Masons, a secret fraternal order. In a scene that calls to mind nothing so much as Harpo Marx, Montresor produces a trowel from beneath his cloak, a sign that he, too, is a mason but of a different, deadly variety.

As the story opens, the men seem more different than alike. Montresor is cold, calculating, sober in every sense of the word. Fortunato greets him with "excessive warmth, for he had been drinking much." Montresor wears a black mask, a short cloak and a rapier or sword, the very image of a distinguished gentleman. Fortunato, on the other hand, is dressed for "the supreme madness of the carnival season" in motley, the jester's costume, complete with ''tight-fitting parti-striped'' clothing and a pointed cap with jingling bells at the tip. A drunken man with bells on his hat seems no match for Montresor, and it is hard to imagine Fortunato as ''a man to be respected, and even feared'' as he sways and staggers and fixates on the prospect of tasting more wine, the Amontillado.

Montresor continues his duplicity. He suggests that Luchesi could taste the wine instead of Fortunato, knowing that the suggestion will make Fortunato all the more eager to taste it himself. He repeatedly fusses over Fortunato's health, proposing that they ought to turn back before the foul air makes his ''friend'' ill, when in fact he intends that Fortunato will never leave the catacombs alive. He emphasizes the ways in which they are opposites: ''You are rich, respected, admired, beloved; you are happy, as once I was. You are a man to be missed. For me it is no matter.''

Up to this point, even the conversation between the two establishes their different purposes. Looking over Montresor's shoulders, the reader is aware of the irony when Fortunato says, ''the cough is a mere nothing; it will not kill me. I shall not die of a cough'' and Montresor replies, ''True true.'' Although Montresor's plans have not yet been revealed, the reader knows with growing certainty that Fortunato will die. When Montresor and Fortunato share the therapeutic Medoc, Fortunato drinks ''to the buried that repose around us,'' and Montresor replies, ''And I to your long life.''

From this point, things begin to change. Montresor's determination to hold himself as unlike Fortunato slips, and he becomes more like him with every step, as the wine works its effect on both of them. ''The wine sparkled in his eyes and the bells jingled. My own fancy grew warm with the Medoc.'' Previously, Fortunato has twice taken Montresor's arm to steady himself as they walk. Now Montresor returns the gesture, ''I made bold to seize Fortunato by an arm above the elbow.'' When they reach the end of the final passageway, Poe presents a flurry of twos: two men in ''the interval between two of the colossal supports'' confronted with ''two iron staples, distant from each other about two feet.'' But as soon as Montresor fastens the padlock on the chain around Fortunato's waist, the two are one.

Now, when Fortunato speaks, Montresor echoes his words. ''The Amontillado!'' Fortunato cries out, and Montresor replies, ''True, the Amontilla-

> **"** When one of Poe's protagonists is wrestling with guilt, Hoffman explains, he sometimes 'doubles his character and then arranges for one self to murder the other by burying him alive.'"

do.'' ''Let us be gone,'' says Fortunato, and Montresor replies, ''Yes, let us be gone.'' ''For the love of God, Montresor!'' cries Fortunato. ''Yes,'' Montresor says, ''for the love of God!'' Montresor becomes unnerved when Fortunato abruptly stops the game, when he refuses to speak any more. ''I hearkened in vain for a reply. I grew impatient.'' Why does Montresor wish Fortunato to keep speaking? Why does he shine his torch inside, hoping for a response? It is when he gets no answer except ''only a jingling of the bells'' that his heart grows sick.

The most chilling moment in the story happens, surely not coincidentally, at midnight (the time when the two hands of the clock are in one place), when the two men transcend human speech and communicate their oneness in another voice. Fortunato begins it with ''a succession of loud and shrill screams, bursting suddenly from the throat of the chained form.'' At first, Montresor does not know how to respond to this communication. He moves ''violently back,'' hesitates, trembles. He waves his rapier around, fearing that Fortunato is coming for him, but is reassured at the touch of the solid walls. ''The thought of an instant,'' the realization that Fortunato is tightly bound, makes Montresor feel safe, and his reaction is dramatic and bizarre: ''I reapproached the wall. I replied to the yells of him who clamored. I reechoed I aided I surpassed them in volume and in strength.'' It is difficult to imagine the sounds produced by two men, enemies and opposites, hundreds of feet underground howling at midnight in a damp stone chamber. Surely the volume and the echoes would not yield two distinct voices, but one grotesque sound. For that moment, the two are one.

After the wall is completed, fifty years pass before Montresor tells the story. What has he learned in the intervening years? Has he felt remorse? For most of the story, Montresor's language is clear and direct, although the formality of nineteenth-century speech may seem difficult to modern readers. In the story's opening paragraph, told fifty years after the crime, the language is uncharacteristically convoluted and opaque: ''A wrong is unredressed when retribution overtakes its redresser. It is equally unredressed when the avenger fails to make himself felt as such to him who has done the wrong.'' Most readers pause over these lines, stopping to sort out the redresser and the redressed from the redressee. If the roles are confusing, it is because in Montresor's mind the lines between avenger and victim are no longer distinct. When Montresor speaks the story's last line, ''In pace requiescat'' (''rest in peace''), is he speaking of Fortunato or of himself? By the end of the story, the two are so connected that it is all the same.

If Poe did intend the two men to be read as twins or doubles, what can he have meant by it? Critics have been pondering this question for over a century and a half. Daniel Hoffman, in *Poe Poe Poe Poe Poe Poe Poe*, explores Poe's theme of ''the fate of the man haunted by his own double, his anima, his weird.'' When one of Poe's protagonists is wrestling with guilt, Hoffman explains, he sometimes ''doubles his character and then arranges for one self to murder the other by burying him alive. In repeatedly telling stories of murderous doubles (''The Tell-Tale Heart,'' ''William Wilson,'' and others), Poe was attempting to deal with his own demons, his own repressed guilt. Poe biographer William Bittner claims that Montresor and Fortunato ''are two sides of the same man Edgar Poe as he saw himself while drinking.'' For Betina Knapp, author of a study titled *Edgar Allan Poe*, the ''shadow figure emerges as a personification of the narrator's hostile feelings and thoughts, symbolizing the repressed instincts of the personality.'' In his criticism and his daily life, Poe ''felt himself striking back, at those forces in society or particularly individuals who might have wronged him.''

Characters encountering and slaying their doubles are found throughout history and throughout the world, from Aristotle's story of a man who could not go out without meeting his ''double'' to *Dr. Jekyll and Mr. Hyde* to Luke Skywalker meeting Darth Vader in Yoda's cave, killing him, and seeing that the face beneath the mask is his own. The Germans have a name for the phenomenon doppelganger, meaning ''double walker'' and psy-

chiatrists have recorded thousands of accounts of people who believe that they have actually encountered mirror images of themselves, usually late at night. Like other archetypal images, the encounter with the double, the other side of oneself, is a powerful image that has attracted and repelled for centuries. Poe anticipated modern psychology with its id, ego and superego by showing through his stories that the monsters outside are nothing compared to the monsters we carry within us.

Source: Cynthia Bily, for *Short Stories for Students*, The Gale Group, 2000.

Leonard W. Engel

In the following essay, Engel discusses Poe's use of enclosures, both figurative and literal, in ''The Cask of Amontillado.''

Edgar Allan Poe used the enclosure device, whether an actual physical enclosure or an enclosure alluded to on the level of image and metaphor, in a highly artistic way. In much of his fiction, and specifically in ''The Cask of Amontillado'' (1846), the device helps to focus the action, assists in plot development, and has a profound impact on the main character, often affecting his personality. In his essay ''The Philosophy of Composition'' Poe remarked, ''A close *circumscription of space* is absolutely necessary to the effect of insulated incident:—it has the force of a frame to a picture.'' A ''circumscription of space,'' that is, an enclosure, I consider to be any sort of physical confinement that restricts a character to a particular area, limiting his freedom. That Poe intended this confinement to have a certain power over narrative action is indicated by the phrases ''insulated incident'' and ''the force of a frame to a picture.'' But confinement in Poe's fiction, I will argue, also has power over a character and often causes him to do things he would not ordinarily do. Such is the case, I believe, with the tale ''The Cask of Amontillado.''

Montresor, the narrator, it will be remembered, unlike the narrators in other tales (such as ''The Tell-Tale Heart'' and ''The Black Cat'') who have murdered their victims and then tried to conceal their bodies, does succeed in concealing his crime, but it has so obsessed his memory and imagination that fifty years after the act, he is able to render an exact, detailed description as though it occurred the previous day. Like the narrator in ''The Black Cat,'' Montresor uses an enclosure to conceal his victim, but Poe places more emphasis on it in "The Cask of Amontillado" by making it a vault which Montresor fashions himself, within his own family catacombs under the city—an enclosure within a series of enclosures. One might argue that Poe uses the same device in "The Black Cat," for the narrator in that tale conceals his wife's body within a wall of his cellar. The main difference lies in the fact that in "The Cask of Amontillado" Poe centers the entire plot on the journey through the catacombs and into the vault in which Fortunato is finally walled up. In the former tale, Poe, while concentrating on the narrator's neurosis throughout the tale, dramatizes the main enclosure at the climax. In "The Cask of Amontillado," the enclosures are more directly related to the narrator's neurosis.

The journey of Montresor and Fortunato through the catacombs becomes gloomier and more ominous with each step. Montresor relates: "We had passed through walls of piled bones, with casks and puncheons intermingling, into the inmost recesses of the catacombs. . . .'The nitre!' I said; 'see, it increases. It hangs like moss upon the vaults. We are below the river's bed. The drops of moisture trickle among the bones. Come, we will go back ere it is too late. Your cough—' 'It is nothing,' he said; 'let us go on.'"

Furthermore, Montresor's language in the following passage emphasizes the enclosure:

> We passed through a range of low arches . . . and . . . arrived at a deep crypt. . . . At the most remote end of the crypt there appeared another less spacious. Its walls had been lined with human remains, piled to the vault overhead, in the fashion of the great catacombs of Paris. Three sides of this interior crypt were still ornamented in this manner. From the fourth the bones had been thrown down, and lay promiscuously upon the earth, forming at one point a mound of some size. Within the wall . . . we perceived a still interior recess, in depth about four feet, in width three, in height six or seven.

When Fortunato, at Montresor's urging, enters this tiny "interior crypt" in search of the Amontillado, Montresor quickly chains him to the granite wall and begins "to wall up the entrance of the niche."

Montresor's last comment and his description of the enclosures indicate a certain relish for the plan, its locale, and the task of walling up his victim. He even pauses at one point to hear more precisely Fortunato's clanking the chain and to take pleasure in it: "The noise lasted for several minutes, during

> "Fortunato, as a character, has little importance; he becomes significant as the object of Montresor's self-hatred, of the projection of his guilt for his aristocratic family's decline."

which, that I might hearken to it with the more satisfaction, I ceased my labors and sat down upon the bones." As the narrator in "The Pit and the Pendulum" is the victim of the enclosure, greatly fearing the pit and its unknown horrors, Montresor in this tale is the homicidal victimizer, fully aware of the horrors of enclosure, enjoying them, and scheming to make them as terrifying as possible.

In spite of his quick and effective work, Montresor pauses twice more before he finishes. The first pause occurs when Fortunato releases a "succession of loud and shrill scream." "For a brief moment I hesitated—I trembled. Unsheathing my rapier, I began to grope with it about the recess: but the thought of an instant reassured me. I placed my hand upon the solid fabric of the catacombs, and felt satisfied. I reapproached the wall. I replied to the yells of him who clamored. I re-echoed—I aided—I surpassed them in volume and in strength. I did this, and the clamorer grew still." The frantic screams of Fortunato momentarily disturb Montresor, until he is reassured by the thought of the locale—the enclosures—and "the solid fabric of the catacombs."

The second disturbance comes when he is nearly finished. He thrusts the torch through the remaining aperture and lets it fall: "There came forth in return only a jingling of the bells. My heart grew sick—on account of the dampness of the catacombs. I hastened to make an end of my labor. I forced the last stone into its position; I plastered it up." At this crucial instant, Montresor tells us, his "heart grew sick"; of course, he is quick to assure us it is because of "the dampness of the catacombs." Although Montresor is obviously fascinated by the deadly enclosure, and uses it with satisfaction in walling up Fortunato, he also experiences moments of horror while within it.

In this story, then, enclosure has a dual aspect. While it is Montresor's main source of delight in planning his revenge, it does create momentary flashes of panic which almost disrupt his carefully planned revenge. One wonders if on a subconscious level Montresor is not trying to isolate, and enclose, a part of himself and a neurosis he hates—symbolized by Fortunato: Once his victim is walled up and Montresor's neurosis is in a sense buried and out of sight, he believes he will probably regain some measure of sanity. But, of course, Poe does not allow him this luxury, for the conclusion of the tale clearly indicates that even though the long dead Fortunato may be buried, Montresor is still obsessed with the details of the crime and can recite them complete and intact after half a century.

Like the narrators of ''The Tell-Tale Heart'' and ''The Black Cat,'' Montresor buries his victim on his premises. But Montresor goes much deeper than the other two narrators, deeper than his cellar, deeper even than his family's subterranean burial ground, though he passes through it to reach the tiny crypt he has prepared for Fortunato. It seems as if he is reaching deep into the past, into his ancestral heritage, to deal with his current problem, Fortunato's insult. Like the other two narrators, he could have disposed of his victim in any number of ways having nothing to do with an enclosure, but he used burial and chose his family's catacombs, even his ancestors' bones, to conceal Fortunato's body: ''Against the new masonry I re-erected the old rampart of bones.'' His act indicates that though he wants to be rid of his victim, he wants him to remain within reach, that is to say, among the bones of his ancestral past.

Fortunato, as a character, has little importance; he becomes significant as the object of Montresor's self-hatred, of the projection of his guilt for his aristocratic family's decline. Montresor says at one point, when his unwitting victim remarks on the extensiveness of the vaults, that ''the Montresors . . . were a great and numerous family,'' implying that they once were but no longer are; and Poe is careful not to mention any immediate family of Montresor.

Like the other two narrators, Montresor, while taking pains to conceal his crime, must needs be found out. However, unlike the other narrators, whose crimes are discovered shortly after they are committed, Montresor's is not found out until he informs the reader of it fifty years afterward. So, although the crime appears successful, the revenge is not, because Montresor has not freed himself from guilt—a fact indicated by his rendering of details which have no doubt obsessed him through every day since the deed. His final words, ''In pace requiescat!'', underscore Poe's irony. Montresor's rest has surely been troubled. Why he has preferred anonymity, while sustaining this obsession during those years, might well be explained by his unconscious fear of the guilt he would, once it was found out, consciously have to accept. And having to accept it might drive him insane, as it does the narrator at the conclusion of ''The Tell-Tale Heart,'' or it might force him to acknowledge the depth of his evil and truly repent—something Montresor is loath to do—as it does the narrator of ''The Black Cat,'' who reveals to the reader that he ''would unburthen [his] . . . soul'' before he dies.

It appears, then, that Montresor is making Fortunato a scapegoat and symbolically enclosing Fortunato, his own identity, in a hidden crypt deep within his own soul—out of sight but certainly not forgotten. A similar view has been expressed by Charles Sweet: ''Montresor's premature burial of his mirror self in the subterranean depths of his ancestral home (house equals mind in Poe) paints a psychological portrait of repression; the physical act of walling up an enemy in one's home duplicates the mental act of repressing a despised self in the unconscious.'' Montresor, Sweet continues, ''buries alive his scapegoat. . . . In Montresor's unconscious mind he is not murdering Fortunato, but burying/repressing that dilettantish side of himself he can no longer endure, that side symbolized by Fortunato.'' The enclosure Poe uses in ''The Cask Amontillado,'' in addition to being the focal point of the plot, providing a journey through a series of enclosures, and adding a sense of pervasive gloom and oppression to the tale, also becomes the central symbol in my interpretation. These enclosures and the crypt in which Montresor buries Fortunato are metaphors for Montresor's obsessive mind and the complex relationship between the reality of his disturbed inner self and his controlled, rational outer appearance. They emphasize his neurosis and symbolize the guilt he wishes to bury. Thus, Poe's enclosures in this enigmatic tale provide it with a thematic unity and an artistic integrity it might not otherwise have.

View of casks or barrels of wine aging in an underground cellar.

Source: Leonard W. Engel, ''Victim and Victimizer: Poe's 'The Cask of Amontillado,''' in *Interpretations: A Journal of Idea, Analysis, and Criticism*, Vol. 15, No. 1, Fall, 1983, pp. 26–30.

James F. Cooney

In the following essay, Cooney discusses the various effects of Poe's ironic plays on religion ''The Cask of Amontillado.''

Although readers of ''The Cask of Amontillado'' have long been aware of the ironies that operate throughout to give special intensity to this tale, an awareness of its Roman Catholic cultural and theological materials adds to the irony and transforms clever trick into an episode of horror.

Throughout the entire episode—its planning, its execution, and its confession—Monsieur Montresor made self-conscious use of cunning, plotting, and irony to wreak his revenge. The French nobleman tells his story of the calmly calculated murder of his Italian aristocratic friend Fortunato. The crime had been perfectly executed; for fifty years now the act has gone undiscovered. Every smallest detail had been so carried out as to satisfy the criminal's two-fold purpose: Montresor would

have revenge without himself getting caught; and, as the avenger, he would make quite sure ''to make himself felt as such to him who has done the wrong.'' Thus he followed the motto on his coat of arms: ''Nemo me impugne lacessit.''

In the course of the narrative we learn how Montresor used the cutting edge of irony to give a surgeon's neatness to his work and to secure the greatest possible delight for himself. With consummate evil he chose the carnival season for his crime. The carnival in question was *Carnevale*, a three days' festivity ending at midnight on Ash Wednesday, during which time, in Catholic cultures, people have one last fling of merriment before beginning the somber Lenten fast. The season afforded a perfect setting for murder: servants were out of the house celebrating, the noise and frenzy of the crowds allowed the murderer to go about his work unnoticed, the high spirits of the season provided an appropriately ironic background for Montresor's playful antics with his victim, and the somber, religious quiet that settled upon the city at midnight was just the right mood for Fortunato's final hour. How appropriate that the victim go to his death in a catacomb while devout Christians were about to gather in churches above to receive blessed ashes, symbol of their mortality, and to hear the warning,

> Montresor relied upon the power of sacramental confession for himself. For Montresor is not simply speaking to a sympathetic friend; he is also making his deathbed confession to a priest."

"Remember man, you are dust and to dust you will return."

But overlying the story is another irony that Montresor is not conscious of, an irony that the reader is only vaguely conscious of, although its presence is felt quite strongly in several places. Basic to appreciating this irony is a correct understanding of sacramental confession. When Montresor killed Fortunato, he counted upon the judgment of God as the final instrument of revenge. He killed his enemy by leading him into sins of pride, vanity, and drunkenness; and without a chance for confession, Fortunato presumably would have been damned with no capacity for striking back in time or eternity. Moreover, to assure his own salvation, Montresor relied upon the power of sacramental confession for himself. For Montresor is not simply speaking to a sympathetic friend; he is also making his deathbed confession to a priest.

Montresor misses the irony of the phrase at the beginning of his confession, "You, who so well know the nature of my soul," with its implication that the penitent had been confessing to this priest for some time, but had not been confessing *all* his sins. In theological terms these were bad confessions because the efficacy of the sacrament hinges upon the sincere disposition and sorrow of the penitent for all his sins. When this is lacking, the sacrament, instead of being an instrument of salvation, becomes an instrument of damnation. Such confessions were sins of sacrilege. Montresor, therefore, has been confessing in vain.

And even now, when on his deathbed Montresor confesses all his sins, he is deluded in thinking himself forgiven. He seems to be unaware, but the reader is not, of the gleeful tone of his confession. Montresor is taking delight in the very telling of his crime—hardly the disposition of a truly repentant sinner. Thus, the "In pace requiescat" with which he finishes his confession is ambiguous. We can see it as a superficial expression of sorrow or a quiet satisfaction in the lasting, unchallenged completeness of his revenge. Here, surely, is the irony of a confession without repentance, an irony that makes the entire plan double back upon the doer.

Finally, Montresor's most serious miscalculation was his total failure to understand the ineffable power of God's mercy. Apparently he had forgotten a fundamental lesson of his catechism, that a person in serious sin—even without sacramental confession—can turn to God, out of love, and in an instant make an "act of contrition" that can win immediate pardon. Fortunato's plea, "For the love of God, Montresor," was directly addressed to his murderer, but implicitly it was a prayer expressing faith in the power of God's loving-kindness. To this, Montresor was deaf; and when the prayer received a merciful hearing in heaven, Montresor's stratagems backfired. Fortunato, lucky as his name suggests, was saved; Montresor, damned. The final effect is one of horror. The ultimate irony is that of a puny creature playing games with God.

Source: James F. Cooney, "'The Cask of Amontillado': Some Further Ironies," in *Studies in Short Fiction*, Vol. XI, No. 2, Spring, 1974, pp. 195–6.

James W. Gargano

In the following essay Gargano explores Poe's subtle use of action and dialogue. Gargano contends that action and dialogue that at first appear "accidental" actually carry a great deal of "connotative value."

"The Cask of Amontillado," one of Edgar Allan Poe's richest aesthetic achievements, certainly deserves more searching analysis than it has received. To be sure, critics and anthologists have almost unanimously expressed admiration for the tale; still, they have rarely attempted to find in it a consistently developed and important theme. Indeed, most criticism of the story has the definitive ring that one associates with comments on closed issues. Arthur Hobson Quinn, for example, pronounces Poe's little masterpiece "a powerful tale of revenge in which the interest lies in the implacable nature of the narrator." More recently, Edward Wagenknecht asserts that the tale derives its value from Poe's "absolute concentration upon the psychological effect."

A few adventurous critics, however, have tried to define the theme of "The Cask of Amontillado" in terms of a split or division within the psyche of the narrator-protagonist or within the author himself. Edward H. Davison has ably related the story to Poe's broad concern with "the multiple character of the self." Davidson concludes that the narrator, Montresor, is capable of becoming two distinct beings with little affinity to each other: "'The Cask of Amontillado' . . . is the tale of another nameless 'I' [*sic*] who has the power of moving downward from his mind or intellectual being and into his brutish or physical self and then of returning to his intellectual being with his total selfhood unimpaired." On the other hand, William Bittner, unconcerned with the division within Montresor, speculates that the "two characters are two sides of the same man—Edgar Poe." Unfortunately, Davidson weakens his judgment by ignoring the role of Fortunato, and Bittner's opinion, if valid, would tell us more about Poe than about Poe's story. Unfortunately, too, Richard Wilbur makes no mention of the tale in "The House of Poe," a brilliant and perhaps seminal essay in which he characterizes the "typical Poe story" as made up of "allegorical figures, representing the warring principles of the poet's divided nature."

In their emphasis upon the psychological "effect" produced by "The Cask of Amontillado," Wagenknecht and others imply that Poe's story has a great deal of art and little or no meaning. In fact, Wagenknecht goes so far as to categorize it with those tales from which Poe deliberately "excludes the ethical element." Once drained of "thought" or serious implication, "The Cask of Amontillado" becomes little more than a remarkably well-executed incident, a literary *tour de force* whose sustained excitement or horror justifies its existence. It degenerates into an aesthetic trick, a mere matter of clever manipulation, and cannot be considered among Poe's major triumphs. Perhaps it is this sense of the work's empty virtuosity which leads W. H. Auden rather loftily to belittle it.

I believe that "The Cask of Amontillado" has discouraged analysis because, uniquely for Poe, it makes its point in a muted and even subtle manner that seems deceptively like realistic objec-

> **Action and dialogue that at first appear accidental or merely horrific appear, upon close examination, to have far-reaching connotative value."**

tivity. Proceeding in a style that Buranelli calls "unencumbered directness," the narrator does not, like the protagonist in "The Tell-Tale Heart," loudly and madly proclaim his sanity; unlike the main characters in "The Imp of the Perverse," "The Black Cat," and "The Tell-Tale Heart," Montresor never suffers the agonizing hallucinations that lead to self-betrayal; moreover, he does not rant, like William Wilson, about his sensational career of evil or attempt, as does the nameless narrator of "Ligeia," an excruciating analysis of his delusions and terrors. Instead, he tells his tale with outward calm and economy; he narrates without the benefit of lurid explanations; he states facts, records dialogue, and allows events to speak for themselves. In short, "The Cask of Amontillado" is one of Poe's most cryptic and apparently noncommittal works.

Yet, though the tale restricts the amount of meaning directly divulged, almost all of its details fuse into a logical thematic pattern. Action and dialogue that at first appear accidental or merely horrific appear, upon close examination, to have far-reaching connotative value. The usual critical presumption that Montresor and Fortunato provide the narrative with a convenient Gothic "villain" and "victim" must give way to the view that they are well-conceived symbolic characters about whom Poe quietly gives a surprising amount of information. In addition, the setting and pervasive irony of the tale do not merely enhance the grotesque effect Poe obviously intends; more importantly, they contribute their share to the theme of the story. In short, "The Cask of Amontillado" is a work of art (which means it embodies a serious comment on the human condition) and not just an ingenious Gothic exercise.

I should like to suggest that Poe's tale presents an ironic vision of two men who, as surrogates of mankind, enter upon a "cooperative" venture that really exposes their psychological isolation. This theme of mock union disguising actual self-seeking intimates that the placid surface of life is constantly threatened and belied by man's subterranean and repressed motives. It also implies that, no matter how beguiling the surface may seem, human division is more "real" than union. Of course, Poe clearly shows the human affinities that make even a pretense of union possible and convincing, but he also reveals his characters' refusal to recognize or acknowledge the binding quality of those affinities. Moreover, as my consideration of the story will seek to prove, Poe suggests that man's inability to act upon these affinities leads to the self-violation that ultimately destroys him.

All the major facets of "The Cask of Amontillado" —action, the calculated contrast between Montresor and Fortunato, and the setting—emphasize the characters' relatedness and differences. In the first of the main incidents, the two men come together only to maintain their psychological separateness; in the second, they undertake an ostensibly common journey, but pursue divergent goals; and in the denouement, when the murderer should emancipate himself from his victim, he becomes psychically attached to him. Moreover, Poe's almost obtrusive point-by-point comparison of the two characters demonstrates that they possess unusual similarities concealed by incompatibilities. Even the masquerade setting subtly establishes the fact that the two men reverse, during the carnival season, the roles they play in "real" life: Fortunato, normally an affluent and commanding man, dwindles into a pitiful dupe, and Montresor, who considers himself a persecuted, social nonentity, takes control of his enemy's destiny and is controlled by it.

The masquerade setting is essential to the meaning of "The Cask of Amontillado." Through it, Poe consciously presents a bizarre situation in which the data of the surface of ordinary life are reversed. Fortunato, we learn, impresses the narrator as a "man to be respected and even feared," a man capable of highhandedly inflicting a "thousand injuries" and "insults." His social importance is more than once insisted upon: "You are rich, respected, admired, beloved." In addition, as a member of a Masonic lodge, he obviously patronizes Montresor: "You are not of the Masons . . . You? Impossible! A mason?" With a touch of self-important loftiness, he admits that he has forgotten, perhaps as something trivial, his companion's coat of

arms. Yet, Fortunato's supremacy dissolves in the carnival atmosphere: though he is a man of wealth and status, he is, for all the abilities implied by his success, an extremely vulnerable human being whose nature is revealed by his costume, that of a fool or jester: "The man wore motley. He had on a tight-fitting parti-striped dress, and his head was surmounted by the conical cap and bells." Absurdly off guard, he has obviously surrendered to the camaraderie of the occasion; he has drunkenly and self-indulgently relaxed his customary vigilance for the trusting mood of the season.

Montresor, on the other hand, is bitterly obsessed with his fall into social insignificance. He announces to Fortunato, with a submissiveness that masks his monomaniacal hatred, "You are happy, as once I was. You are a man to be missed. For me it is no matter." At another point, when his besotted and insensitive companion expresses surprise at the extensiveness of his vaults, he answers with pride: "The Montresors . . . were a great and numerous family." We must remember, too, that his plan to kill Fortunato, deriving from family feeling and a sense of injured merit, is in accordance with his coat of arms and motto. He regards himself as the vindicator of his ancestors, "The human foot d'or" about to crush the "serpent rampant whose fangs are imbedded in the heel." In other words, Fortunato's prosperity has somehow become associated in his mind with his own diminution. His decision to destroy his enemy, pointedly explained in his motto, "Nemo me impune lacessit," ("No one insults me with impunity") indicates that he suffers from a deep dynastic wound. Montresor, then, feels that Fortunato has, by ignoring his ancestral claims, stolen his birth-right and ground him into disgrace.

Yet, during the carnival, he is transformed into a purposive man to be feared. Intellectual and implacable, he designs his evil as if it were a fine art. He facilely baits his powerful adversary with a false inducement; he lures him deeper and deeper into the sinister vaults with cajolery and simulated interest in his health. The preposterous ease with which he manages Fortunato demonstrates how completely he has become the master of the man who has mastered and humiliated him. In the subterranean trip toward the fictitious amontillado, Montresor momentarily regains his birthright and reestablishes his family's importance by giving dramatic substance to the meaning of his coat of arms and motto. Of course, we must ask later whether his triumph is delusive and fleeting or whether, as Davidson declares, he returns to the real world with his ''total selfhood unimpaired.''

The carnival world, then, inverts and grotesquely parodies the actual world. From the beginning of the tale, when Montresor explains the evil motive behind his geniality toward Fortunato, Poe presents a picture of life in which man is bifurcated and paradoxical, dual rather than unified. We see that casual contacts, like Fortunato's meeting with Montresor, may be deeply calculated stratagems; people who greet each other as friends may be enemies; words of kindness and invitation may be pregnant with deceit; helpless gullibility may be allied with talent and firmness; and love may cloak hatred. Everywhere, opposites exist in strange conjunction. One recalls William Wilson's bewilderment as he contemplates the fact that his benign Sunday minister can ''double'' as a cruel teacher on weekdays: ''Oh, gigantic paradox, too utterly monstrous for solution.''

Clearly, the oppositions and disharmonies contained within individual men project themselves into the world and turn it into an ambiguous arena where appearances and words belie themselves. Every aspect of life is potentially deceptive because it has a double face. If universal unity once existed, as Poe speculates in *Eureka*, such harmony no longer prevails in a world where all is only remotely akin but more immediately heterogeneous and in conflict. Significantly, even in the midst of his bitter feud with his namesake, William Wilson entertains the ''belief of my having been acquainted with the being who stood before me, at some epoch very long ago—some point of the past even infinitely remote.'' Yet, he dismisses this insight as a ''delusion'' and persists in his enmity toward the second William Wilson. It is not surprising, then, that man's internal discord recreates ''reality'' in its own image and that single words, like single persons, contain diverse and incompatible meanings. Montresor's wine ''vaults,'' which contain the precious amontillado, become Fortunato's burial ''vaults.'' Fortunato boasts of his membership in a Masonic order, but it is the narrator, who as a different kind of mason, walls up and suffocates his enemy. For Fortunato, Montresor's coat of arms and motto are mere emblems, hardly to be given a second thought, whereas for the latter they are spurs to malevolent action. In one of the most brilliant scenes in the story, the entombed victim's shrieks express his agony; the murderer imitates these shrieks,

but his clamor is a gleeful parody of pain. In fact, both men once utter almost identical sentences to express the contrary emotions of terror and joy:

> ''Let us be gone.'' ''Yes'', I said, ''let us be gone.''
> *''For the love of God, Montresor!''* ''Yes,'' I said, ''for the love of God.''

Poe's irony in ''The Cask of Amontillado'' extends to many details that invest life with an eerie inscrutability. Fortunato, the fortunate man, is singled out for murder. Montresor, ''my treasure,'' locks within himself a treasure of ancestral loathing which impoverishes his nature. Both characters, it soon becomes evident, are intoxicated, one with wine and the other with an excess of intellectualized hatred. Fortunato, on his way to certain death, ironically drinks a toast to ''the buried that repose around us.'' Before his last colloquy with his companion, Montresor expresses a perverse impulse of his being and calls Fortunato ''noble.'' The irony of the last words of the tale, *''In pace requiescat,''* is only too evident. So too is the irony of the method by which the narrator, in ordering his servants to remain at home during his announced ''absence,'' insures that they will be away while he perpetrates his crime safely at home.

Obviously, the ironic pattern of ''The Cask of Amontillado'' adumbrates a world caught in a ceaseless masquerade of motive and identity. Nevertheless, Poe does not naively cleave the world into two irreconcilable antinomies. Instead, he demonstrates that Montresor's dissimulation is an unnatural and unbearable act. For in spite of himself, the narrator's self-divisive behavior affronts his own need for a unified psyche and conscience. After all, he really longs to be what Fortunato is and what he and his family once were. In short, the major ironies of ''The Cask of Amontillado'' are that Fortunato represents Montresor's former self and that the latter deludes himself in imagining that he can regain his ''fortune'' by the violent destruction of his supposed nemesis. Ironically, he turns his energy and genius against himself, against the memory of his lost eminence. Once again, then, Montresor resembles Fortunato in being the dupe of his own crazed obsessions; in the truest sense, he is as much a fool as the wearer of motley. Contrary to Davidson's belief that the narrator recovers his total selfhood after the crime, Montresor is broken on the wheel of a world in which violence is simultaneously an internal and external action. It is in accordance with this principle that the narrator in ''The Black Cat'' feels that in hanging his pet he is ''beyond the reach of the infinite mercy of the Most Merciful and

Most Terrible God.'' Montresor no more achieves his revenge than his victim comes into the possession of the amontillado.

In the final analysis, like so many Poe characters, Montresor fails because he cannot harmonize the disparate parts of his nature and, consequently, cannot achieve self-knowledge. His mind overrules his heart as much as Fortunato's drunken goodfellowship—his trusting heart—has repealed his intellect. Fortunato's ironically meaningful words, ''You are not of the brotherhood,'' imply, on the symbolic level of the tale, that Montresor lives too deeply in his plots and stratagems to have any warm affiliation with mankind; still, though he prides himself that he can commit murder with impunity, he cannot completely eradicate those subconscious feelings which establish—no matter what he wills or intellectually devises—his relatedness to Fortunato. Just as William Wilson's refusal to recognize his ''conscience'' does not eliminate it or deprive it of retributive power, Montresor's intellectualization of his actions does not divest them of their psychological consequences. He remains so divided against himself that, as he consummates his atrocity, it recoils upon him; the purposefulness with which he initiated his plan almost immediately distintegrates. As his victim screams, he momentarily hesitates, trembles, and unsheathes his rapier. With unwitting self-betrayal, he refers to the buried man as the ''noble Fortunato.'' In addition, he confesses that, at the final jingle of his foe's bells, ''my heart grew sick.'' Even though he obtusely attributes his sickness to an external cause, ''the dampness of the catacombs,'' his rationalization should deceive no alert reader. And lastly, his compulsively detailed rehearsal of his crime after fifty years demonstrates that it still haunts and tortures his consciousness.

The ending of ''The Cask of Amontillado'' leaves little doubt as to the spiritual blindness of the protagonist. Montresor resembles many Poe characters who, with no self-awareness, project their own internal confusions into the external world. William Wilson, for example, never understands that his conflict with his strange namesake represents an inner turmoil; with almost his last breath, he declares that he is ''the slave of circumstances beyond human control.'' Certainly, the narrator of ''The Tell-Tale Heart'' fails to discover that the insistent heartbeat he hears and cannot escape is his own rather than that of the murdered old man. To cite a final example, the main character in ''The Black Cat'' never suspects that his mutilation of

Pluto is an objective equivalent of his own serf-impairment. Montresor, I am convinced, should be included in Poe's gallery of morally blind murderers; he does not understand that his hatred of Fortunato stems from his inner quarrel with ''fortune'' itself. Undoubtedly, Fortunato symbolizes Montresor's lost estate, his agonizing remembrance of lapsed power and his present spiritual impotence. With a specious intellectuality, common to Poe's violent men, Montresor seeks to escape from his own limitations by imagining them as imposed upon him from beyond the personality by outside force. But the force is a surrogate of the self, cozening man toward damnation with all the brilliant intrigue Montresor uses in destroying Fortunato.

Source: James W. Gargano, '''The Cask of Amontillado': A Masquerade of Motive and Identity,'' in *Studies in Short Fiction*, Vol. IV, October, 1966 - July, 1967, pp. 119–26.

Sources

Benton, Richard P. ''Poe's 'The Cask of Amontillado': Its Cultural and Historical Backgrounds,'' in *Poe Studies,*, Vol. 29, No. 1, June 1, 1996, pp. 19-21.

Bittner, William. *Poe: A Biography*, Boston: Atlantic Monthly Press, 1962, p. 218.

Buranelli, Vincent. *Edgar Allan Poe,* Boston: Twayne, 1977.

Colton, George. Review of ''Poe's Tales,'' in *American Whig Review*, Vol. 2, September, 1845, pp. 306-309.

Dana, Charles A. Review of *Tales*, in *Brook Farm Harbinger*, Vol. 1, July 12, 1845, p. 74.

Edinburgh Review, Vol. 107, April, 1858, pp. 419-42.

Griswold, Rufus Wilmot. Obituary in *New York Tribune*, Vol. 9, October 9, 1849, p. 2. Reprinted in Carlson, Eric W., *The Recognition of Edgar Allan Poe*, Ann Arbor: University of Michigan Press, 1966, pp. 28-35.

Gruesser, John. ''Poe's 'The Cask of Amontillado','' in *The Explicator*, Vol. 56, No. 3, 1998, p. 130.

Harris, Kathryn Montgomery. ''Ironic Revenge in Poe's 'The Cask of Amontillado','' in *Studies in Short Fiction*, Vol. 6, 1969, pp. 333-335.

Hoffman, Daniel. *Poe Poe Poe Poe Poe Poe Poe*, Garden City, New York: Doubleday, 1972, pp. 221, 224.

Knapp, Bettina L. *Edgar Allan Poe*, New York: Frederick Ungar, 1984, pp. 152- 155, 180.

Poe, Edgar Allan. Review of Nathaniel Hawthorne's *Twice-Told Tales*, originally published in *Godey's Lady's Book*, 1847. Reprinted in *The Portable Poe*, edited by Philip Van Doren Stern, New York: Penguin, 1977, pp. 565-567.

Randall, John H., III. ''Poe's 'The Cask of Amontillado' and the Code of the Duello,'' in *Studia Germanica Gandensia*, Vol. 5, 1963, pp. 175-84.

Rocks, James E. ''Conflict and Motive in 'The Cask of Amontillado,''' in *Poe Newsletter*, Vol. 5, December 1972, pp. 50-51.

Further Reading

Botting, Fred. *Gothic*, New York: Routledge, 1996.
    A clear and accessible introduction to Gothic images and texts in their historical and cultural contexts. Includes a chapter on twentieth-century Gothic books and films.

Buranelli, Vincent. *Edgar Allan Poe*, Boston: Twayne, 1977.
    An overview of the life and work for the general reader, which includes a chronology, a helpful index, and a no-longer-current bibliography of primary and secondary sources.

Carlson, Eric W., ed. *The Recognition of Edgar Allan Poe: Selected Criticism Since 1829*, Ann Arbor: University of Michigan Press, 1966.
    A collection of reviews and commentaries, especially interesting for the remarks by those Poe influenced, including the French poet Charles Baudelaire, Russian novelist Fyodor Dostoevski, and British and American writers including Walt Whitman, William Butler Yeats, and T.S. Eliot.

Howarth, William L., ed. *Twentieth Century Interpretations of Poe's Tales: A Collection of Critical Essays*, Englewood Cliffs, N.J.: Prentice-Hall, 1971.
    The articles in this collection are generally insightful and accessible to the general reader.

Quinn, Arthur Hobson. *Edgar Allan Poe: A Critical Biography*, Baltimore: Johns Hopkins University Press, 1997.
    At over eight hundred pages, this scholarly work is the definitive and insightful, though difficult-to-read, biography.

Silverman, Kenneth. *Edgar A. Poe: Mournful and Neverending Remembrance*, New York: HarperCollins, 1992.
    A psychological approach to Poe's life, focuses on the writer's unresolved mourning as the source of his troubles. Excellent for its description of the literary life of the nineteenth century.

Walsh, John Evangelist. *Midnight Dreary: The Mysterious Death of Edgar Allan Poe*, New Brunswick, N.J.: Rutgers University Press, 1998.
    A factual, not a conjecturing, account of what is known and not known about Poe's last days.

The Daffodil Sky

H. E. Bates

1955

When "The Daffodil Sky" was published in 1955, H. E. Bates was already well known as a prolific writer of short stories and novels. The story itself is the title piece of a collection that has been described as the crowning achievement in Bates's later career. "The Daffodil Sky" and the collection's other stories have received generous praise from reviewers. As testament to their popularity, no less than nine stories from the collection appeared in the 1963 anthology *The Best of H. E. Bates*. The reputation of "The Daffodil Sky" remains high. Critics have applauded the compelling nature of its visual and sensual images, and the story is indeed filled with sights, sounds, and smells which vividly recreate a rainy summer evening in a sooty English industrial town. The characters who populate Bates's story have been admired for their passionate vitality, a feature which has prompted comparisons between them and those in the works of D. H. Lawrence.

Although Bates's story shares general similarities with Lawrence's work, a more notable literary antecedent for "The Daffodil Sky" is Alfred, Lord Tennyson's *Maud* (1855). This poem provided Bates not only with his story's title but also with a pattern for the plot. Just as the nameless protagonist of *Maud* kills the man whom he perceives as an obstacle to his happiness in love, so too does Bates's unnamed young lover kill a potential rival for his love. The literary relationship between Bates and Tennyson lends support to Bates's acknowledged status as a prose poet and underscores the fact that

Bates's subject matter has a universal appeal. "The Daffodil Sky" is about emotions; it is a tale of passion and jealousy, of rage and regret, and it plays out themes of alienation and loneliness which are common to the literature of many ages.

Author Biography

Herbert Ernest Bates was born May 16, 1905 in Rushden, Northamptonshire, England. He left school before the age of seventeen. After brief stints as a reporter and a clerk at a warehouse, he began to establish himself as a writer. His first novel, *The Two Sisters*, appeared in 1926; in the next fifteen years he published eight novels and more than a dozen short story collections. Among the most critically acclaimed works of his early career are his novel *The Poacher* (1935), his short story collections *Something Short and Sweet* (1937), and *My Uncle Silas* (1939).

In 1931 Bates married Marjorie Helen Cox, and they subsequently moved to Little Chart, Kent, England, where they raised four children. Although family life did not have a marked effect on Bates's output as an author, the outbreak of World War II did affect the direction of his work. In the summer of 1941, Bates was commissioned by the Royal Air Force to write works that described the exploits of fighter pilots. Publishing under the pseudonym "Flying Officer X," Bates produced two collections, *The Greatest People in the World* (1942) and *How Sleep the Brave* (1943), which were very popular in England. Other results of Bates's wartime experiences were his novels *Fair Stood the Wind For France* (1944), and *The Purple Plain* (1947), the first of his novels to be adapted to film.

Returning to civilian life after the war, Bates continued to write extensively. Throughout the 1950s some of his most highly praised short story collections appeared, including *Colonel Julian and Other Stories* (1951), *The Daffodil Sky* (1955), *Sugar for the Horse* (1957), and *The Watercress Girl and Other Stories* (1959).

Most of Bates's postwar fiction, however, is written in the novel form. Of his later novels, the five humorous books dealing with the adventures of the carefree Larkin family are the most notable. The first of the Larkin books, *The Darling Buds of May* (1958), was warmly received and was later adapted for television. In his last years, Bates produced a three-volume autobiography, *The Vanished World* (1969), *The Blossoming World* (1971), and *The World in Ripeness* (1972). He was made a Commander of the Order of the British Empire in 1973 and died in Canterbury, Kent, England on January 29, 1974.

Plot Summary

Part I: The Return

"The Daffodil Sky" opens with the story's nameless protagonist arriving by train in an unnamed town. A sign forbidding entry to a footbridge that he used to walk across suggests to him that the town has changed since he was last there. His sense that things have changed is confirmed when he enters a pub that he once frequented and finds a new pinball machine and no familiar faces. Falling into conversation with the barman, the protagonist asks about Cora Whitehead, a woman whom he met when he was twenty-two and who used to frequent the pub. The barman does not know Cora. His repeated response to the protagonist's comments about Cora's occupation and her acquaintances is that it has "been a minute"—that is, a very long time—since any of this information could be verified. One of the patrons, however, knows Cora, and he confirms that she still lives on Wellington Street. The protagonist finishes his drink and leaves.

Part II: Happy Memories

Stepping outside, the protagonist is reminded of the day years before when he first visited the pub. At this point the present fades and gives way to a flashback of past events. As a young farmer bringing a cartload of daffodils to market, the protagonist was caught in a sudden hailstorm one April morning. Running to get into the pub, he collided with Cora. His attraction to her was immediate. Once inside the pub, the protagonist realized that he wouldn't be able to get to market by noon, for he was trapped there by intermittent hailstorms. Cora reassured him that all would be well, and the luck with which Cora claimed to provide him held true. He managed to sell all of his daffodils to the crowds of late shoppers who ventured out to make purchases at the market.

The encounter with Cora did seem to bring luck to the protagonist. Full of life's promise, he replaced his cart with a motorcycle—"a Beardmore combination" which he purchased from Cora's friend,

H. E. Bates

Frankie Corbett—and he subsequently invested in a car. As the affair between the protagonist and Cora blossomed, his luck only seemed to improve. By August, the couple was contemplating purchasing the farmland that the protagonist rented from an aging farmer named Osborne, who was willing to sell on easy terms and at a good price. Their combined funds were insufficient, but Cora suggested that Frankie might help them raise the rest. Cora's offer to help with the purchase prompted the protagonist to propose marriage, and she gladly accepted. His happiness, however, was brief. Six weeks later, on a rainy October night, the protagonist killed Frankie.

Part III: Bitter Memories

The story returns to the present as the protagonist walks slowly up Wellington Street toward Cora's house. The sight of a man walking a dog reminds him of how Frankie had appeared on that October night years earlier, and the present scene gives way once more to a flashback. The protagonist was not surprised to see Frankie, for he had learned from Cora that Frankie exercised his dog each evening. The protagonist became jealous and increasingly suspicious of Cora's relationship with Frankie because Frankie had once been her lover and it had taken her a month of close contact with

Frankie to secure the loan. When he learned that Cora was pregnant, the protagonist's jealousy reached its height because he could not tolerate the thought that the child might be Frankie's. Although he claims that he merely desired a word with Frankie on the fatal night, the protagonist had come prepared for much more:

> He stopped him, and they stood on the pavement and spoke a word or two. He was trembling violently and the air was a confusion of red and black. A few heavier spits of rain came hastily down and Frankie said he was getting wet and hadn't all night to stand there jawing over trifles. ''There's no trifle about this and all I want is a straight answer.'' Then the dog yapped, splashing in a gutter puddle, and Frankie began to swing the crop. He had a sudden blind idea that the swing of the crop was meant for him. A moment later he was hitting at Frankie with a broccoli knife. It was a thin curved knife and he had sharpened it that morning on the grindstone, with Osborne turning the wheel. Then Frankie lashed at him with the crop and then in return he hit out with the knife again. At the fourth or fifth stroke Frankie fell and hit his skull against the iron lip of the gutter, and suddenly there was bright blood in the rain. (Excerpt from ''The Daffodil Sky'')

At the trial which followed, Cora testified—accurately, the protagonist admits—that his jealousy of Frankie had been of the darkest kind.

Part IV: The Meeting

The story returns to the present with the protagonist standing outside Cora's house at 84 Wellington Street. He is confused about why he has come. He realizes that at the age of forty (that is, eighteen years after the events of the flashbacks) he should neither look for a new confrontation nor view himself as the same man whose dreams died so long ago. He knocks on the door, dreading the possibility that he might kill Cora on the spot—an act that would not be regarded as manslaughter, as his attack on Frankie apparently had been.

When the door opens, he finds not Cora but her daughter. He claims to be an old friend but does not offer his name. When he is prevented from leaving by a sudden downpour, she offers him an umbrella and then decides to walk with him to the bus stop. The protagonist is attracted to the girl, for she has her mother's features and temperament. He lets the bus pass and admits that he has nowhere to go, but the girl does not seem surprised. Her friendliness makes his thoughts race. He wants to tell her about himself, yet he also wants to dash off and make a fresh start. The next moment he is in deep despair and feeling lonely. He begins to ask her a question but is cut off by the noise of a passing train. The girl assumes that he wants to ask her out, but he states that he wants a drink and asks her to join him. She accepts, and with the rain apparently ending, the two wander off to the pub.

Characters

Barman

The barman works in the pub that the protagonist frequented in his youth. The barman's repeated comment, "that's been a minute," meaning a very long time, establishes the intimate connection between past and present in the story.

Cora's daughter

See Miss Whitehead

Frankie Corbett

Frankie Corbett is a friend and former suitor of Cora Whitehead. His actions are limited to the flashbacks that dominate the middle of the story. Without appearing in the text, Frankie sells a motorcycle to the protagonist, and he subsequently lends money to the protagonist and Cora to help them purchase a farm. When the loan is being negotiated, Frankie receives considerable attention from Cora, and this fact enrages the increasingly jealous protagonist, particularly after Cora becomes pregnant. When Frankie finally does appear, taking his dog for a walk, he is promptly killed by the protagonist. During their encounter, Frankie is rather annoyed that the protagonist keeps him standing in the rain, and he impatiently dismisses the protagonist's concerns about his relationship with Cora as "trifles." When Frankie raises his cane, apparently to discipline his dog, the protagonist feels threatened and stabs him. After a few blows are exchanged, Frankie falls to the ground, striking his head against the edge of the gutter.

Daughter, Cora's

See Miss Whitehead

Osborne

Osborne is an elderly farmer who rents land to the protagonist. His willingness to sell his farm to the protagonist prompts the protagonist and Cora Whitehead to borrow money from Frankie Corbett.

Media Adaptations

• Although "The Daffodil Sky" is not itself available in other media formats, students might want to view the recent, highly acclaimed television adaptations of Bates's Larkin books to contrast his various tones and styles. The series *The Darling Buds of May* was produced by Yorkshire Television and stars David Jason, Pam Ferris, Philip Franks, and Catherine Zeta-Jones. It is available from Studio BL Home Video (released 1995).

Protagonist

A forty-year-old man, the protagonist has returned to the town where, eighteen years earlier, driven by jealous hatred, he killed Frankie Corbett. The protagonist has returned with the intention of finding and talking to Cora Whitehead, the woman to whom he was engaged at the time of the crime, and the person he blames for his troubles. Nonetheless, his feelings for Cora are ambiguous. His many memories of her are dominated by positive images of her warmth and sensuality. Only when he recalls his jealousy towards her involvement with Frankie or her damning testimony at his trial does he feel any remote sense of dislike toward her.

His mixed emotions are again evident when he finds not Cora but her teenage daughter. He may very well be the girl's father, but because she is so much like her mother he is strongly attracted to her. As a younger man, the protagonist was a creature of variable feelings, as he experienced the heights of hopeful love and the depths of jealous despair. By the story's end, however, the protagonist's emotions appear to be muted, as he would rather have a quiet drink with Cora's daughter than regard her as a substitute for her mother.

Cora Whitehead

Cora Whitehead was the protagonist's lover as a young man. The desire to see Cora compels the protagonist to return to the town where he spent his early adulthood, but Cora only appears in the flashbacks within the story. As a young woman, Cora exerts a powerful influence over the protagonist, for she is attractive and has an uncanny insight into his thoughts. Her relationship with Frankie Corbett, however, disturbs the protagonist. When she admits that Frankie was once her suitor, and then takes a month to secure a loan from him, the protagonist begins to suspect that she is unfaithful. Cora does little to put the protagonist's mind at ease, saying things like ''We want the money, don't we,'' and ''I got to get it the best way I can.'' Her subsequent pregnancy drives the protagonist to distraction and leads to his confrontation with Frankie. At the protagonist's trial, Cora testifies that the protagonist was extremely jealous of Frankie, a statement which the protagonist describes as typical of her ability to know his thoughts.

Miss Whitehead

Miss Whitehead is the daughter of Cora Whitehead. Bearing a striking resemblance to her mother, it is not clear whether her father is the protagonist or Frankie Corbett. It was this issue that led to the protagonist's jealous hatred of Frankie. She answers the door at 84 Wellington Street when the protagonist arrives looking for Cora, and she accompanies him through the pouring rain on his way back to the bus stop. She is coy, and given her likeness to her mother, the protagonist finds her attractive. Her presence in the final section of the story allows the protagonist to master his anger toward her mother and to escape the loneliness and despair he has felt since being incarcerated for the rash act of his youth.

Themes

Time

Given the movement between the events of the past and the present, time and its passage must be counted among the most significant themes in ''The Daffodil Sky.'' The story's treatment of time suggests that past errors must be accepted and cannot be forgotten. For the protagonist, past dreams of success and love are not distant memories. Indeed, he remembers his past ''as if, in the way the barman said, it had been a minute ago.'' Nonetheless, even if he is able to travel back in his mind, the protagonist is always separated from the past by the effects of his youthful mistakes. Frankie Corbett's death and the protagonist's years in jail form an impenetrable barrier between his past hopes and present reality. He can return home, but he can never return to his former life; blaming Cora Whitehead or simply talking to her about past events cannot restore what he has lost. By having the protagonist find Cora's daughter, a substitute for Cora but not the woman who is so much a part of his past, Bates indicates that the past is irrevocably gone. Time has marched on, and any effort to reclaim his lost years, either through confrontation or reconciliation, must be in vain. It is clear at the close of the story, then, that the only option open to the protagonist is to accept the present and to abandon any plan of picking up where he left off.

Alienation and Loneliness

Loneliness and alienation are central themes that grow in importance as the story progresses. At the outset, the protagonist's alienation is not pronounced, although it is evident when he discovers that the pub that he once frequented is now full of unfamiliar faces. His memories of the past indicate that he could be a sociable man, but they also show that his social qualities quickly faded as he began to distrust Cora. With mistrust came an increased distance between them that continued to grow as he fell prey to his jealousy, that all-consuming ''vast dark canker, ugly as death.'' The protagonist's alienation from Cora increased when he thought that she was carrying Frankie's child and reached its height when she testified against him at his trial. His plan, upon his return, is to find Cora and ''to have the last word: perhaps another violent one,'' a clear reference to his fatal meeting with Frankie in which a ''word'' led to murder.

The final meeting in the story, between the protagonist and Cora's daughter, confirms that he is truly a creature of loneliness. Standing next to her in the rain, he ''was aware of an awful loneliness. He felt sick with it. His stomach turned and was slipping out. It was the feeling he had known when they sentenced him.'' The story's close reinforces the themes of alienation and loneliness largely because the events of his past still govern him, and even the promise of friendship with Cora's daughter does not offer any firm hope of happiness or social intimacy.

Choices and Consequences

The intimate relationship between past and present events in the story emphasizes the important theme of choices and consequences. The events of the present inevitably result from the choices that the protagonist made in his youth. His present state could well reflect the promise of his youth if he had chosen to trust Cora's fidelity or had not prepared for his "word" with Frankie by equipping himself with a freshly sharpened knife. Choices—"the little things" that he did as a young man—have far-reaching effects. It is only in hindsight that the protagonist recognizes how one small suspicion led to another and how minor irritants grew to such proportions that they prompted him to commit murder.

At the same time, the protagonist's present actions do not always indicate that he has learned from his earlier experiences. Because he returns with the apparent intention of settling old scores, or at least opening old wounds, other rash choices and unfortunate consequences seem possible. His anxiousness as he waits for Cora shows how close he is to making a foolish decision, for he has "a terrified and blinding idea that if she opened the door he might not be able to restrain himself but would rush straight at her and kill her exactly as he had killed Frankie." The protagonist's subsequent restraint suggests that he now understands something about the nature of choices and consequences. Although he does not wish to live the next eighteen years in the shadow of another ill-considered act, it is not perfectly clear that he has learned a lesson, for his resolve to avoid violence is not truly tested by his meeting with Cora's daughter. In the end, the story leaves the matter open for debate, and it yet remains possible that the protagonist will again make regrettable choices.

Style

Point of View

"The Daffodil Sky" moves between the protagonist's solitary return in the present and his passions and crime in the past. In both the present scenes and the flashbacks Bates employs a limited, omniscient narrator. This type of narrator relates events in the third person ("he," "she," and "they") and offers insight into the minds of a limited number of characters—in this case, the protagonist's alone. This point of view makes the story more engaging than it might be otherwise. In using this approach, Bates blocks out the thoughts of the remaining characters, and he leaves the reader as uncertain about their motivations and attitudes as the protagonist. This uncertainty diminishes sympathy for the protagonist and magnifies the gravity of his crime,

Topics for Further Study

- Research the development of the welfare state in England during the 1940s and 1950s and discuss how "The Daffodil Sky" reflects England during the 1950s.

- Discuss Bates's characterization of women in "The Daffodil Sky."

- Analyze the character of the protagonist. What are his dominant traits? How do they contribute to his fate in both past and present?

- Research the English legal code's definition of murder and discuss why the protagonist in "The Daffodil Sky" was convicted of manslaughter. What evidence is there in the text to support this judgment?

for the reader cannot be certain that he is justified in believing that Cora Whitehead was unfaithful.

If, in contrast, the thoughts of Cora and Frankie Corbett were open to examination and it was clear that the two had engaged in sexual activity, the protagonist would tend to be a more sympathetic character. Under these circumstances, the murder of Frankie could be regarded as the regrettable act of a betrayed lover. The absence of such information, however, makes the murder appear to be the act of an all-too-impulsive and suspicious man. In the end, the truth must remain unknown because the point of view in "The Daffodil Sky" does not permit the reader to form an absolutely flawless picture of events. This ambiguity makes the story itself something like a murder trial, wherein the reader must play the role of a juror who weighs the available evidence before reaching a verdict.

Setting

Both the present and the flashbacks in "The Daffodil Sky" are mostly set in an unnamed town somewhere in the Midlands of England. In his descriptions of the town, which he refers to as black and gritty, Bates captures the essential qualities of an industrial center built around an industry like steel manufacturing. The urban setting disappears briefly when the protagonist takes Cora out to the countryside. This short visit to the peace of the rural world marks the point at which the protagonist is optimistic about his future prospects as a landowner and farmer. The story, however, soon shifts back to the confined world of the town, and its dark, dirty streets make an apt backdrop for the protagonist's jealousy and despair.

The times during which past and present events occur are also unclear, but a sense of the story's time frame is suggested by the protagonist as he talks to the barman in the opening scene, when the protagonist mentions that Cora had lived on Wellington Street "before the war"—that is, sometime before World War II broke out in 1939. Since the protagonist was twenty-two years old at the time and has returned eighteen years later at the age of forty, it seems that the story's present is approximately 1955–the date that "The Daffodil Sky" was published. The lack of specifics about place and time draws further attention to the general ambiguity that dominates the whole story. Like the protagonist himself, the reader is forced to make inferences or educated guesses based on the evidence at hand.

Symbolism

The title of "The Daffodil Sky" points to its two most important symbols. Throughout the story, the sky not only reflects the protagonist's emotions but also prompts him to remember key events from his past. As he disembarks from the train at the outset of the story, the sky is "dusky yellow with spent thunder," but as he nears the pub and his passions rise, the sky takes on an "unnatural stormy glare." The "pure and clear" sky that greets him as he leaves the pub reminds him of the day in his youth when he met Cora—a time when he too was pure and his conscience was clear. Later, the darkening sky brings to mind his encounter with Frankie and mirrors the jealousy he harbored within. A "darkening brown-purple sky" dominates the scene as he broods and waits for Cora to open her door; when he finds Cora's daughter, however, and the crisis of the expected meeting passes, the sky brightens, becoming "pure and empty."

As the sky figures prominently throughout the story, so too do the daffodils, which are clearly symbolic of hope and life's promise. They are a major source of the protagonist's income in his youth and help him smooth the way for his relationship with Cora, for she is taken with the fact that he

smells of flowers. The two major symbols finally intertwine at the story's close. As the protagonist and Cora's daughter walk toward the pub, his passions are calmed, and this inner peace is mirrored by the "great space of calm" overhead. That the scene is now governed by a "daffodil sky" suggests that this state is a merging of personal tranquillity and future hope. Despite this apparently hopeful note at the close, however, ambiguity yet reigns. As Cora's girl lowers her umbrella, she comments, "It'll be hot again tomorrow," and thereby points to the possibility of more stormy weather and heated passions to come.

Historical Context

"The Daffodil Sky" does not directly reflect upon larger social issues, focusing instead on the personal concerns of its protagonist and a handful of other characters. Nonetheless, the story does provide a general image of post-World War II England. Bates's vivid descriptions of the bleak and blackened town in which his story is set reflect the state of England during the 1950s—a nation left diminished both by the cost of its recent war effort and by the loss of its last major overseas colonies. By 1955, when "The Daffodil Sky" appeared, the worst of the daily inconveniences of post-war life—the shortages of food, fuel, building materials, and automobiles—was over.

In order to get the economy back on track, however, England's government had also altered the economy in fundamental ways. Important sectors, including coal production, electrical utilities, health care, and transportation, had been nationalized—that is, taken over and run by the state. Despite these changes and a general improvement in the nation's outlook by 1955, England's post-war economy would never perform as well as those of its major competitors. The reasons for this failure have been hotly debated, but whatever causes are cited, it has become common to regard England at this time as an industrialized nation in decline.

At the middle of the century, England was more heavily urbanized and industrialized than at any time in its past. Roughly four-fifths of the population lived in urban centers, and the various metal industries alone employed four times as many people as agriculture, fishing, and forestry combined. Agriculture itself had also changed, becoming more

Compare & Contrast

- **1950s:** In 1955, the London Clean Air Act puts a ban on burning untreated coal. In 1956, Calder Hall in England begins to produce electricity by means of nuclear fuel

  1992: The Prime Minister of England announces the intention to close 10 coal mines out of 31 mines that are not viable economically.

- **1951:** The population of Britain is 50 million people; the population of London is 8.4 million.

  1990s: In 1992, the population of Britain is 58 million people; in 1991, the population of London is 9 million.

mechanized than ever before and requiring fewer people even as its output increased. The shifts in population distribution and changes in the agricultural sector meant that small-scale farm operations, like that which Bates's protagonist wanted to run in his youth, were less likely to thrive in the 1950s than they had been prior to World War II.

Bates's protagonist accurately notes that the world is a different place when he returns to find Cora. By the mid-1950s, the days when a farmer could hope to get ahead by selling a carload of flowers and produce at the weekly market were largely over.

As the English economy was changing in the 1950s, so too was the relationship between government and citizen. During World War II, many government departments had been created to regulate and ration everything from food to paper; this increase in bureaucratization remained a fact of life in England long after the war's end. New social programs implemented by the government after the war only added to the size of government. These social welfare services were designed to care for more disadvantaged citizens—the sick, the aged, the unemployed, and the poor—by attempting to humanize daily life and ensure that everyone enjoyed certain minimum standards of living. The so-called welfare state, however, was not without its critics. Its services were funded by higher taxes on the wealthy and middle classes. There were also complaints about the state meddling in private affairs. The general distress at increased government interference, inefficiencies, and costs were often

apparent in everyday conversation in local pubs and in English literature written during the 1950s.

Many of the stories in Wyndham Lewis's *Rotting Hill* (1951), for example, focus on the dullness and inefficiency of the welfare state. Clearly, "The Daffodil Sky" is not an overt protest against the welfare state, but it is apparently set against the backdrop of the new English society of the 1950s. As the protagonist heads from train station to town at the outset of the story, he finds that the old footbridge that he once used has been declared unsafe by some unnamed authority. The closed bridge shows him how times have changed and provides an example of an individual's choices being limited through the interference of a faceless bureaucracy.

Critical Overview

There is not an extensive body of critical work devoted to "The Daffodil Sky", but this lack of commentary says less about the story's quality than it does about Bates's reputation in general. Relative to the number of stories Bates produced, there are simply very few studies of them. Two easily identifiable reasons account for this state of affairs. First, Bates was a prolific author. During the 1950s alone he produced four short story collections and many more novels and novellas. Therefore, critics have always had a variety of targets to aim at when discussing his work. (Also, since short stories are by nature limited in size and scope, critics rarely dwell on a single short story by Bates, preferring in general to discuss a number of them in any particular article.)

The second, more troubling reason for the lack of material on "The Daffodil Sky" is that critics have not seen fit to pay a lot attention to Bates's works, despite the fact that they are numerous and popular. The lack of attention Bates's work receives was itself remarked upon by Douglas A. Hughes in his 1982 article, "The Eclipsing of V. S. Pritchett and H. E. Bates: A Representative Case of Critical Myopia." At that time, Hughes deplored the fact that he could not find a single academic essay on Bates's work, and he urged academics to correct this oversight. Apparently, Hughes's advice about Bates was not ignored. By 1984, Dean R. Baldwin could write in his article "Atmosphere in the Stories of H. E. Bates" that Dennis Vannatta had produced *H. E. Bates* (1983), a full-length study of Bates's life and works. Moreover, Baldwin himself would go on to produce his own book, *H. E. Bates: A Literary Life*, in 1987. The quantity of Bates's own work still outweighs the material devoted to it, but the appearance of these studies has gone some distance toward evening the balance.

Despite the scarcity of study on Bates's works, it is still possible to construct a history of the reception of "The Daffodil Sky." Commentary suggests that it has been well regarded since its appearance in 1955. One early reviewer, Edmund Fuller, writing in *The New York Times Book Review*, praises Bates's ability to leave the outcomes of his stories "crowded with possibilities." He notes that there is a "cryptic, pent-up tension" in "The Daffodil Sky." This tension, moreover, is heightened because Bates leaves it to his readers "to divine the meaning" behind the protagonist's encounter with Cora Whitehead's daughter. In *New Statesman and Nation* (1955), another early reviewer of *The Daffodil Sky* collection, Angus Wilson, suggests that the book demonstrates Bates's "penetrating knowledge of people and scenes" and his ability to produce a wide range of stories. Indeed, Wilson's only negative criticism of the collection is that it has a "note of sentimentalism . . . that spoils what would otherwise be perfection."

Recent studies of "The Daffodil Sky" have found much to admire. In *H. E. Bates*, for example, Dennis Vannatta describes *The Daffodil Sky* collection as "Bates's crowning achievement" amongst his later works, and hails these stories for their "assiduous analysis of dangerous passion,

ineffectuality, and loneliness." Commentary on "The Daffodil Sky" itself, moreover, has tended to regard its darker features as worthy of direct praise. Thus, whereas an early reviewer like Edmund Fuller politely referred to the attraction between the story's protagonist and a "daughter of uncertain paternity," Vannatta points straight to "undercurrents of incest and violence."

Similarly, James Gindin, in "A. E. Coppard and H. E. Bates," directs our attention to the question of paternity and incest that hovers over the story, but he also notes the power in its ambiguity. Because nothing is resolved, says Gindin, the story "exists within the slow, heavy, intense feelings" of the protagonist, and "offers a convincing presentation of a man capable of killing for love."

Like Vannatta and Gindin, Deborah Kelly Kloepfer has remarked that Bates toys with the notion of incest. Kloepfer has gone further still, however, and analyzed Bates's extensive use of sexual imagery and noted the many "boundary issues" he explores. She argues that the story is concerned with a variety of violations, from Cora Whitehead's possible infidelity to the protagonist's violation of the law. Even in the limited attention it has attracted, then, "The Daffodil Sky" is clearly a story which evokes in its readers a variety of responses.

Criticism

Robert Eggleston

Dr. Eggleston is an English instructor at Okanagan University College, in Kelowna, British Columbia. In the following essay, he examines Bates's use of description over action and his choice to leave key issues unresolved to heighten tension in "The Daffodil Sky."

Critics often praise H. E. Bates for his ability to describe the world at large in generous detail. He is renowned for creating decidedly visual stories featuring unfailingly accurate descriptions that immediately impress themselves upon the reader's mind. This quality is repeatedly remarked upon not only because Bates is acutely observant of nature and precise and sure in his use of color but also because he is aware of and draws attention to the finer

A daffodil.

distinctions between nearly indistinguishable objects. Yet for all his lavish, almost lyrical treatment of scenes, Bates also tends to be what Edmund Fuller has termed ''an artist of indirection''; Bates might be ''specific about many things,'' but he does not say more than is necessary about his stories' meanings or outcomes. His plots often offer minimal information and leave the reader to fill in the gaps between what is said and what is inferred. This paradox in Bates's method as a short story writer is particularly evident in ''The Daffodil Sky,'' a story which says very little directly and moves forward in an oblique fashion yet speaks volumes about the characters and incidents that it presents.

Bates's reputation as an artist who constructs impressively visual settings is enhanced by ''The Daffodil Sky.'' From the moment his protagonist comes into view, the world which Bates creates is alive with colors, sounds, and smells. Indeed, it is frequently a challenge to decide whether the nameless protagonist or the background against which he is presented should command more attention. The sky, for example, is especially distracting. It is a significant symbol of the protagonist's changing emotions throughout the story and is forever in flux, shifting endlessly from stormy shades of ''dusky yellow'' and ''copper'' through a still more threat-

ening ''darkening brown-purple'' before finally taking on a calmer, brighter appearance of ''rain-washed'' clarity. Beneath the sky, in the industrial Midlands town where the action is set, the streets, the buildings, and the air are gritty and blackened with the smoke of passing trains and heavy industry. The scene Bates evokes is made all the more vivid through his appeals to the sense of touch, in his descriptions of ''hot wet air'' and skin made ''cold and wet with splashes of hail,'' and to the sense of smell, as when he characterizes a back-street pub as filled with odors of ''smoke, stale beer, and cheap strong cheese.''

Although background details are more fully defined than other elements in the story, the characters who populate the foreground are by no means lacking in vitality. The protagonist is both nameless and faceless, but he is not without passions. He has physical desires that draw him irresistibly to Cora Whitehead, and when he is near her he feels ''the flame of her go through him.'' His passions, moreover, show a darker side of his character, for their power can lead him to jealous suspicion and murderous action. He is quick to imagine an illicit affair between Cora and Frankie Corbett and equally quick to kill Frankie when the opportunity arises. The protagonist's irrational impulses, however, are

What Do I Read Next?

- The other stories in Bates's 1955 collection *The Daffodil Sky* provide perhaps the best context for the story itself. They also serve as examples of Bates's mature work as an author of short fiction.

- Bates's 1951 collection *Colonel Julian and Other Stories,* like "The Daffodil Sky," offers examinations of characters who are disappointed, lonely, and despairing.

- *Look Back in Anger,* a play by John Osborne which was first performed in 1956 and published in 1957, examines the marital woes of Jimmy and Alison Porter, a socially incompatible couple who struggle to get by in a town in the Midlands of England.

- Alan Sked's *Britain's Decline: Problems and Perspectives* (Basil Blackwell, 1987) offers a useful introduction to problems associated with defining the social, moral, and economic changes in England since World War II.

- Alfred, Lord Tennyson's *Maud* (1855) is a poem in sections of different meters which treats the relationship between an unnamed protagonist and his beloved Maud. It describes the trials the lovers face, including a fatal duel between the protagonist and Maud's brother, the protagonist's escape from justice, and his ensuing madness.

also balanced by clear-sighted dreams of future success which Bates carefully articulates: "Suddenly all his life seemed to pull him forward like a bounding dog on a leash. . . . He was going to own his own land, his own house, his own poultry or heifers or bullocks or whatever it was he wanted." The dreams themselves are limited in scope, but their nature is perfectly clear.

Such clarity of dreams is even more evident in Cora, who in a practical manner considers the problems inherent in raising the necessary capital to purchase land. Her pragmatism, though, is but one side of her character, for like the protagonist, she is a creature of passion. Her sensual nature, kisses that are "long, soft strokes of her lips," and her physical qualities, "big soft lips," and "masses of heavy red-brown hair," are the details that remain with the protagonist years after their first encounter. Cora is a lover who has no difficulty "finding [the protagonist's] mouth with instinct, without mistake or clumsiness, the first time." Despite her never actually appearing in the story's present, her sensuality (and Bates's description of it) is impressive.

For all of Bates's attention to place and character, the plot in "The Daffodil Sky" does not progress through a series of precisely connected events, nor does it always provide as much information as the reader might like. Instead, in contrast to the rich coherence of its setting, the story's plot is fragmentary, or as Deborah Kloepfer aptly describes it, "stark [and] stripped down." Moving back and forth between present and past, the plot grudgingly provides material sufficient for the reader to construct a picture of the whole.

Yet even if the plot does allow a picture of events to emerge, it also leaves telling gaps that must be bridged by inference or mere guesswork. One conspicuous gap is the matter of Cora's fidelity. The protagonist believes that Cora had an affair with Frankie, but the truth of the issue is not revealed by the story's end. Some passages seem to point to the answer, as when the protagonist stands outside Cora's door, rehearsing for his confrontation with her. At this point, he wants "to ask why in God's name she had had to do a thing like that," but this "thing" is never identified.

With Cora's faithfulness being left in doubt, another issue of equal significance arises: the paternity of Cora's daughter. Again, however, the lack of evidence that prevents a thorough assessment of Cora's relationship with Frankie also obscures matters here. Inference in this instance, even when based on the material at hand, can only provide an unsatisfactory representation of truth. The protagonist might shake wretchedly as if he were struggling with the temptation of making a pass at his own daughter, but it is never fully clear just who is the father of Cora's girl. The imponderables here—and there are others, such as why the protagonist has returned or why he was apparently convicted of manslaughter when his actions had all the marks of premeditation—are the net result of a skeletal plot structure which contrasts markedly with other elements in "The Daffodil Sky."

Ambiguity might well be a characteristic of Bates's short stories in general, but in the case of "The Daffodil Sky" it is possible that obscurity is the result of Bates's efforts to capture the spirit of Alfred Lord Tennyson's poem *Maud* (1855), the work that apparently provided the inspiration for this story. The similarities between "The Daffodil Sky" and *Maud* suggest that Bates had it in mind while writing his story. The broader structure of Bates's story is reminiscent of Tennyson's narrative, for in each work a young man foolishly slays a rival who stands in the way of his love.

More specifically, Bates draws his title from one of the most celebrated passages of Tennyson's poem—a point at which the protagonist invites his beloved Maud to "come into the garden"—and he also picks up a specific image from the same section when he describes several train sheds as looking like "black bats" against the evening sky. The particular subject matter at this point in Tennyson's poem—that is, the invitation from one lover to another to come into the garden—is in essence what Bates's protagonist offers Cora. He is a rural man, a farmer whose plan to purchase a farm provides Cora with the opportunity to escape her urban life and to enter a garden full of daffodils.

That Bates should work from a poetic source is not surprising. In his criticism of the genre he argues that "the short story is a poetic form," and this belief infuses his work to the extent that he has even been described as a prose poet. Poetry by nature is more opaque than prose, and Bates seems to catch that obscurity in the construction of "The Daffodil Sky." Like a poetic work, Bates's story presents a host of possibilities, neither allowing itself to be firmly fixed to any one indisputable meaning nor making its point (for all its use of language to create vivid images) in a straightforward manner. The story is, of course, a prose work; thus, comments about its being "poetic" can never be entirely accurate, but in the absence of a more concrete adjective, the term is quite apt.

Because he chooses to favor description over action and to leave key issues unresolved, Bates turns an otherwise unremarkable narrative into a compelling story. Nothing monumental happens in "The Daffodil Sky," its tension notwithstanding, and in this tense inaction the story leaves a host of unanswered questions in its wake. The uncertainties surrounding his characters' fidelity and paternity, and even those surrounding such legal points as the

> **From the moment his protagonist comes into view, the world which Bates creates is alive with colors, sounds, and smells."**

story raises, provide Bates with an opportunity to multiply possibilities. Like a poet, he can intimate certain ideas—whether unfaithfulness, incest, or any other—without introducing certainties. And, again like a poet, he can prompt his readers to see more in his words than is suggested by their most obvious meanings.

Source: Robert Eggleston, "Overview of 'The Daffodil Sky,'" for *Short Stories for Students*, The Gale Group, 2000.

Theresa M. Girard

Girard is a Ph.D. candidate at Wayne State University who has taught many introduction-to-fiction classes. In the following essay, she examines Bates's descriptions of nature in "The Daffodil Sky," which, she argues, he uses to create a deceptively complex story.

"The Daffodil Sky" appears to be a simple story that is disturbing in its complexity. Bates's style is to present a day in the life of an individual with all of the feelings and nuances that a day can hold. Bates's early works were full of promise, innovation, and ingenuity that marked the modernist movement, but he seldom relied on symbol or metaphor in telling his stories. According to James Gindin, Bates cannot "accurately be called a 'modernist' writer" even though he employed "many of the technical elements ... that are characteristic of what has come to be defined as 'modernism.'" His writing reflects the ordinariness of the individual and all that can entail. "The Daffodil Sky" is an example of the type of story in which Bates excelled.

At the outset, the reader is introduced to a man as he walks into a familiar town. It is obvious that he has not been there in a long time because he remarks on the age of the things he sees. He seems to be warned not to go there by the sky, which has just

> The simplicity in Bates's use of detail, description, and mundane characters serves to emphasize the complexity of the internal struggle all of us must face throughout life on a daily basis."

finished storming but continues to thunder. He approaches the footbridge and again seems to be warned by a sign that says, "Bridge unsafe. Keep off. Trespassers will be prosecuted." As he continues undeterred, he notices how much the town has changed.

The protagonist recalls the day that he met Cora Whitehead and begins to lead the reader into the flashback that contains the real, or embedded, story. He goes to the pub where he first met Cora and, after making small talk about the weather, asks if anyone knows Cora and if she still lives in town. Receiving an affirmative reply, he recalls the day that he first met her and the circumstances that led him to be in that same pub twenty years later. The reader finds out that he peddled daffodils at the market and that he rented the land where he grew the daffodils. The scent of the daffodils on his hands is so strong that Cora notices at once and lifts his hands to her face so that she can inhale the pleasing scent.

The man becomes enamored of Cora; decides to buy the land that he leases; proposes to Cora; and kills a man. The murder is what brings him back to town and to the pub. The murder is the reason so much has changed. He served twenty years in prison for a crime of passion. Cora was the trigger for the crime because she did not stay true to him; it is implied that she had an affair with Frankie Corbett. In fact, Frankie may or may not be the father of Cora's child. The reader never knows. Bates does not seem to think that those details are important to the story. Even the ending of the story lacks information that would satisfy the reader's curiosity.

He goes to Cora's house to confront her and ask her why she testified against him at his trial. Instead,

he meets Cora's daughter, who bears a striking resemblance to her mother. Without saying much more than small talk and with a purposeful avoidance of telling her his name, she walks him to the train station under her umbrella. The storm ends; they agree to get a drink; and the story ends.

Upon reflection, the reader notes that this apparently simple story is complex in its attention to emotion and sensibility. Gindin observes that "dramatic conflict in Bates's stories is seldom depicted with much complexity. More often, the complexity is internalized." This sets up the ultimate conflict. Bates inundates the senses with a myriad of colors and disturbs the sensibilities through the discordant texture of underlying passions and tensions. Gindin states that Bates "radiates the plain man's point of view," and this is clearly seen in "The Daffodil Sky." This unnamed man with "slow, heavy intense feelings . . . offers a convincing presentation of a man capable of killing for love." This slowness of feeling happens to the reader after finishing the story.

Feelings of incompleteness and frustration begin to develop almost as soon as the reader has finished the story. Deborah Kelly Kloepfer writes that "the importance lies perhaps in a recognition of complexity; appearances are deceptive; things both are and are not what they seem." It is through this ambiguity that the reader begins to understand how the main character can represent the "Everyman" of the early Greek plays. The conflict is not in the everyday, mundane activities of day-to-day existence but in the internalized passion that most people spend their lives learning to repress and control. Reflecting on these emotions, the reader learns how it was possible for this simple farmer to lose control for a brief moment and kill in a burst of jealous rage. Kloepfer remarks that Bates shows how "passion short-circuits propriety or reason" and notes stylistic similarities between Bates and D. H. Lawrence.

Bates tried to depict life as he observed it and, according to Gindin, felt that the author should not embroider it. This presentation of life did not extend to nature or "the English countryside which Bates lovingly describes," as stated by Jean Pickering. Gindin picks up on Bates's love of the English countryside and notes in addition that "Bates was . . . sharply observant of all the particulars of nature, [and] superb at describing weather." "The Daffodil Sky" reflects this detail of the country and of nature through Bates's many references to color and weather. Bates provides the mind's eye with a word painting and colors such mundane things as the notice on the footbridge, which he says is written in prussian blue, and the distant bus lights, which he depicts as a strange sharp green. Such attention to detail seems, at first, strange to readers who are used to either reading stories in an abstract, black- and-white manner or inserting colors where and how they see fit. In creating this kaleidoscope of colors, Bates makes this ordinary farmer, who cannot re-member the color of Cora's dress, more remarkable by his plainness.

While Bates reports in his autobiography that A. E. Coppard told him that "the story could learn a great deal from cinematic art in the use of quick cuts close-ups and other techniques with a sharp pictori-al impact" and Gindin acknowledges that film technique influenced Bates's later fiction, there also seems to be a strong musical influence. In particu-lar, the musical form known as the symphonic (or tone) poem is overwhelming in "The Daffodil Sky." The tone poem, as defined by Joseph Machlis, is a piece of music in one movement that in the course of contrasting sections develops a poetic idea, suggests a scene, or creates a mood. Machlis observes that the tone poem is shaped by literary themes and often emphasizes the influence of na-ture. "The Daffodil Sky" mirrors the tone poem by emphasizing descriptions of nature, contrasting ele-ments with the inclusion of flashbacks, and utilizing a natural theme of the controlling sky. Machlis notes that the tone poem evokes all of the senses with an emphasis on sight, just as Bates emphasizes sight through his descriptions of color.

Classical music generally contains a major theme that recurs, in variation, throughout the piece. The overwhelming influence of the sky is the major theme that recurs throughout "The Daffodil Sky." Bates signals changes in mood and tone by the color of the sky, whether it be "a dusky yellow with spent thunder," "an unnatural stormy glare of sky," "a stormy copper glow," "discoloured space of sky . . . leaving it pure and clear," "a bright yellow-green frosty April sky," "mornings that break with pure blue splendour," or the final "calm, rain-washed daffodil sky." The recurring theme is de-scribed by Bates in all of its variation.

Bates does not expand his descriptions into metaphor or personifications of nature. He relates the story in a straightforward fashion that is rife with description and color. Gindin notes that Bates con-

> One of Bates's recurring preoccupations, for which he has been compared to D. H. Lawrence, is the conflict between passion and repression, the ways in which culture and psychological inhibitions strangle natural impulses or, conversely, the ways in which passion short-circuits propriety or reason."

sidered the short story as "the effectively distilled novel" and even praised "his own powers of com-pression by rather grandiosely claiming that he got more 'atmosphere' in a sentence than Thomas Har-dy characteristically managed in a page." His boast seems rather immodest and egotistical, to say the least, but his claims are backed up by comments from Henry Miller, who declared that "Bates al-ways finds time for lengthy descriptions of nature, descriptions which in the hands of a lesser writer would seem boring or out of place." Miller's obser-vations become plainly evident in reading "The Daffodil Sky." The simplicity in his use of detail, description, and mundane characters serves to em-phasize the complexity of the internal struggle all of us must face throughout life on a daily basis.

Source: Theresa M. Girard, "Overview of 'The Daffodil Sky'," for *Short Stories for Students*, The Gale Group, 2000.

Deborah Kelly Kloepfer

Kloepfer is an editorial consultant and author of The Unspeakable Mother: Forbidden Discourse in Jean Rhys and H. D. *In the following excerpt, she gives an overview of Bates's "The Daffodil Sky," focusing in particular on the theme of appearance and reality.*

The story collection *The Daffodil Sky* has been called the crowning achievement of H. E. Bates's later years; the title story both exhibits the hallmarks of his earlier writing and is colored by an increasing maturity, a sensibility altered by World War II, and a recognition of the inescapableness of time's passage.

Like many of Bates's stories, ''The Daffodil Sky'' is highly charged visually, marked by ''the direct pictorial contact between eye and object, between object and reader,'' which Bates admired in Hemingway and discussed in *The Modern Short Story: A Critical Survey*. In the first few paragraphs alone, Bates evokes a spectrum of colors (dusky yellow, prussian blue, ''a strange sharp green,'' ''stencillings of silver,'' ''a stormy copper glow'') not to mention the impact of a farmer's cart full of plums, peas, broccoli, apples, and daffodils. The text is suffused not only with visual images but an intensely sensory contact with the environment: skin ''cold and wet with splashes of hail,'' the smell of ''steam-coal smoke and stale beer and cheap strong cheese,'' the sound of pike ''plopping in the pools of the backwater.''

Much of Bates's work is characterized by stark, stripped down plots which turn on situations rather than on a series of developed events; this is one reason, perhaps, that his short fiction was often more successful than his many novels. ''The Daffodil Sky'' takes place within the space of a few hours, the time frame ruptured by a flashback. The color of the sky is the controlling image, the shuttle that moves back and forth weaving past and present. Bates is known for his striking nature imagery, and here it is the coursing clouds, the discoloured sky, and its sudden clearing ''fresh and brilliant, shot through with pale green fire'' like daffodils, which trigger for the nameless narrator the memories through which his story is revealed.

While waiting out a storm in a pub he once haunted, he asks after Cora Whitehead, a woman he once knew; Bates (whose short fiction, according to the critic Dennis Vannatta, often ''works by inference rather than exposition'') gives the reader no initial clue to the complexity of the narrator's relationship with Cora. He remembers his instant physical attraction to her in a similar rainstorm many years ago—the ''racing flame'' of her ''running hot through his blood and choking his thinking.'' One of Bates's recurring preoccupations, for which he has been compared to D. H. Lawrence, is the conflict between passion and repression, the ways in which culture and psychological inhibitions stran-gle natural impulses or, conversely, the ways in which passion short-circuits propriety or reason.

Indeed, the central event revealed in the flashback is a murder. The narrator, a young farmer, recalls the days when his life seemed full of promise. The man from whom he rented his land proposed to sell him the property; having insufficient funds, he accepted Cora's offer to go in with him on the deal, an offer contingent on the help of a friend of hers, Frankie Corbett. Overcome with the vision of his future, the narrator rather impetuously asked Cora to marry him and then became ''blinded with the stupor of a slow-eating jealousy,'' which intensified with Cora's pregnancy. Unable to tolerate the thought that the child might be Corbett's, the narrator confronted him one night on the street; the ensuing violence between them led to Corbett's death and the narrator, apparently, was sentenced to jail.

The story ends with the narrator returning to Wellington Street to ''have the last word,'' to tell Cora what he thinks of her having testified against him. He is a man of 40 years now, Bates tells us, his dreams long ago ''eaten by the canker.'' A young woman opens the door. The narrator is struck by how little Cora has changed; he feels ''the flame of her stab through him again exactly as it had done on . . . the day of the daffodils.'' Slowly, however, he realizes that this is not Cora but her daughter. It is pouring rain, and the girl, whose mother is not at home, offers to get an umbrella and walk the stranger at her door back to the bridge where he can get a bus. He accepts, and this non-event, so typical in Bates, is the situation upon which the entire story hinges.

The text becomes filled with sexual imagery—the ''rising steam of rain in the air,'' the heat and thickness, his blood beating in ''heavy suction strokes in his throat,'' the girl's arms ''full and naked and fleshy'' like her mother's. She is coy and seductive; he is desperately attracted to her even as he considers telling her who he really is. Looking at the ''haunting yellow sky,'' overcome, sickened by ''an awful loneliness,'' he is, apparently, just about to proposition her when a rather phallic train comes ''crashing and flaring'' under the bridge where they have stopped; the girl waits for it to pass and asks the stranger, whose body is shaking, whether he had intended to ask her out. Instead, the train passed, the storm clearing, he settles for a drink with the girl who is perhaps his daughter, steering clear of the bridge blocked with a notice stating, symbolically,

"Bridge Unsafe. Keep off. Trespassers will be prosecuted."

Clearly there is the suggestion here of incest, only one of the many boundary issues in the story. There are many violations: Cora violates, perhaps, fidelity; the narrator violates the law; reality violates dreams; the present violates the past. Although Bates has been compared to Maupassant, his endings are often more ambiguous than ironic, an ambiguity echoed in the title. The reader is left unsure which sky controls the landscape—the "pure and clear" sky and the "fierce, flashing daffodil sun" of the narrator's youth or the dusky yellow sky "with spent thunder" that the narrator finds upon his return to town. The importance lies perhaps in a recognition of complexity: appearances are deceptive; things both are and are not what they seem; past and present intersect, become confused, coexist. Both inner and outer landscapes are wracked by storms of violence, passion, and loss, but nature also offers the "light of after-storm, . . . a great space of calm, rainwashed daffodil sky."

Source: Deborah Kelly Kloepfer, "The Daffodil Sky," in *Reference Guide to Short Fiction*, edited by Noelle Watson, St. James Press, 1994, p. 679.

Sources

Baldwin, Dean R. "Atmosphere in the Stories of H. E. Bates," in *Studies in Short Fiction,* Vol. 21, 1984, pp. 215-22.

Bates, H. E. *The Vanished World: An Autobiography,* Columbia: University of Missouri Press, 1969.

Fuller, Edmund. "Impressions of Mortality," in *The New York Times Book Review*, July 15, 1956, p. 5.

Gindin, James. "A. E. Coppard and H. E. Bates," in *The English Short Story, 1880–1945*, edited by Joseph M. Flora, Twayne, 1985, pp. 113-41.

Hughes, Douglas A. "The Eclipsing of V. S. Pritchett and H. E. Bates: A Representative Case of Critical Myopia," in *Studies in Short Fiction*, 1982, pp. iii-v.

Machlis, Joseph. *The Enjoyment of Music*, pp. 102-03. New York: W. W. Norton & Co., 1970.

Vannatta, Dennis. *H. E. Bates*, Twayne, 1983.

Vannatta, Dennis, ed. *The English Short Story, 1945-1980*, Twayne, 1985.

Wilson, Angus. A review of *The Daffodil Sky*, in *The New Statesman and Nation*, November 19, 1955.

Further Reading

Baldwin, Dean R. *H. E. Bates: A Literary Life*, Susquehanna University Press, 1987.
   A full- length study of Bates's life containing commentary on many of Bates's works, including the collection *The Daffodil Sky* .

Baldwin, Dean R. "Atmosphere in the Stories of H. E. Bates," in *Studies in Short Fiction*, Vol. 21, 1984, pp. 215-22.
   Comments on the manner in which Bates develops atmosphere in his stories and notes that the atmosphere in many of Bates's works clearly distinguishes them from those of his contemporaries.

Fuller, Edmund. "Impressions of Mortality," in *The New York Times Book Review*, July 15, 1956, p. 5.
   A review of the first American edition of the collection *The Daffodil Sky*, published in 1956, that focuses on Bates's tendency to express ideas in an indirect manner.

Gindin, James. "A. E. Coppard and H. E. Bates," in *The English Short Story, 1880–1945*, edited by Joseph M. Flora, Twayne, 1985, pp. 113-41.
   Argues that Bates's short stories emphasize the plain and ordinary over settings and characters, prefer "country matters" for their subjects, and shun metaphor and symbolism in favor of direct representation of characters and events.

Hughes, Douglas A. "The Eclipsing of V. S. Pritchett and H. E. Bates: A Representative Case of Critical Myopia," in *Studies in Short Fiction*, Vol. 19, 1982, pp. iii-v.
   Observes that Bates's works have not received the attention they deserve and argues that editors of scholarly journals should encourage studies on underrepresented authors such as Bates.

Vannatta, Dennis. *H. E. Bates*, Twayne, 1983.
   A study of Bates's work and life that contains a useful bibliography of primary and secondary sources and discusses the themes, plots, and characterization in some of the stories in *The Daffodil Sky*.

Vannatta, Dennis, ed. *The English Short Story, 1945-1980*, Twayne, 1985.
   The three essays in this collection which cover the years 1945–1970 mention Bates numerous times and cite his short stories as being amongst the most significant examples of the genre produced in post-World War II England.

Wilson, Angus. A review of *The Daffodil Sky*, in *The New Statesman and Nation*, November 19, 1955.
   An early review of *The Daffodil Sky* that praises Bates for the wide range of his stories and faults him for being too sentimental in some of them.

Girl

Jamaica Kincaid

1978

First published in the June 26, 1978, issue of *The New Yorker*, ''Girl'' was the first of what would become more than a dozen short stories Jamaica Kincaid published in that magazine. Five years later, ''Girl'' appeared as the opening story in Kincaid's collection of stories, *At the Bottom of the River* (1983), her first book.

''Girl'' is a one-sentence, 650-word dialogue between a mother and daughter. The mother does most of the talking; she delivers a long series of instructions and warnings to the daughter, who twice responds but whose responses go unnoticed by the mother. There is no introduction of the characters, no action, and no description of setting. The mother's voice simply begins speaking, ''Wash the white clothes on Monday,'' and continues through to the end. Like all of Kincaid's fiction, ''Girl'' is based on Kincaid's own life and her relationship with her mother. Although the setting is not specified in the story, Kincaid has revealed in interviews that it takes place in Antigua, her island birthplace.

When *At the Bottom of the River* was reviewed in major publications, reviewers praised the rhythm and beauty of the language and found the mother-daughter relationship fascinating, especially as it changes and develops throughout the volume. But a few, including the novelist Anne Tyler, found them too opaque. Tyler called the stories ''almost insultingly obscure,'' but still encouraged readers to read the volume and to follow the career of

"a writer who will soon, I firmly believe, put those magical tools of hers to work on something more solid."

Author Biography

Raised in Antigua, a small and beautiful island nation in the Caribbean, Kincaid experienced first-hand the colonialism that affects so many of her characters. Antigua was a colony of Great Britain, when Kincaid was born on May 25, 1949, and given the name Elaine Potter Richardson. Elaine's mother, Annie Richardson Drew, was a believer in obeah, a West Indian religion incorporating magic and ritual. For nine years Elaine was an only child, and felt happy and loved. She began school when she was four, the same year her mother taught her to read. She was a bright student. When her three brothers were born, she felt that her mother turned away from her; a longing for a reconciliation with a distant mother is a recurring theme in Kincaid's work.

Elaine's adolescent years were turbulent. She became aware of various ways that black Antiguans were made to serve the British, and she rebelled, especially at school, where the children were taught English history, geography and literature instead of Caribbean. In June, 1966, at seventeen, Elaine left Antigua to become an au pair in New York. Over the next seven years she worked as an au pair, a receptionist, and a secretary; studied photography; and eventually began a career in publishing. Her first publication was an interview with feminist Gloria Steinem for *Ingenue* magazine. Soon afterward, she changed her name to Jamaica Kincaid, "Jamaica" for the Caribbean country, and "Kincaid" because it "just seemed to go together with Jamaica."

As Jamaica Kincaid, she wrote articles for various magazines and became a staff writer for the *New Yorker* magazine in 1976. She would write more than eighty essays for the magazine in the next decade. One afternoon, after reading an Elizabeth Bishop poem, "In the Waiting Room," Kincaid sat down and wrote the short story "Girl" in one sitting. As she tells it, she found her voice as a writer that afternoon: "I somehow got more confident in what I knew about language. Finding your voice brings great confidence." The story, which is one long sentence spoken by a Caribbean mother to her daughter, appeared in the *New Yorker* in the June 26, 1978, issue, the first of many short stories she

would publish there. It also became the first story in her first book, *At the Bottom of the River*, a collection of ten stories about childhood in the Caribbean. This writing experience taught Kincaid that the Caribbean and her mother would always be her true subjects.

Kincaid married, had two children, moved to Vermont, and continued to write. She has published six books of autobiographical fiction and received numerous awards. Her work has attracted critical as well as popular success, as the writer's voice she found has changed and evolved.

Plot Summary

The story begins abruptly with words spoken by an unidentified voice. "Wash the white clothes on Monday and put them on the stone heap; wash the color clothes on Tuesday and put them on the clothesline to dry; don't walk barehead in the hot sun. . . ." The voice continues offering instructions about how a woman should do her chores, and then about how she should behave: "on Sundays try to walk like a lady and not like the slut you are bent on becoming." At the end of the first third of the story, another voice, signaled by italics, responds, *"but I don't sing benna on Sundays at all and never in Sunday school."* This speaker is presumably the daughter of the main speaker. Without any reply to the daughter, and without missing a beat, the mother continues with her litany. She suggests how to hem a dress "and so to prevent yourself from looking like the slut I know you are so bent on becoming."

As the story progresses, the mother's tone becomes more insistent and more critical. The chores and behaviors are more directly related to a woman's duties to men, such as ironing a man's clothes. The mother again comes back to her earlier admonition: "this is how to behave in the presence of men who don't know you very well, and this way they won't recognize immediately the slut I have warned you against becoming." The lines of advice are loosely grouped into sections of related lines. In a section that recognizes the powers of obeah, a mystical religion based on African beliefs, she cautions the daughter against taking appearances for granted, and explains how to make several medicines to cure disease, bring on an abortion, and catch a man. Finally she shows the daughter how to squeeze bread to tell whether it is fresh. For the second time, the daughter speaks: *"but what if the*

Jamaica Kincaid

baker won't let me feel the bread?'' This time the mother replies to her daughter, ''you mean to say that after all you are really going to be the kind of woman who the baker won't let near the bread?'' With that, the story ends. There is no action, no exposition of any kind, and no hint of what happens to the characters after this conversation.

Characters

Daughter

The daughter is an adolescent or pre-adolescent girl in Antigua, learning from her mother how to be a proper woman. She speaks only twice in the story, voicing impulsive objections to her mother's accusations and warnings.

Mother

The mother is a woman in Antigua who understands a woman's ''place.'' She lives in a culture that looks to both Christianity and obeah, an African-based religion, and that holds women in a position of subservience to men. She recites a catalog of advice and warnings to help her daughter learn all a woman should know. Many of her lines

are practical pieces of advice about laundry, sewing, ironing, sweeping, and setting a table for different occasions. Other harsher admonitions warn the daughter against being careless with her sexuality, ''so to prevent yourself from looking like the slut I know you are so bent on becoming.''

Themes

Mothers and Daughters

Like much of Kincaid's fiction, ''Girl'' is an examination of the relationship between the ''girl'' of the title and her mother. The mother's instruction to ''soak your little cloths right after you take them off'' refers to the cloths woman in many parts of the world use to absorb their menstrual flow and indicate that the girl is a young adolescent. Kincaid has said that all of her fiction is based on autobiography, and that her own relationship with her mother has been difficult since Kincaid was nine years old. In an interview with Selwyn R. Cudjoe she explains, ''the fertile soil of my creative life is my mother. When I write, in some things I use my mother's voice, because I like my mother's voice. . . . I feel I would have no creative life or no real interest in art without my mother. It's really my 'fertile soil.'''

Nearly all of the text of ''Girl'' is the mother's words to the daughter. Although the mother does nearly all of the talking and there is no action or exposition, there is much that can be guessed about the relationship between the two. The mother is preparing the girl to take her rightful place as a daughter and then a wife, and teaches her how to do the chores expected of a woman. If the mother feels that the tasks allotted to a woman are demeaning or subservient, she does not say so, but neither does she describe the satisfactions of her life. She simply shares information about washing, sewing, ironing, gardening, cooking, and making medicine, trying to be objective and thorough. But there is a steady current of suspicion and fear lying under the surface, and the mother is unable to talk very long without something reminding her of the dangers of sex, and of ''the slut you are so bent on becoming.'' When she thinks of sex, and of her daughter's supposed or real flirtation with it, her tone becomes colder, even angry.

The daughter's reaction to her mother's litany can only be imagined, because Kincaid does not reveal it. How would any young teen react to hearing such a long list of suggestions from one's mother? Twice the daughter interrupts with a defensive comment, both times beginning with the word "but." The first time, the mother does not respond, but simply goes on with her speech. The second time, near the end of the story, her growing anger causes her to irrationally hear the daughter's innocent question, *"but what if the baker won't let me feel the bread?"* as confirmation of her suspicions, that the girl is thinking about "sluttish" behavior, that she is going to become "the kind of woman who the baker won't let near the bread."

This conflict between mother and daughter is not unusual. Many mothers, because they know what their daughters may not know—that sexual promiscuity tends to hurt women more than it does men—grow angry and fearful at the thought of their daughters behaving recklessly. However, in this mother's entire long speech there is not a single gentle line, not one word of love or reassurance. The words the mother leaves out reveal as much about the relationship as what she includes.

Culture Clash

Although Kincaid herself has denied that she thought much about politics when she was writing *At the Bottom of the River,* Diane Simmons demonstrates that the wishes of the British colonial powers governing Antigua during Kincaid's youth stand behind many of the lessons of Kincaid's fictional mothers. "As the child in both *At the Bottom of the River* and *Annie John* approaches puberty, the mother increasingly imitates the colonial educational system, which seems bent on erasing all that is native to the child, rewarding only that which imitates the European rulers". Thus, the mother suddenly institutes a number of programs to make a "young lady" out of her daughter.

Clearly the family lives simultaneously in two cultures. They sing *benna* (calypso music), but know enough not to sing it in the European church. They practice obeah, a system of belief derived from Africa, but they also attend Sunday school. They eat bread pudding and doukona, a spicy plantain pudding, but also know how to "set a table for tea." The mother's attempt to train her daughter in the ways of the colonizers ways that will help her be successful but that will turn her against her true self may account for the mother's growing coldness throughout "Girl." She becomes angry because, however dutifully she passes along her knowledge, her heart is not in it. Kincaid remembers her own training with some anger. "I was brought up to be sexless and well-behaved. . . . I was supposed to be

Media Adaptations

- "Girl" is available on audiotape, read by the author. The tape, produced in 1991 by the American Audio Prose Library, is titled *Jamaica Kincaid Reading Annie John (The Red Girl), At the Bottom of the River ("Girl" and "My Mother"), Lucy (Excerpts).*

full of good manners and good speech. Where the hell I was going to go with it I don't know."

Style

Point of View

"Girl" does not have a narrator in the conventional sense, because it does not have action in the conventional sense. There is no event, or series of events, acted out or told about by the characters or by a third-person narrator outside the action. Instead, the story is for the most part one speech delivered by the mother. The mother speaks in the first person referring to herself as "I" when she mentions "the slut I know you are so bent on becoming" and "the slut I have warned you against becoming." Far more important than the pronoun "I," however, is the pronoun "you." The mother directs her speech to her daughter, the "girl" of the title, and every instruction contains either the word "you" ("this is how you set a table for tea") or the implied "you" ("cook pumpkin fritters in very hot sweet oil").

In its handling of point of view, "Girl" is more like a type of lyric poetry called the dramatic monologue than it is like most short prose fiction. The dramatic monologue places one character in a dramatic situation and has her speak to a listener who can be identified but who does not speak herself. Through the words of the speaker, a personality and a conflict are revealed. Of course, "Girl" does have two lines spoken by the listener, the

Topics for Further Study

- Find some examples of poems that are considered dramatic monologues. Examples include ''My Last Duchess'' by Robert Browning and ''The Love Song of J. Alfred Prufrock'' by T.S. Eliot. Do you think ''Girl'' is more like a poem or like a story?

- Investigate the history of African slaves and their descendants in the Caribbean. Compare your findings with what you know about the descendants of slaves in the United States.

- Research the training young women received in the United States in the 1950s, in popular magazines, advice columns, and how-to books. How do the expectations and responsibilities of these young women compare with those of the daughter in ''Girl''? How do they compare with the expectations and responsibilities of young American women today?

- Read Kincaid's first novel, *Annie John*. Some critics have suggested that the novel is in some ways an expanded version of ''Girl.'' Do you agree?

- Find recipes for some of the food mentioned in ''Girl'' and attempt to prepare the using ingredients available locally. What might be learned about a group of people based on what they eat? What could outsiders guess about you from studying the foods you eat?

daughter. These lines, also spoken in the first person, move the story beyond pure dramatic monologue into the realm of fiction, where the exchange between the characters limited though it is becomes the central action.

As Moira Ferguson points out, however, the complete lack of exposition in the story opens up another possibility: ''the entire section could be the daughter's own internal monologue. What if the daughter is simply imagining this oracular, maternal discourse, extrapolating certain worries expressed by the mother in day-to-day asides?'' In that case, the words assumed to be the mother's would be memories of things she has said over time, not necessarily one long speech, and the italicized responses from the girl could be rehearsals for things she might say the next time the mother criticizes. Whether the mother is speaking or the girl is remembering, Kincaid uses the first-person point of view to create immediacy and tension; even with no description of people or places, the reader cannot help but visualize these two women and feel the charged atmosphere between them.

Setting

Although there are no descriptive passages in ''Girl,'' there are several clues to the story's Caribbean setting in the mother's instructions. In the first lines, for example, the mother mentions putting laundry ''on the stone heap'' and ''on the clothesline to dry,'' indicating a way of life without electrical appliances. Later, she tells ''how you make ends meet,'' again indicating relative poverty. The foods she mentions help place the story in the Caribbean: pumpkin fritters, salt fish, okra, dasheen (also called taro, a tropical starchy root), bread pudding, and pepper pot. Kincaid grew up on the island of Antigua, in a home without electricity or running water, and although she does not name the place, in her mind it is set there.

Historical Context

Antigua: British Colony

''Girl'' was first published in *The New Yorker* magazine twelve years after Kincaid left Antigua for New York City. Even at that distance of time and space, Kincaid drew on her experiences growing up in Antigua for the setting and themes of ''Girl,'' as she has done for the rest of her fiction. From the time Kincaid was born in 1949 until she left in 1966, Antigua was a colony of Great Britain. England had gained control of the island in 1667, after thirty years of fighting with the Carib Indians, who inhabited the island, and the Dutch and French, who wished to own it. In 1674 the first great sugarcane plantations were established, and slaves were brought in from Africa to do the work on them; the slaves were freed in 1834, and their descendants make up most of the population of the island. Antigua also became an important naval base for the British, and

Compare & Contrast

- **1978:** Antigua is a semi-independent "Associated State" under British domain, no longer a full colony, but not an independent nation.

  1990s: Antigua, Barbuda, and the uninhabited island of Redonda make up the independent nation of Antigua and Barbuda.

- **1970s:** The economy of Antigua is largely based on farming, particularly fruits, vegetables, cotton and livestock. Its former reliance on sugar production has ended abruptly and catastrophically in the 1960s.

  1990s: The economy of Antigua is based on services, particularly tourism and off-shore banking.

- **1970:** Approximately 41 percent of Antigua's population is fourteen years old or younger.

Many adults leave the country, or die in middle age.

1995: Only 25 percent of the population is fourteen years old or younger. Adults are living longer, and staying in Antigua.

- **1974:** Although Antigua is a small and poor island, it is densely populated. There are 70,000 people, with an average of 412 people per square mile.

  1995: The population of Antigua has decreased to about 65,000 people, as many Antiguans have moved to the United States and elsewhere to escape poverty and to make a better life. The United States has 263 million people, with an average of 71 people per square mile.

---

remained so until the beginning of the twentieth century, when battles between the British and the French for control of the New World waned.

Antigua under the British had a small, wealthy population of whites from Europe, and a large, poor black population descended from imported African slaves. The Carib Indian population had been eliminated. Like her peers, Kincaid attended schools based on the British educational system. The children were taught to speak "proper" English, studied British history, and read and memorized the works of British writers including William Wordsworth and John Milton. They did not learn about the Carib peoples, or about African or even Antiguan history. There were no books by Caribbean writers available.

As a young child Kincaid did not feel the effects of colonialism. In an interview with Donna Perry she comments, "the political situation became so normal that we no longer noticed it. The better people were English and that was life." But as she grew older she began to rebel, as she told Selwyn R. Cudjoe, "When I was nine, I refused to stand up at the refrain of 'God Save Our King.' I

hated 'Rule, Britannia'; and I used to say we weren't Britons, we were slaves."

Because Antigua was so poor, it was easily dominated by Great Britain, and the economy grew worse in the 1960s when the international sugar market declined and Antigua was forced out of the business. However, in 1967, after Kincaid had left for New York, Antigua and another island, Barbuda, became one semi-independent "Associated State." They attained full independence from Great Britain on November 1, 1981.

Antigua: Daily Life

Although it is the wealthiest island in the Eastern Caribbean, Antigua is poor by North American standards, and was even poorer during the time of Kincaid's youth. Most families, like the mother and daughter in "Girl," grew most of their own fruits and vegetables and ate little meat beyond the fish they caught themselves. Foods mentioned in the story were typical: pumpkin fritters, doukona (a pudding made from cornmeal, green bananas, coconut, sugar and spices), and pepper pot (a stew made from spinach-like greens and other vegetables, reheated each day with new ingredients added). Their homes did not have running water or electricity, and they treated illnesses with home-made medicines rather than with doctors and pharmacies.

Many Antiguans, especially the older generations, practice a woman-centered, African-based religion called obeah, similar to voodoo. Even those who are members of Christian churches will often practice obeah as well, using spells and secret medicines when the situation calls for them. Because objects may conceal spirits, believers in obeah do not trust appearances. This lies behind the mother's warning, "don't throw stones at blackbirds, because it might not be a blackbird at all." Kincaid's mother and grandmother practiced obeah, and the writer explained in an interview with Selwyn R. Cudjoe, "I was very interested in it; it was such an everyday part of my life, you see. I wore things, a little black sachet filled with things, in my undershirt. I was always having special baths. It was a complete part of my life for a very long time."

Critical Overview

Because "Girl" and several other Kincaid stories had first been published in the influential magazine *The New Yorker,* when Kincaid's collection *At the Bottom of the River* came out in 1983 it attracted more critical attention than volumes of short stories usually do, particularly for a writer's first book. Early reviewers were drawn to the language of the stories, though some were put off by the overall obscurity. Anne Tyler, writing for *The New Republic,* praised the stories for Kincaid's "care for language, joy in the sheer sound of words, and evocative power." Edith Milton, in *The New York Times Book Review,* also cited the language, "which is often beautifully simple, [and] also adopts a gospel-like seriousness, reverberating with biblical echoes and echoes of biblical echoes." Both writers commented briefly on "Girl" and its theme of the mother-daughter relationship, and David Leavitt, writing for *The Village Voice,* proclaimed, "The tangled love between child and mother, so clearly articulated in "Girl," is the major preoccupation of Kincaid's work."

Though impressed by the language and interested in the themes, early reviewers found the stories in *At the Bottom of the River* needlessly

opaque. Tyler called them "often almost insultingly obscure." Milton wondered "if her imagery may perhaps be too personal and too peculiar to translate into any sort of sensible communication." Barney Bardsley warned in *New Statesman* that the book could be "irritatingly difficult to read unless you let yourself go." Ultimately, however, all of the national reviewers saw promise in the volume and recommended it.

Since that time, "Girl" has been selected for several important anthologies, including *Wayward Girls, Wicked Women: An Anthology of Stories* (1987), *Green Cane and Juicy Flotsam: Short Stories by Caribbean Women* (1991), *Images of Women in Literature* (1991), and *Beyond Gender and Geography: American Women Writers* (1994). Most critical work on Kincaid has focused on her first novel, *Annie John,* considered a richer and more accessible examination of Kincaid's themes.

Kincaid's work has been the subject of two book-length studies, each published in 1994, and each of which analyzes "Girl" as an early articulation of her central concerns. Moira Ferguson's *Jamaica Kincaid: Where the Land Meets the Body* examines the personal and political conflicts in Kincaid's writing. She finds that in "Girl," "the mother-daughter relationship appears to be framed principally in terms of maternal-colonial power, mixed with probable rage and frustration in the daughter. A polyphony of messages fuses with conflicting reactions." Diane Simmons, author of *Jamaica Kincaid,* revisits the sound of Kincaid's language noticed by early reviewers and explains how "Girl" "may be read as a kind of primer in the manipulative art of rhythm and repetition." The mother's speech, she believes, "not only manipulates the girl into receptivity to the mother's condemning view but also teaches the art of manipulation."

One question that has interested readers of *At the Bottom of the River* from the beginning is the nature of the pieces. Though many critics have been content to call the pieces "stories," others have looked for a better term. Barney Bardsley claims, "This is not a story. There is no linear progression, no neat plot. *At the Bottom of the River* is instead a beautiful chaos of images, murky and tactile, which hint at the dreams and nightmares involved as a girl shakes off her childhood." Tyler writes that "this book is more poetry than prose." David Leavitt calls them "prose pieces," and Moira Ferguson consistently calls them "sections." For Simmons

Beaches and coast of Antigua, native land of Jamaica Kincaid.

they are ''dreamlike stories'' or ''surrealistic short stories.''

Kincaid herself has spoken about the voice in her first book. In an interview with Donna Perry she comments, ''I can see that *At the Bottom of the River* was, for instance, a very non-angry, decent, civilized book, and it represents sort of this successful attempt by English people to make their version of a human being or their version of a person out of me. It amazes me now that I did that then. I would never write like that again, I don't think. I might go back to it, but I'm not very interested in that sort of expression any more.''

Criticism

Cynthia Bily

Bily teaches English at Adrian College in Adrian, Michigan. In the following essay, she discusses expectations and opportunities in ''Girl.''

In her 1984 *New York Times Book Review* piece about Kincaid's *At the Bottom of the River*, Edith Milton singles out ''Girl'' as '' the most elegant and lucid piece of the collection,'' and observed that the mother's exhortations ''define in a few paragraphs the expectations, the limitations, and the contents of

What Do I Read Next?

- *Annie John* (1983) is an episodic novel in eight parts by Jamaica Kincaid. Annie John, a young girl living on the island of Antigua in the Caribbean, endures a painful adolescence in which she both adores and hates her mother. As she matures she struggles to come to terms with her parents, her faith, her culture, and her sexuality.

- *At the Bottom of the River* (1983) is Kincaid's first collection of short stories, and the collection in which "Girl" appears. Like "Girl," many of the ten stories about growing up in the Caribbean are told in dreamy, stream-of-consciousness prose.

- *Krik? Krak!* (1996), by Edwidge Danticat, is a collection of nine short stories about women in Haiti. The stories are sad and beautiful, and the volume was a National Book Award finalist.

- *The Penguin Book of Caribbean Short Stories* (1997) collects forty short stories ranging from pre-Columbian myths and legends to stories by Jean Rhys, V.S. Naipaul, Claude McKay and other major twentieth-century writers.

- *Reading Black, Reading Feminist: A Critical Anthology* (1990) is edited by Henry Louis Gates, Jr. In twenty-six essays, this collection traces the history of African-American women's writing in the United States. Works studied include prose and poetry, fiction and nonfiction.

---

an entire life." If this is an accurate assessment and I believe it is, what kind of life does it describe? What will the future hold for the girl is she follows her mother's suggestions?

Many of the instructions give purely practical advice for doing daily chores in a developing nation where running water and electricity are not common. Even in a society where people do not have many clothes, obtaining and maintaining them is hard work, and that work typically falls to women. "Girl" begins with laundry: "Wash the white clothes on Monday and put them on the stone heap; wash the color clothes on Tuesday and put them on the clothesline." Before the one-sentence story is done, the mother will come back to clothing many times, explaining how to buy fabric for a blouse, sew on a button and make a buttonhole, and hem a dress. And of course, women are also responsible for men's clothing, and the mother demonstrates "how you iron your father's khaki shirt so that it doesn't have a crease" and "how you iron your father's khaki pants so that they don't have a crease."

Women are also providers of nourishment, and the mother explains how to grow and prepare different foods. In this family, the girl is expected to catch fish and to "soak salt fish overnight before you cook it." She learns to shop for bread, to grow okra and dasheen, a root vegetable, and to prepare pumpkin fritters, bread pudding, doukona (a cornmeal, banana and coconut pudding), and pepper pot, the staple of poor Caribbean families that involves reheating a large pot of greens with whatever fresh ingredients might be added on a given day. By preparing these humble dishes, a woman can "make ends meet."

The mother rounds out her list of womanly duties with guidance on cleaning ("this is how you sweep a corner; this is how you sweep a whole house; this is how you sweep a yard"), setting a table for any occasion, and making different kinds of "good medicine." In a culture where there is a lot of work to be done, it is important that everyone do a fair share, and this is a woman's share.

Just as important, though, is that the girl learn how to behave in front of other people, especially men. Several of the instructions have to do with how one appears to others, such as the command to "always eat your food in such a way that it won't turn someone else's stomach." A woman must learn to hide her true self, her true feelings, and wear the mask that is right for the occasion: ''this is how you smile to someone you don't like too much; this is how you smile to someone you don't like at all; this is how you smile to someone you like complete-ly.'' Most of all, she must ''try to walk like a lady and not like the slut I know you are so bent on becoming.'' A woman may have thoughts of ''slut-tish behavior'' (by which is meant, I suppose, acting as though she wants or enjoys sex), but ''this is how to behave in the presence of men who don't know you very well, and this way they won't recognize immediately the slut I have warned you against becoming.''

Apparently the mother has learned to do all these things, and they are probably not beyond the girl's capacity either. But if she learns her lessons well, what will she have to look forward to, to be excited about? Where is the pleasure in this life? The litany of instructions in ''Girl'' is a far cry from the advice given to women in today's popular women's magazines, which suggest that taking long aromatherapy baths to regenerate will make one a better mother, or advocate ''making time for yourself.''

Just as important as the advice the mother gives in ''Girl'' is what she leaves out. The advice is practical, ''how to make ends meet.'' There are no instructions for how to make beautiful things, or how to make oneself happy. The Caribbean is celebrated all around the world for its exuberant music, but the only reference to music in the story is to music that must not be made: ''don't sing benna in Sunday school.'' Tourists travel great distances to Antigua to admire its beautiful flowers and birds. In ''Girl,'' the mother refers to flowers only once: ''don't pick people's flowers you might catch some-thing.'' Her one mention of a bird is strangely cautionary: ''don't throw stones at blackbirds, be-cause it might not be a blackbird at all.''

In an early essay in *The New Yorker*, Kincaid described the beauty of Antigua, and explained that Antiguans get up to begin their work very early in the morning, when the island is at its loveliest. In an interview, Kincaid remarked, ''But it wasn't to admire any of these things that people got up so early. I had never, in all the time I lived there, heard anyone say, 'What a beautiful morning.' Once, just the way I read it in a book, I stretched and said to my mother, 'Oh, isn't it a really lovely morning?' She didn't reply to that at all.'' People who live in the midst of rare beauty, it would appear, lose their ability to notice it, to find pleasure in it. A child

> ''The relationship that concerns the mother is the relationship between a man and a woman. If she derives any pleasure or pride from her own experiences with parenthood, she does not reveal it here.''

could be taught to observe and enjoy the natural world for its beauty and elegance, but this daughter will not learn it from this mother.

There are no tender words in the mother's litany. She does not use ''dear'' or any other terms of endearment, or even address the daughter by her name. She gives no advice about how to be a friend, or how to sense which women to confide in. There are no tips about changing a diaper or wiping a tear or nurturing a child in any way; she mentions children only when she shows ''how to make a good medicine to throw away a child before it even becomes a child.'' The relationship that concerns the mother is the relationship between a man and a woman. If she derives any pleasure or pride from her own experiences with parenthood, she does not reveal it here.

Finally, there are no words in the mother's speech about possibilities beyond home and family. She does not speak of school or books, nor of travel, nor of a career. She offers the daughter what she has to offer: a set of instructions for a successful life as the mother understands it and lives it. That Kincaid wanted more is evident. She left Antigua and found a different sort of life for herself, as she explained in an interview with Kay Bonetti in *The Missouri Review*, ''I did not know what would happen to me. I was just leaving, with great bitterness in my heart towards everyone I've ever known, but I could not have articulated why. I knew that I wanted some-thing, but I did not know what. I knew I did not want convention. I wanted to risk something.''

The story ends before we find out what happens to the girl. Does she heed all her mother's advice and become a competent homemaker? Does she follow Kincaid's lead and find something else? If she stays, is her life as joyless as her mother's? If she leaves, can she find a way to create a new family and a new home? What of the mother? If her life is as joyless as it seems, what sense of responsibility compels her to train her daughter for the same life? Kincaid might say that these questions and their answers are irrelevant, that she is revealing a truth about a moment and that should be enough. In an interview with Marilyn Snell in *Mother Jones*, she complains that Americans want pleasant solutions. "Americans find difficulty very hard to take. They are inevitably looking for a happy ending. Perversely, I will not give the happy ending. I think life is difficult and that's that."

Source: Cynthia Bily, for *Short Stories for Students*, The Gale Group, 2000.

Liz Brent

Brent has a Ph.D. in American Culture, with a specialization in cinema studies, from the University of Michigan. She is a freelance writer and teaches courses in American cinema. In the following essay, she discusses the use of language, the mother-daughter relationship and the significance of African cultural heritage in "Girl."

The mother/daughter relationship

Jamaica Kincaid's short story "Girl" is the opening piece in a collection entitled *At the Bottom of the River*. Critics have noted that the use of language in "Girl," as well as in the other stories of this collection, is one of its most notable features. "Girl" is unusual in that it is a short story written in the "second person" voice, meaning that the narrator addresses the reader as "you." The narrator here is a mother giving advice to her daughter, who is the "you" in the story. Kincaid's use of language in this story is key to understanding the nature of the mother/daughter relationship which it conveys. Grammatically, the entire story is a single sentence, which reads like a list or string of statements made by the mother to her daughter. The use of repetition and rhythm renders the mother's words almost hypnotic. In her article "The Rhythm of Reality in the Works of Jamaica Kincaid," Diane Simmons explains that, "in the long, seemingly artless, list-like sentences, the reader is mesmerized into Kincaid's world." She goes on to say that "like the girl to whom the mother speaks, the reader is lulled and drawn in by the chant of motherly admonitions."

The central theme of "Girl," as in many of Kincaid's stories, is the mother/daughter relation-

ship. An important element of the use of language in this story is the sense that the mother's "chant of information and advice" (as Simmons calls it) threatens to completely engulf the girl, leaving her no language with which to formulate her own sense of identity as separate from her mother. Simmons has pointed out that the use of rhythm and repetition in the mother's words "enfolds and ensnares the daughter, rendering the girl nearly helpless before the mother's transforming will." It is as if the mother's incantatory speech pattern is so all-enveloping that it prevents the daughter from asserting any individuality, opinion or will outside of the narrowly defined world of advice and warning her mother has created through her speech. In the two instances in which the girl does attempt to either question her mother's advice or defend herself against her mother's judgement, the rhythm and repetition of the mother's voice only works to overwhelm and engulf this meek voice of dissent.

The power of the mother's words to envelop the daughter within the strict confines of her own set of values and expectations is most apparent in terms of her references to sexuality. What is striking in this piece is the power of the mother's words to impose upon the girl a "sluttish" sexuality which must always be contained and hidden. The mother's "advice" comes in the form of a condemnation for behavior or tendencies the girl herself might not even have considered: "On Sundays try to walk like a lady and not like the slut you are so bent on becoming." The power of this condemnation of the girl's sexuality, perhaps before it has even formed, comes in part from the way in which the mother integrates references to sexuality into advice on even the most mundane tasks: "this is how to hem a dress when you see the hem coming down and so to prevent yourself from looking like the slut I know you are so bent on becoming." The insistence of the mother's repetition of this condemnation gives it all the more power: *"this is how to behave in the presence of men who don't know you very well, and this way they won't recognize immediately the slut I have warned you against becoming."*

The sense that this restricted definition of sexuality which the mother imposes upon the daughter is all-encompassing is most strongly emphasized in the closing lines. What begins as another mundane and harmless piece of advice "always squeeze bread to make sure it's fresh" becomes, upon the daughter's questioning, yet again an opportunity to condemn the girl to the inevitability of becoming a "slut," despite all these warnings. When the daughter, with good reason, asks "but what if the baker won't let me feel the bread?" the mother replies, "you mean to say that after all you are really going to be the kind of woman who the baker won't let near the bread?" As this closing line suggests, the mother's words create a world so all-encompassing that the daughter is unable to escape its judgements.

Growing up female

A good portion of the "chant of information" the mother passes onto the daughter is made up of specific directions on how to carry out the domestic work for which the girl is clearly being trained. The mother's advice concerns such "woman's work" as washing clothes ("Wash the white clothes on Monday and put them on the stone heap; wash the color clothes on Tuesday and put them on the clothesline to dry"); sewing ("this is how to sew on a button; this is how to make a button-hole for the button you have sewed on"); and cleaning house ("this is how to sweep the house; this is how to sweep the yard"), as well as setting the table, ironing and buying fabric. The use of repetition here is suggestive of the repetitive nature of the endless domestic chores which the girl seems condemned to spend her life performing: "this is how you set the table for tea; this is how you set the table for dinner; this is how you set the table for dinner with an important guest; this is how you set the table for breakfast." The tedium implied by this simple repetition mimics the tedium and dullness of the domestic duties the girl is expected to take on.

In addition to the repetitive daily domestic work for which she is training her daughter, the mother also includes messages which assume a role of subservience to a man: "this is how you iron your father's khaki shirt so that it doesn't have a crease; this is how you iron your father's khaki pants so that they don't have a crease." The messages which the mother gives her daughter about relationships with men also include warnings which suggest the potential for violence: "this is how you bully a man; this is how a man bullies you." The potential hazards of sexual relationships with men are also indicated in terms of reference to unwanted pregnancy: "this is how to make a good medicine to throw away a child before it becomes a child." And, despite all the warnings about not being a "slut," the mother also instructs the girl in "how to love a man."

A simple instruction by the mother, toward the end of the story, is suggestive of her underlying motivation in passing on such specific instructions to her daughter. One of the items on her list of

> " The power of this condemnation of the girl's sexuality, perhaps before it has even formed, comes in part from the way in which the mother integrates references to sexuality into advice on even the most mundane tasks ...."

instruction is: "this is how to make ends meet." This statement by the mother in some ways clinches all of her previous statements. The underlying message which the mother imparts to her daughter, through all of these detailed instructions, is a message about how to survive as an African-Carribean woman in a harsh world with limited resources.

Christianity and African heritage

The mother's litany of advice, warning, and condemnation in "Girl" also contains a string of confusing and contradictory messages about the daughter's relationship to her African heritage and culture. On the one hand, the mother insists on warning the daughter against integrating African folk culture into her Christian education. "Is it true you sing benna songs in Church?" the mother asks. As benna songs are African folk songs, the mother's question is designed to warn the daughter against maintaining cultural practices derived from her African heritage.

Yet, on the other hand, the mother's list of advice contains rich elements of this African heritage, which she clearly intends to pass on to her daughter. Thus, while warning against mixing African traditional songs with the Western practice of Christianity, the mother is sure to pass on information based on folk beliefs derived from African culture. As Helen Pyne Timothy explains, in her article "Adolescent Rebellion and Gender Relations in 'At the Bottom of the River' and *Annie John*," "when dealing with the real problems of life," the mother's advice "falls back on the belief in folk wisdom, myth, African systems of healing and bush medicine, the mysteries of good and evil spirits inhabiting the perceived world of nature.'' Thus, the mother's advice includes such folk beliefs as ''don't throw stones at blackbirds, because it might not be a blackbird at all,'' or ''this is how to throw back a fish you don't like, and that way something bad won't fall on you.'' She also includes references to folk medicines or remedies, such as ''this is how to make a good medicine for a cold.''

A rich African-Carribean cultural heritage is also passed on from mother to daughter through the importance of advice and directions concerning food preparation. These elements of the mother's litany add an important element of warmth and nurturing to her warnings and condemnations. Food preparation is described in cookbook style, matter-of-fact detail, such as ''cook pumpkin fritters in very hot sweet oil,'' and ''soak salt fish over night before you cook it.'' Other references to food evoke strong sensory associations, such as ''this is how to make bread pudding'' and ''this is how to make pepper pot.'' In these instances, the mother's insistence on conveying such an overwhelming ''chant of information'' to her daughter takes on a deeper significance in terms of the role of the mother-daughter relationship in the context of African-Carribean cultural heritage. In ''Mothers and Daughters: Jamaica Kincaids' Pre-Oedipal Narrative,'' critic Roni Natov explains that, ''Jamaica Kincaid's fiction focuses on the importance of continuity and community as they are preserved and kept alive by mothers, through their stories and through their connection with their daughters.'' In this way, the mother is maintaining an oral tradition whereby cultural traditions and survival skills are passed down from mother to daughter, and from generation to generation, by way of a rhythmic flow of words such as that conveyed in this story.

Source: Liz Brent, for *Short Stories for Students*, The Gale Group, 2000.

Diane Simmons

In the following excerpt, Simmons discusses the mother's voice in ''Girl,'' which she likens to a manipulative ''chant.''

Kincaid's ''Girl'' may be read as a kind of primer in the manipulative art of rhythm and repetition. The story begins with the mother's voice giving such simple, benevolent, and appropriately maternal advice as ''Wash the white clothes on Monday and put them on the stone heap; wash the color clothes on

Tuesday and put them on the clothesline to dry.'' Like the girl to whom the mother speaks, the reader is lulled and drawn in by the chant of motherly admonitions, which go on to advise about how to dress for the hot sun, how to cook pumpkin fritters, how to buy cloth for a blouse, and how to prepare fish. Seduced in only a few lines, readers, like the listening girl, are caught unaware by an admonition which sounds like the previous, benevolent advice but has in fact suddenly veered in a new direction, uniting the contradictions of nurture and condemnation: ''. . . always eat your food in such a way that it won't turn someone else's stomach; on Sundays try to walk like a lady and not like the slut you are so bent on becoming.'' As the brief, one-sentence story progresses, we come to see that the mother's speech, inviting with nurturing advice on the one hand and repelling with condemnatory characterization on the other, not only manipulates the girl into receptivity to the mother's condemning view, but also teaches the art of manipulation. The mother incorporates into her indictment of the girl's impending sluttishness the task of teaching her how to hide that condition: ''. . . this is how to hem a dress when you see the hem coming down and so to prevent yourself from looking like the slut I know you are so bent on becoming.'' As the contradictions draw closer together—as nurture and manipulation become increasingly intertwined—the language seems to become even more rhythmic.

> . . . this is how you smile to someone you don't like too much; this is how you smile to someone you don't like at all; this is how you smile to someone you like completely; this is how you set a table for tea; this is how you set a table for dinner; this is how you set a table for dinner with an important guest; this is how you set a table for lunch; this is how you set a table for breakfast; this is how you behave in the presence of men who don't know you very well, and this way they won't recognize immediately the slut I have warned you against becoming. . . .

In the last third of ''Girl'' the mother's voice continues the litany of domestic instruction, but added now is comment on a frighteningly contradictory world, one in which nothing is ever what it seems to be. The continued tone of motherly advice at first works to lighten the sinister nature of the information imparted and then, paradoxically, seems to make these disclosures even more frightening; eventually we see that, in a world in which a recipe for stew slides into a recipe for the death of a child, nothing is safe.

> . . . don't pick people's flowers—you might catch something; don't throw stones at blackbirds, because it might not be a blackbird at all; this is how to make

bread pudding; this is how to make doukona; this is how to make pepper pot; this is how to make a good medicine for a cold; this is how to make a good medicine to throw away a child before it even becomes a child; this is how to catch a fish; this is how to throw back a fish you don't like, and that way something bad won't fall on you.

Source: Diane Simmons, "The Rhythm of Reality in the Works of Jamaica Kincaid," in *World Literature Today*, Vol. 68, No. 3, Summer, 1994, pp. 466–72.

Laura Niesen Abruna

In the following excerpt, Abruna discusses Kincaid's use of dream visions and metaphor in her exploration of family life and social structure in the West Indies.

Some of the finest fiction from the West Indies has been written by Jamaica Kincaid. Her fiction, specifically her collection of short stories *At the Bottom of the River*, makes interesting use of dream visions and metaphor as the imaginative projections of family life and social structure in her West Indian society. In the short stories Kincaid explores the strong identification and rupture in the daughter-mother relationship between the narrator and her mother. The process is mediated through metaphor and, when it is threatening, through surrealistic dream visions.

Each of these stories demonstrates tensions in the daughter-narrator resulting from a prolonged period of symbiosis between mother and child, especially because the mother views her daughter as a narcissistic extension of herself. In "Wingless," the narrator dreams the story as a mirror of her own situation and then imagines herself as a wingless pupa waiting for growth. The narrator uses a dream vision to mediate her sense of helplessness as a child dependent on her mother's care and attention.

In this dream, the mother is perceived to be powerful, even more potent than the male who attempts to intimidate and humiliate her. Because the narrator still views her mother as powerful, an incident of potential sexual violence becomes instead an easy victory for the mother:

I could see that he wore clothes made of tree bark and sticks in his ears. He said things to her and I couldn't make them out, but he said them so forcefully that drops of water sprang from his mouth. The woman I love put her hands over her ears, shielding herself from the things he said. . . . Then, instead of removing her cutlass from the folds of her big and beautiful skirt and cutting the man in two at the waist, she only smiled—a red, red smile—and like a fly he dropped dead.

" The many rules, which make the father's circus-going a female impossibility, are experienced by the narrator as unnecessarily restrictive and hostile."

The strong mother is a potential threat of death to those who confront her. But there is also a wonderful parable here of the integrity of the woman who shields herself from assault by refusing to listen to the tree-satyr who is trying to assert his power over her.

The story that best demonstrates the daughter's ambivalent relationship with her mother is "Girl." The voice is the girl's repeating a series of the mother's admonitions:

Wash the white clothes on Monday and put them on the stone heap; wash the color clothes on Tuesday and put them on the clothesline to dry . . . on Sundays try to walk like a lady and not like the slut you are so bent on becoming . . . this is how to hem a dress when you see the hem coming down and so to prevent yourself from looking like the slut I know you are so bent on becoming . . . this is how to behave in the presence of men who don't know you very well, and this way they won't recognize immediately the slut I have warned you against becoming.

The first of the mother's many rules concerns housekeeping. Unlike the girl's father, who can lounge at the circus eating blood sausage and drinking ginger beer, the woman is restricted to household duties. The many rules, which make the father's circus-going a female impossibility, are experienced by the narrator as unnecessarily restrictive and hostile. The mother's aggression is clear in the warnings of the price a girl will pay for ignoring her mother's advice. The penalty is ostracism—one must become a slut, a fate for which the mother is ironically preparing the daughter. The mother's obsessive refrain indicates hostility toward her adolescent daughter, activated when the growing daughter is no longer an extension of the self but a young woman who engenders in the older woman feelings of competition and anger at losing control of her child. Her anger may also result from the pressures felt by every woman in the community to fulfill the restrictive roles created for women. Of the ten stories in the collection, ''Girl'' is the only one told as interior monologue rather than as dream and thus seems to be the least distorted vision. The ambivalence of the mother-daughter relationship is presented here in its most direct form. The reasons for their mutual distrust are very clearly stated: resentment, envy, anger, love.

Source: Laura Niesen Abruna, ''Twentieth-Century Women Writers from the English-Speaking Caribbean,'' in *Modern Fiction Studies*, Vol. 34, No. 1, Spring, 1988, pp. 85–96.

Snell, Marilyn. ''Jamaica Kincaid Hates Happy Endings,'' in *Mother Jones*, Vol. 22, No. 5, September-October, 1997, pp. 28-31.

Timothy, Helen Pyne. ''Adolescent Rebellion and Gender Relations in 'At the Bottom onf the River' and *Anni John*,'' in *Caribbean Women Writers*, edited by Selwyn R. Cudjoe, Wellesley, Mass.: Calaloux Publications, 1990, pp. 233-242.

Tyler, Anne. ''Mothers and Mysteries,'' in *The New Republic*, Vol. 189, No. 27, December 31, 1983, pp. 32-33.

Vorda, Allan. ''An Interview with Jamaica Kincaid,'' in *Mississippi Review*, Vol. 20, No. 8, 1991, p. 15.

Sources

Bardsley, Barney. Review of *At the Bottom of the River*, in *New Statesman*, Vol. 108, No. 2790, September 7, 1984, p. 33.

Bonetti, Kay. Interview with Kincaid, in *The Missouri Review*, Vol. 21, No. 2, August 17, 1998. Available online at http://www.missourireview.org/interviews/kincaid.html.

Cudjoe, Selwyn R. ''Jamaica Kincaid and the Modernist Project: An Interview,'' in *Callaloo*, Vol. 12, Spring, 1989, pp. 397, 402, 408.

DeVries, Helen. Interview, in *Christian Science Monitor*, May 2, 1985, p. 41.

Edwards, Audrey. ''Jamaica Kincaid: Writes of Passage,'' in *Essence*, Vol. 22, No. 1, May, 1991, pp. 86-89.

Ferguson, Moira. *Jamaica Kincaid: Where the Land Meets the Body*, Charlottesville: University Press of Virginia, 1994, p. 18.

Leavitt, David. Review of *At the Bottom of the River*, in *The Village Voice*, Vol. 29, No. 3, January 17, 1984, p. 41.

Milton, Edith. ''Making a Virtue of Diversity,'' in *The New York Times Book Review*, January 15, 1984, p. 22.

Natov, Roni. ''Mothers and Daughters: Jamaica Kincaid's Pre-Oedipal Narrative,'' in *Children's Literature*, Vol. 18, 1990, pp. 1-16.

Perry, Donna. *Backtalk: Women Writers Speak Out*, New Brunswick, N.J.: Rutgers University Press, 1993, p. 132, 133.

Simmons, Diane. *Jamaica Kincaid*, New York: Twayne, 1994, p. 30, 48, 49.

Further Reading

Bloom, Harold, ed. *Jamaica Kincaid: Modern Critical Views*, Philadelphia: Chelsea House, 1998.

Eleven essays of criticism and interpretation, particularly of Kincaid's work after *At the Bottom of the River*. Most of these essays were written for scholarly audiences.

Cudjoe, Selwyn R. *Caribbean Women Writers: Essays from the First International Conference*, Wellesley, Mass.: Calaloux Publications, 1990.

Three dozen essays and interviews about the works and lives of English-speaking women Caribbean writers, as well as overviews of the writing by Spanish-, French-, and Dutch-speaking women. Two pieces explore Kincaid directly, and the others provide context for her work.

Dachner, Don, and Dene Dachner. *A Traveler's Guide to Caribbean History*, Sacramento: Travelers Press, 1997.

An accessible and sensitive overview of the region's historical development, written for the general reader.

Nasta, Shusheila, ed. *Motherlands: Black Women's Writing from Africa, the Caribbean and South Asia*, New Brunswick, N.J.: Rutgers University Press, 1991.

An examination of black women writers and their interpretations of myths of ''motherhood.'' The first two sections of this essay collection are ''Breaking the Silence: New Stories of Women and Mothers'' and ''Mothers/Daughters/Sisters?'' Kincaid's fiction is discussed in the third section, ''Absent and Adopted Mother(land)s.''

A Hunger Artist

Franz Kafka
1924

Franz Kafka's "A Hunger Artist" was first written in 1922 and published in a collection also entitled *A Hunger Artist*. Although Kafka died in 1924, as he was still in the process of correcting the galley proofs, the collection was nevertheless published that same year. "A Hunger Artist" is one of the few manuscripts which Kafka did *not* request that his friends burn or otherwise destroy after his death.

"A Hunger Artist," which takes place in an unspecified time and place, is about a man world-famous for his public performances of the act of fasting, for as much as forty days at a time. Even at the height of his career, the hunger artist is unsatisfied with his work and frustrated by both his manager and his audiences, who never fully appreciate his true talent or the purity of his "art." The hunger artist struggles internally with his sense of dissatisfaction with himself and his feelings of alienation from the world outside the "cage" in which he fasts. As the years go by, the hunger artist's profession goes out of vogue, while audiences move on to newer trends in mass entertainment.

Kafka's stories are often described as fables or parables, and "A Hunger Artist" certainly shares this quality. It is just absurd enough to suggest that its meaning is symbolic rather than literal. As in many of Kafka's stories, "A Hunger Artist" also explores themes of self-hatred, inadequacy, and alienation. "Hunger" becomes symbolic of both a lust for life and a spiritual yearning. The circum-

stance of the protagonist confined in a claustrophobic space is also a common motif in Kafka's work. The hunger artist's "cage" functions as both a refuge from the outside world and a barrier between the artist and the rest of humanity.

Author Biography

Franz Kafka was born into a Jewish family in Prague in 1883. He earned a law degree in 1906 and worked for the Workers Accident Insurance company for most of his adult life. His writing was first published in 1909, and he continued to publish short stories, all written in German, until his death in 1924, shortly before his forty-first birthday. Kafka's literary style is best captured by the term, "Kafkaesque," which has gained broad circulation in common parlance. While this term can mean different things to different people, it is generally used to describe situations which evoke the dark, angstridden, claustrophobic, oppressive, and nightmarish mood of most of his stories.

One of the most significant influences on Kafka's life and work was his domineering father. Kafka's stories often contain themes drawn from the burden of his father's tyranny in his home life, depicting settings of confinement as well as convoluted systems of punishment and other expressions of seemingly all-powerful authority. Nevertheless, Kafka lived with his family for most of his life, moving out for only short intervals. His personal life, meanwhile, was marked by a series of broken and delayed engagements, as well as temporary love affairs.

Kafka has been strongly associated with the city of Prague, as its atmosphere haunts much of his work. He lived in Prague's Jewish ghetto, one of the oldest in Europe, which served as a means of segregating Jews from the rest of the population. Consequently, the ghetto proved a haven of Jewish culture. Kafka once described the ghetto as "my prison cell my fortress."

Although it is never referred to directly, Kafka's Jewish identity in an atmosphere of anti-Semitism is thought to be an underlying theme of his work. His interest in Jewish culture lead him to attend lectures on Judaism as well as to study Yiddish and Hebrew. In the last few years of his life, he lived with Dora Diamont (or Dymant), with whom he considered moving to Palestine. In 1942,

long after Kafka's own death, all three of his sisters, as well two of his lovers, were killed in German concentration camps. Had he lived long enough, Kafka himself would likely have died in a concentration camp as well.

In 1917, Kafka showed the first symptoms of tuberculosis and was in and out of sanitariums for the rest of his life. Shortly before he died, Kafka made requests to both Dora and to his close friend Max Brod to burn all of his unpublished writing. But Brod was wise enough to appreciate the potential contribution of Kafka's work to world literature and made great efforts to edit, translate, and publish much of this material. As a result of Brod's diligence, Kafka, who died in relative obscurity, is now considered to be one of the most important writers of the twentieth century.

Plot Summary

This story is told primarily from the perspective of a "hunger artist," who fasts for up to forty days at a time while sitting in a cage scattered with straw, which is placed on display in a public location, as a form of mass entertainment. In the opening line, the reader is informed that public interest in the "art" of fasting has declined in recent years.

At the height of the hunger artist's career, and of public interest in his performances, things were different. The whole town would "take a lively interest" in his performances; most people made a point of looking at him at least once a day, and the children, most of all, were enthralled by him. To prove that he was not sneaking any food, local men, usually butchers, were assigned to guard the cage at night. The artist was always frustrated by those who made a point of giving him the opportunity to sneak food, which he never did because, "the honor of his profession forbade it." This mistrust of the purity of his art was frustrating to the artist, who preferred those who watched him diligently throughout the night.

The sources of the hunger artist's lifelong dissatisfaction with his performances were many. Since no one could ever really know for sure that he was not cheating, that perhaps he was secretly sneaking food, only the artist himself could fully appreciate the purity of his fasting, as a result of which he was "bound to be the sole completely satisfied spectator of his own fast." But this was not his only source of dissatisfaction. He was also dissatisfied with himself because he found it incredibly easy to fast. Yet he had to "put up with" the fact that no one would believe him that it was so easy, and so "his inner dissatisfaction always rankled." Furthermore, his impresario limited his fasts to forty days. Although the artist was sure he could fast for much longer, the public's attention could not be maintained for longer than that. As a result, the artist never "left his cage of his own free will." Since the end of his fast was a key part of his "performance," the artist had to put up with the impresario's insistence on emphasizing to the audience that the fast had actually been extremely difficult. Worst of all, the artist was forced to eat his first bite of food before the public, as part of the performance, although he had no desire at all to eat. While the crowds were perfectly satisfied with his performances, the artist himself remained "unsatisfied." This all added to his frustration at not being allowed to break his own record with a performance "beyond human imagination."

In all the "rush and glitter of success," the artist failed to notice that his profession had declined in popularity. In fact, "a positive revulsion from professional fasting was in evidence." Audiences had moved on to newer forms of entertainment, as a result of which his career was in rapid decline. When they could no longer deny this change, the artist and the impresario, "his partner in an unparalleled career," went their separate ways, and the artist was reduced to the status of circus sideshow.

For the artist, hiring himself to the circus was the ultimate humiliation. His cage was placed at the entrance to the menagerie so that the only people who noticed him were the crowds waiting impatiently to see the animals. As a result, he was increasingly passed over by his potential spectators. Eventually, even the circus managers forgot him and neglected to change the sign announcing the number of days of his fast.

One day, a circus overseer notices the seemingly empty cage and discovers the hunger artist, on the verge of death, buried in the straw. No one would ever know how long he'd been fasting. A skeletal figure, the hunger artist whispers his last words in the overseer's ear: "I have to fast, I can't help it." When asked why he can't help it, the artist explains, "because I couldn't find the food I liked. If I had found it, believe me, I should have made no fuss and stuffed myself like you or anyone else."

The hunger artist is buried with his straw, and a young panther takes his place in the cage. In the

Franz Kafka

panther, unlike the artist, "the joy of life streamed with ardent passion." Also unlike the hunger artist, who is emaciated and never satisfied, the panther's body is "furnished to the bursting point with all that it needed." The circus spectators "crowded around the cage," and could not stop looking at him.

Characters

Hunger Artist

This story is told primarily from the perspective of the main character, known only as a "hunger artist," a world-famous performer, the "record hunger artist of all time." He travels the world, "performing" his fasts publicly, as a form of mass entertainment. Although the best of the best, the hunger artist continues to be unsatisfied with his performances. Even at the height of his career, he feels that his "work" is never adequately appreciated by his audience, who fail to recognize his true potential. Furthermore, he feels thwarted in his efforts to break his own records, by both the attention span of the public and by the promotional strategies of his impresario (manager). His personal frustrations with his audience and his own "work" are expressive of those felt by many types of artists, who often see their audiences as unable to appreciate their true talent. As the hunger artist ages, his ''art'' goes out of vogue, and he is relegated to an insignificant space in a circus, where he is eventually forgotten by the circus managers and virtually ignored by the crowds, who are more interested in seeing the ''menagerie.''

Impresario

The hunger artist's ''impresario'' is his manager and publicity agent (much as popular musicians today have managers who book their performances and oversee their public image). The impresario, ''his partner in an unparalleled career,'' is clearly a shrewd and invaluable promoter of his work, as well as a buffer between the artist and his audience. Unlike the artist, the impresario's motivation is to develop the artist's career by creating a public image designed to please the crowds. The impresario limits the artist's fasting performances to a maximum of forty days, because he knows that the crowds lose interest after this point. Although the artist's career success is dependent upon the impresario, he is continually frustrated by these limitations, which he sees as a violation of the purity of his art. When it becomes clear that there is no longer a public demand for the art of fasting, the impresario and the hunger artist go their separate ways.

Themes

Alienation & Isolation

''A Hunger Artist'' is the story of one man's feelings of intense alienation and isolation. This state, however, is partly self-imposed, a necessary condition of his ''art.'' The hunger artist spends his fasting performances, and therefore most of his life, in a cage, on display before nameless crowds. Beck has observed that his need to fast is ''symbolic of his isolation from the community of men.'' The cage itself symbolizes the barrier between the artist and the rest of the world. During most of his fasts (which last for up to forty days), the artist sits in a meditative state, ''withdrawing deep into himself, paying no attention to anyone or anything.'' His personal life is therefore almost completely internally, although he is constantly on public display.

Spiritual Yearning

References to spiritual yearning and religious symbolism in ''A Hunger Artist'' are subtle but pervasive. Critic Meno Spann has analyzed the food imagery in Kafka's writing and concluded that ''for Kafka, physical deprivation or hunger represents spiritual hunger and is associated with the 'unknown nourishment' so many of Kafka's characters seek.''

The hunger artist is also described as a religious ''martyr,'' although his martyrdom is based on his own professional frustrations rather than any spiritual enlightenment. At the public spectacle which ended each fast, the impresario ''lifted his arms in the air above the artist, as if inviting Heaven to look down upon its creature here in the straw, this suffering martyr, which indeed he was, although in quite another sense.'' The hunger artist's professional success does not make up for his spiritual emptiness as he spends much of his life ''in visible glory, honored by the world, yet in spite of that troubled in spirit, and all the more troubled because no one would take his trouble seriously.'' Ironically, while fasting is associated with devotion to God, the hunger artist's fasts seem only to exacerbate what Max Brod has maintained to be a central concern of Kafka's writing: ''the anguish and perplexity of modern man in search of God.''

The Joy of Life

In addition to spiritual hunger, the hunger artist also suffers from an inability to engage in ''the joy of life.'' In spite of his professional success, the hunger artist is ''never satisfied.'' Food, for obvious reasons, symbolizes life, and the hunger artist's inability to find ''the food that I liked'' symbolizes his inability to muster a passion for living. The relationship between an appetite for food and a ''passion'' for life in this story is best illustrated by the final image of the panther who replaces the hunger artist in the circus cage. In contrast to the hunger artist, the panther's hearty appetite is a measure of his *joi d'vivire* (joy of life), for ''the food he liked was brought him without hesitation,'' and his ''noble body'' was ''furnished almost to the bursting point with all that it needed.'' In keeping with the panther's satisfaction with his meals, ''the joy of life streamed with ardent passion from his throat.''

Change and Transformation

''We live in a different world now,'' the opening paragraph proclaims. The hunger artist's professional downfall is due to circumstances beyond his control: ''it seemed to happen almost overnight.''

Topics for Further Study

- Kafka's stories have been compared to his contemporary, the painter Edvard Munch (pronounced Moonk). Find a book of prints of Munch's paintings and discuss the ways in which they portray a "Kafka-esque" mood. In what ways do they seem to depict a nightmarish world, similar to that in "A Hunger Artist," in which similar feelings of alienation, entrapment, oppression, self-hatred, and angst are expressed? In what ways is the effect of the visual medium of painting used by Munch different from the effect of the written word used by Kafka's in his stories?

- Kafka and his writing have been strongly associated with the city of Prague. But since Kafka's birth in 1883, Prague has gone through many political, economic, and cultural changes. The national identity of the city has gone from being a part of the Kingdom of Bohemia to the Republic of Czechoslovakia, to occupation by Russia to the Czech Republic. Write a research paper on the history of Prague in the twentieth century. What is Prague like today, in terms of political, cultural and economic conditions? What would it be like to visit Prague as a tourist?

- Kafka's painful relationship with his father has been widely discussed and analyzed. Write a psychological profile of Kafka, based on research into his biography and his published letters. Read his prose piece, "A Letter to His Father," and his story, "The Judgement," both of which are based on his relationship with his father. How has Kafka's family experience influenced his psychology and his writing?

- Kafka's "A Hunger Artist" describes a man who fasts for long periods of time, while on public display, as a form of mass entertainment. But over the centuries, human beings have fasted for a variety of reasons, from religious and political protest to health to eating disorders. Research and discuss the various practices of fasting humans have undertaken, why they have done so, and what effect they have had on the person fasting and those around her or him.

- Think of a particular artist or artistic style in any area of popular American culture today which seems to express "Kafka-esque" sensibilities. This could be a particular musician or musical style, a particular film or filmmaker, a particular television show, a comic book character, or visual artist (such as painter or sculptor). Discuss the ways in which this example from popular American culture refers to contemporary issues and concerns while expressing "Kafka-esque" sensibilities and themes, such as alienation, entrapment, oppression, self-hatred, and angst.

- Write an original short story of your own in a "Kafka-esque" style. You do not need to write about similar topics or story lines. Rather, try to write a contemporary story based on your own ideas, but which captures a similar mood of anxiety, oppression, angst, darkness, entrapment and alienation. This could be a Kafka-esque parable, in which the main character is an animal with a human psychology, but which is ultimately a commentary on society or humanity. Or it could capture a sense of the absurd which Kafka often portrays, containing elements of both cynicism and humor.

Times are changing and the form of entertainment he provides is no longer popular with the masses, who have moved on to "other more favored attractions." In fact, his "art" comes to be despised, as "everywhere, as if by secret agreement, a positive revulsion from professional fasting was in evidence." The artist's frustration with the whole world is partly due to his feeling that these inevitable cultural changes are simply unfair. He can hardly accept that he has been outmoded.

The Suffering Artist in the Modern World

The artist's sense of alienation is partly a function of his lifelong struggle over the feeling that no one but he himself fully understands and appreciates his art. As one critic has explained, the hunger artist represents "a symbol or allegory of the suffering artist in society." He alone knows the truth about his accomplishments: "to fight against this lack of understanding, against a whole world of nonunderstanding, was impossible." "Just try to explain to anyone the art of fasting! Anyone who has no feeling for it cannot be made to understand it." He in fact blames the "whole world" for not granting him the "satisfaction" he feels her deserves: "It was not the hunger artist who was cheating, but the whole world was cheating him of his reward."

Style

Point of view

"A Hunger Artist" is written from a third-person limited perspective, meaning that the narrator is an abstract voice, not a character in the story. But the story is told mostly from the perspective, or point-of-view, of the hunger artist. Only in the final paragraph, as the hunger artist is dying, does the narrational perspective broaden out.

Imagery and Symbolism

Hunger. The most prominent symbolic motif in "A Hunger Artist" is hunger. This "hunger" motif is characterized by the hunger artist's lifelong feelings of dissatisfaction. No matter how successful and famous he becomes, the hunger artist remains "unsatisfied" and "troubled in spirit." Hunger symbolises both a lust for life and a spiritual yearning. The Hunger Artist's dying admission is that, "I have to fast, I can't help it. . . . I couldn't find the food I liked. If I had found it, believe me, I should have made no fuss and stuffed myself like you or anyone else." His inability to find the food that he likes is symbolic of his inability to engage in "the joy of life" or find spiritual fulfillment.

The Cage. The hunger artist spends most of his life sitting in a display "cage." The image of the cage strewn with straw, set finally at the entrance to the "menagerie" in a circus, draws a parallel between the hunger artist and the caged animals in the circus. When he is particularly frustrated by his audience's questions, the hunger artist would "shake the bars of his cage like a wild animal." The setting of the "cage" is also reflective of the settings of entrapment and images of claustrophobia in a number of Kafka's stories where the main character (whether animal or human) is confined to, or nearly imprisoned in, a single room or other cage-like location. In this case, it represents not just a literal cage, but a psychological and spiritual cage of his own making. In other words, he freely chooses to maintain a profession which bars him from humanity and the flow of life, its physical, social and even spiritual pleasures.

The Panther. The powerful image that ends this story, that of the panther who replaces the hunger artist in his cage at the circus, brings together the symbolic implications of the hunger imagery which runs throughout the story. Unlike the hunger artist, whose body is emaciated, and who lives in a figurative as well as literal cage, on the verge of starvation and death, the panther's "noble body, furnished almost to the bursting point with all that it needed, seemed to carry freedom around with it." Furthermore, unlike the hunger artist, whose lack of appetite symbolizes a lack of lust for life, in the panther "the joy of life streamed with such ardent passion from his throat that for the onlookers it was not easy to stand the shock of it." Finally, the hunger artist, while literally free (he chooses to be put in a cage), is a prisoner of his own mind; the panther, by contrast, while held in captivity, carries "freedom" within his own body.

Allegory and Parable

Allegory. Allegory is the general term used to describe stories in which the meaning is not so much in the literal elements of the story, but is to be understood on a symbolic level, hidden or buried beneath the surface meaning. The *Encyclopaedia Britannica* defines allegory as expressing "spiritual, psychological, or abstract intellectual concepts in terms of material and concrete objects." In allegories, the details of the story "are found to correspond to the details of some other system or relations." The *Encyclopaedia Britannica* states that Kafka's stories represent "the most original use of allegory in the 20th Century." Kafka's use of allegory is particularly enigmatic as his stories are "not susceptible of any single or precise interpretation." "A Hunger Artist," with it's absurd premise that fasting is in fact an "art," which for the hunger artist is central to all of life's dilemmas, invites the reader to search for a greater meaning than simply the internal thoughts of a hunger artist. The central symbol of "hunger," for instance, suggests themes of spiritual, social, psychological and existential yearnings.

Parable. "A Hunger Artist" can more specifically be described as a type of allegory called a "parable." Kafka's use of parable has been described in the *Encyclopaedia Britannica* as "one of the most enigmatic in modern literature." While this story clearly invites us to search for a deeper or more abstract meaning, it leaves us with no sense of certainty about what that meaning might be.

Absurdism

This story shares a quality of "absurdism" practiced by a number of writers in the twentieth century, of which Kafka is one of the foremost. According to the *Encyclopaedia Britannica*, the absurd element of a story is that of "the tragicomic nature of the contemporary human image and predicament," and is primarily represented through images of the "grotesque." The hunger artist builds his profession on his ability to display his own emaciated body as a "grotesque" form. At the point of death, he is hardly a human figure. His life of alienation from human society and perpetual dissatisfaction with himself and others is depicted as "tragic." But this story also has an element of humor which gives it an absurd quality. While sympathizing with the hunger artist's feelings, how can one not break into a wry smile at the very notion of fasting as an "art" which can be "performed" as a source of entertainment? How can one not experience a nagging feeling that perhaps the hunger artist is taking his art a little too seriously?

Historical Context

The Hunger Artists

It may come as a surprise that "A Hunger Artist" is partially based on the real historical phenomenon of "professional fasting." While most critics have failed to note this, Breon Mitchell, in his article, "Kafka and the Hunger Artists," has brought to light the history of a world famous "hunger artist" whose coverage in local newspapers may have inspired Kafka's story. Mitchell points out that "almost every detail" of Kafka's story corresponds to "the actual profession of fasting for pay." He states that, "The correspondence with reality is, in fact, so close that Kafka could not possibly have written the tale without some direct or indirect knowledge of the best-known hunger artists of his time."

The phenomenon of "professional fasting" lasted from 1880-1922, roughly the years of Kafka's lifespan. The first professional fast was accomplished by Dr. Henry Tanner, an American who was said to have gone for forty days under medical observation without food. The most famous of his European imitators was Giovanni Succi, on whom Kafka's story was most likely based. Giovanni "performed" fasts at least 30 different times, for periods of up to 30 days, in various European cities. Many imitators followed in the path of Anderson and Succi, achieving varying levels of success as professional fasters.

Although not in cages, these hunger artists were generally displayed in some form of confinement. Like Kafka's hunger artist, some of them even sold photographs of themselves at various stages of previous fasts. However, in general, these professional fasters had normal body types and looked relatively healthy (not the least bit emaciated) both before and after their fasts. In light of this, Kafka may have combined a different type of entertainer with the professional fasters in creating his character. Claude Ambroise Seurat, "The Living Skeleton," whose anatomy was excessively bony and skeletal, was exhibited in "freak show" type performances, very different from that of the professional fasters.

With the development of twentieth-century forms of mass entertainment, the place of "hunger artists" had indeed declined by the time Kafka wrote his story. And, in fact, this decline occurred simultaneously with the newer practice in circus entertainment of displaying wild animals, often big cats such as lions and leopards. Mitchell concludes that "from beginning to end, Kafka's tale accurately reflects an actual development in the history of European popular culture."

Prague's Caf Life and Literary Salons

Prague boasted an active caf culture during this time, where artists and intellectuals met at informal "salons." The Caf Continental, of which Kafka was a regular attendant, was a well-known location for one such salon. Others he frequented included the Caf Arco, Caf Central, and the Caf Louvre. Max

Compare & Contrast

- **1883-1924:** At the time of Kafka's birth in 1883, the city of Prague was ruled under the Hapsburg Empire, as part of the Kingdom of Bohemia. World War I, however, brought about significant changes in Prague's national identity. The War, which began with the assassination of the Archduke Ferdinand, resulted in the collapse of the Hapsburg Empire. During the first two years after the War, Prague became the capitol of the newly formed Republic of Czechoslovakia. As part of this new Republic, Prague changed from a city dominated by German language and culture to one dominated by Czech language and culture.

  1990s: With the end of the Cold War, signified by the tearing down of the Berlin Wall, Prague was released from communist rule and made the capitol of the newly formed Czech Republic. As part of the Czech Republic, Prague has undergone a major transformation. There is now a free market, tourism, relaxing of censorship, and the welcoming of American enterprises, such as MacDonald's, into the city.

- **1883-1924:** Though not widely recognized during his lifetime, Kafka was well-respected within his small literary, intellectual circle in Prague, who were aware of his considerable talents. Kafka published his first prose pieces at the age of 25 in *Hyperion*, a journal edited by his close friend Max Brod. Throughout his brief life, he continued to publish in journals, as well as several small volumes of his stories. He died in relative obscurity, many of his stories and novels still unpublished. A number of his unpublished manuscripts were destroyed during a Nazi raid on his companion Dora Diamont's apartment, and his work was not made available in Prague until a decade after his death.

  1990s: Franz Kafka is indisputably one of the most important and influential writers of the twentieth century. However, in regard to the *meaning* of his stories, there is little in the way of critical consensus. Perhaps as a result, there is no sign of retreat on the part of critics from adding to the mounds of published critical material on Kafka.

- **1883–1924:** Prague boasted an active caf culture during Kafka's lifetime, where artists and intellectuals met as informal ''salons.'' The Caf Continental, of which Kafka was a regular attendant, was a well-known location for one such salon. More organized forums for literary discussion were various literary meetings and clubs. Kafka became associated with the ''Prague Circle,'' an internationally recognized literary society of German-Jewish authors.

  1990s: Since the end of the Cold War, the city of Prague's association with Kafka has become a tourist attraction. The area of the city which was once Kafka's loved and hated Jewish ghetto has become an American-influenced tourist trap, complete with Kafka T-shirts, souvenirs and guided tours. As David Zane has cynically, although perhaps realistically, described this phenomenon, Kafka is now ''finding his place amidst the KITSCH.'' Zane goes on to explain that, ''After years of ignoring him or treating him as a pariah, the new Czech Republic is finally discovering its strange Jewish son, no longer a threat and suddenly BANKABLE, as a tourist attraction.'' He concludes, ''the irony would not be lost on him.''

Brod, Kafka's friend and editor, described these meeting places as ''free and open to ideas, crammed together in four or five rooms, smoky, stifling, thick with the fumes of mocha coffee.'' More organized forums for literary discussion were various literary meetings and clubs. Kafka became associated with the ''Prague Circle,'' an internationally recognized literary society of German-Jewish authors.

German Literary Movements

While Kafka never explicitly subscribed to any particular literary movement, he was associated with the fashionable literati of his day and his writing is now understood as representative of several schools of literature. Prominent schools of thought in the early part of the twentieth century included Expressionism and Symbolism, both of which Kafka is now considered a key example. Expressionism, according to the *Encyclopaedia Britannica*, was the "key movement in German literature" in the World War I era. The expressionist style "emphasized the inner significance of things and not their external forms." Kafka's influence by, and contribution to, expressionism took the form of a "negative vision," in which "with the stark clarity of a nightmare, he depicted the horror and uncertainty of human existence." Like expressionism, the symbolist movement emphasized the inner world, creating a literary style described as dream-like or nightmarish.

Prague

At the time of Kafka's birth in 1883, the city of Prague was ruled under the Hapsburg Empire, as part of the Kingdom of Bohemia. World War I, however, brought about significant changes in Prague's national identity. The war, which began with the assassination of the Archduke Ferdinand, resulted in the collapse of the Hapsburg Empire. During the first two years after the war, Prague became the capitol of the newly formed Republic of Czechoslovakia. As part of this New Republic, Prague changed from a city dominated by German language and culture to one dominated by Czech language and culture. However, because he spoke Czech as well as German, Kafka was able to keep his job, even though he was the "token" Jew in his company.

Jews in Prague

During Kafka's lifetime, Prague was "a city of three peoples." In 1900, the city of a half-million people was populated mostly by Czechs. Germans, however, while only about six percent of the population, made up the dominant culture of Prague. At five percent of the population, the Jews in Prague spoke German and identified themselves with German culture. Most Jews, however, like Kafka, lived in Josefov, the Jewish "ghetto," a walled-off section of the city which served to maintain segregation of Jews from the rest of the population.

Many Jews at this time, like Kafka's father, were assimilationist, meaning that they largely ignored their Jewish identity in hopes of blending into the dominant German culture. However, anti-Semitism from both Czechs and Germans meant that neither accepted the Jews as their own. As a result, Jews in Prague were always seen as the scapegoats of either ethnic group in times of crisis, and waves of anti-Semitic rioting swept through the Jewish ghetto in times of national unrest. The Czech population, for instance, went through waves of nationalist sentiment, during which they targeted the Jews as the most visible and hated element associated with German culture. Other riots on the part of anti-Semitic German sentiments also swept through the ghetto.

Critical Overview

Kafka's Lifetime

Though not widely recognized during his lifetime, Kafka was well-respected within his small literary, intellectual circle in Prague, the members of whom were aware of his considerable talents. Kafka published his first prose pieces at the age of 25 in *Hyperion*, a journal edited by his close friend Max Brod. Throughout his brief life, he continued to publish in journals, as well as several small volumes of his stories.

Posthumous Publications

Kafka was one of those classic literary figures who lived and wrote in relative obscurity, only to be hailed as one of the foremost writers of his century years after his death. Shortly before his death, Kafka requested that his female companion, Dora Diamant, burn all of his unpublished writing, echoing a similar request to his close friend Max Brod. Brod, however, was wise enough to see the potential importance of Kafka's work to international literature and subsequently acted against his friend's dying wish. Brod spent years organizing and editing Kafka's many manuscripts, which were generally in fragments and multiple drafts with chapters unnumbered and out of order, assigning them titles, and seeing that they were translated and published.

The Nazi Regime

During the Reign of Adolph Hitler, Kafka's writing was both reviled and celebrated, depending on which part of the world one is referring to. In

Nazi Germany, where Kafka's three sisters and two of his lovers perished in concentration camps, Kafka's surviving work was unavailable; anything which didn't escape the Holocaust with Max Brod was destroyed or banned. Max Brod escaped the Holocaust in 1939, with Kafka's work in tow, and eventually settled in Palestine. Many more of the late Kafka's manuscripts, however, left in Prague with his female companion Dora Diamant, were destroyed in 1933 during a Nazi raid on her apartment. None of Kafka's publications were available in Prague for ten years after his death. In France and the English-speaking world, meanwhile, Kafka was gaining international notoriety (thanks to Max Brod).

The Post-War Era

During the post-War era, Kafka's work was once again available in Germany and Austria, where it became an important influence on German literature. But, under the communist regime that ruled Prague after 1948, Kafka's work did not fare so well. The dominant artistic school of "socialist realism" dictated a style of writing which was completely "realistic," in the sense of maintaining the values of socialist ideals. Of course, Kafka's surreal parables did not conform to this aesthetic, and his work was accused of expressing bourgeois decadence. But for those living under this regime who managed to get a hold of a smuggled copy of his book *The Trial,* Kafka did indeed seem to be representing a realistic image of the nightmarish and oppressive bureaucracy which characterized the Russian system of government. This even furthered the government's reasons for banning his work. Nonetheless, Kafka's literary reputation throughout the world was becoming widespread and influential.

The 1960s

From 1963-1968, Kafka's work did enjoy a brief period of renewed legitimacy in his homeland, based on the efforts of a group of intellectuals to redeem him in the eyes of Czech communists. In 1968, however, a series of events referred as "Prague Spring," during which Russian tanks rolled into Prague against ardent protest by its citizens, once again lead to the banning of Kafka's books.

The 1990s

With the end of the Cold War, signified by the tearing down of the Berlin Wall, Prague was released from communist rule and made the capitol of the newly formed Czech Republic. The city's association with Kafka has since become a tourist attraction, and the area of the city which was once Kafka's loved and hated Jewish ghetto has become an American-influenced tourist trap, complete with Kafka t-shirts, souvenirs and guided tours. As David Zane Mairowitz has cynically, although perhaps realistically, described this phenomenon, Kafka is now "finding his place amidst the KITSCH." Zane Mairowitz goes on to explain that, "After years of ignoring him or treating him as a pariah, the new Czech Republic is finally discovering its strange Jewish son, no longer a threat and suddenly BANKABLE, as a tourist attraction." He concludes, "the irony would not be lost on him."

International Literary Reputation in the Late 20th Century

Franz Kafka is indisputably one of the most important and influential writers of the twentieth century. However, as to the *meaning* of his stories, there is little in the way of critical consensus. As Franz R. Kempf explains, "Kafka critics only agree on one thing, and that is that they are not in agreement." Perhaps as a result, there is no sign of retreat on the part of critics from adding to the mounds of published critical material on Kafka. A noteworthy addition to this stockpile is a series of new translations of his novels *The Trial* and *The Castle,* published in 1998, based on newly restored and re-edited editions of the original manuscripts and edited by Breon Mitchell.

Criticism

Liz Brent

Brent has a Ph.D. in American Culture from the University of Michigan. In the following essay, she discusses possible interpretations of "A Hunger Artist" in light of key factors in Kafka's life.

"Kafka's Hunger, Kafka's Art"

Kafka was a master of the enigmatic. In his book, *Everyone's Darling: Kafka and the Critics of His Short Fiction,* Franz R. Kempf states that, "Kafka critics only agree on one thing, and that is that they are not in agreement." Kempf points out that Kafka valued this resistance in his work to specific interpretations, as he "understood writing to be a consciously created ambiguity." Walter Benjamin has even asserted that Kafka "took all

What Do I Read Next?

- *Franz Kafka: The Complete Stories* (1971) includes some of Kafka's most notable stories, such as "Before the Law," "The Judgement," "The Metamorphosis," and "In the Penal Colony."

- *The Trial: A New Translation, Based on the Restored Text* (1998) is a recent translation and is said to be a more accurate rendition of Kafka's original manuscript. The story is about Joseph K., who is interrogated by unidentified government officials and accused of an unnamed crime. He becomes entangled in a legal and bureaucratic maze from which there seems to be no exit.

- Max Brod's *Franz Kafka, a Biography* (1937) is an early biography by Kafka's close friend and literary executor.

- *Letters to Friends, Family and Editors* (1977) contains selections from Kafka's extensive letter-writing.

- *Kafka's Clothes: Ornament and Aestheticism in the Habsburg Fin de Siecle* (1992), by Mark Anderson, discusses Kafka's social milieu of fashionable Prague intellectuals at the turn of the Century.

- Klaus Wagenback's *Franz Kafka: Pictures of a Life* (1984) is a book of photographs from Kafka's life, family, and home town of Prague.

---

conceivable precautions against the interpretation of his writings." Even Kafka himself, Kempf explains, "found his work to be incomprehensible."

Yet, while Kafka's work resists definitive interpretation, there has been no end to the critical material written about Kafka and his work. In his book *Introducing Kafka*, David Zane Mairowitz claims that, "no writer of our time, and probably none since Shakespeare, has been so widely over-interpreted and pigeonholed." Kafka's work, interpreted and over-interpreted by countless critics over the decades is described by Kemp as "the kaleidoscopic carnival of Kafka criticism." A brief discussion of some of the possible interpretations of "A Hunger Artist" in light of Key themes in Kafka's life will provide a glimpse of several of the many patterns of meaning created by this "kaleidoscope."

As "ambiguity" is "the very core of Kafka's art," his stories invite us to speculate about possible meanings or interpretations, without providing a sense of certainty that any one reading is the reading. Kafka's work, therefore, is best interpreted while keeping in mind this built-in ambiguity. Entertaining several possible interpretations, without having to choose one as the definitive "meaning"

of a Kafka story, produces the richest and most meaningful way of discussing his work.

Kafka's Hunger

As an allegory, "A Hunger Artist" employs many symbolic motifs which, although interrelated, may be examined separately. The motif of "hunger," for example, takes on a highly symbolic, yet ambiguous, significance in the story. Surprisingly, however, this story is also based on the real historical phenomenon of "professional fasting." While most critics have failed to note this, Breon Mitchell, in his article, "Kafka and the Hunger Artists," has brought to light the history of a world famous "hunger artist" whose coverage in local newspapers may have inspired Kafka's story. Mitchell points out that "almost every detail" of Kafka's story corresponds to "the actual profession of fasting for pay."

The phenomenon of "professional fasting" lasted from 1880 to 1922, roughly the years of Kafka's life span (1883-1924). The first professional fast was accomplished by Dr. Henry Tanner, an American who was said to have gone for forty days under medical supervision without food. The most famous of his European imitators was Giovanni

> To add to this, Kafka experienced hunger, during the six months he spent in Berlin, due to astronomical inflation resulting in 'the total uncertainty of his material existence."

Succi, on whom Kafka's story was most likely based. Giovanni "performed" fasts at least 30 different times, for periods of up to 30 days, in various European cities. Although not in cages, these hunger artists were generally displayed in some form of confinement. Mitchell states that, "The correspondence with reality is, in fact, so close that Kafka could not possibly have written the tale without some direct or indirect knowledge of the best-known hunger artists of his time."

But the fact that "hunger artists" were a real historical phenomenon does not lessen the legitimacy of the story's allegorical meanings. Rather, it adds depth to our understanding of the richness of Kafka's story. As Mitchell suggests, "A Hunger Artist" is both "the powerful literary testament to an inner world," and a means of "linking his own sense of spiritual solitude and artistic mission to figures from the margins of history."

Kafka himself had significant experiences of hunger during the course of his life, due to both illness and poverty. "A Hunger Artist" was written in the last two years of Kafka's life, during which time he was in and out of sanitariums and suffered a variety of treatments for tuberculosis of the larynx. To add to this, Kafka experienced hunger, during the six months he spent in Berlin, due to astronomical inflation resulting in "the total uncertainty of his material existence." He and his female companion Dora Diamant were nearly desperate for food, which only further compromised Kafka's failing health.

Because of the location of the illness in his throat, Kafka was barely able to eat, drink or even speak toward the end of his life. Although he had originally written "A Hunger Artist" before this stage of his illness had set in, it can easily be seen as partly inspired by Kafka's various health and diet regimes over the course of 17 years of tuberculosis. Like the hunger artist, it became increasingly difficult for him to "find the food that I liked." As he himself was, in effect, starving to death, Kafka was still correcting the galley proofs for "A Hunger Artist" at the time of his death in 1924, two months before the story was published.

The symbolic significance of "hunger" in "A Hunger Artist," however, goes well beyond any literal referent. Hunger in this story suggests symbolic references to spiritual yearning. References to spiritual yearning and religious symbolism in "A Hunger Artist" are subtle but pervasive. Critic Meno Spann has analyzed the food imagery in Kafka's writing and concluded that "for Kafka, physical deprivation or hunger represents spiritual hunger and is associated with the 'unknown nourishment' so many of Kafka's characters seek."

Understanding Kafka's religious orientation helps us to make sense of this symbolism. Although he did not practice it as a religion. Kafka developed a great interest in studying his Jewish culture. As with most religions, many Jewish rituals and traditions revolve around food. Fasting is an equally important ritual during the holiday of Yom Kippur. Evelyn Torton Beck has suggested that the hunger artist's fasting suggests "a grotesque distortion of the fasting associated with Yom Kippur, which, ironically, is intended to have the opposite effect of bringing Jews together before God." The hunger artist fasts for periods of 40 days, a time period evocative of biblical events. After Noah built his ark, it rained for 40 days and 40 nights. After escaping slavery in Egypt, the Jews wandered in the desert for 40 years.

The hunger artist's fasting and lifelong sense of dissatisfaction is in part symbolic of a hunger for spiritual fulfillment. The hunger artist is also described as a religious "martyr," although his martyrdom is based on his own professional frustrations, rather than any spiritual enlightenment. At the public spectacle which ended each fast, the impresario "lifted his arms in the air above the artist, as if inviting Heaven to look down upon its creature here in the straw, this suffering martyr, which indeed he was, although in quite another sense." The hunger artist's professional success does not make up for his spiritual emptiness, as he spends much of his life "in visible glory, honored by the world, yet in spite of that troubled in spirit, and all the more troubled because no one would take his trouble seriously."

Ironically, while fasting is associated with devotion to God, the hunger artist's fasts seem only to exacerbate what Max Brod has maintained to be a central concern of Kafka's writing: "the anguish and perplexity of modern man in search of God."

The meaning of the hunger symbolism in this story is best illustrated by contrasting the hunger artist to the panther who replaces him in the circus cage. In contrast to the hunger artist, whose mouth and throat rarely admit sustenance, the panther eats heartily, and carries "freedom" in his "noble body," and "the joy of life streamed with ardent passion from his throat." Whereas the panther's hearty appetite is associated with "freedom" and the "joy of life," the hunger artist's fasting and inability to find "the food that I liked" is manifest in an emaciated body, "troubled in spirit," and bereft of any sense of the "joy of life."

Kafka's Art

Many critics have interpreted Kafka's "A Hunger Artist" as an allegory in which the hunger artist serves as a symbol of "the suffering artist in society." His dying words, "I always wanted you to admire my fasting," express the hunger artist's inner torment and lifelong feelings of alienation. This stems primarily from the distance between his own appreciation for the purity of his art and a modern world concerned only with newer forms of mass entertainment. The hunger artist's internal vision of himself as a virtuoso "artist" is perpetually at odds with his public image. While his impresario limits his fasts to a maximum number of 40 days, he longs for the opportunity to "beat his own record by a performance beyond human imagination." Yet, even at the height of his career, his enthusiastic audiences all over the world fail to appreciate "the honor of his profession"; they are always in doubt as to whether or not he may be a fraud, sneaking morsels of food to sustain himself through the fasts. Only the artist himself knows for certain that his fast has been "rigorous and continuous." And so, he suffered to be "the sole completely satisfied spectator of his own fast."

A closer look at Kafka's own personal experience as a writer will illuminate the significance of such an interpretation, for Kafka has come to be known as the quintessential "suffering artist" of the twentieth century. Kafka's suffering came in many forms, not least of which were his parents' neutral reaction to his minor successes and his own inner torment stemming from self-doubt about the quality of his writing. Kafka suffered from his parents' complete lack of appreciation for his talents. When he proudly handed his father a bound copy of his first published collection of short stories, he was met with indifference and told to set it on his father's nightstand. Any attempts to impress upon them the importance of his writing must have been futile, as the hunger artist knows: "Just try to explain to anyone the art of fasting! Anyone who has no feeling for it cannot be made to understand it."

Furthermore, their dismissive attitude towards their son's needs as a writer contributed in part to the terrible conditions under which Kafka wrote—in a small, cramped household with no privacy and dominated by the almost continual sounds of his father's habitual yelling. His bedroom was between that of his parents and the central room of their apartment, so that he was subjected to almost constant noise as he struggled to write during his free time after work. In addition to writing at night, Kafka developed an ability to tune out the chaos around him, which David Zane Mairowitz has referred to as "a kind of self-hypnosis," much as the frustrated hunger artist escapes from the unappreciative crowds by sitting in a meditative state, "withdrawing deep into himself, paying no attention to anyone or anything."

Although Kafka is now indisputably one of the greatest writers of the twentieth century, he met with only marginal success during his lifetime and died in relative obscurity. While his talent was appreciated by the small coterie of writers and intellectuals with whom he was associated, his publications were few and his circle of admirers small. Kafka wrote "A Hunger Artist" at the end of a five-year period during which he refrained from all writing intended for publication. As Joachim Unseld has discussed in *Kafka: A Writer's Life*, attempts to publish his work had become "futile," and he spent much of this time receiving medical treatment for the Spanish Flu. But in January of 1922, Kafka began moving into a "new creative phase." By that Spring, he had completed "A Hunger Artist," which was accepted for publication in the fall. This minor success "signified a landmark in the history of his publications"; his "self-esteem as a writer" was boosted and he began to see himself as a professional. Even so, he described the finished story as "'bearable' presumably the most positive description the author could elicit in evaluating his own work."

Kafka's internal self-doubt about the quality of his work was most famously expressed through his written requests to both his female companion Dora Diamont and his friend and editor Max Brod that they burn all of his unpublished manuscripts upon his death. However, the suspicion that Kafka may have secretly counted on his friends reluctance to carry out such a wish has been suggested by the writer Jorge Luis Borges in the comment that, "If he really wanted a bonfire, why didn't he just strike the match himself?"

The dual interpretations of "A Hunger Artist" as a parable of both the "suffering artist in modern society," and, as Brod maintained, "an elaborate quest for an unreachable God," can be brought together by an understanding of how Kafka himself viewed the relationship between his writing and spiritual fulfillment. As quoted by Unseld, Kafka's companion Dora Diamont expressed the strong connection between writing and spirituality for Kafka: "For him literature was something holy, absolute, uncompromising, something great and pure." And the *Encyclopaedia Britannica* states that Kafka understood "his writing and the creative act" to be "a means of redemption," a "form of prayer."

Unlike the hunger artist, who's "art" was out of vogue by the time of his death, Kafka's art did not come into vogue until nearly 40 years after his death. The hunger artist dies behind the times while Kafka died ahead of his time.

Source: Liz Brent, for *Short Stories for Students*, The Gale Group, 2000.

Paul Neumarkt

In the following essay, Neumarkt explores the effect a "borderline" existence has on the human psyche, focusing on the isolation of the title character in "A Hunger Artist."

Kafka's collection of short stories which has come down to us under the heading of *Ein Hungerkuenstler* represents the author's last creative production. In each of these stories the ego finds itself largely isolated; yet, there are varying degrees of relatedness by means of which the ego gauges its isolation. In "A Hunger Artist," Kafka has carried this predicament to its most plausible conclusion. The aim of this paper is to explore a psyche exposed to the vicissitudes of a border-line existence. By dwelling on the potential of this unique phenomenon in terms of individuation, I will try to elucidate its concomitant triumph, and pitfalls within the wider framework of the collective setting as it affected Kafka's personality.

The Hunger Artist's "Liebestod"

"A Hunger Artist" may be divided into two parts. The first is dominated by the "contract" between the hero and his impresario while the second deals with the period between the dismissal of the impresario and the death of the Hunger Artist. This division is not arbitrary but closely follows the course of the particular neurosis in this story in which the pathological background remains paramount.

Students of the psyche are aware of the fact that neuroses are seldom cured in a sense that they are completely removed. What usually happens is that the neurosis is outgrown and loses some of its acute gravity, as the patient moves on to different situational settings. In this process of reorientation, the neurosis is displaced, or better, deprived of its natural habitat and thus relegated to a dormant state for an indefinite period of time. The possibility of reactivation, however, remains an ever present challenge to the ego sphere. If the advance of the neurosis is not expertly checked, the condition may worsen to an extent that makes it impossible for the person to extricate himself. The psychic dilemma of the Hunger Artist lies in his inability to transcend his pathological setting towards new goals, or as we would say in colloquial terms, to come to grips with his neurosis by putting it in its proper place. This pathological streak in his psyche pervades the entire story like a *basso ostinato* that reverberates mightily throughout the composition.

We are dealing here with the Leitmotif of a "Liebestod," that is, flirtation with the finality of death. If "the instinct to eat . . . is one of the most elementary of man's psychic instincts," we must *ipso facto* assume that the hero's abstinence from food is his own, mainly unconscious choice in his preparation for death, even as he has consciously chosen the profession of Hunger Artist. His protracted exercises in going hungry constitute, in fact, a process of self-dissolution which bears the distinctive mark of nostalgic regression. The longing to consummate "marriage" with death is, however, constantly thwarted by the letter of the "contract" which forbids the fast to go beyond its forty-day limit. This is an indication that defensive, that is, positive forces within the psyche are still active and strong enough to frustrate any sudden surprise move by the ever present destructive elements. The Tristan and Isolde syndrome we are dealing with in this context has a Wagnerian tone. The chromatic, tension-evoking technique of the musical scale appears in Kafka as a literary device. Each time the fast is interrupted by the impresario, it is as if the Hunger Artist has been cheated out of his natural propensity to complete the cadence on a note of final rest. The "contract" is the lease of life, the *modus operandi*, that remains in effect as long as the association between the artist and impresario is not questioned. Thus the show will go on, for the "impresario . . . is present in every man, the essence of the forces that inevitably and without question cling on to life." The setting is existential. Being means being with others, and as such is a sort of contractual assurance that the performance will continue. The possibility of upheaval, that is, of a severe disturbance of the delicate psychic balance with a sudden swing to the dialectical alternative is, as I have pointed out elsewhere, an ever present challenge. Kafka is only too aware of this psychological insight, for no sooner has the Hunger Artist taken leave of the impresario—termination of contract is implicit within each such formal agreement—than the show is fatefully interrupted, and the final marriage with death is about to be consummated. Herbert Tauber alludes to the negative forces as the "falsity of the forces deriving from the negative." However, the term 'falsity' in its contextual association with the negative, is a psychological misnomer. The negative contents of the psyche are just as formidable as reality itself and can never be discounted, as anyone dealing with matters of the unconscious must be aware of.

The trauma of the Hunger Artist furthermore harbors a synchronistic element which is not causally related to his very being: the refusal of the collective to let him continue the fast to his heart's desire. His yearning is "to set the world agape," to fulfil himself in this world which, however, is utterly disinterested in his private desires. "Kafka realized," states Harry Slochower, "that the laceration of individuality could be circumvented only by communal attachment." The trauma of this realization, however, lies in the very essence of "this hopeless Kafkaesque world of blind necessity . . . this absurd world." The human stage and its background which is the *sine qua non* of the genuine artist, is suddenly transmogrified into a circus setting with the cage of the Hunger Artist being hardly discernible among the animal stables that hold the attraction of the audience during the intermission. While he is actually begging for a pittance of attention, he has the bitter experience that his cage is "strictly speaking only an obstacle in the path of the stables" around which the people throng. In this synchronistic juxtaposition of artist and world, the

> " In his early years, Kafka was apparently driven into identification with his mother who, at this early stage of the novelist's life, appeared to his imagination as a young beautiful girl whom he desires to rescue from her exploiter husband."

latter is completely unrelated to his efforts. The dilemma of the Kafkaesque personality is that "he finds no reliable witness" for his despair. This is reminiscent of the world of Camus' *The Stranger* from which the dialectical struggle has vanished. "Each event of this absurd world is simultaneously real and unreal, possible and impossible." The meaningful causal relationship between the artist and his world has irrevocably been supplanted by a non-causal, hence, indifferently synchronistic coexistence between actor and stage, or as Slochower states: "Kafka reaffirms the paradox of co-existing opposites."

The phenomenon of a "Liebestod" or a nostalgic regression in its encounter with the "contractual," that is, life-affirming postulates leads us further to the assumption that there may be a latent homosexual tendency within Kafka's personality. The contract with the impresario, the father-figure, who makes decisions for the Hunger Artist, is terminated as soon as the absurdity of his circus-existence has dawned upon him. Hand in hand with the collapse of the meaningful outside world goes the unconscious rejection of the father image and its substitution by contents indigenous to the maternal, pleromatic sphere. It is at this particular juncture that the latent homosexual tendency within Kafka can be discerned.

Latent Homosexuality

It is not that highly ambivalent relationship of the artist with his father which is psychologically most relevant here, but his intricate, psychic reaction vis-a-vis his mother. While outwardly there is a classical oedipal potential in this particular setting, it would be misleading to analyze it merely as such because the actual resultant is not the author's marriage with the mother, or a mother-like figure, but his rejection of marriage as a suitable solution for himself. The reason for this may be gleaned from Kafka's entry into the diary dated 1911: "I was . . . able to spend a good deal of time before falling asleep in imagining that some day, a rich man in a coach and four, I would drive into the Jewish quarter, with a magic word set free a beautiful maiden who was being beaten unjustly, and carry her off in my coach." If we take into consideration the fact that his mother "was untiringly busy helping his father in his business, and most probably irreplaceable," the aforementioned daydream about the rescue of the beaten girl becomes psychologically pertinent. Freud states that in "all male homosexual cases the subjects had had a very erotic attachment to a female person, as a rule to their mother, during the first period of childhood, which is afterwards forgotten." While the presence of a strong father would generally be beneficial for the adolescent to favor a proper decision in the selection of his object from the opposite sex, in this particular case, Kafka's father assumes archaic, monstrous dimensions and is thus instrumental in bringing about the opposite result. In his early years, Kafka was apparently driven into identification with his mother who, at this early stage of the novelist's life, appeared to his imagination as a young beautiful girl whom he desires to rescue from her exploiter husband. The mother for whose care and loving kindness he yearned, but whose love he was deprived of by his brutal father who virtually held her captive in his ghetto, i.e. business establishment, is no longer the object of his pity on a conscious level. Not the mother, but he himself, by way of identity substitution, is the one to bear the brunt of his father's ruthlessness. Freud suggests that "the boy represses the love for the mother by putting himself in her place, by identifying himself with her, and by taking his own person as a model through the similarity of which he is guided in the selection of his love object. He thus becomes homosexual." While I do not infer that Franz Kafka was actively homosexual, there remains the suggestion of such latent propensity in his psychic disposition. This is manifested by his frequent need to rationalize the merits and demerits of marriage as a solution for himself. Thus in a letter of November 1912 to Miss F., a young woman whom he, for a while, seriously considered as an eligible marriage partner, he conjectures that marriage was entirely impractical as far as he was concerned: "I must be alone a great deal. All that I have accomplished is the result of being alone. . . . Fear of being tied to anyone, of overflowing into another personality. Then I shall never be alone anymore. . . . Single I might perhaps one day really give up my job. Married, it would never be possible." One year later, in a letter, dated September 1913, Kafka writes: "The very idea of a honeymoon fills me with horror." In all this rationalization he is, however, not unaware that there is some imbalance in his psychic makeup that thwarts all his attempts to consummate marriage. Thus, with reference to the daydream in which he, now a man of twenty-eight, saw himself as a rescuer of the beautiful maiden, there is the dawning realization that his daydreams, "this silly make-believe . . . probably fed only on an already unhealthy sexuality." If Kafka's dilemma is seen within the context of the "Liebestod" syndrome, activated by nostalgic regression and characteristic of the uroboric incest motive, the assumption of latent homosexuality is adequately substantiated. Kafka's border-line psyche is the tightrope walk of an ego in isolation. However, the tightrope walker must never permit himself—on a conscious level—to trip into the path of no return, because he is ever bound to cross the dangerous path anew in his never ending game of brinkmanship. Kafka was well aware of his predicament. In a letter to Max Brod, in 1913, he reports a short-lived episode with a Swiss girl. Again his yearning is blunted by his psychosexual dilemma which Kafka, in terms of border-line experience, expresses so aptly in the words: "always the longing to die and yet keeping oneself alive, that alone is love." Kafka's awareness of his "unhealthy sexuality" may be considered a safety valve which prevented him from crossing the border-line into the sphere of psychosis. Within the depth of the psyche, there are no clear cut borders and the analyst is forever in a quandary because he can never be "quite certain that a neurosis never steps beyond the danger-line." Kafka's awareness at times reached dimensions that might leave even the trained observer awestruck, as in the quasi casual conversation between the Inspector and the Hunger Artist:

> I. "You are still fasting? . . . Will you ever stop? H.A. "I have always wanted you to admire my going hungry." I. "Well we admire it." H.A. "But you shouldn't admire it." I. "All right, then we don't admire it . . . but why shouldn't we admire it?" H.A. "Because I have to go hungry, I can't help it." I. "And why can't you help it?" H.A. "Because I . . . have never found the right food to suit my taste. If I had . . . I would have made no fuss and gorged myself as you and the rest of your kind."

The absurdity of this situation lies in the utterly uncoordinated synchronicity of artist and world. Since it cannot be visualized within a dialectical frame of reference, it forces the creative personality into a state of uncontested awareness of desolate, moribund isolation. It lies furthermore in what Max Bense defines as simultaneity of the "real and unreal, possible and impossible," in the dilemma of craving for admiration, yet simultaneously rejecting it as soon as it is expressed. Even on this level of border-line existence, however, the psyche puts up as much of a defensive counter-force as it can muster under the circumstances. If the process of harnessing the archaic, negative forces is to serve the life affirming mechanism of defence, it must relate meaningfully to the individual in question.

Fasting: Isolation and Relatedness

If fasting is reflective of the ego in a state of unqualified isolation, then it is, in its widest possible application, simultaneously an expression of the author's relatedness to the world around him, a relatedness which evidently bears no longer the mark of collective standards but of a baroque, silhouetted reflection of the ego, cut loose from the common roots of life. In other words: the concept "meaning" has ejected its inherently collective content and, in terms of moral standards, is reduced to a thoroughly subjective, questionable abstract. Kafka is well aware of this psychic condition. In his story "Investigations of a Dog" the author states: "For today I still hold fasting to be the final, and most potent weapon of research. The way goes through fasting; the highest if it is attainable, is attainable only by the highest effort, and the effort among us is voluntary fasting. . . . My whole life as an adult lies between me and that fast, and I have not recovered yet." Kafka's confession may appear as if he were postulating fasting as a "most potent weapon of research." This is, no doubt, a neat bit of rationalization by means of which the conscious ego would justify its existence. The quoted exchange between the Inspector and the Hunger Artist stresses that the isolation depicted in this story is a finality, lacking an alternative. Van Gogh expresses himself in a similar vein in a letter to his brother Theo: "either fast or work less, and add to this the torture of loneliness." Thus fasting becomes a means of breaking away from the path of loneliness. In fact, it is within the process of creativity that the artist may go hungry without being aware of it. In this state of transcendence of the material stratum, in this state of weakened physical existence the artist, quite paradoxically, may reach the maximum

in terms of productivity. Loneliness as used by Van Gogh and in an implied manner by Kafka, is the exact antonym of isolation, because the latter, within the context of fasting, is the conscious expression of the individual in terms of conative experience, while the former fundamentally reflects a state of deficiency within the individual's collective psyche. Isolation in this reference is the very existential setting of the artist. It is, as I have tried to demonstrate, a synchronistic datum that leaves the personality in a state of uncontested awareness of irreconcilable alienation.

Our "Overburdened Memory"

Kafka appraises this development appropriately when he states: "I can only see decline everywhere . . . I do not mean that earlier generations were essentially better than ours, but only younger; that was their great advantage, their memory was not so overburdened as ours today." We may not relegate this apercu to the realm of a *bon mot* or chance remark. The artist quite aptly points his finger at a contemporary malaise, namely our "overburdened memory." The pathological symptoms concomitant with exaggerated stress on man's intellectual faculty could not but be seen as a danger signal by Kafka's sensitive psyche. It is for this reason that he warned: "they [our fathers] did not know what we can guess at contemplating the course of history: that change begins in the soul before it appears in ordinary existence." Psychologically speaking, Kafka hints here at the phenomenon of dissociation with reference to the conscious psyche, a process which, in terms of distortion and violence, will undoubtedly exact a more exorbitant price in the future than we are already paying now, if the necessary steps to check this "progress" are not taken in time. At the present stage there is little use for the unconscious, since we pursue the cult of consciousness to the exclusion of all else. Our true religion is a monotheism of consciousness, a possession by it, coupled with a fanatical denial that there are parts of the psyche which are autonomous. Actually, we are still possessed by autonomous, subliminal contents. What once used to be associated with the name God is today known as phobia, compulsion etc. The gods have become diseases.

From the vantage ground of such psychological introspection, Kafka had reason to acknowledge the changes that had started to register in his psyche long before they had reached down to and had become part of the level of experience of the social world. What affected him immediately and intimately would manifest itself in mass-hysteria, psychosis, and other expressions of insanity engulfing mankind as a whole. The psychogenesis of schizophrenia is alluded to by Kafka. If the pathogenesis of schizophrenia were to be stripped of its professional jargon and shifted to a more literary form of expression, I cannot think of a better example than Kafka's description of the overflowing river that ''loses outline and shape, slows down the speed of its current, tries to ignore its destiny by forming little seas in the interior of the land, damages the field, and yet cannot maintain itself for long in its new expanse, but must turn back between it banks again, must dry up wretchedly in the hot season that presently follows.''

There are two definite, mutually exclusive elements in this somewhat rustic scene. There is the unbridled, destructive force of the water following its gradient down the path of annihilation. This unconscious drive, represented here by the rushing stream was referred to above as ''flirtation with death,'' and may be identified as an integral part of the regression syndrome. There are, however, on the other hand, the defensive forces that almost simultaneously counter the brute, insensitive element until it has been subdued and summoned back to its natural boundaries. This rather conscious reaction that calls the entire array of positive reserve into action against the threat from the sinister depth of the unconscious has been associated with the life-affirming potential of the ''contract.'' The breaking asunder of the huge body of water into small inland-seas constitutes, aside from its symbolical representation, the dissociation and disintegration of the ego complex.

Here, Kafka's reference to the ''overburdened memory'' gives us a clue. If, as I have stressed, the ego sphere is inflated into a monotheism of consciousness, we have *ipso facto* denied the existence of the ''tremendum,'' the autonomous, subliminal contents prevalent in the human psyche. What happens is this: The individual having declared the ''tremendum'' to be dead ''should find out at once where this considerable energy . . . has disappeared to. It might reappear under another name, it might call itself 'Wotan' or 'State' or something ending with -ism, even atheism, of which people believe, hope and expect just as much as they formerly did of God. If it does not appear under the disguise of a new name, then it will most certainly return in the mentality of the one from whom the death declaration has issued. Since it is a matter of tremendous

energy, the result will be an equally important psychological disturbance in the form of a dissociation of personality. It is as if one single person could not carry the total amount of energy, so that parts of the personality which were hitherto functional units instantly break asunder and assume the dignity and importance of autonomous personalities.''

We are dealing here with what Janet has called ''abaissement du niveau mental'' (reduction of attention). When this etiological requisite is posited, the individual has reached the critical stage where the ego cannot successfully counter the onslaught of the powerful subliminal forces. That Kafka envisaged the possibility of a fateful crossing of the border-line without the alternative of return is suggested in the last part of ''A Hunger Artist.'' Theoretically, at least, that is, within the framework of the story, the author made the possibility of no return a viable alternative. The dismissal of the impresario is the first danger signal in so far as it spells the end of the period associated with the ''contract,'' the symbolical guaranty that the ego defences are fit to ward off any intrusion from the subliminal strata. With the removal of this last safety measure, the existential setting of the Hunger Artist is no longer dominated by the ego complex since it has been divested of its supremacy. In terms of expenditure, the hero of the story has paid in full for his unbridled desire to continue the fast. His death constitutes the final atonement of the artist in relation to the community whose tenets he has violated. This is the literary device by means of which the *dramatis persona* can bow out of his performance. The real hero, however, the author behind the uncompromising figure of the Hunger Artist, the man of flesh and blood, is not quite so negative as his literary figure. He is aware of the possibility of returning to his previous *modus operandi*. This is indicated by the receding water that ''must turn back between its banks again.''

A thorough perusal of Kafka's work will furthermore confirm my suspicion that Kafka was fully aware of the danger inherent in his border-line existence.

Kafka's ''A Little Woman'' and ''First Sorrow''

In his story ''A Little Woman,'' in which the process of alienation touches on the very psychic balance of the author himself, the synchronicity no longer reflects the artist as an island of psychic manifestations. But unlike the Hunger Artist who crosses over into the sphere of oblivion, the hero in

"A Little Woman" establishes a *modus operandi* this side of the danger-line. He is, of course, aware of his predicament he must live with day in and day out, but has come to understand that one cannot stray off the beaten track or flaunt the capricious whims of society with the hope of going unnoticed for any length of time. Thus the author states with plausible confidence: "From whatever standpoint I may look at it my opinion remains unshaken. If I keep this matter [the questionable relationship with his feminine counterpart] under cover, I will be able to continue living in this world." A similar, strong desire not to carry the dissociation of his psychic makeup to an extreme is depicted in "First Sorrow," a short story in which the trapeze artist maintains his existence by physical isolation. He makes his abode high up in the dome structure of the circus and refuses to come down or to have any truck with his fellow workers. The flight of the trapeze artist into his self-chosen "splendid isolation" is, however, not to be looked at as a psychic finality, because the world below—his co-workers and audience—are at all times visible and within earshot, hence at the lowest perimeter of his conscious awareness. This ambivalent situation is part of the Kafkaesque absurdity as well. He can't live with the community, and can't perform without it. The flood-lit vaulted roof above, representative of the sphere of ego consciousness, does not provide for repressive tendencies as such. Thus his "overburdened memory," or in psychological terms, his dissociated existential setting has forced him to live in constant awareness of his absurd state of affairs. The border-line is ever dangerously near, but so are cast and audience to whom he is obligated under "contract." As a result, his delicate psychic condition is kept in a precarious balance.

In sum: The study of the literary masterpiece "A Hunger Artist" has revealed a number of danger zones to which the ego in isolation is prone. There is the particularly grave threat implicit in the "Liebestod" syndrome which initiates the process of nostalgic regression. There is furthermore the Kafkaesque absurdity, a setting which is thoroughly a causal, hence to be grasped in terms of synchronicity only. The implication of latent homosexuality which is intimately tied up with the regressive propensity of Kafka's psyche, and his constant need to rationalize his dilemma are additional phases in this never ending game of brinkmanship. Added to this is the threat to the psyche from utter dissociation due to modern man's "overburdened memory," a gentle reminder to our present day world that the breaking

asunder of the ego sphere may engulf humanity in the psychotic darkness of chaos. This legacy of doom transmitted by the artist, due to his exposed station in life, is countered by the life-affirming, psychic contents, represented symbolically by the "contract," the concrete expression of public approval that checks excessive, individual appetites. Thus, the individual can never completely escape the scrutiny of the society that sets his limits. In fact, the process of individuation is only possible because of the *a priori* existence of the undifferentiated state of the sphere of collective consciousness. With this realization, Kafka creates a *modus vivendi* for himself that enables him to skirt the dangerous border-line, the vicissitudes of which the ego in isolation is constantly exposed to.

Source: Paul Neumarkt, "Kafka's 'A Hunger Artist': The Ego in Isolation," in *American Imago*, Vol. 27, No. 2, Summer, 1970, pp. 109–21.

R. W. Stallman

In the following excerpt, Stallman explores the multiple levels of meaning in "A Hunger Artist," proclaiming that it is one of the "greatest short stories of our time."

"A Hunger-Artist" epitomizes Kafka's theme of the corruption of interhuman relationships, as one of his critics defines it. It is one of his perfections, if not his best story, and it belongs surely with the greatest short stories of our time.

The present essay attempts to open up the cage of Kafka's meaning in "A Hunger-Artist," But first, as a starting point for our analysis, here is the story at its literal plane, a matter-of-fact account stripped of interpretation:

> The story is about a once-popular spectacle staged for the entertainment of a pleasure-seeking public: the exhibition of a professional "hunger-artist" performing in a cage of straw his stunt of fasting. His cage's sole decoration is a clock. His spectators see him as a trickster and common circus-freak and therefore they expect him to cheat, to break fast on the sly. But fasting is his sole reason for existing, his life purpose; not even under compulsion would he partake of food. For him, to fast is the easiest thing he can do; and so he says, but no one believes in him. Because the public distrusts him, he is guarded—usually by three butchers—and prevented from fasting beyond a forty-day period, not for humane reasons, but only because patronage stops after that time. His guards tempt him with food and sometimes mistreat him; yet they breakfast on food supplied at his expense! A great public festival celebrates his achievement, and thus he is "honored by the world." But when he is removed

> The plight of the hunger-artist in his cage represents the plight of the artist in the modern world: his dissociation from the society in which he lives."

from his cage he collapses in a rage, not from hunger, but from having been cheated of the honor of fasting on and on and on and of becoming thus "the greatest hunger-artist of all time." Though emaciated almost to the point of death, he quickly recovers and after brief intervals of recuperation performs again and again.

Nowadays, however, he has been abandoned for other spectacles. People visit his cage in the circus tent, but only because it is next to the menagerie. His spectators are fascinated by the animals. All's changed: there is, apparently, no clock, and the once beautiful signs to announce the purpose of his act have been torn down. Now no tally is kept of the number of fasting days achieved. There are no guards. "And so the hunger-artist fasted on without hindrance, as he had once dreamed of doing . . . just as he had once predicted, but no one counted the days; no one, not even the hunger-artist himself, knew how great his achievement was and his heart grew heavy." Thus the world robs him of his reward. Indifference replaces admiration and on this note he expires. He is buried with the straw of his cage and replaced by a panther, who devours fiercely the food he naturally craves. The people crowd about his cage.

We notice that the facts in this "matter-of-fact" account are not in themselves complete or sufficient, and that our attempt to take them at their matter-of-fact or literal level is quite impossible. They seem to compete with each other and to thrust us beyond their literal properties into the plane of their allegorical significance. That clock seems to be simply a clock; it does not apparently represent anything else. And yet no literal meaning can be ascribed to that bizarre clock. It strikes the hour just like a real clock, but (so to speak) it does not appear to tick. The life of this hunger-artist is unclocked. He exists outside time, and periodically he survives starvation sieges no ordinary man could endure. (Actually, a calendar would be the logical means for reckoning the artist's fasting days.) As for the other facts, these objects likewise suggest symbolic significance. It is impossible to reduce Kafka's facts to a single self-consistent system of meaning. The trouble is that his meanings emerge at several planes at once, and the planes are interconnected. No complete paraphrase is possible.

We cannot confine Kafka's meaning to a single circle of thought. The plight of the hunger-artist in his cage represents the plight of the artist in the modern world: his dissociation from the society in which he lives. By this reading of the story, "A Hunger-Artist" is a sociological allegory. But we can also interpret the hunger-artist to represent a mystic, a holy man, or a priest. By this reading the story allegorizes in historical perspective the plight of religion. A third possible interpretation projects us into a metaphysical allegory: the hunger-artist represents spirit, man as a spiritual being; the panther, in contrast, represents matter, the animal nature of man. If the story is translated into metaphysical terms, the division is between the spiritual and the physical; into religious terms, between the divine and the human, the soul and the body; into sociological terms, between the artist and his society. Kafka's blueprint—the groundplan of ideas upon which he has built this structure of parables—is toolmarked with these three different systems of thought.

Consider first the story as an allegory of the dilemma of the artist. He is set in contrast to the multitude. The people who attend his exhibitions of fasting cannot comprehend his art. "Just try to explain the art of fasting to someone! He who has no feeling for it simply cannot comprehend it." The artist starves himself for the sake of his vision. He has faith in his vision, faith in himself, and integrity of aesthetic conscience. As the initiated alone understood, "the hunger-artist would never under any circumstances, not even under compulsion, partake of any nourishment during the period of fasting. His honor as an artist forbade such a thing." It is his vision, solely this, which nourishes him. Of course the artist can "fast" as no one else can do. It's not everyone who is an artist. We concede, "in view of the peculiar nature of this art which showed no flagging with increasing age," the claim he makes of limitless capacity for creating works of art. But if his public is devoid of any sympathetic understanding of the artist and of his art, if his public has no faith in him, how then can he cling to this faith in himself? It is because his public is an unbeliever that the artist is in a cage (the cage symbolizes his isolation). Society and the artist—each disbelieves in the other. And so the artist comes to disbelieve, finally, in himself; he cannot survive in isolation.

The hunger-artist is emaciated because of the disunity within himself, which is the result of his dissociation of soul from body, and because of the disjunction between himself and his society. It is his denial of the world of materiality that is the source of his gnawing doubt and ''constant state of depression.'' He repudiates half of life, and the multitude repudiate him. The public reject the emaciated body of the artist for the healthy body of the panther—they reject art for life itself. These two occupants of the cage, the purely spiritual and the purely bestial, represent, then, the dual nature of man. The people outside the cage, with whom he is also contrasted, crave the same food as the panther. For them, as for the beast, their joy in living issues from their throat—and from their belly. These human and bestial beings represent the sensuous physical realm of matter. They are all-flesh, whereas the hunger-artist is no-flesh. In the one we have pure matter; in the other, pure spirit. But the hunger-artist, as pure soul, is a failure. Though he is apparently free from those gnawing dissatisfactions which our purely physical appetites create in us again and again, nevertheless he is not entirely free from the claims of the body, from the claims of matter, from the claims of the world in which he lives. At the same time that he denies the evil natural social world he longs for some recognition of his fasting from the public; he wants the people to crowd around his cage. Finally, ''though longing impatiently for these visits [of the people on their way to the eagerly awaited stalls], which he naturally saw as his reason for existence, [he] couldn't help feeling at the same time a certain apprehension.'' He apprehends the truth that he who is the faster cannot be ''at the same time a completely satisfied spectator of his fasting.'' He sees that an existence of pure spirituality is impossible to man. He sees that this insatiable hunger with which he, as artist or as mystic, is possessed is at bottom only the sign of his maladjusted, and therefore imperfect, soul.

Complete detachment from physical reality is spiritual death. This statement sums up the meaning of ''A Hunger-Artist'' insofar as the story is an allegory about the nature of man. What is man, matter or spirit? The story might be described as a kind of critique of this philosophical problem. Spirit and matter—each is needed to fulfill the other. At the moment of his death the hunger-artist recognizes his failure as an artist or creator. For this superannuated artist there is no possibility of resurrection because in our present-day world not spirit but matter is recognized. That matter has today

triumphed over spirit is recognized by the dying hunger-artist as he confesses his secret. I had to fast, he admits, because I could find no food to my liking. Fasting, you see, was my destiny. But '''if I had found it [i.e., food to my liking], believe me, I should have caused no stir, I should have eaten my fill just as you do, and all the others.' Those were his last words, but in his glazed eyes there remained the firm, though no longer proud, conviction that he was still fasting.'' Here, then, is the key to his enigma. Cut off from the multitude, the artist performing his creative act (his fasting) has to die daily and be daily reborn. This is a martyrdom, but for what purpose? The creative artist cannot also be his own public; he dies when no one cares that he and his art should live. Devotion to an aesthetic or spiritual vision cannot be an end in itself. Pure creativeness is impossible, even as absolute spirituality is impossible. The creative imagination must feed upon all reality. For art is but a vision of reality. The artist, no less than the mystic-faster, must live in the world of mundane life. Art requires the material conditions of life, and these conditions nourish it. Life is at once the subject of art and its wellspring.

It is the clock in the hunger-artist's cage that triumphs over the artist. It is time that triumphs over the very one who denies the flux of time, which is our present reality. The clock in his cage is a mockery of the artist's faith in the immortality of his creative act or vision, a mockery of his faith in his art as an artifice of eternity. The tragedy of Kafka's hunger-artist is not that he dies, but that he fails to die into life. As he dies he seeks recognition from those whom he has all his life repudiated: '' 'I always wanted you to admire my fasting,' said the hunger-artist.'' It is his confession that spirit has no absolute sovereignty over matter, soul has no absolute sovereignty over body, and art has no absolute sovereignty over life. . . . Kafka's hunger-artist represents Kafka's doctrine: ''There is only a spiritual world; what we call the physical world is the *evil* in the spiritual one, and what we call *evil* is only a necessary moment in our endless development.'' ''A Hunger-Artist'' is a kind of critique of this doctrine. Matter here triumphs over Spirit.

Throughout the story the author laments the passing of our hunger-artists, their decline and extinction in our present-day civilization. But nonetheless throughout the story all the logic is weighted against this hunger-artist's efforts at autarchy. In his last words we are given his confession that the artist must come to terms with life, with the civilization in which he lives, the world of total reality. "Forgive me, all of you," he whispers to the circus manager, as though in a confessional before some priest. And they forgive him. They forgive him for his blasphemy against nature. The hunger-artist seeks Spirit absolutely; he denies the *"evil* natural social world" at the same time that he longs for it. And this is his dilemma, even as it is ours. It is not possible for man to achieve a condition of pure spirituality, nor again is it possible for him to achieve a synthesis of spirit and matter. As the agent of divine purity the hunger-artist is a failure. His failure is signified, for instance, on the occasion when he answers the person who has explained his emaciation as being caused by a lack of food: he answers "by flying into a rage and terrifying all those around him by shaking the bars of his cage like a wild animal." This reversion to the animal divests him momentarily of the divine, and it also betrays the split-soul conflict within him. His location next to the menagerie serves as reminder that the claims of the animal body are necessary claims upon the soul and cannot be denied. And this is true even though matter is wholly evil (i.e., "the evil odors from the stalls," etc.); complete separation from reality can never be obtained. (Compare the idea of "complete detachment from the earth" as it figures in "The Burrow.") Pure Spirit is as vacuous as Pure Matter.

In the same way that Kafka's sets of facts can be translated into allegorical terms at the philosophical and aesthetic levels of meaning, so too in terms of the religious allegory the multiple meanings of his facts overlap. Our post-Renaissance world has discarded the philosopher, the artist, and the mystic. The hunger-artist as mystic-faster is dead. Call him priest or artist, he has been rejected by the "pleasure-seeking multitude" and replaced by other amusements; for instance, by the exhibition of a live panther. It was different in times past. For example, in the Middle Ages and in the Renaissance he "lived in apparent glory, honored by the world." Then he had his patron. (The patron of the artist was the impresario.) He had his critics, the butchers who guarded him out of the public distrust of his creative act. And he had his historians, the attendants who recorded his creative act or kept count of his remarkable performances. In those times he was at least admired for his achievements as an imitator of life. . . . But what a poor imitation of real life he presented! In those times he was at least celebrated (albeit, not without hypocrisy), honored by rituals conscientiously enacted upon

appointed fast days. Consider this hunger-artist as mystic-faster or priest. At one time, everyone attended his services daily. Regular subscribers sat, as in church pews, "before the small latticed cage for days on end." Everyone pretended to marvel at his holy fast. Actually, however, not one worshiper had faith. Nevertheless, despite this sham of faith in him, he submitted again and again to crucifixion by these pretenders to faith. He was a martyr for his divine cause. The multitude, because "it was the stylish thing to do," attended his "small latticed cage"—they attended it as they might a confessional box. But the multitude, since it does not understand what Faith is, has no sin to confess. The hunger-priest hears no confession. (Ironically it is he who, in dying, confesses.) In short, all mankind—apart from a few acolytes to his cult, disbelieves this Christ who many times died for man's sake. And when he dies, see how these disbelievers exploit the drama of his death. Here is Kafka's parody on the drama of the Virgin mourning the loss of her Son.

> But now there happened the thing which always happened at this point. The impresario would come, and silently—for the music rendered speech impossible—he would raise his arms over the hunger-artist as if inviting heaven to look down upon its work here upon the straw, this pitiful martyr—and martyr the hunger-artist was, to be sure, though in an entirely different sense. Then he would grasp the hunger-artist about his frail waist, trying as he did to make it obvious by his exaggerated caution with what a fragile object he was dealing, and after surreptitiously shaking him a little and causing his legs to wobble and his body to sway uncontrollably, would turn him over to the ladies, who had meanwhile turned as pale as death.

The ladies who so cruelly sentimentalize over his martyrdom represent sympathy without understanding; a sympathy which is devoid of understanding is mere self-sentiment. One of the ladies weeps—but not for him. She breaks into tears only in shame for having touched him. "And the entire weight of his body, light though it was, rested upon one of the ladies, who, breathless and looking imploringly for help (she had not pictured this post of honor thus), first tried to avoid contact with the hunger-artist by stretching her neck as far as possible, and then . . . she broke into tears to the accompaniment of delighted laughter from the audience. . . ." It is a mock lamentation that these two Marys perform. What a difference between the theme of the Virgin mourning the loss of her Son as treated in Kafka's parody and as depicted in the famous *Avignon Pieta* or in Giotto's *Lamentation.*

It is thus that the religious and the metaphysical and the aesthetic meanings of ''A Hunger-Artist'' coincide: (1) Christ is truly dead. Our post-Renaissance world has discarded the act of faith from its reality. (2) For the mystic, as for the artist, there is no resurrection because today not spirit but matter alone is recognized. And as we have seen, it is recognized, this triumph of matter over spirit, even by the dying mystic, who ends a skeptic and a defeatist (not unlike Kafka himself): I had to fast, because I could find no food to my liking. Fasting is my destiny. But '' 'if I had found it, believe me, I should have caused no stir, I should have eaten my fill just as you do, and all the others.' Those were his last words, but in his glazed eyes there remained the firm, though no longer proud, conviction that he was still fasting.''

Source: R. W. Stallman, '''A Hunger Artist,''' in *Franz Kafka Today*, edited by Angel Flores and Homer Swander, The University of Wisconsin Press, 1958, pp. 61–70.

Glatzer, Nahum N., ed. *Kafka: The Complete Stories*, New York, Schocken Books, 1971.

Kempf, Franz R. *Everyone's Darling: Kafka and the Critics of His Short Fiction*, Camden House, Colombia, S.C., 1994, pp. 1-4.

Mairowitz, David Zane and Robert Crumb. *Introducing Kafka*, Cambridge, England, Totem Books, 1994, pp. 5, 17, 73, 154, 175.

Mitchell, Breon. ''Kafka and the Hunger Artists,'' in *Kafka and the Contemporary Critical Performance*, edited by Alan Udoff, Indiana University Press, 1987, pp. 238, 248, 251, 252.

Spann, Meno. *Franz Kafka,* Boston: Twayne, 1976.

Stern, J. P., ed. *The World of Franz Kafka*, New York, Reinhart and Winston, 1980.

Udoff, Alan, ed. *Kafka and the Contemporary Critical Performance*, Indiana University Press, 1987, pp. 1, 3.

Unseld, Joachim. *Kafka: A Writer's Life*, Ariadne, Riverside, CA, 1994, pp. 225, 230, 235, 237, 238, 262, 264.

Sources

Beck, Evelyn Torton. *Kafka and the Yiddish Theater: Its Impact on His Work*, University of Wisconsin Press, 1971, pp. 200-202.

Britannica Online [database online] , Chicago, Ill.: Encyclopaedia Britannica, Inc., 1999- [cited 2 June 1999], available from Encyclopaedia Britannica, Inc., Chicago, Ill., s.v. ''Allegory,'' ''The Art of Literature: DRAMA: Comedy: KINDS OF COMEDY IN DIVERSE HISTORICAL PERIODS: The absurd,'' ''The Art of Literature: NARRATIVE FICTION: Fable, parable and allegory,'' ''German Literature: The 20th century: MAJOR LITERARY TRENDS AND CONDITIONS,'' and ''Kafka, Franz.''

Brod, Max. *Franz Kafka: A Biography,* Schocken Books, 1937.

Carter, F. W. ''Kafka's Prague,'' in *The World of Franz Kafka*, edited by J. P. Stern, New York, Reinhart and Winston, 1980, pp. 31-32, 34-35.

Further Reading

Beck, Evelyn Torton. *Kafka and the Yiddish Theater, Its Impact on His Work*, University. of Wisconsin Press, 1971.
     Discusses Kafka's life and work in relation to dramas of the Yiddish Theater which Kafka frequently attended.

Gilman, Sander L. *Franz Kafka: The Jewish Patient*, Routledge, New York, 1995.
     Discusses Kafka's life and work in relation to perceptions of tuberculosis during his lifetime, as well Kafka's perceptions of his own body as Jewish, male, and suffering from tuberculosis.

Wagenback, Klaus. *Kafka's Prague: A Travel Reader*, Overlook, Woodstock, NY, 1996.
     Literally a tourist guide to the contemporary city of Prague for the Kafka devotee. Includes many photos and suggested walking tours of cites significant to Kafka's life and work.

The Life You Save May Be Your Own

Flannery O'Connor

1953

Like much of Flannery O'Connor's short fiction, "The Life You Save May Be Your Own" is set in the American South and contains characters whose most notable feature seems to be their ordinariness. Through imagery, dialogue, and moments of revelation, O'Connor explores the themes of morality and religion, both frequent concerns in her work. The story evoked critical praise upon its publication in the *Kenyon Review* in the spring of 1953. Within the sparse, apparently simple plot of the story, O'Connor constructs a world torn between renewal and emptiness, natural beauty and crass materialism, compassion and cruelty. In the end, O'Connor's protagonist must choose between these extremes and attempt to experience the grace of God's love.

Author Biography

Flannery O'Connor's parents had an effect on their only daughter in ways that were both fruitful and tragic. O'Connor was born in 1925 to a prominent Georgia family of devout Roman Catholics—an anomaly in the largely Protestant South. This intensely religious milieu played a major role in O'Connor's evolution as a writer. She attended schools in Savannah and Milledgeville and confronted tragedy at age fifteen when her father died of lupus, a degenerative disease which attacks the body's vital organs. O'Connor later entered Geor-

gia State College for Women (now Georgia College), majored in social sciences, and spent her spare time writing and drawing for student publications. She began writing and publishing short fiction in earnest when she entered the graduate writing program at Iowa State University, which she completed in 1947.

O'Connor started work on her first novel, *Wise Blood*, while living at a writer's colony in upstate New York. She later lived in New York City and Connecticut with Sally and Robert Fitzgerald, fellow Catholics who shared many of O'Connor's literary interests and who later wrote about her. This rather artistic lifestyle came to an abrupt end when, at age twenty-five, O'Connor herself suffered an attack of lupus. She moved back to Georgia to live with her mother on a dairy farm and continued to write, publishing *Wise Blood* in 1952, the story collection *A Good Man Is Hard to Find* in 1955, and a second novel, *The Violent Bear It Away*, in 1960. Her most famous stories, "A Good Man Is Hard to Find" (1953) and "The Life You Save May Be Your Own," were both written during this period. She received numerous awards, grants, and citations for her work.

Despite persistent health complications, O'Connor continued to write fiction and nonfiction, displaying a sharp wit and penchant for self-mockery. She spent her final years being cared for by her mother and hired helpers, who likely resembled many of the impoverished characters that appear regularly in her fiction. O'Connor also enjoyed painting and raising exotic birds, motifs that are evident in her writing. She finally succumbed to lupus in August 1964 at age 39. *Flannery O'Connor: The Complete Short Stories* was published in 1971 and won the National Book Award. With two novels and thirty-one stories to her credit, O'Connor remains one of the most important short fiction writers of the twentieth century.

Plot Summary

Part I: Meeting

An old woman and her daughter sit quietly on their porch at sunset when Tom Shiftlet comes walking up the road to their farm. Through carefully selected details, O'Connor reveals that the girl is mute, that the old woman views Shiftlet as "a tramp," and that Shiftlet himself wears a "left coat sleeve that was folded up to show there was only

Flannery O'Connor

half an arm in it." The two adults exchange curt pleasantries. "I'd give a fortune to live where I could see me a sun do that every evening," Shiftlet states, looking at the sunset, to which the woman coolly answers, "Does it every evening." Shiftlet surveys the run-down farm and inquires about a rusted automobile, which has not worked in years. "Nothing is like it used to be, lady," Shiftlet observes. "The world is almost rotten." Again the woman's response is abrupt: "That's right." Their disturbing conversation continues along the same lines, with additional important allusions to nature. Shiftlet then reveals that he is a carpenter, which suggests that he may be of some use to Mrs. Crater around the farm. Shiftlet's occupation identifies him with Jesus Christ, who was also a carpenter.

Mrs. Crater offers him shelter in exchange for work but warns, "I can't pay." Shiftlet says he has no interest in money, adding that he believes that most people are too concerned with money. Sensing not only a handyman but a suitor for her daughter, Mrs. Crater asks if Shiftlet is married, to which he responds, "Lady, where would you find you an innocent woman today?" Mrs. Crater then makes known her love for her daughter, adding, "She can sweep the floors, cook, wash, feed the chickens, and hoe." Mrs. Crater is clearly offering her daughter's hand to Shiftlet. For the moment, however, he simply decides to stay on the farm and to sleep in the broken-down car.

Part II: Resurrection

Once Shiftlet moves into the Crater's farm, he fixes a broken fence and hog pen, teaches Lucynell how to speak her first word (''bird''—a recurring symbol in O'Connor's fiction), and, most importantly, repairs the automobile. ''With a volley of blasts it emerged from the shed, moving in a fierce and stately way. Mr. Shiftlet was in the driver's seat. . . . He had an expression of serious modesty on his face as if he had just raised the dead.'' At this moment, when Shiftlet most clearly appears to be the bearer of heavenly powers, Mrs. Crater offers Lucynell to him. He replies, however, by stating, ''It takes money,'' suggesting that he is perhaps changing and becoming more interested in money. Soon he compares the human spirit to an ''automobile,'' and his smile turns into ''a weary snake.'' Earlier allusions to nature's beauty have given way to nature's darker side. In her desperation to gain Shiftlet's services and marry off her daughter, Mrs. Crater offers Shiftlet a small sum. In this symbolically important car, the three of them drive into town, and Shiftlet and young Lucynell are married. Shiftlet's once mournful philosophical inquiries suddenly become bitter now that he has taken a wife and some money. The newlyweds then set off on their honeymoon.

Part III: Abandonment

The newlyweds stop at a diner, and in the middle of eating, Lucynell passes out. ''She looks like an angel of Gawd,'' says the boy serving food at the diner, to which Shiftlet simply responds, ''Hitchhiker.'' He pays for lunch and abandons Lucynell.

Afterwards Shiftlet ''was more depressed than ever'' and he ''kept his eye out for a hitchhiker.'' As a storm is breaking in the sky, Shiftlet sees a road sign that reads, ''Drive carefully. The life you save may be your own.'' Shiftlet then offers a ride to a boy who did not even have his thumb out.

Shiftlet tries to make conversation, telling stories about his sweet mother, who is—as the boy at the diner called Lucynell—''an angel of Gawd.'' But the boy does not buy Shiftlet's sentimentality. ''My old woman is a flea bag and yours in a stinking polecat,'' he snaps, before leaping from the car. Shocked, Shiftlet ''felt the rottenness of the world was about to engulf him,'' exclaiming, ''Oh Lord! Break forth and wash the slime from the earth!'' The rain finally breaks, with a ''guffawing peal of thunder from behind and fantastic raindrops, like tin-can tops, crashed over the rear of Mr. Shiftlet's car.'' Shiftlet speeds off to Mobile, Alabama.

Characters

Lucynell Crater

Lucynell Crater is Mrs. Crater's mute daughter who eventually marries Tom Shiftlet. Though she is almost entirely silent, she plays a pivotal role as a symbol of innocence, an ''angel of Gawd'' whom Shiftlet rejects, forcing him to confront his own emptiness.

Mrs. Crater

An old, toothless woman trying to marry off her mute daughter and secure Shiftlet's services as a handyman, Mrs. Crater is abrupt and manipulative. She speaks of her undying love for her daughter while trying to pass her off on Shiftlet, whom she attempts to win over with material goods. Even her name suggests the emptiness of her character. At the end of the story she appears to have been outsmarted by Shiftlet, who has taken both her car and her daughter.

Tom T. Shiftlet

The pivotal figure in the story, Shiftlet is a one-armed drifter who wanders into the Crater family's life. Shiftlet even admits that he may be lying about his real name. This ambiguity has led to divergent critical readings of Shiftlet as a character. Presented at first as a lost, Christ-like figure who asks poignant questions and appreciates nature's beauty, Shiftlet can be viewed as either corrupted by Mrs. Crater's opportunism, or as a sinister and calculating figure who feigns naivete to gain access to the Crater family's possessions. The latter interpretation is supported by his name, which suggests a ''shifty'' nature. By the story's conclusion, Shiftlet is spiritually bereft. He has opted for the emptiness of the nomadic lifestyle that led him to the Craters in the first place.

Themes

Search for the Meaning of Life

When Shiftlet approaches the Crater's farm, it is not clear what type of person he is. What is apparent is that he is searching for something. By marrying Lucynell and then abandoning her, he has missed an opportunity to experience redemption (an event symbolized by the "guffawing peal of thunder" and his anguished plea to God at the end of the story). Shiftlet has failed to bring meaning into his transient life. He entered the Craters's lives as a lonely wanderer, and he leaves it the same way.

Given the gradually increasing interest he shows in money and Mrs. Crater's automobile, perhaps Shiftlet believes that such material possessions might bring meaning to his life. By the end of the story, he has obtained these things, as well as a wife who can perform household chores and who, as a mute, "can't sass [him] back or use any foul language," as Mrs. Crater tells him. But none of these things bring meaning into Shiftlet's life. He wanders on towards Mobile (notice the double meaning of the town's name), where he will likely continue to live a life devoid of significance.

Moral Corruption

While on the surface, the automobile and wedding gift in "The Life You Save May Be Your Own" seem unimportant, they in fact reveal a world in which money has become more important than people or spiritual peace. From the beginning, it is clear that Mrs. Crater is seeking to lure Shiftlet into her home so that she can gain his services—first as a carpenter, and then as a husband for her daughter. This causes Mrs. Crater (whose name suggests emptiness) to treat her own daughter as little more than an object to be traded.

While Shiftlet seems initially unconcerned with money, he is soon inquiring about the automobile, as well as cash for a wedding. (His name suggests that he is capable of such a "shift.") Like Mrs. Crater, he also abandons Lucynell, mistakenly believing, perhaps, that a car—which he admits he has always wanted but has never been able to afford—will fulfill his needs. O'Connor's morally corrupt characters, who prize cars and money over human relations, are capable of self-deception but not self-fulfillment. In the end, Shiftlet cannot avoid the fact that he is once again empty and wanting.

Media Adaptations

- "The Life You Save May Be Your Own" was filmed for television in 1957 as a segment included in "Playhouse of Stars" and starred Gene Kelly, Agnes Moorehead, and Janice Rule. This adaptation has a different ending than O'Connor's story.

God and Religion

Closely related to the moral corruption of Shiftlet and Mrs. Crater is their inability to embrace everyday manifestations of God's grace. Indeed, both surrender Lucynell, who is referred to as an "angel of Gawd." In doing so, each trades a symbol of God's presence for material comfort. It is this very absence of religious redemption that has led to Shiftlet's nomadic life and Mrs. Crater's lack of compassion. A road sign warns Shiftlet, "the life you save may be your own." Embracing Lucynell would have offered him an opportunity to grasp at some form of salvation or atonement—one that Mrs. Crater has apparently already yielded. Shiftlet even makes one final desperate attempt by offering a ride to a young boy. But the boy scolds Shiftlet, who is bluntly reminded of the lack of a religious presence in his rootless existence.

Nature and Its Meaning

"The Life You Save May Be Your Own" opens with a "piercing sunset" but ends with a "cloud descended . . . over the sun, and another, worse looking, crouched behind" the car driven by Shiftlet. A thunderous storm breaks; Shiftlet's eyes are "instantly clouded over with a mist of tears," and he feels "that the rottenness of the world was about to engulf him." The light and illumination of the sun has been replaced by a dangerous and threatening storm. These are two examples of O'Connor's use of natural imagery in this story.

Such imagery serves as a function both of O'Connor's plot and her characterization. Mrs. Crater is initially seen "shading her eyes" from the

Topics for Further Study

- Research aspects of Christian theology—specifically, passages or stories from the Bible—and compare them with the themes in O'Connor's story. Start with Jesus's disruption of the market in the temple or Judas's betrayal of Jesus.

- Research the automobile's effect on American society in the early 1950s. Include such aspects as the way it was advertised on television and in magazines to demonstrate its effect on our modern lifestyle and culture. Based on your research, how might readers from the 1950s have greeted O'Connor's somewhat critical depiction of the automobile in "The Life You Save May Be Your Own"?

- Is O'Connor's depiction of young Lucynell Crater insensitive to people with disabilities? Why or why not?

---

light of the sun and later standing "as if she were the owner of the sun," whereas Shiftlet is initially awed by its beauty. Mrs. Crater tries to deflect the sun, while Shiftlet seems to want to understand its powers. This is confirmed later when, after a "fat moon appeared in the branches of the fig tree as if it were going to roost there with the chickens," Shiftlet says that "a man had to escape to the country . . . where he could see the sun go down every evening like God made it to do." This lush passage, connecting the moon, plants, and animals, further suggests the important presence of nature in O'Connor's story and the way in which she uses it to suggest Shiftlet's longing. Even the first word he teaches Lucynell is "bird."

While attempting to persuade Shiftlet to marry Lucynell, Mrs. Crater refers to Shiftlet as a "poor disabled friendless drifting man." This appears to be where Shiftlet's "shift" of attitude begins to take place. Natural allusions point the way. "The ugly words settled in Mr. Shiftlet's head like a group of buzzards," and his smile becomes "a weary snake waking up by a fire." Nature remains present, but it

is more threatening, foreshadowing Shiftlet's abandonment of Lucynell. After he leaves Lucynell at a diner, a sinister storm breaks. The storm seems to have a double meaning; Shiftlet pleads for the storm and asks it to "wash the slime from the earth." Such salvation eludes Shiftlet, but as all of O'Connor's complex allusions to nature suggest, nature can be both a pleasure and a threat, a guiding light or sinister shadow. This is consistent with O'Connor's view of her characters, who are capable of either saving or condemning themselves.

Style

Point of View

O'Connor employs a detached yet observant third-person narrative in "The Life You Save May Be Your Own." Shiftlet is a stranger without a fixed identity who wanders into the Craters's lives. He soon moves in with them and takes an interest first in the Craters's automobile and then in Lucynell, Mrs. Crater's mute daughter. Shiftlet and Lucynell are married, but he abandons her at a roadside diner.

While Shiftlet clearly emerges as the central character, O'Connor offers enough glimpses into both his and Mrs. Crater's psyche to provide insight into their motivations. For example, the reader learns that Shiftlet "always wanted an automobile but he had never been able to afford one before." This passage, late in the story, confirms his desire for the automobile and the importance he places on money and material goods. Furthermore, O'Connor includes careful details in several descriptive passages which establish the natural world as an important aspect of the story. The reader might not perceive such details if the story were narrated from the point of view of one its characters.

The characters' dialogue works in tandem with her descriptive passages to reveal their moral emptiness. For example, the cold, abrupt way that Mrs. Crater responds to Shiftlet's elaborate soliloquies on sunsets and innocent women suggests that she intends to land Shiftlet as a husband for Lucynell. Readers may note that the initial discussion between Shiftlet and Mrs. Crater is odd, even unrealistic, moving casually from philosophy to human nature to the weather. Such jarring dialogue should be read closely because it reveals aspects of both characters' personalities. It also suggests a certain fantastic quality that is consistent with much of O'Connor's fiction and elevates her stories above a fixed time and place, giving them a mythic timelessness.

O'Connor's reserved tone also plays a part in achieving this quality. Rarely does she intrude into the narration, pointing the reader neither in one way nor the other. O'Connor's subtle tone requires the reader to pay close attention to the details that she provides. Given O'Connor's detached narrative point of view, when a disturbing line like ''The world is almost rotten,'' is spoken by Shiftlet, readers should assume that this is more than just a casual observation.

Setting

O'Connor's short fiction is steeped in the culture of the American South, and ''The Life You Save May Be Your Own'' is no exception. The landscape—rural farmland that is seemingly isolated from ''the real world''—heightens the timelessness, or disconnection from a specific time or era, of O'Connor's fiction. The Craters and Shiftlet make a quick appearance in the nearby town so that Lucynell and Shiftlet can be married, and the only other setting used in this story is the highway, where the newlyweds stop at a roadside diner.

Setting is important in one key area: the character's voices. They speak with a fairly strong Southern dialect, using local slang and occasionally broken English. The effect, however, can be disturbing, since such important issues are often discussed using this seemingly flawed language. ''There's one of these doctors in Atlanta that's taken a knife and cut the human heart . . . out of a man's chest and held it in his hand,'' Shiftlet says at one point, ''and studied it like a day old chicken, and lady . . . he don't know no more about it than you or me.'' This odd, powerful imagery is made stronger because it is revealed using such language.

Symbols and Imagery

O'Connor uses symbols and imagery to significant effect in this story. Some recurring images and symbols include Christ, nature, physical ailments, and the automobile. When the reader is first introduced to the protagonist, for example, Shiftlet forms ''a crooked cross'' against the sky. He is also a carpenter. Thus, he appears to be a Christ figure, but since he has only one arm, it may be that he is a flawed Christ. Indeed, all three characters are physically disabled: Shiftlet is without an arm, Mrs. Crater is without teeth, and Lucynell is unable to speak. All of these physical features may reflect the difficulties of the human condition, which is made

worse by both Shiftlet's and Mrs. Crater's refusal to embrace Lucynell, the manifestation of God's grace (or ''angel of Gawd,'' as she is called) in the story.

Nature is perhaps the most pervasive symbol in this story. It is used as both a positive contrast to the crass materialism of Shiftlet and Mrs. Crater and as a negative foreshadowing technique. For example, after Shiftlet chooses to pursue his greed, the tone of the story grows darker. Both nature and Lucynell, who is closely linked with nature in the story, are depicted as victims of the automobile which Shiftlet resurrects.

Historical Context

Unlike many other works of fiction, which explicitly address historical events or implicitly attempt to wrestle with aspects of a particular historical era, much of O'Connor's fiction—including ''The Life You Save May Be Your Own''—has a timeless quality to it. Aside from small details, such as the presence of an automobile, this story could just as well have been published in 1853 as in 1953. There is no mention, for example, of the Korean War or the post-World War II flight to the suburbs, important American social phenomena which took place in the early 1950s. Similarly, O'Connor does not appear to be making any explicit statements about the changing role of women in American society through either Lucynell or Mrs. Crater. In short, O'Connor's stories are dominated by spiritual rather than historical or political themes. Nonetheless, some of the themes which appear in this story do lend themselves to a historical perspective.

Postwar Affluence and the Rise of the Automobile

When placed in the context of post-World War II America, this story can be seen as an implicit critique of an increasingly wealthy and mobile America that has become more concerned with money than with individuals. A key symbol in this story is the automobile, which was rapidly changing American lifestyles in the early 1950s. Suburbs were popping up all across the country and highways and expressways were being constructed, all because of the impact of the automobile. O'Connor uses the Craters's old automobile, which Shiftlet repairs, as a symbol of his connection to material goods and his lack of compassion towards Lucynell,

Compare & Contrast

- **1950s:** In 1950, the U.S. produces 6.7 million automobiles and sells over 13 million used automobiles. In 1956, The Federal Aid Highway Act proposes the construction of approximately 42,500 miles of roads, particularly interstate freeways, to connect major cities. The federal government is to pay for 90 percent of the proposed 33.5 billion effort.

  1990s: With approximately 70 percent of the Interstate Highway System having been finished by 1976, the system is now essentially complete. In urban centers it provides major arteries for daily commuting traffic. However, it is now worn from use and in need of repair and continuous upgrading.

- **1952:** The U.S. Atomic Energy Commission explodes a hydrogen nuclear fusion bomb at its testing site at the Eniwetok proving grounds in the Pacific. In the following year, the U.S.S.R. will explode a hydrogen bomb designed by Soviet physicist Andrei Sakharov.

1989: The Berlin Wall, built in 1961 and separating Democratic West Germany from Communist East Germany, is torn down. In the next two years, NATO (the North Atlantic Treaty Organization) and Warsaw Pact countries will agree to reduce their military armaments, the leaders in Russia will agree to give up the monopoly of power held by the Communist party, and Russia will lose control over 15 of its member republics.

- **1953:** O'Connors's character Shiftlet mentions the removal of a human heart by a doctor, but the first transplant of a human heart is 14 years in the future.

  1999: There are approximately 2,300 heart transplants performed in the U.S. each year. Approximately 73 percent of patients with transplanted hearts survive for 3 years after their surgery. Approximately 85 percent of patients with transplanted hearts can return to work or participate in some pleasurable activity, including certain sports.

---

whom he abandons at a diner before driving off to Mobile.

O'Connor connects Shiftlet's obsession with the automobile with his inability to attain some form of redemption through Lucynell, who is referred to as an "angel of Gawd." Observers of American society who are aware of America's growing obsession with the automobile during the 1950s can read "The Life You Save May Be Your Own" as a warning: If, like Shiftlet, we become too materialistic, if we abandon relationships with God and our fellow human beings, we will all lose our ability to experience religious grace. That Shiftlet sleeps in the car is linked by O'Connor to the coffins in which ancient monks used to sleep. Mrs. Crater observes, "They were not as advanced as we were." But "advanced" may be used ironically here, suggesting that with their pure lifestyle of religious devotion the monks were more "advanced" than a

society obsessed with constant mobility. In this sense, the automobile does become a kind of modern day "coffin," leading these characters to a kind of death. Even the story's foreboding title comes from a road sign which Shiftlet sees and which was a common sight along highways in the 1950s. O'Connor herself, speaking cynically of a television version of the story which was broadcast in 1957, said: "Mr. Shiftlet and the idiot daughter will no doubt go off in a Chrysler and live happily ever after." O'Connor was not only criticizing television's tendency to change dark endings into happy ones but was touching upon the importance of automobiles to her audience.

Relations between Women and Men

Some critics have suggested that "The Life You Save May Be Your Own" relies upon gender roles that men and women historically have been expected to play. Specifically, Mrs. Crater is rooted to responsibility. She cares for her farm and Lucynell, pays the bills, and even arranges Shiftlet's and Lucynell's wedding. Shiftlet, on the other hand, in the tradition of Herman Melville's Ishmael (from *Moby Dick*) and Mark Twain's Huckleberry Finn (from *The Adventures of Huckleberry Finn*) is a wanderer with no discernible ties. His desire to obtain the Craters's automobile while seeking to abandon both Mrs. Crater and Lucynell seems to be a reflection of his desire to move on without becoming tied to women, who represent roots and entanglement in civilized society. In this reading, men are allowed a freedom that women are not.

Critical Overview

Critics recognized the importance of "The Life You Save May Be Your Own" immediately after it was published in the literary journal *Kenyon Review* in the spring of 1953. That year the story was included in the annual collection of exemplary short fiction published to honor the memory of the short story writer O. Henry. Critics have seen this story as a nearly paradigmatic example of O'Connor's almost obsessive concern with religious themes—specifically, an individual's ability to find opportunities for salvation and redemption in everyday life.

Initial critical reaction to "The Life You Save May Be Your Own" was largely positive, though some critics were not quite sure what to make of O'Connor's alternately ordinary and grim story. Highlighting the ambiguities and difficulties present in O'Connor's stories, with their odd characters and often harrowing endings, the *New Yorker* went so far as to suggest that O'Connor's collection *A Good Man Is Hard to Find*—in which "The Life You Save May Be Your Own" was reprinted—was meaningless and without depth. *Time* magazine, meanwhile, while acknowledging the skill in O'Connor's narrative style, also found in it a certain amount of "arty fumbling." Still, the *New York Times* deigned O'Connor's collection the work of an "extraordinarily accomplished short story writer," praising the author's originality and noting, as others did, her use of "grotesque horror." The reviewer also called attention to O'Connor's singularly disturbing vision of life, acknowledging that O'Connor's stories "were not a dish to set before most readers," but adding that those "who are attracted by it will admire it immensely."

Since the original publication of "The Life You Save May Be Your Own," its reputation, like O'Connor's, has grown in stature. Critics have expanded upon the theological reading of the story and have discovered or incorporated such themes as feminism and anti-materialism as well as its place in the Southern literary tradition.

Criticism

Tom Deignan

Deignan is a teaching assistant in American Cultural Studies at Bowling Green State University. In the following essay, he traces the theme of Christian anti-materialism in "The Life You Save May Be Your Own," finding it "a cautionary tale of twisted priorities and excessive materialism which is consistent with a rich body of thought in American history."

While Flannery O'Connor builds several important themes into "The Life You Save May Be Your Own," the anti-materialist aspect of the story deserves special attention because it fits into what could be characterized as the anti-materialist strain in American intellectual history.

Since the founding of the republic, prominent and common Americans alike have experienced conflicting emotions regarding material wealth. After the late eighteenth-century American Revolution, John Adams, the second president of the United States, wondered how it would be possible "to prevent luxury from producing ... extravagance, vice and folly?" Such American thinkers as Adams were concerned that the pursuit of wealth would lead to laziness, sin, and moral corruption and might eventually undermine the values of the revolution itself.

Nonetheless, the pursuit of wealth was deeply ingrained into the American nation. It should be noted that issues of taxation were as important as acts of violent repression in fanning the flames of the American Revolution. In the 1780s, a French immigrant named Michel-Guillaume-Jean de Crevecoeur penned a famous group of letters, one of which has come to be known as "What is an American?" In this essay, de Crevecoeur directly links American freedom with the ability to create wealth. Of the American, he writes, "the rewards of his industry follow with equal steps the progress of

"Tops" Roadside Diner, 1952, an example of one of the many diners that sprang up alongside American highways in the years after World War II.

his labour; his labour is founded on the basis of nature, self-interest; can it want a stronger allurement?'' To de Crevecoeur, the essence of American freedom was the opportunity to work hard and reap the plentiful benefits. Thus, in Adams's skepticism and de Crevecoeur's optimism can be seen the two points of view of a conflict with which Americans, in many ways, still have not come to terms.

This conflict was certainly on the mind of the American essayist and philosopher Ralph Waldo Emerson when he delivered a speech entitled ''The American Scholar'' in the 1840s. ''Perhaps the time is already come,'' Emerson said, ''when the sluggard intellect of this continent will look from under its iron lids and fill the postponed expectation of the world with something better than the exertions of mechanical skill.'' Emerson was suggesting that America had expended so much energy mastering entrepreneurial pursuits that it was failing to meet its intellectual potential in poetry, philosophy, and the arts.

Emersonian anti-materialism found an even more radical spokesman in Henry David Thoreau, who lived on the shores of Walden Pond in Massa-

What Do I Read Next?

- *The Catcher in the Rye*, by J. D. Salinger, and *Rabbit, Run*, by John Updike, also explore the search for meaning in a seemingly empty and cruel world. Salinger's novel was published in 1952 and is particularly interesting since its main character, Holden Caulfield, is a teenager. Updike's novel was published several years after O'Connor's story. Both of these novels are set in the Northeast, rather than the South.

- James Joyce published several stories and novels which depict religion quite differently than do O'Connor's stories. His novel *Portrait of the Artist as a Young Man* and some of his stories in *Dubliners* often depict religion as oppressive.

- "The Church and the Fiction Writer" is included in *Mystery and Manners*, a collection of O'Connor's essays and prose. This piece explains O'Connor's concern with what she called the "added dimension" of religious spirituality in her fiction.

- O'Connor's other fiction complements this story. Her works include two novels, *Wise Blood* (1952) and *The Violent Bear It Away* (1960). All of her short fiction was reprinted in *The Complete Stories*.

- *As I Lay Dying*, a novel by William Faulkner published in 1930, is another example of Southern Gothic fiction. Told from several different perspectives, it follows a family's journey to another county to bury their dead wife and mother.

- Nathanael West's *Miss Lonelyhearts* was one of O'Connor's favorite novels. Published in 1933, It explores dark religious themes and imagery in its story of a newspaper advice columnist who becomes entangled in the lives he writes about.

- The theological and philosophical essays of French Catholic intellectual Pierre Teilhard de Chardin influenced O'Connor throughout her career.

---

chusetts for two years because he grew so disenchanted with the industrial outlook of his fellow New Englanders. "Most men . . . are so occupied with the factitious cares and superfluously coarse labors of life that its finer fruits cannot be plucked by them," Thoreau wrote in *Walden*. Americans, he added, spend too much time "laying up treasures which moth and rust will corrupt and thieves break through and steal."

Thoreau is an important figure to understand when assessing O'Connor, since both find significance in nature. To Thoreau, natural beauty is worth much more than money; lakes, mountain ranges, and the star-filled skies are the "true coins from heaven's own mint." As for industrial progress in the name of profit, Thoreau cynically commented: "We do not ride on the railroad; it rides upon us." Like Thoreau, O'Connor contrasts objects from the material and the natural worlds in "The Life You Save May Be Your Own" and suggests that her

characters' obsessions with the former prevents them from appreciating the latter.

Despite the impassioned pleas of such thinkers as Thoreau and Emerson, however, industrialists became popular folk heroes in the late nineteenth century, while men, women, and children often worked more than fourteen hours a day. The most egregious example of trading humanity for profit, of course, is the institution of slavery in the South, which subjected thousands of African Americans to brutal labor and humiliation and was the main cause of the American Civil War.

Through the 1870s and 1880s, which Mark Twain derisively labeled the "Gilded Age," workers and industrialists frequently squared off, with the industrialists usually emerging as the victors. One of the reasons for this was the unique importance of profiteering in America, which elevated the importance of wealth and ingenuity like no other

---

> "O'Connor's full, vivid description of the Crater farm culminates in Shiftlet's longing to connect in some way with God, clearly suggesting that he is a character in search of a religious experience."

country. Steel baron Andrew Carnegie is often credited with preaching a "gospel of wealth," a phrase which elevates a moneyed lifestyle to a religious level. In the 1870s, author Horatio Alger wrote book after book in which a young boy down on his luck would suddenly—through charity, hard work, and good fortune—come into his fortune, again supporting the notion that the American dream is one with a dollar sign. While these attributes—part myth, part reality—were instrumental in turning America into one of the world's great economic powers, there was always an opposing faction which wondered if we were paying too great a price for our national prosperity.

Much of O'Connor's fiction reflects the concerns of this cynical, questioning faction, and a close reading of "The Life You Save May Be Your Own" indicates why. Like nature, the role of religion is also important in both O'Connor and the anti-materialist movement in American culture. Many Americans have felt that obsession with money and material goods blinded people to their duties towards others and made them selfish and greedy, encouraged crime, and generally distanced them from religious dedication. Even the turn-of-the-century Socialist Eugene V. Debs, often vilified as an un-American radical, rooted his critique of American capitalism in Christian philosophy. "It is easier for a camel to go through the eye of a needle, than for a rich man to enter into the kingdom of God," Jesus said in Mark 10:25. Some version of this biblical gospel, whether spoken through Emerson or Debs, has usually served as an anti-materialist counter to the "gospel of wealth." This is where O'Connor fits in.

In this story, O'Connor's critique of materialism centers around her main character, Tom Shiftlet, and his desire to obtain the Craters's automobile. O'Connor's criticism is particularly sharp given the context of the story, which was published in 1953, when many Americans were purchasing their first automobiles and hitting the roads to "see the U.S.A. in their Chevrolet," to paraphrase a popular television commercial of the time. Even such beatnik authors as Jack Kerouac, who published *On the Road* in 1957 while O'Connor was still writing, viewed the automobile as a vehicle of flight from stifling middle-class values.

Nonetheless, for O'Connor, Shiftlet's desire for the automobile indicates a hollowness within him, just as Mrs. Crater's desire to use Shiftlet's carpentry skills and his availability as a mate for her daughter reveal her own emptiness. Each character is willing, for the sake of some form of material comfort, to dehumanize not only Mrs. Crater's mute daughter Lucynell but themselves as well, shunning religious grace (whether represented in nature or Lucynell) for common goods.

Even before the automobile is introduced, O'Connor echoes Thoreau in establishing the importance of the natural landscape, which is presented as a purified contrast to a corrupted world. At first Shiftlet seems to celebrate nature; he is a man who would "give a fortune to live where I could see me a sun do that every evening." As Thoreau did, Shiftlet contrasts a "fortune" in money with the beauty of the natural world. Later, he ruefully remarks that "all most people were interested in was money."

Mrs. Crater, on the other hand, is wheeling and dealing from the very beginning. She even stands "as if she were the owner of the sun" and offers only cold, clipped responses to Shiftlet's rhapsodic appreciation of the sunset and the mountains. She is more interested in his marriage prospects and his household skills.

O'Connor then provides the reader with carefully selected details to highlight the prominence of nature in this story. "A fat yellow moon appeared in the branches of the fig tree as if it were going to roost there with the chickens. [Shiftlet] said that a man had to escape to the country to see the whole world and that he wished he lived in a desolate place like this where he could see the sun go down every evening like God made it to do."

O'Connor's full, vivid description of the Crater farm culminates in Shiftlet's longing to connect in some way with God, clearly suggesting that he is a character in search of a religious experience. The natural world, O'Connor suggests, is capable of moving Shiftlet closer to this experience. But Mrs. Crater breaks the mood with a blunt question: "Are you married or single?" Hinting that Lucynell is available, she says of her daughter, "She can sweep the floor, cook, wash, feed the chickens, and hoe. I wouldn't give her up for a casket of jewels." Not only does Mrs. Crater depict Lucynell as little more than a domestic machine, but she is completely unconvincing in her assertion that she would never give her daughter up. Note also that another comparison using currency ("jewels") is being made, this time regarding not nature but a human being.

By now, though, Shiftlet has noticed the car and has offered not only to fix it but to accept Mrs. Crater's offer to sleep in it. "[T]he monks of old slept in their coffins," Shiftlet responds, eerily linking the car to a symbol of death. Mrs. Crater then says "They wasn't as advanced as we are." But Mrs. Crater's response may be ironic. By inserting the image of stoic, noble monks, O'Connor seems to be contrasting their lives of devotion with these two lives of greedy pursuit. The monks, within O'Connor's value system, are perhaps more "advanced." Furthermore, Shiftlet's desire for the car just might lead him to some sort of death.

Shiftlet repairs the car and fixes several other broken items around the Craters's rundown farm. He even teaches Lucynell to speak her first word which, consistent with the prominence of the natural world in O'Connor, is "bird." In a powerful scene, as Shiftlet tries to get the car moving, "Lucynell was sitting on a chicken crate, stamping her feet and screaming." In slurred language, she yells the word that Shiftlet has taught her. However, "her fuss was drowned out by the car." Lucynell, as the embodiment of innocence and good and the victim of these two connivers, is linked in this scene with nature, yet it is interesting to note that her "fuss" is "drowned out by the car." This suggests the power of machines (and humans, of course) to block out or crush innocence, nature, even other human beings entirely, through machinery. To paraphrase Thoreau, Shiftlet does not ride the car, the car rides him, as well as those around him. But he cannot yet see this. In the driver's seat he wears "an expression of serious modesty on his face as if he had just raised the dead." Indeed, in Shiftlet's materialist mind, this is almost a religious experience.

By now, Mrs. Crater has stated explicitly that Lucynell would make a fine wife for Shiftlet, to which he replies, "It takes money." The two of them haggle, and the ugly bargaining over humanity requires O'Connor to insert darker imagery. "You don't need no money," Mrs. Crater tells Shiftlet, "there ain't any place in the world for a poor disabled friendless drifting man." These "ugly words settled in Mr. Shiftlet's head like a group of buzzards." He later adds that "a man is divided into two parts, body and spirit," and the spirit—that which we assume to be most linked to religion and nature—"is like an automobile." Shiftlet has staked his claim. In his crass materialism he is no better than Mrs. Crater. She offers him money, the car, and Lucynell; he accepts, and his smile becomes "a weary snake waking up by a fire."

It is important to note that O'Connor lets her characters choose their own fate. She is always exploring duality; thus, nature, like people, can be both a positive or negative symbol, good or bad, redeemed or condemned. Shiftlet's pivotal choice—to refer to his new bride, who is called "an angel of Gawd," as merely a "hitchhiker" and abandon her—reveals that he has turned his back on redemption.

When he does this, deep in the sky "a storm was preparing . . . as if it meant to drain every drop of air from the earth before it broke." Nature has turned on Shiftlet as he turned on Lucynell, who was at various times linked to both nature and God—that is, the forces that could have filled the hole in Shiftlet's life. Even Shiftlet seems to instinctively realize that he has made a mistake, so he tries to ignore the road signs which provide the story's title and searches for another hitchhiker. He finds one, but his passenger merely compounds Shiftlet's problems, making him feel "that the rottenness of the world was about to engulf him." He makes a plea to God, and the storm breaks, but his choice has been made. The rain falls, but it eludes him, perhaps even menaces him. So he steps on the gas and "with his stump sticking out the window he raced the galloping shower into Mobile." In choosing the car and mobility, greed and selfishness, Shiftlet—at least for now—has eluded nature and God's grace. In this way, O'Connor's story becomes a cautionary tale of twisted priorities and excessive materialism which is consistent with a rich body of thought in American history.

Source: Tom Deignan, "Overview of 'The Life You Save May Be Your Own,'" for *Short Stories for Students*, The Gale Group, 2000.

Brian Abel Ragen

In the following excerpt, Ragen provides an overview of O'Connor's ''The Life You Save May Be Your Own,'' and examines the character of Shiftlet, particularly with regard to the themes of freedom and responsibility.

O'Connor makes her fullest use of the automobile and all that is associated with it in *Wise Blood*, but the car and the traditions linked with it are also prominent in some of the short stories. In ''Parker's Back,'' O. E. Parker plays the role of the ever-moving American. He escapes from his mother and from the God preached in the revival tent, and then travels the world without any goal, first on board ship, like Ishmael, then wandering through the country in a beat-up truck. He has not meant to ''get himself tied up legally'' with a woman. But Parker has the good fortune to have his wanderings ended by Sarah Ruth. Sarah Ruth—the domesticating woman—opposes the tradition of endless escape: ''One of the things she did not approve of was automobiles.'' In ''The Life You Save May Be Your Own'' an automobile is at the center of the action, and the central character, Mr. Shiftlet, has a great deal in common with the heroes of the traditions I have described.

Shiftlet takes his place in the long line of ever-moving males escaping from entanglements contrived by women. When he first appears he is a traveling man—a tramp. He comes out of nowhere. He just appears on the road before Mrs. Lucynell Crater's desolate farmhouse one day. He gives his name and tells Mrs. Crater where he is from, but then he lets on that it may all be a lie:

> A sly look came over his face. ''Lady,'' he said, ''nowadays, people'll do anything anyways. I can tell you my name is Tom T. Shiftlet and I come from Tarwater, Tennessee, but you never have seen me before: how you know I ain't lying? How you know my name ain't Aaron Sparks, lady, and I come from Singleberry, Georgia, or how you know it's not George Speeds and I come from Lucy, Alabama, or how you know I ain't Thompson Bright from Toolafalls, Mississippi?''

Like many American heroes, Mr. Shiftlet, or whoever he is, can create himself by choosing a name. He rattles off in a moment as many names as Huck Finn or Natty Bumppo use in the course of their long journeys. Shiftlet also says that he has had a number of jobs in his ''varied life'':

> He had been a gospel singer, a foreman on the railroad, an assistant in an undertaking parlor, and he had come over the radio for three months with Uncle

Roy and his Red Creek Wranglers. He said he had fought and bled in the Arm Service of his country and visited every foreign land . . . .

He is also a carpenter. Shiftlet has, in fact, tried almost as many callings as Emerson's sturdy lad from New Hampshire or Vermont. He can, in the fashion of the American Adam, constantly create himself anew.

Shiftlet, however, is not entirely new and fresh. He carries in his body the evidence that he must have a past. In his left coat sleeve there is only half an arm. He is not Adamic in his newness and perfection, but already maimed by some history. The missing arm points up the contrast between Shiftlet and the Adamic role he plays in much the same way that Ahab's wooden leg shows the difference between the captain and the Adamic Ishmael. Ishmael acknowledges no injury, no past, and no goal, and he bears a name of his own choosing. Ahab, however, is burdened with an evil name he did not give himself, and his wooden leg is a constant reminder of his past, and, at the same time, of the goal of his voyage. Melville and O'Connor both use the missing limb to mark a character who is not new or innocent. Shiftlet's deformity is also an outward sign of his spiritual state: before the story ends it is clear that Shiftlet is more crippled in soul than in body.

When Shiftlet comes down the road, Mrs. Crater is sitting on the porch with her idiot daughter. While he approaches she remains motionless. She only rises when he is actually in her yard. The contrast between motion and stability expresses much of the difference between the old woman and the young man. Mrs. Crater sits. She is fixed to one place, her farm. She has her daughter Lucynell for a companion. She is burdened with the responsibility for both the farm and the daughter. Shiftlet is alone, unencumbered, and moving.

Mrs. Crater sees things she wants in Shiftlet. The farm is rundown and needs attention, and she is willing to trade food and a place to sleep for carpentry work. (While Shiftlet is talking she is wondering ''if a one-armed man could put a new roof on her garden house.'') But, more importantly, she is ''ravenous for a son-in-law.'' She needs a man who will care for the daughter, as well as tend the farm, and begins dropping hints to Shiftlet about the subject during their first conversation.

Shiftlet is faced with the danger that besets the moving man in our tradition: women who would encumber him with responsibilities and end his travels. Mrs. Crater wants a man who will stay put. ''Any man come after her [Lucynell] 'll have to stay around the place.''

While Mrs. Crater is sizing up her visitor as a possible son-in-law, Shiftlet also has his eye on something he wants. Almost the first thing he notices is the ''square rusted back of an automobile.'' It is on his mind from the beginning. As Mrs. Crater is introducing herself, he is thinking about what make and year the car in the shed is. While she is telling him that any man who wants her daughter will have to stay around the place, his eye is ''focussed on a part of the automobile bumper that glittered in the distance.''

Having discovered what each wants from the other, Shiftlet and Mrs. Crater begin bargaining. Mrs. Crater gives Shiftlet a place to stay—the backseat of the car, where he sleeps with his feet out the side window. Shiftlet begins making the repairs Mrs. Crater wants, and teaches Lucynell to say her first word. He then announces that he is going to make the car run, and Mrs. Crater suggests he teach Lucynell another word: ''sugarpie.'' Soon the negotiations become more direct:

> The next day he began to tinker with the automobile and that evening he told her that if she would buy a fan belt, he would be able to make the car run.
>
> The old woman said she would give him the money. ''You see that girl yonder?'' she asked, pointing to Lucynell. . . ''if it was ever a man wanted to take her away, I would say, 'No man on earth is going to take that sweet girl of mine away from me!' but if he was to say, 'Lady, I don't want to take her away, I want her right here,' I would say, 'Mister, I don't blame you none. I wouldn't pass up a chance to live in a permanent place and get the sweetest girl in the world myself. You ain't no fool,' I would say.''
>
> ''How old is she?'' Mr. Shiftlet asked casually.
>
> ''Fifteen, sixteen,'' the old woman said. The girl was nearly thirty but because of her innocence it was impossible to guess.
>
> ''It would be a good idea to paint it too,'' Mr. Shiftlet remarked. ''You don't want it to rust out.''
>
> ''We'll see about that later,'' the old woman said.

He wants the car moving; she wants a man who will live in a permanent place; it is all very clear.

Both Mrs. Crater and Mr. Shiftlet talk a great deal about Lucynell's innocence. Shiftlet asks early on ''where you would find an innocent woman today?'' Mrs. Crater has the answer—her baby girl whom she wouldn't give up ''for a casket of jewels.'' The American tradition makes a great deal of innocence—the innocence of boys and boyish men.

> ❝ Shiftlet's deformity is also an outward sign of his spiritual state: before the story ends it is clear that Shiftlet is more crippled in soul than in body.''

O'Connor shows innocence only in a helpless feebleminded girl. The traveling man is as corrupt and conniving as the stationary woman.

When the bargain is finally complete, Shiftlet gets a painted car and some cash as well. Money has been one of the things on Shiftlet's mind since he arrived—early on he tells Mrs. Crater that ''there's some men that some things mean more to them than money''—and he contrives to get the promise of money for a wedding trip before he agrees to the marriage. In their final negotiations, Shiftlet and Mrs. Crater again argue over moving and staying put. Shiftlet says he cannot marry unless he has the money to take his wife ''on a trip like she was somebody. I mean take her to a hotel and treat her. I wouldn't marry the Duchesser Windsor unless I could take her to a hotel and giver something good to eat.'' To Mrs. Crater, taking a trip does not make sense: it is having a place to stay that matters:

> Lucynell don't even know what a hotel is. . . . Listen here, Mr. Shiftlet, . . . you'd be getting a permanent house and a deep well and the most innocent girl in the world. You don't need no money. Lemme tell you something: there ain't any place in the world for a poor disabled friendless drifting man.

As Shiftlet keeps talking, Mrs. Crater sees what the price will be,

> ''Listen, Mr. Shiftlet,'' she said ''my well never goes dry and my house is always warm in the winter and there's no mortgage on a thing about this place. You can go to the courthouse and see for yourself. And yonder under that shed is a fine automobile.'' She laid the bait carefully. ''You can have it painted by Saturday. I'll pay for the paint.''

Once Shiftlet knows he will get the car, the deal is settled. All that remains is some dickering over how much cash Shiftlet will get for his trip. Shiftlet gets the offer raised from $15 to $17.50, but that is as far as Mrs. Crater will go. ''That's all I got so it isn't any use you trying to milk me. You can take a lunch.''

While Mrs. Crater talks of the advantages of staying in one place with a deep well and the most innocent girl in the world, Shiftlet talks about why a man has to move.

> "Lady, a man is divided into two parts, body and spirit.''
>
> The old woman clapped her gums together.
>
> "A body and a spirit,'' he repeated. "The body, lady, is like a house: it don't go anywhere; but the spirit, lady, is like an automobile: always on the move, always . . .''

It is at this point that Mrs. Crater realizes that she will have to throw in a painted car. "I'm only saying a man's spirit means more to him than anything else,'' Shiftlet continues while asking for the money for his trip. "I got to follow where my spirit says to go.'' The woman talks about having a place to stay and the man about being able to move.

"A *man* is divided into two parts, body and spirit''; "a *man's* spirit means more to him than anything else.'' Shiftlet's division between the moving spirit and the unmoving body seems to apply to men only. Women, who stay put, are perhaps less spiritual than the men who move when the spirit says go. If this is Shiftlet's theory, it puts him again into the mainline of the American tradition, in which only men are capable of escaping the traps of society and its responsibilities and finding fresh, new, innocent selves by escaping into the wilderness or down the road.

As Mrs. Crater's farm, with its responsibilities and its deep well, is feminine, the car is masculine and attracts all of Shiftlet's attention. The old car has not moved since the farm has been in the hands of women—"The day my husband died, it quit running.'' Automobiles, like moving itself, are linked with masculinity. And Shiftlet keeps emphasizing that he is a man: after he reels off the list of names that might be his, he says, "Maybe the best I can tell you is, I'm a man.'' When he says he can fix anything on the farm he again proclaims, "I'm a man.'' And when he strikes his deal with Mrs. Crater he explains what a man is like and what a man needs. Shiftlet keeps emphasizing the masculine role he plays, and the car is certainly part of it.

Once the car is painted and all is settled, Shiftlet and Mrs. Crater and Lucynell drive into town for the wedding. The ceremony at the courthouse leaves Shiftlet discontented.

As they came out of the courthouse, Mr. Shiftlet began twisting his neck in his collar. He looked morose and bitter as if he had been insulted while someone held him. "That didn't satisfy me none,'' he said. "That was just something a woman in an office did, nothing but paper work and blood tests. What do they know about my blood? If they was to take my heart and cut it out,'' he said, "they wouldn't know a thing about me. It didn't satisfy me at all.''

"It satisfied the law,'' the old woman said sharply.

"The law,'' Mr. Shiftlet said and spit. "It's the law that don't satisfy me.''

The law could hardly satisfy him. It means involvement and entanglement with society—anything but the freedom to be always on the move. Shiftlet, like the heroes of the running-male tradition in American literature from Deerslayer on, is opposed to the law. They, like Shiftlet, are all antinomians, and proclaim their doctrine by always moving on, fleeing the law, just as they flee women and home.

Once the unsatisfactory ceremony is complete, and they have stopped at the farm to drop off Mrs. Crater and pick up their lunch, Shiftlet drives away with Lucynell. Shiftlet does not say a word as he leaves, and Mrs. Crater, who is clutching the car as she says her good-byes, only lets go when the car pulls out. Once he is on the road, Shiftlet begins to feel the joy of motion.

> Although the car would go only thirty miles an hour, Mr. Shiftlet imagined a terrific climb and dip and swerve that went entirely to his head so that he forgot his morning bitterness. He had always wanted an automobile but he had never been able to afford one before. He drove very fast because he wanted to make Mobile by nightfall.

For a moment, Shiftlet's spirit is satisfied.

The satisfaction does not last long. He soon becomes "depressed in spite of the car.'' Shiftlet's new wife seems to be the cause of his depression, for it descends on him after he has "stopped his thoughts long enough to look at Lucynell in the seat beside him.'' The woman and the responsibility she represents ruin the pleasure of driving. After about a hundred miles, Shiftlet stops at a diner. Lucynell rests her head on the counter and falls asleep as soon as she sits down. Shiftlet tells the boy behind the counter to give her her ham and grits when she wakes up. "'Hitchhiker,' Mr. Shiftlet explained. 'I can't wait. I got to make Tuscaloosa'.'' He drives off, having avoided the entanglements of women.

Once on the road again, Shiftlet is even more depressed. He decides that he wants company. "There were times when Mr. Shiftlet preferred not to be alone. He felt too that a man with a car had a responsibility to others and he kept his eye out for a hitchhiker.'' Finally he picks up a boy standing at the side of the road with a suitcase.

Once he has a companion, Shiftlet feels no better.

> The child held the suitcase on his lap and folded his arms on top of it. He turned his head and looked out the window away from Mr. Shiftlet. Mr. Shiftlet felt oppressed.

The hitchhiker is a wandering male like Shiftlet himself, and Shiftlet tortures him with talk about running away from women. In the most sentimental fashion, he talks about mothers—''I got the best old mother in the world so I reckon you only got the second best''—and says ''I never rued a day in my life like the one I rued when I left that old mother of mine.'' By this point the boy's hand is on the door handle. Shiftlet ends, ''My mother was an angel of Gawd. He took her from Heaven and giver to me and I left her.''

This talk drives the boy to rage. He jumps out of the car after yelling at Shiftlet, ''You go to the devil! . . . My old woman is a flea bag and yours is a stinking pole cat!'' He does not want to hear about the blessedness of women while he is making his escape from them. Shiftlet, however, seems almost free of the guilt for abandoning a woman with which he torments his passenger. He talks about leaving his old mother, who was ''an angel of Gawd,'' soon after abandoning Lucynell at the diner, and hearing the boy behind the counter say that Lucynell ''looks like an angel of Gawd.'' Thanks to her idiocy, Lucynell is as close to angelic innocence as a person can be; while mothers, like Mrs. Crater, are as involved in sin as the rest of humanity. Shiftlet's sentimental talk about mothers points up the real quality of the act he has committed.

After the boy is gone, Shiftlet drives on. The day has been hot and sultry and a storm has been brewing. As Shiftlet's car moves down the road, the clouds begin to descend.

> Mr. Shiftlet felt that the rottenness of the world was about to engulf him. He raised his arm and let it fall again to his breast. ''Oh Lord!'' he prayed. ''Break forth and wash the slime from this earth!''

As if in answer to his prayer, the storm descends on Shiftlet himself.

> After a few minutes there was a guffawing peal of thunder from behind and fantastic raindrops, like tin-can tops, crashed over the rear of Mr. Shiftlet's car.

Very quickly he stepped on the gas and with his stump sticking out the window he raced the galloping shower into Mobile.

Shiftlet seems to be fleeing from the divine wrath he has invoked. That the skies respond to Shiftlet's prayer with guffawing thunder is appropriate: ''Why do the heathen rage?. . . He that sitteth in the heavens shall laugh; the Lord shall have them in derision'' (Psalm 2:1,4). Shiftlet flees God, just as he flees women. He tries to escape both by always moving on. That his destination is Mobile can hardly be accidental. His goal is to be always mobile, always moving, and in this he is like many American heroes.

He is also like them in the direction of the journey. Mr. Shiftlet is heading West. Like the frontiersmen, like Natty Bumppo going out to the prairie, like Huck Finn lighting out for the territory, Shiftlet follows the course of the setting sun. ''The Life You Save May Be Your Own'' opens with Shiftlet watching the sun set over Mrs. Crater's farm. His first words to Mrs. Crater are, ''Lady, I'd give a fortune to live where I could see me a sun do that every evening.'' Mrs. Crater assures him that it does it every evening. She means that the sun sets over her three mountains every day; her sunsets take place only on her farm. Shiftlet, however, seems to be attracted by the dream of the golden West. After he has abandoned Lucynell, he drives off into the West, and the sun begins to set directly in front of the automobile.

Shiftlet's goal, finally, is the freedom of the open road, but he hides his true character as much as possible. The real attraction movement has for him only appears clearly once or twice—when he first gets the car moving and when he drives away from Mrs. Crater's farm. For most of the story he dissembles. He presents his air of ''composed dissatisfaction as if he understood life thoroughly.'' He prays at the end though he is running from God. He praises women—in his talk about an innocent women and his old mother—but he is running from them. He plays a number of roles in the story, and plays them convincingly enough to get what he wants. To put it another way, he creates himself anew several times. The figure of the Confidence Man is not altogether separate from the figure of the innocent, moving male—Huck Finn, for instance, is constantly lying and assuming new identities—and Shiftlet joins the two.

One of the roles Shiftlet plays is that of Jesus himself. There is a fair amount of incongruous

Christ-imagery in "The Life You Save May Be Your Own." As Shiftlet watches the first sunset, he extends his arms so that "his figure formed a crooked cross." He is a carpenter. And his resurrection of the automobile seems almost miraculous: when he drives the repaired car out of the shed for the first time, he wears "an expression of serious modesty on his face as if he had just raised the dead." He is in many ways an Anti-Christ: he offers what must seem like salvation to Mrs. Crater and Lucynell but brings disaster on them instead.

He is, in fact, almost diabolic. In a letter to John Hawkes, O'Connor wrote that Meeks in *The Violent Bear it Away* is "like Mr. Shiftlet of the Devil because nothing in him resists the Devil" (*The Habit of Being . . .*). "The Life You Save May Be Your Own," is a story of grace resisted. In Mrs. Crater and Lucynell, Shiftlet is presented with an opportunity for a real sacrifice, an opportunity to love unlovable people. Shiftlet refuses it in order to remain free and mobile. In escaping from female entanglements, he is not preserving his innocence, but rejecting a chance to redeem his sinful self. The roadside sign he passes warns him to "Drive Carefully. The life you save may be your own." Shiftlet is trying to save only his own life—while he is given the chance to at least improve Lucynell's or Mrs. Crater's. But "He that loveth his life shall lose it; and he that hateth his life in this world shall keep it unto life eternal" (John 12:25). The wickedest and most abandoned characters in O'Connor's stories are those, like Mr. Shiftlet and the Bible salesman in "Good Country People," who keep moving and never have to face God.

Source: Brian Abel Ragen, "The Automobile and the American Adam," in *A Wreck on the Road to Damascus: Innocence, Guilt, & Conversion in Flannery O'Connor*, Loyola University Press, 1989, pp. 55–106.

Mark G. Edelstein

In the following excerpt, Edelstein offers an interpretation of the use of satire in O'Connor's "The Life You Save May Be Your Own." Edelstein also examines the theme of man's perversity in the character of Shiftlet.

Whenever anyone bothers to ask why modern satire is so poor or why there is so little of it, the usual reply is that satire depends upon the general acceptance of certain values or standards of behavior and that contemporary society lacks such values and

standards. This explanation is not very satisfying, however, for even if the assumption is correct that the satirist must rely upon widely shared values, the fact is that contemporary men do still hold some values in common, and such values could be used as the basis for satire.

Perhaps one can find a better answer to this question of modern satire by considering Northrup Frye's statement that "satire demands at least a token fantasy, a context which the reader recognizes as grotesque, and at least an implicit moral standard, the latter being essential in a militant attitude toward experience" [*Anatomy of Criticism*, 1957]. If, as I believe, the contemporary satirist can fulfill the second requirement, can employ a moral standard that is acceptable to his readers or that he can convince his readers to accept, then it may well be the other requirement, the fantasy, that is the real problem.

At a time when reality seems both fantastic and grotesque, as it does to many people today, then the satirist's fantasy may strike us as different from the real world only in the degree of grotesqueness, and the satire is likely to sound redundant to us. But the fact that reality now seems to satirize itself does not mean that the modern satirist is out of business. It simply means that the satirist's fantasy, the grotesque world which he depicts, cannot merely be an exaggeration of the real world's grotesqueness. The satirist must create his own world in order to make the fantasy work, that is, in order to maintain the necessary distance and the necessary difference between the content of his work and the object of his attack. This world must be related to our world and yet distinct from it, not necessarily more fantastic than our world but fantastic in a different way. The itinerant preachers, Bible salesmen, and "good country people" of Flannery O'Connor's fiction constitute just such a world, and through these people O'Connor brilliantly satirizes contemporary man.

The making of a satirist is a complex affair, involving much more than simple disapproval or dislike of the world as it is, and I do not mean to imply that O'Connor decided to change the world through satire and invented a grotesque world for that purpose. Rather, I think that O'Connor actually saw man as grotesque, not grotesque in the way others have seen him, but grotesque because he tries so hard to escape from his own salvation; and the stupidity of this infuriated her to the point where much of her writing *had* to be satire. In the story "A

Temple of the Holy Ghost,'' the cook asks the difficult young girl why her attitude toward other people is so ''ugly,'' and the child can only reply, in utter exasperation, ''Those stupid idiots.'' O'Connor's own ugliness of attitude, her relentlessly harsh view of man, is born of the same exasperation. O'Connor's view of man as grotesque may have developed before her religious ideas or independently of them, but this view eventually merged with her ideas so that man's rejection of God became both the ultimate symbol and the most important instance of man's incredible perversity and stupidity.

Although most people would admit that there are elements of satire in her works, O'Connor is not generally thought of as a satirist. This is not because people have misunderstood her attitudes toward man, but is due, rather paradoxically, to the fact that as satire her work is much more successful than it should be. O'Connor's satire is not based on the kind of moral standard her readers might readily accept but on a religious perspective that should, theoretically, render her satire ineffective among all non-believers. If God does not exist, then there is nothing perverse about man's rejection of God and, therefore, no real ground for O'Connor's satire. But the satire *is* effective, and the reason for this is that quite surprisingly and quite against our will O'Connor manages to convert us. O'Connor is no gentle Christian lady; she drags us forcefully into her world and *makes* us believe by the very nature of that world. The conversion may be short-lived, but it is none the less real; for the more we read of O'Connor, the more we see the startling similarities between ourselves and her grotesque atheists and hypocrites. We must believe in God simply in self defense; for to reject God, once we have been drawn into O'Connor's world, is to reveal the same kind of perversity that strikes us as so ludicrous in her characters. . . .

O'Connor satirizes both man's perversity and his perversion; he is grotesque both in the act of turning away from God and as a result of that act. The theme of man's perversity is an undercurrent in most of the stories, but it is most plainly a subject of satire in ''Wise Blood,'' where Hazel Motes tries frantically to escape his own deepest beliefs, and in ''The Life You Save May Be Your Own,'' a story almost entirely devoted to this satiric attack. The ''hero'' of this story, Tom T. Shiftlet, seems at first glance to be merely a vicious, heartless hypocrite, a man who would marry a woman's mentally retarded

> O'Connor satirizes both man's perversity and his perversion; he is grotesque both in the act of turning away from God and as a result of that act."

daughter and then desert her on their honeymoon just to get his hands on the mother's car. But Shiftlet is more than this, or perhaps less than this, for he is also an utter fool. In taking the almost worthless old car, he not only gives up ''a permanent house, a deep well and the most innocent girl in the world,'' but also gives up his own salvation, for O'Connor describes the girl as an ''angel of Gawd.'' Here, as in most of her other stories, O'Connor underlines the fact of man's perversity by showing that he is surrounded by the manifestations of God in nature. The sun, birds, mountains, sky, and moon all reflect God's presence, but they fail to make any real impression on the obtuse Shiftlet. He is so totally perverse that he can hardly appreciate the truth of his own hypocritical words; and when he understands the truth, he cannot apply it. He speaks frequently of God and the spirit, but he acts as though neither exists. At one point he states that he is a ''moral intelligence'' and is then ''astonished himself at this impossible truth.'' Needless to say, he does not let this realization stand in the way of his greed.

After Shiftlet abandons the girl in a restaurant, he picks up a hitchhiker, a boy running away from home. In characteristic fashion, not only does Shiftlet try to dissuade the boy from leaving home as he himself drives the boy away, but also he speaks of how wrong he was to leave his own mother, whom he describes in terms directly applicable to the girl, while he has not the slightest intention of turning back. At the end of the story, as a storm is about to begin, Shiftlet calls on God to ''Break forth and wash the slime from this earth''; but as the first drops of rain touch the back of his car, Shiftlet steps on the gas and races the storm into Mobile. When he is actually confronted with the purification and redemption that he has called for, he can hardly move fast enough to escape it.

The title of the story alludes to a sign that Shiftlet sees as he drives along. The sign warns: "Drive Carefully. The Life You Save May Be Your Own," and the satiric point here is most obvious, for Shiftlet has earlier compared the soul to an automobile. His failure to care about anyone else is ultimately a failure to care about himself, about his own salvation. He does not "save his own life," but O'Connor clearly wants us to see that he could have, that the possibility was definitely before him. We see Shiftlet as a fool turning down a gift of ultimate worth for junk, for nothings; and at the same time we see that Shiftlet is not much more of a fool than other men who turn from God to materialism, who fail to see the truth that is always plain as a roadsign before them. . . .

If the modern satirist wants to stir up his readers about evils or failings or absurdities that the reader is already very aware of, then he must find some way to surprise the reader, to shock him out of the complacent attitude he has been forced to develop because he has seen no alternative to those evils and failings and absurdities. O'Connor is successful as a satirist because she does surprise us consistently by the very peculiarity of her characters. She does not try to show man his own face but the face of a stranger, a comic and grotesque face that bears a disturbing resemblance to his own.

Source: Mark G. Edelstein, "Flannery O'Connor and the Problem of Modern Satire," in *Studies in Short Fiction*, Vol. 12, No. 2, Spring, 1975, pp. 139–44.

Albert J. Griffith

In the following excerpt, Griffith examines the use of religious parallels and the thematic significance of the Christ archetype in O'Connor's "The Life You Save May Be Your Own."

Christ crops up so frequently as a character in modern literature that every sophisticated reader nods knowingly when an author takes pains to point out that a certain character bears the initials J. C., is Thirty-Three Years Old, or Once Worked as a Carpenter. When a character has a Defeat on Friday, the mythwise reader can guess that the same character will rise to Triumph on Sunday. Writers as diverse as Dostoyevsky and Tennessee Williams, Steinbeck and Graham Greene, Faulkner and Nathanael West have all produced recognizable Christ figures, often in metamorphoses perverse enough to shock a pagan Ovid. But identifying a latter-day

incarnation is one thing; understanding its artistic function is often a more complex problem.

No modern writer illustrates this problem better than the late Flannery O'Connor, who once even transfigured Christ in a strutting peacock on a Georgia farmyard. "When fiction is made according to its nature, it should reinforce our sense of the supernatural by grounding it in concrete observable reality," she once theorized, [*America*, XCVI, March 30, 1957] and applied her own theory by plopping Christ archetypes down among the good country people of her stories, in clay field, dark wood, pig parlor, wherever they happened to be. The thematic significance of the mythic device is, however, sometimes obscure and puzzling.

The frequently anthologized story, "The Life You Save May Be Your Own" (from *A Good Man Is Hard to Find*, 1955), provides an example of the difficulties that one may encounter. Ample clues, beginning with the words *life* and *save* in the title, will tip off any college sophomore who has ever read any quarterly review criticism that Religious Parallels abound. The author introduces the reader at once to a Mr. Shiftlet, who is coming up the road to a "desolate spot" where an old woman and her mute and retarded daughter live. The old woman recognizes at once that the seedily-dressed, one-armed stranger is a tramp and "no one to be afraid of." With long black hair that hangs flat from a part in the middle, the tramp seems to be a young man with a paradoxical "look of composed dissatisfaction as if he understood life thoroughly." When the woman greets him, he swings both his whole and his short arm up slowly so that they indicate "an expanse of sky" and his figure forms a "crooked cross."

After this, Miss O'Connor allows progressively less doubt about the identification. Mr. Shiftlet quickly begins to expound on the beauty of the sun for contemplation, the rottenness of the world, the mystery of the human heart, and the purpose man was made for. He is coy about his name, even suggesting that Tom T. Shiftlet is just a pseudonym. "Maybe the best I can tell you is, I'm a man; but listen lady," he says ominously, "what is a man?" He admits, however, that he is a carpenter and has been in the past a gospel singer, a foreman on the railroad, an assistant in an undertaking parlor, a radio broadcaster, and a visitor to every foreign land, all burlesque disguises for a messianic role. He insists that there is not a broken thing he cannot fix;

and he asserts, with ''sullen dignity'' and with emphasis on ''the immensity of what he was going to say,'' that he is a man with ''a moral intelligence.''

The action of the story, without ever for an instant abandoning its authentic regional realism, furthers the symbolic suggestiveness by a close series of semi-comic parallels to the Christian myth. Thus Mr. Shiftlet begins to teach the Christian doctrine of human dichotomy: ''The body, lady, is like a house: it don't go anywhere; but the spirit, lady, is like a automobile: always on the move.'' He shows his disdain for the body when he rejects the old woman's offer for ''a permanent house and deep well and the most innocent girl in the world,'' and he shows his concern for the spirit (''I'm only saying a man's spirit means more to him than anything else'') when he restores an old car on the farm to running condition—a car that had quit running the day the old woman's husband (the old Adam?) died (fell into Original Sin?). The restoration of the automobile (which he has, with liturgical appropriateness, painted green, the color for hope) is indeed the crucial action of the narrative, with the aura of a miracle about it: ''He had an expression of serious modesty on his face as if he had just raised the dead.''

The simple-minded daughter of the old woman, named Lucynell Crater just like her mother, now emerges into symbolic prominence. She joyfully learns from Mr. Shiftlet her first word—*bird*, which in the mythic context readily suggests the promised Paraclete. After dickerings between the older woman and Mr. Shiftlet, the threesome drive into town, where Mr. Shiftlet marries the daughter. The pair are thereby removed from the house (which Mr. Shiftlet has identified with the body) and carried away in the automobile (which he has identified with the spirit). The winning of the innocent girl is not without cost to Mr. Shiftlet, however; he must submit to the ritual shedding of blood—here literally plausible in the required pre-marital blood test. ''That didn't satisfy me none,'' Mr. Shiftlet says, insisting that nobody can know a thing about him even if his heart were cut out. When the old woman reminds him that the blood shedding satisfied the law, he replies: ''It's the law that don't satisfy me.''

Up to this point, the Christian correspondences of the narrative have an almost allegorical neatness: the messiah comes in character as the friendless, homeless man to a desolate country and an empty people (as the name Crater suggests), gradually

> " If Mr. Shiftlet thus turns out to be neither Christ nor Christ's reverse image, he must be merely *like* Christ--though presumably like Christ in some thematically significant way."

reveals himself as the Son of Man, teaches the primacy of the spiritual, proves both the identification and the doctrine by the raising of the dead (the car), sheds his blood to satisfy the law, and carries away the innocent soul whom he teaches to pray for the Paraclete. Unfortunately for neatness, however, the story does not end here. Mr. Shiftlet starts off for Mobile on a wedding trip, but abandons his white-garbed bride asleep at a lunch counter called The Hot Spot, only paying for a meal to be given her when she wakes up. Depressed, he sets out on the road again and picks up a boy hitchhiker whom he lectures about the worth of mothers and the sorrow of running away from home. The boy angrily rejects Mr. Shiftlet's advice, tells him ''You go to the devil,'' leaps out of the car, and leaves Mr. Shiftlet feeling that the ''rottenness of the world'' is about to engulf him. ''Oh, Lord,'' Mr. Shiftlet prays, as the story ends, ''break forth and wash the slime from this earth!''

What does Miss O'Connor mean by this bizarre turn of events? At first, one might suppose that the myth is still being reenacted: The Hot Spot could well be the hell harrowed by Christ's descent; the meal left for the girl might be a Eucharistic commemoration. But the story exists first of all on a literal level, and the tone of the literal details is all wrong for supporting the supposition that Mr. Shiftlet is a true reincarnation of the historical Christ. The authentic Christ does not abandon the souls he weds, as Shiftlet—whose very name suggests both apathy (''shiftless'') and unconcern (''let shift'')— does. If he is not the real Christ, is Mr. Shiftlet then a pseudo-Christ, perhaps even an anti-Christ? Miss O'Connor is indeed capable of using the Christ figure in either way: in "The Lame Shall Enter First," Sheppard, the counselor who tries to play the Good Shepherd with a reform school parolee, is a perfect example of the pseudo-savior; in *Wise Blood*, Hazel Motes, the backwoods youth who attempts to form "The Church Without Christ," is her prototypical anti-Christ. Yet Mr. Shiftlet never completely reverses his Christ-like role, for he keeps some sense of "responsibility to others," even after callously abandoning Lucynell, and he prays at the end for divine ablution.

If Mr. Shiftlet thus turns out to be neither Christ nor Christ's reverse image, he must be merely *like* Christ—though presumably like Christ in some thematically significant way. There is one sense, of course, in which all men—"the least of my brethren"—are traditionally identified with Christ in the concept of the Mystical Body, and Miss O'Connor has used the Christ figure this way in other stories (notably the Polish refugee in "The Displaced Person," the hermaphrodite freak in "A Temple of the Holy Ghost," and the delinquent girl in "The Comforts of Home"). But the detailed correspondences between Shiftlet's life and the life of Christ suggest more than this sort of anagogical similarity: they suggest a common vocation, the vocation to live the mobile life of the spirit, to follow (in Mr. Shiftlet's own words) "a moral intelligence." Mr. Shiftlet, then, seems to represent modern man called to follow the pattern of Christ, a pattern that is unfortunately often followed imperfectly and incompletely. Mr. Shiftlet fails in his vocation when he abandons the sleeping girl, a point which the unexpected climax can now be seen to make clear.

The key to the interpretation is the detail singled out for emphasis by the title of the story. After Mr. Shiftlet leaves The Hot Spot, Miss O'Connor writes: "There were times when Mr. Shiftlet preferred not to be alone. He felt too that a man with a car had a responsibility to others and he kept his eye out for a hitchhiker. Occasionally he saw a sign that warned: 'Drive carefully. The life you save may be your own.'" The sign is obviously intended to have implications on the religious level, recalling familiar Christian epigrams about the paradoxes of saving and being saved, giving and receiving, dying and living. To the man with a car (symbolically, spirit or moral intelligence), it is a clear admonition to essential charity and prudence.

The dialogue with the runaway boy reveals the gradual impact of the sign on Mr. Shiftlet's conscience. As Shiftlet talks of rueing the day he left his own mother, he is thinking in actuality of the abandonment of Lucynell—a fact made evident when he refers to his old mother as an "angel of Gawd," the exact phrase in which The Hot Spot attendant described Lucynell. The boy's profane rejection of this sentiment forces Mr. Shiftlet to recognize his own flaw in the loveless boy. The shock of failure leads to his anguished prayer and to an answering shower from heaven, as a turnip-shaped cloud (suggesting, perhaps, the stylized figure of the Pentecostal dove) descends on him and spurs him on to his destination, Mobile, symbolically the kinetic haven of the ever-moving spirit.

"For me the meaning of life is centered in our Redemption by Christ," Miss O'Connor once asserted; "what I see in the world I see in its relation to that." [*The Living Novel: A Symposium*, ed. Granville Hicks, 1957] Mr. Shiftlet, too, is seen in this relationship. As a man who seeks the spiritual, Miss O'Connor seems to say, Mr. Shiftlet leads a meaningful life only insofar as his life corresponds with the pattern set by Christ; when he departs from the pattern, becomes shiftless or lets others shift for themselves, he falls into depression and despair. Only recognition of the failure brings hope of final grace by which he can save others and in so doing save himself.

Source: Albert J. Griffith, "Flannery O'Connor's Salvation Road," in *Studies in Short Fiction*, Vol. 3, No. 3, Spring, 1966, pp. 329–33.

Further Reading

Desmond, John F. "The Shifting of Mr. Shiftlet: Flannery O'Connor's 'The Life You Save May Be Your Own,'" in *Mississippi Quarterly*, Vol. 28, No. 1, Winter, 1974-75, pp. 55-9.
    A close reading of Shiftlet's character, in which the author argues that his motivations devolve during the course of the story from good to bad.

Gentry, Marshall Bruce. *Flannery O'Connor's Religion of the Grotesque*, University Press of Mississippi, 1986, pp. 112-18.
    A reading of the religious themes and O'Connor's use of the Grotesque in "The Life You Save May Be Your Own."

Giannone, Richard. *Flannery O'Connor and the Mystery of Love*, University of Illinois Press, 1989, pp. 54-7.
    A study on O'Connor, which concentrates on Shiftlet's denial of spiritual grace.

Kessler, Edward. *Flannery O'Connor and the Language of the Apocalypse*, Princeton University Press, 1986, pp. 141-47.
    Through analysis of language in O'Connor's fiction, Kessler develops a largely negative reading of "The Life You Save May Be Your Own," finding the story unnecessarily ambiguous and shallow.

Westling, Louise. *Sacred Groves and Ravaged Gardens: The Fiction of Eudora Welty, Carson McCullers, and Flannery O'Connor*, University of Georgia Press, 1985, pp. 144-55.
    This work identifies O'Connor with two other Southern writers and pursues her work from a feminist rather than a religious perspective.

Whitt, Margaret Earley. *Understanding Flannery O'Connor*, University of South Carolina Press, 1995, pp. 52-6.
    A general introduction to the themes of "The Life You Save May Be Your Own" as well as to O'Connor's life and other works.

The Man That Corrupted Hadleyburg

Mark Twain

1899

"The Man That Corrupted Hadleyburg" first appeared in *Harper's Monthly* in December 1899. Harper Brothers publishers reprinted the story in 1900 in the collection *The Man That Corrupted Hadleyburg and Other Stories and Sketches*. Twain wrote the story in 1898 while he lectured in Europe, and the manuscript, which is held by the Pierpont Morgan Library in New York City, was written almost entirely on the stationery of Metropole Hotel in Vienna. Twain had hoped that a lecture tour would help him recover recent financial losses, which resulted from investing heavily in the unsuccessful Paige typesetting machine. Along with his financial burdens, Twain was depressed after his daughter Susy died, and he also was concerned about the failing health of both his wife Olivia and his youngest daughter Jean, who suffered from epilepsy. Hence, critics often interpret "The Man That Corrupted Hadleyburg" in relation to Twain's personal discontent, attributing the story's pessimistic tone and its theme of disillusionment with human nature to his own misfortunes during the 1890s.

Many critics discuss the town of Hadleyburg as a "microcosm of America," comparing the activities and personalities of the townsfolk to various features of the American character. Whether Twain based Hadleyburg on an actual place or constructed it as a fictional symbol remains unclear, although various American towns have claimed to be the model for Hadleyburg. Critics often debate whether

"The Man That Corrupted Hadleyburg" represents a story of revenge or of redemption. Some critics emphasize the revenge theme, pointing to the hypocritical characterizations and the deterministic tone of the story. Others analyze "Hadleyburg" in terms of a revised "Eden" myth, citing the moralistic theme that demonstrates the possibility of salvation. Commentators often identify the mysterious stranger as a Satan figure. Like the Satan of seventeenth-century poet John Milton's *Paradise Lost*, the stranger leads the town to a "fortunate fall," but critics disagree whether he is an agent of moral destruction or rejuvenation.

Author Biography

The son of John Marshall Clemens, a judge, and Jane Lampton Clemens in Hannibal, Missouri, Samuel Langhorne Clemens (1835-1910) adopted the pseudonym Mark Twain when he began to write professionally. Before beginning his literary career, Clemens held diverse jobs, ranging from riverboat pilot and occasional gold-miner to journeyman printer and journalist. He spent much of his early adulthood traveling up and down the Mississippi River by steamboat and throughout the western frontier with his brother Orion, who became Nevada's secretary of territory in 1861.

Clemens's earliest works include a series of letters published in regional newspapers that reported the risk and adventure of life on the frontier. Sensing America's appetite for "news," especially the sensational kind, Clemens often peppered his reports with outlandish hoaxes and tall tales, which often caused controversy as readers assumed they were true. A headline Clemens wrote in 1853 for his brother's Hannibal newspaper, *Journal*, evinces his penchant for irony, comedy, and good-natured satire: "Terrible Accident! 500 Men Killed and Missing!" He explains in the subsequent article, "We had set the above head up, expecting (of course) to use it, but as the accident hasn't yet happened, we'll say 'To be continued.'" Clemens first signed his pen name in 1863 to his "Carson City Letters" series that appeared in Virginia City's *Territorial Enterprise*. In 1865, Clemens as Twain published "Jim Smiley and His Jumping Frog," his first short story.

Astounding for both its quantity and quality, Twain's work is best known for its humorous rendering of human imperfection. While his early novels, short stories, essays and public lectures poke fun at human fallibility with delight and good nature, his later writings assume a moralistic tone, including such works such as *What is Man?* (1898), the collected fragments that were to make up *The Mysterious Stranger* (1916), and "The Man That Corrupted Hadleyburg" (1899). Critics detect an underlying "deterministic" philosophy in his later works. Determinism asserts that humans refuse to accept their inherently sinful nature, which inevitably leads to a moral fall. Pointing to the edifying benefits of sin, some critics read stories like "The Man That Corrupted Hadleyburg" as an expostulation of "the fortunate fall" myth. Scholars often attribute Twain's gloomy outlook at the time to personal troubles. Recently bankrupted by investments in the failed Paige typesetting machine, Twain lost his daughter Susy to meningitis in 1896, while he was in Europe on a lecture tour to satisfy his creditor's demands. Critics also sense optimism in his later moralistic writings. Similar in this respect to his earlier works, he notes in his *Autobiography* that solid morals always inform worthy and lasting humor. Otherwise, humor is merely "decoration" and "fragrance." Twain writes: "Humor must not professedly teach, and it must not professedly preach, but it must do both if it would last forever."

Plot Summary

Part 1

An omniscient narrator opens the story with a description of Hadleyburg, U.S.A., as "honest," "upright," and very proud of its "unsmirched" reputation. The town enjoys national renown for protecting every citizen against all temptation from infancy through death. Appropriately, the town motto reads "Lead us not into temptation." The tale then segues to the bitter thoughts of an "offended stranger," who has nursed a grudge against the town during the past year for an unnamed, unrequited offense. Rather than murder the one or two individuals responsible, the stranger plots vengeance to "comprehend the entire town, and not let so much as one person escape unhurt."

The "mysterious, big" stranger puts his scheme into action when he delivers a sack of gold coins, supposedly worth $40,000, to the home of Mary and Edward Richards, who is a cashier at the Hadleyburg bank. Alone when the sack arrives, Mary panics

Mark Twain

then notices a note attached to the sack. The note explains that some time ago a financially and morally bankrupt ex-gambler arrived in Hadleyburg, where a citizen gave him twenty dollars and sage advice. Ironically, the stranger amassed a fortune by gambling with those twenty dollars. He now wants to repay his benefactor whose identity can be determined by repeating the words of advice that he spoke so long ago, which are disclosed in a document within a sealed envelope inside the sack. The stranger's note concludes by asking the Richardses to find the man and to conduct their search either privately or publicly. However, if they choose a public method, all claims must be forwarded to Reverend Burgess, whom the stranger authorizes to open the sealed envelope and verify a match.

Alarmed by the prospect of theft, Mary explains the situation to Edward when he comes home. Edward jokes about burning the letters and keeping the money to themselves, but he promptly goes to the newspaper office to advertise the sack. He favors the public method because neighboring towns will envy Hadleyburg for being deemed worthy to safeguard such a huge sum of gold. Edward and Mary conjecture that the anonymous citizen is the deceased Barclay Goodson. In the course of their speculation, Edward reveals a few

secrets about "honest" Hadleyburg. Barclay Goodson and Reverend Burgess, respectively, became the most hated men in town, due in part to Edward's cowardice. As it happens, Burgess was falsely accused of committing an unnamed deed, which ruined his reputation. Edward knew Burgess was innocent but withheld the information that would have cleared him because Edward feared public reproach against himself. Still, Edward felt guilty about his role in bringing scandal to Burgess, so he advised Burgess to leave town until the crisis passed. Meanwhile, Edward convinced the townsfolk that Goodson withheld the self-incriminating information. Shocked by Edward's revelations, Mary wavers between outrage and acceptance but ultimately supports her husband's actions. They alternately indulge in fantasies about keeping the money and self-reproach for entertaining such "awful" thoughts, when Edward decides to cancel the advertisement. Meanwhile, the printer Mr. Cox, the only other person in town aware of the sack, has spent a similar evening with his wife. He, too, decides to stop the ad and meets Edward at the newspaper office, but they are too late to prevent the notice from appearing in the next day's paper. The men return to their respective homes, where both couples bicker over the right course of action, wavering between greed and self-condemnation.

Part 2

As news about the mysterious sack of gold in Hadleyburg spreads across the country during the next morning, the town celebrates this new confirmation of its honesty, prompting the townsfolk to suggest that "Hadleyburg" be listed in the dictionary as a synonym for "incorruptible." Pride soon turns into contention as the townsfolk begin to guess at the contents of the envelope. Absorbed in thought and irritable, Mary comes across a letter that she had received earlier from a Howard L. Stephenson, who identifies himself as an associate of Goodson. The letter contains the precise wording of the advice enclosed within the mystery envelope and identifies the late Goodson as the man who spoke it to the stranger. In the letter, Stephenson reports that Goodson generally loathed Hadleyburg but spoke "favorably" of two or three families residing there. He vaguely recalls that Goodson sometimes mentioned a "great service" done for him by someone perhaps named Edward Richards. Stephenson indicates that the man who offered his service to Goodson is the "legitimate heir" of the gold. Since he is uncertain about the details of the good deed and the exact identity of the do-gooder, Stephenson appeals to Edward's honesty and sense of honor to refresh his memory, adding that he fully expects an honest man to relinquish his claim if an error has been made. Finally, he reveals Goodson's advice: "YOU ARE FAR FROM BEING A BAD MAN: GO, AND REFORM."

Mary is elated but not for long, as Edward tries to recall the details of his good deed. After eliminating a series of possible scenarios that include saving his soul, property, and life, Edward "dimly" recalls "rescuing" Goodson from marrying a woman (Nancy Hewitt) who had a "spoonful of Negro blood in her veins." Satisfied with this sketchy memory, he reconstructs the details of the event.

The mood in Hadleyburg improves markedly by the next day. Eighteen other couples have received a similar letter from "Stephenson," with the exception that the name of the respective recipient replaces Edward's. Each husband reconstructs a dubious account of their "service" to Goodson, and each wife dreams of a future of luxury. All the couples accordingly forward their claims to a perplexed Burgess.

Part 3

The residents of Hadleyburg and curious visitors gather at the town hall to learn the identity of the sack's rightful owner. As instructed, Burgess presides over the meeting. He offers warmly enthusiastic praise of the town's honesty and thanks the stranger for giving them this opportunity to display their virtue, as each claimant silently rehearses his humble acceptance speech. Burgess reads the first claim and identifies Deacon Billson as its owner. As the crowd cheers, Lawyer Wilson objects and charges Billson with plagiarism. Burgess concedes that he also has a claim from Wilson, which he reads aloud and finds the same piece of advice, "You are far from being a bad man. Go, and reform." A vigorous debate ensues, when the tanner points out that Billson's claim differs by including the extra word very. At the urging of the crowd, Burgess opens the sack to retrieve the sealed envelope. Instead, he finds two envelopes, and one of them is labeled, "Not to be examined until all written communications which have been addressed to the Chair—if any—have been read." Burgess opens the unmarked envelope, which contains a note that reads, "Go, and reform—or, mark my words—some day, for your sins, you will die and go to hell or Hadleyburg—

TRY AND MAKE IT THE FORMER." The note exposes the greed of the claimants and the hypocrisy of the town.

The crowd erupts in pandemonium over the claimants's deceit, when Burgess announces that he has additional claims. One by one, he slowly reads the names of the other claimants. The crowd delights in the public humiliation of the town's upstanding members. Edward tries to stop the proceedings and relieve his guilt, but Burgess interrupts him and continues reciting the rest of the names. Resigned to impending humiliation, Edward and Mary wait for their names to be called. Burgess, however, concludes after reading only eighteen claims. As the crowd cheers the sole virtuous couple, Edward and Mary cringe as their hypocrisy settles around them.

Burgess then opens the second envelope, which reveals the entirety of the stranger's scheme as well as a suggestion that the gold be used to establish a "Committee on Propagation and Preservation of the Hadleyburg Reputation." The coins, however, are merely gilded slugs. The crowd decides to auction the counterfeit coins and donate the proceeds to Edward, the "one clean man left." A stranger, "who looked like an amateur detective gotten up as an impossible English earl," escalates the bidding and purchases the sack for $1282. He declares that he will stamp the coins with the slogan "Go and reform" along with the names of the eighteen claimants, when Dr. Clay Harkness offers the man forty thousand dollars for the sack. The crowd approves the deal, singing "You are f-a-r from being a b-a-a-d man-a-a-a-a-men!"

Part 4

After receiving payment from Harkness, the stranger writes four checks in the amount of $1500 and one for $34,000, each payable to "Bearer." Keeping one of the smaller checks for himself, he delivers the rest to the Edward along with a note extolling their honesty, which proved that he failed to "corrupt the whole town." Later, Edward receives a message from Burgess explaining that he refrained from naming him during the proceedings as a gesture of gratitude for Edward's advice to leave town before news of his scandal broke. Reminded of his cowardice and stung by guilt, Edward burns the checks.

As time passes, Edward and Mary become sick and paranoid. They believe that Burgess knows about Edward's cowardly silence, and that his gratitude masks a sarcastic accusation. Nearing death, they murmur bits of the truth while their nurses circulate rumors. Edward asks Burgess to visit him before he dies. Confessing his past and present cowardice, Edward tells a roomful of admirers that Burgess had refrained from naming Edward at that fateful town meeting, and "the dying man passed away without knowing that once more he had done poor Burgess a wrong."

During the town's next election, Harkness uses the counterfeit coins as a campaign gimmick to unseat the incumbent Pinkerton, whose name was stamped on them along with the other duped claimants. Harkness wins by a landslide. His first official act is to change the town's name and to delete the word not from its motto, thereby establishing "an honest town once more."

Characters

John Wharton Billson

Billson is a Deacon with the nickname "Shadbelly." He is the first of the nineteen claiming ownership of the sack. When Burgess reads his name, the crowd doubts that Billson could have been so generous, shouting: "*Billson*! Oh, come, this is *too* thin! Twenty dollars to a stranger-or *anybody-Billson*"; Wilson falsely accuses him of plagiarism.

Reverend Burgess

The letter attached to the sack authorizes Burgess to break the seals of the sack and the enclosed envelope. Unaware that Edward Richards concealed information that could have cleared him of wrongdoing in a previous scandal, Burgess regards Edward as his savior for advising him to leave town. Burgess repays his perceived debt by not announcing Edward's name at the town meeting, which leads everyone to believe that Edward is the only truly honest man in town. After the stranger gives the Richardses the proceeds from the auction, Burgess sends them a note that accounts for his action at the town meeting. On his deathbed, Edward burns Burgess once more, since he confesses that Burgess purposely withheld Edward's name at the town meeting.

Mr. Cox

Mr. Cox is the printer of the town's newspaper. He is the second person to learn about the gold sack when Edward Richards submits the advertisement to him. Cox dutifully forwards the information to the central office, but hurries back to stop it, hoping to keep the money for himself. At the office, he meets Edward, who has the same idea, but they are too late, since the newspaper printing schedules changed that day, and the clerk submitted the information earlier than usual. Like the Richardses, the Coxes argue about the haste with which they decided to publicly advertise the sack, reasoning that had they only waited, they could have quietly kept the money for themselves.

Barclay Goodson

At the time the story begins, Barclay Goodson is dead. The town surmises that only Goodson was generous enough to give a stranger twenty dollars. Though he once lived in Hadleyburg, he was not born or raised there. He scandalized the town in the past. Although Mary Richards calls him the "best-hated" man in town, Goodson was wrongfully accused of informing Burgess that news of his scandal was about to break. While Goodson generally regarded Hadleyburg as an "honest" town, he also thought it was "narrow, self-righteous, and stingy." He was supposed to marry Nancy Hewitt, but he broke the engagement at the implicit behest of the community who discovered that she had a "spoonful of Negro blood."

Jack Halliday

A minor character, Jack Halliday provides ironic commentary on present events in Hadleyburg. He is described as a "loafing, good-natured, no-account, irreverent fisherman, hunter, boys' friend, stray-dogs' friend, typical 'Sam Lawson' of the town." According to the narrator, Halliday "noticed everything." He also guides the reader through the foolish behavior of the town, indicating by humorous conjectures that Deacon Billson was happy because a neighbor broke his leg, and that Gregory Yates rejoiced when his mother-in-law died. His "insider" perspective reveals the town's hypocrisy despite its virtuous reputation. Halliday's observations about town life echo the ironic tone of the omniscient narrator.

Dr. Clay Harkness

"Dr." Clay Harkness appears briefly at the end of the story as a charlatan doctor and political candidate. One of the "two rich men" in town, he made his fortune by patenting a popular medicine. Displaying a "strong appetite" for money, Harkness intends to campaign against Pinkerton in an upcoming legislative election. If elected, he would plan the route for a new railway and reap the financial rewards. He purchases the worthless sack of gilt slugs for $40,000 from the stranger who had bought it at auction after the town meeting. During his campaign, Harkness distributes the fake coins—after stamping the names of the eighteen hypocrites on them—to remind the town especially of Pinkerton's compromised reputation. He wins the election by a landslide.

Nancy Hewitt

Mentioned only once, Nancy Hewitt is a minor character who does not appear in the story. According to Edward, she was supposed to marry Goodson, who broke the engagement for unknown reasons. The townsfolk later "discovered" that she had a "spoonful of Negro blood." Edward believes that he passed on this information to Goodson, the "great service" that justifies his claim to the sack of gold. Hewitt's presence in the narrative also implies the racist sentiment of the town.

Offended Stranger

"Mysterious" and "big," the offended Stranger is the man that corrupts Hadleyburg. Little else is known about him. Bearing a grudge against the town for an unnamed insult, the stranger carries out a plan that exposes the town's famous "incorruptible" honesty as a sham. His plot begins when he delivers a sack of fake gold to the Richardses, which throws the town into a greedy frenzy. Critics often identify the Stranger as a Satan figure, since his mischief centers around his "fiendish sack" and brings him "evil joy." He also might be the "Henry L. Stephenson" whose signature appears on the claimants's letters. He also might by the stranger who purchases the sack at auction for $1282 and

suggests stamping the names of the greedy townsfolk on the gilt slugs to remind everyone of their foolish greed.

Omniscient Narrator

An *omniscient*, or all knowing, narrator tells the story of "The Man That Corrupted Hadleyburg." The narrator knows the innermost thoughts and emotions of the characters and tells the reader their motives and desires. For instance, the manner in which the narrator details Edward's recollection of "saving" Barclay Goodson informs the reader that Edward's account is fictional and exaggerated. Here, the narrator also alludes to the frailty of human nature and its will to justify self-deceit in the face of temptation. Similarly, the narrator reports Mary's thoughts and struggles as she decides whether to keep the money. The narrator appears to empathize with the characters since he knows their agony and self-reproach, which encourages the reader's empathy. Through the narrator's ironic tone, the reader becomes aware of "the secret" of Hadleyburg, but also must be wary of adopting the narrator's point of view, since it may be unreliable.

Pinkerton

Hadleyburg's banker and one of the "two rich men" in town, Pinkerton is described as "little, mean, smirking, oily." Rubbing his "sleek palms" together, he boasts that the sack of gold certifies Hadleyburg's honest reputation. Among the nineteen claimants, he too receives a letter from "Stephenson" and forwards a claim to Burgess. Near the end of the story, Pinkerton loses the election to "Dr." Clay Harkness, who distributed fake coins stamped with Pinkerton's name. Though no guiltier than the rest, Pinkerton is perhaps singled out for this heightened humiliation because of his professional association with money.

Edward Richards

A hard-working man of modest means, Richards is Hadleyburg's bank cashier and one of the "nineteen principal citizens" of the town. Though some of these residents acquired their status through wealth and power, Edward's respectability appears to be based on strength of character. Though he and his wife are poor, Mary is comforted that "we have our good name." At the start of the story, Edward

Topics for Further Study

- As a critique of "community," "The Man That Corrupted Hadleyburg" demonstrates the dangerous consequence of a "herd mentality." Do you agree or disagree with Twain's representation of American communities and the spirit of the nation as a whole, as oppressive and inhibitive to individualism? In your opinion, what is more important, individual expression or group cooperation? Use concrete examples from national or local history or current events to support your argument.

- Discuss how today's society is influenced by communal values. Does society today encourage and tolerate individual views and opinions, or is it as rigid and close-minded as Twain's Hadleyburg? Perhaps it is a combination of these characteristics. Use quotes from newspaper and magazines where possible. You can also choose an excerpt from literature and analyze the community it describes. Use textual evidence.

- Great detail is given about the opinions of the Hadleyburgians, what they believe and whom they hate. What are omitted are the viewpoints of the victims of this powerful public judgment. What are the so-called outcasts, Goodson and Burgess, thinking? Write a version of events from either or both of their points of view. You may choose to name the "sin" these men supposedly committed.

- Hadleyburg can be understood as a microcosm of America and the story has been interpreted as warning adhering too closely to "nationalism." Using historical, literary, and other resources define "nationalism." Focusing on one or two events that are popularly understood as nationalistic, explain whether nationalism as you define it is a beneficial, productive force or a dangerous and oppressive one. You can contrast two events to discuss how nationalism changes according to the situation and need.

- Earl F. Briden argues that interpretations of "The Man That Corrupted Hadleyburg" as a "fortunate fall" story are mistaken. He cites the various obstacles to such an interpretation. For instance, in his other writings, Twain recognizes the fortunate fall philosophy as an excuse for "sinning one's way to moral security." The story teaches commercial not moral lessons. The residents' shame represents a superficial response to "getting caught," not deep penitence. Psychologically unstable people like the Richards are unable to learn moral lessons from their experiences. Briden also offers Tom Sawyer's argument against fortunate fall philosophy from *Tom Sawyer Abroad* (1892-94). Tom states that lessons learned from life "ain't no account, because the thing don't happen the same way again—and can't." Using textual evidence from the story, related works by Twain or other relevant literary works, argue for or against one or more of the points delineated by Briden. You may also choose to compare the Briden's various points and note contradictions or expand on them.

---

has little aspirations for material gain. Although he grumbles about working hard, it is a "moment's irritation" and a simple kiss from Mary cheers him up. His first reaction to the sack of gold reflects his sense of honesty. He advertises the sack in order to bolster the town's reputation for honesty, but Edward entertains notions of keeping the money for himself. He complains: "Always at the grind, grind, grind, on a salary—another man's slave, and he sitting at home in his slippers, rich and comfortable." Though well intentioned at heart, Edward fears public disapproval. This fear explains his cowardice, particularly during Burgess's scandal, when he withheld evidence and let Goodson take the blame for Burgess's absence. At the town meeting, Edward again submits to his fear of public opinion, cowering in silence and shame as the crowd praises his virtue. Edward eventually owns up to his cowardly deeds n his deathbed, and in the process damages Burgess's reputation again.

Mary Richards

A minor character, Mary is the "dutiful wife," who supports her husband's dubious logic and actions. Introduced as a model of female Christian piety, Mary is Edward's wife, whose morality also is shaped by public opinion and applied in the spirit of practicality. For example, when she learns that Edward withheld the truth about Burgess, she wavers between condemning and excusing him. As she discovers his other lies, she rationalizing her husband's behavior on a relative scale of moral conduct.

Howard L. Stevenson

Non-existent, Stephenson is merely a fictitious persona conjured by the offended stranger to facilitate his corruption of Hadleyburg. The signature of "Howard L. Stephenson" appears on the letters sent to the nineteen claimants, each of whom believes he is the sole recipient. Each letter reveals the identity of the person who gave twenty dollars to the stranger (Goodson) as well as his advice, the conditions which satisfy a claim to the gold. The letter suggests that Stephenson was Goodson's guest. It also relates Goodson's true opinion of the town. Part of the offended stranger's ruse, the letter tells each recipient that Goodson mentioned him by name for doing him some "great service," which entitles him to the gold. The letter-writer concludes that he is "almost sure" of the name Goodson mentioned, so he appeals to their fabled honesty to satisfy his inquiry.

Tanner, Hatter, Saddler, and the Mob

These characters form the crowd that gathers at the town hall. With their cheers and jeers, they typify a "mob." Expressing strong opinions, they act in unison to shame everyone into agreeing with their perspective. Joyous in the misfortunes of others, the mob ridicules the nineteen claimants. The power of a mob works by intimidation, which plays on an individual's fear of exclusion.

Thurlow G. Wilson

The second to claim ownership of the sack, "Lawyer Wilson" appears at the town meeting. As Billson "humbly" accepts it, Wilson charges him with plagiarism, claiming that Billson sneaked into his office and read the note while he was away from his desk. He uses this lie to explain the presence of two claims that seem identical. At first the crowd sympathizes with him, but Wilson eventually becomes an object of ridicule when Burgess reveals there are more claims. Earlier, Wilson and his wife plan a pretentious "fancy-dress" ball upon receipt of Stephenson's letter.

Gregory Yates, L. Ingoldsby Sargent, Nicholas Whitworth, and Others

Mentioned at the town meeting, these characters have submitted claims for the gold. Each one deceitfully attempts to claim ownership and suffers the consequences of public humiliation.

Themes

Hypocrisy

Several narrative elements render the honest reputation of Hadleyburg suspect from the beginning. The narrator describes a town that "care[s] not a rap for strangers or their opinions," while a couple of its residents so severely offend a stranger that he feels compelled to wreck revenge against the whole town. After the stranger delivers the sack of gold to the Richardses, Mary becomes anxious about theft, exclaiming, "Mercy on us, and the door not locked!" She regains composure only after she "listens awhile for burglars." The suspicion, fear, and malice evinced by these events belie the town's "unsmirched" honesty and suggest that an imperfect reality lurks beneath the surface. The real nature of Hadleyburg becomes apparent as the story progresses. In the privacy of their homes the townsfolk slander each other, revealing the mutual hatred that exists in the community. For instance, Goodson ranks as the "best-hated," followed by Burgess. Edward's silence not only causes an undeserved scandal for Burgess, but his deception also leads the townsfolk to blame Goodson for Burgess's rapid departure from the town. In addition, Edward hides his involvement in the scandal from Mary, because he fears that she would expose him. He even admits that he only warned Burgess after he was sure that his actions were undetectable. Edward says, "[A]fter a few days I saw that no one was going to suspect me [of warning Burgess], and after that I got to feeling glad I did it." Edward's revelations to Mary suggest that even before the tempting sack of gold appeared, a complex web of self-interest and deceit ensnared Hadleyburg that contradicts its boastful claims of thorough integrity. Hypocrisy, not honesty, defines the town's character, since the residents preach honesty but practice self-interest and deceit.

Morality, Ethics and the Innateness of Human Sinfulness

The story of Hadleyburg teaches a moral lesson to both characters and readers alike. The town's secrets raise a series of moral questions. For instance, would the Richardses have been right to keep the gold since it would not have "hurt" anybody? Was it ethical for Edward to conceal the evidence that could have cleared Burgess? Mary justifies her husband's actions by reasoning that they could ill-afford to bring public disapproval upon them. Furthermore, she claims that as long as Burgess did not "know that [Edward] could have saved him . . . that makes [withholding the information] a great deal better." Edward soothes his guilty conscience by warning Burgess of impending trouble, but only when he ensures that "no one was going to suspect me." Such decisions demonstrate the self-serving interests of human nature, which tends to make unethical choices when confronted by difficult situations, and as Edward's character illustrates, cowardice further complicates a lack of ethical conviction. Besides Edward and Mary, other townsfolk succumb to the same temptation offered by the sack of gold, including the Coxes, the Wilsons, and the Billsons. In this way, the story represents an honest, universal response of human nature to the temptation of "easy" money. Although the residents of Hadleyburg are not consciously predisposed to sin, their collective response suggests the innate weakness of human nature.

The Eden Myth and the "Fortunate Fall"

Critics have described "The Man That Corrupted Hadleyburg" as a story of "the fortunate fall." In other words, the moral regeneration comes through learning from past mistakes. Thematically similar to the biblical story of Adam and Eve and John Milton's *Paradise Lost*, the town's debacle results in improved understanding, or as Mary says, protected and untested virtue is as sturdy as a house of cards. Although the townsfolk lose their "Eden," in the process they learn a practical means to achieve honesty. After their hypocrisy is exposed,

Hadleyburg will seek out temptation in order to test and solidify their virtue, which the town's modified motto indicates: "Lead us into temptation." The reformed town realizes that its survival depends on trading its smug standard of honesty for an authentic, provable version.

Individual versus Society

Mary and Edward's dilemma in "The Man That Corrupted Hadleyburg" illuminates the influence of communal values on the lives of individuals, especially how those values override individual judgment. The town hall scene dramatizes the destructive and seductive nature of conforming to a group identity. Assuming a "mob" or "herd" mentality, the crowd condemns or praises at the least provocation. For instance, when Wilson's accuses Billson of plagiarism, the crowd erupts and "submerge[s] Wilson] in tides of applause," but as soon as they hear of Wilson's fraud, they break into a "pandemonium of delight" and applause becomes ridicule. In "The Role of Satan in 'The Man That Corrupted Hadleyburg,'" Henry Rule likens the crowd's behavior each time it starts jeering loudly to the unthinking and impulsive behavior of the "automatic dog" that "bark[s] itself crazy." Rule's comparison places the crowd's reactions on the level of animals, which instinctively respond to any external stimuli.

Despite the unappealing portrait of the Hadleyburg community as a mob, the townsfolk discourage nonconformity, as in the cases of Burgess and Goodson. On the other hand, conformity reaps benefits, as in the case of the Richardses, who yield to public opinion and net $38,500! Twain ironically represented the real cost of Mary and Edward's "success" by describing their anguished consciences and consequent decay into physical and psychological frailty. Although the story seems to discourage conformity to communal standards, it neither condones the pursuit of individualism. Instead, the story turns a cynical eye toward conditions of American society, which advocates individuality and liberty in principle, but in actuality limits personal freedoms under the guise of community standards. In "The Lie that I Am I: Paradoxes of Identity in Mark Twain's 'Hadleyburg,'" Earl F. Briden and Mary Prescott claim that the story attempts "to embody a turn-of-the-century American society in which . . . a personal, original, and undetermined, freely-willing selfhood could scarcely be found.''

Style

Verbal Irony

Commonly and simply referred to as ''irony,'' verbal or rhetorical irony hinges on discrepancies between reality and the words a writer or speaker uses to represent reality. A fictional character may or may not be aware of the contradictions, but the meaning of the text often depends on the reader recognizing them. According to the *Bedford Glossary of Critical and Literary Terms*, ''Irony is commonly employed as a 'wink' that the listener or reader is expected to notice so that he or she may be 'in on the secret.''' If such effects are consistent throughout the text, *ironic tone* characterizes the narrator or speaker's voice. *Satire* frequently uses irony, which produces, but is not limited to, comic effect.

In ''The Man That Corrupted Hadleyburg,'' the exaggerated descriptions of the town as ''most honest,'' ''upright,'' and ''unsmirched'' identify the ironic tone of the narrator's voice, especially as the reader recognizes that this model of virtue has deeply offended a stranger and makes Mary feel threatened by burglars. The story contains numerous contradictions between the reality of Hadleyburg and its reputation for virtue. Early examples include Edward's quiet history of lying, Mary's generally disdainful opinion of the neighbors, and their conjecture that only Goodson, born and raised outside of Hadleyburg, could have been generous enough to give a stranger twenty dollars.

The narrator uses a neutral journalistic tone to report the ridiculous, self-serving and hypocritical behavior of the townsfolk. His tone produces a comic effect that emphasizes the contradiction between the town's reputation and reality. For instance, when Edward struggles to remember his ''great service'' to Goodson, the narrator reports: ''Thereafter during a stretch of two exhausting hours [Edward] was busy saving Goodson's life.'' Highlighting the visions of rampant greed that con-

sumed Hadleyburg after the nineteen residents received their letters from Stephenson, the narrator tells how each wife ''put in the night spending the money . . . an average of seven thousand dollars each . . . ''

Among the residents of Hadleyburg, only Jack Halliday notices of the town's hypocrisy and assumes the ironic tone of the narrator. He observes the town's fluctuating moods as they brood over the gold sack, seeing how they take pleasure in others' misfortunes, such as the injury of a neighbor or the death of a mother-in-law. Halliday guides the reader through the verbal irony of the text, particularly by his ability to see through hypocrisy and to tell the difference between the town's reputation and its reality.

Dramatic Irony

A type of *situational irony*, dramatic irony registers differences between what the characters know and what the reader knows as well as differing levels of information available to characters at any give point in a story. Like verbal irony, the discrepancy produces a comic effect. Verbal and dramatic irony often combine forces to heighten the writer's intent. For instance, partially informed characters make remarks unaware of the full meaning those words convey.

Like the verbal irony of ''The Man That Corrupted Hadleyburg,'' dramatic irony underscores the hypocrisy of the town. Numerous plot devices feature dramatic irony, including the nineteen letters from Stephenson, the ''favor'' Burgess erroneously grants Edward by not naming him, and the applause showered upon the guilty Richardses for their honesty. Throughout the various twists and turns of the plot, the omniscient narrator keeps the reader informed of the ''real'' situation in Hadleyburg by means of dramatic irony.

Dramatic irony among the characters allows Burgess to exact his own subtle revenge on the townsfolk. Although he seemingly expresses no anger or bitterness about his scandalous past, Burgess avenges himself during the town meeting and only he and the reader is privy. Knowing beforehand that he has claims from nineteen prominent residents of Hadleyburg, he announces them one by one and feigns surprise at each name. Burgess purposely pauses between each name to give them the ignominy due them. Perhaps Burgess relishes the opportunity to humiliate the people that turned against him. In addition, Burgess's advance knowledge about who submitted claims infuses verbal irony into his opening speech at the meeting, "Today your purity is beyond reproach . . . there is not a person in your community who could be beguiled to touch a penny not his own." Both Burgess and the reader can recognize the ironic tone of his hyperbolic praise.

Parable

The literary form of "The Man That Corrupted Hadleyburg" closely resembles the parable. According to the *Bedford Glossary of Critical and Literary Terms*, a parable is "a short, realistic, and illustrative story intended to teach a moral or religious lesson." A parable is a specific type of allegory. Whereas allegories convey multiple meaning on various levels-for instance, the obvious, surface tale means one thing but a deeper, symbolic story means something else-parables tell realistic stories in response to particular situations.

On its surface, "The Man That Corrupted Hadleyburg" tells a story about the demoralizing forces at work in an ordinary American town at the turn of the century. The motivations and desires of the townsfolk typify those of an average American community. The townsfolk's tendency to deceive, be greedy, and serve self-interests suggest parallels to the general behavior of American society, specifically to the character of American society in the 1890s. In "The Lie That I Am I: Paradoxes of Identity in Mark Twain's 'Hadleyburg,'" Briden and Prescott discuss the opposing aims of individualism and communal cooperation that inform the Puritan ethic which helped to shape the American society. In his story, Twain dramatized the disastrous consequence of this struggle.

Critics also interpret "The Man That Corrupted Hadleyburg" in terms of the Eden myth, in which Hadleyburg represents Eden. Edward and Mary become Adam and Eve figures, the offended stranger becomes the snake or Satan, and Goodson representing God. In "The Role of Satan in 'The Man that Corrupted Hadleyburg,'" Rule describes Hadleyburg as an "ironic Eden"—a paradise already "fallen" into sin—which an ironic Satan

visits in order to restore rather than condemn. Rule asserts that American society became "diseased by hypocrisy and money-lust," similar to immoral Babylon rather than wholesome New Canaan, the model for America's early settlers. Hadleyburg symbolizes the status of humankind after the fall into sin.

Historical Context

"The Gilded Age"

In Twain's lifetime, the America experienced astounding industrial progress and unprecedented social ills. Andrew Carnegie, Cornelius Vanderbilt, John D. Rockefeller, and other so-called "robber barons" made fortunes developing the American steel, railroad, and oil industries. While they strengthened America's industrial power and ushered the nation into the modern world, they grew their monopolies at the expense of smaller companies and the interests of ordinary workers by successfully influencing the President and Congress.

Although a few prospered enormously, average Americans paid a price for progress. America's agricultural economy gradually shifted toward industry, as unemployed farmers began migrating to the cities. The modern city emerged in this era, along with a host of urban ills: overcrowding, unsanitary living conditions that bred disease, and poverty. Most laborers worked at factories for low wages and usually in dangerous conditions. Unable to live on their parents' meager incomes, children also went to work at factories.

Twain coined the phrase "The Gilded Age" to describe the period of American history from the 1860s through the 1890s. This phrase resonates with the image of the gilt slugs in "The Man That Corrupted Hadleyburg." Although Twain did not explicitly address specific social and political problems in his story, he dramatized the theme expressed by the adage "All that glitters is not gold." The people of Hadleyburg learn the consequences of pursuing illusions. As the nineteen claimants demonstrate, it often leads to ruin. Their self-imposed humiliation over a worthless sack of gilt lead

Compare
&
Contrast

- **1844:** Samuel Morse sends his first message over telegraph.

  1876: Alexander Graham Bell invents the first "speaking telegraph" machine, or telephone. Advances in communications technology shrink the geographical distance between regions, which allows Americans to view themselves as a nation.

  1990s: The Internet and the World Wide Web become household words. With the click of a "mouse," individuals connect with people all over the globe. The development of fiber optics in communications technology makes high quality, overseas calling inexpensive and convenient. The world is often described as a "global village."

- **1860s-1880s:** The American railroad industry standardizes and consolidates routes, which facilitates movement of freight and passengers between different regions. In 1886 railroads adopt a standard gauge. In 1883 the American Railway Association establishes four national times zones (Eastern, Central, Mountain, and Pacific) to standardize train schedules.

  1976: Regular commercial flights of the British-French supersonic transport plane, the Concorde begin. Breaking the sound barrier, the Concorde's maximum cruising speed is 1,354 miles per hour. Traveling west, time of arrival is hours earlier than time of departure. For example, a departure from London at 6 p.m. arrives in New York at 4 p.m. the same day.

- **1860s-1890s:** "The Gilded Age," a phrase coined by Twain, describes a period of industrial progress and wealth, during which a few industrialist prosper while the majority of Americans work in unsafe factories for low wages. Corruption, scandal, and bribery pervade Washington, D.C., as "big business" interferes with the legislative process.

  1992-2000: William Jefferson Clinton serves as President. America experiences a period of unprecedented economic growth. The Clinton administration predicts a budget surplus of $9.5 billion for 1999 and estimated to grow to $1.1 trillion by 2010. In 1999, the nation struggles with moral questions in the wake of Clinton's "inappropriate" sexual relations with an intern.

- **1886:** Haymarket Riots in Chicago. Workers demonstrate for safer conditions and an eight-hour workday. Largely due to the violent nature of the riots, the workers fail. In 1918, the Supreme Court reverses the Keating-Owen Act (1916), which regulated child labor. The eight-hour workday and six-day workweek become the standard for U.S. factories during World War I. Employers concede to workers' demands as increased mechanization increases productivity.

  1990s: Multinational corporations allegedly exploit foreign labor to gain competitive advantage in a global marketplace. For instance, Asian workers earn low wages producing shoes that retail for over $100.

---

serves to warn a nation obsessed with material wealth and "progress" of the human cost involved.

The Birth of a Nation

With the consolidation of railroads and advances in communication America began to consider itself a true nation. In 1869 the first transcontinental railroad was completed, and by 1886 all railroads adopted a standard gauge. Switchovers between regional lines became seamless, which simplified the movement of freight and passengers across the country. In 1844 Samuel Morse invented the telegraph, and in 1876 Alexander Graham invented the "speaking telegraph," or the telephone. The advent of new technology in transportation and communication helped break down regional differences, which created a sense of community and a national identity among people living in the United States.

Critics identify Hadleyburg as a microcosm of America society, representing both the strengths and weaknesses of the nation. Hadleyburg also benefits from contemporary developments in print technology. By advertising the stranger's money-bag in the newspaper, word spread across the country. The mass production of the printed word let Hadleyburg brag about its honesty on a national scale. The narrator claims that "the name of Hadleyburg the Incorruptible was on every lip in America, from Montreal to the Gulf, from the glaciers of Alaska to the orange-groves of Florida; and millions and millions of people were discussing the stranger and his money-sack." Through the printed word the mutual interests of a community extend beyond the boundaries of a single locale, which eventually shaped a national American identity in the minds of Twain and his contemporaries.

However, rapid communication also comes with drawbacks. A small town communicates not only its successes to the world via newspapers and telephone lines but its failures as well. Critics point out the oppressive nature of community in "The Man That Corrupted Hadleyburg," noting the disastrous effects of "slavish" attention to public opinion. In this way, Hadleyburg embodies the inherent dangers of conforming to preconceived notions of national identity.

Critical Overview

"The Man That Corrupted Hadleyburg" received mixed reviews when it first appeared in *Harper's Monthly* and later in the collection *The Man That Corrupted Hadleyburg and Other Stories and Sketches*. Despite the range of critical estimations of the story, the magazine version of the story enjoyed a wide audience and earned Twain about $2000. Many commentators detected a movement away from Twain's trademark humor and light-hearted satire toward a moralizing didactic tone. A reviewer for *Living Age* states: "Mark Twain at his best is as good in his own line as any living writer of English prose . . . The snag on which he now seems most apt to run his vessel is that of edification. He is too fond of being didactic, or pointing morals, of drawing lessons, of teaching the old world how to conduct its affairs." This reviewer longs for the "gleams of the

old humor" and "outbursts of the old daring" that marks Twain's previous literary efforts and recommends that Twain return to his successful style of "gleaming humor," "daring exaggeration," and "vivid and 'full-steam ahead' narration." On the other hand, William Archer of the *Critic* defended the moralistic tone of his story: "Perhaps you wonder to find Mark Twain among the moralists at all? If so, you have read his previous books to little purpose. They are full of ethical suggestion." Archer praised "The Man That Corrupted Hadleyburg" for delivering a "sermon that sticks." Citing Twain's story as a perfect parable, Archer explained that the appeal of a parable lies in its dramatic content, illustrating a lesson in an enjoyable fashion.

Scholars usually situate "The Man That Corrupted Hadleyburg" within the context of Twain's other so-called "serious fiction." Late in his life, Twain addressed various philosophical and political issues in both his essays and fiction. His contemporaries often balked at these forays into the sober side of literature. "Mark Twain, ardent patriot as he is, has an inability to put himself in the situation of a foreigner or of one who lived in another generation than the present," remarked the reviewer for *Living Age*. "He is conspicuously defective in the historic sense; and one who is defective in the historic sense had best keep his views on politics to himself." Still, Twain himself viewed humor as more than mere entertainment. In *Mark Twain: A Study of the Short Fiction* (1997) Tom Quirk quotes Twain as saying, "Humor must not professedly teach, and it must not professedly preach, but it must do both if it would last forever."

Numerous critics have admired the literary structure of "The Man That Corrupted Hadleyburg" for its "economy" and "efficiency." Archer claimed, "A more tight-packed piece of narrative art it would be hard to conceive." Quirk remarked, "The prose is wonderfully cadenced, but it is stripped for action and running headlong toward some undisclosed end." Commentators usually appreciate the town hall meeting as "pure dramatic comedy." According to Quirk, Twain "approached the Hadleyburg story sometimes with the instincts of a dramatist and sometimes with the calculated intellectual interests of a philosopher, and throughout with the spontaneous trust that the tale would tell itself."

In the latter half of the twentieth century, many critics approach "The Man That Corrupted Hadleyburg" in terms of the ethical implications of

What Do I Read Next?

- *Genesis 1-3, The Old Testament* contains the story of Adam and Eve, the Original Sin, and their expulsion from the Garden of Eden. "Hadleyburg" is often interpreted as an allegory of this story.

- *The Awakening* (1899) by Kate Chopin, published the same year as "Hadleyburg," provides a woman's point of view on the oppressions of community. The protagonist, Edna Pontellier, struggles with traditional expectations of a wife and mother. In her rigid society her attempts to break boundaries results in tragedy.

- *The Yellow Wallpaper* (1899) by Charlotte Perkins Gilman explores in eye-opening detail the alarming consequences of societal oppression of women whose desires transgress patriarchal norms.

- *The Scarlet Letter* (1850) by Nathaniel Hawthorne relates the story of Hester Prynne, a Puritan woman who bears a minister's child out of wedlock. Refusing to reveal the father's name, she is forced to wear a red letter "A" as punishment. This novel is a deep exploration of the often-malicious motives of collective identity and community.

- *A Hazard of New Fortunes* (1890) by William Dean Howells explores the psychological struggles of a self-made American millionaire who finds his financial interests at odds with his social conscience. Howells was a close personal friend of Twain and one of his most ardent literary admirers.

- *Paradise Lost* (1667) by John Milton is an epic poem describing the fall of humankind. The poem views the original Fall as fortunate and ultimately redemptive and develops Satan's character in detail. Critics argue that Milton created a sympathetic portrait of him, likening the archfiend to a tragic hero. The poem also introduces the idea of a Satan who unwittingly performs God's will. Difficult read for younger readers.

- "Jim Smiley and His Jumping Frog" (1865) by Mark Twain is considered the story that launched Twain's literary career. The work exemplifies his humorous style and features the "frame narrative" or story-within-a-story that became one of his hallmarks. The story also uses the "anti-genteel" narrator that frequently appears in his work.

- *The Adventures of Huckleberry Finn* (1885) by Mark Twain is considered one of his masterpieces, and it exemplifies his humorously ironic style and simultaneously addresses historical issues.

- "The Cask of Amontillado" (1846) by Edgar Allen Poe, a classic "revenge story", has been identified as a source for "Hadleyburg." The tone and meaning of Poe's macabre story is much more somber and fatalistic.

---

the story, debating whether Twain advocated a deterministic philosophy, a moralistic code, or some combination of both. Some critics find that "The Man That Corrupted Hadleyburg" expresses the inherent sinfulness of human nature, while others emphasize that moralistic impulses inform the story, highlighting the freedom of choice available to the characters as well as the ethical implications raised by the ironic narrator. However, commentators on both sides puzzle over the basic contradictions of these philosophies. Quirk considers Twain's story as an "absurdist's nihilistic parable, full of misfired messages, dramatizing the impossibility of accurate understanding and communication." Quirk adds that the only philosophical consistency in this story is its inconsistency, a symptom of the instability of human nature that Twain so vividly captured. Some critics interpret "The Man That Corrupted Hadleyburg" as an amalgam of literary motives and styles that define Twain as a mature

Old church with steeple, c. 1900, a symbol of the religious character of the people scrutinized in "The Man That Corrupted Hadleyburg."

writer. In *The Authentic Mark Twain* (1984) Everett Emerson analyzes the story as an expression of "inconsistent" determinism that presupposes limited freedom of choice. Though things are indeed "ordered," as Edward Richards recognizes, the presence of freedom of choice allows for flexibility in the cosmic order. Other critics discuss "The Man That Corrupted Hadleyburg" as a uniquely American story, dramatizing the essential conflict between individualism and communal cooperation that has molded the American character since Puri-

tan times. The story has also been recognized for its critique of materialism.

Criticism

Yoonmee Chang

Yoonmee Chang is a Ph.D. candidate in the English Department at the University of Pennsylvania. Her dissertation focuses on class and labor issues in Asian American literature. In the following essay, she discusses Mark Twain's "The Man That Corrupted Hadleyburg" as an exploration of nation formation and a critique of the attendant ills generated by a strong sense of "community."

America celebrated the 400th anniversary of its discovery in 1893 with the lavish Columbian Exposition in Chicago. The Exposition was part of a nascent tradition, starting with London's Crystal Palace in 1851, which grandly boasted its nation's culture, science and industry to itself and the world. Central to the exposition was the concept of the "nation," that there was a unified cultural, political and geographical entity to speak of. The idea of the "nation" is a powerful ideology, uniting diverse race and class groups along common, abstract goals and moral tenets. History has demonstrated that goals and tenets that come be recognized as "national" or as comprising "nationalism" are so sacred that citizens are willing to die for them. Historians and literary critics have noted that it is often when the internal cohesion of "nations" are threatened, that such grandiose productions like the Columbian Exposition appear. Large-scale, ideological projects like this, at best, hope to reunify fragmenting parts and, at worst, manufacture an artificial, public perception of national unity.

Late nineteenth century America, in which Mark Twain wrote "The Man That Corrupted Hadleyburg" (1899), was just such a fragmented era. It was a period where America-as-nation began to be concretely imagined, as advances in transportation and communication linked distant regions. But it was also a time when that unity was thrown into question as the common American citizen realized that her low-paid, back-breaking work was mainly contributing to the outlandish wealth of a few powerful men. For the average laborer, her "nationalist" dedication to building up American industry reaped paltry personal rewards. Mark Twain was no stranger to the paradoxes of contemporary society. He is credited with coining the phrase, "The Gilded Age" to describe a time (1860s to 1890s) when America's sparkling and powerful industrial facade thinly concealed a phalanx of social and political ills. In "The Man That Corrupted Hadleyburg," he provides a localized account of the process of American nation-building and then moves on to critique the Hadleyburgians as examples of blind and mechanistic adherents of potentially invidious communal ideologies like "nation."

With Samuel Morse's invention of the telegraph, Alexander Graham Bell's creation of the

"Advances in print technology allow the Hadleyburgians to understand themselves as both a local community and part of a larger 'nation' comprised of a cluster of such communities."

telephone, and the consolidation of the regional railroad lines, America ceased to be a series of loosely linked, disparate geographical regions. Within minutes an order for coal or meat products, transported in recently invented refrigerated train cars, could be placed across North America. For a reasonable price an individual could travel by rail anywhere across the continent in the comfort of a Pullman, or sleeping train car, invented by George Pullman in 1864. Geographical distances were shrinking much in the same way as advanced technology today has fashioned the world into a "global village." What nineteenth-century residents of the United States were experiencing was the birth of America as a nation.

Advances in print technology allow the Hadleyburgians to understand themselves as both a local community and part of a larger "nation" comprised of a cluster of such communities. Benedict Anderson in *Imagined Communities* (1983) argues that it is precisely the development of print-capitalism that caused individuals to perceive themselves as part of a community. In particular, the form of the newspaper, widely circulated, rapidly consumed, and reporting both local and "national" events in the vernacular, assumes that its readers are part of a larger group who read and care about the same news. This audience comprises the basic unit of community. In addition, by giving them a glimpse of the events in other regions, for instance in "national" sections of local editions, newspapers link their readers' and their particular community to a constellation of other communities and audiences. Through the narrative created by the newspaper, these various communities perceive themselves as living life simultaneously, for instance, while Hadleyburgians are announcing the birth of a baby, the Brixtonites may be celebrating the election of a new mayor. The aggregate of these linked, simultaneously living communities forms a "nation." Importantly, there are other bonds through which communities can be linked, based on shared geography, history, language, and cultural and religious practices; Hadleyburg understands itself to be similar to Brixton but not to Caracas.

Anderson's analysis of the relationship between print-capitalism and community formation is played out in "The Man That Corrupted Hadleyburg." The printed word unites the Hadleyburgians in a community of that both celebrates and despises itself. The nineteen claimants share such similar-if not identical-responses to the stranger's first note, and later Stephenson's secret-bearing letters, that they could be said to be acting as a collective whole, a community. Each husband fabricates a dubious account of the "great service" bestowed on Goodson and each wife fantasizes about holding fancy parties. In an earlier stage when only the Coxes and Richardses knew about the sack, Twain described their actions and conversations as "seeming plagiarisms of each other." To be sure, Hadleyburg had been behaving as a community even before the arrival of the sack and the notes, as evidenced by their group condemnation of Goodson and Burgess.

As a unified, local community, the Hadleyburgians also understand themselves as connected to the larger "national" body. Edward Richards's immediate reaction to the stranger's note is to print it in the newspaper, gleefully anticipating the "noise it will make" in "mak[ing] all the other towns jealous" that Hadleyburg was entrusted with such a sum of money. The unnamed newspaper has quite a far-reach, exaggeratedly so. By "breakfast-time next morning the name of Hadleyburg the Incorruptible was on every lip in America, from Montreal to the Gulf, from the glaciers of Alaska to the orange-groves of Florida; and millions and millions of people were discussing the stranger and his money-sack." As Anderson demonstrates, communities understand themselves as discrete and unique but simultaneously linked to similar groups who have assumed interests in their news, "national" news as it were. The stranger's note printed in the newspaper serves just this purpose. Proud of its unity by virtue of its unassailable honesty, Hadleyburg differentiates itself as a unique and unified community while linking itself to related communities under the rubric of the "nation." Significantly, as widespread as Hadleyburg's news

is, it stops at the boundaries of the United States as Twain's contemporaries understood it. By circumscribing the news within the four "corners" of Montreal, Alaska, Mexico and Florida, Twain maps out the borders of what he considers to be the American nation.

The printed word also unites Hadleyburg in contempt. As Burgess reveals that there is more than one note claiming ownership of the sack, the community roars in ridicule. The consensus of derision builds as Burgess reads the nineteen names one by one. In "The Lie that I am I: Paradoxes of Identity in Mark Twain's 'Hadleyburg,'" Earl Briden and Mary Prescott interpret the Hadleyburgians as unthinking duplicates who slavishly serve public opinion. The God that they worship is "everybody." In this kind of community, individualized selfhood is illusory and each citizen finds him and herself blindly performing "repetitive, automatic, duplicated" actions that deterministically push them forward to a predictably ignoble end. Even their nationally acclaimed honesty is merely a means to "communal self-approval" as the town is "motivated to perpetuate not the empirical reality [of its honesty] but the reputation for it."

The town hall scene in Part 3 offers a clear demonstration of "herd mentality." Briden and Prescott discuss the robotic Hadleyburgians who are seduced or intimidated by it-better to be part of the jeering mob than its victim. The undifferentiated crowd is roused by the least provocation, capriciously alternating between praise and contempt (for instance in the case of Wilson). Except for the nineteen claimants, the citizens do not have individual names but are generically labeled, for instance "the hatter" or "the tanner." Even the nineteen claimants-the Billson, Wilson, Wilcox, Cox-seem to be duplicates of each other as Briden and Prescott point out. In other words, the underbelly of Hadleyburgian unity is a degenerate and even malicious herd mentality that punishes those, like Goodson and Burgess, who refuse to serve it. The result is a stupefied group intellect, or lack of it, that seeks to homogenize the opinions and desires of its members.

This dangerous homogenizing power of community was a prevalent problem in Twain's America. As the nation grew larger and more diverse, encompassing individuals of different ethnic backgrounds and economic classes who emigrated from various countries, the social and political unification of its citizens became problematic. Lisa Lowe writes in *Immigrant Acts* (1996) that recruiting diverse citizens into a generic course of "nationalism" is a powerful ideological technique. For instance, at the turn of the nineteenth century, immigration increased at a dramatic rate. These new Americans were prime targets for exploitation by big business. With limited networks and language abilities, and sometimes a fear of being returned to their country of origin, many immigrants accepted substandard wages and conditions. They frequently lived on factory premises in unsanitary, overcrowded hovels provided by the employer who profited enormously from his teams of pennies-per-hour workers. Why did American workers tolerate this treatment?

These new Americans were often seduced by the "American dream," the still ubiquitous myth that if one only works hard, one will no doubt achieve prosperity. This myth was supported by the popular Horatio Algers dime novels of the day and widely told rags-to-riches stories of industrial magnates like Andrew Carnegie. This myth of the American dream is an ideology, that is, a powerful abstract concept that aligns diverse individuals towards a common goal for the benefit of the powerful few. Those in power can be the military, the national government, capitalist leaders or a cooperation of several such groups. The "American dream" is one of the sacred tenets of this nation and its ideological power is evident in its ability to convince individuals to accept debased qualities of life, like the immigrant workers discussed above. Nationalistic behavior in this case is believing in the fictive American dream, continuing to work for pennies in the hopes of achieving it, and disseminating this ideology to other (would-be) Americans. The spread and success of this ideology perpetuates a situation where individuals bewilderingly subjugate themselves to exploitation for the sake of a nebulous idea of "nation."

The above example provides a historical illustration of the Hadleyburgians unquestioning and slavish adherence to communal ideals. This kind of rigid group mentality defuses rebellion either by recruiting resisters for an abstract, and perhaps empty, common goal or punishing them severely for their insurgence, using images of past rebels, like Goodson and Burgess, to intimidate them. In this way, a community, and in the larger sense a nation, assumes the power to homogenize minds and inhibit individual thought. Lowe writes, "The national institutionalization of unity becomes the measure of the nation's condition of heterogeneity." In other words, when a nation "threatens" to

become diverse and pluralistic, it tends to disseminate ideas and even policies of sweeping and unifying nationalism in order to stanch such diversification. Hadleyburg as a microcosm of America represents this kind of homogenizing process. In light of the town hall proceedings, the town motto probably should read: "Agree with the group or be destroyed by it." The Richardses are well versed in this doctrine, as shown by their inability to disabuse the crowd of its error when it congratulates them for being the only "clean" ones left. The Richardses choose to waste away and die rather than go against the community's opinion.

The town hall scene serves as an ever-relevant warning against degenerate, malicious, but seductive mob mentality. Despite the so-called "redemption" of the town at the end of the story, at least nineteen lives are destroyed by the consensus of the community. Perhaps the nineteen claimants "deserved" their fate, but the community also ruined Burgess and Goodson's lives simply because they went against the grain. Hadleyburg, as both microcosm and part of the nation, represents the dangerous effects of cultural homogenization and blind allegiance to communal values.

Source: Yoonmee Chang, for *Short Stories for Students*, The Gale Group, 2000.

Jack Scherting

In the following essay, Scherting asserts that Poe's "The Cask of Amontillado" served as inspiration for Twain.

"I cannot praise a fugitive and cloistered virtue, unexercised and unbreathed, that never sallies out and sees her adversary, but slinks out of the race, where that immortal garland is to be run for, not without dust and heat. Assuredly we bring not innocence into the world; we bring impurity much rather; that which purifies us is trial." These well-known lines from Milton's *Areopagitica* (1643) may have provided Mark Twain with the thematic element for his story "The Man That Corrupted Hadleyburg" (1899). But the structural similarities between Twain's story and Poe's "The Cask of Amontillado" (1846) are close enough to suggest that Poe's work was a much stronger and more immediate influence.

In the first place, both tales concern men seeking revenge for some unspecified insult. Poe's narrator, Montresor, explains his motive: "The thou-

> In Twain's story, we also find that the avenger exploits the vanity of the citizens of Hadleyburg to execute his plan."

sand injuries of Fortunato I had borne as I could, but when he ventured upon insult, I vowed revenge.'' In Twain's version, the corruptor (known only as Stephenson) relates the cause of his grievance as follows: ''I passed through [Hadleyburg] at a certain time, and received a deep offense which I had not earned.''

Second, both of these men are willing to defer vengeance until they can find a suitable means of exacting it—one which will cause the offending victims to suffer and, at the same time, leave them aware of the agent of their suffering. ''*At length* I would be avenged,'' says Montresor, ''this was a point definitely settled—but the very definitiveness with which it was resolved precluded the idea of risk. I must not only punish, but punish with impunity. A wrong is unredressed when retribution overtakes its redresser. It is equally unredressed when the avenger fails to make himself felt as such to him who has done the wrong.'' Likewise, in Twain's story we learn that Hadleyburg's nemesis has nursed his grudge for a long time before he finally devised a suitable plan of action: ''All through his wanderings during a whole year he kept his injury in mind, and gave all his leisure moments to trying to invent a compensating satisfaction for it.'' And in his final letter to the citizens of Hadleyburg, the ''corruptor'' expressed a criterion for revenge much like Montresor's: ''Any other man would have been content to kill one or two of you and call it square, but to me that would have been inadequate; for the dead do not suffer.''

Third, in exacting revenge both Montresor and Stephenson use identical means to achieve their ends: they exploit human vanity by challenging the reputation of their victims. Montressor appeals to Fortunato's ego to gull him into the wine cellar: ''He had a weak point—this Fortunato—although in other regards he was a man to be respected and feared. He prided himself on his connoisseurship in

wine.'' In Twain's story, we also find that the avenger exploits the vanity of the citizens of Hadleyburg to execute his plan. ''You were easy game,'' Stephenson gloats, ''you had an old and lofty reputation for honesty, and naturally you were proud of it—.'' Moreover, the characters in the two stories lure their victims into uncompromising situations with tempting bait—in Poe's, it is a cask of rare wine; in Twain's, a stack of gold bars. Both avengers reveal themselves when they have finally tricked their victims into situations from which they cannot extract themselves. Fortunato is chained to a wall, and the citizens of Hadleyburg are committed to conflicting claims for the gold bars which are in reality gilded lead.

Finally, in addition to these parallel patterns in the plots of the two stories, there is also a textual similarity to indicate that Poe's story influenced Twain's. Mottoes are used to complement the themes of both stories. Montresor's coat of arms is inscribed ''*Nemo me impune lacessit*'' (No one attacks me with impunity,) and Hadleyburg's official town seal contains the words ''LEAD US NOT INTO TEMPTATION.'' (The *not* was deleted after the ''corruptor'' made his point).

The two stories were written from different points of view and to create different literary effects; however, these parallels still suggest that Twain had read Poe's work and that the story served in a sense as a prototype for ''The Man That Corrupted Hadleyburg.'' While writing, Twain was probably not even conscious that he was incorporating important elements of Poe's tale into his own; nevertheless, these elements are there and stand as another example of Poe's seminal influence on later authors. Much to his embarrassment, Twain himself was made aware of the subtle manner in which previous reading often determines the pattern of an author's current writing project. In his *Autobiography*, he related a case in point concerning his unconscious plagiarism of the dedication in a volume of Oliver Wendell Holmes's poems. Twain's remarks on the matter provide a fitting conclusion for this paper. Twain observed. . . .

that all our phrasings are spiritualized shadows cast multitudinously from our readings; that no happy phrase of ours is ever quite original with us; there is nothing of our own in it except some slight change born of our temperament, character, environment, teachings and associations; that this slight change differentiates it from another man's manner of saying it, stamps it with our special style and makes it our own for the time being; all the rest of it being old, moldy, antique and smelling of the breath of a thousand generations of them that have passed it over their teeth before!

Source: Jack Scherting, "Poe's 'The Cask of Amontillado': A Source for Twain's 'The Man That Corrupted Hadleyburg,'" in *The Mark Twain Journal*, Vol. XVI, No. 2, Summer, 1972, pp. 18–19.

Helen E. Nebeker

In the following essay, Nebeker extends critic Henry B. Rule's discussion of the role of Satan in "The Man That Corrupted Hadleyburg," arguing against Rule's assertion that the "man" of the title refers to Satan.

Regarding Professor Henry B. Rule's article "The Role of Satan in "The Man That Corrupted Hadleyburg'" (*Studies in Short Fiction*, Vol. 6, Fall, 1969), I suggest that his thesis can be strengthened and extended by taking a second look at the identity of the Corrupter. The assumption prevails that the Man of the title is naturally the Stranger alias Stephenson, or by extension, as Mr. Rule so carefully develops, Satan. However, in contradiction, and completely supported by the text of the story, I believe that the reference is not to Satan but to another who is fully revealed as the story unfolds. This premise takes Mr. Rule's explication one step further, both in his treatment of Twain's "determination to rehabilitate Satan's character" and in his belief that "man is nothing more than a machine that responds . . . to outside stimuli." It further adds dimension to his discussion of the Eden myth.

To absolve Satan of the guilt of being the Corrupter and thus participate in rehabilitating his reputation, we must note the careful detail by which Twain indicates the initial moral bankruptcy of Hadleyburg. Mary, left with the gold, flies to lock the door, to pull the window-shades and then stands listening for burglars, in this most honest of towns. Later, she tells her husband "it is fast getting along toward burglar-time." Then successively we learn that Edward is envious and covetous, that Mary cannot conceive of her husband having done a generous deed, that Edward has permitted Reverend Burgess to bear the blame for a crime he did not commit. We hear Mary condone her husband's act; we note her snobbery when she says of Burgess," ". . . he is always trying to be friendly with us, as little encouragement as we give him. . . . I wish he wouldn't persist in liking us so. . . ." And in this same conversation, we see the mean spirits of the Wilsons and the Wilcoxes and the Harknesses, as

> "Twain could not have pled Satan's case more powerfully than he does in this story where the Great Gambler, already flung from Heaven by a vengeful God, finds himself the tool of a 'benevolent' Providence."

we will later see the same faults in the other "caste-brothers."

Furthermore, even Jack Halliday, the "natural" man, is not generous and joyous but mean and petty, a man who rejoices in his townspeople's unhappiness and who becomes "dissatisfied with life" when they appear happy again. And Barclay Goodson, the "one good generous soul in this village" emerges even more tarnished. He calls the people, "to the day of his death," ". . . honest, narrow, self-righteous, and stingy." He tells them to "go to hell." He is the "best-hated man," a "soured bachelor" and a "frank despiser of the human species" until ". . . Heaven took Goodson."

Certainly, in view of these details, Satan can be, in no real sense, the Corrupter. He can be that only in a secondary way of offering the catalyst of gold, which will, ironically, result in regeneration rather than the destruction that has been his goal.

Now at this point I begin to differ with Mr. Rule. Satan is, indeed, "the tempter who speeds Hadleyburg to its fall by the lure of gold," but he is not "the ruler of this world." He, himself, has no free agency; he cannot determine the outcome of his scheming. This bitter, brooding, evil stranger, motivated by his desire for vengeance, can act only as a force for moral regeneration. He is as bound by his nature ("made as I am," he says) as are any of his victims. Twain could not have pled Satan's case more powerfully than he does in this story where the Great Gambler, already flung from Heaven by a vengeful God, finds himself the tool of a "benevolent" Providence. As Mary so vehemently exclaims, "Ordered! Oh everything's *ordered*. . . ." or as Edward sighs, "It—well, it was ordered. *All things* are.'' And we, the readers, are able to see clearly that this applies even to Satan himself. Satan is not the Great Corrupter; he is merely a pawn.

What, then, does all this presage? How are we to identify the Corrupter, remain true to the text, and strengthen and extend Mr. Rule's thesis? Simply by seeing all of the factors already developed herein in terms of a Calvinist ethos which Twain both knew and detested. Generally stated, that interpretation of God and man goes something like this: The Great Creator, offended (as was the Stranger) by his creations, Adam and Eve, seeks revenge (as does the Stranger) and fully effects it (as the Stranger cannot) by driving these, his children, from Eden, condemning them to a corrupt, mortal life. Henceforward, according to Calvinist doctrine, fallen man must dwell in absolute depravity, victim of his own evil nature, unable to save himself, predestined to eternal hell-fire, unless he is *divinely elected*, by Providence through Grace, for salvation—a blessing reserved for a select few. Hence man, in his very origin is corrupt, and God, in condemning man to his fallen nature has become the Great Corrupter.

Now to substantiate my thesis contextually. The Richards—representative of all their "castebrothers''—are the general run of mankind. Carnal, weak, tempted, they are victims of their corrupt human nature. Barclay Goodson (God's Son), appointed as an instrument for their redemption, is a narrow, carping, condemning misanthrope (created in His Father's image?) who has in him no power unto redemption and lies "in his grave. . . .'' Thus, if man ever had a chance, he muffed it by offending his Saviour who seems, in Twain's hands, far more mortal than heavenly. God has further betrayed his mortal creatures by having them taught to pray from their birth, "Lead us not into temptation,'' thus assuring their destruction when temptation does occur.

Satan, then, is left apparently unchecked in his efforts to demoralize man. But the Great Corrupter corrupts even this Master of Evil, perverting his destructive plans to a regenerative force—but in dreadful form. For Satan, feeling most un-Satanlike respect for the "virtue'' of the Richards, acts to reward the old couple, with money, of course, bringing them to their death from guilt and despair. Thus the human, weak, but essentially guiltless man and his wife are completely destroyed, as they further injure Burgess, at once the most innocent and the most wronged.

The horror deepens when we realize that "Dr.'' Clay Harkness, "one of the two very rich men'' actually profits from the debacle. Although he has been one of the nineteen, by fortuitous circumstances (Grace and Providence), he takes advantage of the whole hoax and, in the words of Twain, "Harkness' election was a walk-over.'' Twain's malicious satire on the Calvinist doctrine of salvation of the "divinely elected,'' without reference to merit, must be obvious.

Now, the explanation of America as Fallen Eden is inescapable. For man, by nature corrupt, can never, even in a new world, resist temptation—especially in the form of gold or materialism. So the noble experiment is doomed from the outset and man and Eden fall, victims of the Great Corrupter.

Source: Helen E. Nebeker, ''The Great Corrupter or Satan Rehabilitated,'' in *Studies in Short Fiction*, Vol. VIII, No. 4, Fall, 1971, pp. 635–37.

Henry B. Rule

In the following essay, Rule argues that ''The Man That Corrupted Hadleyburg'' is an Edenic analogy, casting Satan in the role of the ''man'' of the title of the story.

''I have always felt friendly toward Satan,'' Twain wrote in his *Autobiography*. "Of course that is ancestral; it must be in the blood, for I could not have originated it.'' Perhaps it was "ancestral,'' for Twain described in another passage of his *Autobiography* his mother's sympathy for Satan. He wasn't "treated fairly,'' she claimed. After all, he was just a sinner, like the rest of us. Sinful man cannot save himself by his own efforts; his hope lies in "the mighty help of pathetic, appealing, imploring prayers that go up daily out of all the Churches in Christendom and out of myriads upon myriads of pitying hearts. But,'' she asked, "who prays for Satan?'' It is doubtful that Jane Clemens caused many of her fellow Presbyterians to relent in their hardened attitudes toward Satan. But her son, Sam, apparently heard her and decided to do something about this injustice. In his article "Is Shakespeare Dead?'' Twain said that when he was seven years old he asked his Sunday-school teacher, Mr. Barclay, a stone-mason, to tell him about Satan. Mr. Barclay was willing to set forth the five or six facts concerning Satan's history, "but he stopped there; he wouldn't allow any discussion of them.'' Upon hearing that Sam was thinking about a biography of Satan, Mr. Barclay was "shocked'' and made the boy stop writing. Mr. Barclay's victory was temporary, however, for Twain never relinquished his determination to become Satan's biographer. Among his writings in which Satan plays the lead role are "Letters to Satan," "Sold to Satan," "A Humane Word for Satan," "Letters from Earth," "That Day in Eden," and the two major works of his old age— "The Man that Corrupted Hadleyburg" and *The Mysterious Stranger.*

Twain's interest in Satan bore its most remarkable fruit in the year 1898. In that year he avowed his determination to rehabilitate Satan's character, began the first version of *The Mysterious Stranger,* and finished "The Man that Corrupted Hadleyburg." His resolution to rescue Satan from centuries of slander was candidly expressed in his article "Concerning the Jews." In this article Twain declared that he had "no prejudice" against Satan and admitted that he even leaned "a little his way, on account of his not having a fair show": "All religions issue bibles against him, and say the most injurious things about him, but we never hear *his* side. We have none but the evidence for the prosecution, and yet we have rendered the verdict. . . . As soon as I can get at the facts I will undertake his rehabilitation myself, if I can find an unpolitic publisher." Acting upon his determination to restore Satan's character, Twain jotted in his notebook the plot outline for the first version of *The Mysterious Stranger:* "Story of little Satan Jr. who came to Hannibal, went to school, was popular and greatly liked by those who knew his secret. The others were jealous and the girls didn't like him because he smelled of brimstone. He was always doing miracles—his pals knew they were miracles. The others thought they were mysteries." The final version of *The Mysterious Stranger* was laid in a sixteenth-century Austrian village rather than in the Hannibal of Twain's youth. But for his best Satan, story. "The Man that Corrupted Hadleyburg," Twain *did* return to the scene of his earlier masterpieces—the small village in the American hinterland—only this time the innocent vision of boyhood is supplanted (there are no children in "Hadleyburg") by the disillusioned gaze of adulthood.

A good deal of critical attention has focused on the ethical and philosophical import of "Hadleyburg," but little on its allegorical ingenuity, and to miss this aspect of the story is to miss much of its satirical and moral force. The purpose of this essay is to examine "Hadleyburg" as another example of the Eden myth that, as R. W. B. Lewis in his *The American Adam* has demonstrated, is so prominent in the American literary tradition. When

> **"** In Twain's treatment of the Eden myth, Satan plays the role of savior rather than corrupter. The Eden of Hadleyburg, microcosm of America, is already corrupted by greed and deceit before Satan arrives on the scene. **"**

one recognizes that "the mysterious stranger" in the story is Satan, then Hadleyburg becomes an ironic Eden that is diseased by hypocrisy and money-lust—an Eden that is symbolic of the fallen hopes of the American forefathers for a new paradise on Earth where mankind could begin afresh in peace and brotherhood and Godliness. In Twain's treatment of the Eden myth, Satan plays the role of savior rather than corrupter. The Eden of Hadleyburg, microcosm of America, is already corrupted by greed and deceit before Satan arrives on the scene. Although his initial motivation may have been revenge, the result of Satan's machinations is to lead Hadleyburg, perhaps without his volition, to some degree of moral reformation.

The character of the stranger in "Hadleyburg" is the same as that of Satan in the Bible and in folklore. His *strangeness,* his non-human difference, is suggested at the beginning of the story by a repetition of the word *stranger* . Hadleyburg "had the ill luck to offend a passing stranger." Mrs. Richards is "afraid of the mysterious big stranger" when he enters her house. He introduces himself to her with the words, "I am a stranger." (*ibid.*) In the letter that he leaves with her, he declares, "I am a foreigner," and his confession as to why ("made as I am") he cannot gain his revenge by merely killing the citizens of Hadleyburg also stresses his foreignness or strangeness. In the past, he was "a ruined gambler"—a reference to the greatest gamble of all time, Satan's foiled rebellion against Jehovah; he even thinks in gambling terms: "Yes, he saw my deuces *and* with a straight flush, and by rights the pot is his." Now, his home is in Mexico, land of fiery heat, and he is several times associated with hell-fire. When he arrived at his plan to corrupt Hadleyburg, his whole head was ''lit up with an evil joy''; and the guilty Richards remarks upon receiving a note from him, ''It seems written with fire—it burns so.'' Like the Satan in the Book of Job, he is a wanderer (''all through his wanderings''). Like the Satan in Genesis, he is the master of disguises; the disguise that he chooses for his appearance at the town-hall meeting (''an impossible English earl'') suggests Prince Satan's aristocratic lineage as does also the name Stephenson (Greek *stephanos,* a crown) that he signs to the letter addressed to the nineteen principal citizens of Hadleyburg.

His dominion over Hadleyburg (Hadesburg?) is Satanic in its method and extent. He is the trickster and schemer of Christian and biblical fame. This ''bitter man and revengeful'' spent ''a whole year'' laying his snare for the men of Hadleyburg. He is the father of lies who leads Richards to tell his first lie to his wife and who unmasks the lie that the whole town had been living. He is the tempter who speeds Hadleyburg to its fall by the lure of gold, for he knows that in Hadleyburg ''the love of money is the root of all evil''; as he slyly tells the citizens at the town-hall meeting, ''I have dealings with persons interested in numismatics all over the world.'' The ease with which he manipulates the Hadleyburgians through their greed proves him to be ''the ruler of this world.'' The town-hall meeting is ''the synagogue of Satan'' or the Devil's Mass of Christian folklore: ''The house droned out the eight words in a massed and measured and musical deep volume of sound (with a daringly close resemblance to a well-known church chant),'' ending with ''a grand and agonized and imposing 'A-a-a-a-men!''' The pious folk of Hadleyburg have given themselves over to Satan and have become his ''children.''

The names of the other main characters suggest their symbolic roles in Twain's fable. Richard's name implies that he is a ''son of riches'' who yearns for the wealth of his master, Pinkerton the banker. His first words in the story disclose his envy of Pinkerton: '''I'm so tired—tired clear out; it is dreadful to be poor, and to make these dismal journeys at my time of life. Always at the grind, grind, on a salary—another man's slave, and he sitting at home in his slippers, rich and comfortable.''' Even his given name Edward (Anglo-Saxon *ead* riches and *weard* guardian = guardian of riches) suggests his social status as well as his occupation at the bank. On the other hand, Twain places the Reverend Mr. Burgess (historically, his name de-

notes a freeman of a borough who owed special duties to the king and had special privileges) somewhere in between the position of those within the boundaries of Hadleyburg society, like the Richardses, and a true outsider, like Jack Halliday. His speech at the town meeting shows that he believes in the shibboleths of Hadleyburg, and as a minister he had held in the past an important position in society. But the fact that he has been cast out of Hadleyburg society because of the accusation of some crime that he didn't commit allows him a certain freedom from the narrow code of Hadleyburg, and he is able to perform the virtuous and sacrificial act of perjuring himself in order to save the Richardses from disgrace. Jack Halliday's name connotes his freedom from the pressures of Hadleyburg's business community. He is the only man in town who maintains a ''holiday'' mood as he jokes and laughs at the principal citizens throughout their vacillations from ''holy happiness'' to sad and sick reverie. Apparently, he was born outside of Hadleyburg respectability. He is a kind of ''natural'' man or grown-up Huck Finn, this ''loafing, good-natured, no-account, irreverent fisherman, hunter, boy's friend, stray-dog's friend.'' It is ironic that these two outsiders—the ruined minister and the no-account loafer—are chosen to be the leaders of the town-meeting, a tribute to their moral superiority.

The name of Goodson (God's son) reveals his role as Christ in the world of Hadleyburg. His alienation from society is due neither to force nor to birth, but to his own moral conviction. He is the most hated man in town, for he sees through its sanctimonious cant. But everyone knows privately that he is the ''one good generous soul in this village'', and Satan points out (while making a pun) that he was the only man in Hadleyburg who ''would give away twenty dollars to a poor devil.'' If we keep in mind the significance of Goodson's name, then the attempt of Richards (the son of riches) to save the soul of Goodson (the son of God) becomes highly ironic. Goodson's moral force, mysterious origin, and spiritual destination are suggested when Satan admits that at first he was afraid that Goodson might mar his plan to corrupt Hadleyburg, for ''he was neither born nor reared in Hadleyburg. . . . But heaven took Goodson'' (*ibid.*). Goodson's propertyless state and the hatred of the village philistines for him are also in the Christ tradition, but his defiance and bitterness do not conform to the character of the meek and loving Christ in the Gospels. However ''years and years ago'' (as long ago as 2,000 years?) he had been a man of love rather than hate. In his youth, Goodson had been in love with a girl named Nancy Hewitt, but ''the match had been broken off; the girl died''; and Goodson became ''a frank despiser of the human species.'' The etymology of the sweetheart's name—Nancy (diminutive-variant of Anna, from the Hebrew *hannah*, grace) Hewitt (diminutive-variant of Hugh, Teutonic for spirit) reveals the spiritual or heavenly quality of Goodson's love. Twain strongly suggests in the story that the broken engagement and the girl's death were due to the village gossip ''that she carried a spoonful of negro blood in her veins'' (*ibid.*). The love of Goodson for this racially mixed girl, therefore, recalls the love of ''the heavenly bridegroom'' for mankind in general, and the broken engagement and the death of the girl may represent Twain's despairing conviction that the love of Christ is doomed in the world of Hadleyburg. ''God's son'' has gone to heaven, and Satan has a clear field.

The true god of the Hadleyburgians is Mammon, one of Satan's chieftans, not the God of love to whom they pray in church. The piety of Mrs. Richards, who plays the role of Eve in Twain's allegory of the Fall, is completely ineffectual as protection against the golden temptation of Satan. When Satan knocks on her door, she is piously reading the *Missionary Herald*, but as soon as he leaves her alone with the gold-sack, her tranquility is shattered. At first she weakly struggles against its fatal attraction and mutters a few prayers, but she soon finds herself kneeling in worship at the golden altar of Satan: ''She turned the light down low, and slipped stealthily over and kneeled down by the sack and felt of its ridgy sides with her hands, and fondled them lovingly; and there was a gloating light in her poor old eyes.''

The picture of poor Mrs. Richards kneeling before the sack of gilded coins is a blistering satire on the place of wealth in the Protestant fundamentalism of the citizens of Hadleyburg. Twain depicts the gross adulteration of virtue by money, piety by wealth, in the minds of these pious folk with beautiful irony in their unconscious language. ''What a fortune for the kind man who set his bread afloat upon the waters!'' exclaims Mrs. Richards upon reading Satan's first letter. In his speech to his townspeople, Rev. Burgess unwittingly accentuates the relationship between piety and profit in the minds of the Hadleyburgians by his mixture of Christian and commercial terminology. The town's ''reputation'' for honesty, he declares, is ''a treasure of priceless value,'' and he predicts that ''under Providence its value will become inestimably enhanced.'' He then rises to a climax: ''Today there is not a person who could be beguiled to touch a penny not his own—see to it that you abide in this grace.'' And the audience responds, ''We will! We will!'' The religious words *providence* and *grace* acquire a new ironic intensity when one recognizes that they refer to the guidance and inspiration, not of God, but of Satan. Satan is the ruler of Hadleyburg. The irony becomes even more sardonic when, in a parody of the Puritan doctrine of inherited sin, the minister urges his townspeople to transmit their reputation ''to your children and to your children's children.''

Fallen Hadleyburg is a microcosm of fallen America. Rather than the new Canaan, the Kingdom of God in the wilderness that the forefathers had envisioned, America had become the new Babylonia devoted to the golden altar of Mammon. ''I am grateful to America for what I have received at her hands during my long stay under her flag.'' confesses Satan with a fine sense of irony. The scene at the beginning of the town-hall meeting for Devil's mass) constitutes an acid satire on American greed. Flags—emblems of national honor and pride—are everywhere: ''The platform at the end of the hall was backed by a showy draping of flags: at intervals along the walls were festoons of flags; the gallery fronts were clothed in flags; the supporting columns were swathed in flags; all of this,'' says Twain in what appears to be a pun, ''was to impress the stranger [*i.e.*, Satan], for he would be there in considerable force, and in a large degree he would be connected with the press'' (Twain's low opinion of newspapers is well known). At the center of this patriotic display sits the gold-sack ''on a little table at the front of the platform where all the house could see it.'' The whole audience rivets its attention on it ''with a burning interest, a mouth-watering interest, a wistful and pathetic interest . . . tenderly, lovingly, proprietarily. . . .'' The scene is a brilliant satire on national avarice; and what makes the satire even more effective is the revelation that the ''gold'' discs are lead covered with gilt—a perfect symbol for the falsity of what Twain called ''the gilded age'' and its pursuits.

The one thing in this ironic Eden of Hadleyburg that is more precious than gold is the town's ''reputation'' for honesty. The false and empty pride of Hadleyburg in its honesty represents the apple that Eve plucked—''the very apple of your eye'', as Satan described it to the Hadleyburgians—and anticipates its fall. Hadleyburg values its reputation for honesty mainly for business reasons: "the mere fact that a young man hailed from Hadleyburg was all the recommendation he needed when he went forth from his natal town to seek for responsible employment." The true substance of Hadleyburg's honesty is indicated by Mrs. Richard's words as soon as she realizes that she is alone with a sack of gold: "Mercy on us, and the door not locked!" Filled with anxiety, she flies about locking the door and pulling down window shades. It is their reputation for honesty that the Hadleyburgians treasure, not its reality. Some of the most cutting ironies in the story spring from the incongruity between private deed and public appearance. When Satan at the town-meeting speaks of the "invulnerable probity" of the Richardses, they "blush prettily; however," Twain adds sardonically, "it went for modesty, and did no harm." Any act is permissible as long as it is performed in the dark. "Oh, bless God, we are saved!" cries Mrs. Richards when Burgess fails to read their test-remark. Salvation for these pious people consists of keeping their sins hidden from public view. Edward Richards is so fearful of public opinion that he repents of his one act of virtue—his warning to Burgess of the town's plan to ride him on a rail. "Edward!" gasps his wife Mary. "If the town had found it out—" "Don't! It scares me yet to think it. I repented of it the minute it was done." Obviously, the apple (*i.e.,* Hadleyburg "honesty") in this Eden is ready to drop from the weight of its own corruption. Satan's purpose is to force the inhabitants to eat this bitter fruit of their hypocrisy.

To accomplish this aim, that master engineer, Satan, manipulates his weak and foolish Edenites with superhuman precision. The mechanical actions of the dog in the audience at the town-hall is an amusing image of the automatic reflexes of the Hadleyburgians to Satan's relentless stratagems: when the crowd rises to its feet, so does the dog; when the crowd roars, the dog barks "itself crazy." The Richardses constantly have the feeling that their actions are controlled by a force outside of themselves, but they are too weak to resist. "Do you think we are to blame, Edward—*much* to blame?" Mary asks. "We—we couldn't help it, Mary. It—well, it was ordered. *All* things are", Edward answers truthfully enough, although he would have been shocked to know that his actions were "ordered" by Satan, not God. Man is nothing more than a machine that responds automatically according to outside stimuli—this is the philosophy of man described in Twain's "bible," *What is Man?* writ-

ten the same year as "Hadleyburg," and in many respects an enlightening commentary on the short story. Satan has no need to perform crude miracles; all he has to do is to activate the human mechanism with the desire for wealth and the need for the approval of his fellows and set it on its track. Each human piston goes through its cycles with perfect timing. When Edward puts on his hat and leaves his house "without a word," he doesn't need to communicate his intentions to his wife: both have arrived at the same conclusion in silence. In the meantime, Cox, the newspaper editor, and his wife go through the same series as did the Richards: elation and pride, fidgety silence, unspoken agreement, and departure. Richards and Cox meet at the foot of the printing-office stairs; again there is no need for words; but Satan has timed their mechanical reflexes so precisely that they meet just two minutes too late to spoil his plan. Later, the rest of the nineteen principal citizens go through the same intricate series of maneuvers as does their "caste brother Richards." Each puppet has been cast in the same mold, and Satan knows exactly which lever to pull or button to push to accomplish his ends.

This picture of robot man is grim and pessimistic, but not without hope. In *What is Man?* Twain states that in man's "chameleonship" lies "his greatest good fortune." The human machine cannot change from within, but the influences that dominate it can be changed. The duty of government, therefore, should be to lay "traps for people. Traps baited with *Initiatory Impulses toward high ideals.*" That is exactly what Satan does in "Hadleyburg": he *traps* his victims into reform. The lies of the Father of Lies are an agency of truth. He weaves a snare of lies about the Hadleyburgians to force them to recognize that they have been living a monstrous lie.

Immediately after Satan sets into motion his machinations, the moral reformation of the Richardses begins. His stratagems lead this pathetic, middle-aged Adam and Eve to know the truth about themselves. Mary, who subscribes to the *Missionary Herald*, is very soon convinced that charity does not begin at *her* home by the realization that her husband lacks the generosity to give "a stranger twenty dollars." They both become aware that the only person in the town capable of an act of such magnanimity was the hated outcast Goodson. Edward must admit to Mary that the town's hostility toward Burgess stems from an injustice and that he hasn't the courage to right the wrong. Stripped of illusions concerning themselves, they can see the town in its true light. "Edward, it is my belief that this town's honesty is as rotten as mine is; as rotten as yours is," Mary confesses. Treading the well-worn path of Puritan regeneration, the Richardses are led first to a perception of their own sinfulness and then to a public confession. Whether or not Edward dies in a state of grace, his death-bed confession does have three beneficial results: (*1*) it enables him to die under the illusion, at least, that he is "a man, and not a dog"—like the automatic dog in the town-hall audience; (*2*) it at last clears Burgess of the crime that the town had charged against him; and (*3*) it completes the destruction of the false pride of the town by revealing that its last respected important citizen had also sinned.

It is safe to conclude, therefore, that Satan is Hadleyburg's greatest benefactor. In addition to his arsenal of therapeutic lies, he has one other mighty weapon against humbuggery—laughter. When Satan traps the Hadleyburgians into facing the shattering discrepancy between their pious pretentions and their secret venality, they explode into roars of whole-hearted laughter that sweeps away their hypocrisy. The change of the motto of the town from "Lead us not into temptation" to "Lead us into temptation" proves that the experience has had a lasting effect. As Satan in *The Mysterious Stranger* points out: ". . . your race, in its poverty has unquestionably one really effective weapon—laughter. Power, money, persuasion, supplication, persecution—these can lift at a colossal humbug—push it a little—weaken it a little, century by century; but only laughter can blow it to rags and atoms at a blast. Against the assault of laughter nothing can stand." The pious citizens of the town are quite unaware of the ironic application of their chant as Satan leaves the town-hall: "You are f-a-r from being a b-a-a-d man—a-a-a-a-men!" Satan's original motive may have been revenge, but the result of his labors is to bring Hadleyburg to an understanding of its corruption so that it can reform. That he reveres virtue can be seen in his apology to Edward: "I honor you—and that is sincere, too."

Satan as man's benefactor is a fairly common idea in nineteenth-century literature. The cynical Mephistopheles in Goethe's *Faust*, of which Twain owned several translations, is clearly an unwitting servant of God; his duty is to stimulate man's discontent so that he will constantly strive for a higher ideal. Other books that he read—*The Gods* by Robert G. Ingersoll (who was one of Twain's

heroes), and *La Sorciere* by Jules Michelet (which Twain probably read in preparation for his *Personal Recollections of Joan of Arc*) defend Satan and his devils as humane and civilizing forces in the world. Most likely, however, Twain's characterization is derived from the Bible, which he had memorized as a boy during many weary Sabbaths. Many Biblical passages depict Satan as a servant of God whose functions are to test man's faith, punish his wickedness, and purge his flesh "that his spirit may be saved." Perhaps Satan's major service to man is to chasten his pride. This is the role that he employs to bring about the fortunate fall of the Eden of Hadleyburg. Saint Paul himself was aware of Satan's usefulness as a means of humbling man's pride: "And to keep me from being too elated by the abundance of revelations, a thorn was given me in the flesh, a messenger of Satan, to harass me, to keep me from being too elated" (I Cor. 12:7). Possibly this and similar passages in the Bible, in addition to the encouragement of his kindhearted mother, inspired little Sam at the age of seven to rescue Satan from nineteen centuries of Christian defamation. "Hadleyburg" is the finest product of that long endeavor.

"Hadleyburg" is far superior to *The Mysterious Stranger*, the other major Satan story of Twain's old age. It is more subtle, more wittily devious in its presentation of Satan and mankind and their relation to one another. "Hadleyburg" achieves the unity of tone and aesthetic distance that satire and irony require, while *The Mysterious Stranger* violently alternates between the vulgar antics of a P. T. Barnum side show and the nakedly ferocious tirades of a world-hating, self-hating old man. Twain himself once described the reason for the artistic failure of *The Mysterious Stranger:* ". . . of course a man can't write successful satire except he be in a calm judicial good-humor . . . in truth I don't ever seem to be in a good enough humor with anything to *satirize* it; no, I want to stand up before it & curse it, & foam at the mouth,—or take a club & pound it to rags & pulp." For once, while writing "Hadleyburg," Twain found the emotional restraint to create a work of art. Standing alone among the products of his old age for the neatness and precision of its form and the richness of its allegorical ironies, "Hadleyburg" might be compared to two other American treatments of the Eden myth—Hawthorne's "Young Goodman Brown" and Melville's *Billy Budd*.

Source: Henry B. Rule, "The Role of Satan in 'The Man That Corrupted Hadleyburg,'" in *Studies in Short Fiction*, Vol. VI, No. 5, Fall, 1969, pp. 619–29.

Sources

Anderson, Benedict. *Imagined Communities: Reflections on the Origin and Spread of Nationalism*, revised edition, New York: Verso, 1991.

Archer, William. "The Man That Corrupted Hadleyburg-New Parable," in *The Critic*, Vol. 37, November, 1900, pp. 413-415.

Briden, Earl F. "Twainian Pedagogy and the No-Account Lessons of 'Hadleyburg,'" in *Studies in Short Fiction*, Vol. 28, No. 2, 1991, pp. 125-134.

Briden, Earl F. and Prescott, Mary. "The Lie that I Am I: Paradoxes of Identity in Mark Twain's 'Hadleyburg,'" in *Studies in Short Fiction*, Vol. 21, No. 4, 1984, pp. 383-391.

Emerson, Everett. *The Authentic Mark Twain: A Literary Biography of Samuel L. Clemens*, Philadelphia: University of Pennsylvania Press, 1984.

Lowe, Lisa. *Immigrant Acts,* Duke University Press, 1996.

Quirk, Tom. *Mark Twain: A Study of the Short Fiction*, New York: Twayne, 1997.

Murfin, Ross, and M. Ray Supryia. *The Bedford Glossary of Critical and Literary Terms*, New York: Bedford, 1997.

Review of *The Man That Corrupted Hadleyburg and Other Stories*, in *Living Age*, Vol. 227, December 15, 1900, pp. 695.

Further Reading

Briden, Earl F. "Twainian Pedagogy and the No-Account Lessons of 'Hadleyburg,'" in *Studies in Short Fiction*, Vol. 28, No. 2, 1991, pp. 125-34.

Argues against "fortunate fall" interpretations of "Hadleyburg," delineating obstacles presented in the narrative for such readings.

Briden, Earl F. and Mary Prescott. "The Lie that I Am I: Paradoxes of Identity in Mark Twain's 'Hadleyburg.'" in *Studies in Short Fiction*, Vol. 21, No. 4, 1984, pp. 383-91.

Discusses the contradictory pressures of individualism and social conformity, identifying the consequences for characters who "slavishly" seek social approval.

Emerson, Everett. *The Authentic Mark Twain: A Literary Biography of Samuel L. Clemens*, Philadelphia: University of Pennsylvania Press, 1984.

Comprehensive biography of Clemens and the development of his persona "Mark Twain," detailing his literary career.

Quirk, Tom. *Mark Twain: A Study of the Short Fiction*, New York: Twayne, 1997.

Concise three-part analysis of Twain's major short stories in their historical context, comprising Twain's biography, excerpted works, critical essays, and chronology. A solid introduction to Twain's stories.

Rucker, Mary E. "Moralism and Determinism in 'The Man That Corrupted Hadleyburg,'" in *Studies in Short Fiction*, Vol. 14, 1977, pp. 49-54.

Outlines the thematic debate surrounding the story, emphasizing the incompatibility of both schools of thought to show that neither theme informs "Hadleyburg."

Scharnhorst, Gary. "Paradise Revisited: Twain's 'The Man That Corrupted Hadleyburg,'" in *Studies in Short Fiction*, Vol. 18, No. 1, 1981, pp. 59-64.

Examines the "moralism versus determinism" debate, explicating "Hadleyburg" in terms of Milton's influence and the "fortunate fall" myth.

The Management of Grief

Bharati Mukherjee
1988

"The Management of Grief" is a poignant fictional account of one woman's reaction to the 1985 bombing of Air India Flight 182. It was first published in 1988 in the collection *The Middleman and Other Stories*, winner of the 1988 National Book Critics Circle Award. "The Management of Grief" tells the story of Shaila Bhave, an Indian Canadian Hindu who has lost her husband and two sons in the crash. In third person narration, Shaila recounts the emotional events surrounding the event and explores their effects on herself, the Indian Canadian community, and mainstream Euro-Canadians. The clumsy intervention of a government social worker represents the missteps of the Canadian government in the general handling of the catastrophe.

Mukherjee herself had a deep personal response to the crash, having lived in Canada from 1966 to 1980 with her husband, Clark Blaise. She was enraged by the Canadian government's interpretation of the crash as a foreign, "Indian" matter when the overwhelmingly majority of the victims were Canadian citizens. In a book-length investigation and account of the incident, *The Sorrow and the Terror*, co-written with Blaise, Mukherjee pieces together the bombing and events leading up to it, charging the government with ignoring clear signs of Khalistani terrorism cultivated on Canadian soil. Mukherjee argues that the government dismissed the escalating Indian Canadian factionalism (e.g. Canadian Khalistanis vs. Canadian Hindus) as a "cultural" struggle that would be best settled among

the "Indians." She blames Canada's official policy of "multiculturalism," which ostensibly encourages tolerance and equality but effectively fosters division and discrimination across racial boundaries.

The Sorrow and the Terror is a moving, non-fictional precursor to "The Management of Grief," articulating the human costs of the escalations of intra-ethnic Indian conflict whose reach does not exempt the country's North American emigrants. As Shaila laments: "We, who stayed out of politics and came half way around the world to avoid religious and political feuding, have been the first in the New World to die from it."

Author Biography

Bharati Mukherjee was born in Calcutta, India on July 27, 1940. Her father was a renowned chemist with connections around the globe. She and her two sisters were educated in India, England and Switzerland. At the age of three she spoke English along with her native Bengali. Mukherjee received her B.A. in English Literature from the University of Calcutta in 1959 and an M.A. in English and ancient Indian culture from the University of Baroda in 1961. She received her M.F.A. and Ph.D. from the University of Iowa in 1963 and 1969 respectively. In 1964 she married Clark Blaise, a fellow writer in the Iowa Writers Workshop. The "culture shock" of the midwest, not to mention America in general, profoundly affected Mukherjee; many of her works, like *Jasmine* (1989) and *The Middleman and Other Stories* (1988), dramatize the uniqueness of the immigrant's struggle in the "heartland."

Mukherjee's academic resume is impressive: she has taught literature and writing at Marquette University, the University of Wisconsin-Madison, McGill University, Skidmore College, Mountain State College, Queens College and Columbia University. She is now Distinguished Professor at the University of California at Berkeley. She is also an award-winning writer of both fiction and non-fiction. Her first novel, *The Tiger's Daughter* (1975), was a finalist for the Governor General's Award of Canada, and *The Middleman and Other Stories* (1988) won the National Book Critics Circle Award for fiction that year.

Mukherjee remembers Canada bitterly as an angry, racist nation. In a 1989 interview with *The Iowa Review*, she remarks that in her nearly 15 years of residence there, the country never ceased making her feel like a "smelly, dark, alien other." Mukherjee blames Canada's policy of "multiculturalism" for engendering this atmosphere of thinly veiled racism. "The Management of Grief" speaks out against the social ills generated by this policy. In this story, the tragedy of the Air India Flight 182 brings the racial divisions of Canadian society into sharp relief. Shaila Bhave's perspective is much like Mukherjee's own, criticizing the government for dismissing the catastrophe as an "Indian" incident when over 90% of the passengers were Canadian citizens. The clumsy treatment of crash victims' relatives by Judith Templeton, the government social worker, represents mainstream culture's ignorant perception of ethnic citizens as "not quite," second-class, Canadians.

Plot Summary

"The Management of Grief" opens with the chaos at Shaila Bhave's Toronto home. Her house is filled with strangers, gathered together for legal advice, company, and tea. Dr. Sharma, his wife, their children, Kusum and "a lot of women [Shaila] do[esn't] know" are trying to make sense of the crash of Air India Flight 182, simultaneously listening to multiple radios and televisions to catch some news about the event. The Sharma boys murmur rumors that Sikh terrorists had planted a bomb. Shaila narrates the scene from a haze, speaking with detached, shell-shocked calm. The Valium she has been taking contributes to her stable appearance, but inside she feels "tensed" and "ready to scream." Imagined cries from her husband and sons "insulate her" from the anxious activity in her house.

Shaila and Kusum, her neighbor and friend, are sitting on the stairs in Shaila's house. Shaila reminisces about Kusum and Satish's recent housewarming party that brought cultures and generations together in their sparkling, spacious suburban home: "even white neighbors piled their plates high with [tandoori]" and Shaila's own Americanized sons had "broken away" from a Stanley Cup telecast to come to the party. Shaila somberly wonders "and now . . . how many of those happy faces are gone." Implicitly Shaila feels "punished" for the good success of Indian immigrant families like hers and Kusum's. Kusum brings her out of her reverie with the question: "Why does God give us so much if all along He intends to take it away?"

Shaila regrets her perfect obedience to upper-class, Indian female decorum. She has, for instance, never called her husband by his first name or told him that she loved him. Kusum comforts her saying: "He knew. My husband knew. They felt it. Modern young girls have to say it because what they feel is fake." Kusum's first daughter Pam walks into the room and orders her mother to change out of her bathrobe since reporters are expected. Pam, a manifest example of the "modern young girls" that Kusum disdains, had refused to go to India with her father and younger sister, preferring to spend that summer working at McDonald's. Mother and daughter exchange harsh words, and Pam accuses Kusum of wishing that Pam had been on the plane, since the younger daughter was a better "Indian." Kusum does not react verbally.

Judith Templeton, a Canadian social worker, visits Shaila, hoping Shaila can facilitate her work with the relatives of the deceased. Judith is described as young, comely and professional to a fault. She enlists Shaila to give the "right human touch" to the impersonal work of processing papers for relief funds. Judith tells Shaila that she was chosen because of her exemplary calm and describes her as a "pillar" of the devastated Indian Canadian community. Shaila explains that her seemingly cool, unaffected demeanor is hardly admired by her community, who expect their members to mourn publicly and vocally. She is puzzled herself by the "calm [that] will not go away" and considers herself a "freak."

The story moves to Dunmanus Bay, Ireland, the site of the crash. Kusum and Shaila are wading in the warm waters and recalling the lives of their loved ones, imagining they will be found alive. Kusum has not eaten for four days and Shaila wishes she had also died here along with her husband and sons. They are joined by Dr. Ranganathan from Montreal, another who has lost his family, and he cheers them with thoughts of unknown islets within swimming distance. Dr. Ranganathan utters a central line of the story: "It's a parent's duty to hope." He scatters pink rose petals on the water, explaining that his wife used to demand pink roses every Friday. He offers Shaila some roses, but Shaila has her own gifts to float — Mithun's half finished model B-52, Vinod's pocket calculator, and a poem for Vikram, which belatedly articulates her love for him.

Shaila is struck by the compassionate behavior of the Irish and compares them to the residents of

Bharati Mukherjee

Toronto, unable to image Torontonians behaving this open-heartedly. Kusum has identified her husband. Looking through picture after picture, Shaila does not find a match for anyone she knows. A nun "assigned to console" Shaila reminds her that faces will have altered, bloated by the water and with facial bones broken from the impact. She is instructed to "try to adjust [her] memories."

Shaila leaves Ireland without any bodies, but Kusum takes her husband's coffin through customs. A customs bureaucrat detains them under suspicion of smuggling contraband in the coffin. In her first public expression of emotion, Shaila explodes and calls him a "bastard." She contemplates the change in herself that this trauma has wrought: "Once upon a time we were well-brought-up women; we were dutiful wives who kept our heads veiled, our voices shy and sweet."

From Ireland, many of the Indian Canadians, including Shaila, go to India to continue mourning. Shaila describes her parents as wealthy and "progressive." They do not mind Sikh friends dropping by with condolences, though Shaila cannot help but bristle. Her grandmother, on the other hand, has been a prisoner of tradition and its gender expectations for most of her life. She was widowed at age sixteen and has since lived a life of ascetic penitence and solitude, believing herself to be a "harbinger of bad luck." Shaila's mother calls this kind of behavior "mindless mortification." While other middle-aged widows and widowers are being matched with new spouses, Shaila is relieved to be left alone, even if it is because her grandmother's history designates her as "unlucky."

Shaila travels with her family until she is numb from the blandness of diversion. In a deserted Himalayan temple, Shaila has a vision of her husband. He tells her: "You must finish alone what we started together." Knowing that her mother is a practical woman with "no patience with ghosts, prophetic dreams, holy men, and cults," Shaila tells her nothing of the vision but is spurred to return to Canada.

Kusum has sold her house and moved into an ashram, or retreat, in Hardwar. Shaila considers this "running away," but Kusum says it is "pursuing inner peace." Shaila keeps in touch with Dr. Ranganathan, who has moved to Montreal and has not remarried. They share a melancholy bond but are comforted to have found new "relatives" in each other.

At this point, Judith has done thorough and ambitious work observing, assessing, charting and analyzing the grief of the Indian Canadians. She matter-of-factly reports to Shaila that the community is stuck somewhere between the second and third stage of mourning, "depressed acceptance," according to the "grief management textbooks." In reaction to Judith's self-congratulatory chatter, Shaila can only manage the weak and ironic praise that Judith has "done impressive work." Judith asks Shaila to accompany her on a visit to a particularly "stubborn" and "ignorant" elderly couple, recent immigrants whose sons died in the crash. Shaila is reluctant because the couple are Sikh and she is Hindu, but Judith insists that their "Indian-ness" is mutual enough.

At the apartment complex, Shaila is struck by the "Indian-ness" of the ghetto neighborhood; women wait for buses in saris as if they had never left Bombay. The elderly couple are diffident at first but open up when Shaila reveals that she has also lost her family. Shaila explains that if they sign the documents, the government will give them money, including air-fare to Ireland to identify the bodies. The husband emphasizes that "God will provide, not the government" and the wife insists that her boys will return. Judith presses Shaila to "convince" them, but Shaila merely thanks the couple

for the tea. In the car Judith complains about working with the Indian immigrants, calling the next woman "a real mess." Shaila asks to be let out of the car, leaving Judith and her sterile, textbook approach to grief management.

The story ends with Shaila living a quiet and joyless life in Toronto. She has sold her and Vikram's large house and lives in a small apartment. Kusum has written to say that she has seen her daughter's reincarnation in a Himalayan village; Dr. Ranganathan has moved to Texas and calls once a week. Walking home from an errand, Shaila hears "the voices of [her] family." They say: "Your time has come, . . . Go, be brave." Shaila drops the package she is carrying on a nearby park bench, symbolizing her venture into a new life and her break with an unproductive attachment to her husband and sons' spirits. She comments on her imminent future: "I do not know where this voyage I have begun will end." Nevertheless, she "drops the package" and "starts walking."

Characters

Shaila Bhave

Shaila is the central character of "The Management of Grief." Her third person voice narrates the story and offers poignant reflection, provocative implications and subtle irony. Her tone can be described as understated and detached, but it is by no means dispassionate. Like the appearance of calm that masks her "screaming" within, the even, often soothing tone of the narrative voice stretches thinly over Shaila's rage and pain. She is shell-shocked by the rapid succession of devastating events.

Shaila's husband and two sons have been the killed in the crash of Air India Flight 182. Some consider her callous and insensitive for not openly grieving, but Judith Templeton, the government social worker, hears that she is a "pillar" of the community and solicits her help. Shaila scorns Judith's textbook methods of "managing" grief but agrees to play the cultural liaison out of politeness. Shaila wishes she could "scream, starve, walk into Lake Ontario, [or] jump from a bridge." She considers herself a "freak," helplessly overtaken by a "terrible calm."

Like many others, Shaila harbors hopes that her family is still alive. She travels to Ireland to identify and possibly recover the bodies of the deceased. When called by the police to identify a body thought to be her son, Shaila insists that it is not him. She is unable to provide a positive identification of any of her family members.

From Ireland, Shaila goes to India. Her ''progressive'' parents encourage her to avoid falling into self-destructive depression and mourning, the ''mindless mortification of her grandmother.'' She is discomfited by Sikh friends who pay their condolences and admires her parents' unprejudiced attitude, noting that in Canada the crash will likely revive Sikh-Hindu animosity. In a Himalayan temple, Shaila sees Vikram in a vision. He commands her to ''finish alone what we started together.'' Taking this as an injunction to resume a forward moving life, she returns to Canada. Unlike many of the others, Shaila does not remarry. She assumes that friends and relatives in India avoid matching her up because of her ''unlucky'' history (her grandmother's husband died when he was nineteen). For this, Shaila is relieved.

Shaila accompanies Judith to a ghetto tenement to visit a helpless Sikh couple whose sons have died in the crash. Shaila is struck by the poverty and concentrated ethnicity of their apartment building. Just as Shaila could not bear to identify any of the bodies in Ireland, the couple refuses to sign Judith's documents, even though they entitle them to relief funds. Despite Judith's urgings, Shaila does not press them to sign, remembering Dr. Ranganathan's adage: ''It is a parent's duty to hope.'' They leave the apartment without signatures, and in the car Shaila can no longer tolerate Judith's complaints about ''stubborn'' and ''ignorant'' Indian Canadians, recalcitrant textbook subjects, and asks Judith to stop so that she can get out.

Shaila has made a tolerable life for herself with the profits from the sale of her and Vikram's house. But she is living joylessly and mechanically; she ''waits,'' ''listens,'' and ''prays.'' She is falling prey to the ''mindless mortification'' of her grandmother. The turning point is when Shaila hears the voices of her ''family.'' They tell her: ''Your time has come ... Go, be brave.'' Shaila drops the symbolic ''package'' on a park bench and ''starts walking'' toward a life of healing and hope.

Vikram Bhave

Vikram is Shaila's husband and is killed in the Air India crash. In a vision, he tells Shaila: ''You're beautiful'' and more importantly, ''What are you doing here? ... You must finish alone what we started together.'' He appears to her healthy and whole, ''no seaweed wreathes in his mouth'' and speaking ''too fast, just as he used to when we were an envied family in our pink split level.''

Vinod and Mithun Bhave

Shaila and Vikram's two sons, Vinod and Mithun, were also killed in the crash. Vinod was going to be fourteen in a few days. His brother, Mithun, was four years younger. The boys were going down to the Taj with their father and uncle for Vinod's birthday party.

Elderly Couple

Because their sons have been killed in the crash, the elderly couple that Judith and Shaila visit are entitled to government relief funds, including air-fare to Ireland. They speak little English and live in a tenement building inhabited by Indians, West Indians, and a ''sprinkling of Orientals.'' Judith Templeton has visited them several times, imploring them to sign government documents that will entitle them to the funds. Because they are poor and unable to write a check, their utilities are being cut off one by one. Notwithstanding, they refuse to sign Judith's papers. The husband places his faith in God, uttering : ''God will provide, not [the] government.'' The wife believes her sons will return to take care of them.

Kusum

Kusum has lost her husband, Satish, and her unnamed second daughter in the plane crash. She had moved into the well-to-do Toronto suburb with her family, across the street from Shaila and Vikram, less than a month before the crash and hosted a welcoming party to celebrate their success. She is with Shaila in Ireland identifying bodies and hoping for life. Her husband's body is discovered and she takes it in a coffin to India. When Kusum moves back to India to follow a life of mourning, Shaila accuses her of ''running away.'' Kusum responds that this is her way of finding ''inner peace.'' She writes Shaila at the end of the story to inform her that she has seen her husband and daughter. On one pilgrimage she spotted a young girl who looked exactly like her deceased daughter. Noticing Kusum staring at her, the young girl yelled ''Ma!'' and ran away. Kusum alludes to suicide in Ireland when she remarks to Shaila at Dunmanus Bay: ''That water felt warm.''

Pam

Pam is Kusum's oldest daughter and would have been on the plane had she not refused to visit India. Pam is represented as irreverent and "westernized." She works at McDonalds, preferring "Wonderland" to Bombay, and is "always in trouble," "dat[ing] Canadian boys and hang[ing] out in the mall, shopping for tight sweaters." Her lifestyle and attitude strain her relationship with her traditional Indian mother, who in a moment of self-pitying despair blurts: "If I didn't have to look after you now, I'd hang myself." Deeply hurt by this remark ("her face goes blotchy with pain"), Pam retorts: "You think I don't know what Mummy's thinking? *Why her?* That's what. That's sick! Mummy wishes my little sister were alive and I were dead!" She later heads for California to do modeling work or open a "yoga-cum-aerobics studio in Hollywood" with the insurance money. She ends up in Vancouver, working at a cosmetics counter "giving makeup hints to Indian and Oriental girls." She sends Shaila "postcards so naughty I daren't leave them on the coffee table."

Dr. Ranganathan

Dr. Ranganathan is a well-to-do and respected electrical engineer who has also lost his family in the crash. The reader is introduced to him when he meets Shaila and Kusum searching for hope on the southwestern coast of Ireland. He suggests to the women that survivors may have been able to swim to uncharted islets and gives Shaila hope that both her sons may have survived given that "[a] strong youth of fourteen . . . can very likely pull to safety a younger one." He succors a sobbing Kusum and offers the story's central phrase: "It's a parent's duty to hope," continuing that "It is foolish to rule out possibilities that have not been tested. I myself have not surrendered hope." He has taken pink roses from someone's garden and scatters them on the water in memory of his wife. She had demanded that he bring her pink roses every Friday. He would bring them and playfully reproach: "After twenty-odd years of marriage you're still needing proof positive of my love."

Dr. Ranganathan accompanies Shaila to look through photographs of recovered bodies, offering her the comfort of a "scientist's perspective." Understanding Shaila's psychological defenses, he looks at the pictures for her and does not force her to make positive identifications. He identifies the boys thought to be Vinod and Mithun as the Kutty brothers, bringing Shaila great relief.

Back in Canada, Dr. Ranganathan continues to be a source of comfort for Shaila. Both have not remarried and he calls Shaila twice a week from Montreal. He considers himself and Shaila as "relatives," joined together by race, culture and now this mournful event. He takes a new job in Ottawa but cannot bear to sell his house in Montreal, choosing rather to drive 220 miles a day to work. His grief also prevents him from sleeping in the bed he shared with his wife, so he sleeps on a cot in his large, empty house. Describing his house as a "temple" and his bedroom as a "shrine," Dr. Ranganathan, for all the comfort he offers to others, is also crippled by his pain.

At the end of the story, Dr. Ranganathan moves to Texas to start a new life, a place where "no one knows his story and he has vowed not to tell it." He continues to call Shaila, but only once a week.

Satish

Satish is Kusum's husband who died in the plane crash.

Shaila's grandmother

Though only briefly mentioned, Shaila's grandmother has an important effect on Shaila's sense of self. She is portrayed as a traditional Brahmin woman who unquestioningly fills her role as wife and female, in other words, as a submissive and second-class citizen. Her husband, Shaila's grandfather, died of diabetes when he was nineteen, leaving his wife a widow at age sixteen. Considering herself a "harbinger of bad luck," she shaved her head and lived in self-imposed suffering and seclusion.

Shaila's Mother

Having been raised by an "indifferent uncle" in the presence of a morbid and depressed mother, Shaila's mother becomes a "rationalist" and an enemy of "mindless mortification." She encourages her daughter to rebound quickly from the crisis, still calling her son-in-law by his casual Anglicized name, "Vik." Reminding Shaila of the uselessness of her grandmother's wasted life, she tells her: "You know, the dead aren't cut off from us!" and "Vikram wouldn't have wanted you to give up things." To Shaila's discomfort, her "progressive" parents receive condolences from Sikh neighbors, refusing to "blame communities for a few individuals." Later, in the family's travels to the Himalayas, Shaila does not tell her mother about her vision of Vikram, knowing that she "has no patience with ghosts, prophetic dreams, holy men, and cults."

Dr. and Mrs. Sharma

This couple is one of the few guests at Shaila's house that are mentioned by name. Dr. Sharma is the treasurer of the Indo-Canada Society and offers Shaila help in legal and financial matters. His wife, pregnant with her fifth child, offers general comfort and admonishes her husband not to bother Shaila with "mundane details." They are respected members of the Indian community and provide leadership to the group of anxious and confused friends and relatives of the victims gathered at Shaila's house.

Judith Templeton

Judith Templeton is a Canadian social worker whose job is to contact the relatives of the crash victims and offer government aid. Her task is daunting because many of the people she visits speak little English and are wary of government employees and their confusing documents. Judith asks Shaila to help her bridge this cultural gap, suggesting that as an Indian, Shaila has the "right human touch." Judith is described as cool, stiff, professional and insensitive: "She [Judith] wears a blue suit with a white blouse and a polka-dot tie. Her blond hair is cut short, her only jewelry is pearl-drop earrings. Her briefcase is new and expensive looking . . . She sits with it across her lap . . . her contact lenses seem to float in front of her light blue eyes."

Judith's insensitivity to the Indian Canadians is not, however, malicious. She is represented as emotionally and psychologically stunted, only understanding human suffering through textbooks. In one of her conversations with Shaila, she remarks that according to "textbooks on grief management," most of the Indian Canadians are stuck between "stage two" and "three." This dispassionate description strikes Shaila as typical of Judith's impersonal and professional relationships with deeply suffering individuals. Judith has created charts and pages of analyses which appear to Shaila to be terribly inadequate accounts of the tragedy. After a frustrating visit to an elderly couple, Judith complains vocally about the Indians' "stubbornness and ignorance" which is "driving her crazy." When she begins prattling about the next "client," a woman who is a "real mess," Shaila can no longer bear to offer Judith her polite help and gets out of the car.

Themes

Gender Roles and Cultural Tradition

The crash of Air India Flight 182 brings radical changes to its victims' families' lives. In "The Management of Grief" Mukherjee focuses on its effects on women. Women are confronted with the problem of mourning; do they need to observe the self-sacrificing mourning rituals and decorum of "proper" Indian widows, even in the "new world" of Canada? Shaila and Kusum are opposing models of behavior; Kusum succumbs to her culture's expectation that she will dedicate her life to her dead husband (by not remarrying and living a life of asceticism) while Shaila struggles with these oppressive cultural demands, finally rejecting them.

Shaila imagines that she hears Vikram and her sons crying out to her: "Mommy, Shaila." Their cries are telling: Shaila's main roles are that of mother and wife. The patriarchal conventions of the majority of the world (women stay home, cook and tend the children etc.) are compounded by the specific "regulations" of Indian culture. For instance, Shaila has never called her husband by his first name or told him that she loved him, as is proper of an upper-class Indian woman. The emotions wrought by the crash lead Shaila to call into question her blind obedience, up until now, to Hindu female decorum. The tragedy of the crash makes the unseen but ubiquitous veil of female oppression palpable, challenging the affected women to break free.

As Indian wife and mother, Shaila is expected to follow mourning traditions. The Hindu widow cannot remarry, is prohibited from wearing certain hair decorations and jewelry, and is restricted in her choice of dress. In short, she is meant to spend the rest of her life despairing over the loss of her husband, denying her own social and sexual needs, and even doing penance as if somehow responsible for her husband's death. Shaila's grandmother has always been an example of such self-sacrifice: she shaves her head, thereby obliterating any trace of vanity or sexual appeal, and lives in self-imposed seclusion. She is so devoted to mourning that she forsakes her infant daughter, passing on her upbringing to an "indifferent uncle." Growing up in such a somber atmosphere, Shaila's mother has learned to be "progressive" and "rational," rejecting her mother's "mindless mortification" and urging Shaila to do the same. To encourage Shaila to "get on with her life," her parents remember

Topics for Further Study

- Throughout her work and personal search for identity, Mukherjee has drawn a line between the "immigrant" and "expatriate." In her introduction to *Darkness* (1985), she rejects the "aloofness of expatriation" for the "exuberance of immigration." What is the difference between immigrants and expatriates? What are their attitudes towards their new country? Select a story or a section of a novel from Mukherjee's work and discuss whether the characters fulfill Mukherjee's (or your own) conception of immigrant and expatriate.

- "The Management of Grief" offers a glimpse of the mourning rituals of Hindu women. Research in fuller detail the mourning rituals of Indian cultures (e.g. Hindu, Muslim, Sikh). Are these rituals different for men and women? Examine your own culture's mourning rituals. Do they have varying expectations according to gender?

- In *The Sorrow and The Terror*, Mukherjee and Blaise carefully differentiate radical Khalistani groups from Sikhs in general. They emphasize that it is erroneous to blame the bombing of Air India Flight 182 on Sikhs when only a small, violent group of Khalistanis were responsible. They also bemoan the media stereotype of Indians as terrorists. Research the Khalistani movement, paying attention to the work of non-violent groups. How has the media contributed to their stereotyping as violent terrorists?

- Mukherjee has been both criticized and praised for being an *assimilationist*. What is assimilation? Research this concept using history, literature, or current events and discuss its pros and cons.

- Mukherjee has praised America's "melting-pot" mentality. Yet across the nation, more and more "ethnic-towns" are emerging. In this way, the American landscape is beginning to resemble Canada's "mosaic." Discuss how contemporary America fits or does not fit into Mukherjee's image of the melting-pot. In your opinion, which model is better, the mosaic or the melting pot? Use specific examples from literature, history or current events to substantiate your argument.

- Mukherjee and several other writers do not support "hyphenated" status. That is, they do not consider themselves Indian American or Chinese American, but simply American. What is your opinion of this "hyphenated" status? Does the hyphen devalue the immigrant's claim to this country, or does it duly honor her ancestor's culture? Use excerpts from literature, history and current events to support your argument.

Vikram by his casual westernized name, "Vik," and tell her that he "wouldn't have wanted you [Shaila] to give up things."

Shaila's parents want her to stay in India so that they can pamper her with luxuries and travel. As "progressive" as they are, they do not see that Shaila needs to return to Canada to "finish" what she and Vikram started. In deciding to return, Shaila resists binding ideas about both gender and culture. She is not just "Indian" any more, but Indian Canadian, and must return home (Canada) to foster and develop her complex, hybrid identity. Kusum,

on the other hand, returns to India and in a sense becomes more "Indian" than before, pursuing a life of ascetic piety and travel to holy sites. Shaila views this as a regression into traditional culture and gender roles, accusing Kusum of "running away" and "withdrawing from the world." Like Shaila's grandmother, Kusum also forgets about her living daughter to succumb to the "mindless mortification" expected of Hindu widows.

Shaila articulates the change she is going through when Kusum is detained at the airport on suspicion of smuggling contraband in her husband's coffin.

Surprising herself, Shaila explodes and calls the customs officer a ''bastard.'' She reflects on her transformation: ''Once upon a time we were well-brought up women; we were dutiful wives who kept our heads veiled, our voices shy and sweet.'' This is the clearest indicator that the trauma has unmoored traditional, upper-class Indian women like Shaila from the safety of their patriarchally imposed decorum. But even though, unlike Kusum, Shaila breaks free from these limits, the process is quite a struggle. After selling her and Vikram's house and moving into a small apartment in downtown Toronto, Shaila lives a mechanical, joyless life. For a long time, she is haunted by visions of her lost ones. In this way, Shaila has also fallen prey to a kind of ''mindless mortification,'' repressed by her memories and her longing for the past. Like Kusum, she is living in a kind of paralyzing self-denial and has not made the brave venture into self-fulfillment. Only at the end of the story, interestingly at the behest of her ''family's'' voices, does Shaila finally break free, symbolically discard the package, and treat herself to a life of her own. Ironically, the tragedy is the agent of productive transformation, forcing Shaila to reexamine her patriarchally bound life.

Collective Identity versus Personal Identity

The tragedy of Flight 182 forges a new bond between Indian Canadians. As Shaila says of the afflicted, ''We've been melted down and cast as a new tribe.'' While providing much needed comfort, this new community bond has its pitfalls, especially when it is stretched beyond its effective limits. This is most apparent in Judith Templeton's uneducated perception that all ''Indians'' are the same. Based on this misunderstanding, she enlists Shaila to give the ''right human touch'' to her government mandated visits to victims' relatives. But as Shaila explains, all Indians are not the same: the elderly Sikh couple might be uncomfortable with Shaila because she is Hindu (the religious affiliations are often marked by surnames). Judith takes no heed, thinking that ''Indian-ness'' is a sufficient and common enough bond. Though Shaila and the couple do manage to communicate, Mukherjee makes it clear that they communicate on the basis of their mutual loss, not their mutual ''Indian-ness.''

As a result of Indian Canadians being lumped together as a group, individuals lose their personal identity. They are considered as part or representative of a group rather than as unique individuals with diverse needs. Collective identity is substituted for personal identity. Members of one's own ethnic groups also perpetuate this notion. The story opens up with a group of Indian Canadians gathered at Shaila's house. As she narrates, there are ''a lot of women I don't know.'' The group has gathered under the assumption that their common ethnicity not only brings them together in a support network but is itself a source of comfort. This is not the case for Shaila, who feels alienated and ''ready to scream.'' Even though they are of the same ethnicity, the strangers in her kitchen do not attend to her individual needs.

Although the story portrays the Irish as warm and sympathetic, it also highlights their assumption that all Indians are alike. Because Dr. Ranganathan has stolen roses from somebody's garden, an Irish newspaper urges: ''When you see an Indian person . . . please give them flowers.'' While this gesture strikes Shaila as deeply compassionate, there is some criticism of the Irish conception that Indian Canadians are a generic group with a strong liking for flowers. As the reader knows, Dr. Ranganathan's floating of the pink roses has nothing to do with his ''Indian-ness'' but is a memorial to a very personal and unique ritual he shared with his wife.

''Melting Pot'' versus ''Mosaic'': Assimilation versus Multiculturalism

''The Management of Grief'' supports a vision of assimilation. Although the word ''assimilation'' in today's parlance has negative connotations, Mukherjee's conception as expressed in this story is progressive and productive. In particular, it is positioned against the idea of ''multiculturalism,'' Canada's official cultural policy. In interviews and other writings, Mukherjee has criticized Canada's vision of its country as a ''mosaic,'' preferring the ''melting pot'' model of America. Canada's Ministry of Multiculturalism recognizes and protects immigrants' rights to preserve their ethnic customs. While this sounds generous in theory, the real-life result is the emergence of divided ethnic communities that are reluctant to communicate with each other. Mukherjee and others have characterized these communities as ''ethnic ghettoes'' that discourage new immigrants from creatively adapting to a strange land or even just learning English. While providing important networks and mutual comfort, these mono-ethnic communities separate new immigrants from mainstream life and severely limit their life choices.

The criticism of these ethnic ghettoes is most evident in the description of the elderly Sikh couple's neighborhood. Even Shaila, an Indian Canadian who has close contacts with the Indian Canadian community, is taken aback by the unmistakably "Indian" smell of the apartment building: "[E]ven I wince from the ferocity of onion fumes, the distinctive and immediate Indian-ness of frying ghee." She is equally astonished by the women waiting for buses in saris and boys playing cricket (a British sport popular in Britain's former colonies) in the parking lot. In other words, she is struck by the distilled Indian-ness of this small bit of Canada. The non-English speaking elderly couple, with their fear of Canadian documents and the white people who bear them, are representative of the fear and limits under which immigrants restricted to ethnic communities live.

The so-called recognition and support of diverse communities engenders an attitude of separatism. For example, the mainstream Euro-Canadians who run the government may be hesitant to get involved in the Chinese Canadian or Caribbean Canadian community, perceiving their "issues" to be culturally specific and best handled among "themselves." Mukherjee argues in *The Sorrow and the Terror* that the Canadian government's lackadaisical response to the crash was the result of this kind of separatist perception of the incident as an "Indian" matter. As Shaila's house guests strain to find radio and TV news about the crash, Shaila "want[s] to tell [them] we're [Indian Canadians] not that important." She realizes that as an "Indian" matter, the tragedy does not warrant the full dedication of national resources.

As the sympathetic protagonist, Shaila offers a more productive model of Indian Canadian living. She resists falling into the trap of tradition like Kusum, who becomes more Indian than an Indian. She also rejects her parents' implicit desire that she stay in India and be comforted by the familiarities of "home." Shaila has accepted Canada as her new home and, as Vikram exhorts, must finish there what they started together. Her dropping of the package also signals her release from being stuck in mind-numbing mourning and its associations with oppressive "Indian-ness." She says "A wife and mother begins her life in a new country, and that life is cut short." Rather than figure out how to be that same Indian wife and mother, she ventures out into a new direction.

Style

Social and Cultural Critique

In a 1989 interview with *The Iowa Review*, Mukherjee criticizes contemporary American fiction for "exist[ing] only in a vacuum of personal relationships." She believes that "[a] social and political vision is an integral part of writing a novel, or being a novelist." In light of these comments, "The Management of Grief" must be understood through a social-political lens. While it is a deeply moving exploration of Shaila Bhave's individual response to the Air India crash, it is also a critique of Canada's racialized society and its inadequate attempts at "handling" the tragedy. In this way, the story is more than a personal narrative, it is a *politicized* account, offering a social, cultural and political critique.

Through the story, Mukherjee criticizes the Canadian policy of multiculturalism. A superficial reading may fail to discover this subtle critique. The word is briefly but pointedly articulated when Judith Templeton calls on Shaila. Shaila's first words to her are "Multiculturalism?" referring to the Ministry of Multiculturalism that sent her. Judith's misunderstanding of the Indian immigrants and the several culture clashes that ensue are indicative of mainstream Euro-Canadians' ignorance about Canadian immigrants. Judith refers to the Indian Canadians as "them" and "lovely people," in other words, definitively different from the mainstream she represents. But as different as "they" are from "her," "they" are all the same. Judith fails to differentiate among Indians, asking Shaila, a Hindu, to go with her to visit a Sikh couple, oblivious and unconcerned that Hindus and Sikhs have a history of antagonism, exacerbated by rumors that Sikhs bombed Flight 182.

Remembering Mukherjee's comments about the political responsibility of fiction, the miscommunication and awkwardness between Shaila and

Judith, and Judith and the Indian Canadians, can be interpreted as a microcosmic representation of the tensions between mainstream Canadians and ethnic Canadians in general. In one sense, Shaila could be read as the voice for Mukherjee's political views, though her character is not limited to this function. In another brief but pointed statement, Shaila brings up the government's sloppy investigation of the case because of the opinion that this is an "Indian," not Canadian, matter. When Judith tells Shaila that "[w]e" [the Canadian government] do not want to make mistakes," Shaila wryly replies: "More mistakes, you mean."

Shaila also expresses a criticism of patriarchal Indian traditions. By framing her individual experience in the larger context of Indian cultural mores, the story uses Shaila's personal struggle to free herself from her the crippling memories of her past life to symbolize a break from oppressive cultural traditions, particularly those that constrain women. The stagnant life of self-abnegation and mournful clinging to memories is the expected behavior of an Indian widow. By refusing to give in to this stultifying tradition, Shaila frees her personal spirit, but also symbolically rejects oppressive and outdated cultural mores. The association of a certain kind of "Indian-ness" with personal oppression is highlighted by Shaila's grandmother's lifetime of "mindless mortification." Kusum follows in this tradition, neglecting the living (both Kusum and Shaila's grandmother forsake their daughters) in order to choose a life of self-denial and personal repression. Shaila is "trapped between two modes of knowledge" but her ultimate return to Canada and dropping of the symbolic "package" implies that she has rejected personal stagnation and the patriarchal Indian traditions associated with it.

Point of View

The perspective in "The Management of Grief" is Shaila's and allows the reader to understand the world as she sees it. This narration may be called "third person limited" as the reader is privy to Shaila's deepest thoughts but does not have access to any other character's thoughts. The intimate revelation of thought and motive provides justification for Shaila's judgment of people and events. For instance, when Shaila tells Kusum that she is "running away" by going back to India to follow a religious life of mourning, we understand Shaila's logic from her description of the "mindless mortification" of her grandmother.

But this point of view has its limitations also. While it allows the reader to identify closely with, or reject, the main character, it flattens the point of view of the other characters. Kusum, for example, explains that going back to India will help her find "inner peace," but the reader is not given any way to understand her logic, only Shaila's rejection of it. In this way, limited third person narration can obscure opposing views, depriving the reader of alternate interpretations of events.

Narrative Tone: Understatement and Detachment

The tone of the story's third person narration can be described as melancholy and subtle. While the story has great emotional impact, that impact works through *understatement* and *detachment*. Shaila's account is almost journalistic in tone, neutrally reporting events. But the weightiness of tragedy behind the narration belies Shaila's unaffected tone. The poignancy of the story is derived not from any outright declarations of misery, but from the readers' recognition of Shaila's voice as speaking from a tenuous, shell-shocked calm.

Understated tones can give increased credibility to opinions or social critiques. Consider, for instance, testimonies of individuals convinced of government conspiracy or alien invasions. Accounts spoken in calm and rational tones tend to be more believable than emotional, raving harangues that make the speaker look unreliable because of instability. Compare headlines in tabloids that shout excited claims, "Woman Gives Birth to Ape!" versus matter-of-fact headlines in respected newspapers that report "Scientists Combine Primate and Human DNA." Thus, when Shaila softly comments that the Canadian government is mishandling the investigation, or that the reason that the crash is not well broadcast is "we're [Indian Canadians] not that important," her criticisms of mainstream attitudes are not likely to be dismissed as the rants of a radical political agitator. Her controlled attitude offers an interesting contrast to the agitated and violent behavior of the terrorists who are rumored to be responsible for the crash. Shaila's only overt display of emotion is at the airport when she calls the customs official a "bastard." But she herself is surprised at her uncharacteristic outburst and, while not wholly regretting it, ponders it as indicative of a deep change.

Similarly, a detached tone can give the narrative voice greater credibility in describing volatile, politically charged events. Shaila's detached tone is especially effective because she maintains an emotional distance in the face of a devastating personal loss. Importantly, Shaila's calm is only a mask for the "screaming" inside. On the other hand, Shaila's detached attitude may be construed as callousness; Shaila comments to Judith that some of the "hysterical Indians" are appalled by her lack of outward emotion.

Historical Context

Air India Flight 182 and Khalistan

"The Management of Grief" dramatizes the complex emotional response of those affected by the crash of Air India Flight 182 on June 12, 1985. All 329 passengers and crew members on board were killed when a bomb in the front luggage compartment exploded, hurtling the plane into the North Atlantic ocean, 110 miles southwest of Ireland's coast. The flight was headed to New Delhi and Bombay and had departed from Toronto and Montreal.

Investigations have suggested that the bomb was planted by a Canadian based Khalistani network devoted to their kinsmen's historical struggle to secede from India. Khalistanis are a sect of Sikhs, one of the three major religious groups of India, along with Hindus and Muslims. These religious groups live in varying degrees of harmony and contention, often sharing spoken language and elements of culture, but also engaging in violent confrontations over religious differences.

In 1947 the British partitioned the Indian subcontinent into India and Pakistan to give Muslims their own country (Pakistan). Having closer relations to Hindus than Muslims, most Sikhs in the new Pakistan migrated to the Indian side of the border after the partition. A large community of Sikhs occupy Punjab, an Indian state bordering Pakistan on the northwest. Sikh movements for independence have been ongoing since the 19th

century, but it was in 1971 that the name "Khalistan," based on the Punjabi word *khalsa* meaning "pure," was created to invoke a separate Sikh state. Its founder, Dr. Jagjit Singh Chauhan, drew up elaborate maps of the imagined country, appropriating much of Punjab; he issued passports and currency and established legislative bodies like the "Khalistan House" and the "Council of Khalistan."

Except for a few militant supporters, "Khalistan" was not taken seriously until Indira Gandhi's raid on the Golden Temple, a Sikh shrine and administrative site, June 4-7, 1984. Under increasing tensions and the military buildup of the Golden Temple, Mrs. Gandhi ordered its "extirpation." At least 2700 people, mostly Sikhs, were killed in the massacre, including the Sikh leader and priest, Jarnail Singh Ghindranwale. Mrs. Gandhi was assassinated by her Sikh bodyguards a few months later. The devastating events brought many moderate Sikhs into the radical Khalistani militant cause. The bombing of Flight 182 is thought to have been planned as a one year anniversary memorialization of the Golden Temple massacre. It is important to emphasize that not all Sikhs support the creation of Khalistan, nor do they participate or condone the often violent measures employed by Khalistani groups. After the discovery of Khalistani involvement in the bombing, many Sikhs dissociated themselves from the Khalistani movement.

Khalistanis in Canada

The Air India bombing and the related explosion at Tokyo's Narita Airport (a bomb planted in CP Air Flight 003 prematurely exploded in the baggage handling section, killing two baggage handlers and injuring four) were traced to a Khalistani fundamentalist living in Duncan, British Columbia, Inderjit Singh Reyat. On February 5, 1988, eight charges were brought against him, mostly related to the Narita bombing. Singh was being closely monitored by the CSIS (Canadian Security Intelligence Service, the Canadian equivalent of the FBI) and was spotted in early June of 1984 testing explosives off a highway in Duncan, British Columbia. Singh was associated with the Babar Khalsa ("Pure Tigers"), a militant North American Khalistani cell. In 1991 he was convicted of manslaughter for the Narita bombing.

In *The Sorrow and the Terror*, Mukherjee and Blaise note that religious-political commitment is

Compare & Contrast

- **1970:** 13% of Canadians are bilingual in English in French.

   1991: After $ 2.5 billion is spent to promote bilingualism, as part of the larger effort to support multiculturalism, there is only a 3% increase in English and French bilinguals.

- **1971:** Prime Minster Pierre Trudeau enacts the Act of the Preservation and Enhancement of Multiculturalism in Canada, popularly known as the Canadian Multiculturalism Act.

   1990s: The Canadian Council of Christians and Jews conducts a public opinion poll on the perception of multiculturalism. Their report, published in the December 14, 1993 *The Globe and the Mail*, is headlined "Canadians Want Mosaic to Melt . . . Respondents believe immigrants should adopt Canada's values." The report states that Canadians are becoming "increasingly intolerant" of ethnic groups' demands and favor a "homogenization" of Canadian society. In 1992, the federal government conducts its own opinion poll, reporting that 46% of polled Toronto residents felt that there were too many "visible minorities" in the city, particularly Arabs, blacks, and Asians. In 1994, the federal government conducts another opinion poll which reports a 21% increase in immigrant intolerance. Now, 67% of polled Toronto residents complain that there are too many immigrants in the city, which in 1994 had a 38% immigrant population, the largest in Canada.

- **1914:** The *Komagata Maru* is detained and quarantined in a Vancouver port. Of the 376 passengers on board, all from Asia and many of Sikh background, only 22 are allowed to land. The rest are rejected on grounds of possible contagion. In an attempt to get its passengers off board, the ship remains docked for two months, during which time it is refused the transmission of food, water, passengers, and garbage. One young male Sikh is removed from the ship and presented as a "test case" for eligibility for Canadian entry. The courts reject him and the *Komagata Maru* is ordered to return to Asia.

   1930s: Canada charges standard landing fees of $25 - $50 to Americans, depending on whether they are black or white, while Asians are charged "head taxes" of $200 to $250.

   1993: Herbert Grubel, a member of the conservative Reform Party and Professor of Economics at Simon Fraser University, declares new immigrants are a burden to Canadian society (reported in the October 15, 1993 *The Globe and the Mail*). John Tillman, also a member of the Reform Party, calls women and minority groups "parasites of society" (*The Globe and Mail*, October 29, 1993).

- **1986:** Employment Equity Act enacted in Canada. Sets up quotas to increase employment of women, aborigines, visible minorities, and the disabled in federal jobs.

   1993: *Job Mart*, an Ontario Public Service employment listing, posts an ad that reads: "The competition is limited to the following employment equity designation groups: aboriginal peoples, francophones, persons with disabilities, racial minorities and women." Political groups are outraged at this blatant expression of "reverse" discrimination.

---

often more fervent in countries of emigration than in India itself. In fact, they interpret the political activism that led to the Flight 182 bombing as having been fostered entirely on Canadian soil. Mukherjee and Blaise attribute the radical Khalistani presence to the structure of Canadian immigration law in the 60s and 70s, which engendered Sikh communities of working class background concentrated in British Columbia. In contrast, Hindu emigration was Ontario-centered and generally constituted by the professional-managerial class. These class differences and the glaring material discrepancies between Hindu and Sikh in the "new world" fueled their tradition of enmity. Mukherjee and Blaise suggest that Canadian Khalistani leaders prey on financially and socially struggling immigrants, offering them a sense of belonging and strong leadership, thereby redirecting their frustrations over Canadian social inequalities to their Indian and Indian Canadian countrymen. They also appeal to second-generation immigrants who perhaps have never been to India, but nurse romantic fantasies about Sikh independence.

The leadership of Sikh groups in Canada consists of middle-class, professional "family men." One interviewed Khalistani leader in New York, who was making a six figure income, told Mukherjee and Blaise: "Six days a week I work for Reagan [this was 1988]. Seventh day, for Khalistan." Another leader invited them to his comfortable suburban home and introduced them to his well-adapted children, who were probably unaware that their father was quite literally a "weekend warrior." At the time of the bombing, there were several prominent Sikh organizations in North America dedicated to an independent Sikh nation, not all of which employed terrorist tactics: the World Sikh Organization (WSO - members are usually middle-class professionals), Khalistan Youth (a moderate group that disbanded in 1986 to protest other groups' endorsement of violence), the International Sikh Youth Federation (ISYF) and Babar Khalsa (both groups have slightly different political and religious ideals, but both are committed to violence). Competition for prestige and money among these groups often exacerbates violent actions.

Critical Overview

"The Management of Grief" was virtually universally acclaimed in North America. It is the poignant, closing story of Mukherjee's 1988 collection *The Middleman and Other Stories*, which won the National Book Critics Circle Award for fiction that year. Not all the stories in *The Middleman* received unmitigated praise; one reviewer disdained the collection's overall obsession with "sleaze spiced with

violence" (Gillian Tindall in "East Meets West and Writes It" in *The Times*, April 26, 1990). Mukherjee and her supporters respond that such "unsavory" events and topics are the reality of North American immigrants. They praise Mukherjee for having the courage to honestly represent such realities in all their raw brutality.

In *Middleman*, Mukherjee writes from the point of view of several ethnicities: Vietnamese, Caribbean, Afghanistani, and Phillipino, to name a few. Johnathan Raban writes in the June 19th, 1988 *New York Times Book Review*, that these immigrants explode stereotypes; they are "not tired, huddled or even poor." In contrast, they are daring and full of bravado, operating small businesses, legal and illegal, or jetsetting on American Express cards. Though Mukherjee claims affinity with writers like Bernard Malamud, Raban insightfully notes that her immigrants are not the "introspective and overmothered sons of the ghetto." Their "lives are too urgent and mobile" to be nostalgic for a lost "home" and "they hit the page in full flight, and ... move through the stories as they move through the world, at speed, with the reader straining to keep up with them." Despite the often less than perfect outcomes of these protagonists' lives, many ending in violence and murder, "[e]very story ends on a new point of departure. People are last seen walking though an open door ..."

"The Management of Grief" is different in tone from the majority of stories in *Middleman*. It is somber, understated and melancholy, but in accordance with Raban's analysis, closes on the optimistic note of an "open door," however bittersweet. Consistent with Mukherjee's preference for America's "melting pot" ideal over the Canadian "mosaic," the story ends on a note of productive and progressive adaptation, a life of dynamic combination of "old" and "new" cultures. Shaila's hope-filled choice at the end of the story is contrasted with those of others who find comfort in reverting back to "Indian-ness" in their time of crisis.

The story was also praised for highlighting and memorializing the effects of the Air India Flight 182 crash. "The Management of Grief" was the offspring of her non-fiction account of the crash, *The Sorrow and the Terror* (1987), co-authored with husband, Clark Blaise. In both works, Mukherjee criticizes the Canadian government's handling of the event, connecting their attitude of

Robot submersible SCARAB II retrieved Air India flight 182's cockpit voice recorder from a depth of 6,700 feet of water in the Atlantic Ocean.

negligence and dismissal to the national policy of multiculturalism. This policy, Mukherjee argues, encouraged the nation to see the crash as an ''Indian'' event, inextricable from the exotic machinations of terrorism, when over 90% of the passengers were Canadian citizens. This kind of nationally sanctioned compartmentalizing of people by race is exemplified in the figure of Judith Templeton.

The ''open door'' Mukherjee supports in this and the other stories of *Middleman* implicitly expresses an assimilationist ideal. While this word often has the negative connotations of mimicry and

cultural betrayal, Mukherjee is more concerned with assimilation's positive aspects, urging immigrants to be creatively adaptive and resilient in their new environment. They have, after all, left a country for a chance to change and transform, not to stagnate in familiar modes of behavior. She contrasts her resilient, dynamic immigrants with expatriates who, with psychological and political ties to the ''homeland,'' pine for an impossible and romanticized image of ''home.'' As she writes in the introduction to *Darkness*, ''Indianness is now metaphor.'' She herself had fashioned her identity as an expatriate during her years in Canada (1966-1980) and did not fully appreciate and embrace the "exuberance" of immigration until she left the "mosaic" for America's "melting pot."

But while new worlds force a change on its immigrants, these immigrants also engender transformations in mainstream culture. As Mukherjee comments in a 1989 interview with *The Iowa Review*, the relationship between the immigrant and her new country is like "two-way traffic." Though she has lived a decade in Canada and continues to be concerned with Canadian topics, she has settled in America, moving to New York in 1980. Having declared American citizenship, she considers herself not as an ethnic writing about ethnic characters, but as an American writing about Americans.

Mukherjee has been criticized for what are perceived to be regressive ideas about gender. She was sharply criticized by *Ms.* magazine in their review of *Wife* (1975) for its representation of women as submissive. Mukherjee wryly remembers a line from the review: "*Ms.* magazine had a review which said, 'Some books can be allowed to die, but others have to be killed'" (from 1989 *Iowa Review* interview). *Jasmine* (1989), a novel developed from the short story of the same name in "Middleman" was similarly criticized because the main character, "Jasmine," seems only to be able to find her identity through a series of husbands or live-in lovers. However, Mukherjee counters that her characters are not mere mouthpieces of feminist theory. In fact, they are excluded by color and class from the white, middle-class dominated feminist movement. Instead, she portrays these immigrant women's "in-between" realities that may well disturb the privileged feminist theorists pontificating from their sheltered university positions. Mukherjee has vocally criticized "feminist imperialists" who mandate how "third world" women should behave. She points out in the *Iowa Review* interview that the feminism "being offered by the *Ms.* magazines are not at all appropriate [for women of color and poor women]; they just don't work in their lives, they don't ring true for their psychologies." Fakrul Alam paraphrases Mukherjee in a 1990 interview: "She claims that she would much rather show them [women] in the process of acquiring the power that would enable them to control their fates than make them mouthpieces of white, upper-class feminist rhetoric."

Criticism

Yoonmee Chang

Yoonmee Chang is a Ph.D. candidate in the English Department at the University of Pennsylvania. She is currently working on her dissertation, which explores class and labor issues in Asian American literature. In the following essay, she interprets Mukherjee's story as part of a critique of Canada's controversial policy of multiculturalism.

"Multiculturalism?" is Shaila's brief and somewhat enigmatic response to Judith Templeton's introduction in Bharati Mukherjee's "The Management of Grief." Judith is the social worker sent by the Ontario government to "reach out" to the families of the victims of Air India Flight 182. She enlists Shaila to give the "right human touch" to her work, in other words, to act as the cultural liaison between a Euro-Canadian government and its ethnic citizens. Shaila's response indicates that Judith's work is partially decreed by the national Ministry of Multiculturalism or Ontario's provincial equivalent. Enacted in 1971, by Prime Minster Pierre Trudeau, the Canadian Multiculturalism Act announced:

> It is hereby declared to be the policy of the Government of Canada to . . . recognize and promote the understanding that multiculturalism reflects the cultural and racial diversity of Canadian society and acknowledges the freedom of all members of Canadian society to preserve, enhance and share their cultural heritage. (quoted from Neil Bissoondath, *Selling Illusions: The Cult of Multiculturalism in Canada*, 1994)

The non-specific yet self-righteously benevolent language obscures the political motivations behind the act (namely appeasing the secession oriented Quebecois) and makes it a flexible, easy to manipulate tool in political battles that hinge on varying interpretations of the general language. Not surprisingly then, the Multiculturalism Act has proliferated, rather than resolved, a phalanx of petty political-cultural battles. For instance, in 1990, a group of outraged RCMPs (Royal Canadian Mounted Police) presented a 210,000 name petition to their Commissioner for allowing Sikh members to wear turbans on duty. The doctrine of multiculturalism plays a contradictory and central role in this conflict: does it support the Sikhs officers' right "to preserve, enhance and share their cultural heritage," or can it be invoked to protect non-Sikhs' own "freedom of religion." The vexed answer to both questions is "yes." This is just one of the

What Do I Read Next?

- *Darkness* (1985) by Bharati Mukherjee is Mukherjee's first collection of short stories. It includes an interesting introduction by the author sketching out her conception of ''immigrant'' versus ''expatriate.''

- *Jasmine* (1989) by Bharati Mukherjee is an outgrowth of the short story ''Jasmine'' in *The Middleman and Other Stories*. The story of a young woman who immigrates to America after her husband is killed by political terrorism in India. She goes through an agonizing but ultimately fulfilling process of personal development as evinced by her name changes from the dense, unpronounceable ''Jyoti'' to the spontaneous and casual ''Jas'' and finally to the stable midwestern, ''Jane Ripplemeyer.''

- *Junglee Girl* (1995) by Ginu Kamani is a collection of short stories about the hold of oppressive Indian traditions on young women's awakening sexuality. ''Junglee'' is derived from the Sanskrit root ''jungle'' and is often used as an epithet to describe a reckless and uncontrollable woman. The work also touches upon intra-ethnic tensions among Indians.

- *Leave it to Me* (1997) by Bharati Mukherjee is Mukherjee's latest novel. His work heavily explores the theme of violence, which Mukherjee has commented is central and necessary to an immigrant's experience, whether it be physical or psychological.

- *Masala* (1993) directed by Srinivas Krishna is a bleakly humorous film account of the effects of the Air India bombing on a young man, Krishna, who has lost his entire family in the crash. Humorously criticizes Canada's clumsy policy of multiculturalism stereotypical image of Sikhs as violent terrorists.

- *Of Customs and Excise* (1991) by Rachna Mara is a piece of short fiction exploring the conflict between rapidly westernizing second-generation children and their tradition-holding parents. Focuses on the cultural oppression of women.

- *Selling Illusions* (1994) by Neil Bissoondath is a personal critique of Canada's official policy of multiculturalism. Novel writer Bissoondath argues in the same vein as Mukherjee that multiculturalism creates ethnic ghettoes, political and social divisiveness and a strata of second-class citizens.

---

inadequacies of the ambiguous policy. A survey of the recent conflicts it has engendered reveals it as Canada's Frankenstein. Novelist Neil Bissoondath writes: ''As a political statement it [the 1971 Multiculturalism Act] is disarming, as a philosophical statement almost naive with generosity. Attractive sentiments liberally dispensed — but where, in the end do they lead?'' (*Selling Illusions*).

The Air India crash brought the racialized structure of Canada's social, political and economic structures into sharp relief. Shortly after learning of the tragedy, the then Prime Minister, Brian Mulroney, sent condolences to the Prime Minister of India at the time, Rajiv Gandhi. As the majority of the passengers on the Delhi and Bombay bound plane were Canadian citizens of South Asian ancestry, this action was, on the one hand, a compassionate cross-cultural gesture. But in light of the subsequent delayed and lackadaisical Canadian investigation, the gesture took on a politically charged meaning. It soon became all too clear that Canadian leadership, despite the Canadian citizenship of the victims, considered the crash an ''Indian'' event.

As such, it was not worthy of the sincerest efforts or dedicated resources of the federal government. The bombing remained unresolved for 12 years, during which time more than 100 tapes of evidence were ''accidentally'' destroyed or lost

---

> A dominant theme in her
> work is the criticism of such
> immigrants who suffer
> arduous and often violent
> journeys into America or
> Canada, only to settle in
> isolated, insulated ethnic
> ghettoes where opportunities
> are as narrow as in the
> 'homeland' they left."

(according to the *The Toronto Star*, June 5, 1995). The government refused persistent demands for a public inquiry, claiming that it would interfere with the criminal investigation, and conceded in 1991 to an internal inquiry in the CSIS's (Canadian Security Intelligence Service) botched procedures. A leading suspect, Talwinder Singh Parmar, was not named until ten years after the crash and at that time, he had been dead for nearly three years. Yet the CSIS had been tracking Parmar, a leader of a Canadian Khalistani radical cell, the Babar Khalsa ("Pure Tigers"), for years. In fact they were monitoring him until six days before the bombing and even witnessed him detonating "test" bombs off a Vancouver highway with Inderjit Singh Reyat, a Barbar Khalsa associate, who was charged in 1991 with manslaughter for the related Narita Airport bombing. In 1995, the RCMP announced a $1 million reward for information leading to arrests in connection with the Air India bombing, but the action — "too little, too late" — was scorned as a clumsy, belated attempt to recognize the Canadian victims ten years after the fact. In 1997, the RCMP announced that it was about to charge six Khalistani terrorists for the bombing.

The tragedy is "unhoused" as Deborah Bowen writes in "Spaces of Translation" (*Ariel*, Vol. 28, No. 3, July, 1997). Mukherjee's non-fictional account of the crash, *The Sorrow and the Terror*, co-written with husband and Canadian citizen, Clark Blaise, poses the provocative question: "Why was the Canadian government slow to dedicate its political, social, and psychological resources to the crash that killed 280 Canadian citizens of South Indian ancestry?" Like Shaila's in "The Management of Grief," Mukherjee and Blaise's response is: "Multiculturalism."

Since multiculturalism encourages cultural practices to be "preserved" and "enhanced," Canadian immigrants encounter few incentives to transform their lives and identities. Under its rubric, various "ethnic-towns" have emerged (e.g. Chinatown, Sikh communities, Hindu communities). Today, an Indian can travel straight from Delhi to Vancouver or Toronto, and ensconce herself in one of the many Sikh or Hindu communities, depending on her affiliation, get a job in an Indian store or agency catering to Indians, continue to dress in Indian clothes, and have easy access to Indian groceries. All this without a drop of English. Mukherjee views this kind of immigrant life as cultural stagnation. A dominant theme in her work is the criticism of such immigrants who suffer arduous and often violent journeys into America or Canada, only to settle in isolated, insulated ethnic ghettoes where opportunities are as narrow as in the "homeland" they left. This is expressed in the repulsion Shaila feels when she visits the elderly Sikh couple with Judith. The apartment building is a veritable Indian and West Indian ghetto with a "sprinkling of Orientals." The women at the bus stop are all dressed in saris and the "ferocity of onions" which denote the "distinctive and immediate Indian-ness of frying ghee" makes Shaila uncomfortably aware that Canada and its multiculturalism is encouraging the wholesale transplant of "chunks" of India. One could argue that this enclave of Toronto "Indian-ness" is a felicitous manifestation of Canada's atmosphere of free cultural practice. But what to make of the poverty?

The dire reality of most ethnic "communities" is that they are poverty-laden, urban ghettoes. Despite the eye-candy they provide for tourists, the majority of residents in places like Chinatowns around the "western" world live alarmingly below the poverty line. The scope of this essay cannot address the forces that link spatial ethnic communities with poverty, but it is generally apparent that these communities and poverty are structurally linked, and that life in such ethnic ghettoes is severely delimited. While such "communities" can initially provide comfort, information, and networks to newly landed immigrants, the preservation of these spaces as proper, appropriate, and perhaps the only suitable habitation for ethnic immigrants perpetuates their ghettoization. With little incentive to learn English and adapt to mainstream cultural practices, immigrants who chose to "preserve" their culture in this way deprive themselves of the skills necessary to personal and professional advancement that often demands they step outside the ethnic ghetto. In the case of Canada, the government supports such ghettoization under the banner of multiculturalism, protecting these poverty and crime-stricken enclaves as "natural" "expressions" of culture.

By privileging the "there" over the "here," Canada, as a result, has become a land of "us" and various "thems," with the Euro-Canadian dominated political body still holding power. Moreover, the multiculturalist recognition of diverse cultural practices has provided a convenient excuse to deny protection to all its citizens, especially those of color. Mukherjee and Blaise charge that the government had deep and detailed knowledge of Khalistani terrorist activities in Canada, including Parmar and Reyat's "bomb practice" in Duncan, British Columbia, 19 days before the bombing. They accuse the Canadian government of dismissing the import of such information because Khalistani radicalism was after all, an "Indian" matter. And Indian matters are best settled in the Indian community along Indian rules.

An analogous case is invoked by Bissoondath in *Selling Illusions: The Cult of Multiculturalism in Canada* (1994). In 1994, Quebec judge, Raymonde Verreault, ruled a lightened sentence for a Muslim man charged with sexual assault (23 months in prison instead of the prosecution's requested four years). Over a period of two and a half years, the man repeatedly sodomized his eleven year old stepdaughter, refraining from vaginal intercourse to preserve her virginity, thereby keeping her eligible for marriage by traditional Muslim standards. The judge claimed that the man "spared" the young girl by respecting his cultural tenets and that these tenets must duly be respected and recognized by the Canadian court. As Bissoondath remarks, this reasoning is perverse and absurd. More disturbingly, it points up the deeply inimical potential of multiculturalism. The judge effectively deprives a segment of the Canadian population of the full protection of Canadian law on the basis of race and ethnicity while hiding under the supposedly humanistic policy of multiculturalism. Had the victim been a white girl, it would be difficult to imagine the judge favoring the Muslim man's cultural mores over the girl's personal right to protection under Canadian law. Along the same lines, had the victims of the Flight 182 been British or white Canadian, the

government response and investigation may have been more devoted. Mukherjee and Blaise argue that it is precisely this negligence of its minority citizens that made Canada the perfect incubator for radical Khalistani terrorism. Where else but Canada to develop and execute violent, political plans under the guise of "cultural practice"?

"The Management of Grief" critiques Canada's policy of multiculturalism and its invidious consequences in many ways: through Shaila's repulsion at the Indian ghetto she visits, as mentioned, the proliferation of Judith's insensitive and ignorant comments about her work with "them," and through the negative portrayal of Kusum's return to India. The measure of the characters' "Indian-ness" is adumbrated through their mourning style, or as the title suggests, how they manage their grief. Extreme and destructive "Indian-ness" is embodied by Shaila's grandmother. When her young husband died, she, at age sixteen, sequestered herself in mourning, denying all her personal needs like a proper Hindu widow. She even neglected to raise her infant daughter, who was consequently passed on to an uncle. Shaila's parents exhort her not to fall prey to a similar "mindless mortification." Kusum follows this path. After recovering her husband's body and taking it to India for burial, she embarks on a life of itinerant, religious asceticism, searching for the reincarnated faces of her lost ones. Like Shaila's grandmother, Kusum has abjured the living, similarly disregarding the needs of her surviving daughter, Pam. Shaila accuses her of "running away" and withdrawing from her daughter and the world. Importantly, Kusum's personal and psychological regression is paired with oppressive aspects of Indian culture. In this way, engagement in this kind of life-paralyzing mourning is metonymic of a similarly unproductive revival of traditional Indian ways that may have no bearing on an Indian immigrant's Canadian life.

Shaila, on the other hand, ultimately rejects such oppressive paralysis/Indian-ness, though it is a slow and painful process. Like Kusum, she returns to India to receive the succor of her "homeland." Her parents do not want her to follow the fate of her grandmother, but they are happy to have her stay in India to be coddled by their affection and luxuries. But Shaila recognizes that succumbing to such a lifestyle, however seductive, is neither recovery nor progress. She asks a vision of her husband: "*Shall I stay?*" He replies: "*What are you doing here? . . . You must finish alone what we started together.*" From this moment Shaila realizes that in order to recover a forward moving life, she must return to Canada. Implicit in this realization is that Canada, not India, is her homeland.

By rejecting a life of mind-numbing mourning, self-deprivation associated with oppressive aspects of "Indian-ness," Shaila gestures towards a transformative, productive vision of recovery and life. In the last line of the story, Shaila narrates that she has dropped a "package" and "started walking," ostensibly in a literal and symbolic new direction. If this direction is the opposite of Kusum and her grandmother's "mindless mortification"/retreat into Indian-ness, Shaila's life will likely favor negotiating the challenges of mainstream Canadian life, discarding the burden of a repressive, insular Indian one. Her choice to be Canadian Indian with a stress on the Canadian defies the national policy of multiculturalism which would remand their ethnics to psychological and geographical ghettoes.

It is possible to criticize Mukherjee and her characters as "assimilationist." Though this word is freighted with negative and troubling connotations, the cultural vision that Mukherjee supports does not necessarily require a wholesale abdication of one's ancestors' culture. It is important to note that she does not laud assimilation for its inherently superior qualities, but as a resistant alternative to the ghettoizing nature of multiculturalism. Assimilation is a remedy, not a final solution. In her introduction to *Darkness* (1985), Mukherjee writes that for years she haughtily considered herself an "expatriate," psychologically and politically connected to India, with Canada's multiculturalism feeding her attitude. But moving to America and experiencing its so-called "melting-pot" philosophy, she realized that immigration was "exuberance" and expatriation, a mere aloof and ironic defense mechanism. Thus to support "assimilation" is not to be a cultural traitor, but to refuse being cast as a racialized, second-class denizen of the ethnic ghetto, excluded from the white, mainstream structures which are the repositories of advancement and power. Assimilation is tactical. As Bissoondath writes: "My history, my past, my 'roots' — the people, places and events that have shaped me — are an integral part of myself. Just as no one can take them away, so I cannot rid myself of them. This does mean, though, that I must be their prisoner (*Selling Illusions*). On a general level, "The Management of Grief" uses the plane crash to symbolize the inevitably failed and destructive nature of trying to return to India. The survivors are resilient characters like Shaila or Kusum's daughter, Pam, who "survives" precisely because she prefers to stay in Canada rather than visit the mythic "homeland." Both Pam and Shaila's life as immigrants embracing the "new" world are by no means glamorous. Both have undergone severe emotional trauma and Pam is living on less than enviable means as a makeup counter salesperson. Their lives are merely dynamic, creatively adaptive and bittersweet.

Source: Yoonmee Chang, for *Short Stories for Students*, The Gale Group, 2000.

Diane Andrews Henningfeld

Diane Andrews Henningfeld is an associate professor at Adrian College. She holds a Ph.D. in literature and writes widely for educational publishers. In the following essay, she examines Mukherjee's use of contrasts and unbridgeable gaps in "The Management of Grief."

Bharati Mukherjee's short story, "The Management of Grief" serves as the final story in the 1989 collection *The Middleman and Other Stories*. Mukherjee won the National Book Critic Circle Award for fiction for this collection, and in 1989, the story appeared in *The Best American Short Stories, 1989*, edited by Margaret Atwood and series editor Shannon Ravenel. Critics have continued to review the collection favorably.

Jonathan Raban, for example, in *The New York Times Book Review*, June 19, 1988, writes that Mukherjee's "writing here is far quicker in tempo, more confident and more sly than it used to be." However, although many critics and scholars comment on the quality of the collection as a whole, and although they also investigate closely a number of the stories, few have written specifically on "The Management of Grief." It seems that most literary critics prefer to concentrate on stories that seem more characteristic of Mukherjee's work. Nevertheless, reviewers like Elizabeth Ward in the *Washington Post*, July 3, 1988, call "The Management of Grief" "a quietly stunning story. . . ."

"The Management of Grief" is the story of how one woman copes (and does not cope) with the deaths of her husband and two sons in an airplane crash. It seems apparent that Mukherjee developed the idea for this story while working on a nonfiction, book-length study of the 1985 Air India crash near Ireland, a book she co-authored with her husband Clark Blaise. On board the plane were hundreds of Indo-Canadians, traveling between Toronto and India. According to Ann Mandel in *The Dictionary of Literary Biography*, Mukherjee attributes the crash to ''[r]acism, prejudice and ethnic estrangements born of multicultural policy.'' Mukherjee blames the Canadian government in large part for its failure to address the issues of Sikh terrorism, leading to the planting of bombs in the Air India jetliner. Mandel further writes, ''Particularly moving are the portraits of those who died and of the other victims, those who still remember the dead and who now ask both for justice and for honor.'' Certainly, these portraits, shifted and fictionalized, find their way into ''The Management of Grief.''

The story, however, is more than a series of portraits. Mukherjee skillfully builds ''The Management of Grief'' on a series of contrasts and unbridgeable gaps. As Avrinda Sant-Wade and Karen Marguerite Radell assert in ''Refashioning the Self: Immigrant Women in Bharati Mukherjee's New World,'' ''Mukherjee weaves contradiction into the very fabric of the stories: positive assertions in interior monologues are undermined by negative visual images; the liberation of change is undermined by confusion or loss of identity; beauty is undermined by sadness.'' Through the protagonist Shaila Bhave, a member of the Toronto Indian community who loses her husband and her two sons in the crash, the reader stands poised between contradictions, balanced between two worlds. As Fakrul Alam suggests in his book *Bharati Mukherjee*, Shaila is a person in the middle, thematically linking the story to the other stories in the collection *The Middleman and Other Stories* .

Early in the story, Shaila reports on the scene in her house as members of the Indian community gather to receive news about the tragedy that has overtaken them. She tells the reader, ''Two radios are going in the dining room. They are tuned to different stations.'' This very early image helps to establish a sense of duality. Each radio reports the same event, but in different words. A listener would have to choose to listen to one radio or the other to make sense of the story being reported. The two radios together, their words out of synch with each other, produce meaningless noise. Shaila, numbed and distant from the event itself, finds herself unable to make sense of the tragedy. Instead, she seems to be trapped between the two radios, trapped between worlds.

Initially, it appears that the two worlds are India and Canada. Kusum's daughters Pam and her sister highlight the gap between the two. Pam, the older

> Of course, the greatest division of all in the story is the unbridgeable gap between the living and the dead."

sister, decides to stay in Canada for the summer, choosing to work at Wonderland (a Canadian amusement park) rather than visit her grandparents in Bombay. Pam ''dates Canadian boys and hangs out at the mall, shopping for tight sweaters.'' Her younger sister, on the other hand, chooses traditional Indian values and boards the ill-fated flight to Bombay with her father.

Likewise, Mukherjee emphasizes the contrast between Indian and Canadian culture through the introduction of the character Judith Templeton, the government social worker sent to help the Indians ''manage'' their grief. Templeton tries to recruit Shaila to help her with this task, placing Shaila in the middle between the government and her fellow immigrants. Mukherjee's portrayal of Judith Templeton slices to the heart of her own discontent with the Canadian's government failure to understand Indian culture. As Alam argues, ''Judith is basically well-meaning but ultimately ill-equipped to 'manage' the grief of the Indo-Canadian community because of the cultural distance separating her from them.'' By failing to recognize that Shaila's outward calm is a signal of internal upheaval, Judith reveals her own lack of understanding of the people she is trying to help. Her mistaken assumption that Shaila is managing well places Shaila in an impossible situation. Like the two radios, Indian and Canadian cultural assumptions play in Shaila's ears until she is unable to make sense of her own grief or her role in the healing process.

Another important dichotomy in the story is that between the genders. The men and the women handle their grief differently, with the women wishing that they could commit suicide and the men trying to provide explanations for the tragedy. In India, during the months following the crash, the men who have lost their wives find that their living relatives quickly line up new families for them: ''Already the widowers among us are being shown new bride candidates. They cannot resist the call of custom, the authority of their parents and older brothers. They must marry; it is the duty of a man to look after a wife." However, the women's families do not try to arrange marriages for them. As Shaila reports, "No one here thinks of arranging a husband for an unlucky widow."

Mukherjee also suggests that there are two radically different ways to respond to grief: a return to life, or a retirement from life. Dr. Ranganathan, an engineer who has resisted his relatives' efforts to remarry him, represents the gradual, active return to life. At first, this return to life manifests itself by a change in jobs, although he is still unable to change his home. Eventually, he not only changes jobs and homes, he changes careers, and moves from Montreal to Texas to start life in a place "where no one knows his story." Shaila's neighbor Kusum, on the other hand, represents the other response to grief. She leaves Toronto and moves to an ashram, or retreat, in India. She relies on a swami for advice and counsel. Through her retreat from the world, Kusum finds serenity. She is in contact with her dead husband and believes that she hears her daughter singing while on a pilgrimage. Again, Mukherjee places Shaila in the middle of these two extreme positions. Shaila returns to Toronto, determined to do as the spirit of her husband has instructed her: "You must finish alone what we started together." Although she actively attempts to return to life by writing letters to "the editors of local papers and to members of Parliament" so that they will acknowledge that the crash was an act of terrorism, at the same time, she retreats from active life, shunning Judith Templeton and living alone with the memories of the dead.

Of course, the greatest division of all in the story is the unbridgeable gap between the living and the dead. Throughout the story, Mukherjee contrasts the living with the dead. In the second paragraph of the story, Mukherjee introduces Dr. Sharma's wife, "monstrously pregnant," who is the mother of four boys. One of the boys walks through the scene at this moment and Shaila recognizes him by his "domed and dented forehead." Such reference reminds readers that Shaila's boys, too, must have literally "dented foreheads," the result of the trauma of the crash. Further, the picture Shaila keeps in her mind of her boys and her husband, as they were alive, prevents her from identifying their bodies when presented with the bloated corpses of several victims. Readers are unable to determine if the corpses truly are Shaila's sons. Does her need to think of them as living

prevent her from recognizing their corpses, or are these not her sons at all, as she asserts?

Shaila again finds herself suspended between two worlds, the world of the living and the world of the dead, not knowing how to join either fully. "I am trapped between two modes of knowledge," she says. "At thirty-six, I am too old to start over and too young to give up. Like my husband's spirit, I flutter between worlds." While Kusum learns to live with her grief by identifying with the dead, and Dr. Ranganathan by identifying with the living, Shaila tells the reader, "I wait, I listen, and I pray, but Vikram has not returned to me. The voices and the shapes and the nights filled with visions ended abruptly several weeks ago." This suggests that Shaila has been occupying the land of the living during the day while seeking the land of the dead at night. Even her downtown apartment locates Shaila in the middle, "equidistant from the Ontario Houses of Parliament and the University of Toronto."

As the story closes, Shaila reports, "I heard the voices of my family one last time. *Your time has come*, they said. *Go, be brave.*" Shaila's response is to begin walking. Although the ending is inconclusive because neither Shaila nor the reader know where she is heading, it is at least a sign that she is moving from the middle. The closing words of the story are also the closing words of the collection: "I do not know which direction I will take. I dropped the package on a park bench and started walking." These words leave the reader with a sense of movement, a sense that Shaila no longer stands motionless and trapped between worlds, but rather walks toward her unknown future, finishing what she and her husband started in a new land, a new world.

Source: Diane Andrews Henningfeld, for *Short Stories for Students*, The Gale Group, 2000.

Deborah Bowen

In the following essay, Bowen discusses Mukherjee's depiction of how the various cultural groups in "The Management of Grief" deal with tragic loss, "translating" grief according to their cultural experience.

The word "translation" comes, etymologically, from the Latin for "bearing across." Having been borne across the world, we are translated men. It is normally supposed that something always gets lost in translation; I cling, obstinately, to the notion that something can also be gained. SALMAN RUSHDIE, *Imaginary Homelands*

In the final article of the special January 1995 issue of *PMLA* on "Colonialism and the Postcolonial Condition," Satya Mohanty observes that "vital cross-cultural interchange depends on the belief that we share a 'world' (no matter how partially) with the other culture, a world whose causal relevance is not purely intracultural." There are occasions on which such a shared world is traumatically imposed upon diverse groups of people. If ever there were an occasion for a human compassion that transcends boundaries of race and culture in the need for vital cross-cultural interchange, the Air India crash of 1985 surely must have been it—an occasion when the attempt to be "borne across" the world was itself "translated" in a particularly macabre way. During the spring and summer of 1995, the anniversary of this disaster brought it back into the Canadian news, specifically because the belief that "its causal relevance [was] not purely intracultural" had led some people to continue to fight for a Royal Commission of Inquiry into an unresolved crime.

The initial tragedy of the plane's destruction was, in the eyes of many, compounded by the fact that the Canadian government treated the event precisely as an Indian intracultural tragedy, not immediately relevant to the ordinary Canadian citizen. Bharati Mukherjee and her husband Clarke Blaise published a book about the disaster in 1987. They pointed out that over 90% of the passengers on the plane were Canadian citizens. They described the disaster as, politically, an "unhoused" tragedy, in that Canada wanted to see it as an Indian event, and India wanted to see it as an "overseas incident" that would not train an international spotlight on the escalated Sikh-Hindu conflicts in India. In the last sentence of that book, *The Sorrow and The Terrror*, one of the bereaved requests, "Mr. Clarke and Mrs. Mukherjee, tell the world how 329 innocent lives were lost and how the rest of us are slowly dying." Blaise and Mukherjee declare in their introduction that in researching the book they spoke with a wide range of people directly and indirectly involved with the tragedy; "mainly, however, we have visited the bereaved families and tried to see the disaster through their eyes" (xii). It was perhaps in order to manage the grief involved in such seeing that Mukherjee found it necessary to write not just *The Sorrow and The Terror* but also the short story "The Management of Grief," which appears in her 1988 collection *The Middleman.*

It is a story about the effects of the Air India disaster on Toronto's Indian community and specifically on the central character and narrator,

> **"**Shared ethnicity is in itself no guarantee of the presence of 'the right human touch.' In the story, the customs officer at Bombay airport, who is presumably Indian, is as obnoxious an example of petty officialdom as one might hope to avoid, and unlike Judith he is therefore treated to vociferous anger from Shaila."

Mrs. Shaila Bhave, who loses her husband and her two sons in the crash. Because she is rendered preternaturally calm by the shock, she is perceived by the government social worker, Judith Templeton, as "coping very well," and as "a pillar" of strength, who may be able to help as an intermediary—or, in official Ontario Ministry of Citizenship terms, a "cultural interpreter" —between the bereaved immigrant communities and the social service agencies, though of course she has had no training. Shaila wants to say to Judith but does not, "I wish I could scream, starve, walk into Lake Ontario, jump from a bridge." She tells us, "I am a freak. . . . This terrible calm will not go away." In fact, then, the "pillar" and the "temple" are both unstable; figured as tottering buildings in a collapsing of hierarchy, both women are initially beyond knowing what to do. Death is the great leveller, even of the social worker's neocolonial benevolence. "I have no experience with a tragedy of this scale," says Judith; and Shaila interjects, "Who could?" When Judith suggests that Shaila's apparent strength may be of practical help to others who are hysterical, Shaila responds. "By the standards of the people you call hysterical, I am behaving very oddly and very badly, Miss Templeton. . . . They would not see me as a model. I do not see myself as a model." Instead, she says, "Nothing I can do will make any difference. . . . We must all grieve in our own way."

Judith is caught between worlds; she does not know how to translate the grief she shares with Shaila and the Indian community into cultural specifics that will be acceptable to both Indian and Western modes of thought. Shaila is initially caught, too, between different impulses coming from different cultural models which she has internalized within herself. The question of how to effect moral agency while practising the acceptance of difference is in both instances a tricky one. Satya Mohanty addresses the question of the immobilizing effects of difference by proposing a revisionary universalist perspective. "Given the relativist view of pure difference, difference can never represent genuine cross-cultural disagreement about the way the world is or about the right course of action in a particular situation" because cultures are seen as "equal but irredeemably separate." Edward Said had already taken an overtly polemical stance against such separateness, at the end of *Culture and Imperialism:*

> No one today is purely *one* thing. . . . No one can deny the persisting continuities of long traditions, sustained habitations, national languages, and cultural geographies, but there seems no reason except fear and prejudice to keep insisting on their separation and distinctiveness, as if that was all human life was about. Survival in fact is about the connections between things.

But the practical question remains intransigent: how are such connections to be made?

Mohanty argues that "[g]enuine respect depends on a judgment based on understanding, arrived at through difficult epistemic and ethical negotiations"; otherwise, "the ascription of value (and of equality among cultures) is either meaningless or patronizing." Mohanty proposes what he calls a "post-positivist 'realism'" of socially negotiated knowledge, undergirded by a moral universalism: "Perhaps the most powerful modern philosophical ally of modern anticolonial struggles of all kinds is this universalist view that individual human worth is absolute; it cannot be traded away, and it does not exist in degrees." Such a universalist claim concerns a basic capacity for agency shared by all humans; it *invites* cultural articularization but does not *depend* upon it for support of the underlying claim, and thus provides "the strongest basis for the multiculturalist belief that other cultures need to be approached with the presumption of equal worth." Perhaps this is not to say more than Gayatri Spivak, quoting Derrida—"there are no rules but the old rules." But then, perhaps this is to say something quite momentous. Universalism has had a bad press, associated as it has been with a manipulative essentialism and the blindnesses of liberal humanism to inherent racism, sexism, paternalism, phallocentrism, Eurocentrism, and all those other distressing -isms from which we in the late-twentieth-century West are anxious to dissociate ourselves. But perhaps a universalist ethic always already underlies much of our ism-rejection: on what other basis do we respect difference? On what other basis do we assume worth?

In Mukherjee's story, the assumption of moral universalism is a necessary precursor to the problems of negotiating social knowledge. Judith wants to help exactly because she is presuming the equal human worth of the Indian bereaved. But Mukherjee addresses questions of cultural particularization head-on by showing how inadequately translatable are institutionalized expressions of concern: as Judith says to Shaila when she is trying to persuade her to help, "We have interpreters, but we don't always have the human touch, or maybe the right human touch." This distinction between "the human touch" and "the right human touch" is crucial: one is universal, the other particular. The grief is transcultural; the management of grief is not. Thus it is that grief shared rather than managed may have more chance of adequate translation.

Here is how the issue could be formulated: a shared world: the trauma of violent death; a universal: the experience of grief; a cultural, even intracultural particularization: grief "in our own way." For the bereaved relatives in Mukherjee's story, this grief is figured as "a long trip that we must all take." The story enacts a kind of diaspora through death, a doubling of cultural displacement for those immigrants whose chosen initial passage was to Canada, and who must now embark on a voyage out grimly parodic of those earlier "civilizing missions" of the colonizers, journeying first to Ireland, to identify the wreckage from the ocean, then to Bombay, to mourn and reassess in the mother-country, and thence back to step-mother Canada, to find another new identity.

Both in Mukherjee's story and in the non-fiction account of the tragedy, the people most able to connect viscerally with the grief of the bereaved are the Irish, off whose shores the plane went down. They have the quintessentially "human touch." They weep with the bereaved; strangers hug strangers in the street; once one mourner has picked flowers from a local garden to strew on the ocean, a newspaper article asks residents to please give flowers to any Indian person they meet. All this really happened. Such transcultural expressions of erapathetic connectedness, however impractical, construct an equal and opposite subjectivity; even the difference between the Eastern mode of management, the "duty to hope", and the Western, the spelling out of grim knowledge and the request to "try to adjust your memories", is rendered tolerable by grief so obviously felt and shared and by a compassionate regard for the privacy of pain. In fact Blaise and Mukherjee suggest in *The Sorrow and The Terror* that there may also have been a kind of cultural knowledge at work here, in that the Irish, as a chronically subalternized people who have first-hand experience of terrorism, may have been particularly sensitive to a tragedy like the Air India disaster.

The practical distinction between universal human emotions and their particular cultural manifestations seems to be one that a writer like Neil Bissoondath does not clearly draw, when he declares that "Culture, in its essentials, is about human values, and human values are exclusive to no race." The visceral connection made between the Irish and the Indians would seem to support Bissoondath's view. But Mukherjee does not allow the reader to be lulled into sentimentality by such a connection: she presents the reader also with the dissonance between Shaila and Judith. More useful here is Homi Bhabha's distinction between "the semblance and similitude of the symbols across diverse cultural experiences," including death, and "the social specificity of each of these productions of meaning." In Shaila and Judith, Mukherjee figures the problems of this social specificity: how does one translate even shared grief into practical action? What is more, this is a story in which the characters are not merely "shuttling between the old and the new world," as Mukherjee has remarked of her characters elsewhere. She does not allow the reader a straightforward binarism between Shaila and Judith; here there are also differences within the "old" culture—differences of sensibility and differences between different generations and belief-systems.

Shared ethnicity is in itself no guarantee of the presence of "the right human touch." In the story, the customs officer at Bombay airport, who is presumably Indian, is as obnoxious an example of petty officialdom as one might hope to avoid, and unlike Judith he is therefore treated to vociferous anger from Shaila. Even though "[o]nce upon a time we were well brought up women; we were dutiful wives who kept our heads veiled, our voices

shy and sweet", the universal human experience of grief can be so extreme as to free such a woman from the patriarchal customs of her culture into the beginnings of an effective moral agency. The women get the coffins through the customs, despite the official's officiousness. That is, grief neither shared nor decorously managed may itself translate into a power of cultural resistance.

Moreover, when Shaila finds herself "shuttling" between Indian and Western modes of managing grief, the sense of being "trapped between two modes of knowledge" is not unlike what she had experienced within her Indian upbringing, which had pitted the irrational faith of her grandmother against the nonsense rationalism of her mother. In Bombay after the rituals of death are over, Shaila struggles: "At thirty-six, I am too old to start over and too young to give up. Like my husband's spirit, I flutter between worlds." Shaila's response at this point is to make her journey one of "courting aphasia"—dancing, riding, playing bridge. She is in any case paradoxically "luckier" than some: because the bodies of her family did not surface from the wreckage, she is marked as *un*lucky, and therefore does not have parents arranging a new husband for her. In a wry reversal of patriarchal oppression, she has widowers, "substantial, educated, successful men of forty," phoning her and saying, "Save me. . . . My parents are arranging a marriage for me." Most will succumb, because "they cannot resist the call of custom" that decrees it is "the duty of a man to look after a wife." But Shaila returns to Canada alone: in the end, she is saved by faith—by visions and voices, by the irrational world of temple holy men and prophetic dreams.

"[O]n the third day of the sixth month into [her] odyssey, in an abandoned temple in a tiny Himalayan village," her husband appears to her and tells her two things: "You're beautiful," and "You must finish alone what we started together." Like other travellers, Shaila returns to her starting-place "translated" in more than physical being: she returns to Canada with "something . . . gained"—with a personal affirmation and a mission. It is through the universalizing power of grief that she experiences metaphysical intervention and the freedom to choose even between different Indian behaviors within her own cultural background. Thus in her translating and her translation, the narrator not only experiences the aporias inherent in attempts to communicate between cultures; she also recognizes the gaps in her own cultural constructedness. These gaps are traversed most powerfully in the story not by Mohanty's cognitive negotiations—Judith trying so hard to understand—but by the metaphysical "translations" of mystical experience: the voices and forms of the longed-for dead who comfort the living and direct them through their grief. This unapologetic introduction of the metaphysical is of course, on Mukherjee's part, in itself a "writing back" to the poststructuralist theorists of the West. Back in Canada, Shaila is surrounded by the spirits of her deceased family who, "like creatures in epics," have changed shapes and whose presence brings her both peace and rapture. But what is the shape of her mission?

Initially on her return she gets involved in trying to help Judith help the bereaved. She realizes that she has become Judith's confidante. As Judith's management skills lead her to compile lists of courses on bereavement, charts of how the relatives are progressing through the textbook stages of grief, lists of "cultural societies that need our help," Shaila tells her politely that she "has done impressive work." She goes with Judith to translate for her to an elderly Sikh couple who had been brought to Canada two weeks before their sons were killed in the crash, and who refuse to sign any of the papers which would secure them money, lodging, and utilities, because they are afraid, and proud. The interchange is laced with the ironies of half-translation, mistranslation, and non-translation. Because Shaila is Hindu and the couple are Sikh (something she, though not Judith, has recognized from their name), there are already unspoken stresses. Shaila stiffens involuntarily, and remembers "a time when we all trusted each other in this new country, it was only the new country we worried about." In Toronto as in India, Mukherjee explores the doublenesses and duplicities of intracultural differences. The Indian characters in Canada are united by their grief at the very moment that they are also divided by their fear and suspicion of those supposedly of their community who have caused that grief: Sikh extremists were likely responsible for the bombing. It is only when Shaila identifies herself to the Sikh couple as another of the bereaved, and not merely a translator, that real communication begins between them. The common reference provides a shared world; nevertheless, the cultural particularizations erect barriers, and those separating Judith from the Sikh couple are all but insuperable, because her neo-colonial expressions of concern inadvertently enact a recolonization. Shaila is drawn more to the Sikh couple's obstinate and impractical hopefulness

than to Judith's anxious and bureaucratic goodwill. After all, Shaila too has lost sons. After all, the Sikh couple too are managing their grief.

The scene is interwoven with Shaila's awareness of the difficulties of translation: "How do I tell Judith Templeton?" "I cannot tell her"; "I want to add"; "I wonder"; "I want to say"; "I try to explain." But in the end, reading without words the elderly Sikh couple's stubborn dignity, their determination to fulfil their cultural duty to hope, she asks to be let out of Judith's car on the way to the next appointment. Judith asks, "'Is there anything I said? Anything I did?' I could answer her suddenly in a dozen ways, but I choose not to. 'Shaila? Let's talk about it,' I hear, then slam the door." Words will not do. Words cannot enable the Sikh couple to appreciate Judith's concern; words here can construct only a kind of cultural enmeshment, *Judith*'s mode of managing grief. Mukherjee seems in this moment of decisive action to be making an equal and opposite point to that of Gayatri Spivak when she writes, "If the subaltern can speak, then, thank God, the subaltern is not a subaltern any more." Sometimes silence itself may be a choice, against both subalternity and forced assimilation, a kind of "claiming ownership of one's freed self," as Mohanty puts it. Hybridity is not of itself necessarily productive: Ella Shohat has distinguished between the hybridities of forced assimilation, internalized self-rejection, political co-optation, and social conformism, as well as creative transcendence. If, to use E.D. Blodgett's formulation, we posit translation as a threshold, a kind of "ur-language" or "langue" that is between languages, preventing assimilation while allowing for interpretation, then Shaila lives on this threshold in her dealings both with Judith and with the Sikh couple; and it is her choice to translate into silence.

In fact, the relationship to one's own language is also problematized in this story. One of Shaila's first responses to news of her husband's death is to lament that "I never once told him that I loved him" because she was so "well brought up." Her bereaved friend Kusum says, "It's all right. He knew. My husband knew. They felt it. Modern young girls have to say it because what they feel is fake." This distinction between words and feelings reinforces the notion of a prelinguistic realm of universal capacities. But later in Ireland Shaila lets drift on the water a poem she has written for her husband: "Finally he'll know my feelings for him." Not that her feelings are fake; rather that words are a survival technique, a management tool for her, just as, at the beginning of the story, the woman who got the first news of the crash must tell her story "again and again." After the second diaspora and return, Dr. Ranganathan, alone in Montreal, having lost his whole huge family, calls Shaila twice a week as one of his new relatives: "We've been melted down and recast as a new tribe" in which "[t]alk is all we have." Eventually he accepts "an academic position in Texas where no one knows his story and he has vowed not to tell it. He calls me now," says Shaila, "once a week." Inside the tribe, he chooses speech, outside, silence; each is a means of survival, a mode of agency.

At the end of the story, Shaila's voyage is still incomplete. She accepts the mission to "go, be brave," received through the final message of the other-worldly voices of her dead family; she "drop[s] [her] package on a park bench and start[s] walking"; but she tells us that "I do not know where this voyage I have begun will end. I do not know which direction I will take." The story is encircled in unknowing: it opens, "A woman I don't know is boiling tea the Indian way in my kitchen. There are a lot of women I don't know in my kitchen, whispering, and moving tactfully." Where that first unknowing conveyed shock and repressed hysteria, the last unknowing figures acceptance and reconstruction, another journey, willingly undertaken beyond the pages of the story. Acceptance and reconstruction: Judith would recognize these words, the last two stages of her textbook description of the management of grief. She might not, however, recognize their manifestation in Shaila, who hears voices, who drops packages, for whom grief is ultimately managed more through *meta*physical translations than physical ones. True, she has sold her pink house for four times what she and her husband had paid for it; she has taken a small apartment downtown; she has plenty of money from her husband's careful investments; she is even looking for a charity to support. In Western terms, it seems that she has managed her grief very well. But this alone would be what Bhabha calls colonial mimicry; it is not where the story ends.

Grief must in the end also manage Shaila—almost, stage-manage her. If grief shared rather than managed is the most effectively translated, it is perhaps appropriate to point to the doubleness of Mukherjee's title. "The Management of Grief" can mean "how people manage grief," or "how grief manages people"—in other words, "grief" in this phrase can be understood as grammatical object or subject of the action of managing. Moreover, the phrase can be read as what Roland Barthes calls a "structure of jointed predication" in which the translator figures as the fulcrum, the pre (and post) position "of." This little word itself contains and signifies the space of translation, whose function is to hold substantive concepts together, a liminal space, an almost unnoticed minimal word signifying possession—in this case, possession of the ability to construct the self.

Thus when Shaila hears the voices of her family giving her her mission, "I dropped the package on a park bench and started walking." Interpreting for propositional meaning, a reader might wonder if she is going mad. If so, what happens now? Does she get home for supper? If not, who finds her? Looking for symbolic meaning, a reader might think that it is now that the most personal journey begins, in privacy and solitude. But a postcolonial reading is likely to note the performative structure of the text, and to recognize the tension between these two interpretations—the cognitive and the phantasmatic, the rational and the intuitive—as precisely that experienced both interculturally and intraculturally by Shaila as translator throughout the story. We know that she got back to her apartment: the story is composed in such a way that she is telling us about the final moment of insight a week after it happened. She is herself the fulcrum, the translator and the translation, undoing the traditional oppositions between West and East, reason and faith, physical and metaphysical. She is settled in a good apartment, and she walks off the page. Nor is this merely a West-East difference of response: Shaila's mother and grandmother themselves represented this same difference. Shaila is a figure for productive cultural hybridity. Standing on the translator's threshold, looking in both directions, she comes to possess the power to understand her liminality as itself a space for "effective (moral) agency" (Mohanty).

The phrase "space of translation" is Bhabha's: in discussing the language of critique, he suggests that such language is effective

> to the extent to which it overcomes the given grounds of opposition and opens up a space of "translation": a place of hybridity, figuratively speaking, where the construction of a political object that is new, neither the one nor the other, properly alienates our political expectations, and changes, as it must, the very forms of our recognition of the "moment" of politics.

In Mukherjee's story, Shaila journeys into figuring just such a language of critique, just such a place of hybridity, and she stands at a new and unexpected political "moment": the immigrant translator who learns how to be translated, how to inhabit the productivity of the threshold. The package that she drops stands synechdochally for the weight both of her grief and of her translator's role. Having journeyed thus far in her odyssey, she leaves behind the weight of translating as she steps beyond the narrative into her own translation: she "started walking." In moving from translator to translation she breaks open the management of grief, each part of the substantive proposition falling away from her because the preposition has taken upon itself its own self-possession. Through this figure, Mukherjee suggests that, despite the cultural misunderstandings inescapably exposed in a transcultural tragedy, the experience of being "borne across"—or through—grief itself opens up a space of translation in which, as Salman Rushdie hopes, "something can also be gained": Shaila deconstructs apparently opposing modes of knowledge into a productive hybridity without denying either of them. Shaila thus becomes in herself an embodiment of Mohanty's "understanding, arrived at through difficult epistemic and ethical negotiations." No longer "fluttering between worlds," Shaila reinscribes herself through self-translation, and possesses her own space beyond the page, outside the sentence, a space of moral agency where the place of both words and silences is a chosen one.

Mukherjee has written of "colonial writers" like herself that "[h]istory forced us to see ourselves as both the 'we' and the 'other,'" and that this kind of training has enabled her to inhabit a "fluid set of identities denied to most of my mainstream American counterparts." In a similar way, she chooses to write of immigrant characters for whom re-location is a positive act requiring "transformations of the self." This story suggests that such an embracing of hybridity can actually be empowered by the experience of grief, because grief first exposes an inner world irrevocably divided and estranged by loss, a world from which there is no turning away, and then acts as a form of energy to enable the dislocated mourner in the task of management, reconstruction, and translation into acceptance. In writing out of the political and personal tragedy of the Air India crash, Mukherjee achieves a particularly fine figuring-forth of such transforming hybridity; I would argue that this is because the universal nature of grief is a powerful if complex force for change, cultural resistance, and moral choice. It is partly because such transcultural grief is still at work that two years ago a million dollar reward was offered by the RCMP for information leading to the prosecution of the six prime suspects in "the worst terrorist act involving Canadians." Indeed there are many mourners who hold to the strong hope that their grief may yet translate into a Royal Commission of Inquiry into the Air India crash, even though it is more than a decade after the fact.

Source: Deborah Bowen, "Spaces of Translation: Bharati Mukherjee's 'The Management of Grief,'" in *ARIEL: A Review of International English Literature*, Vol. 28, No. 3, July, 1997, pp. 47–60.

Sources

Alam, Fakrul. *Bharati Mukherjee*, New York: Twayne, 1996.

Bissoondath, Neil. *Selling Illusions: The Cult of Multiculturalism in Canada*, Ontario: Penguin, 1994.

Connell, Michael, Jessie Grearson, Tom Grimes. "An Interview with Bharati Mukherjee," in *The Iowa Review*, Vol. 20, No. 3, Fall, 1990, pp. 7-32.

Mandel, Ann. "Bharati Mukherjee," in *Dictionary of Literary Biography*, Vol. 60, Gale, 1987.

Mukherjee, Bharati. *Darkness*, Ontario: Penguin, 1985.

Mukherjee, Bharati and Clark Blaise. *The Sorrow and the Terror*, Ontario: Penguin, 1987.

Raban, Jonathan. A review of *The Middleman and Other Stories*, in *The New York Times Book Review*, June 19, 1988, pp. 1, 22-23.

Sant-Wade, Arvindra, and Karen Marguerite Radell. "Refashioning the Self: Immigrant Women in Bharati Mukherjee's New World," in *Studies in Short Fiction*, Vol. 29, No. 1, Winter, 1992, pp. 11-7.

Tindall, Gillian. "East meets West and Writes It," in *Times*, April 26, 1990.

Ward, Elizabeth. "Notes from a new America," in *Book World—The Washington Post*, July 3, 1988, p. 9.

Further Reading

Alam, Fakrul. *Bharati Mukherjee*, New York: Twayne Publishers, 1996.
    A concise critical study of the various stage of Mukherjee's fiction writing, and her psychological transformation from expatriate to immigrant.

Bissoondath, Neil. *Selling Illusions: The Cult of Multiculturalism in Canada*, Ontario: Penguin, 1994.

A convincing, personal and political argument against Canada's official policy of multiculturalism.

Connell, Michael, Jessie Grearson, Tom Grimes. "An Interview with Bharati Mukherjee," in *The Iowa Review*, Vol. 20, No. 3, Fall, 1990, pp. 7-32.
A casual and informative interview with Mukherjee and husband Clark Blaise. Conducted in the Thanksgiving of 1989, shortly after the publication of *Jasmine*. Mukherjee and Blaise discuss a range of Mukherjee's work including non-fiction co-authored with Blaise, *Days and Nights in Calcutta* (1977) and *The Sorrow and the Terror* (1987). Mukherjee also discusses her political and personal vision of fiction writing.

Dhawan, R. K., ed. *The Fiction of Bharati Mukherjee: A Critical Symposium*, New Delhi: Prestige Books, 1996.
A collection of critical essays that covers the span of her fiction up until 1996. Separated according to work, with sections devoted to *The Tiger's Daughter* (1972), *Wife* (1975), *Darkness* (1985) and *The Middleman and Other Stories* (1988), *Jasmine* (1989), and *The Holder of the World* (1993).

Frideres, James S., ed. *Multiculturalism and Intergroup Relations*, Westport, Conn.: Greenwood Press, 1989.
A collection of critical essays discussing the issues plaguing multiculturalism in Canada and the United States.

Mukherjee, Bharati and Clark Blaise. *The Sorrow and the Terror*, Ontario: Penguin, 1987.
A moving and thorough reconstruction of the bombing and possible events leading up to it, including interview of relatives of the victims and terrorism-linked Khalistani agitators. Criticizes Canada's policy of multiculturalism and differentiates the radical pro-Khalistani faction from Sikhs in general.

Nelson, Emmanuel S., ed. *Bharati Mukherjee: Critical Perspectives*, New York: Garland Publishing, 1993.
A diverse collection of critical essays on Mukherjee's work with introduction by Nelson.

The Minister's Black Veil: A Parable

Nathaniel Hawthorne

1836

Nathaniel Hawthorne's "The Minister's Black Veil" first appeared in 1836 in the journal the *Token*. It was published anonymously, along with several other tales that Hawthorne had submitted. These tales met with critical acclaim, and their anonymous author, writing of unique American experiences, was praised as a genius. In 1837 "The Minister's Black Veil" was included in *Twice Told Tales*, a collection of short stories published under Hawthorne's own name.

Author Biography

Nathaniel Hawthorne was born on July 4, 1804 in Salem, Massachusetts, the second of three children born to Nathaniel and Elizabeth Hathorne. (Their son added the "w" to the family name when he began his writing career.) In 1808, his father, a ship's captain, died of yellow fever in the distant port of Surinam. Shortly thereafter, four-year-old Nathaniel moved with his mother and two sisters, Elizabeth and Maria Louisa, from their home on Union Street to the house next door belonging to the Mannings, his mother's family. In the Manning household, Hawthorne's keen intelligence was noted and nurtured; in fact, his maternal relatives hoped that he would eventually attend college. At

the age of sixteen, Hawthorne demonstrated a flair for journalism when he wrote and printed the *Spectator*–an intra-family newsletter he wrote with his sister that functioned as a kind of correspondence between the Mannings in Salem and an uncle who was overseeing the family lands in Raymond, Maine.

In 1821, Hawthorne entered Bowdoin College in Maine, and he proved to be a competent, but not always industrious, scholar. While there, he became acquainted with Franklin Pierce, who would later become the fourteenth president of the United States. Another classmate of Hawthorne's was Henry Wadsworth Longfellow, soon to be one of America's most acclaimed poets. As his time at Bowdoin drew to a close, Hawthorne wrote a letter to his mother expressing his lack of enthusiasm for the professions of law and medicine. He proposed that he should become a writer, asking his mother to imagine the pride she would experience at seeing his name in print and at hearing his works generally praised.

After graduating from Bowdoin in 1825, Hawthorne returned to the Manning residence and lived a life of relative isolation that lasted for some eleven years. During this period he wrote *Fanshawe*, a novel that took as its subject matter his days at Bowdoin, and published it at his own expense in 1828. However, fearing that the novel was inadequate, he stopped its publication and burned all the copies of it that he could find. "Young Goodman Brown" was written circa 1836 and "The Minister's Black Veil," was published in 1837 in the collection *Twice Told Tales*. It was also during this time that Hawthorne studied New England history and discovered that one of his Puritan ancestors had ordered the whipping of a Quaker woman, and another had served as a judge in the Salem witch trials of 1692. Many critics believe that the guilt Hawthorne felt over his family history prompted him to explore the evil of man and original sin in works such as "Young Goodman Brown" and "The Minister's Black Veil."

After 1830, several of Hawthorne's short stories appeared in various literary journals. Hawthorne, though, was frustrated with his literary career, not only because it paid so little but also because he had always desired recognition as the writer of a collection of tales, hoping to imitate the successful literary career of Washington Irving. Hawthorne finally achieved this critical recognition

with the publication of *Twice Told Tales* in 1837, but the financial rewards were still not enough to support him. Hawthorne married Sophia Peabody in 1842. The couple moved to Concord, Massachusetts, where they stayed for three years before returning to Salem.

Even before the publication of *Twice Told Tales,* Hawthorne had tried his hand at other jobs in order to make a living. He had served as the editor for a short-lived magazine, written a series of children's stories, and worked as a measurer in the United States Customs House in Boston. He joined the ill-fated farming commune at Brook Farm, an enterprise that combined intellectual and physical labor, only to leave in disappointment after six months. With the help of Franklin Pierce, Hawthorne procured the position of Surveyor for the Customs House in Salem, a position he held from 1846 to 1848.

The publication of *The Scarlet Letter* in 1850 occurred during the same time of Hawthorne's controversial discharge from his customs position. Hawthorne had been granted that position by a Democratic administration, and when the Whigs won the national election, local party members demanded that those appointed by the Democrats be removed from their jobs. Hawthorne was disappointed that some of his neighbors and friends turned against him during this time. This controversy—added to the publicity over the book's content—boosted sales, and the Hawthornes were able to move back to Concord. After publishing several more successful novels, serving as the American consul to Liverpool from 1853 to 1857 under Franklin Pierce, and touring Europe for several years, Hawthorne returned to Concord, Massachusetts in 1860. He died on May 19, 1864 while vacationing with his old college friend, Pierce.

In 1837 Hawthorne had written to Longfellow "that there is no fate in this world so horrible as to have no share in either its joys or sorrows." He went on to say, "For the last ten years, I have not lived, but only dreamed of living." It seems that not even the years of his ultimate success could eradicate the experience of his early days as a writer. Always somewhat reclusive, Hawthorne projects his private world in his narratives, portraying many of his characters as dispassionate observers of the dark recesses of the soul, unable to participate in life's "joys and sorrows."

Nathaniel Hawthorne

Plot Summary

Part I: Hooper Dons the Veil

As the story opens, the congregation of a small church in Milford, Connecticut is arriving in their best clothes to attend Sunday service. The sexton, a person responsible for maintaining the church, is ringing the bell that announces the service will soon begin. His ringing stops abruptly when he is startled by the Reverend Mr. Hooper emerging from his quarters with a veil of black crepe that covers his whole face and leaves only his mouth and chin exposed.

In the minds of the parishioners, Mr. Hooper is a young and self–disciplined parson who has never acted irrationally before. They are bewildered by his present behavior, believing that either he has lost his wits or he has committed some terrible sin. An excited hush greets Mr. Hooper as he walks to the pulpit. He has never been a terribly effective orator, but, on this day, he delivers a sermon concerning "secret sins" that every man harbors and would hide from his fellow man and even God Himself. The congregation is dramatically moved by the combination of the sermon and the inexplicable black veil, each parishioner feeling as if Mr. Hooper has penetrated to his or her very soul. They cannot

wait to flee the oppressive atmosphere of the church and feel the bright sunshine outside. No one wants to walk with Mr. Hooper, and one of the parishioners who always invites Mr. Hooper to dinner fails to do so on this occasion. As the Reverend Mr. Hooper enters his quarters he turns and casts a "sad smile" on the curious congregation.

Part II: The Funeral and the Wedding

At the later service, the black veil has the same impact on the parishioners. After the service is over, Mr. Hooper officiates at the funeral of a young lady. When Hooper leans forward to utter some final words into the face of the deceased, the veil falls away, and he clutches it back into place as if afraid the corpse might see his features. One superstitious old lady swears that when he did this, she saw the corpse shudder. As the mourners leave the church, one of them looks back furtively, convinced that Hooper and the deceased were walking hand in hand, this eerie conviction seconded by others present.

Later that evening, one of the most popular couples in town is to celebrate their wedding. The parishioners anticipate the arrival of Parson Hooper, convinced that the earlier wearing of the veil was just a passing fancy, expecting that he would be his old mildly amusing and comfortable self. When he arrives with the veil still covering his face, he casts a funeral-like atmosphere over what should be a joyous occasion, prompting some there to imagine that he had brought the spirit of the dead girl from the funeral for the purpose of some unholy or otherworldly marriage. As he raises his glass of wine to toast the newly married couple, Hooper glimpses his own veiled face in the mirror and is struck by the same sense of evil he has evoked in his parishioners. Horrified, he runs out into the darkness of the night.

Part III: Requests for an Explanation

In the ensuing days, the black veil is all the congregation can talk about. The fascination with Hooper's eccentricity extends even to the young schoolchildren. This young boy wears a black veil and frightens his playmates so badly that the boy scares even himself. Since the Reverend Mr. Hooper has always been ready to listen to the advice and concerns of his congregation, a group is selected to approach the parson and inquire as to the meaning and purpose of the veil. When this select group comes into Hooper's presence they are tongue-tied and cannot ask him. If the veil were only removed, they say, they could have advanced to the point. Since it was not, they leave in ignorance, deciding that the issue of the veil is better left to the consideration of a church counsel, or even the consideration of a group of churches uniting in a general synod.

Elizabeth, the woman to whom Hooper is engaged to be married, is not frightened or put off by the veil, and she asks Hooper, directly, the question the others could not. She asks him to remove the veil and then explain why he put it on in the first place. When he replies that he cannot, she asks him at least to remove the mystery from his words. As he explains that he has vowed to wear the veil forever, as a "type and symbol," she is suddenly unnerved by his willingness to give up the most meaningful of human relationships for the sake of that veil, and is finally struck by its symbolic horror. She asks him one last time to remove it, and he again refuses. When she leaves in dismay, he displays, again, that sad smile, both amazed and amused that a simple piece of cloth could intrude so heavily upon human happiness.

Part IV: A Summary of Hooper's Persistence

It soon becomes evident that Mr. Hooper intends to keep wearing the veil, despite his discomfort with the reactions of his parishioners, many of whom cross the street to avoid him while certain others make it a point of honor to confront him, in order that they might brag about their courage later. It upsets him that small children run from him. Also, he is disappointed that he has to give up his customary walks to the cemetery because of those who always hide behind the gravestones trying to see behind the veil as he leans over the gate.

Rumors continue to circulate that he has committed some terrible and unpardonable sin. Yet, in a way, he has become a more effective minister. Many of those he had converted to his own religious faith insist upon his presence at the moment of their deaths, as if they believe the veil has given him an intimate understanding of life's mysteries.

Part V: The Deathbed Scene

The Reverend Mr. Hooper lives this lonely life for many years. On his own deathbed, the Reverend Mr. Clark, a young and energetic parson who has come from the nearby town of Westbury to comfort Hooper, asks if he might remove the veil before Hooper dies. Perhaps misunderstanding Hooper's ambiguous answer, the Reverend Mr. Clark reaches toward the veil, but Hooper clutches it to his face

and prevents it from being removed. Hooper, at last, offers to those assembled around him an explanation for his wearing of the veil:

> "'Why do you tremble at me alone?' cried he, turning his veiled face round the circle of pale spectators. 'Tremble also at each other! Have men avoided me, and women shown no pity, and children screamed and fled, only for my black veil? What, but the mystery which it obscurely typifies, has made this piece of crepe so awful? When the friend shows his inmost heart to his friend; the lover to his best-beloved; when a man does not vainly shrink from the eye of his Creator, loathsomely treasuring up the secret of his sin; then deem me a monster, for the symbol beneath which I have lived, and die! I look around me, and, lo! on every visage a Black Veil!''" (Excerpt from "The Minister's Black Veil: A Parable")

The Reverend Mr. Hooper accuses everyone of veiling their innermost secrets and desires. The black veil symbolizes this masking. His explanation, though, is somewhat dissatisfying, since readers might wonder why Hooper insists upon wearing that worldly symbol in the afterlife. As the story ends, Hawthorne leaves readers with the grim image of Hooper lying in his coffin with the black veil still firmly fixed to his face.

Characters

Rev. Mr. Clark

The Reverend Mr. Clark is a young and enthusiastic minister from the nearby town of Westbury, who is summoned to Milford to attend the dying Reverend Mr. Hooper. Knowing that "the veil of eternity" is about to be lifted from his worldly existence, Clark asks Hooper if he can remove the veil that he has stubbornly worn for many years. When Hooper desperately clings to that veil, Clark cries, "Dark old man! . . . with what horrible crime upon your soul are you now passing to the judgment?" Clark is then witness to Hooper's dying claim that everyone in life wears a veil of secret shame that isolates him from the rest of the world. Hooper's veil is different only in that his is visible.

Elizabeth

Elizabeth is engaged to the Reverend Mr. Hooper, the minister who has, for some unknown reason, taken to wearing a mysterious black veil over his face. At first, Elizabeth is not affected by the horror that the veil seems to evoke in others. She considers it to be only a piece of crepe cloth hiding the face for which she has acquired some affection. But she, too,

Media Adaptations

- A sound recording of "The Minister's Black Veil: A Parable" has been created by Robert H. Fossum as part of the Nineteenth Century American Writers Series, with Fossum as Lecturer. Deland, Florida, Everett/Edwards, 1971; available on cassette.

- In another sound recording, "The Minister's Black Veil: A Parable" can be heard as read by Basil Rathbone, Caedmon TC 1120, 1197, (1960); available on vinyl.

- Many of Nathaniel Hawthorne's stories and novels are set in seventeenth-century Puritan New England. Here, Lillian Gish and Lars Hanson portray the Puritan characters Hester Prynne and Arthur Dimmesdale in the 1926 film version of Hawthorne's novel *The Scarlet Letter.*

finally feels the veil's unsettling power when Hooper refuses her request to remove it. He explains to her that the veil might serve equally well as either a symbol of mourning or a symbol of sorrow for the secret sin he is accused of harboring. Even though Elizabeth breaks off the engagement, she proves herself to be Hooper's steadfast friend by nursing and supporting him at the hour of his death.

Father Hooper
See Rev. Mr. Hooper

Mr. Hooper
See Rev. Mr. Hooper

Parson Hooper
See Rev. Mr. Hooper

Rev. Mr. Hooper
The Reverend Mr. Hooper is a minister in the small town of Milford, Connecticut, who shocks his congregation by appearing at Sunday services with a black veil covering nearly his entire face—only his mouth and chin are exposed. He wears this veil throughout the service to the dismay and bewilderment of his parishioners. Hooper is engaged to be married to Elizabeth, but abandons his marriage plans when she insists that he remove the veil or adequately explain its meaning. He can do neither. The mystery of the black veil isolates Hooper from his parish and his community, and this isolation is evident in his despairing cry to Elizabeth: "Oh! you know not how lonely I am, and how frightened, to be alone behind my black veil." Despite the loneliness the veil causes him to experience, he never removes it. As he is dying, he explains that he has worn the veil as an outward symbol of humankind's hoarding of secret sins. Hooper hides his face with the mysterious black veil even into death.

Themes

Alienation and Loneliness
The moment that the Reverend Mr. Hooper, a parson in the small town of Milford, puts on the black veil that he is to wear for the rest of his life, the influence of the veil becomes evident. As he delivers his first sermon wearing the veil, his congregation gets the uncanny sensation that it is not really their beloved Parson Hooper. After the service, those who usually vie for the prestige of accompanying Hooper out of the church do not do so, and a parishioner who always invites Hooper to dinner fails to invite him on this occasion. The veil so isolates him from the companionship of others that it denies him even the happiness of a marriage with Elizabeth, to whom he admits the veil's unhappy effects: "Oh! you know not how lonely I am, and how frightened, to be alone behind my black veil. Do not leave me in this miserable obscurity forever!" That miserable obscurity only intensifies as he adamantly continues to wear the veil, despite the pain he experiences when, again and again, certain people cross the street to avoid him, and children quit playing and run away at his approach.

Doubt and Ambiguity
The black veil is a symbol fraught with doubt and ambiguity, but critics disagree what it symbol-

Topics for Further Study

- The Reverend Mr. Hooper's preoccupation with secret sin suggests that truly embracing Calvinist theology as Puritans did would lead to a rather grim outlook on life. Research the communities of early American Puritan colonies. Did the members of these Puritan communities constantly remind one another of Original Sin and lead bleak lives of suffering and isolation like Hooper?

- Hawthorne calls his short story a parable. In addition to the story of Mr. Moody provided by Hawthorne in the footnote, could Hawthorne have been alluding to biblical mentions of veils? Read Exodus 34:30-33, in which Moses wears a ''vail'' to shield his followers from the blinding glory of his face, which radiates as a result of his having been in God's presence for forty days and forty nights. Read also II Corinthians 3:7-18, in which St. Paul explains why Moses really wore the veil. Do these biblical accounts shed any light on Hooper's black veil?

- Hawthorne's ancestors were involved in both the persecution of Quakers and the execution of people convicted of witchcraft in Salem, Massachusetts, in 1690. Research either of these events. You may want to read *The Crucible* by Arthur Miller; *The Salem Witch Trials* by Earle Rice, Jr.; or *Neighbors, Friends, or Madness: The Puritan Adjustment to Quakerism in Seventeenth-Century Massachusetts Bay* by Jonathan M. Chu. How did Puritans treat people who were different from them? What similarities are there between Mr. Hooper and others the Puritans disliked?

izes. Upon Hooper's first appearance in the black veil, one woman in his congregation declares that the veil symbolizes the Parson's madness. Other parishioners who consider themselves wise suggest that there is no mystery to the veil at all; the Reverend Mr. Hooper has only strained his eyes the night before in intense studies by lamplight. But as he continues to wear the black veil, the parishioners offer other explanations of its symbolism.

At its least mysterious, Hooper's veil is explained as a symbol of mourning for some lost soul. At its most mysterious, Hooper's veil is explained as a symbol of some great and unpardonable sin that Hooper himself has committed. Doubt and ambiguity exist not only for characters in the story who try to read the black veil's symbolism, but also for modern readers of Hawthorne's tale. In trying to penetrate the mystery of the black veil, modern readers are helped neither by the author's footnote to the subtitle nor by Hooper's dying accusation. The footnote to the subtitle suggests that the story be read as a parable wherein Hooper's veil is not unlike the veil worn by the clergyman Mr. Joseph Moody,

as a symbol of sorrow for the accidental killing of a friend. But the footnote also says, ''In his case, however, the symbol had a different import.'' As Hooper lies dying, he accuses all men of veiling themselves from God and other men. But if his own black veil has been worn as a symbol of that shared sin or weakness, the reader might still question why Hooper insists upon wearing the veil after he is dead and has gone to his eventual judgment before God.

Guilt and Innocence

With his dying words, Hooper asks that his behavior be judged until others have examined their own consciences and found themselves free of sin. Those sins prevent people from communicating fully and openly with others and with God. Hooper has worn the black veil of ''secret sin'' visibly on his face while others wear that black veil on their souls. As a symbol, Hooper implies, the black veil represents a shared human weakness in the inescapable tendency to commit and hide sin. This implication is reinforced by the topic of the sermon Hooper delivers when he first appears wearing the black veil. ''The subject had reference to secret sin, and those sad mysteries which we hide from our nearest and dearest, and would fain conceal from our own consciousness, even forgetting that the Omniscient can detect them.'' In Christianity, this shared tendency to sin is called Original Sin, an imprint of guilt inherited from Adam and Eve, who sinned against God and then tried to hide from Him. No one is born innocent of Original Sin, and no one escapes the mark of guilt of which Hooper's black veil is representative.

Moral Corruption/Sin

Many critics believe that the Reverend Mr. Hooper wears the black veil, at first, to teach his congregation a lesson about acknowledging the presence of Original Sin in each and every parishioner. His continued wearing of the veil, however, is a morally corrupting influence on Hooper since it leads him to the sin of excessive human pride. Had Hooper immediately explained to the congregation the significance of the black veil, the lesson he meant to impart would have been clear. Instead, he wears the black veil for the rest of his life, never offering an explanation until he is on his deathbed. And even then, the explanation is not as clear and direct as it might have been.

Moreover, the black veil isolates him from the religious community to whom he should minister with affection and concern. He takes great pride both in having discovered the dark secrets of the soul and in parading that discovery in front of the congregation. His isolation and suffering are, perhaps, only tolerable in his sense of moral superiority, and he puts his own continued sense of moral superiority ahead of the concerns of his congregation. Ironically, the black veil, which was initially meant to represent secret sin, comes to represent Hooper's own sin of pride, and conceals the very thing it was meant to expose.

Style

Point of View

In ''The Minister's Black Veil: A Parable,'' the Reverend Mr. Hooper shocks his congregation in Milford, Connecticut, by appearing at Sunday services wearing a black veil that shrouds his face. He wears this veil the rest of his life and insists upon wearing it into the grave. The story is told from the point of view of an unknown narrator who describes the events of the story in the third person. This narrator is omniscient, that is, the narrator seems to know more about the motivations of the characters than they might know about themselves. In addition to describing events and reporting dialogue between characters, the narrator supplies the reader with a sense of the characters' thoughts and feelings. For example, it is the narrator who reveals Hooper's sense of horror at observing his veiled semblance in a mirror while toasting the newlywed couple. It is also the narrator who describes the sense of revulsion and horror that Elizabeth finally experiences, realizing that the veil will never be removed from her beloved's face.

The narrator sometimes frames events by indicating how they should be interpreted. For example, even as it is described that the corpse of the recently deceased young lady shuddered at the approach of Hooper's veiled face, the narrator implies that this account not be taken too seriously, since ''A superstitious old woman was the only witness of this prodigy.''

Setting

The story is set in the small town of Milford, Connecticut. Aside from the observation that the church and the graveyard seem to mark the extent of Hooper's world, the story does not seem dependent on the setting for its significance. It is interesting to note, however, that Hawthorne may have actually visited Milford in his preparation for writing *Twice Told Tales*, the collection of sketches in which ''The Minister's Black Veil'' appears. These collections of sketches or short stories were popular in nineteenth-century America, perhaps because the diverse and unique settings they offered were representative of the geographic and social diversity of America itself.

Structure

The structure of ''The Minister's Black Veil'' is easily divisible into five parts. The first part describes the reaction of Hooper's congregation to his appearance in the black veil and to the sermon he delivers. The second part recounts the events and describes the atmosphere of the funeral and the wedding later that day. The third part presents two attempts to elicit an explanation of the veil from Hooper, first by an authorized and select group of parishioners, and then by Elizabeth. The fourth part summarizes Hooper's isolation and suffering as he lives out his life and approaches death. The fifth part is the deathbed scene, in which he finally touches on the significance of the black veil as a symbol of "secret sin." The secret sin of the story's final part mirrors the secret sin upon which Hooper sermonizes in the first part. The structure of the story, then, reinforces the reading of the veil's meaning.

Symbols/Symbolism

A symbol, simply defined, is an object that is understood to represent some concrete and tangible object while, simultaneously, representing one or more abstract ideas. The black veil that the Reverend Mr. Hooper wears certainly fits this definition. Several of the characters in the story remark that the veil is simply a piece of black crepe cloth, yet, at the same time, this simple piece of crepe instills a sense of horror in those who observe it because it represents the more abstract ideas of death, mourning, and the hidden secrets of the soul. But as with many things, when the black veil is designated as a symbol, it accumulates more and more abstract ideas. For example, some critics read the black veil as symbolic of Original Sin and of Hooper's excessive pride. Since to study the black veil is to learn its many diverse symbolic values, its significance is not easily apparent. It becomes a symbol that, in one of its abstractions, recalls the idea of symbolism itself. It becomes a symbol of symbols.

Figurative Language

Figurative language uses common terms to metaphorically express an unfamiliar idea in familiar terms. This is different from literal language that uses precise, factual terms to express exactly what is meant. Two examples from "The Minister's Black Veil" help illustrate this difference. When Hooper runs terrified from the wedding reception after glimpsing himself in the mirror, Hawthorne writes, "For the earth, too, had on her Black Veil." Hooper wears a literal veil on his face. The earth, in the shades of night, wears a figurative one. When Hooper refuses Elizabeth's request that he remove the veil and explain its significance, she says, "Your words are a mystery too . . . Take away the veil from them, at least." Since he will not remove the literal veil from his face, she asks him, metaphorically, to remove the metaphoric language that hides the literal meaning of his words.

Parable

A parable is a short and concise tale which usually expresses a moral or religious message in terms of something that is easily understood. Hawthorne subtitles "The Minister's Black Veil" as "A Parable." He footnotes this subtitle with a brief account of another minister named Mr. Moody, who lived in York, Maine, approximately eighty years before the events of Hawthorne's story take place. Mr. Moody wore a black veil to symbolize the sorrow he felt at being involved in the accidental killing of a friend, and Hawthorne tells us that, although the eccentric behaviors of Mr. Moody and Mr. Hooper might be the same, the import or significance of the veils is not. Hawthorne is perhaps suggesting to the reader that the black veil as a symbol of secret sin is better understood when compared to the black veil as a symbol of the more easily understood loss of a loved one.

Historical Context

When "The Minister's Black Veil" was first published in the periodical the *Token* in 1836, America was still a relatively new country struggling to form a national identity distinct from that of England. Americans no longer needed to channel all of their energies into survival; they now had the freedom to engage in and develop a whole host of cultural activities.

Ralph Waldo Emerson had long been exhorting the American public to cultivate its own unique identity. For example, in "Self-Reliance," he says, "Insist on yourself; never imitate." Many Americans were upset that so many people in the fledgling United States still looked to England for examples of great literature and dismissed American literary

Compare & Contrast

- **1850s:** Puritanism is still a strong influence in New England life.

  1999: With the influence of the Moral Majority waning, many clergyman and cultural observers debate the role of religion in politics.

- **1850s:** Americans continue to move west. The population of the northern states exceeds the population of the south by one million. Slave-holding states seek to expand their influence in the new territories, such as California and Utah. A compromise reached in 1850 holds the peace for a decade, but slavery becomes a major and confrontational domestic issue dividing North and South.

  1999: Differences between northern and south-

ern states remain, but not at constitutional levels. Slavery has long been abolished but many blacks suffer from racism. Foreign policy issues lead the political agenda as America seeks to maintain and extend its international influence.

- **1850s:** As a rejection of Calvinistic sobriety, many middle-class people dabble in hydropathy, hypnotism, and phrenology, but these are still seen as alternatives to mainstream religious belief and medical therapies.

  1999: Proponents of alternative medicines such as reflexology and aromatherapy present them as whole belief systems and substitutes for orthodox religion.

---

efforts as inferior. Evert Augustus Duyckinck, editor of a journal that published some of Hawthorne's early work, laments this state of literary affairs. He writes in an 1841 issue of his journal *Arcturus*, ''In his own peculiar walk of fiction and sentiment, there is perhaps no author who could supply to us the few natural beautiful sketches of Nathaniel Hawthorne. Of the American writers destined to live he is the most original, the one least indebted to foreign models or literary precedents of any kind, and as the reward of his genius he is the least known to the public.'' Duyckinck is stressing the point that the American public did not honor America's authors, and, like so many others, he is calling for this situation to be remedied.

In 1820, Washington Irving had become a celebrity in both England and America with the publication of his *The Sketch Book of Geoffrey Crayon, Gent*. This work offers a series of individual and diverse tales connected by the framing story of a traveler, and Irving was to write several more successful collections of this type. Hawthorne wanted very much to be known as the writer of a collection of short stories about his New England experience, hoping to imitate the successes of Irving. In 1837,

Twice Told Tales was published with Hawthorne's name on the title page, and he finally realized the critical claim he had so desired.

Irving perhaps adopted the literary format he did as a matter of necessity. His elaborate and distancing framework—Irving pretends to have discovered a sketch book belonging to Geoffrey Crayon who, in turn, records tales told to him by others—is almost an apology for the seeming audacity of an American writer proclaiming to the world that American experiences were interesting and important. Hawthorne adopted the literary format of Irving because it was the one literary tradition that had been established in America, one that had brought its author prominence. Still, there is a correspondence between these collections of tales and the national identity forming in America. Just as the individual tales in the collection were connected in a loose unifying framework, the individual colonial experiences of Americans were loosely connected in the confederation of states which had become a unified nation.

Having discovered his own connections to the early Puritan intolerance of Quakers and the persecutions of the alleged witches in Salem, Hawthorne refocused the Puritan experience in colonial America through his own perspective. In an 1850 article entitled "Hawthorne and his Mosses, by a Virginian Spending the Summer in Vermont" which appeared in *Literary World*, Herman Melville, a contemporary and eventual neighbor of Hawthorne's, wrote a review of *Mosses from an Old Manse*, a subsequent selection of tales written by Hawthorne in 1846. Referring to the Calvinist sense of Original Sin in Hawthorne, Melville writes that the gloom in Hawthorne's soul is "blackness, ten times black."

The darkness of the soul that Hawthorne connects with Calvinism is evident not only in "The Minister's Black Veil" but also in several of his other stories and novels, most notably "Young Goodman Brown" and *The Scarlet Letter*. It is not clear whether Hawthorne meant to justify the severity of his Puritan ancestors or condemn Puritan/Calvinist theology entirely, but it is clear that he wove the threads of Puritanism into the fabric of America, many modern readers getting their only understanding of Puritanism through Hawthorne. "The Minister's Black Veil" has a specific geographic setting in Milford, Connecticut, but is set in no specific time, almost as if it is deliberately suspended somewhere between the earliest of colonial American times and the nineteenth-century America in which Hawthorne wrote.

Critical Overview

Criticism of "The Minister's Black Veil" has mainly explored the meaning of the veil worn by the Puritan minister, the Reverend Mr. Hooper. Some see the veil as a physical reminder of a specific sin committed by Hooper. Others view Hooper as a Christian martyr wearing the emblem of Original Sin. Still others believe that Hooper's donning of the veil is a sin of pride. More recent criticism has focused on the veil as a "symbol of symbols," a deliberate ambiguity that is not meant to be resolved, but only to call attention to itself.

In his portrayal of the isolated Puritan minister in this story, Hawthorne reveals his fascination with

Puritanism in colonial America prompted by the discovery that his earliest ancestors were Puritan figures publicly involved with both the harassment of the Quakers and the persecution of the alleged Salem witches. In drawing on his own understanding of the "Puritan experience" in America, Hawthorne introduces the themes of alienation and loneliness, doubt and ambiguity, guilt and innocence, pride, and the moral corruption of sin. These themes receive their most extended treatment in "Young Goodman Brown" and *The Scarlet Letter*, but they are evident in nearly all of Hawthorne's works.

Hawthorne's work has been favorably received throughout the years. When his first short stories began appearing anonymously in literary journals, their author was praised as a man of genius, a uniquely American author who might rival the authors of England. In 1841 Evert Augustus Duyckinck, a man familiar with Hawthorne's previous work and the editor of a journal called *Arcturus*, praised "The Minister's Black Veil" because it demonstrated "an ingenious refinement of terror, wrought with none of the ordinary machinery of gloom." According to Duyckinck, Hawthorne's story represented "a metaphysical exposition of the dark places of the human soul."

In 1842 Edgar Allan Poe, a writer contemporary with Hawthorne, offered a mixed review of Hawthorne's *Twice Told Tales* in the May issue of Graham's, calling them the product of a "truly imaginative intellect, restrained and in some measure repressed, by fastidiousness of taste, by constitutional melancholy, and by indolence." In short, Poe believed that Hawthorne was a truly gifted writer, but a lazy one who relied too much on mystery for his stories' effects. Poe believed that he had figured out the mystery of "The Minister's Black Veil." He speculated that the veil was a symbol of the minister's own private sin, and contended that Hooper had had an illicit relationship with the young lady whose funeral he attends.

Following Poe's example, many critics see Hooper's black veil as a symbol of his private shame for some wicked deed or impure desire, and some fairly recent criticism has projected Hooper's private shame onto Hawthorne. For example, in his 1966 publication of The *Sins of the Father*, Frederick Crews suggests that Hooper, along with several of Hawthorne's other characters, represents Haw-

American country church in the winter, c. 1875.

thorne's own fear of sexual intimacy. He writes, "It could be plausibly argued ... that Hooper has donned the veil in order to prevent his marriage." Still other critics, taking their cues from the story itself, suggest that the black veil represents the Christian idea of Original Sin, the unavoidable inclination in all of humankind to sin and to hide that sin in the inner recesses of the soul.

In 1955 a new trend in the criticism of Hawthorne's story emerged with William Bysshe Stein's essay "The Parable of the Antichrist in 'The Minister's Black Veil.'" Stein argues that Hooper's veil prevents him from interacting with his parishioners in the loving way ministers were expected to act. As a minister, Hooper acts in a way that is exactly opposite to the example Christ had taught, and the veil becomes a symbol of Hooper's gross negligence in addressing the needs of the religious community he is supposed to serve. In isolating Hooper from his congregation and signaling Hooper's sense of moral superiority, the black veil can be seen as a symbol of excessive human pride.

Explanations of the black veil's significance seemed to culminate in Stein's suggestion that it was an anti-Christian symbol, but in 1969 W. B. Carnochan, in "'The Minister's Black Veil': Symbol, Meaning, and the Context of Hawthorne's Art,'' introduced the notion that Hooper's black veil functioned as a ''symbol of symbols,'' since its meaning could never be ultimately determined. Carnochan writes, ''As language gives a meaning to experience but also comes between the subject and any direct perception or recreation of that experience, so does the veil.'' The veil suggests some symbolic meaning but, at the same time, prevents the possibility of any final pronouncement about that meaning. Considerations of the black veil's significance can only refer the reader to a horizon of possible interpretations, one of which is unresolved ambiguity. According to Carnochan, the veil both reveals and conceals meaning, for if Hooper's veil were to be lifted from his face, its significance would disappear since the veil can only communicate meaning when it is hiding something. When it no longer hides meaning, it ceases to be a symbol, and the reader cannot get beyond the impasse that the veil has become a symbol for something that can never be revealed.

Like Stein's earlier work, Carnochan's interpretation of the black veil seemed to offer the last word in criticism of ''The Minister's Black Veil.'' After all, what can be said about the black veil once its symbolic mystery has been pronounced insoluble? In 1992, William Freedman suggested a new and interesting interpretation of the veil in his ''The Artist's Symbol and Hawthorne's Veil: 'The Minister's Black Veil' Resartus.'' He expounds on Carnochan's work by asserting that Hawthorne was intrigued by the unlimited possibilities of the artistic symbol.

According to Freedman, the veiled Hooper can be likened to the veiled Hawthorne, both producing a similar impact on their reading audience. Just as the townspeople of Milford try to penetrate the mystery of Hooper's veil, the readers of Hawthorne's tale try to penetrate the mystery of the artistic symbol. In seeing the veil as only a piece of cloth, the character Elizabeth represents the simple reader who cannot go beyond the literal. She understands the veil's allegorical dimensions only when Hooper finally forces her to do so. In his last-minute attempt to remove the veil and reveal its ultimate meaning at Hooper's impending death, the Reverend Mr. Clark represents the naive reader who expects that lifting the veil will reveal its simple allegorical meaning. Just as the veil hides Hooper's face, the artistic symbol hides the author's self, and it is the effects that these symbols produce in their readers that are interesting to examine.

Criticism

Timothy Montbriand

Montbriand teaches writing and literature at Oakland University and St. Mary's College in Michigan. In the following essay, he refutes popular interpretations of the veil in Hawthorne's story, suggesting that the meaning of the veil is not found by looking into it, but in looking out of it, as the character Hooper does.

In ''The Minister's Black Veil,'' Hawthorne calls the reader's attention to the veil as an obvious symbol, and critics have dutifully responded to the call. Criticism of Hawthorne's story has proceeded on the assumption that the veil hides something and is donned by Hooper to send a message to the congregation. But critics have overlooked another effect of the veil, which not only hides the face of the wearer from view but also colors his view of the world. Hooper is a Puritan minister who has realized the full significance of the Calvinist theology he preaches, a theology which embraces the idea of *predestination*. God has arbitrarily destined an ''elect'' group of people to the glory of heaven and has destined a ''reprobate'' group of people to an eternity of damnation. Since this sorting is done by divine decree, there is nothing man can do to alter his ultimate fate. The most worrisome aspect of this theology, perhaps, is that a person never knows whether he or she is a member of the elect or the reprobate designation.

Hooper is struggling with doubts about his own salvation, and the beginning of that struggle is marked by the moment he first dons the veil. Forever after that, he must, necessarily, see the world in a different way, for his preoccupation with his eternal destiny cuts him off from fully participating in the joys of the world around him. The veil represents his isolation; it does not cause it. Critics have been, as it were, on the wrong side of the veil. They have been trying to penetrate its mystery rather than looking through it as Hooper does. The veil is meant neither to communicate a message to Hooper's congregation nor to represent some fault in Hooper, as so many critics have argued.

Interpretations of the black veil as a representation of some fault in Hooper follow three identifiable trends: the veil as a marker of some specific crime Hooper has committed; the veil as the embodiment of Original Sin, humanity's tendency to

What Do I Read Next?

- In Nathaniel Hawthorne's "Young Goodman Brown" (1835), the title character witnesses what appears to be a witches' sabbath, at which he recognizes several notable people from his hometown. His experience is more illusory than real, but afterward, Young Goodman Brown shies away from the evil he perceives in the townspeople, an evil which may be his own sense of guilt projected onto others.

- Nathaniel Hawthorne's *The Scarlet Letter* (1850), a tale of Puritan hypocrisy and repression, relates the story of Hester Prynne, who is accused of adultery and is forced to wear the letter "A" on her breast as a sign of that indiscretion. Hester will not reveal the name of her lover, the preacher Arthur Dimmesdale, and Dimmesdale does not admit his involvement with her until just before he dies and is safely beyond the reach of social sanction.

- Perry Miller's *The New England Mind: From Colony to Province* (1953) is an in-depth study of the Puritans in colonial and early American times. Miller dispels many of the myths about Puritan society, many of which were generated by the memory of the Salem witchcraft trials and perpetuated by authors like Hawthorne.

- In *The Antinomian Controversy 1636-1638: A Documentary History* (1968), David D. Hall records the experiences of Anne Hutchison. Anne Hutchinson "went against the law" of her Boston congregation, accusing New England preachers of being too mechanical in their preaching. She argued that individuals should be allowed to interpret Scripture according to the inspiration they received from it. This kind of thinking was intolerable for New England ministers, and they banished her to Rhode Island. Hall provides the records of her courtroom examination.

---

transgress against the laws of God; and the veil as a signal of Hooper's excessive pride. As an example of the first trend, Edgar Allan Poe announced, somewhat triumphantly, that he had figured out the mystery of "The Minister's Black Veil." Hooper's veil was a badge of shame for the illicit relationship he had had with the young lady whose funeral is described in the story. Poe bases this assertion on some rather flimsy evidence from the story itself—the superstitious old woman's report that the corpse of the deceased girl had shuddered when Hooper drew near her and the premonition of several mourners that Hooper and the dead girl were walking hand in hand.

The second trend of interpretation takes its cue from Hooper's deathbed statement and the subject matter of the first sermon he delivers while wearing the veil. Both address the secret sin that men harbor in their hearts. The suggestion is that Hooper wears the black veil in order to inform his parishioners about or to remind them of the guilt that stains every one of their souls and the weakness that inclines them to hide their sins from themselves, other men, and even God. But if Hooper's intention really is to communicate some message to his congregation, he could have done it much more effectively than he does—if, in fact, he does at all. He waits until he is on his deathbed to say anything about the veil, and even then he speaks rather ambiguously. He might have worn the veil for a short time, explaining its significance simply and directly. The fact that he does not do so affirms that his intention is not to inform his congregation about Original Sin, but only to acknowledge its presence in himself. If he were accusing his followers of hoarding sin, it is logical to assume that he would exhort them to confess that sin. But he does not follow this logical course, because he realizes that, according to a strict interpretation of Calvinist theology, confessing one's sins does not affect one's predestined course.

The third trend in interpretation is closely linked to the second. It assumes that the black veil was initially meant to communicate a message to Hooper's parishioners. The black veil becomes a symbol of Hooper's sin of excessive pride when he continues to wear it and gets caught up in thinking that he is morally superior because he is the conveyor of such an important message. E. Earle Stibitz ingeniously connects the two levels of the veil's meaning: "Out of the first level of meaning, the calling of attention to the truth of man's proneness to the sin of concealment, rises the second level, the minister's sin in making his veil demonstration all-important; and this second level, with its irony, absorbs the first, creating a dominant theme." The "dominant theme" to which Stibitz refers is less the result of an ironic coexistence between the first and second levels of interpretation than the mistaken assumption upon which both rest—the assumption that the veil is intended to somehow enlighten the congregation.

The greatest condemnation of Hooper, leveled by those who see the veil as a symbol of pride, is that he is a bad shepherd to his flock because he neglects them as he becomes more and more preoccupied with his moral mission. These critics even include Hawthorne in their condemnation of Hooper's pride. Nicholas Canaday, Jr. argues that "the author's severe moral judgment of Mr. Hooper" is not as evident as it might have been because Hawthorne was constrained by "the subtlety of the portrait," "the brevity of the tale," and "the limited cast of characters." On the contrary, far from portraying Hooper as a creature of pride, Hawthorne portrays him as one of abject humility, the humility he experiences in his isolation and agony of doubt. More importantly, Hooper cannot be accused of neglecting his congregation. As a Puritan minister aware of the Calvinist notion of predestination, he knows that his parishioners are predestined to either heaven or hell; there is nothing he can do to help them.

Although the Calvinist interpretation of the veil seems somewhat bleak, there is evidence to suggest that Hawthorne may have been reflecting the hstorical and cultural context of the time in which "The Minister's Black Veil" was written. Hawthorne had become fascinated with Puritanism when he discovered that two of his earliest ancestors in America had been important figures in two very controversial and deplorable historical incidents—the expulsion of the Quakers from Massachusetts, and the Salem witchcraft trials.

> " The veil represents Hooper's isolation; it does not cause it."

Alluding to Hawthorne's Calvinist interests, Herman Melville wrote that Hawthorne's soul had a gloomy side that evidenced "blackness, ten times black." More importantly, Hawthorne was writing at a time when American authors were trying to forge an identity that was completely American, and this identity would have had to incorporate, somehow, the shaping influence of Puritan colonists and the Calvinist theology they embraced. It is not unlikely to suggest that Hawthorne was reflecting, in works like *The Scarlet Letter*, "Young Goodman Brown," "The Birthmark," and "The Minister's Black Veil," a cultural concern with the influence Calvinism's more severe tenets might have on America's future. After all, New England's first colonists had come to America to establish a religious community free from religious persecution. It does not seem odd to find a nineteenth-century writer like Hawthorne weaving early Puritan attitudes into the fabric of American life.

Certain evidence from the text supports the idea that the black veil represents a new or renewed doubt about his predestined soul. In the earliest description of Hooper's veil, the narrator says that it "probably did not intercept his sight, farther than to give a darkened aspect to all living and inanimate things." The veil tinges his view of not only worldly things but also spiritual things since "it threw its obscurity between him and the holy page, as he read the Scriptures; and while he prayed, the veil lay heavily on his uplifted countenance." Symbolically, the veil denies him meaningful and complete access to God's presence in both Scripture and prayer. Realizing that he can never be certain whether God has elected or damned him taints a clear and uncomplicated view of worldly and spiritual things.

On the first day that Hooper wears the veil, he turns to enter the parsonage after having delivered his sermon on secret sin. Before he enters, "A sad smile gleamed faintly from beneath the black veil, and flickered about his mouth, glimmering as he disappeared." Canaday suggests that Hooper's smile is diabolical in each of its seven additional appearances in the story: "once when he receives the delegation of parishioners, three times in the important central scene with Elizabeth, once as he contemplates the rumors that the veil has given him supernatural powers, once on his deathbed just before he pronounces his final moralizing statement about the veils of men in general, and finally as it lingers on his corpse lying in the coffin. The import of this smile, which is condescending and self-satisfied, is crucial as a symbol of his spiritual pride."

If all of these occasions are examined, however, it becomes clear that each specifies a time when Hooper realizes that others are trying desperately to penetrate the mystery of the veil. The smile is not a diabolical one; it is a smile of resignation to the reality that he is cut off from the joys of friendship and a smile of amused sadness at seeing others struggle to understand the meaning of an emblem that is not meant for them.

Hooper's veil is an intensely personal emblem, much like the one worn by Mr. Joseph Moody of York, Maine. Hawthorne subtitles his story "A Parable" and explains, in a footnote to this subtitle, that Mr. Moody was a cleric who had been involved in the accidental killing of a friend some eighty years earlier. Several critics have difficulty with the parable, feeling that it obscures rather than clarifies the meaning of Hooper's black veil. Edgar A. Dryden examines the use of parable in the Bible and concludes that parables were used to inform the worthy and to amuse the ignorant while diverting them from the truth. Rather than having the specific purpose of clarifying meaning, parables are like "veils that serve the double purpose of revealing and concealing meaning."

No doubt, Dryden is influenced in his analysis by the earlier work of W. B. Carnochan, who writes that "the veil, creating meaning and simultaneously hiding it, invites speculation and resists it." However interconnected these remarks about parables and veils are to the larger question of the indeterminacy of symbolism and language, they do not help very much in explaining the meaning of Hooper's black veil. If read correctly, Hawthorne's footnote to the subtitle does help to clarify the meaning of Hooper's veil. The veils of both Mr. Moody and Mr. Hooper are to be looked out from and not looked into. It might be assumed that Mr. Moody does not wear his veil in order to call attention to it; he wears it because it provides him a darker view of the world befitting his changed attitude toward life. Similarly,

Mr. Hooper does not wear his veil in order to gain the opportunity to preach a moral message; he wears it because intense and internal doubt about his salvation has changed his attitude to both social and spiritual life.

One last question remains to be answered: Why does Hooper wear the veil into his grave and to his final judgment? If the veil were meant to represent a specific crime, Original Sin, or excessive pride, these things could not be hidden from an all-knowing God. The veil represents not what Hooper would hide but what is hidden from him. He cannot lift the veil himself. Only God can do that at the final judgment when He reveals to Hooper where his soul will spend eternity.

Source: Timothy Montbriand, "Overview of 'The Minister's Black Veil,'" for *Short Stories for Students,* The Gale Group, 2000.

William Freedman

Freedman is a professor of English at the University of Haifa, Israel. In the following excerpt, he offers his interpretation of the veil as a symbol of Hawthorne's own alienation as an artist and his ultimate failure of imagination.

. . . In Carnochan's view, "The Minister's Black Veil," is less a parable of hidden guilt than an exercise in the complex employment of the artistic symbol, and, ultimately, a tale about the nature of such symbols. The principal effect of the veil is "to avert explicit statements of what it stands for." Creating meaning and simultaneously hiding it, inviting speculation and resisting it, the veil not only "conceal[s] what is behind it, but is a sign of that concealment." It is, in short, a "symbol of symbols":

> Because the meaning of the veil consists only in what is hidden, meaning is lost in the very act of revelation. It is in this that the veil serves as 'type' and 'symbol' of types and symbols in their general nature. As language gives a meaning to experience but also comes between the subject and any direct perception or recreation of that experience, so does the veil. (Carnochan)

These are Carnochan's points about the veil and they are, in my view, extremely well taken. But they are also brief and partial, leaving much to be said, because Carnochan is more interested in the veil as a clue to Hawthorne's ultimate disintegration as a symbolist, hence as a writer, than in the veil-as-artistic-symbol in the tale. His observations must be extended and many others added if we are to grasp not only the full richness of this symbol of symbols, but also its implications for the artist who wears it. My view of the parable is that it carries autobiographical import more for the artist's dubious present than for his declining future, that it speaks of Hawthorne's adoption of the symbolic method (the donning of the veil), of the power of that alteration of his literary "face," and of its price. Appearing first in *The Token* for 1836, "The Minister's Black Veil—A Parable" is one of Hawthorne's earliest symbolic tales. It speaks, I think, of the nature of the symbol he had begun to explore after his earlier failure with *Fanshawe* (1828) and other relatively or baldly realistic fictions, and of its effects not only on his real and imagined readers, but on the artist as well.

The veil, like the artistic symbol it represents, invites a round of tentative interpretations, all based inevitably on surmise. But its chief significance lies not in these "readings," surely not in its "ultimate meaning," which may or may not be revealed, but in its power to stimulate such efforts and in the still more potent emotional effects it produces in those who behold it. Some of the townspeople are amazed, others awed; some are fearful or intimidated, others perplexed or defensively wise, while yet others are inspired or made hopeful. For all the emphasis on interpretive hypotheses—and there is much—there is as much or more on the accompanying emotional impact. And both, of course, are characteristic of the symbol, the latter more profoundly than the former. Symbols, as D. H. Lawrence remarks [in his introduction to *The Dragon of the Apocalypse*, by Frederick Carter, 1920], "don't 'mean something.' They stand for units of human *feeling*, human experience. A complex of emotional experience is a symbol. And the power of the symbol," like the power of the minister's veil, "is to arouse the deep emotional self, and the dynamic self, beyond comprehension" (Lawrence). The "strangest part of the affair," remarks a physician, "is the effect of this vagary, even on a sober-minded man like myself" (Hawthorne).

The emphasis on this effect, I believe, reflects Hawthorne's larger concern with the literary symbol as he had begun to employ it in this and other short works. He is preoccupied here with the question of interpretation and effect, tantalized, it seems, by the radiant power of his new instrument. Like ideal readers or critics in relation to a story, the townspeople are obsessed with the veil, intrigued by its possible meanings, overwhelmed by its spiritual

> By refusing revelation and provoking an endless battery of possible interpretations and responses, the minister carries Hawthorne's message that the only truth that stands affirmed in the veil is the truth of the artistic symbol's boundless resonance and evocative force."

and emotive power. Like readers cut off from the author or intimidated by him, "not one ventured to put the plain question to Mr. Hooper, wherefore he did this thing". But eventually, like naive readers unable to control their curiosity and simplistically trustful that the author is the final arbiter of his own meanings (a trust, by the way, that, if we share it, finally reduces the rich tale to the shallowness of the minister's own death-bed fulmination), a few approach him. Futilely, of course, for the creator will not reveal his intentions.

The ultimate naive reader, however, is the minister's fiancee. A simple literalist who perceives none of the symbolic import that perplexes and mortifies the others, Elizabeth "could discern nothing of the dreadful gloom that had so overawed the multitude": to her "it was but a double fold of crape ...." Such a reader would have the author renounce his symbol and return to the realist's simpler perception of the world (which she has never transcended), undarkened and uncomplicated by the veil. Rejecting her entreaty, the minister echoes the sentiment of Carlyle's Professor Teufelsdroeckh in [Thomas Carlyle's] *Sartor Resartus*, a work written but two years earlier than "The Minister's Black Veil," and one whose views on symbolism, so close to that of the parable, may suggest an influence. "Small is this which thou tellest me," declares the Professor,

> that the Royal Sceptre is but a piece of gilt-wood; that the Pyx has become a most foolish box, and truly, as

Ancient Pistol thought, 'of little price.' A right Conjuror might I name thee, couldst thou conjure back into these wooden tools the divine virtue they once held. (Carlyle)

Hawthorne is such a conjurer, of course, as is Hooper. Both conjure back into the simple materials of literature and earth a power beyond. They do so, as Teufelsdroeckh recommends, by planting ''into the deep infinite faculties of man, his Fantasy and Heart'' (Carlyle)—Hooper by means of the veil, the artist by means of the symbol the veil represents. And it is here that Elizabeth, experiencing what both the minister and the artist hope for, feels its effects at last, as its terrors fall around her. Only now does she sense what the physician's wife had remarked earlier: the power with which person and context can invest the otherwise barren tools of art's ministry. ''How strange,'' the wife had mused, ''that a simple black veil such as any woman might wear on her bonnet, should become such a terrible thing on Mr. Hooper's face!'' The observation is crucial, for it suggests that, like the symbol—indeed like all language—the veil has no detachable or intrinsic significance. The meanings it carries and the impact it generates, finally to Elizabeth as well, are dependent on the user, on the context, and on the inferred intentions of its use. It is when the minister rejects the invitation to removal and literal rendering and, offering evocative symbolic hypotheses for her to ponder, returns the burden of feeling and reflection to this ''reader,'' that she becomes aware of these forces and feels the shuddering impact of the symbol.

''In a symbol,'' remarks Carlyle, ''there is concealment and yet revelation.'' And the veil, both as symbol and as symbol of . . . , is a concealment that is a revelation of concealment. To the minister and the sinners who become his disciples, it is a concealment revelatory of the universal masking of secret sin (''lo! on every Visage a Black veil!''). For the reader it is a concealment that reveals concealment as the only viable meaning. In this tale, in all of Hawthorne's best symbolic work, perhaps in all fiction and language, the veil as veiling or veiledness is itself the message. The ambiguity and mystery of the concealing veil become themselves the meaning, suggesting the inaccessibility of determinate meaning or truth.

The meaning of a (Hawthorne) story is found not behind its signs or symbols, but in the fact and experience of impenetrability, the realization that no interpretation will suffice. The veil again is a symbol of symbols, more broadly a symbol of the symbolistic resonance of signs. ''Speech,'' as Teufelsdroeckh affirms, ''is great, but not the greatest.'' For ''Speech is of Time, Silence [like the symbol and the veil] is of Eternity'' (Carlyle . . .). The Professor's point about the silent power of the symbol—that ''Thought will not work except in Silence''—is the parable's point about the veil: namely, that speech, the minister's earlier sermons unaccompanied by the veil, is relatively effete as a stimulant of profoundest thought and recognition. In the symbol, on the other hand, ''in many a painted Device or simple Seal-emblem, the commonest Truth stands out to us proclaimed with quite new emphasis'' (Carlyle). As it does for Hooper, whose sermons assume unprecedented power.

What we see in Hawthorne's tale, of course, is that the moral message of the veil, if indeed there is one, is not disclosed until the minister's death, if even then. The power and consequently the point of the veil lies not in its meaning, its ''common Truth,'' for were it so, Hooper would surely have proclaimed it sooner. Rather, by refusing revelation and provoking an endless battery of possible interpretations and responses, the minister carries Hawthorne's message that the only truth that stands affirmed in the veil is the truth of the artistic symbol's boundless resonance and evocative force. The important truth of the veil is not the universality of concealed sin, for that revelation is too long postponed to be of consequence to most of its observers. The veil speaks far more eloquently of what Carlyle calls ''The incalculable influences of Concealment'' that account for ''the wondrous agency of Symbols''.

That the meaning of the veil is in the veil itself and not in any hidden referent seems confirmed by the pointlessness of the Reverend Mr. Clark's last-minute effort to raise the veil in search of its meaning. ''Before the veil of eternity be lifted,''' urges Clark at Hooper's bedside, ''let me cast aside this black veil from your face!' . . . And thus speaking . . . bent forward to reveal the mystery of many years.'' If Elizabeth is the naive literalist who believes at first that the veil is a mere object rather than a sign or symbol, the Reverend Clark is the simple allegorizer who looks for single meanings directly behind the given sign. The effort is futile, of course, not because Hooper resists it, but because the raising of the veil would reveal only a face and nothing of the veil's meaning. The minister clasps the veil to his face not because its removal would reveal the hidden meaning behind it, but because such an act would remove veil and all meaning together.

Hawthorne emphasizes the point in a fine ambiguity that introduces and casts doubt on the minister's deathbed revelation, which has too often been accepted as the "true meaning" of the veil. "What, but the mystery which it obscurely typifies has made this piece of crepe so awful?" asks the minister. Readers have assumed—and been led to assume—that the mystery he speaks of is revealed in the ensuing tirade on the loathsome treasuring up of secret sin.

But there is another way to read the minister's question, one that seals the concealed meaning of the veil as artist's symbol, hence as essential mystery, as tightly as Hooper's disclosure seems to shut the door on further queries into what this sign signifies. For what has made this piece of crape so aw[e]ful is precisely "the mystery" it obscurely typifies. The veil, in other words, typifies not *a* mystery to be disclosed, but mystery itself, and it does so by typifying obscurely, in a way that perpetually tempts and frustrates the assignation of all meaning beyond itself.

Such a reading of "The Minister's Black Veil" raises again the familiar question of Hawthorne's view of the role and power of the artist and, through that, the nearly threadbare controversy over his attitude toward the minister's donning and wearing the veil. For if the veil is the artist's symbol, then Hooper is a kind of symbolizing artist, the author himself perhaps. Like Hawthorne before he discovered the awesome power of the literary symbol, Hooper was a good but "not an energetic" preacher who "strove to win his people . . . by mild persuasive influences, rather than to drive them thither [to heaven], by the thunders of the Word." When he adopts the symbolic method by donning the veil, however, a telling change is felt in his oratory. The sermon he now delivers is marked by "the same characteristics of style and manner," the same unthundering quietness.

> But there was something, either in the sentiment of the discourse itself, or in the imagination of the auditors, which made it greatly the most powerful effort that they had ever heard from their pastor's lips . . . . A subtle power was breathed into his words.

As it was into Hawthorne's own written words, and it is not too much, I think, to suggest that "The Minister's Black Veil—A Parable" is itself the fictive equivalent of the minister's sermon. Its subject too "had reference to secret sin"; it too is "tinged rather more darkly than usual with the gentle gloom" of its author's temperament; and it too, Hawthorne may well have felt, was his most powerful effort to that time.

That "The Minister's Black Veil" is, as the full title indicates, "A Parable," places it in the same category with Hooper's sermon on secret sin—a veiled reference to the veil—and with the veil itself as a bearer of veiled messages. Hawthorne and the minister, in other words, are identified as preacher/artists. Both deliver texts whose subject is the veil and whose parabolic meaning is concealed until the deathbed "revelation," which at once retroactively casts at least putative meaning on both the minister's sermon and the tale that contains it. It is only here that we encounter the allegorical message of the veil and recognize the veil as the hidden referent of Hooper's dark sermon. Hawthorne as artist offers the symbol in search of single meaning. Hooper, the double craftsman, presents a similar challenge in his veil while offering in his sermon-as-veiled-parable meaning in search of attachment to the floating symbol of the veil.

By donning the veil, Hooper becomes what Hawthorne would come to feel himself, more and more strongly as he developed and perfected his symbolic art: a removed and judging observer who felt he could penetrate the mystery of other souls while remaining invisible. The veil conceals the minister's face as effectively as a tale, particularly a veiled symbolic tale, conceals its author and his intent. It hangs before his face, covering everything but the mouth and chin, leaving free, in other words, the speaking organ only. It enables him to preach far more effectively than before, and it causes the members of his magnetized congregation to shrink uneasily from his eye, "which they felt to be fixed upon them with an invisible glance." Passing from the uninspired realism of his earlier work to the eerily suggestive power of the symbolic tales, we feel, with Elizabeth and his congregation, the effects of the veil that is a symbol of symbols.

For Hawthorne, we know, there is a price to be paid for the artist's mission and his remotely scrutinizing insight: the price of personal isolation, the punishment as well as the privilege of the seer who sees and remains himself unseen. The minister, of course, pays the artist's price for his power. He has "changed himself into something awful . . . by hiding his face" and peering, like Hawthorne, through his obscure and somber tales, through a veil that gave "a darkened aspect to all living and inanimate things."

Like the poet Coverdale in *The Blithedale Romance* where the veil is again a focal symbol; like the scientific researchers of the soul that darken his fiction; and like Hawthorne's guilty conception of the writer that these figures typify, Hooper is ''a man apart from men,'' separated from the world by his ''dismal shade.'' He is separated too, and as a result, from happiness, lonely and frightened behind his black veil, where he gropes ''darkly within his own soul [and gazes] . . . through a medium that saddened the whole world''. Like Hawthorne's image of the minister ''gazing darkly within his own soul,'' the Hawthorne given us by critics and biographers experienced ''the perpetual turning in of the mind upon itself, the long introspective brooding over human motives'' that probed the soul's secret impulses and laid bare its dark workings. ''I have made a captive of myself and put me into a dungeon,'' he wrote to Longfellow in 1837,

> and now I cannot find the key to let myself out—and if the door were open, I should be almost afraid to come out. . . . [There] is no fate in this world so horrible as to have no share in either its joys or sorrows. For the last ten years, I have not lived, but only dreamed about living. (''To Henry Wadsworth Longfellow'')

''[Without] thy aid,'' he wrote to his wife Sophia in 1840,

> my best knowledge of myself would have been merely to know my own shadow—to watch it flickering on the wall, and mistake its fantasies for my own real actions. Indeed, we are but shadows—we are not endowed with real life, and all that seems most real about us is but the thinnest substance of a dream— till the heart is touched. (''To Sophia Peabody Hawthorne'')

This closing phrase, if it is more climax than afterthought, seems to support Malcolm Cowley's hypothesis that Hawthorne's work declined in the final years of his life not, as many have argued, because of his claustrophobic preoccupation with the shadows of his imagination, but because the affections of his heart and his emergence into the too bright world blocked his access to the source of his hermetic inspiration. It was, after all, after his heart was touched by Sophia, his time by the demands of wife and family, his insulated privacy by the demands upon a public figure, that his imagination and his art began to fail.

But whatever the cause of his artistic decline, there is a poignant connection between the suspected vacuity of the symbol and Hawthorne's anxiety about the vaporous insubstantiality of the isolated self. In a private world where fantasies are mistaken for human actions and where all that seems most real is but the faint immateriality of a dream, symbol and reality merge in their common lack of substance. The self that wants reality is reflected in the symbol devoid of meaning or reference. Both exist in solitude, draped in the shadow that is all the reality they possess.

While I do not wish to venture into the controversy over the tale's implicit judgment of the minister and his art, whether Hooper is a devoted martyr, an inhuman anti-Christ, or some hybrid form between, I will offer an addendum that touches on the question. The veil, as we have traditionally read the minister's deathbed translation, is the symbol not of human sinfulness, but of the refusal of its revelation, the ''loathsome . . . treasuring up'' that conceals what should be made manifest. ''When the friend shows his inmost heart to his friend; the lover to his best-beloved; when man does not vainly shrink from the eye of his Creator . . . ,'' declaims the minister, ''then deem me a monster. . . .''

There is more to this denunciatory confession than at first appears; implicit self-accusation stirs beneath the seeming self-exoneration and projection. On one level, ''*then* deem me a monster'' invites merely nominal condemnation. The minister alone will continue to wear the veil symbolic of sin's furtive concealment when others have opened their sinfulness to divine and human view. Only at this barely imaginable time will he be monstrous, and then but metaphorically, for his veil is but an emblem of the crime it represents. Indeed, by wearing the veil, the minister exalts himself, becomes, it seems, a kind of Just Man by publicizing on his own face the secretiveness others practice but deny. The minister is as yet no monster, not only because others share his defect but, equally paradoxically, because he achieves in his exposure at least partial absolution from the sin he exposes to view.

And yet, as the minister/artist takes on the character of the symbol he employs, in the very act of exposing the souls and hidden sinfulness of others, Hooper, like the artist, also partakes of the infection he perceives. As the artist falls into isolation in the demanding task of its description, becoming the distanced judge of those whose judgmental detachment he condemns, so Hooper, in the obfuscation of his message, becomes tangled in what he would merely emblemize. Like the power of the purloined letter, hidden by a different sort of minister, the power of the symbol, as of the veil, lies not in its use but its concealment.

"With the employment [of the letter]," Poe's narrator observes, "the power departs." And similarly, the conclusive ascription of any given meaning to the veil or symbol drains the potency bonded to its mystery. By withholding until the moment of his death the presumed meaning of his symbol, Hooper maintains his lifelong grip upon his "readers," but at another price. For in concealing from them the secret of his veil, he turns the symbol into the moral reality it allegedly signifies. The minister's act implicates him in the crime of concealment that the veil symbolizes and condemns. The symbol has become its meaning, the artistic or symbolizing act a patch of the moral as well as existential darkness it illumines.

It is in this sense among others that "a preternatural horror was interwoven with the threads of the black crape." And it is for this reason that "the black veil involved [the minister's] . . . own spirit in the horror with which it overwhelmed all others." The minister's frame, which is also that of the artist and the narrative, shudders when he glimpses his veiled figure in the looking-glass, not merely for its emblematic potency, but because of the enmeshing tangle of doing and being that twines Ahab to the whale. The "Veil" as fiction, which, like the veil, is a parable finally only of its mystery, weaves the artist into the incriminating veil of his own separating mystification.

Source: William Freedman, "The Artist's Symbol and Hawthorne's Veil: 'The Minister's Black Veil' Resartus," in *Studies in Short Fiction*, Vol. 29, No. 3, Summer, 1992, pp. 353–62.

W. B. Carnochan

In the following excerpt, Carnochan presents his interpretation of the veil as symbol, emphasizing that Hawthorne uses it in the story to explore the nature of all such symbols.

"The Minister's Black Veil," one of Hawthorne's early tales (1836), has a reputation as one of his best. It has had less attention than, say, "Rappaccini's Daughter" or "My Kinsman, Major Molineux," no doubt because it is in some ways less problematic and is a less bravura piece than are they. Still the story presents its own kind of difficulties, and there is no critical unanimity among its readers. On one view the Reverend Mr. Hooper is a saintly figure, calling his people to repentance in the manner of an old testament prophet; on another view he is a victim of monomaniac obsession, one of Hawthorne's unpardonable sinners or, even, a type of antichrist. Between these extremes, opinion shades off to a less monochromatic center. But interpretation of the story generally rests on some moral assessment or explanation of the minister's symbolic self-veiling. The mystery is conceived as one to be *solved*, just as Poe conceived it when he argued that the minister had committed a "crime of dark dye" against the "young lady" whose burial is described. What Poe calls a defect—"that to the rabble its exquisite skill will be *caviare*"—he surely thinks a virtue: he is happy in the discovery of concealed evidence, from which he infers a romantic solution more congenial to his taste than the merely generalized didacticism of the "moral" that the minister pronounces at his death. I shall argue, to the contrary, that neither solutions, like Poe's, nor moral estimates, like many a critic's and even the minister's own, are essential. The story, I believe, is concerned above all with the veil as a symbolic object, pointing toward questions that cluster about the notion of a symbol itself. Beside these questions, the moral character of the minister who wears the veil is relatively a minor matter.

If so, this early story has a more important place than it is usually given in Hawthorne's canon: like *The Scarlet Letter*—which is *about* the letter of its title, just as this story is about the veil—"The Minister's Black Veil" has to do with the materials of Hawthorne's own art in proportion as it has to do with the nature of symbolic meaning. Thinking about this story, we need to remember all the while the abortive history of Hawthorne's last romances and the altogether desolate end of his literary life—where we get, as Hyatt H. Waggoner has said [in *Hawthorne: A Critical Study*, 1963], "no merely technical failure, and no turning to new subjects that he did not know how to handle, but a failure at the very center, a failure of meaning." This failure of meaning is a failure of the symbolic process: the relationship, always for Hawthorne a difficult matter, between symbol and reference breaks down entirely, and the course of his artistic life can be roughly plotted in terms of this disintegration. "The Minister's Black Veil" stakes out the ground on which Hawthorne was to struggle with the angel of destruction.

Even to ask the bald question, "What does the veil stand for?" implies the difficulty of giving any answer. Perhaps it is just as well, however, to frame the question in a way that makes the difficulties apparent. In any case, the Hawthornian business of false leads and doubtful clarifications is under way from the very start of the tale. In an introductory

> **So the veil, creating meaning and simultaneously hiding it, invites speculation and resists it."**

note, we hear about ''another clergyman in New England, Mr. Joseph Moody, of York, Maine, who died about eighty years since'' and who ''made himself remarkable by the same eccentricity that is here related of the Reverend Mr. Hooper.'' Then, still with an air of being helpful and direct, Hawthorne offers what seem to be distinctions: ''In his case [Moody's], however, the symbol had a different import. In early life he had accidentally killed a beloved friend; and from that day till the hour of his death, he hid his face from men.'' But what sort of distinctions are these? And how precisely are Moody and Hooper different cases? The explanation, on a closer look, turns out not to be an explanation at all. Of what is Mr. Moody's veil a ''symbol''? Grief, surely; but we do not know the ''accidental'' means by which he killed his friend, nor do we know except in a general way why he hid his face from men. We are faced with an ''ambiguity of sin or sorrow,'' as much as in Hooper's case. Hawthorne's note—like the veil itself—obscures as much as it reveals. Still, despite the falseness of its reassurance, there is something of the genuine in it, too; it is in keeping, as I want to show, with the whole point of the tale that Hooper's mysterious veil has a counterpart in reality. Here again it is like the scarlet letter with its counterpart that Hawthorne finds in the custom house and is at such pains to be precise about (''By an accurate measurement, each limb proved to be precisely three inches and a quarter in length''). Each fictional symbol is attached to a fact in the real world.

We can try another question, a little less blatant: what does Hooper's veil stand for in its own context? Because the minister's dying speech sounds a dominant note, or seems to, it is easy to go there first of all:

> ''When the friend shows his inmost heart to his friend; the lover to his best beloved; when man does not vainly shrink from the eye of his Creator, loathsomely treasuring up the secret of his sin; then deem me a monster, for the symbol beneath which I have lived,

and die! I look around me, and, lo! on every visage a Black Veil!''

Coming as it does at the end, this looks like summary and conclusion. But that is as deceptive as the authoritative air of the opening footnote. If we throw caution aside and take this last pronouncement as conclusive, the story is that parable of hidden guilt which it is usually supposed to be—and also, I think, a less interesting story than it really is. Hooper's final piety, his deathbed utterance with its implied confession, all this needs to be taken dramatically—as a formal setpiece—and with the reservations appropriate to so pat a gesture. It is the end, or almost the end, of the story—but not the whole of it. We need not, in fact cannot, let it go as a drama of clandestine sin. Granted that Hawthorne was concerned, deeply so, with that theme; but here it is concealment and mystery, not guilt, that concerns him most, and that makes the difference.

The very nature of the veil itself is to avert explicit statements of what it stands for, or at least to throw them immediately in doubt. It is not just that ''the meaning of the symbol is ambiguous''; that would tell us little we did not always know. Rather the strange quality of the veil is that not only does it conceal what is behind it, it is a sign of that concealment; it both symbolizes and generates what is symbolized, is its own symbol—and, in its self-containment, is in one sense beyond interpretation, i.e., beyond any rendering in referential terms. But to ''mean'' is a function of the human, to ''be'' a function of the divine; a symbol, humanly speaking, implies something symbolized that is not only itself. So the veil, creating meaning and simultaneously hiding it, invites speculation and resists it. No one ever dares ask Hooper why he wears the veil. The deputation from the church, sent to ''deal with Mr. Hooper about the mystery''—how obviously inappropriate is the commercial dealing with mystery—never comes to the point: ''Were the veil but cast aside, they might speak freely of it, but not till then.'' Because the meaning of the veil consists only in what is hidden, meaning is lost in the very act of revelation. It is in this that the veil serves as ''type'' and ''symbol'' of types and symbols in their general nature. As language gives a meaning to experience but also comes between the subject and any direct perception or re-creation of that experience, so does the veil. ''In a Symbol,'' says Carlyle (as Professor Teufelsdroeckh) [in *Sartor Resartus*], ''there is concealment and yet revelation.'' Hooper's veil embodies the paradox.

In this setting the common Hawthornian tactic that F. O. Matthiessen calls [in *American Renaissance*, 1941] "the device of multiple choice" and Yvor Winters [in *Maule's Curse*, 1938] "the formula of alternative possibilities" works to special advantage. The tactic is uncomplicated: merely that of offering several explanations of events or symbolic circumstances and apparently leaving the reader, according to his own lights, to accept the one that suits him best. "The reader may choose," says Hawthorne, among the several theories proposed to explain the mark (if there was one) "imprinted" in the Reverend Mr. Dimmesdale's flesh. But the formula is really designed to prevent, not to encourage, speculation. We are intended *not* to choose; it is difficult to suppose that Donatello has furry ears, but it is damaging to suppose that he doesn't. And, by the same token, it is damaging to limit the extensions of the veil to this one or to that. It is not one veil but every veil. It is the glass through which we see darkly; Hooper appears in the pulpit "*face to face* [my emphasis] with his congregation, except for"—a grim irony—"the black veil." Elsewhere it is associated with the darkness of night that obscures the visible world, or with "the veil that shuts in time from eternity." Sometimes it turns Hooper away from the mirrors of self-knowledge: "In truth, his own antipathy to the veil was known to be so great, that he never willingly passed before a mirror, nor stooped to drink at a still fountain, lest, in its peaceful bosom, he should be affrighted by himself." He resists the last knowledge that he is hidden even from himself. But, still elsewhere, the veil itself becomes a magic mirror, reversing the world of normal experience in its transfiguring presence: the funeral of the young woman is transformed to a marriage ("I had a fancy," says one observer—giving Poe the lead he was looking for—"that the minister and the maiden's spirit were walking hand in hand"), and the "cold fingers" and "deathlike paleness" of a bride at her wedding change the ceremony into a dance of death. For the veil all things are possible; its extensions come naturally from its primary character as a symbol of symbols, hence capable of all their protean changes. If we cannot eliminate the human fact of reference, still we need not commit ourselves to other versions of the absolute and insist on singleness of reference; since a single correspondence cannot be finally established, that way lies either delusion or skepticism and despair.

To insist on a single meaning or explanation is in fact to be like the townspeople of the story, who speculate upon the reasons for Mr. Hooper's veil: "A few shook their sagacious heads, intimating that they could penetrate the mystery; while one or two affirmed that there was no mystery at all, but only that Mr. Hooper's eyes were so weakened by the midnight lamp, as to require a shade." In this case we are specifically not asked to choose—the technique has not yet crystallized into a "formula" of alternative possibilities—and we do well to profit from the absence of advice. The alternatives available are each intended to be unacceptable: on one hand, to be identified with the "sagacious" few who think they can penetrate the mystery; on the other, to deny the mystery altogether. Either choice is self-defeating. But "sagacious" readers have not been wanting.

In truth, however, they have better reasons than any we have seen so far. Misguided prying into the mystery by "all the busybodies and impertinent people in the parish" is one thing; the case of Elizabeth, betrothed to Mr. Hooper, looks more doubtful. Her plea that Hooper take off the veil and reveal his secret to her is a sympathetic one; probably it is her presence that accounts for the view of Hooper as a malevolent spirit: "As his plighted wife, it should be her privilege to know what the black veil concealed." The scene that follows between Elizabeth and Hooper is a strange one, however. To her request that he "lift the veil but once," he answers that it cannot be. The feeling aimed at seems to be that the veil in literal fact *cannot* be removed; it is not, we are made to think, a volitional matter. But Elizabeth bids Hooper farewell, and the strangeness is especially in Hooper's response: "But, even amid his grief, Mr. Hooper smiled to think that only a material emblem had separated him from happiness, though the horrors, which it shadowed forth, must be drawn darkly between the fondest of lovers." On one hand it is "only a material emblem," on the other it seems to be everything; but symbol and thing symbolized, however (other than itself) that may be interpreted, are felt as concordant with one another. And there seems to lie the motive for Elizabeth's reappearance to nurse Hooper at his death—"no hired handmaiden of death, but one whose calm affection had endured thus long in secrecy, in solitude, amid the chill of age, and would not perish, even at the dying hour." The long endurance of a "calm affection" comes unexpectedly after Elizabeth's abrupt farewell in the earlier scene; the assertion of fidelity, in the presence of mystery is no easy one for Hawthorne to make, and the narrative lacks cohesion at the point of greatest strain. An assertion, nonetheless, there is: to keep faith is to accept the fact of human meaning behind the veil—even though that meaning, in the nature of things, is hidden to the eye.

But the phantom lure of knowing the unknowable is not so easily set aside. Mr. Hooper's veil and the efforts—Elizabeth's well-intentioned ones, the townspeople's vulgar and impertinent ones—to discover what lies behind it anticipate the veils and masks and efforts to "penetrate their mystery" that are so important in Hawthorne's later fiction. They make a large subject, beyond the reach of this paper. Also beyond the reach of this paper are the details of Hawthorne's decline. But this generalization may be risked: it is the possibility of faith—by that I mean a habit of mind more crucial than any specifically religious belief, the failure of which is sometimes supposed to account for Hawthorne's fate as an artist—that is for him ever more in doubt. The vain hope of lifting the veil and the fears of what might be found there (or, really, what might not be found there) become obsessive and, in the long run, paralyzing to the imagination. . . .

Despite Elizabeth's fidelity and despite the wan hope in that "faint, sad smile, so often there, [that] seemed to glimmer from its obscurity, and linger on Father Hooper's lips" as he dies, no one is likely to mistake the mood of the tale. Elizabeth's affection, revealed so late, scarcely relieves the gloom, and the last word is still the veil: "The grass of many years has sprung up and withered on that grave, the burial stone is moss-grown, and good Mr. Hooper's face is dust; but awful is still the thought that it mouldered beneath the Black Veil!" The veil survives the changes of time after its meanings have turned to dust. Acceptance was not Hawthorne's lot, nor was the unreflective life, whose matter-of-factness he sometimes catches sight of with a touch of longing and reproduces here in the accents of the village, at the beginning of the tale:

> "Are you sure it is our parson?" inquired Goodman Gray of the sexton.

> "Of a certainty it is good Mr. Hooper," replied the sexton. "He was to have exchanged pulpits with Parson Shute, of Westbury; but Parson Shute sent to excuse himself yesterday, being to preach a funeral sermon."

"Certainty" is for the unthoughtful, acceptance for the faithful; for Hawthorne, there will be only the gathering pressure of questions not to be answered and meanings not to be found. In its fine rhetorical adjustment of means to ends, "The Minister's Black Veil" is among Hawthorne's best stories; in mood and substance it is grimly prophetic of what was to come.

Source: W. B. Carnochan, "'The Minister's Black Veil,'" in *Nineteenth-Century Fiction,* Vol. 24, No. 2, September, 1969, pp. 182–92.

E. Earle Stibitz

In the following excerpt, Stibitz presents his interpretation of Hawthorne's handling of irony in the story, focusing on the Reverend Mr. Hooper's alienation from the rest of humankind.

Because Hawthorne is always very much the same and yet also surprisingly varied, one way of understanding "The Minister's Black Veil," as with any Hawthorne tale, is to read it not only as the unique work of art that it is, but as a tale comparable to others by Hawthorne, viewing it in the context of his essentially consistent thought and art as a whole. Such a reading of "The Minister's Black Veil" yields an unambiguous meaning. Hawthorne, with his usual assumption of the reality of personal evil, presents on one level his fundamental belief in man's proneness to hide or rationalize his most private thoughts or guilt. This is the "parable" (of the subtitle) that the Reverend Mr. Hooper seeks to preach with his wearing of the veil. On another level, Hawthorne reaffirms his equally constant belief that man is often guilty of pridefully and harmfully exalting one idea, frequently a valid truth in itself, to the status of an absolute. This is the sin Hooper commits by his self-righteous and self-deceptive insistence upon wearing the veil.

The second level grows out of the first and remains dependent upon it, a structural pattern repeated in varying ways in each major division of the story. Furthermore, this organic relationship of the two levels is ironic. Hooper in his stubborn use of the veil parable of one sin is unconsciously guilty of a greater one—that of egotistically warping the total meaning of life. This irony is compounded in that Hooper's sin is a hidden one—hidden not only from his fellows but from himself. He thus unintentionally dramatizes the very sin of secrecy that he intentionally sets out to symbolize. The central symbol of the veil keeps pace with this added irony: in addition to standing for man's concealment or hypocrisy and for Hooper's own sin of pride with its isolating effects, it stands also for the hidden quality of the second sin. All told, "The Minister's Black Veil" is less ambiguous and more unified because it is more ironic than has usually been recognized.

The interpretations various critics have made of "The Minister's Black Veil," taken as a whole, offer three basic points of view. First is the interpretation that the veil indicates some specific crime by Mr. Hooper. This is Poe's view [in his review of *Twice-Told Tales*] and is one concurred in by Leland Schubert and in part by R. H. Fogle, who holds that a crime by the minister remains an ambiguous possibility in the story. A second view, and the one most widely held, rejects the idea of personal wrongdoing and sees the veil simply as a device chosen by the minister to dramatize a common human failing: man's refusal to show to anyone his inner heart with its likely load of private guilt. Among the critics that have subscribed to this view are Newton Arvin, Gilbert Voigt, Randall Stewart, and Mark Van Doren. Some of the critics who hold generally to this view concern themselves, in addition, with the effect of the veil upon the minister. The third view holds that there is something fundamentally wrong in the minister's wearing of the veil. W. B. Stein is a vigorous exponent of this view, arguing that the story is one of a man of God turned antichrist, especially in Hooper's failure to follow Paul's II Corinthians injunction to ministers to let love be the principle of the relationship with their congregations. Mr. Fogle, basically representative of this view, argues for two meanings. There is the explicit meaning of the veil as a symbol of man's secret sin, with Hooper as Everyman bearing his lonely fate in order to demonstrate a tragic truth; and there is the implicit one of human unbalance, with Hooper's action out of all proportion to need or benefit. The story, says Mr. Fogle, remains ambiguous with the discrepancies in meaning unresolved—albeit an effective lack of resolution. A footnote to Mr. Fogle's argument is Mr. Walsh's comment on the minister's dubious smile, a recurrent element in the story. The smile, always linked with light, though consistently faint, stands in opposition to the veil, always linked with darkness, and produces, says Mr. Walsh, a fundamental ambiguity. Both Mr. Stewart and Mr. Van Doren, in general discussions of Hawthorne's tales, imply that Hooper is perhaps guilty of some spiritually wrong attitude.

That Hooper is in some way in the wrong seems an inescapable conclusion from any careful reading of the story, but some qualification is called for in each of the criticisms presenting this third view. Mr. Stein's low estimate of Hooper must in general be accepted, but because of Hawthorne's humanistic emphasis in this story as well as elsewhere it is very difficult to see Hooper as an antichrist; Mr. Stein

> **" Actually, by focusing attention, including the minister's own concern, on the general sin of human concealment the veil has made effective the hiding of the more important personal sin."**

makes Hawthorne too orthodox. And the argument for the II Corinthians analogue remains speculative. What Mr. Fogle says about the minister's unbalance is valid, but perhaps less so his judgment about the meaning of the tale as a whole. Against his claim of "discrepancies," of a basic ambiguity, must be asserted the essential unity of the tale. The irony is strongly unifying, not only in tone but also in meaning. Hawthorne here is his usually detached self, but this artistic distance is not noncommittalism. In general too much has been made of Hawthorne's ambiguity in theme. Often he employs ambiguity in details and is ambiguous in total philosophy revealed, but only very rarely does ambiguity qualify a specific theme. Finally, Mr. Walsh's assumption, in his point of ambiguity in the smile-light and veil-dark imagery, that Hawthorne uses light to suggest something spiritually positive, is acceptable. But most readers will not find the smile a true smile or the light clearly light, as the faintness of the whole image makes evident; there is a peculiarly mixed quality about the smile itself—indeed something ironic.

The ironic meaning of "The Minister's Black Veil," is incorporated in and, in part, is created by its vertical or logical structure. Out of the first level of meaning, the calling of attention to the truth of man's proneness to the sin of concealment, rises the second level, the minister's sin in making his veil demonstration all-important; and this second level, with its irony, absorbs the first, creating a dominant theme. An analysis that seeks to offer evidence of this unity of form and meaning can best be presented by following the horizontal or chronological structure of the tale—the successive divisions of its narrative development. Narrative sequence and timing are very important here and have usually been neglected in the religious and philosophical discussions of the story. There are five divisions: (1) the first appearance of Hooper wearing the veil at the Sunday morning service; (2) Hooper's appearances at the funeral and at the wedding on the same Sunday; (3) the unsuccessful effort of a deputation from the congregation, and of Elizabeth, his fiancee, to reason with him about the veil; (4) a summary picture of Hooper's life from the time of these efforts to his death; (5) the deathbed scene. In each of these divisions the two levels of meaning are ironically united to produce a singleness of theme.

At the beginning of the first division the minister is revealed as experiencing a twofold alienation—from man and from God. Because of the strange veil the members of the congregation sense the minister's distance, and he, in turn, sees them darkly. Also the veil comes between him and God as he reads the Scripture and as he prays. That Hooper's estrangement is the first point established in the story suggests the central importance of the minister's second-level sin. In Hawthorne, isolation of one kind or another is consistently presented as the result of sin, and at times as being something very close to sin itself, a sin frequently linked with intellectual or spiritual pride. Here Hooper's alienation argues that the wearing of the veil is in some way profoundly wrong. And under this second level of meaning lies the more briefly developed first level, the veil as the symbol of hidden guilt, which is introduced by the sermon with its condemnation of secret sin.

Not only are the two levels thus established but so also is their ironic relationship. While the one sin is consciously preached (through veil parable and sermon), the second sin is unconsciously embodied (through the minister's egotistic assumptions and actions). Emphasis is upon the minister's pride that leads him to make the truth of man's hypocrisy the only Truth and brings him to force his idea upon the consciousness and conscience of his congregation. For example, though the sermon is supposedly praised as one of the most powerful that the minister has preached, the minister himself is described as creeping upon the members of the congregation behind his awful veil and discovering the hoarded iniquity of each one. In this, Hooper is close to Hawthorne's most damning sin—"the human invasion of the sanctity of the human heart," to use Dimmesdale's description of Chillingworth's sin. That Hooper is acting professionally increases rather than lessens the sin, for as a minister he should have been spiritually more sensitive. Indeed he is like a number of other Hawthorne sinners who ". . . in their attempt to assume the role of God . . . naturally give their allegiance to Satan, and subsequently find themselves contributing to that very imperfection which they had originally wished to eliminate." The irony here is heightened in that the spiritual wrongdoing pictured by the minister in his sermon describes precisely what he is soon guilty of—hiding his sin "from his nearest and dearest, and from his own consciousness."

In the second division, two contrasting yet representative events of life, a funeral and a wedding, dramatize the meaning of the veil on both levels with their continuing ironic tension. At the funeral, the veil for the only time in the story is a truly appropriate emblem. Apart from its somberness it is appropriate (if we accept the idea of the minister's prayer) because the truth of human secretiveness is one that human beings most fully realize when they are confronted with death. Yet even now the incidents that Poe believed linked the minister with the dead girl in some specific crime—for example, his fear that she will see his face—indicate that the wearing of the veil is not entirely right. As often, Hawthorne uses such ambiguous details to enrich the meaning and heighten the tone of the narrative rather than to establish its main direction. These details underscore the meaning already revealed by emphasizing the unnaturalness of Hooper's action, and they heighten the tone by pointing up the ironic discrepancy between the supposedly helpful intent of the minister and the actual spiritual result.

The unbalance of Hooper in his isolation from normal life and love is strongly in evidence at the wedding, where his wearing of the veil brings fear and doubt, a markedly different effect from the feeling of quiet cheerfulness and sympathy he formerly evoked on such occasions. Hooper's use of the veil to instruct his parishioners religiously has resulted in their spiritual impoverishment in that human love has been diminished. To Hawthorne this is a loss of something holy, for throughout his writings the acceptance or rejection of human love usually marks the choice of salvation or damnation. Mr. Hooper faces this choice and is damned by choosing to live by an idea rather than by human love. His unrepentant insistence upon his abstracted idea as central to life violates the warm reality of human existence.

The irony of Hooper's action is humorously symbolized by the prank of the village youngster who in imitation of the minister puts a black handkerchief over his face and so frightens his playmates that he creates a panic in his own mind. The presence of this satiric element, comparable to the dog's chasing its tail in "Ethan Brand," indicates that Hawthorne has a definite point of view and does not intend the story to be ultimately ambiguous. The two levels of meaning are not allowed to stand in uncommitted balance; ironic tension unites them, the first being subsumed into the second.

In the third division, the story comes to its climax with the two futile attempts to break through the wall of isolation that the minister has erected, one attempt by members of the congregation, the other by Elizabeth, his fiancee. Although the two-level irony is present in each of these efforts, the first underscores more the validity of the veil symbol as intended by the minister, the second, the fact of his sin in making the veil idea all important. Even though Mr. Hooper, heretofore, has been almost too amenable to congregational advice, a deputation of parishioners fails in its mission to question him about the veil. Feeling its symbolic truth, the visitors sit speechless before him, aware that his glance goes into their guilty hearts. But as before with the sermon the effect is less than good, for the minister's attitude and action are essentially unkind. It is not the parishioners' guilt alone that alienates them, for we are told that the minister's veil hung down over his heart. Hooper has changed from exhibiting too great submissiveness to displaying an opposite unbalance, the stubbornness of an essentially weak person obsessed with an idea.

In the succeeding scene, Hooper's response to Elizabeth's questions about the veil and his resistance to her pleas to lay it aside constitute a rejection of her love. Her patient efforts to draw him from his vow to wear the veil as a "type and symbol" meet his gentle but insurmountable obstinacy. In Hawthorne, as suggested earlier, the way to salvation is most frequently the acceptance of human love. Hooper fails to take this way. And his reaction to Elizabeth's tears reveals the sharp irony of his attitude, for it is not the hidden-sin meaning of the veil that causes her grief and terror, as he egocentrically thinks, but the rejection of her love and the irredeemable alienation demonstrated by his refusal, even for a moment, to lift the veil.

Hawthorne's description of the minister as gentle, melancholy, and sad and the quiet style of the story throughout tend to hide the fact that we are face to face with an unbalanced and unredeemed sinner. Although Hawthorne does not dwell upon the antecedent cause of Hooper's "fall," some elements of causation are evident and help to illuminate his character and clarify the irony of the tale. The minister is shown as an essentially weak man, poorly prepared by his unmarried solitude, his somewhat morbid temperament, and his professional position to deal in a stable way with an absorbing religious idea that harmonizes with his personal and vocational prejudices. He finds false strength in a kind of fanaticism, which strength destroys him as a balanced human being.

The fourth and penultimate division of the story offers chiefly the results of the events and attitudes already presented, with the ironic pattern of the previous divisions repeated. Here on the dominant second level is the minister's continued isolation, with the veil as a sign of his peculiar sin; on the first level is the account of his work as a minister, with the veil as a valid symbol of the general sin of human duplicity.

Hooper continues to stand abnormally alone in the community. The veil so envelops him with a cloud of sin or sorrow that neither love nor sympathy can reach him, and he fumbles obscurely within his own heart. But the veil also has the supposedly good result of making him an effective minister by enabling him to enter into the dark emotions of agonized sinners. Still this ability is a dubious good, and the terms "efficient" and "awful power," used to describe the minister's spiritual work, are not entirely flattering. Nor is it praise when the author speaks of the terror rather than consolation that Hooper brings to sinners who come to him for help. His awareness of the truth of hidden sin and sorrow ought to enable him not just to enter the lives of his parishioners but to enter comfortingly; however, when with evident irony he egocentrically insists upon the mechanics of the veil, he largely destroys this good potentiality.

The final division of the story, the account of Hooper's death, continues the ironic and unifying relationship of the two levels of meaning. Quantitatively the emphasis is again upon the second level, for of about a thousand words all except a hundred or so are used to picture the minister's intractability in wearing the veil on into death. Organically, this is the emphasis, too, for the irony of his action while depending upon the hidden-sin aspect so absorbs it that the story as it comes to a close is unambiguously one.

Although various persons, including Elizabeth, attend Hooper's dying moments, he is spiritually alone. Hawthorne leaves little doubt that this loneliness is the result of the minister's unbalanced action; an idea has supplanted life and love: "All through life that piece of crape has hung between him and the world; it has separated him from cheerful brotherhood and woman's love, and kept him in that saddest of all prisons, his own heart; and still it lay upon his face, as to deepen the gloom of the darksome Chamber, and shade him from the sunshine of eternity." In these closing moments of his life, his monomania is so powerful that even amid his convulsive struggles and amid the wanderings of his mind he is desperately careful to keep the veil over his face. And it is still upon his face when he is buried, a token of his final lack of repentance.

Particularly demonstrative of the ironic union of the two levels of meaning is Hooper's delayed defense of his wearing the veil by saying that everyone around him has on his own black veil. The veil is no longer merely a symbol of the fact of hidden sin or sorrow, but it is also, more dominantly, a symbol of Mr. Hooper's prideful adherence to a destructive idea—the sin of a spiritual egotism that enables him to see the mote in another's eye and blinds him to the beam in his own. The irony has become even more complex than this, for things have gone full circle, and added to the double symbolism is the fact that the veil now stands for a new *hidden* sin. Actually, by focusing attention, including the minister's own concern, on the general sin of human concealment the veil has made effective the hiding of the more important personal sin. For the reader of Hawthorne's story, of course, the veil is now the means of communicating the total irony of the minister's action and of establishing the single meaning that the author wishes to convey.

Source: E. Earle Stibitz, "Ironic Unity in Hawthorne's 'The Minister's Black Veil,'" in *American Literature*, Vol. XXXIV, No. 2, May, 1962, pp. 182–90.

Sources

Canaday, Nicholas, Jr. "Hawthorne's Minister and the Veiling Deceptions of Self," *Studies in Short Fiction*, Vol. 4, No. 1, Fall, 1966, 135-42.

Dryden, Edgar A. "Through a Glass Darkly: 'The Minister's Black Veil' as Parable," in *New Essays on Hawthorne's Major Tales*, edited by Millicent Bell, Cambridge: Cambridge University Press, 1993, pp. 133-50.

Melville, Herman. Excerpted in Faust, Bertha. "Hawthorne's Contemporaneous Reputation: A Study of Literary Opinion in America and England 1828-1864," dissertation, University of Pennsylvania, 1939, p. 63.

Stein, William Bysshe. "The Parable of the Antichrist in 'The Minister's Black Veil,'" in *American Literature*, Vol. 27, November, 1955, pp. 386-392.

Further Reading

Canaday, Nicholas, Jr. "Hawthorne's Minister and the Veiling Deceptions of Self," *Studies in Short Fiction*, Vol. 4, No. 1, Fall, 1966, pp. 135-42.
> Canaday argues that Hooper's donning of the veil reveals his excessive pride, a sin which Hawthorne criticizes in his character more than critics have realized.

Crews, Frederick. *The Sins of the Fathers: Hawthorne's Psychological Themes*, Oxford University Press, 1966, pp. 106-11.
> Crews explores issues of sexual intimacy in Hawthorne's work. He maintains that Hooper wears the veil as a pretext for breaking off his marriage to Elizabeth.

Dryden, Edgar A. "Through a Glass Darkly: 'The Minister's Black Veil' as Parable," in *New Essays on Hawthorne's Major Tales*, edited by Millicent Bell, Cambridge University Press, 1993, pp. 133-50.
> Dryden examines Hawthorne's footnote to the subtitle and finds that, instead of clarifying the meaning of Hooper's veil, the parable of Mr. Moody only makes that meaning more obscure.

German, Norman. "The Veil of Words in 'The Minister's Black Veil,'" *Studies in Short Fiction*, Vol. 25, No. 1, Winter 1988, pp. 41-7.
> German traces the Greek and Latin origins of several words Hawthorne uses frequently in close proximity, arguing that Hawthorne was consciously punning for the appreciation of those who were as well versed in classic language as he was.

Stein, William Bysshe. "The Parable of the Antichrist in 'The Minister's Black Veil,'" *American Literature*, Vol. 27, November, 1955, pp. 386-92.
> Stein condemns the Reverend Mr. Hooper as a preacher who has neglected the needs of his congregation in his pursuit of the singular message which only he is morally good enough to understand.

Turner, Arlin. *Nathaniel Hawthorne: A Biography*, Oxford University Press, 1980, 457 p.
> Turner provides the reader with a comprehensive biography of Hawthorne's life, enlivened by his use of extensive quotations from Hawthorne and his family.

Neighbour Rosicky

Willa Cather
1928

"Neighbour Rosicky," written in 1928 and collected in the volume *Obscure Destinies* in 1932, is generally considered one of Willa Cather's most successful short stories. In it, she returns to the subject matter that informed her most important novels: the immigrant experience on the Nebraska prairie. Unlike *My Antonia* and *O Pioneers!*, two novels which compellingly explore the frontier experiences of young and vigorous immigrant women, "Neighbour Rosicky" is a character study of Anton Rosicky, a man who, facing the approach of death, reflects on the meaning and value of his life. In tracing Rosicky's journey from Bohemia to Nebraska, Cather explores the intimate relationship between people and the places they inhabit. Though the story considers the pain of separations, "Neighbour Rosicky" also celebrates the small triumphs of life. Written not long after the death of her father, the story reflects a new maturity in Cather's treatment of loss. Critics often remark on the story's graceful acceptance of death's inevitability. Like many of the novels and stories that Cather wrote in the decades after World War I, "Neighbour Rosicky" also criticizes the unthinking materialism that marked the 1920s. Though some early critics found her approach sentimental, critics in later decades tended to applaud Cather's portrait of an immigrant farmer whose honesty, integrity, and emotional depth help him achieve a meaningful and happy life for himself and for his family.

Author Biography

Willa Cather was born in 1873 in Virginia, where her family lived in a small farming community. In 1884 her father, Charles Cather, decided to join his parents on the Nebraska Divide. The family lived for a year and half on the prairie among settlers from Bohemia, Scandinavia, France, Russia, Germany, and Denmark. Settler life on the Nebraska prairie would figure prominently in much of her writing, including two of her best-known novels, *O Pioneers!* (1913) and *My Antonia* (1918), as well as the story ''Neighbour Rosicky'' (1928). However, Charles Cather did not share his family's fondness for working the land and soon moved them to a nearby town of Red Cloud, Nebraska. There he worked in a real estate and loan office. Though comfortable, the family never grew prosperous. Cather later described her father as a ''Virginian and a gentleman and for that reason he was fleeced on every side and taken in on every hand.''

While in Red Cloud, Cather studied medicine and put on amateur theatricals until, with the full support of her father, she entered the University of Nebraska in 1891. There she began to write short stories for the first time and wrote articles and reviews for the *Nebraska State Journal.* These experiences led to her first job as a writer in Pittsburgh, Pennsylvania. In Pittsburgh, where part of ''Paul's Case'' is set, Cather edited a woman's magazine called *Home Monthly* and taught high school English and Latin. She lived and traveled with her friend Isabelle McClung. In 1905 she published her first book of short stories, *The Troll Garden,* which included ''Paul's Case.'' A year later she went to New York City to become managing editor for *McClure's* magazine. She worked in New York until 1912, when she retired on the advice of her friend and fellow writer Sarah Orne Jewett, who encouraged Cather to ''find [her] own quiet centre of life.''

From 1912 until her death in 1947, Cather wrote a number of successful novels, including *O Pioneers!*, *My Antonia*, and *One of Ours*, for which she won the Pulitzer Prize in 1922. She was also a prolific writer of short stories; after *The Troll Garden*, she published three more volumes of stories: *Youth and the Bright Medusa* (1920), *Obscure Destinies* (1932), in which ''Neighbour Rosicky'' appears, and *The Old Beauty, and Others* (1948). Like many of her contemporaries, Cather became disillusioned with social and political institutions after the First World War. An attitude of hopelessness often permeates her novels and stories, particularly after 1922. Critics have suggested that her turn toward historical subjects—nineteenth-century New Mexico in *Death Comes for the Archbishop* (1927) and seventeenth-century Quebec in *Shadows on the Rock* (1931)—reflects a growing need to retreat from contemporary life.

Plot Summary

I

''Neighbour Rosicky'' begins at the office of Dr. Ed Burleigh where Anton Rosicky learns that he has a bad heart. Readers also learn that Rosicky, a farmer on the Nebraska prairie, is a native of Bohemia, a region in what is today Slovakia. He is sixty-five and has a wife and six children as well as an ''American'' daughter-in-law. The doctor urges Rosicky to cease doing heavy farming chores.

After Rosicky leaves his office, Dr. Burleigh remembers how he breakfasted at the Rosicky farm the previous winter after delivering a baby for a rich neighbor. His warm welcome there causes Burleigh to reflect that good people such as the Rosickys never seem to get ahead; but he concludes that perhaps they enjoyed their life all the more.

II

As Rosicky leaves the doctor's office, he starts home but pauses by the ''snug and homelike'' graveyard that lies on the edge of his hayfield. It is snowing, and Rosicky remembers that winter means rest for the fields, the animals, and the farmers.

When he reaches home, Rosicky tells Mary that his heart ''ain't so young.'' Mary recalls that Rosicky has never treated her harshly in all their years of marriage, which has been successful because they both value the same things. The section ends with a story about how they refused to sell their cream when approached by a creamery company, preferring to give the cream to their own children instead of someone else's.

III

In section III, Rosicky has taken the doctor's advice to relinquish the heavy chores to his sons. He spends his time in his "corner" patching his sons' clothes and reminiscing. He remembers his first days in New York City, when he came to America at the age of 20 and worked in a tailor shop. In the evening he went to school to learn English. His wages were adequate, but he never saved any money and instead loaned it to friends, went to the opera, or spent it on "the girls." Soon, however, Rosicky became restless. On the Fourth of July, Rosicky "found out what was the matter with him." He realized that, in the city, he was living in an unnatural world without any contact with earthly things. He began to think about going west to farm. He left New York when he was thirty-five to start a new life in Nebraska.

IV

Rosicky is worried about his son Rudolph, who rents a farm not too far from Rosicky's. Rudolph has recently married Polly, a woman from town whom the Rosickys describe as "American," meaning her parents are not recent immigrants. Polly has found the transition from being a single woman living in town to married life on a farm difficult. Because Rosicky is afraid that Polly's unhappiness will prompt Rudy to abandon the farm for a job in the city, Rosicky decides to loan his son the family car, suggesting that he and Polly go into town that evening. The section ends when, on his way home, Rosicky stops to look at "the sleeping fields" and "the noble darkness."

V

It is the day before Christmas and Rosicky, sitting by the window sewing, is reminded of his difficult years in London when he was always dirty and hungry. That evening, Rudolph worries about trouble ahead if the winter is too harsh for the crops. Mary responds by telling the story of how, one Fourth of July, the heat and wind destroyed their crops. Instead of despairing, Mary explained, Rosicky decided to have a picnic in the orchard. The storytelling continues when Rosicky describes one particular Christmas in London when he discovered a roasted goose that his poor landlady had prepared for the next day's meal and hidden in his corner of the room. Before he realized what he had done, Rosicky had devoured half of the goose. Horrified, he wandered the city in despair before meeting some wealthy Czechs who generously gave him money to replace the goose. Shortly after this incident, Rosicky left for New York. Polly is moved by

Willa Cather

this story and tells Rudy she wants to invite his family to their farm for New Year's dinner.

VI

In the final section of the story, Rosicky reflects on the future of his children. He hopes that they don't suffer "any great unkindness[es]." When spring comes, Rosicky decides to pull thistles from Rudolph's alfalfa field while his sons tend the wheat. The heavy labor causes another heart attack and Polly, calling him "Father" for the first time, comes to his aid. While she nurses him, Rosicky subtly asks Polly if she is pregnant. She suddenly feels that no one had ever loved her as deeply as Rosicky. Rudolph and Polly take Rosicky home, where he dies the next morning.

The story concludes when Dr. Burleigh, driving to the Rosicky farm one evening, stops by the graveyard where Rosicky is buried:

> For the first time it struck Doctor Ed that this was really a beautiful graveyard. He thought of city cemeteries; acres of shrubbery and heavy stone, so arranged and lonely and unlike anything in the living world. Cities of the dead, indeed; cities of the forgotten, of the "put away." But this was open and free, this little square of long grass which the wind for ever stirred. Nothing but the sky overhead, and the many-

colored fields running on until they met the sky. The horses worked here in summer; the neighbours passed on their way to town; and over yonder, in the corn-field, Rosicky's own cattle would be eating fodder as winter came on. Nothing could be more undeath-like than this place; nothing could be more right for a man who had helped to do the work of great cities and had always longed for the open country and had got to it at last. Rosicky's life seemed to him complete and beautiful. (Excerpt from ''Neighbour Rosicky'')

Characters

Dr. Ed Burleigh

Dr. Burleigh is an unmarried doctor in the small farming community where the Rosickys live. A young man, but ''solemn'' and already getting gray hairs, Dr. Burleigh provides the reader with the initial view of Rosicky as a happy and untroubled man. This view is deepened and qualified as the story progresses. Cather uses Burleigh to provide a frame for the story. Just as he introduces readers to Rosicky, Burleigh also provides a way for readers to say farewell to him, when, at the end of the story, Dr. Burleigh stops by the graveyard where Rosicky is buried and thinks once again about his neighbor.

Lifschnitz

Lifschnitz is the poor German tailor for whom Rosicky worked in London. He spoke a little Czech, so when he and Rosicky met by chance, he discovered how poor the young man's circumstances were and took him into his home and shop. Lifschnitz lived with his wife and five children in a small three-room apartment and rented out a corner of the living room to another waif, who was studying violin.

Miss Pearl

Miss Pearl is a young town woman who works as a clerk at the general store. Rosicky waits for her to be free to wait on him; she knows ''the old fellow admired her, and she liked to chaff with him.'' The story gives two clues that she is conscious of style: she plucks her eyebrows, and she interprets Rosicky's remark about not caring much for ''slim women like what de style is now'' as aimed at her.

Anton Rosicky

Anton Rosicky, the protagonist of the story, came to Nebraska to work as a farmer. Originally from Bohemia, Czechoslovakia, he experienced country life as a boy when he went to live on his grandparents' farm after his mother died. At eighteen he moved to London, where he worked for a poor German tailor for two years. At twenty he made his way to New York, again working as a tailor until at thirty-five he decided he needed to get out into the country and work on the land. Having saved enough money to buy his own farm, he has lived happily, if modestly, on his farm with his wife and six children.

The story begins when sixty-five-year-old Rosicky learns from his doctor that he has a bad heart. This news causes him to reflect on his life and the choices he has made. As the story reveals more about Rosicky and what he values, it becomes apparent that Rosicky's heart is anything but bad. Rather, Rosicky embodies the ideal of the good man. He works hard but still finds the time to enjoy life's pleasures, including his pipe and coffee. More importantly, he is emotionally astute and is able to touch people profoundly. Cather is careful to point out that Rosicky's qualities have not prevented him from making mistakes, but his generosity makes him wholly capable of redressing those wrongs. After his death, Rosicky, who is buried in a small graveyard near the farm, remains connected to both the human community and the natural world.

John Rosicky

John, Rosicky's youngest son, is about twelve years old. He takes care of the horses after his father returns from town.

Josephine Rosicky

Josephine is Rosicky's youngest child and only daughter. It is she who sets an extra place for Dr. Burleigh at the breakfast table when he stops in after a house call.

Mary Rosicky

Mary is Anton Rosicky's wife; she is fifteen years younger than her husband. Also from Czecho-slovakia, Mary exhibits a warm generosity and exuberant enjoyment of simple pleasures. The narrator comments that ''[w]ith Mary, to feed creatures was the natural expression of affection.'' Her nurturing gift is also apparent in her house plants—Dr. Burleigh marvels that her geraniums bloom all year. She is the natural complement to Rosicky: ''she was rough, and he was gentle''; he is from the city, and she is from the country. Their marriage succeeds because ''they had the same ideas about life.''

Polly Rosicky

Polly, one of four daughters of a widow, is the wife of Rosicky's son Rudolph. She is thin, blonde, and blue-eyed, and she ''got some style, too,'' as Rosicky notes. Unlike her husband, to whom she has been married less than a year, Polly grew up in town and is not the child of immigrants. These differences make her feel somewhat awkward around Rudy's family—she calls her father-in-law ''Mr. Rosicky'' and is ''stiff and on her guard'' with Mary, whose occasional gifts of bread or sweets she is not quite comfortable receiving. Rosicky notes that ''an American girl don't git used to our ways all at once.'' Polly sometimes feels lonely living in such an isolated area. Once a store clerk, she misses the social contacts she had at her job and in her church choir, and she is touched by Rosicky's kindness toward her. When Rosicky has a heart attack after raking thistles in the hayfield, it is Polly who nurses him through it. This is the first time in the story that she calls him ''Father,'' and he is the first person she allows to know of her pregnancy. Afterward, while he is sleeping, it strikes her that ''nobody in the world . . . really loved her as much as old Rosicky did.''

Rudolph Rosicky

Rudolph is Rosicky's oldest son and Polly's husband. About twenty years old, he is described as a ''serious sort of chap'' and a ''simple, modest boy,'' but ''proud.'' Although he and Polly were just married in the spring, he ''had more than once been sorry he'd married this year.'' This statement of regret comes immediately after a reference to the crop failure of the past year, but other references indicate there is also trouble with his marriage itself. Both Rosicky and his wife are afraid that Polly will grow too discontented with farm life and that her discontent will spread to Rudolph or start trouble in their marriage. He works his rented farmland, but he struggles with money, toying with ideas of going to the city to work for the railroad or a packing house for a more secure income. Before he married, he worked at the Omaha stockyards for a winter to earn money. Rudolph is not eager to take handouts, as when his father offers him a dollar to spend on ice cream and candy for Polly, but instead is personally generous—a man who ''would give the shirt off his back to anyone who touched his heart.'' He feels

less experienced and less worldly than his wife and her sisters.

Rudy Rosicky

See Rudolph Rosicky

Zichec

Zichec, a young Czech cabinet-maker, was Rosicky's friend and roommate in New York. He played the flute, and he and Rosicky often went to the opera together.

Themes

Goodness

What does it mean to be a good man? This is a fundamental question posed by ''Neighbour Rosicky'' and one of its major themes. Cather depicts Anton Rosicky, who must come to terms with his own mortality during the course of the story, as a man of integrity who has found value in an ordinary life on a modest farm. Generosity, a capacity for pleasure, sympathy, and hard work comprise some significant virtues of the good man. According to the story, Rosicky is also a man who maintains a lively interest in the world around him and who can communicate his good fellowship almost wordlessly to others. His capacity to forge connections with the people around him and his ability to understand and appreciate the land constitute Rosicky's goodness.

Wealth and Poverty

Closely linked to the idea of goodness is the issue of wealth, since Cather is careful to point out that Rosicky's ''success'' has nothing to do with material wealth. Rosicky is out of debt, but he is not a rich man. His inability to ''get ahead,'' however, is seen as one of his strengths. ''[M]aybe you couldn't enjoy your life and put it into the bank, too,'' muses Dr. Burleigh early in the story. Later, Rosicky offers his own ideas about material comforts to his sons: ''You boys don't know what hard times is. You don't owe nobody, you got plenty to eat an' keep warm, an' plenty water to keep clean. When you got them, you can't have it very hard.'' Though wealth is not considered a virtue in this

Topics for Further Study

- Research the various groups of immigrants who came to the United States during the first part of the twentieth century. Who were they? Why did they leave their homelands? Where did they settle? What jobs did they perform? When did your family arrive in the United States? Can you link their history to larger patterns of immigration to or migration within the United States? Though you will want to use your school library to gather background information, you should also interview older members of your family. Like Rosicky, they might have memories they wish to share with you.

- ''Neighbour Rosicky'' was written just before the Great Depression. During the early 1930s especially, farmers faced many hardships, including foreclosures on their farms. In addition, long periods of drought turned the usually fertile plains of the United States into a ''dust bowl,'' and many families fled their farms seeking better conditions elsewhere. By investigating the conditions farmers faced in the thirties, think about whether Rosicky's dream that his children remain and farm his land was likely to come true. Do you think that Rudolph and Polly remained on the farm? What might their life have been like if they had? If they had not?

- Though Cather celebrates the contributions that immigrants made to the growth and development of the United States, many American citizens remained suspicious and distrustful of foreign influences. In 1919, at the direction of Attorney General A. Mitchell Palmer, people suspected of subversive activity were arrested and jailed, often without cause. Many were immigrants active in labor movements. Research the Palmer Raids of the early twenties. How does the fear and distrust of foreigners caused by the raids contrast to the portrayal of foreigners in ''Neighbour Rosicky''?

story, neither is poverty. Rosicky's own hard times in London have left him with painful memories. In addition, the fact that Rosicky owns his own farm is seen as a valuable achievement for an immigrant from a country where landowning was reserved only for people of a certain privileged class.

City and Country

The different experiences that Rosicky faces in the city and in the country help to explain his deep attachment to the natural world and comprise another important theme in ''Neighbour Rosicky.'' In this story, the open expanses of the Nebraska prairie are contrasted with the enclosed spaces of cities like London and New York. Rosicky experienced both the best and the worst of the modern cities. He believes that while farm life might mean enduring occasional hardships, country people ''weren't tempered, hardened, sharpened, like the treacherous people in cities who live by grinding or cheating or poisoning their fellow-men.'' For Rosicky, city life means a life of unkindness and a life divorced from living and growing things.

Cycle of Life

Rosicky's impending death is closely linked to the agricultural cycles that define life on a farm. A field of wheat must be planted in the spring, tended in the summer, harvested in the fall, and left fallow for the winter. Rosicky, at sixty-five, is still in many ways a robust and lively man, and it is clear that he will be missed by the people in his life. But Rosicky himself recognizes the need for winter—or death—to come for all things when he muses on the falling snow: ''It meant rest for vegetation and men and beasts, for the ground itself; a season of long nights for sleep, leisurely breakfasts, peace by the fire.'' When Rosicky returns to the earth at the end of the story, he completes the cycle of life that defines the natural world, and his death is made meaningful.

Generosity and Greed

Generosity in ''Neighbour Rosicky'' takes many forms and is a major theme of the story. While Anton Rosicky's generosity is especially important and earns him the title of ''neighbour,'' all of the members of the Rosicky family display a natural generosity and spontaneous affection. Mary, for instance, loves to feed both people and creatures. She also takes great pleasure in the success of others. Dr. Burleigh believes this is a rare quality in a woman and he is touched by Mary's concern for him. Rudolph, too, displays generosity when he expresses concern over a pregnant woman he saw lifting heavy milk cans. Rosicky displays his generous spirit many times in the story, when he buys candy for the women or loans the family car to Rudy and Polly. But his most poignant display of generosity occurs through the pain of his heart attack, when Rosicky is able to reach out to Polly and touch her. As a result, she relinquishes her natural reserve long enough for Rosicky to see her own capacity for tenderness.

Memory and Reminiscence

Much of ''Neighbour Rosicky'' consists of memories and reminiscences—primarily, but not exclusively, those of Anton Rosicky. In the story, reminiscences help readers understand what Rosicky values and why. Since Rosicky is facing his own mortality, reminiscing becomes especially important to him, and he recalls several pivotal moments in his life. He shares some of these memories with his family, especially when he wants to pass along a lesson to his sons or to Polly. By recalling and sharing his memories, Rosicky is able to come to terms with the hardships he had in life; he is able to weave those individual years into the larger pattern of a lifetime and share his wisdom with members of his family.

Style

Narration and Point of View

''Neighbour Rosicky'' is narrated through an omniscient narrator; that is, a speaker who is not a part of the action of the story and who has access to the thoughts and feelings of all the characters. Through this narrator the reader enters the consciousness of several different characters and sees the world from their *point of view*. For instance, the story begins from Dr. Burleigh's point of view, and he provides readers with some crucial information about the Rosickys through his memories of past events. The story concludes from Burleigh's point of view as well, and his point of view functions as the story's narrative frame. Some critics have suggested that Burleigh's point of view is unreliable; they believe that his assessment of the story's characters or action is at times incorrect or flawed. Other critics believe that this framing device provides an objective balance to the story.

Most of the story, however, is narrated from the point of view of Rosicky, who participates in the story's present and also reminisces about the past. The story provides cues to help the reader follow these shifts in time. When Rosicky is about to think about a particular day in New York City many years ago, readers are told that ''Rosicky, the old Rosicky, could remember as if it were yesterday the day when the young Rosicky found out what was the matter with him.'' The narration and point of view in ''Neighbour Rosicky'' serve to weave the past together with the present.

Setting

The main setting of ''Neighbour Rosicky'' is a small farm on the Nebraska prairie in the 1920s, but Cather shifts at times to New York City about thirty years earlier and to London, some years before that. These shifts in setting are crucial to the story's concern with the contrast between country life and city life. The country is portrayed as open and free, a place of opportunity that can sustain the people who live on the land. By contrast, the city is portrayed as lifeless and confining: ''they built you in from the earth itself, cemented you away from any contact with the ground.'' Cather's idealization of the country and distrust of the city has led critics to identify some of her novels and short stories (like ''Neighbour Rosicky'') with the *pastoral* tradition in American letters. Though it originally described a literary style developed by the Greek poet Theocritus (c. 308-c. 240 BC), pastoralism—the idealized portrayal of country life—remained a vital literary tradition for many centuries. Cather's pastorals tend to celebrate the perfection of the Nebraska prairie.

Structure

The most significant challenge Cather faced in constructing this story was weaving together memories of past events with the present action of the story. ''Neighbour Rosicky'' is divided into six sections; each section reveals a significant detail about Rosicky's life. In section I, readers learn that Rosicky has a bad heart; in section II Mary is introduced; in section III Rosicky remembers his carefree days in New York; in section IV he loans Rudolph and Polly the car; in section V Rosicky remembers his painful days in London; and in section VI he dies.

Cather also uses significant days to organize the action of the story. On the Fourth of July in New York, ''the young Rosicky'' realizes that he must leave the city; many years later in Nebraska, Rosicky celebrates the Fourth of July by having a picnic even though his crop has just failed. Similarly, the reader observes Rosicky's experience of two different Christmases: one in London and one in Nebraska, forty-five years later. The contrasts between these different holidays serves as a way for Rosicky, and the reader, to measure the progress of the character's life.

Finally, Cather frames the story with allusions to the graveyard where Rosicky is eventually buried. At the beginning of the story, Rosicky stops to contemplate the graveyard's comfort and homeliness. At the end of the story, Dr. Burleigh stops to contemplate the graveyard's connection to the unconfined expanse of prairie.

Imagery

Two closely related images in ''Neighbour Rosicky,'' are the motif of hands and the motif of sewing. Though Cather carefully describes Rosicky's physical appearance early in the story, her descriptions of his hands take on special significance. Like Rosicky, they are communicative, reassuring, warm, and clever. In section IV, Rosicky's ''reassuring grip on her elbows'' touches Polly deeply; in section VI, his hands become a kind of symbol for his tenderness and intelligence. Because the human hand can convey what the heart feels, Rosicky's hands become something more than mere appendages, they express his essential goodness.

Rosicky often sits and sews in his corner by the window when he thinks about his life. Although he is usually patching his sons' clothes, sewing in ''Neighbour Rosicky'' is intimately related to the activity of remembering. Rosicky patches together his sons' clothes in the same way that he patches together parts of his past. Sewing can also be linked to the work of the imagination, and so to the activity of the writer. Rosicky's patching, mending, and reminiscing resemble the work a writer performs when creating a piece of fiction.

Historical Context

The Farming Crisis

Although it was not collected in *Obscure Destinies* until 1932, Cather wrote ''Neighbour Rosicky'' in 1928, just one year before the Stock Market Crash of 1929 plunged the country into the Great Depression, an economic crisis that affected millions of Americans. Before 1929, during the administration of Calvin Coolidge in particular, the country's economy was vigorous and prosperous. One important exception to this prosperity, however, was the American farmer. After World War I, European markets were restricted by new tariffs, and American farmers could not sell the food they were producing. As a result, many farmers experienced an economic crisis long before the Stock Market Crash. The price of wheat, for instance, fell from $2.94 a bushel in 1920 to 30 cents a bushel in 1932. While Cather does not explicitly allude to the farming crisis in the Midwest during the 1920s, she is careful to point out that although Rosicky planted wheat, he also grew corn and alfalfa. In fact, he is quite concerned over his alfalfa fields at the end of the story and considers this crop, not his wheat fields, to be an essential one.

Materialism

For Cather, the 1920s represented a time of crass materialism and declining values. In 1924 President Coolidge declared that ''the chief business of the American people is business,'' a philosophy which dominated the country's political and social agendas. The tensions between labor and industry were severe. Rosicky, Cather tells the reader, ''was distrustful of the organized industries that see one out of the world in the big cities.'' Many authors during this period responded to the 1920s with disillusionment. F. Scott Fitzgerald considered the consequences of American affluence in his novel *The Great Gatsby*; Sinclair Lewis criticized social conformity and small-town hypocrisy in novels like *Babbitt* and *Dodsworth*. While critics have

Compare
&
Contrast

- **1920s:** Farms are run by individual families who view the farm as a means of making a living close to the land and away from the commercialism of the city.

  1990s: Farms may be run by individual families or by farming corporations, but the emphasis is often on farming as a business. Farms are worked with huge diesel-powered tractors pulling wide cultivators or several disc plows in combination.

- **1920s:** Rosicky gives Rudolph a dollar for "ice cream an' candy" and possibly the cost of a movie.

  1990s: The total for these items would be between fifteen and twenty dollars for two people.

- **1920s:** Rosicky gets some kind of prescription from Dr. Burleigh for his heart, but that is the last mention of his medication. When he has a heart attack, there is only Polly with her hot compresses to care for him.

  1990s: People take nitroglycerin and aspirin among other things for heart problems; emergency medical help is available by dialing 911 to summon an ambulance; heart bypass surgery is common; there are approximately 2,300 heart transplants performed in the U.S. each year, and approximately 73 percent of patients with transplanted hearts survive for three years after their surgery.

---

debated whether or not Cather adequately examined the roots of American materialism, she clearly values Rosicky's rejection of the heartless pursuit of money. After 1929, the country became more wary of identifying its interests with the interests of big business. Throughout the 1930s, economic reform programs were established to help working people and farmers who were suffering under the Depression.

Multiculturalism

Recent critical attention to Cather has pointed to the ways in which her work brings into focus the multicultural heritage at the heart of the American Midwest. Like her novels, "Neigbour Rosicky" celebrates the spirit, imagination, and determination of America's immigrant population. Millions of displaced and homeless Europeans journeyed to America, particularly after World War I. Many remained in urban centers such as New York, Boston, and Chicago and labored at jobs like the ones Rudolph considers—jobs working on railroads or in the slaughterhouses. A significant number of immigrants, however, sought out new opportunities to own and farm land on America's frontier. True to this pattern of migration, Rosicky arrives in New York and spends fifteen years there before seeking a

new life in Nebraska. While "Neighbour Rosicky" focuses on the history of one Czech family in Nebraska, Cather's other stories and novels detail the lives and contributions of diverse ethnic groups.

Critical Overview

When "Neighbour Rosicky" was published, it was greeted with generous enthusiasm. Henry Seidel Canby pointed out in the *Saturday Review of Literature* that "Cather's achievement . . . lies in her discovery and revelation of 'great souls' inside the commonplace human [being] called . . . Neighbour Rosicky." Clifton Fadiman, writing in the *Nation*, found "Neighbour Rosicky" a fine example of Cather's subtle craftsmanship. By contrast, Peter Quennell, writing for the *New Statesman and Nation*, found the story sentimental and unimpressive. Another interesting exception to the story's generally positive reception was Granville Hicks's essay "The Case against Willa Cather," which appeared in the *English Journal* in 1933. Because he supported the kind of literary realism that "examine[s] life as it is,'' Hicks found that the romantic and nostalgic aspects of Cather's work ''isolated [her] from the social movements that were shaping the destiny of the nation.'' In writing about ''Neighbour Rosicky'' in particular, Hicks argued that Cather ''exaggerates the security of the country'' in her depiction of Anton Rosicky's devotion to the land. Hicks's essay represented a point of view held especially by the social realists of the American left in the 1930s, who believed that writers should directly represent social and economic issues.

While Hicks criticized Cather's literary treatment of the land, commentators writing in the post-Depression years have generally applauded it. Writing about ''Neighbour Rosicky'' in 1951, David Daiches argued that its ''earthiness almost neutralizes its sentimentality, and the relation of the action to its context in agricultural life gives the story an elemental quality.'' In '''Land' Relevance in 'Neighbour Rosicky,''' Sister Lucy Schneider suggested that the land symbolizes the possibility of transcendence; writer Hermione Lee praised Cather's ''celebration of old-fashioned American agrarian values . . . and [her] belief in land-ownership as better for the soul than urban wage-earning.'' Other critics, like Kathleen Danker and Dorothy Van Ghent, focused on Cather's pastoralism, which Danker defined as the ''retreat from the complexities of urban society to a secluded rural place such as a farm, field, garden, or orchard, where human life is returned to the simple essentials of the natural world of cyclical season.''

Many commentators on this story have noticed the special affinity between Rosicky and the earth. In an article from 1979, Edward J. Piacentino noticed how Cather uses imagery to connect Rosicky to the land. He pointed out that even Rosicky's triangular-shaped eyes suggest the shape of a plow. In her book *The Voyage Perilous: Willa Cather's Romanticism*, published in 1986, Susan J. Rosowski linked ''Neighbour Rosicky'' to the nineteenth-century American poet Walt Whitman, whose poem cycle *''Leaves of Grass''* influenced many American writers, including Cather. Rosowski maintained that

> ''Neighbour Rosicky'' is as Whitmanesque as was *O Pioneers!*. In 1913 [the year *O Pioneers!* was published] Cather announced the affinity with her title and then spelled it out with her conclusion—''Fortunate country, that is one day to receive hearts like Alexandra's into its bosom, to give them out again in the yellow wheat, heat, in the rustling corn, in the

shining eyes of youth!'' In 1928 the affinity is relaxed, natural, unobtrusive—yet nonetheless present as powerfully as ever. Like Whitman, Anton Rosicky bequeathed himself to the dirt to grow from the grass he loved.

Critics too, have tended to agree on the story's precise balancing of opposites to achieve a kind of harmony or unity. Marilyn Arnold in particular emphasized the many dualities that are brought into a special rapport in this story: ''city and country, winter and summer, older generation and young, single life and married life, Bohemians and Americans.'' By contrast, Jacquelynn S. Lewis suggested that these oppositions produce instead a ''brand of aloneness'' peculiar to Cather's characters.

In recent years, several critics have suggested that, in 1928, ''Neighbour Rosicky'' provided a new vision of the American Dream. Merrill M. Skaggs declared that the story redefined success, stating that Rosicky ''becomes the model neighbor because he has made himself a life in which 'he had never had to take a cent from anyone in bitter need.''' Loretta Wasserman suggested that Cather's allusions to the Fourth of July are unusually patriotic. She argued that Cather's attention to this holiday demonstrates her commitment to ''the original Jeffersonian American dream of the yeoman farmer, independent and virtuous.''

Criticism

Bonnie Burns

Burns is a writing specialist at Emmanuel College, and her areas of special studies include film studies and nineteenth-century British literature as well as gay and lesbian studies. In the following essay, she discusses the balances between life and death in Cather's ''Neighbour Rosicky.''

With her portrayal of Anton Rosicky, a Bohemian farmer on the Nebraska prairie in the 1920s, Willa Cather returns to the settings and themes of her early fiction. Like *O Pioneers!* and *My Antonia*, ''Neighbour Rosicky'' explores both the literal and symbolic importance of the land to the people who settled on the plains in the first decades of the twentieth century. Cather's sympathetic interest in the struggles and triumphs of the immigrants who domesticated the great prairies of the Midwest is keenly alive in this story about one farmer's gentle cultivation of his land and his home. Though

A farm near Beatrice, Nebraska, the state where Willa Cather spent part of her childhood and where some of her stories, including "Neighbour Rosicky," are set.

"Neighbour Rosicky" marks Cather's return to the great themes of her early fiction, critics agree that the story displays a new maturity of vision.

Cather's biographer, E. K. Brown, attributes Cather's mature vision to the fact that she wrote "Neighbour Rosicky" shortly after her father's death. Cather had always been attracted to the *elegiac* mode. An elegy is a poem of mourning and reflection written on the occasion of someone's death. Cather can be called "elegiac" because she often used her fiction to reflect on the meaning of death and separation. In "Neighbour Rosicky,"

Anton Rosicky faces his own impending death after the doctor tells him he has a bad heart. The knowledge that he soon will be leaving behind everything that he cherishes causes him to reflect on the important events that have marked his life. Though she is writing a story about death, Cather's deft handling of her subject matter transforms sorrow into celebration; the permanence of the land makes the brevity of life meaningful.

Critics have almost unanimously pointed to the story's careful balancing of life and death. In her book *Willa Cather's Short Fiction*, for instance,

What Do I Read Next?

- *O Pioneers!*, Cather's second novel, was written in 1913. Set in Nebraska in the late nineteenth century, the novel tells the story of a group of immigrants who settled there and met, loved, and parted. The novel provides a rich and detailed look at pioneer life.

- *My Antonia*, Cather's fourth novel, written in 1918, anticipates the themes that dominate "Neighbour Rosicky." Narrated by Jim Burden, a farm boy on the Nebraska plains at the end of the nineteenth century, the novel recounts his memories of Antonia Shimerda, a Bohemian farm girl who survives various hardships to thrive in the new land.

- *The Professor's House*, which Cather wrote in 1925, tells the story of a middle-aged professor at a Midwestern university who must come to terms with the melancholy that has haunted his life. Embedded in the professor's story is the story of Tom Outland's adventures on the mesa in the American southwest.

- *Death Comes for the Archbishop* was written the year before "Neighbour Rosicky," in 1927. In this novel, Cather turns to the landscapes, myths, and histories of the southwestern United States to weave an episodic tale of the French missionary Archbishop Lamy, who came to America in the mid-nineteenth century. Though a departure from her early novels, it is considered one of Cather's finest achievements.

- *The Grapes of Wrath*, by John Steinbeck (published 1939; Pulitzer Prize, 1940), is set in the Great Depression and traces the migration of an Oklahoma farming family from their Dust Bowl-ravaged farm to California. There the family faces hardships of an exploitive migrant farm worker system.

- *Winesburg, Ohio* (1919), by Sherwood Anderson, is a novel comprising many interconnected short stories which tell of the hopes, defeated ambitions, earnest attempts at genuine communication, and sweetness of life in a small Midwestern farming town.

- *Main Street* (1920), by Sinclair Lewis, is set in a Scandinavian-settled small town in Minnesota during the early twentieth century. This groundbreaking novel, called by many critics the foremost literary work to express the "revolt from the village" in American literature, is a scathing treatment of small-town materialism and dullness.

- The poem "East Coker," by T. S. Eliot, is part of the poet's acclaimed *Four Quartets* (1943). This poem is a meditation upon the cyclical nature of life, the nature of religious belief, and the approach of death, with the poem informed by Eliot's Christian vision.

Marilyn Arnold observes that "[d]eath is neither a great calamity nor a final surrender to despair, but rather, a benign presence, anticipated and even graciously entertained. It is the other side of life, and comes ... as a natural consequence of 'having lived.' It is a reunion with the earth for one like Rosicky who has lived close to the land." Indeed, at the end of the story Dr. Burleigh observes, after Rosicky's death, that "Rosicky's life seemed to him complete and beautiful." Since the story's

publication, critics have attempted to define precisely what contributes to this sense of completeness. Many critics consider Cather's attention to the defining power of agricultural cycles to be central to the story's measured acceptance of death. In *Willa Cather: A Critical Introduction*, David Daiches argues that "the relation of the action to its context in agricultural life gives the story an elemental quality." However, Arnold points out that unity in "Neighbour Rosicky" is also "defined in human terms, a wholeness and completeness that derives from human harmony and caring.''

In ''Neighbour Rosicky,'' Cather establishes an accord between the natural world and the human one, between the inflexible facts of material existence and the human ability to transcend them. Cather strikingly illustrates the intimate connection between the human and the natural world through the image of the graveyard which occurs twice in ''Neighbour Rosicky'': once at the beginning of the story and once at its conclusion. When Rosicky first learns that he has ''a bad heart,'' he stops by the graveyard on the way home from town and considers its finer points:

> It was a nice graveyard, Rosicky reflected, sort of snug and homelike, not cramped or mournful,—a big sweep all round it. A man could lie down in the long grass and see the complete arch of the sky over him, hear the wagons go by; in summer the mowing-machine rattled right up to the wire fence. And it was so near home. Over there across the cornstalks his own roof and windmill looked so good to him that he promised himself to mind the Doctor and take care of himself. He was awful fond of his place, he admitted. He wasn't anxious to leave it. And it was a comfort to think that he would never have to go farther than the edge of his own hayfield. The snow, falling over his barnyard and the graveyard, seemed to draw things together like. And they were all old neighbours in the graveyard, most of them friends; there was nothing to feel awkward or embarrassed about.

Imagining this small cemetery as ''snug and homelike,'' and finding consolation in its nearness to his own farm, Rosicky dwells on the pleasures of domestic life. Unwilling as yet to leave the home he has made for himself and his family, Rosicky is comforted by the fact that the graveyard is just at ''the edge of his own hayfield.'' As he watches, the falling snow seems to draw his farm and the cemetery even closer together. He considers those who have been buried there ''old neighbours.'' Rosicky's vision of death is softened by his ability to imagine it as a part of his domestic world—the world of family and neighbors, of comfort and pleasure.

This initial vision of death as a kind of home-coming helps Rosicky, and the reader, cope with the story's impending conclusion: Rosicky's death. Cather returns to the image of the graveyard at the end of the story when Dr. Burleigh stops there after Rosicky's death to contemplate the cemetery's beauty:

> [T]his was open and free, this little square of long grass which the wind for ever stirred. Nothing but the sky overhead, and the many-coloured fields running

> In 'Neighbour Rosicky,' Cather establishes an accord between the natural world and the human one, between the inflexible facts of material existence and the human ability to transcend them."

on until they met that sky. The horses worked here in the summer; the neighbours passed on their way to town; and over yonder, in the cornfield, Rosicky's own cattle would be eating fodder as winter came on. Nothing could be more undeathlike than this place.

As Arnold points out, ''this particular graveyard . . . is not a place where things end, but where they are completed.'' This sense of completion, however, depends on relinquishing the comforts of domestic tranquility for the transcendence of the natural world. The image of the graveyard at the end of ''Neighbour Rosicky'' remains slightly wild, ''open and free.'' Rosicky has left his home and family behind him and has returned to the ''grass which the wind for ever stirred.'' In her book *The Voyage Perilous: Willa Cather's Romanticism*, Susan J. Rosowski observes that Cather's ability to connect the human and the natural in these scenes depends on her capacity to join ''one person's life'' to something ''universal.'' Rosowski points out that in this final passage ''one family's fields run into endless sky; a single man has merged with all of nature.'' This vision of the graveyard as a place of transcendence seems quite different from Rosicky's vision of the graveyard as ''snug and homelike.'' Cather begins and concludes ''Neighbour Rosicky'' with these two images because she would like her readers to see the connections between the human and the transcendent. In her analysis of the story's concluding images, Rosowski observes that ''this is a graveyard that is a part of life, where the fence separating the living from the dead is hidden with grass, where some neighbors lie inside and other neighbors pass on their way to town.'' The delicate balance between the human world and the natural one has been maintained, even, or perhaps especially, in death.

Other images throughout "Neighbour Rosicky" suggest that the "snug" boundaries of a single human life and the unboundedness of a transcendent natural world are deeply interconnected. In "The Agrarian Mode in Cather's 'Neighbour Rosicky'," Edward J. Piacentino argues that Rosicky symbolizes "the land, agricultural life, and agrarian values." He notes that even Rosicky's hands are described as warm and brown and observes that "[w]armth, in this sense, relates to the vital heat needed by the brownish-red soil in the developmental process of the vegetative cycle." Rosicky's hands are mentioned in many different contexts throughout the story. Rosicky's "reassuring grip" on Polly's elbows as he insists that she leave the duty of cleaning her kitchen to him and enjoy herself in town is one example among many of Rosicky's almost magical ability to touch the lives of those around him.

Another way that Rosicky expresses his generosity through his hands is by sewing. A tailor in his youth, Rosicky often patches his sons' clothes while musing over his past life. A domestic activity usually associated with female labor, sewing in "Neighbour Rosicky" is related to the other activity Rosicky performs with his hands, his labor as a farmer. The resonances between "sewing," using a needle to stitch together fabric, and "sowing," planting a field with seed, bring together quite forcefully the domestic and the natural worlds.

Perhaps because Rosicky is at the end of his life, we never see him actually sowing a field. Rather, as Piacentino and others have pointed out, we see him laboring to protect the fields he has already planted. Piacentino argues that "Rosicky's death comes after he overexerts himself cutting thistles that have grown up in his son Rudolph's alfalfa field. His death . . . can be seen as a labor of love for restoring the proper conditions for productive vegetation." Rosicky's sewing signals his desire to reflect and reminisce, sewing together the details of his previous experiences into a whole cloth—an entire picture. In a sense, his sewing restores "the proper conditions" for remembering a life. Both activities, sowing and sewing, producing and remembering, are vital to the human. And both of these activities are performed by the human hand.

In one of the most moving passages in "Neighbour Rosicky," Cather celebrates the capacity of the human hand to perform the tasks necessary to sustain both the human and the natural world. When Rosicky suffers a heart attack, Polly, his American daughter-in-law, finds him between the barn and the house and helps him back into the comfort of a domestic setting where she nurses him until his pain subsides. Throughout the story Polly has been reserved and wary, unwilling to get too close to Rosicky even though she cares for him deeply. In "Character and Observation in Willa Cather's *Obscure Destinies*," Michael Leddy has pointed out that "it would be impossible to imagine Rosicky's life as complete and beautiful if he were to die without coming close to his daughter-in-law, without the assurance that Polly has 'a tender heart.'" What touches Polly finally is, of course, Rosicky's hand:

> After he dropped off to sleep, she sat holding his warm, broad, flexible brown hand. She had never seen another in the least like it. She wondered if it wasn't a kind of gypsy hand, it was so alive and quick and light in its communications. . . . Rosicky's [hand] was like quicksilver, flexible, muscular, about the colour of a pale cigar, with deep, deep creases across the palm. . . . [I]t was a warm brown human hand, with some cleverness in it, a great deal of generosity, and something else which Polly could only call "gypsy-like,"— something nimble and lively and sure, in the way that animals are.

> Polly remembered that hour long afterwards; it had been like an awakening to her. It seemed to her that she had never learned so much about life from anything as from old Rosicky's hand. It brought her to herself; it communicated some direct and untranslatable message.

Though he dies because he labors to save an alfalfa field, Rosicky continues to live in the legacy, "direct and untranslatable," that he leaves to Polly. It is a legacy of tenderness and determination, of hope and realism. Rosicky's life is complete—especially since Polly's life can now begin.

Source: Bonnie Burns, "Overview of 'Neighbour Rosicky,'" for *Short Stories for Students*, The Gale Group, 2000.

Merrill M. Skaggs

In the following excerpt, originally presented at the Brigham Young University's Willa Cather Symposium in September 1988, Skaggs offers an interpretation of Cather's "Neighbour Rosicky" and praises Cather's "courage to affirm a new route to . . . the American dream of success."

In "Neighbour Rosicky," one of her best short fictions, Willa Cather characteristically manages to establish plot, character, and theme in the compact scope of her opening sentence. The sentence reads, "When Doctor Burleigh told neighbour Rosicky he had a bad heart, Rosicky protested." We learn here that the story's central concern is a bad heart, that the heart belongs to a man named Rosicky whose neighborliness defines him, and that Rosicky protests the diagnosis, thereby providing an action for the narrative. The story, we are forewarned, will reveal how Rosicky prepares himself and others to cope with bad hearts, and to understand the nature of good ones. We spot in the phrase a *double entendre*. Thus the story begins with the deftly woven and double-stranded intricacies we anticipate in Cather's major work.

The modified name used as title, of course, calls a reader's attention emphatically to the major character. Cather never tired of using realistic names that supplied a wider suggestiveness. She also expected sophisticated readers to catch literary overtones within her texts. Often her names make an important statement about character, and Rosicky's—pronounced in Nebraska with the accent on the second syllable—is no exception. Pronounced as Cather learned it, *Rose-sick-y* suggests the famous Blake poem ''The Sick Rose.'' That poem, in turn, supplies the given conditions of the story by summarizing Rosicky's physical predicament and his reasons for resistance to Doctor Burleigh:

> O Rose, thou art sick.
> The invisible worm
> That flies in the night
> In the howling storm
> Has found out thy bed
> Of crimson joy,
> And his dark secret love
> Does thy life destroy.

Rosicky is dying. Having heard the truth in the opening sentence, however, he sets out to prepare all who are important to him for the lives they will live without him. His first act is to put his house in order by making purchases that are of good enough quality to outlast him. His second is to purchase candy for his women to sweeten the moment when he must announce his bad news. The third is to prepare himself for his end by looking carefully, on his way home, at the graveyard in which he will be buried. As snow falls softly ''upon all the living and the dead,'' Rosicky surveys the cemetery. Unlike James Joyce's sadder Gabriel Conroy in ''The Dead,'' Rosicky finds the cemetery to be ''snug and homelike, not cramped or mournful''—a good place to lie with ''old neighbours . . . , most of them friends.'' Best of all, ''it was a comfort to think that he would never have to go farther than the edge of his own hayfield.'' Rosicky concludes simply that in connection with his own death, ''there was nothing to feel awkward or embarrassed about.''

> ❝ What makes 'Neighbour Rosicky' great is that the story provides a new set of definitions."

For several reasons, this story can be considered a *tour de force*. For one, it immediately suggests it will end with death, and thereafter keeps readers engrossed in spite of that threatening promise. For another, this consistently upbeat tale continues to hold an admiring public in a century that has associated value with ambiguous and darker shades of irony. A third reason, however, is that Cather creates in her character study of a simple man a story that is *itself* complex and multifaceted in form, without once undercutting a reader's admiration for Rosicky. The feat seems more astonishing the longer you look at it.

By its final sentence, the story has unequivocally established the fact that Rosicky's life has been ''complete and beautiful.'' This life's final stages include a good, affectionate and hardworking wife, a family Rosicky can get some comfort out of, a farm unencumbered by debt, a neighborhood containing people who return his affection. His end appears to be deserved. Rosicky is a man with a gleam of amusement in his triangular eyes, a contented disposition, a gaily reflective quality, ''city-bred'' and delicate manners, and a clear (though by no means conventional) sense of what a man does and does not do. Significantly, he is known not to be a ''pusher'' but in fact is characterized by a willingness to indulge himself. He is as considerate of others as of himself. He does not envy and refuses to take hard times hard. He not only remembers his good times but also creates them for himself.

Rosicky seems to love women generally, and his wife Mary specifically. For Mary, he has become an extension of herself: ''They had been shipmates on a rough voyage and had stood by each other in trying times. Life had gone well with them because, at bottom, they had the same ideas about life. They agreed, without discussion, as to what was most important and what was secondary.'' They had agreed ''not to hurry through life, not to be always skimping and saving.'' The key to Mary's enduring affection for Anton, however, is that "he had never touched her without gentleness."

This capacity for loving women gently and well is hinted at when Rosicky goes to the general store. After his fateful doctor's appointment, he waits patiently to be attended by the pretty young clerk who always waits on him and with whom he flirts mildly, for their mutual enjoyment. The small incident is worth noting, especially since no small incidents are trivial in Cather's fiction. The Rosicky marriage holds up so well, we infer, because the husband, fifteen years older than his wife, has known women before her and has learned how to treat them in his youth. In the five happy years he spent in New York as a young man, we read, he was self-indulgent, enjoyed all his favorite pleasures, and never saved money, for "a good deal went to the girls." He obviously learned enough to know that women appreciate receiving special attention. He learned some necessary cautions as well, and concluded, "the only things in his experience he had found terrifying and horrible [were] the look in the eyes of a dishonest and crafty man, of a scheming and rapacious woman."

The delayed marriage shapes Rosicky's attitude to his whole family:

> Perhaps the fact that his own youth was well over before he began to have a family was one reason why Rosicky was so fond of his boys. He had almost a grandfather's indulgence for them. He had never had to worry about any of them—except, just now, a little about Rudolph.

His son Rudolph is a problem partially because he and his wife Polly have married so young that they must do a lot of their life-learning on each other. Yet Rosicky's special sensitivity to women is nowhere better dramatized than in his interactions with his daughter-in-law. He accurately infers that Polly, a town girl, must be lonely and increasingly discontent as an isolated farm wife. So Rosicky tactfully coaches his son about how to keep her happy: "I don't want no trouble to start in Rudolph's family. When it starts, it ain't so easy to stop." He suggests that Rudolph treat Polly as if they were courting, take her to town for a movie and an ice cream, and then he even provides the car and the money the outing requires, while he himself stays to clean up Polly's kitchen after supper. Rosicky knows how to give a treat and why treats are important. Because he is specially attentive, he first guesses that Polly is pregnant, before her husband or mother or mother-in-law know of it—intimate knowledge indeed. But, of course, the experienced capacity for such guesswork partially explains his own happy marriage.

As a member of a communal family, Rosicky enjoys his greatest triumphs. In that context he has also endured his most painful defeat. We are reminded very early that Rosicky has a past. That past includes so sore a spot that he has been able to reflect on it only in the last days of his life; for his two years in London were so great a misery that "his mind usually shrank from [it] even after all this while." As a hungry, dirty, harassed, exploited London tailor's apprentice, Rosicky once betrayed a woman's trust in a way that makes him writhe. He tells of the debacle on his last Christmas Eve. The tale emerges as a gesture of trust and concern for Polly and Rudolph, who are experiencing hard times of their own. But the contrasting Christmas Eves thus juxtaposed become one set of the doubled holidays Cather uses as a structuring device.

When young Rosicky lived in London, he subsisted by working for a tailor and sleeping in a curtained-off corner of his employer's apartment. When Christmas approached, his employer's wife arranged a surprise for her household and on Christmas Eve hid a cooked goose under the box in Rosicky's corner; it was the safest place available in her hungry family's quarters. That night Rosicky, hungry himself, followed his nose, found the bird, and characteristically indulged in a small advance bite. He thereafter ended up eating at least half the bird. Distraught with guilt and dismay over his betrayal of trust, he then ran out to the street contemplating suicide. But, accidentally, he heard wealthy patrons talking in Czech as they emerged from a fine restaurant. He approached them and begged them as "fellow countrymen" to give him enough money to replace the goose. Their money not only saved Christmas but also paved the way for Rosicky to get to New York, and to eventual good fortune.

The first point of this episode is that Rosicky's bitterest memory involves his betrayal of an extended family community; for he knows "how hard dat poor woman save to buy dat goose, and how she get some neighbour to cook it dat got more fire, an' how she put it in my corner to keep it away from dem hungry children . . . . An' I know she put it n my corner because she trust me." The second point is that he has enough faith left in fellow humans, even after he himself has played Judas, to throw himself, in emotional extremis, on the mercy of strangers. The third point is that it is the ladies of the group who rescue him, feed and comfort him, after which "both of dem ladies give me ten shillings." Thus having sinned by the worst betrayal he can imagine, he finds forgiveness and plenty. Community is re-established and the next day "we all sit down an' eat all we can hold."

Willa Cather had an affinity for doubling effects and used them regularly as part of her techniques to expand the implications of a story. With her Christmases past and present, she suggests both the best and the worst of both past and present. Rosicky tells of his past London memory because of his present gnawing concern for Rudolph and Polly. Yet both Christmases end happily, and Rudolph and Polly run home arm in arm to plan for the first familial New Year's Eve.

In Cather country one pair of doubles deserves another. In contrast to the winter's high holiday is the summer's, and the Fourth of July proves as significant for Rosicky's life as does Christmas. After five happy years in New York, Rosicky remembers sitting miserably on one Fourth, "tormented by a longing to run away." He decides that the trouble with big cities was that "they built you in from the earth itself, cemented you away from any contact with the ground." He resolves to get back to the land and eventually gets to Nebraska and to his own farm. On his second memorable Fourth of July, however, he confronts in Nebraska the worst disaster the land can supply. At this point, he is past running. What Rosicky does in this most dramatic adversity defines him.

In his second summer trial, a heat wave burns up all his crops in a few hours. In the literal heat of this disaster, with no retreat possible, Rosicky suggests fun and frolic. He kills two chickens for supper, spends the afternoon splashing with his sons in the horse tank, and then at sundown takes his family outside for a picnic; his reasoning—"No crop this year. . . . That's why we're havin' a picnic. We might as well enjoy what we got." His wife adds, "An' we enjoyed ourselves that year, poor as we was, an' our neighbours wasn't a bit better off for bein' miserable."

While the two Christmases function to define Rosicky's response to familial and community bonds, his Fourth of July turning points appropriately become his personal Independence Days. In the first, he decides to relinquish one acceptable life in the city for another life near the earth. In the second, he decides when the earth fails him that he will rejoice and be glad. Thus he illustrates what makes him

what he is: he loves himself, his family, his life, and his fun. Under the most adverse circumstances, "everything amused him."

What makes "Neighbour Rosicky" great is that the story provides a new set of definitions. Rosicky himself, our definition of a good man, can be summarized best in the phrase he "had a special gift for loving people." The good life is defined almost as succinctly: "You don't owe nobody, you got plenty to eat an' keep warm, an' plenty water to keep clean. When you got them, you can't have it very hard." The good family is depicted as one that can share its pleasures in mutual concern and affection. And the keys to Rosicky's brand of good fortune are as simple: no envy; self-indulgence; and a "habit of looking interested"—Cather's highest accolade. As a result of having these things, Rosicky can state as a simple fact, "We sleeps easy." But Rosicky is important above all as a "neighbour." His obligations as a neighbor are not defined in this story by what he is rich enough to give; rather, Rosicky becomes the model neighbor because he has made himself a life in which "he had never had to take a cent from anyone in bitter need,—never had to look at the face of a woman become like a wolf's from struggle and famine."

What does this story signify? First, its writer's courage to portray a loving man whole, and lovingly. But its significance also includes that writer's courage to affirm a new route to, or definition of, the American dream of success. With such an appealing definition, we can only hope the story eventually influences a national community.

Source: Merrill M. Skaggs, "Cather's Complex Tale of a Simple Man, 'Neighbour Rosicky,'" in *Willa Cather: Family, Community, and History (The BYU Symposium)*, edited by John J. Murphy with Linda Hunter Adams and Paul Rawlins, Brigham Young University Humanities Publications Center, 1990, pp. 79-83.

Michael Leddy

Leddy is an assistant professor of English at Eastern Illinois University. In the following excerpt, he examines the disparity of perspectives between the observer and the narrator in Cather's "Neighbour Rosicky."

The organization of *Obscure Destinies* works along more complex lines that involve not only thematic but narrative elements as well. Cather's trilogy centers on acts of observation and narration, on the discrepancies between the perceptions of an observing character and the perceptions of a fictional narrator, and on acts of narrative compensation that make up for what observers fail to see. Such compensation is in strikingly different ways a distinctive feature of the first two stories of *Obscure Destinies* , "Neighbour Rosicky," and "Old Mrs. Harris," and it is Cather's forsaking of the compensating narrator that accounts for much of the atmosphere of sadness and loss in "Two Friends." Thus the narrative organization of *Obscure Destinies* involves not the repetition of a single narrative situation but three variations on the possibilities of observation and narration. In arranging the three stories as she does, Cather shapes *Obscure Destinies* so that the volume moves toward obscurity and darkness, from a life that is complete, beautiful, and intelligible to lives that are incomplete, isolated, and puzzling; from the compensations of narrative art to painful loss; from a fictional narrator who sees all to an observing character who is left, literally and figuratively, in the dark.

The narrative situation of "Neighbour Rosicky" centers on the discrepancies between the perceptions of Doctor Ed Burleigh and those of the narrator. Doctor Burleigh is the principal observer; the narrative begins with farmer Anton Rosicky visiting him in his office and closes with the doctor stopping by Rosicky's grave and concluding that Rosicky's life was "complete and beautiful." Cather's readers have been rather generous in their appraisals of the doctor's relation to Rosicky and his family: Stouck suggests that the doctor's "appreciative presence . . . gives accent to the richness and fullness of their lives" [David Stouck, *Critical Essays on Willa Cather*, edited by John J. Murphy, 1984]; Arnold, while noting that the doctor is "something of an outsider," goes on to say that he "understands, perhaps even better than Rosicky's family, the completeness and beauty . . . of the man's life" [*Willa Cather's Short Fiction*, 1984]. But "something of an outsider" begins to sound like an understatement when one considers just how much an outsider the doctor is and how little authority his perspective has. He has known Anton Rosicky for many years and has a "deep affection" for his wife Mary; he is quick to appreciate how "generous and warm-hearted and affectionate" the Rosickys are, yet in relation to the family he is essentially an admiring and very occasional observer. A visit from the doctor is an event; his last seems to have been a year before the present time of the story, when he came by unannounced for breakfast after delivering a baby nearby and Mary found it "a rare pleasure to feed a young man whom she seldom saw." As an infrequent visitor, the doctor tends to a doting appreciation of the Rosickys, delighting in their warm kitchen, their good, strong coffee, their hearty laughter, the "natural good manners" and the absence of "painful self-consciousness" in the boys; it is his perspective that is responsible for what Daiches calls the "incipient sentimentality" of the story [*Willa Cather*, 1951]. Obviously, the doctor does not have the chance to see son Rudolph angry, face red and eyes flashing, taking the gift of a silver dollar from his father "as if it hurt him." More importantly, he knows nothing of the problems the Rosickys have with their new American daughter-in-law, Polly, remarking to Rosicky during the office visit that Rudolph and Polly's marriage "seems to be working out all right." Rosicky keeps the problems all in the family, replying only that Polly is a fine girl with spunk and style, but it is not working out all right at all. Rosicky's wife, Mary, lies awake, afraid that Polly will make her husband discontented with farming; Rosicky shares her fears; Polly is sensitive about being married to a foreigner and misses the society of the store, the church choir, and her sisters; Rudolph at times regrets having married this year and resents his wife's stiff, guarded demeanor. Doctor Burleigh's summary evaluation of Rosicky's family displays the strength and weakness of his perspective, a sure grasp of the family's goodness coupled with blindness to any possibility of trouble: "My Lord, Rosicky, you are one of the few men I know who has a family he can get some comfort out of; happy dispositions, never quarrel among themselves, and they treat you right. I want to see you live a few years and enjoy them."

But the narrator of "Neighbour Rosicky" sees all and speaks with an authority that could only come from having observed Rosicky and his family at every moment, an authority expressed in two adverbs of frequency—"always" and "never"— that figure prominently in the descriptions of Rosicky and his family, suggesting their firm sense of custom, their consistency of character. As Rosicky heads home from his visit to Doctor Burleigh, for instance, the narrator notes that he always likes to drive through the High Prairie, that he never lunches in town, that Mary always has some food ready for his return. The boys, of course, always go to town in the family Ford on Saturday night. The adverb "never" often suggests the Rosickys' extraordinary consistency; indeed, Anton's character is constituted largely by what he has never done. He has never raised his voice to Mary; he and Mary have never disagreed about what to sacrifice; he has never touched his wife without gentleness. That Doctor Burleigh's lone "always" and "never" should miss their marks is a measure of the difference between the perspectives of the doctor and the narrator. Rosicky did not always long for open country as the doctor believes. He left the nightmare of London not for open country but for another city, New York, where he lived happily for five years. The problems with Polly and Rudolph give the lie to the doctor's claim that the Rosickys "never quarrel among themselves."

The narrator of "Neighbour Rosicky" compensates for Doctor Burleigh's limited perspective by presenting what the doctor does not see—the trouble in Rosicky's family and the bond that develops between Rosicky and his daughter-in-law as she cares for him on the day before his death: her spontaneous exclamation "Father," her disclosure that she is probably pregnant (Rosicky, not her husband Rudolph, will be the first to know), and the time that passes while she holds Rosicky's hand, a time that is "like an awakening to her." The relationship is crucial. It would be impossible to imagine Rosicky's life as complete and beautiful if he were to die without coming close to his daughter-in-law, without the assurance that Polly has "a tender heart" and that "everything [would come] out right in the end." What Cather's readers seem to have missed is that as Doctor Burleigh knows nothing of the problems between Polly and her in-laws, so too he knows nothing of their resolution. He is away in Chicago when Rosicky dies and has not seen the family since his return; no one could have told him what happened between Polly and Rosicky. Moreover, there is a strong implication that neither the doctor nor anyone else will ever know what happened; the only witnesses are the two people involved, and they remain silent.

Thus, when in the last paragraphs of "Neighbour Rosicky" Doctor Burleigh stops his car to meditate upon the graveyard in which Anton Rosicky is buried, his affirmation of Rosicky's life becomes entirely problematic: "Nothing could be more undeathlike than this place; nothing could be more right for a man who had helped to do the work of great cities and had always longed for the open country and had got to it at last. Rosicky's life seemed to him complete and beautiful."

No doubt one wants to give unqualified assent: of course such a life is complete and beautiful. But such a judgment is not based, as Doctor Burleigh's

> "Doctor Burleigh's summary evaluation of Rosicky's family displays the strength and weakness of his perspective, a sure grasp of the family's goodness coupled with blindness to any possibility of trouble...."

is, only on the fact that Rosicky finally reached the open country that he had (not always) longed for; it is based on all that the doctor has not seen: the family's problems and the moment that binds Polly to Rosicky, the moment that allows the reader to say with Doctor Burleigh, but with an enlarged frame of reference, that Rosicky's life is complete and beautiful. Doctor Burleigh is right but for an insufficient reason; to read the final sentence as a ringing affirmation is to ignore the disparity between the perspectives of observer and narrator. . . .

Source: Michael Leddy, "Observation and Narration in Willa Cather's *Obscure Destinies*," in *Studies in American Fiction*, Vol. 16, No. 2, Autumn, 1988, pp. 141-53.

Marilyn Arnold

In the following excerpt, Arnold gives an overview of Cather's "Neighbour Rosicky" and examines Cather's use of integrating devices to create a sense of balance, wholeness, and unity in the story.

The first story in the collection [*Obscure Destinies*], "Neighbour Rosicky," may have been written as E. K. Brown believes, in "the early months of 1928, when her [Cather's] feelings were so deeply engaged by her father's illness and death" [*Willa Cather: A Critical Biography*, 1953]. It is generally agreed that the portrait of Anton Rosicky is a composite picture of both Antonia's (Annie Pavelka's) husband and Charles Cather, Willa's father. Excruciating though the loss of her father must have been, Cather does not use "Neighbour Rosicky" to vent bitter feelings about death and loss. Rather, she makes the story an expression of acceptance and faith. In "Neighbour Rosicky" death is not a confinement, nor is it a rupture with life; it is, instead, a final liberating union of a human being with the earth. As a rule, Cather took death hard; yet, Rosicky's death seems somehow more a continuation than a severance, and nothing to be feared or fretted over. Rosicky has simply gone home, as perhaps Charles Cather had gone home.

There is a quiet perfection about ''Neighbour Rosicky'' that almost defies comment. Surely, it is one of the stories for which Willa Cather will always be remembered. Nothing is out of place, everything counts, and the tone is maintained consistently. What one senses in reading the story is harmony, unity, and completeness in both life and art. One of the story's thematic accomplishments is a strong sense of acquiescence, of bowing to things that must be, of enjoying the good rather than grieving over the ill. No blind idealist, Rosicky has a total understanding of what is worthy and what is not, and his one desire as an old man is to convey that understanding to his children. Through a lifetime of sorting out values he has acquired a sense of balance, a healthy perception of the other side of things, and a great tolerance for variety.

Cather seems to be looking, especially now, for a way to organize experience, not just in art but in life as well. She is using art to generate a comprehensive vision that can reconcile and make whole the vast number of disparate elements that constitute a human life. Particularly with *Obscure Destinies*, she seems to be trying to fit Nebraska into her life's larger scheme, a life spent variously—in Europe, in the American city, and on the prairie. Rosicky is a character who brings together all of those aspects of Cather's experience. In ''Neighbour Rosicky'' Cather uses memory as an integrative device, and the winter Rosicky spends indoors tailoring and carpentering in deference to his ailing heart is a highly reflective one for him. Rosicky's attitude toward the past, so different from the ambassador's in ''On the Gulls' Road'' and Harriet Westfield's in ''Eleanor's House,'' is clearly the attitude endorsed by Cather. Rosicky does not look longingly at the past—indeed, he had known loneliness and terrible poverty in the past—but he sets it gently against the present and is grateful.

The picture of Rosicky's past gradually materializes as Cather weaves the various strands of his life and memory into a pattern, moving carefully and repeatedly from present to past and then back to present again, from earth to city and back to earth again. Rosicky's mother died when he was a young-

ster, and for a time he lived with his grandparents who were poor tenant farmers. On the death of his grandmother, however, he was returned to his father and stepmother. A hard woman, she made his life such an agony that finally his father helped him get away to London. Unfortunately, the cousin whom he sought there had already moved to America, and the young man was stranded penniless in a foreign land.

This was ''the only part of his youth he didn't like to remember.'' But remember it he does, and on the day before Christmas his mind reaches back to the meager, starving years he spent in London, shivering in the wretched home of a poor tailor who took him in off the streets out of pity, but who had little to give him but a corner to sleep in. He was filthy always, and his quarters were infested with bugs and fleas. Rescued almost miraculously by some of his countrymen one bleak Christmas Eve, Rosicky made it to New York and got a job with a tailor. For the most part he remembers the New York years as good years, full of jolly times with friends and frequent exposures to the opera (at standing room prices). For a time ''Rosicky thought he wanted to live like that for ever.'' But gradually he grew restless and began drinking too much, drinking to create the illusion of freedom. Then one day, appropriately the Fourth of July, he discovered the source of his trouble. Not only was the city empty in midsummer, but its ''blank buildings'' seemed to him ''like empty jails'' in ''an unnatural world'' that ''built you in from the earth itself.'' It was then that he decided to go west and reestablish ties with the soil.

Still another piece of Rosicky's past is revealed through the memory of his wife, Mary. She recalls one terribly hot Fourth of July when Rosicky came in early from the fields and asked her to get up a nice supper for the holiday. He took the boys, just little fellows then, and dunked them in the horse tank; then he stripped off his own clothes and climbed in with them, playing and frolicking in a way that made a passing preacher raise his pious eyebrows. It was not until later as they picnicked under the linden trees that Mary noticed how the leaves were all curled up and thought to ask about the corn. He told her it was all gone, roasted by midafternoon, and added, ''That's why we're havin' a picnic. We might as well enjoy what we got.'' So while the neighbors grieved and spent a miserable year, the Rosickys made out and managed to enjoy the little they did have.

Just as in its concern with the unity of experience this story carefully balances past and present, so it also balances life and death. A mood of spiritual equanimity pervades Rosicky's life and death, and death comes *for* him in the same sense that it comes for Jean Latour in *Death Comes for the Archbishop*. Death is neither a great calamity nor a final surrender to despair, but rather, a benign presence, anticipated and even graciously entertained. It is the other side of life, and comes, as Latour says, as a natural consequence of "having lived." It is a reunion with the earth for one like Rosicky who has lived close to the land.

Cather creates this sense of balance between life and death, a balance that lends unity to experience, at least partly through structure and symbolic landscape. The story opens with a consultation in Doctor Ed's office in which Rosicky learns that his heart is going bad. On his way home in the wagon he pauses at the small graveyard which nestles comfortably on the edge of his hay fields, especially cozy in the lightly falling snow. Aside from the Rosicky home itself, the most important setting in the story is that little graveyard. Cather introduces it early, and she ends the story there—bringing both her story and Rosicky's life full circle. Still pondering the news about his heart, Rosicky contemplates the view of his own fields and home from the graveyard. Though he admits that he "wasn't anxious to leave," Rosicky sees death and the graveyard as unifying, completing aspects of life. To him the graveyard is "sort of snug and homelike, not cramped or mournful,—a big sweep all round it." Life continues to hum along nearby, and home is close. "The snow, falling over his barnyard and the graveyard, seemed to draw things together like. And they were all old neighbours in the graveyard, most of them friends; there was nothing to feel awkward or embarrassed about". The winter snow itself is symbolic of death, for it too carries an element of the "mysterious"; it too means "rest for vegetation and men and beasts."

At the conclusion of the story, after Rosicky is dead, Doctor Ed starts one evening for the farm to see the family. He pauses by the graveyard as Rosicky had done some months earlier, remembering that his old friend is there in the moonlight rather than over on the hill in the lamplight. His thoughts echo Rosicky's thoughts the night the old farmer had stopped his horses to watch the snow fall on the headstones and on the long red grass. He, like Rosicky, feels something "open and free" out here

> " Cather seems to be looking, especially now, for a way to organize experience, not just in art but in life as well. She is using art to generate a comprehensive vision that can reconcile and make whole the vast number of disparate elements that constitute a human life."

with just the "fields running on until they met that sky." And he senses that this particular graveyard, unlike the dismal cemeteries of cities, is not a place where things end, but where they are completed. He sees a mowing machine where one of Rosicky's sons and his horses had been working that very day; he thinks of the "long grass which the wind for ever stirred," and of "Rosicky's own cattle" that "would be eating fodder as winter came on"; and he concludes that "nothing could be more undeathlike than this place." Ed feels a sense of gratitude that this man who had lived in cities, but had finally wanted only the land and growing things, "had got to it at last" and now lay beneath its protective cover. The story's conclusion sums up the man: "Rosicky's life seemed to him complete and beautiful."

In a multitude of other ways Cather achieves a sense of balance and wholeness in the story. Often she does it through contrasting or pairing opposites: city and country, winter and summer, older generation and younger, single life and married life, Bohemians and Americans. Not infrequently opposites are paired in a single sentence through a character's natural thought processes. For example, of herself and Rosicky Mary thinks, "He was city-bred, and she was country-bred. . . ." She is aware that their life together "had been a hard life, and a soft life, too." Once the family has been warned about Rosicky's condition, they rush to his aid whenever he starts some manual task. In response, Rosicky sometimes even speaks in balanced rhetoric, complaining that "though he was getting to be an old man, he wasn't an old woman yet." And the narrator mentally balances Rosicky's older self against his younger self, observing that "the old Rosicky could remember as if it were yesterday the day when the young Rosicky found out what was the matter with him." Cather also achieves a marked sense of equilibrium by balancing two halves of sentences against each other. The technique seems quite deliberate because some paragraphs are made up almost wholly of compound sentences. For example, although the first sentence in the following paragraph is not based on structural coordination, the rest are; and the achievement of balanced antithesis is felt in both subject and form:

> On that very day he began to think seriously about the articles he had read in the Bohemian papers, describing prosperous Czech farming communities in the West. He believed he would like to go out there as a farm hand; it was hardly possible that he could ever have land of his own. His people had always been workmen; his father and grandfather had worked in shops. His mother's parents had lived in the country, but they rented their farm and had a hard time to get along. Nobody in his family had ever owned any land,—that belonged to a different station of life altogether. Anton's mother died when he was little, and he was sent into the country to her parents.

The pattern is the same for the concluding sentences in the paragraph.

But finally, perhaps the most important kind of balance in "Neighbour Rosicky" is more abstract, a balance defined in human terms, a wholeness and completeness that derives from human harmony and caring. Probably nowhere else has Cather drawn a more sublime picture of oneness and understanding than in the relationship between Rosicky and Mary, a relationship anchored in mutual love and in a value system that always keeps its priorities straight: "They agreed, without discussion, as to what was most important and what was secondary. They didn't often exchange opinions, even in Czech,—it was as if they had thought the same thought together. A good deal had to be sacrificed and thrown overboard in a hard life like theirs, and they had never disagreed as to the things that could go." When a creamery agent comes to tempt them to sell the cream off the milk they drink, they agree without discussion that their children's health is more important than any profit they might realize from skimming cream. Yes, people like the Rosickys do not get ahead much in worldly terms, Doctor Ed reflects, but "maybe you couldn't enjoy your life and put it into the bank, too." As Rosicky intimates

to his favorite clerk in the general store, in a home as harmonious as theirs, "We sleeps easy."

Rosicky's unifying influence extends also into the somewhat troubled lives of his son Rudolph and Rudolph's wife, Polly, a town girl who has found farm life lonely and Bohemians a little strange. Rudolph is ready to leave the land and look for work in the city. Rosicky is worried about Rudolph and Polly, but is finally able to enclose them in the healing warmth of his remarkable capacity for love. Polly learns a little about that capacity when Rosicky slips over one Saturday night with the family car and sends her and Rudolph off to a movie in town while he cleans up their supper dishes. She has just a passing urge then to lay her head on his shoulder and tell him of the lonesomeness a town girl feels when stuck in the country. She learns still more the Christmas Eve he describes his last Christmas in London. Then, finally, the two of them are brought into complete harmony the day he rakes thistles to save his alfalfa field and suffers a heart attack. She leads him into her house and cares for him tenderly, understanding at last his ability to touch another life and make it whole. After hot-packing his chest until the pain subsides, she sits by the bed and holds his "warm, broad, flexible brown hand" in hers. From that hand comes a revelation that is "like an awakening to her. It seemed to her that she had never learned so much about life from anything as from old Rosicky's hand. It brought her to herself; it communicated some direct and untranslatable message." This is the culminating experience of the story, a sacred moment of oneness for both Rosicky and Polly. She really knows now the meaning of love, and he knows that he can count on her. For the first time, she has called him "Father."

Watching the Rosickys over the years, grateful to visit a home where the kitchen is warm and lively and the food plentiful and wholesome—and where the laughter is ready and the comeback easy—Doctor Ed is himself a device for sustaining wholeness in the story. Something of an outsider even though Mary claims him for her own, Ed provides the appreciative eye that encompasses the Rosicky family phenomenon. Standing close enough to feel the radiated warmth, he frames the miracle. Artistically, the story is unified and whole, completing not only itself but in some respects *My Antonia* as well. Ed understands, perhaps even better than Rosicky's family, the completeness and beauty, as he calls it, of the man's life. Whoever Rosicky touched was graced by that wholeness—from the girl with the funny eyebrows in the general store to Polly, and to Ed himself. A work of art can be like that, restoring a sense of unity to experience. "Neighbour Rosicky" is like that.

Source: Marilyn Arnold, in *Willa Cather's Short Fiction*, Ohio University Press, 1984, pp. 135-40.

Edward J. Piacentino

In the following excerpt, Piacentino offers an interpretation of Cather's "Neighbour Rosicky," particularly with regard to the themes of Agrarianism. Piacentino also examines Cather's use of imagistic descriptions.

"Neighbour Rosicky," a story claimed to be "among the finest of Willa Cather's works," "a kind of pendant, or coda, to her classical pastoral *My Antonia*," was written in 1928, shortly after Cather's father's death, and became the first of three stories collected in *Obscure Destinies* (1932). This endearing story has been somewhat generally and briefly analyzed by several of Cather's critics, but no one has thoroughly examined its rich agrarian texture, even though a few commentators have hinted at its presence. David Daiches has properly observed that the story's "earthiness almost neutralizes its sentimentality, and the relation of the action to its context in agricultural life gives . . . [it] an elemental quality." [*Willa Cather: A Critical Introduction*, 1951] John H. Randall, noting that "Neighbour Rosicky" describes the demise of the pioneer epoch, has viewed the story as a symbolic archetype, a portrait of the "earthly paradise, the yeoman's fee-simple empire founded in the garden of the Middle West." [*The Landscape and the Looking Glass: Willa Cather's Search for Value*, 1960] And Dorothy Van Ghent, in her study in the University of Minnesota Pamphlets on American Writers series, has accurately remarked, "There is in this tale that primitive religious or magical sense of relationship with the earth that one finds in Willa Cather's great pastoral novels." [*Willa Cather*, 1964]

Certainly, one does not have to read with much insight or perception to realize that Anton Rosicky intensely loves and appreciates the land, agricultural life, and agrarian values. The story affirms this repeatedly. Throughout, Cather accents the old man's admiration of and fondness for the agrarian simplicity of the Nebraska prairie, particularly through Rosicky's outspoken aversion to the world of urbanized mechanization and convenience. We are told, for instance, that Rosicky does not like cars, girls with unnatural eyebrows ("thin India-ink

> *". . . 'Neighbour Rosicky' is a fine work of conscious literary artistry, artistry that is partly reflected through Willa Cather's consistent selection and arrangement of references affirming and reaffirming the agrarian spirit."*

strokes"), or town food. Moreover, he believes that it is "extravagant" to eat any meals in town. In condemning town food, his wife Mary remarks to Dr. Ed Burleigh, the family physician, that he will ruin his health by eating at a hotel.

At other times, Cather points to the naturalness of the Rosicky family to affirm and to complement her preference for agrarian values. For example, very early in the story, it is said that Rosicky's five sons, who range from twelve to twenty years, exhibit "natural good manners," as evidenced in their caring for Dr. Burleigh's horse when he arrives at their farm, in their helping him off with his coat, and in their showing him genuine hospitality during his visit. In this same scene Cather describes Rosicky's wife Mary and states, "to feed creatures was the *natural* expression of affection,—her chickens, the calves, her big hungry boys." In short, as Dr. Burleigh, through whose consciousness the narrative is filtered, reflects, the Rosickys are "generous," "warmhearted," and "affectionate."

As an urban dweller during his early years in America, Rosicky rarely found evidence of these affirmative human qualities. In one of the story's several flashbacks, Rosicky, recalling a Fourth of July holiday in New York City when he worked in a tailor's shop there, vividly remembers this city as a place where "they built you in from the earth itself, cemented you away from any contact with the ground . . .—an *unnatural* world . . . ." Moreover, in pondering the fate of his children (at the time of the narrative, his oldest son Rudolph is contemplating migration to a city in search of more prosperous opportunity), Rosicky facilely decides that subsistent existence in the country is preferable to any apparent material advantages city life may offer:

> They would have to work hard on the farm, and probably they would never do much more than make a living. But if he could think of them staying here on the land, he wouldn't have to fear any great unkindness for them. Hardships, certainly; it was a hardship to have the wheat freeze in the ground when seed was so high; and to have to sell your stock because you had no feed. But there would be other years when everything came along right, and you caught up. And what you had was your own. You didn't have to choose between bosses and strikers, and go wrong either way. You didn't have to do with dishonest and cruel people.

This kind of affirmation, affirmation of "human relationships rather than success and accomplishments," to quote critic David Stouck, is clearly implied in the story's use of vital, organic imagery. Among the positive images Stouck cites are the blooming geraniums and bountiful food in the Rosicky kitchen, the child that is to be born to Rudolph and Polly, and, at the close of the story, the "undeathlike" country graveyard where Rosicky is buried, with Rosicky's horses working in a nearby field and his cattle eating fodder as winter approached.

Even more affirmative, it seems to me, are Cather's poignantly imagistic descriptions of Rosicky that verify the existence of a conscious harmony between Rosicky and the land. In most of the passages describing Rosicky's physical features, Cather consistently employs color imagery suggestive of the soil that provides his livelihood. The story's initial description, for instance, notes that on Rosicky's "brown face," "he had a *ruddy* colour in smooth-shaven cheeks and in his lips, under his long *brown* moustache" (my italics, here and following). A short time later as Rosicky is leaving the doctor's office, he holds out his "warm *brown* hand" to Dr. Burleigh. And near the end, after Rosicky's stroke, Polly, his daughter-in-law, holds his "warm, broad, flexible *brown* hand," "alive and quick and light in its communications," which to her seems "very strange in a farmer". Also, his neck, Cather points out, was "burned a *dark reddish brown.*" And finally, as Polly and Rosicky are talking just after his stroke, Polly notices not only the warmth of his hand but "the twinkle in his *yellow-brown* eyes" as well, a fine detail that again illustrates the emerging pattern of Rosicky's description in terms of nature's earthy colors. In many of the same passages quoted above, the warmth of Rosicky's hands is also stressed, warmth that may be interpreted within an agrarian context. Warmth, in this sense, relates to the vital heat needed by the brownish-red soil in the developmental process of the vegetative cycle.

Besides combining images of the soil's color scheme and the life-giving heat that it must have for germination, Cather, in her descriptions of Rosicky, occasionally associates him with other images that fittingly suggest characteristics of agricultural implements or of cultivated farm land. A good illustration is the description of Rosicky's eyes, which are "large and lively, but the lids were caught up in the middle in a curious way, so that they formed a triangle"—the shape of a plow, an essential implement for a man of the soil. In addition, there are several passages pointing out the creases in Rosicky's forehead, neck, and hands: "His brown face was creased but not wrinkled"; "his forehead . . . was "naturally high and crossed by deep parallel lines"; his neck had "deep creases in it"; and, according to Polly, his hand "was like quicksilver, flexible, muscular, about the colour of a pale cigar, with deep, deep creases across the palm." These details may, of course, be coincidental, but nevertheless if the wary reader is willing to use his imagination, it is not difficult to perceive a possible connection between these creases and the furrows that a plow shapes on farm land.

Another feature of "Neighbour Rosicky" that complements the story's agrarianism is the occasional use of poetic figures that seem to establish an association between Rosicky and the land. Rosicky's moustache, for example, "was of the soft long variety and came down over his mouth like the teeth of a buggy-rake over a bundle of hay." Or to highlight his persistence, toughness and durability gained from farm life, Cather notes, "his back had grown broad and curved, a good deal like the shell of an old turtle." Most important, his natural simplicity, his dedication to the land and farming, is summed up very aptly in a standard organic image: "He was like a tree that has not many roots, but one taproot that goes down deep."

Significantly, Rosicky's death comes after he overexerts himself cutting thistles that have grown up in his son Rudolph's alfalfa field. His death, among other things, can be seen as a labor of love for restoring the proper conditions for productive vegetation, an act with an implicit ulterior motive of persuading his disgruntled son to recognize the value of a livelihood gained from the land. Furthermore, Rosicky, it seems, accepts death stoically, an event that John Randall perceptively recognizes as "timely and welcome when it comes after a full life, in its proper place in the sequence of the vegetation cycle.'' Finally, in the agrarian tableau that concludes the story, Dr. Burleigh, as he muses near the country graveyard where Rosicky is buried, seems to encourage this line of interpretation. He stresses the ebullient quality of ongoing life that is exhibited in the vast, open, ''many-coloured fields'' surrounding and adjacent to the graveyard—all a part of an harmonious organic totality: ''Nothing could be more undeathlike than this place; nothing could be more right for a man who had helped to do the work of great cities and had always longed for the open country and had got to it at last. Rosicky's life seemed to him complete and beautiful.''

In sum, ''Neighbour Rosicky'' is a fine work of conscious literary artistry, artistry that is partly reflected through Willa Cather's consistent selection and arrangement of references affirming and reaffirming the agrarian spirit. These agrarian references complement the story's central thematic focus, importantly giving it an idyllic flavor, which provided in the late 1920s, when it was first published as well as in the uncertain present of our own times, a tender and captivating expression of our persistent, sometimes latent yearning for a return to a simpler, natural existence.

Source: Edward J. Piacentino, ''The Agrarian Mode in Cather's 'Neighbour Rosicky,''' in *The Markham Review*, Vol. 8, Spring, 1979, pp. 52–4.

Sources

Brown, E. K. and Leon Edel. *Willa Cather: A Critical Biography*, New York: Knopf, 1964, p. 275.

Canby, Henry Seidel. Review, in *The Saturday Review of Literature,* August 6, 1932, p. 29.

Daiches, David. *Willa Cather: A Critical Introduction*, Ithaca, N.Y.: Cornell University Press, 1951, p. 158.

Danker, Kathleen A. Cited in *A Reader's Guide to the Short Stories of Willa Cather,* edited by Sheryl L. Meyering, New York: G. K. Hall & Co., 1994.

Fadiman, Clifton. Review, in *The Nation,* August 3, 1932, p. 107.

Hicks, Granville. ''The Case against Willa Cather,'' in *Willa Cather and Her Critics,* edited by James Schroeter, New York: Cornell University Press, 1967, pp. 139-147.

Lee, Hermione. ''Cather's Bridge: Anglo-American Crossings in Willa Cather,'' in *Forked Tongues?,* edited by Ann Massa and Alistair Stead, London: Longman, 1994, pp. 38-56.

Murphy, John J., ed. *Critical Essays on Willa Cather*, Boston: G. K. Hall, 1984.

Quennel, Peter. Review, in *The New Statesman and Nation,* December 3, 1932, p. 694.

Randall, John H., III. *The Landscape and the Looking Glass: Willa Cather's Search for Value*, Westport, Conn.: Greenwood Press, 1960.

Rosowski, Susan J. *The Voyage Perilous: Willa Cather's Romanticism*, Lincoln, Nebraska: University of Nebraska Press, 1986, pp. 190-95.

Schneider, Sister Lucy. ''Land' Relevance in 'Neighbour Rosicky,''' in *Kansas Quarterly,* 1968, pp. 105-110.

Van Ghent, Dorothy. *Willa Cather*, Minneapolis: University of Minnesota Press, 1964.

Wasserman, Loretta. *Willa Cather: A Study of the Short Fiction,* Boston: Twayne, 1991, p. 55.

Further Reading

Canby, Henry Seidel. Review in *The Saturday Review of Literature*, August 6, 1932, p. 29.
    This is an early review of *Obscure Destinies* which praises Cather's realism.

Danker, Kathleen A. ''The Passing of a Golden Age in *Obscure Destinies*,'' in *Willa Cather Pioneer Memorial Newsletter*, Vol. 34, pp. 24-8. Cited in *A Reader's Guide to the Short Stories of Willa Cather*, edited by Sheryl L. Meyering, New York: G. K. Hall & Co., 1994.
    Danker pays particular attention to pastoralism in ''Neighbour Rosicky,'' offering a useful definition of the term and explaining the ways it can be applied to Cather's work.

Fadiman, Clifton. Review in *The Nation*, August 3, 1932, p. 107.
    Clifton praises Cather's craftsmanship and purity of style in ''Neighbour Rosicky.''

Hicks, Granville. ''The Case Against Willa Cather,'' in *The English Journal*, November, 1933. Reprinted in *Willa Cather and Her Critics*, edited by James Schroeter, New York: Cornell University Press, 1967, pp. 139-47.
    A social realist, Hicks was critical of Cather's nostalgic and idealized notion of life on the land.

Quennell, Peter. Review in *The New Statesman and Nation*, December 3, 1932, p. 694.
    Quennell offers one of the few critical opinions of *Obscure Destinies* and finds ''Neighbour Rosicky'' weak and indistinct.

Schneider, Sister Lucy. ''Land' Relevance in 'Neighbour Rosicky,''' in *Kansas Quarterly*, 1968, pp. 105-10.

Schneider discusses Cather's land-philosophy and suggests that Rosicky symbolizes the elemental and traditional.

Wasserman, Loretta. *Willa Cather: A Study of the Short Fiction*, Boston: Twayne, 1991, p. 55.
Wasserman examines Cather's allusions to patriotic holidays and suggests that she is attempting to redefine the American dream.

The Overcoat

Nikolai Gogol
1842

One of the most influential short stories ever written, Nikolai Gogol's "The Overcoat" ("Shinel") first appeared in 1842 as part of a four-volume publication of its author's *Collected Works* (*Sochinenya*). The story is considered not only an early masterpiece of Russian Naturalism—a movement that would dominate the country's literature for generations—but a progenitor of the modern short story form itself. "We all came out from under Gogol's 'Overcoat'" is a remark that has been variously attributed to Dostoevsky and Turgenev. That either or both might have said it is an indication of the far-reaching significance of Gogol's work.

Gogol's writings have been seen as a bridge between the genres of romanticism and realism in Russian literature. Progressive critics of his day praised Gogol for grounding his prose fictions in the everyday lives of ordinary people, and they claimed him as a pioneer of a new "naturalist" aesthetic. Yet, Gogol viewed his work in a more conservative light, and his writing seems to incorporate as much fantasy and folklore as realistic detail. "The Overcoat," which was written sporadically over several years during a self-imposed exile in Geneva and Rome, is a particularly dazzling amalgam of these seemingly disparate tendencies in Gogol's writing. The story begins by taking its readers through the mundane and alienating world of a bureaucratic office in St. Petersburg where an awkward, impoverished clerk must scrimp and save in order to afford a badly needed new winter coat. As the story

progresses, we enter a fairy-tale world of supernatural revenge, where the clerk's corpse is seen wandering city streets ripping coats off the backs of passersby. Gogol's story is both comic and horrific—at once a scathing social satire, moralistic fable, and psychological study.

Author Biography

Nikolai Vasilievich Gogol-Yanovski (who later dropped the second part of his hyphenated name) was born in Russia in 1809. He was by all accounts a driven, moody individual. Extremely sensitive to the opinions of others, he could be crushed by the slightest negative criticism and then swell with confidence from positive feedback. Yet he was most strongly motivated, it seems, by his own search for spiritual meaning.

Gogol aspired to become a civil servant. At age 19 in 1828 he left his widowed mother on his family's modest farm in the Ukraine and made the journey to St. Petersburg in search of a government job. He found one in ten months, but by then young Gogol was already disenchanted with public service and set on pursuing a literary career. Using money from his mother and a pseudonym, Gogol arranged to publish a long poem (''Hans Kuechelgarten'') he had written in the then popular German Romantic style. When the poem received only two reviews, both unfavorable, Gogol promptly burned all remaining copies and fled to Germany with still more of his mother's money.

He fared better on his return to St. Petersburg six months later, when he began writing a volume of comic folktales set in his native Ukraine. *Evenings on a Farm near Dikanka* (*Vechore na khutore bliz Dikanki*) was published in 1831 and immediately won acclaim for its young author, bringing him to the attention of celebrated poet Alexander Pushkin and influential critic Vissarion Belinsky. With encouragement from his two new literary mentors, Gogol began the most productive period of his life. From 1831 to 1836 he wrote two highly successful collections of stories, *Mirgorod* and *Arabeski*, and a play, *The Government Inspector* or *Revizor*, which has come to be seen as one of the greatest comedies ever written for the Russian stage.

Public reaction to *The Government Inspector* after its 1836 premier, however, apparently sent Gogol on another downward spin. Initial reviews of the play—in which the central character is a drifter who is mistaken for a government inspector by the residents of a provincial town and showered with bribes until the real official arrives—were in fact mostly favorable, though some expressed offense at the prevalence of dishonest characters. Czar Nicholas I himself attended the premier and was so delighted that he ordered his ministers to see it. Even with the Czar's blessing, however, Gogol felt threatened enough to flee the country again, this time for nearly twelve years.

During this second self-imposed exile, Gogol began writing an epic novel, *Dead Souls* (*Mertvye dushi*), which was to be his *magnum opus*—a sweeping portrait of the whole of Russia. In 1842, Gogol published a first volume of *Dead Souls*, as well as a four-volume edition of his *Collected Works* (*Sochinenya*) in which his famous story ''The Overcoat'' made its first appearance.

By this time, however, Gogol seemed to be facing an intensifying spiritual crisis. He became obsessed with the notion that the second volume of *Dead Souls* must accomplish nothing less than the moral regeneration of the Russian people. He returned to Russia in 1848, still unsatisfied with his great work and increasingly uncertain of his abilities. In 1852, already weakened by long hours of work, he embarked upon a particularly severe fast for Lent, hoping to achieve spiritual cleansing. The result was that Gogol fell into a coma and died four weeks before his forty-third birthday. Just ten days earlier, he had burned the only existing manuscript of the second volume of *Dead Souls* in his fireplace.

Plot Summary

''The Overcoat'' is the story of Akaky Akakievich Bashmachkin, an impoverished clerk who has toiled for a number of years in an unspecified department within the huge government bureaucracy in St. Petersburg. The tale is told by an unnamed narrator with a tendency to digress and editorialize. Critics have disagreed about how closely the narrator should be identified with Gogol and about how much sympathy the author intended his readers to feel for Akaky the clerk. In any case, the tone of the narration is at various times condescending, compassionate, humorous and nightmarish.

The narrator begins with a fairly thorough introduction of the story's main character, including a broadly comic aside on the origin of his name (which bears a similarity to the common childhood term for feces, ''kaka''). We learn that Akaky is zealously devoted to the tedious, low-level work of a copyist and that he has been passed over for promotion because the prospect of being given even the simplest editorial responsibility overwhelms him with fear. Akaky's office-mates make fun of him relentlessly, a situation he usually accepts without a word, preferring to carry on as if nothing were happening. In a passage often cited to illustrate the story's thematic concern with compassion and the universal brotherhood of mankind, the narrator describes how one of Akaky's rare outbursts in response to the constant teasing—''Leave me alone! Why do you insult me?''—affects one of his coworkers:

> [T]here was something touching in [Akaky's] words and in the voice in which they were uttered. There was a note in it of something that aroused compassion, so that one young man, new to the office, who, following the example of the rest, had allowed himself to tease him, suddenly stopped as though cut to the heart, and from that time on, everything was, as it were, changed and appeared in a different light to him. Some unseen force seemed to repel him from the companions with whom he had become acquainted because he thought they were well-bred and decent men. And long afterward, during moments of the greatest gaiety, the figure of the humble little clerk with a bald patch on his head appeared before him with his heart-rending words: ''Leave me alone! Why do you insult me?'' and with those moving words he heard others: ''I am your brother.'' (Excerpt from ''The Overcoat,'' translated by Constance Garnett)

The plot of ''The Overcoat'' does not really begin to move forward until some four pages into the story, when it is revealed that Akaky's old and threadbare overcoat, no longer able to withstand St. Petersburg's viciously cold winters, must be replaced. The local tailor, Petrovich, convinces the reluctant Akaky that his old coat is beyond repair and begins making a very modest new one for him. Akaky must undergo severe deprivations in order to save enough money for the coat, and the process ends up taking months. When Akaky finally arrives in his office wearing the new coat, the entire department notices and his coworkers half-mockingly insist on a celebration in his honor. Akaky is embarrassed but also proud, and he accepts an invitation to a party given by his superior that evening. Akaky happily wears his new coat to the occasion but feels out of place at the party—though he enjoys himself somewhat after his coworkers cajole him into getting a little drunk.

Nikolai Gogol

At the night's end, however, on his walk back to his own less affluent neighborhood, Akaky is assaulted by a band of ruffians who steal the new coat right off his back. The incident occurs right in front of a policeman, who does nothing and claims that he assumed Akaky's assailants were simply his friends.

From this point on, Akaky begins to deteriorate rapidly. In trying to report the crime and seek restitution, he asserts himself and ''for the first time in his life trie[s] to show the strength of his character.'' Yet, his efforts go nowhere and he receives no real help from those around him. A police commissioner even casts suspicion on Akaky by asking what he was doing out so late at night in the first place. Akaky misses work for the first time, and though his coworkers take up a collection to buy him a replacement coat, they only manage to raise a trifling sum. Finally, Akaky finds the courage to ask for assistance from a relatively high-level bureaucrat, referred to by the narrator as ''the Person of Consequence.'' This man, however, proves to be petty and arrogant, and, instead of helping, he lectures Akaky on the importance of going through the proper bureaucratic channels. Akaky, unable to withstand the ''severe reprimand'' he receives, faints immediately and the next day falls ill. With no apparent hope of recovering either his overcoat or his dignity, he becomes delirious and dies within a few days.

In its final pages, as the narrator himself points out, ''our little story unexpectedly finishes with a fantastic ending.'' Akaky's corpse is seen wandering in various neighborhoods of St. Petersburg stealing overcoats off the backs of passersby. As the corpse eludes policemen, panicky rumors spread until the corpse eventually confronts and steals an overcoat from the ''Person of Consequence.'' Greatly disturbed by the incident, the ''Person of Consequence'' runs directly home to his family vowing to practice better morals, and begins to treat his underlings with a little more consideration. The supernatural revenge complete, the story returns to the realm of reality with the images in its closing paragraph, in which a policeman witnesses another assault. This time, however, the assailant—who escapes into the night—is too tall to have been the avenging corpse and fits more closely the description of the man who had stolen Akaky's coat.

Characters

Akaky Akakyevich
See Akaky Akakievich Bashmachkin

Akaky Akakievich Bashmachkin

Akaky Akakievich Bashmachkin, the impoverished clerk and protagonist of the story, is one of the first appearances in modern literature of the ''little man''—the poor, meek soul overwhelmed by dehumanizing forces in an increasingly technological and bureaucratized society. In introducing him, the story's narrator describes him as ''a clerk of whom it cannot be said that he was very remarkable.''

Akaky is a short, balding man with a bad complexion whose world seems to be defined by the tedious and solitary job of copying the various trivial documents he is given by his superiors. He has performed this work for uncounted years in an unspecified governmental department in St. Petersburg, even taking it home to complete at night. The prospect of a promotion that might give him the simplest editorial responsibility fills him with such fear that he once told a superior, ''No, I'd rather copy something.'' A passive person, Akaky usually responds to the constant teasing of his coworkers by

silently carrying on with his work and pretending that nothing is happening.

When he finds himself thrust into the center of attention after buying himself a new winter coat, the self-effacing clerk actually begins to feel a sense of pride. His newfound ability to assert himself is intensified after the coat is stolen: in trying to report the crime and seek restitution, as the narrator comments, ''Akaky Akakievich for the first time in his life tried to show the strength of his character.'' In the end, however, this test of character overwhelms him, and his personality disintegrates. Akaky becomes incoherent and dies more or less as a result of a ''severe reprimand'' that he receives from the General. The final image we have of him is that of a walking corpse, for in death he finally obtains some of the justice that eluded him in life.

General
See Person of Consequence

Important Personality
See Person of Consequence

Narrator

Though not directly involved in the events of the story, the narrator is a very strong—and controversial—presence. The ambiguous picture of the narrator that emerges through his many digressions poses some of the most important interpretive dilemmas in the story: How closely should the narrator be identified with Gogol? What is the narrator's attitude toward the other characters in the story?

The narrator's point of view could be described as omniscient or authorial because it is privy to more information than any other character in the story and has access to the characters' innermost thoughts and feelings. On the other hand, there are moments when the narrator's awareness seems limited. He (or she) seems to rely on rumor, for example, in reporting the exploits of Akaky's corpse. The narrator's frequent use of awkward, pompous-sounding phrases like ''as it were'' and ''so to speak''— that also characterize the language used by the bureaucrats in the story, including ''The Person of Consequence'' and Akaky himself—suggests that the story is being told by just another office drone like them. In some passages, such as the lengthy aside on the origin of Akaky Akakievich's name, the voice of the narrator sounds as mocking and sarcastic as those of Akaky's cruel office mates. In other passages, the narrator is more sympathetic, as in the description of Akaky's plea to be left alone by his co-workers.

Person of Consequence

"The Person of Consequence" is a petty official Akaky consults for help in retrieving his stolen overcoat. In introducing him, the narrator paints him as the epitome of all that is pretentious and inconsequential in the strictly hierarchical bureaucracy of Russia's government. Though his authority is only a few levels higher than Akaky's, this man is so intimidating to Akaky that his "severe reprimand"—a tirade about the importance of going through appropriate bureaucratic channels—leads to Akaky's fainting, falling ill, and eventually dying.

"The Person of Consequence" reappears in the final part of the story as he is confronted by and loses his own overcoat to Akaky's avenging corpse. On his way to visit a mistress at the time, the official rushes home to his wife and children vowing to practice better morals, and from then on, he treats his underlings with a little more kindness.

Media Adaptations

- "The Overcoat" was made into a film of the same title in 1959 by Russian actor Alexei Batalov. This faithful adaptation was shot in black and white and is available in video format with English subtitles. The film represents an important turning point in the history of Soviet film making, as it reflects a shift away from the overtly political/historical films that had been predominant since the revolution. It won a "Best Foreign Film" award in 1965.

Themes

The Human Condition

The universal human need for compassion is a central theme in "The Overcoat." Akaky Akakievich and others in the story deny their connection to the rest of humanity, but ultimately fail. This view of the human condition is embodied in the early passage in which the narrator describes the lack of compassion with which Akaky is treated by his coworkers: in one of Akaky's rare pleas to be left alone by his tormentors, a newer office mate unexpectedly hears, "I am your brother." The overcoat becomes a symbol for both a basic human need that unites us as well as our tragic tendency to deny that need. The coat is stolen by men supposedly mistaken for Akaky's friends. His efforts to retrieve the coat are thwarted by the hierarchical bureaucracy that encourages people to deny their common bonds and to treat one another without compassion. The story's "fantastic" ending underscores the interconnectedness of all humanity as Akaky's corpse returns to seek vengeance by stealing overcoats from random passersby and from "The Person of

Consequence" himself. Only after the tables have been turned by this supernatural visitation can "The Person of Consequence" recognize the error of his treatment of Akaky and others.

Alienation

The prevalent theme of alienation is closely tied to the story's rendering of the human condition. Akaky Akakievich has no close friends and is so alienated from those around him that he usually seems unwilling—or unable—to communicate at all. The anonymous, dehumanizing bureaucracy in which Akaky works epitomizes and perpetuates alienation. Difference in bureaucratic rank is an impediment to communication for both Akaky, who is intimidated by authority, and "The Person of Consequence," who feels obliged to insist on proper protocol. Akaky's total immersion in his copyist's job keeps him in isolation and further impairs his ability to communicate, as he becomes fixated on mere language fragments—the shapes of letters, and isolated words and phrases.

Language and Meaning

In addition to its pernicious, alienating effects on individuals, bureaucracy in "The Overcoat" also undermines language itself and its function as a medium for meaningful communication. The narrator's digressive way of telling the story, frequently

Topics for Further Study

- One famous passage in "The Overcoat" describes how one of the clerks in the office is touched by Akaky Akakievich's protest against the teasing from his fellow workers. This passage has been the subject of considerable debate: it seems to suggest that we should feel sympathy for Akaky, but many readers disagree. What do you think?

- What is the role of the narrator in this story? How would the story have been different if it were told in the third person? How much like or unlike Gogol do you think the narrator is?

- One definition of "allegory" is: "a method of telling a story in which characters and events are meant to represent moral or spiritual concepts more significant than the actual narrative itself." To what extent does "The Overcoat" fit this definition?

- Research the philosophical debates in Russia in the 1830s and 1940s between the "Slavophiles" and the "Westernizers." In his lifetime Gogol was associated with the "Westernizers" (represented by Gogol's friend Vissarion Belinsky). Some later readers, however, see Gogol's work as more in keeping with the ideas of the "Slavophiles." Based on "The Overcoat," in which of these two camps would you place Gogol? If you had been a participant in these debates, how would you have reacted to "The Overcoat"?

---

using meaningless phrases like "as it were" and "so to speak," seems infected with the self-conscious and pompous culture of the bureaucratic office. Akaky's troubles with language begin before he can even speak, when he is christened with his absurd, repetitive and slightly off-color name. His mother, after rejecting equally absurd suggestions from the child's godparents (who are, not coincidentally, a head clerk in the Senate and the wife of a police official), decides to name the child after her husband (also a government clerk): "His father is Akaky; let the son be Akaky, too." As he lay dying, Akaky is reduced to speaking "a medley of nonsense," which though obscene at times is also interspersed with the occasional "your Excellency," the appropriate polite form of address to a superior.

The Supernatural

The return of Akaky's corpse introduces a "fantastic" element into a story otherwise grounded in a realistic, contemporary setting and the mundane life of a clerk. Other aspects of the story could be described as exaggerated or absurd—Akaky Akakievich's name, and a bureaucratic reprimand so severe that it sends someone to his deathbed—but the story's ending is unique and, as the narrator comments, "unexpected." The supernatural intervention of Akaky's corpse appears in the story as the only means for redemption: by turning the tables on "The Person of Consequence," the corpse not only avenges Akaky but brings about his victim's acknowledgment of his own humanity as well. While not an explicitly religious image, Akaky's corpse seems to embody many of Gogol's spiritual concerns in an interesting—perhaps profane—twist on Christian mythology.

Style

Prose

Russian literature before the 1830s had been comprised almost entirely of poetry, while prose was reserved primarily for official documents, correspondence, histories, and journals. So Gogol's use of prose for literary purposes is in many ways one of his most lasting and significant contributions. Prose seems appropriate, of course, for telling the story of a simple clerk like Akaky Akakievich. The long and sometimes rambling sentences used by the narrator reflect Akaky's awkward personality, as well as the dull, bureaucratic milieu around him.

Narrative Perspective and Tone

The story is told from the perspective of an unnamed first person narrator who is not directly involved in the events of the story but is aware of (and, to varying degrees, sympathetic with) the characters' thoughts and emotions. For many present-day readers accustomed to short stories beginning *in medias res* (i.e., as the action has already begun), ''The Overcoat'' seems to adopt a leisurely pace initially as the character of Akaky Akakievich, his family background, and the St. Petersburg setting in which he lives and works are all introduced. Gogol uses the opening section of the story not only to set the scene, but to establish a particular narrative voice as well. By turns sarcastic, humorous, poignant, and disturbing, Gogol's narrator tells the story in a way that both entertains and instructs— with enough distance to provide critical commentary and yet enough dramatic intensity to draw readers in and not seem preachy.

Setting

The story's setting, amongst office-workers in contemporary St. Petersburg, must have seemed startling to Russian readers of Gogol's time, who were used to literature that described adventures amongst noblemen in pastoral and aristocratic settings. The setting in ''The Overcoat'' plays a role that is almost more important than that of any of the story's characters. The cold winter weather of St. Petersburg requires Akaky to buy his new coat, and the ''cold'' treatment he receives at the hands of the bureaucracy in which he exists finally kills him. The dehumanizing, anonymous and self-conscious atmosphere of the government offices that so dominate St. Petersburg in the story is conveyed in the very first sentence by the narrator's decision not to identify the name of the specific department. Akaky's home is described as cold, dark, and dreary, and his neighborhood, especially in contrast to that of the head clerk at whose home Akaky attends a party, is similarly bleak and dangerous.

Symbolism

For all the story's emphasis on stark realism in its depiction of St. Petersburg, ''The Overcoat'' operates on a symbolic level as well. Many elements—including the anonymous ''everyman'' nature of the character Akaky and the ''fantastic'' reappearance of his corpse near the end—give the story a fairy tale or dreamlike quality, suggesting that the whole narrative has a kind of symbolic significance. As the story's title indicates, Akaky's overcoat is an important, multilayered symbol. On one level, the coat represents a basic human need common to all residents of St. Petersburg in winter; at the same time, the overcoat in the story also seems to stand for the stifling status-oriented attitudes that envelope Russian society. Akaky is ridiculed for wearing his old threadbare overcoat, and though his new coat gives him entree into his coworkers' social circle, Akaky fails to make any real connection with them. When Akaky's corpse returns to strip an overcoat from ''The Person of Consequence,'' what is taken away is the pretension that had kept ''The Person of Consequence'' from acknowledging his common bond with Akaky and the rest of humanity.

Historical Context

Nikolai Gogol lived during one of the most tumultuous periods of Russian history. It was a time when the strict censorship was imposed on writing and teaching; yet many writers were expressing new ideas that were openly critical of the status quo. Though there were some hostile reviews of Gogol's work, most were favorable and his writings were never actually repressed by censors during his lifetime. Nevertheless, the atmosphere of scrutiny under which writers lived and worked was never comfortable for the sensitive Gogol, and he felt the need to leave his country on two occasions. Though his friends urged him to return, Gogol stayed away for twelve years during the second of these self-imposed exiles.

Events in December of 1825, a few months before Gogol's seventeenth birthday, would be a harbinger of trouble to come. A group of idealistic young aristocrats with vaguely defined notions of democratic reform attempted to overthrow the czarist government. Czar Alexander I had just died from eating poisoned mushrooms in the Crimea and there was some delay before his younger brother Nicholas would be installed as the new leader of

Compare & Contrast

- **1840s:** Russia is impacted by two political factions: the ''Slavophiles,'' who support Russian culture and advocate an isolationist view; and the ''Westernizers,'' who view Russia's future in light of Western Europe.

  1990s: With the breakup of the Soviet Union, Russia and the surrounding republics that once made up the Soviet Union look to the United States and the European community. Yet some Russians advocate a return to Communism and isolationism as a result of economic failures and food shortages.

- **1840s:** Gogol and other Russian authors struggle to develop a Russian school of literature.

1990s: Russian authors of the mid- to late-nineteenth centuries are highly regarded all over the world. Gogol, Dostoevsky, Turgenev, and others have had a great influence over subsequent Russian authors and world literature.

- **1840s:** Censorship of literary and journalistic work is commonplace under the Czarist regime.

1990s: Russia is an open society after the fall of Communism and the repeal of harsh repressive laws that had been in place for many years.

---

the country's vast empire. The revolutionaries (''Decembrists,'' as they were later called) were poorly organized and the new Czar was able to crush their revolt quickly. Nevertheless, Nicholas I—and the country as a whole—was badly shaken by the incident, and the new Czar would assert his authority with increasing rigidity throughout his thirty-year reign.

After the Decembrist revolt, Nicholas I completely revised the administrative structure of the Russian government. He removed aristocrats from government office and replaced them with professional military men. He established six new government departments, including a secret police that would all report to him and through which he would manage important economic and political matters. The government bureaucracy to which young Gogol applied for a job in 1828 was in turmoil: many of its officials were new in their jobs and there was a great deal of mistrust and fear due to the presence of the zealous new Czar's spies.

Abandoning work as a public servant for a literary career, however, did not remove Gogol from an atmosphere of contentiousness and instability. Despite Nicholas I's tightened control over

the press and education, many Russian intellectuals continued to criticize the Czar and to debate amongst themselves, eventually splitting into two main camps. The ''Slavophiles,'' who tended to support autocracy but favored free speech and an end to serfdom, held that the Orthodox Church and other aspects of Russian culture made it unique and superior. ''Westernizers,'' on the other hand, believed Russia's progress to be dependent on liberal government and the adoption of ideas and technology from western Europe. Vissarion Belinsky, a prominent literary critic from the Westernizer's camp, was impressed by Gogol's early work and hailed the young author as a pioneer of a new, progressive aesthetic.

One could argue, however, that Gogol had as much in common with the more conservative Slavophiles as with Belinsky and the Westernizers. While Gogol was interested in western Europe— and lived there for a time—he was very proud of his Ukranian/Russian roots. The work that first attracted Belinsky's attention to Gogol (*Evenings on a Farm Near Dikanki*), for example, was a collection of stories based on traditional Ukranian folktales that had a very Russian flavor. Gogol later became involved with the Russian Orthodox Church, and his growing conservatism eventually alienated Belinsky.

Ultimately, of course, Gogol cannot be assigned entirely to either camp. It is difficult to say whether it was the authoritarian censors of the Czar or the polarized community of Russian dissident intelligentsia that drove Gogol to leave Russia for so long. Gogol wrote "The Overcoat" during the longer of his two self-imposed exiles—in an effort, perhaps, to capture something quintessentially Russian from a perspective outside of Russia.

Critical Overview

When Nikolai Gogol's story "The Overcoat" appeared as part of his multivolume *Collected Works* in 1842, Gogol's prestige amongst the contentious Russian literary critics of the day was relatively secure. It was a time of rigid censorship and sometimes vindictive reviews, but Gogol had already won the support of powerful allies, including the famous (though recently deceased) poet Alexander Pushkin and prominent critic Vissarion Belinsky. More importantly perhaps, the Czar himself seemed to look favorably on Gogol's work. In fact, Gogol's harshest critic may have been Gogol himself. Halfway through a self-imposed twelve-year exile from Russia, he was beginning a period of intense self-doubt and spiritual uncertainty that would last for the remaining ten years of his life.

"The Overcoat" and most of Gogol's other works have enjoyed both critical and popular success in Russia and elsewhere since their first appearance. Following Belinsky's interpretation, Gogol came to be seen as an originator of Russia's naturalist school of literature. As distinct from a rhetorical or romantic tradition epitomized by Gogol's friend and mentor Pushkin, Belinsky saw in Gogol's work a new approach emphasizing the realistic depiction of social problems as a means to foster progress. This naturalist approach would have tremendous influence on Russian novelists in the second half of the nineteenth century (e.g., Turgenev, Dostoevski, and Tolstoy), and then be elevated in the Soviet era to the status of state doctrine—"Socialist Realism."

Belinsky and other readers of "The Overcoat" in Gogol's day believed that the author displayed deep sympathy for the story's beleaguered main character and that he hoped to inspire reform on behalf of poor clerks and others. When Gogol appeared to espouse different ideas in his 1847 *Selected Passages*, Belinsky was especially shocked and disappointed: "Why, if you had made an attempt on my life," he wrote to Gogol, "even then I would not have hated you more than I do for these shameful lines." Belinsky theorized that Gogol's personality somehow contained two separate people: one was a brilliant artist who served the highest humanitarian and political ideas, and the other was a philosopher who, lacking basic intelligence and decency, deserved to be ignored.

Subsequent critics have sought alternatives to Belinsky's "Two Gogols" theory, but most have addressed questions pertaining to which political beliefs are expressed in Gogol's writing, what degree of sympathy he shows for his characters, and whether or not Gogol himself was rational and coherent.

At the beginning of the twentieth century, a group of Russian writers and intellectuals called the "Symbolists" suggested a new way of understanding Gogol's work. Pointing to the frequent appearance of the "half-fantastic" in Gogol's writing, the Symbolists believed that Gogol was not concerned with depicting external reality or political issues. Rather, they saw his stories as symbolic portraits of internal psychological struggles. Akaky's overcoat, for example, could represent a mask enabling the character to disguise his spiritual destitution. The views of these symbolist writers, however, were not well received by Soviet Marxist literary critics, and soon the only interpretations published in Russia described Gogol as a politically engaged social realist.

On the international scene—particularly in Western Europe and America—Gogol's work has continued to receive a great deal of critical attention and diverse readings. More recent scholars have tended to see more ambivalence expressed in Gogol's work toward characters from the lower classes, like Akaky Akakievich, and to find in his stories suggestions of the conservative religious views he held late in his life. Gogol's work is seen as a major influence on the twentieth-century Austrian writer, Franz Kafka. Early in his career, the American/Russian-expatriate author Vladimir Nabokov devoted himself to writing a major study of Gogol. Gogol's high literary reputation is secure, with his writing seen today as an early inspiration for literary modernism and for the short story form itself.

Scene from a Times Film Corp. adaptation of Nikolai Gogol's story "The Overcoat."

Criticism

Michael Sonkowsky

Sonkowsky has taught English at the University of Pennsylvania. In the following essay, he examines the "multiplicity of meanings" in Gogol's short story and asserts that it "[sheds] light . . . on modern life as it is experienced everywhere."

"The Overcoat" was the last short story Nikolai Gogol ever wrote, and many consider it to be his finest. Even setting aside his other literary accomplishments—writing a great stage comedy (*The Inspector General*) and the first great epic Russian novel (*Dead Souls*)—it is difficult to overestimate the importance of Gogol's work in introducing the short story as a literary form in Russia.

Beginning in 1831 with the publication of a collection of tales set in his native Ukraine (*Evenings on a Farm Near Dikanka*) and culminating in 1842 with the appearance of "The Overcoat," Gogol developed a new form that is still in use today by writers in Russia and elsewhere. In more than a century and a half since "The Overcoat" first appeared, it has inspired diverse interpretations and raised many unanswered questions about its eccen-

What Do I Read Next?

- Gogol's story "The Diary of a Madman" ("Zapriski sumassehdshago"), published in 1835, also makes use of the motif of a garment as a status symbol. The story is written in the form of a diary that records the mental deterioration of its writer. At one point the writer, another poor government clerk, believes himself to be the King of Spain, Ferdinand VIII. When he decides to reveal his identity in public, he reasons, "If only I could get hold of a royal mantle of some sort. I thought of having one made but tailors are so stupid. . . . I decided to make a mantle out of my best coat which I had worn only twice. . . . I had to cut my coat to ribbons with the scissors since a mantle has a completely different style."

- "The Nose" ("Nos") is another of Gogol's short stories which first appeared in his 1842 *Collected Works*. Also a satire of bureaucratic life in St. Petersburg, "The Nose" takes a more absurdist or surreal approach than "The Overcoat." It is the story of a minor bureaucrat who struggles to retrieve his nose after it apparently abandons him and takes on the role of a bureaucrat with a higher rank.

- *The Government Inspector* (*Revizor*) is Gogol's famous stage comedy, first performed in 1836. It is the story of a drifter who is mistaken for a government inspector by the residents of a small provincial town and showered with bribes until the real official appears. Despite its obvious satire of Russian bureaucracy, Czar Nicholas I loved the play and ordered all his ministers to see it. It has been one of the most highly acclaimed Russian plays ever since.

- *Notes from Underground* is a novella written by the great Russian novelist Fyodor Dostoevsky in 1864. Reminiscent of Gogol's work—"The Diary of a Madman" in particular—*Notes from Underground* is a darkly humorous first person narration of a bureaucrat whose sanity is questionable.

- "The Metamorphosis," a story written by Franz Kafka in 1915, shows a great deal of Gogol's influence. It is a disturbingly surreal and satirical depiction of Gregor Samsa, a poor office worker who wakes up one day to find himself transformed into an insect.

- "Gogol's Wife" is a short story published in 1961 by Italian avant-garde writer Tommaso Landolfi. Well-known as a critic and translator of Russian literature, Landolfi creates a fictional narrative to explain the mystery surrounding Gogol's love life. The real Gogol never married and there is little evidence that he ever felt romantic attraction toward anyone. In "Gogol's Wife," Landolfi makes up some evidence—in the form of an account from a fictional acquaintance/biographer of Gogol's—that suggests that Gogol had a very bizarre love life indeed.

---

tric author. Gogol has been seen as both a progressive social critic and a conservative religious idealogue. He has been called the father of realism in Russian literature, but also a romantic and even, by Vladimir Nabokov, a "fantast." The ambiguities of Gogol's work are a reflection of the tumultuous times in which he lived and may, in fact, be an important source of the power in the new literary form he helped to establish.

One of the great coincidences in the history of literature is that the modern short story form first emerged in two different places on opposite sides of the world at virtually the same time. While Gogol was publishing the first Russian short stories, American writers Nathaniel Hawthorne and Edgar Allan Poe were establishing the same new literary form in their country. Hawthorne began writing sometime after graduating from college in 1825 and published his first collection of stories in 1837 (*Twice-Told*

> To study it is to begin to examine a tradition of writing that continues to grow and to shed light not just on Russian culture, but on modern life as it is experienced everywhere."

Tales). Poe published short stories in various journals throughout the 1830s and perhaps wrote his greatest story in 1839 (''The Fall of the House of Usher'').

During these years, America and Russia were both considered somewhat remote, far from the centers of literary activity in the great capitals of western and central Europe. The early pioneers of the short story looked to these European cities for inspiration, encouragement and even protection—as would generations of Russian and American writers to come—but they also sought to convey experiences linked in identifiable ways to their own native countries. In addition to the language and setting these writers used, the short story form itself seemed to reflect some of the isolated and fragmented nature of life in the two rapidly changing countries of America and Russia. The short story has endured as a literary form and has thrived in many different cultures partly because it is uniquely suited to portraying aspects of modernity that would characterize much of the twentieth century.

The most immediate precursor of the modern short story may be the common folktale or fable. Amongst Romantic intellectuals from the generation preceding the first short story writers, folktales—along with a general interest in the innate wisdom of ''common folk''—were in vogue. The Grimm brothers published their famous collections of folktales gathered from German peasants in 1812 and 1815. Gogol, Hawthorne, and Poe all incorporated narrative elements reminiscent of folktales, but their stories tended to be set in reality. The fantastic elements are portrayed as intrusions into a world familiar to most of the stories' contemporary readers—a world populated not by princesses and witches, but by office clerks and small-town ministers.

At the beginning of Gogol's ''The Overcoat,'' the narrator takes great care initially in describing the setting in which the story takes place. Even if the main character (Akaky Akakievich) has a strange name and is a bit extreme in his obsessive work habits, St. Petersburg is easily recognizable in the story—as are its cold winters, large bureaucratic offices and dark streets that cross through neighborhoods of different social classes. The narrator feels obliged to pause and give warning to the readers before introducing the relatively bizarre concept of an animated corpse in search of vengeance: ''But who could have imagined that this was not all there was to tell about Akaky Akakievich, that he was destined for a few days to make his presence felt in the world after his death, as though to make up for his life having been unnoticed by anyone? But so it happened, and our little story unexpectedly finishes with a fantastic ending.''

The ''fantastic ending'' is a focal point for much of the ambiguity that has kept critical debate about the story alive for so long. The political reform-minded critics of Gogol's day saw the return of Akaky's corpse as a kind of progressive call to arms and as a way for Gogol to underscore the story's message of social criticism. Thus, they interpreted the ending in much the same way as one reads a moral at the end of a fable.

To some later critics, the story's ending seemed less ''tacked on.'' They pointed to other elements in the story that can be seen as bizarre or unusual—the miraculous way in which the new overcoat seems to transform Akaky and win acceptance for him amongst his coworkers, for example. These critics argued that the entire story could be interpreted as a symbolic depiction of human emotions or psychological states. For them, the return of Akaky's corpse was the symbolic resurfacing of repressed guilt—an image to represent the feelings of remorse connected with treating someone like Akaky with insufficient compassion. Still other critics have seen Akaky's ''resurrection'' as a reworking of the Christian myth—an indication that Gogol meant to offer his story to readers as a means for their redemption.

''The Overcoat'' is able to encompass a multiplicity of meanings in part because, unlike a fairy tale or fable with a moral lesson explicitly stated at the end, it is told by a first-person narrator who is as unable as any reader to give the final, authoritative statement of the story's significance. Gogol's contemporaries tended to assume that the first-person pronoun in the story simply referred to Gogol himself. Subsequent readers, however, have noticed ways in which Gogol distances himself from the narrator and creates the impression that the story is being told by another St. Petersburg office-worker. For example, like other characters in the story, the narrator tends to use the somewhat formal language interspersed with meaningless little phrases like ''as it were'' and ''so to speak.'' Toward the end of the story, as the narrator describes the indifference with which people in St. Petersburg responded to Akaky's death, he confesses that he too has been remiss: ''Who came into [Akaky's] wealth God only knows; even I who tell the tale must admit that I have not bothered to inquire.''

Does Gogol intend for us to feel sympathy for Akaky's plight and anger toward the system that makes it so difficult for poor clerks to afford basic necessities such as a new winter coat? Has the author created a symbolic portrait of the workings of the human mind racked by guilt and denial? Or is the story best understood as an expression of its author's concern over the spiritual well being of his countrymen and an attempt to point the way to redemption? Gogol's story leaves any or all of these possibilities open. In so doing, the story shows us something about human experience in a world characterized by radically competing ideas and large bureaucratic structures—something as true in Gogol's day as it still is today.

One commentary on the genre of the short story points out that although not every short story is set in a city, ''. . . in a way the modern short story is an expression of the life led in the modern city, with its estrangement and anonymity and its special awareness.'' As one of the first short stories to give such prominence to a large urban setting, ''The Overcoat'' is obviously an early milestone in this important contemporary literary form. To study it is to begin to examine a tradition of writing that continues to grow and to shed light not just on Russian culture, but on modern life as it is experienced everywhere.

Source: Michael Sonkowsky, ''Overview of 'The Overcoat,''' for *Short Stories for Student*, The Gale Group, 2000.

R. A. Peace

In the following excerpt, Peace offers an interpretation of Gogol's ''The Greatcoat'' (''The Overcoat''), particularly in regard to Gogol's narrative technique, verbal devices, and use of humor.

''The Greatcoat'' is the story of an impoverished civil service clerk, in St. Petersburg, who by dint of great sacrifices manages to buy himself a new coat, but is robbed of it the very first evening he wears it. He tries to get it back by going to see a highly-placed official who gives him such a reprimand that the poor clerk falls ill and dies. Later his ghost haunts St Petersburg, stealing coats; it is only laid to rest when it has taken the greatcoat of the highly-placed official himself.

The story is often regarded as having initiated a whole tradition of Russian realism. 'We have all come out of Gogol's greatcoat' is a remark allegedly uttered by Dostoevsky (though this attribution is suspect). Yet in what sense can a story with a ghost sequence be called realistic? By realism Russian critics in the nineteenth century often meant 'critical realism,' implying that a writer by portraying society 'realistically' was thereby expressing criticism of it. On the face of it the plot of ''The Greatcoat'', as outlined, does suggest a social theme and it cannot be denied that criticism is implicit in Gogol's treatment of the police (in particular his laughter at the inept constables). Veneration of rank and the insolence of authority (the 'Important Person') are presented with implied censure. Yet, as regards his poverty, the authorities in Akakii Akakievich's own department are not responsible for his plight. The director gives him a much higher bonus than he had expected when he needs the money for his coat. Afterwards the assistant chief clerk invites him to a party, partly in honour of his coat. Nor can it be argued that the civil service has turned Akakii Akakievich into the automation that he undoubtedly is. Indeed, he seems to have been born to his role and we learn that he had once been given more interesting work but had proved incapable of it.

Nor is it entirely true that he is portrayed sympathetically. If the other clerks poke fun at him, they do little more than the narrator of the story himself; for in spite of his strictures on those writers who mock titular councillors, he nevertheless constantly presents his own hero as a figure of fun, with a neck that reminds him of a toy plaster-kitten, and the strange ability always to find himself under a window when rubbish is being thrown out. . . .

The opening paragraph of ''The Greatcoat'' should be a warning to the reader. It is long, involved and absolutely irrelevant to the story itself. In fact the opening paragraph is a sort of verbal arabesque which goes nowhere, except back to its

> " It is typical of Gogol to take his reader on a long aside which will go nowhere. As a form of humour it may be compared to the shaggy dog story, where the joke is not <u>for</u> the listener but <u>on</u> the listener."

original starting point: from 'In one of our government departments' to '. . . a certain department.'

It is typical of Gogol to take his reader on a long aside which will go nowhere. As a form of humour it may be compared to the shaggy dog story, where the joke is not *for* the listener but *on* the listener. It is, of course, a dangerous game to play with a reader, who can always terminate the joke by putting the book down. Moreover, such a joke implies a latent hostility towards the reader. Yet if the anecdote in the opening paragraph about the police inspector has any point at all, it is to suggest quite the reverse, namely that readers (especially those in official positions) are only too prone to show hostility towards authors.

The narrator of the story is, of course, not Gogol himself. It is someone who is very naive, not at all well educated, and who as a teller of a story is incredibly inept. He repeatedly concentrates on inessential and often absurd details, at the expense of the plot itself—and in this sense the opening paragraph is a foretaste of what is to come. (The inept narrator is a favourite device with Gogol, and this type of tale—a story told by an illiterate narrator—is quite common in Russian literature).

But although the narrator is naive, the narrative, in effect, is not: it is full of hints, innuendoes, puns and verbal tricks of all sorts. It is through these that the tale really unfolds, and in a way which gives hidden depth to a seemingly shallow surface.

One of the great ironies of this style is that the naive narrator requires a sophisticated reader, a reader who is sensitive, not to the possibilities of personal libel, as those whom Gogol mocks in the opening paragraph, but one who is sensitive to words and tone and word-play.

Naive ambiguity is a constant feature of the narrative technique in ''The Greatcoat''. There are many puns which communicate a waywardness and playfulness of tone to the narrative, yet their contribution is not so much to the humour of the story as to the external presentation of the inner world of the central character, a man who is himself obsessed by the outward form of words, their graphic contours, only because their real content and function eludes him. The pun is precisely this: a word taken at face value which nevertheless has a hidden content beneath its deceptive surface. The verbal play has more meaning than is at first apparent, and the relationship between facade and interior is not only the central 'device' of ''The Greatcoat'', it is the architectural principle which informs its shape.

There is a great deal of verbal play at the opening of the story, (i.e., the whole of the introductory section ending with the play on the word 'councillor'). In introducing Akakii Akakievich the narrator places exaggerated importance on the naming of his hero, whereas his formative years are merely bridged by a verbal formula: 'The child was christened. At which he began to cry and he pulled such a face as though he sensed beforehand that he would be a titular councillor.' Almost immediately after this we find him already long established in the office as a copy clerk: '. . . so that later people became convinced that he had obviously been born into the world ready-made, in a uniform and a bald path on his head.' His christening seems to pre-ordain his profession and his profession seems to have been entered on at birth.

This emphasis on his christening and lack of interest in his formative years suggests that his name is far more important than his life in determining his character. In particular the origin of the surname is treated with naive seriousness:

> The civil servant's name was Bashmachkin. From the very name itself one can see that at some time it had been derived from a shoe; but when, at what particular time and in what way it was derived from a shoe—nothing of this is known. Both his father and his grandfather, and even his brother-in-law, all Bashmachkins through and through, used to walk about in boots, changing the soles only three times a year.

The whole of this explanation is patently absurd, if taken at its surface meaning. Yet, on another level, it suggests a whole train of semantic ambiguities which are picked up and developed later in the story, and in such a way as to reveal the psychological problems of Akakii Akakievich himself.

In the first place the verb 'derived' is taken quite literally, (the all important qualification 'word' which ought to precede 'shoe' is omitted) so that our hero's name appears to have come directly from an article of footwear—a shoe (just as later it will be suggested that he has almost got married to a greatcoat). Through his surname the hero is thus directly identified with a mere casing of the human body.

The narrator compounds the absurdity by asserting that all Akakii Akakievich's family wore boots, and gives the irrelevant information that they had the soles replaced only three times a year. (The saving of his soles will later figure prominently in Akakii Akakievich's economies needed to acquire the coat.) The list of Akakii Akakievich's relatives, who, according to the narrator, are all genuine Bashmachkins includes 'even a brother-in-law' (*i dazhe shurin*) despite the fact that, as this is a relationship by marriage, he could not possibly be a genuine Bashmachkin as the narrator claims. Yet the inclusion of this brother-in-law is absurd in an even more profound sense. Russian relationships by marriage are very precise, and *shurin* can only mean 'wife's brother.' For Akakii Akakievich to have a '*shurin*,' he must also have a wife, but a wife is no more in evidence than these other relatives with whom he is here credited. Akakii Akakievich is completely alone. This little verbal puzzle, therefore, tangles the 'shoe from which his name is derived, with the relatives from whom he is actually derived (his father and his grandfather) and ties them in with a figure to whom he can only be related by a sexual bond (the brother-in-law).

The theme of the wife, who is non-existent but implied, appears again when the narrator gives examples of his 'down-trodden' existence, such as the teasing to which he is subjected at the office:

> They would relate, right in front of him, various stories concocted about him. They said about his landlady, an old woman of seventy, that she beat him, and they would ask him when their wedding would be. They would scatter paper on his head, calling it snow.

The motif of the 'shoe' is prominent in the picture which stirs a vague sexual awakening in Akakii Akakievich, and the detail seems intentional, for virtually the same picture is described at the end of "The Nose", but without the mention of a shoe. At a later stage a shoe will also link this picture with his landlady. Thus the 'shoe,' from

which his outward identification (his name) is derived, suggests a latent sexual motif in much the same way as does that other item of apparel, his other outward form, the greatcoat.

Akakii Akakievich's progress through St. Petersburg may be interpreted as a journey in self-exploration: it is certainly a progress towards light. He moves away from his own badly-lit part of the city, past the lighted window with its erotic picture to the apartment of the civil servant who has invited him; 'the assistant chief clerk lived in great style; there was a lantern shining on the staircase.'

The fact that Akakii Akakievich is at first overawed is again suggested by Gogol's external method of psychological portrayal. Akakii Akakievich is reduced to the status of an object among other objects:

> On entering the hall Akakii Akakievich saw on the floor a whole row of galoshes. Among them in the middle of the room stood a samovar, noisily emitting clouds of steam. On the walls hung nothing but greatcoats and capes, among which there were several which even had beaver collars or velvet lapels.

It seems significant that he is confronted with footwear and greatcoats. The only thing which appears to have life in this ante-room is another inanimate object—the samovar. Real life once more, it seems, is going on elsewhere: for on the other side of the wall he can hear the noise of the party. The guests have already been assembled for some time.

Nevertheless the occasion has been held partly to honour Akakii Akakievich's new coat. He is accepted by this society, and his greatcoat is rapturously admired, even though there are better ones hanging up in the hall. 'Then, of course, everybody dropped him and his coat and turned, as is the custom, to the whist-tables.' After all, Akakii Akakievich is not really at home in these surroundings. He tries to creep away, but is made to stay for supper and two festive glasses of champagne. It is after midnight when he escapes. He finds his coat, 'which, not without regret, he perceived was lying on the floor.' He carefully shakes it, and goes down to a still lighted street. Here, sexual promptings (inexplicable to the narrator) once more well up within him:

> Akakii Akakievich went along in a gay mood, and for some unknown reason he was even almost on the point of running up behind some lady or other, who went past like lightning, and every part of whose body was full of unusual movement. However, he stopped at once and went on as before very slowly, amazed himself at this unaccountable burst of speed.

His progress now, however, is away from light and conviviality towards the dark, shuttered emptiness of his own quarter of the town.

On his outward journey he had been *looking* for the first time in his life. Now, as he crosses a dark square, where a light seems 'at the world's end' and 'it is as though there is a sea around him,' our explorer closes his eyes—and is robbed of his greatcoat by men with moustaches. Thus he is brutally deprived of the promise of that fuller life which had been offered to him so briefly and so tenuously.

He goes home to his landlady and the details of his return seem to reproduce in ironical terms the elements of the picture in the lighted window which had earlier aroused such strange stirrings within him:

> The old lady, the landlady of his apartment, hearing the terrible knocking at the door, hurriedly jumped out of bed and with a shoe on only one foot, ran to open the door, holding her nightshirt to her bosom out of modesty.

The landlady, as we know, has already been associated with the marital status of Akakii Akakievich by the clerks at the office, who teased him about marrying her and scattered 'snow' on his head. Now, when he comes back covered in real snow, his landlady, like the woman in the picture, confronts him with 'a shoe on one foot' and a hint of sexual titillation ('holding her nightshirt to her bosom, out of modesty'). But the 'man at the door' is not the dandy with the side whiskers and beautiful beard; it is the dishevelled Akakii Akakievich, with what little hair he has in complete disarray.

So Akakii Akakievich is thrown back on his seventy-year-old landlady, by the 'light' of whose candle he used to work in the evenings (after first having taken off his underwear to economise on laundry!). On her advice he goes to the police, but the district superintendent seems to think that the loss of the coat is in some way connected with its owner's dissolute life:

> The district superintendent received the story of the theft of the coat somehow in an exceedingly strange way. Instead of turning his attention to the main point of the matter, he began to question Akakii Akakievich as to why he was returning home so late, and hadn't he called in at some disorderly house or other?

Here, as elsewhere in the story, the significance of the coat is interpreted not in terms of the obvious, but in terms of a suggested sexual theme. The hint is present even on his death-bed, for he keeps asking his landlady to drag a coat-thief out from under his blankets.

If in the opening section of ''The Greatcoat'' verbal play is an important device for establishing motifs which are to be developed in the central section of the story, now in the final section (the ghost sequence) verbal play has a similar function. There is a recurring pun on the concepts of 'dead' and 'alive.' The police are ordered to apprehend the '*dead man* dead or alive.' One of them apparently succeeds, but loses the ghost because he pauses to take snuff of a quality 'which even a dead man couldn't stand,' and from that time on the police 'got so frightened of dead men, that they were even fearful of arresting the living.' Finally, there is an 'apparition' at the end of the story, who when challenged by a policeman, shows him a huge fist 'such as you would not find on the living.'

All this seems like humour directed at the police, who throughout the story have shown themselves to be particularly inept, but there is also a serious intention behind the word-play. The ghost is first introduced as 'a dead man in the form of a civil servant' (*mertvets v vide chinovnika*). Later he is simply referred to as the 'dead man-civil servant' (*chinovnik-mertvets*). The verbal play on 'dead' and 'alive' is therefore a motif pointing to the artistic function of the story's fantastic ending; it raises the whole question of '*chinovnik-mertvets*.'

When he was alive, Akakii Akakievich was in reality more like a 'civil servant in the form of a dead man.' The promise of an awakening into life, flimsy though it may have been, was cruelly taken from him by men with moustaches. When he has died he returns as a 'dead man in the form of a civil servant' to avenge himself and, by one of those ironies in which the story abounds, he proves to be more effective as a dead man, than he was when alive.

It is typical of Gogol that this inversion to which the central character is subjected should also be reflected in the external world around him. When earlier Akakii Akakievich was going through the streets of St. Petersburg, the narrator was insistent that everything in the city was so muddled in his head that he could not remember names; now, when his hero appears as a ghost, he is very meticulous about giving the precise location of each appearance. In the first instance a real man was going through a spiritual city; in the second a spirit man is haunting a concrete and actual city.

It is only after the ghost has robbed the 'important person' of his greatcoat that this unquiet spirit is finally laid, and the whole incident is presented with the same ironic parallelism of detail which has been noted elsewhere in the story. The important person, having just learned of the death of Akakii Akakievich, goes to a party to cheer himself up. (Akakii Akakievich had been to a party before he lost his coat.) Here (like Akakii Akakievich before him) he has two glasses of champagne. He feels in a gayer mood, and just as Akakii Akakievich had then, for some unknown reason, wanted to chase after a woman in the street, so the important person now entertains thoughts of an amorous nature:

> The champagne put him in a mood for special measures; that is he decided not to go home yet, but to call on a certain lady of his acquaintance, Karolina Ivanovna, a lady who appeared to be of German extraction, and for whom he felt an entirely friendly relationship.

Here, as in the earlier incident with Akakii Akakievich, the narrator shows himself to be naively uncomprehending about the sexual motivation of his characters.

Whereas Akakii Akakievich had been making the first tentative gestures in the direction of life, the important person has long had it firmly in his grasp. He takes an active part in the evening gathering as a man among equals; on leaving the party he is going to a real mistress; and moreover, unlike Akakii Akakievich, he also has a family:

> But the important person, although he was quite content with the family affection he received at home, considered it fitting to have a lady-friend in another part of town for friendly relationships. This lady-friend was not a whit better or younger than his wife. But such puzzles do exist in the world, and it is not for us to judge them.

It seems poetic justice that the ghost should rob this 'man of substance' of his greatcoat at this precise moment. The effect is cathartic: the ghost is laid, and the general himself becomes a much better person.

The story ends with yet another ironic twist. Another ghost is seen and it is believed to be the ghost of Akakii Akakievich, but it is really an 'apparition' and when challenged by a particularly inept policeman it threatens him with a fist not unlike that of the man who had stolen Akakii Akakievich's greatcoat in the first place and had showed him a fist 'the size of a civil servant's head.' The policeman leaves the apparition alone:

> The apparition was, however, much taller and wore really enormous moustaches, and turning its steps, as it seemed, towards the Obukhov Bridge, it completely disappeared in the darkness of the night.

Even Akakii Akakievich's credibility as a ghost, it seems, is being challenged by those men with moustaches and the whole story ends on a note of darkness.

Source: R. A. Peace, "Gogol: 'The Greatcoat,'" in *The Voice of a Giant: Essays on Seven Russian Prose Classics*, edited by Roger Cockerell and David Richards, University of Exeter, 1985, pp. 27–40.

Carl R. Proffer

In the following excerpt, Proffer examines the major critical viewpoints regarding Gogol's short story and suggests that "the real meaning of the story is then that life, even when it shrinks to almost ridiculous proportions, in the end triumphs over death."

Some critics have seen in Akaky Akakievich a humiliated and insulted human being who invokes our pity by his cruel lot and who makes us understand that, despite his insignificance, he is also "our brother." In order to prove their point, these critics cite what is usually called the "humane passage," in which Gogol presents the timid protest of his outraged hero and ponders the profound impression that these words make on a young colleague

> Leave me alone, gentlemen. Why do you insult me?— There was a strange note in the words and in the voice in which they were uttered: there was something in it that touched one's heart with pity. Indeed, one young man who had only recently been appointed to the department and who, following the example of the others, tried to have some fun at his expense, stopped abruptly at Akaky's mild expostulation, as though stabbed through the heart; and since then everything seemed to have changed in him and he saw everything in quite a different light. A kind of unseen power made him keep away from his colleagues whom at first he had taken for decent, well-bred men. And for a long time afterwards, in his happiest moments, he would see the shortish Civil Servant with the bald patch on his head, uttering those pathetic words, "Leave me alone! Why do you insult me?" And in those pathetic words he seemed to hear others: "I am your brother."

It should be noted that the critics who stress the pitiful fate of this little man and the fact that this humiliated being is "our brother" are at the same time inclined to see only the "humane passage" and to forget the remainder of the story. M. and R. Hoffmann bluntly deplore the fact that Gogol was not satisfied with the theft of the overcoat as sufficient cause for Akaky Akakievich's death, but that he also found it necessary to introduce the episode with the "important person." The fantastic ending of the story, according to them, is all the more out of place in that it destroys the impression of the whole "and transforms this *realistic* and *tragic* story into a fantastic tale of a very questionable nature." [Modeste and Rostislav Hofman, *Gogol: Sa vie et son ouevre*, 1946] In fact, they readily admit that the story as such does not interest them: "The major interest in 'The Overcoat' lies not in its subject, nor in its development, but in a new theme which slips in rather timidly, a theme which inspired the novelists of the second half of the nineteenth century to compose their vast symphonies. When the colleagues of Akaky Akakievich made fun of him, his voice echoes weakly, imploring pity for all of the unhappy, humiliated, oppressed and dispossessed creatures of this world . . ."

There exists, then, a critical viewpoint which places the highest value on the "humane passage" and stresses the humiliating destiny of the little civil servant, who implores our pity and our recognition of his worth as a human being. In addition, there is also a viewpoint which sees Akaky Akakievich as a ridiculous character of inferior human status, and which says that throughout the story Gogol stressed only the ridiculous insignificance of his hero. This criticism sees the "humane passage" only as an episode grafted onto the story, an abstraction by which the author vainly strove to add a moving and ethical touch to a commonplace and cruel story. Nearly all of the discussions of "The Overcoat" which we have read fall between these two points of view.

We know of only one study which attempts to resolve the paradox of the humiliated and pitiful man who is still our brother, and the ridiculed and inferior "dead soul," to use Vyacheslav Ivanov's expression. This is Driessen's study which emphasizes both the pitiful banality of this character and his tragic fight for happiness and the defense of an ideal. [F.C. Driessen, *Gogol als novellist*, 1955] At the same time, Driessen notes that there are two "humane passages" and he tries to integrate them as well as the story's fantastic ending into the narrative. According to Driessen, the two passages accent the tragic in Akaky Akakievich's life and raise the comic to the level of humor. The fantastic ending is tied, by its form, to the preceding part of the story; it contains the same themes (the theft of the overcoat, the evening party, the romantic adventure). In addition to his emphasis on the relationship

between the two perspectives, Driessen refers to a first draft which shows that Gogol originally wanted to entitle his tale "The Story of a Civil Servant who Stole Overcoats." It can, therefore, be assumed that initially the little civil servant's theft of overcoats was the main theme of the story. If this is so then the fantastic ending must be of major significance. It shows how Akaky Akakievich, by stealing overcoats after his death, avenges himself on the bureaucratic world which had trampled underfoot his human dignity. That world was dead. Akaky Akakievich alone guarded the flame of life no matter how small. The real meaning of the story is then that life, even when it shrinks to almost ridiculous proportions, in the end triumphs over death. . . .

In short, as a factual narrative the story has ended, just as Gogol himself stresses: Akaky Akakievich had died and was buried and a new employee sat in his place. If the epilogue is nonetheless integrated into the story, it is because it still plays a role in evoking Bashmachkin's character; it brings to light the urgency and desperation of his appeals for help, his forays against the world of policy and bureaucracy in the tragic moments of his existence, when he fought to regain his lost happiness.

> But who could have foreseen that this was not all about Akaky Akakievich, that he was destined to make quite a stir for some days after his death, as if in recompense for a life that had passed completely unnoticed.

Thus Gogol begins the final part of his narrative. Indeed, all these people from whom Akaky sought recourse in his distress and who then made fun of him—in the end, they all seem affected by the violence of his appeal and protest, especially the "important person." Not without good reason does Gogol say that the fantastic epilogue was written from the perspective of this character. In his anguished imagination, as in that of others who had seen Akaky in his misery, the little civil servant takes on a grandiose shape; he becomes an enormous and menacing figure. The ghost of the late Bashmachkin appears as a grotesque contrast to the timid civil servant of real life. Yet by this exaggeration Gogol shows us, in effect, how in spite of everything, Bashmachkin left an indelible mark by his fight against the misfortune which crushed him, just as it crushes the conquerors of this world.

If we weigh the different elements, it appears that Akaky Akakievich is characterized by a combination of comic, grotesque, tragicomic and tragic elements. The comic elements at the beginning of the story make us see in Akaky a man whose physical and psychic vitality finds itself in some ways annihilated by all kind of circumstances which automatize him completely. A stubborn and bizarre Bashmachkin who is totally unassimilated into society emerges before us. From the first "humane passage" Gogol deepens the comic aspects in Akaky's personality. He shows us that the mechanical side of Akaky's life may be the result of a state of mind completely distracted and absorbed by an ideal, the effect of an extraordinary zeal which makes Akaky devote himself completely to a task which he judges to be sacred, to such an extent that he forgets everything else. Gogol makes it clear that the mechanical side of his activities is partly the result of his childlike spirit. (Cf. the fact that he often talks like a child, repeating the same meaningless particles, while expressing something very precise.) The grotesque elements characterize Akaky Akakievich as a man who constantly lives anxiously and austerely for a ridiculous goal. The tragicomic elements emphasize the poverty and drabness of his fate. The tragic elements finally present the man who little by little realizes the futility of his asking help from the officials. He rebels against this bureaucracy which refuses to listen to his appeal and which then, indifferent to his happiness, crushes him with its formality and vanity.

There has been some question concerning the relation of the two "humane passages" to the rest of the story. By mixing the serious and ludicrous, these two passages point to the pitiful humility and the human dignity of Akaky Akakievich. The first passage anticipates the story's development; the second makes the meaning of the events stand out and at the same time accentuates Bashmachkin's defeat which puts him in the class of the tsars of this world and constitutes a transition to the fantastic epilog. This grotesque counterpart of the story also contributes to the presentation of Bashmachkin's character; it clarifies retrospectively or rather, shows through some of the other characters' feverish imagination, Akaky Akakievich's moving and sad rebellion against the world of bureaucracy.

Source: Carl R. Proffer, "Practical Criticism for Students," in *From Karamzin to Bunin: An Anthology of Russian Short Stories*, edited by Elizabeth Trahan, Indiana University Press, 1969, pp. 12–17.

Carl R. Proffer

In the following excerpt Proffer examines the Symbolist, Formalist and Freudian interpretations of Gogol's short story. He also discusses Gogol's style, deeming him a "verbal gymnast."

> The ghost of the late Bashmachkin appears as a grotesque contrast to the timid civil servant of real life. Yet by this exaggeration Gogol shows us, in effect, how in spite of everything, Bashmachkin left an indelible mark by his fight against the misfortune which crushed him, just as it crushes the conquerors of this world."

[Gogol] is rightly regarded as Russia's foremost verbal gymnast. Tongue-twisting names, rhymes, and puns spring up like clowns. Using metaphor and metonymy to turn people into toe-nails or noses, he works more transformations than a drunken Roman mythologist. His prose is poetic and onomatopoetic—rhetorical figures abound, rhythmic and phonetic considerations help determine each phrase. Pushkin's favorite punctuation is the period. Gogol's is the semicolon; and at first glance, the profusion of dependent clauses and qualifications may bring to mind a fishing reel's backlash. Many of Gogol's old-fashioned contemporaries considered him a vulgarian, both because of his inelegant subject matter and the "non-literary" vocabulary which he introduced (colloquialisms, bureaucratese, dialectisms, jargon, and neologisms); but with time his lexical salmagundi, syntactical intricacies, and sometimes shaky grammar became "estheticized," and his style was imitated by writers as different as Dostoevsky, Saltykov-Shchedrin, Remizov, Bely, and Abram Tertz.

"The Overcoat" (1842) was Gogol's last story. Partly because it was published in a four-volume collection of his works—and in the same year as *Dead Souls*—his contemporaries paid little attention to it. I say this because one of the folklore items among teachers of Russian literature is the belief

> " Using metaphor and metonymy to turn people into toe-nails or noses, Gogol works more transformations than a drunken Roman mythologist."

that Belinsky's interpretation of the story has been followed by all socially-oriented critics, but in fact Belinsky wrote no critique or analysis of "The Overcoat." He did not "interpret" Gogol's best story. Most Russians take it as a philanthropic tale. Indeed, the entire philanthropic trend of Russian literature, with "little men" as heroes, has been traced back to Pushkin's "The Station Master" and Gogol's Petersburg stories. Dostoevsky's remark, which he did not make (and which is not true), that "We all came from under Gogol's 'Overcoat'" is reprinted in almost every literary history written in the last seventy years. The first axiom of this theory, variations on which are used by every Soviet critic, is that Gogol was a realist.

Following the lead of V. V. Rozanov, the Russian Symbolists preferred to emphasize the non-realistic aspects of Gogol's work, his hyperbole and fantasy. They suggest it is impossible to sympathize with such grotesque humanoids as Akaky. The second assault on the philanthropic interpretation came from the Formalists. Boris Eichenbaum interpreted the story simply as an excuse for unfolding the verbal material. According to him, Gogol's switching from the comic to the pathetic to the ironic is all a game—acoustical play on the part of a narrator who mugs and mimes, changing his voice unexpectedly to entertain the listener. Akaky Akakievich's remark, "Leave me alone, why do you insult me" and the passage about the clerk who was so touched by these words are not meant to arouse pity—they are there simply to shatter the comic play and create a grotesque contrast in intonation. The sterility of this part of Eichenbaum's analysis results from the theoretical straight-jacket which the Formalists sometimes mistook for armor in their revolt against the sociological critics. In reaction to Soviet criticism, most Western scholars have expanded on the Symbolist or Formalist views of "The Overcoat." For example, [Chizhevskij]

claims that the story does not attack social evils or defend underdogs; its theme is the development of a passion for a nothing (an idea first suggested by Apollon Grigoriev). Since Akaky sees the coat as a wife, Chizhevskij interprets it as a parody of romantic love stories. Critics of Formalist inclination like to see parodies in everything because it emphasizes the *literariness* of a work as opposed to its bases in real life. While Chizhevskij's article contains several ridiculous assertions (e.g. that Petrovich is the devil), he does offer some sophisticated stylistic analysis. For example, the adverb *dazhe* (even) is used dozens of times, often illogically. It intensifies where there is no need of intensification. Chizhevskij hypothesizes that the use of "even" projects Akaky's "view from below" through the narrator. Akaky is such a limited, insignificant creature that he sees ordinary things as strange, grand, and beyond his sphere.

One man's heresy is another man's cliche, as is seen by the different attitudes (in communist countries and in western ones) toward the assertion that Gogol is not a realist. It seems clear to us that Tolstoy and Flaubert are poles away from Gogol, that his "realism" is the literary analogue of Potemkin's villages. His sometimes microscopic description is designed to trick the reader; when you step back a little you see that things are much vaguer than they seemed. The student should note some of the features of style which help create this impression. For example, the narrator staggers from omniscience to senility in the same paragraph—although usually the things which he cannot remember (the date the coat is finished) are not important anyway. Digressiveness is not a characteristic of realistic style, and the Sternian divagations of the narrative begin after only two words. Compare the final version of the opening to this early (1839) draft:

> In the department of taxes and collections [*podatej i sborov*] which, incidentally, is sometimes called the department of frauds and nonsense [*podlostej i vzdorov*], not because there were in fact frauds there, but because Mssrs. the civil servants like to joke just as much as military officers do—thus, in the department. . . .

The fungi-like growth of "irrelevant" details is characteristic of Gogol's work on the successive versions. Often the reader is so hypnotized by the details that he forgets to question absurdities "such as the bland assumption that 'full-grown young pigs' commonly occur in private houses," says Vladimir Nabokov, referring to the last paragraph of the story.

Following hints by Bely, James Woodward has carefully catalogued a number of specific devices which Gogol uses to blur reality, to make things indefinite: affirmative statements which are immediately made dubious by qualifications, a plethora of adversative conjunctions (but, however, nevertheless, etc.) used to introduce comments which cast doubt on the veracity of statements in previous clauses, negative statement (''not without pity,'' ''not without terror''), direct and indirect questions, a profusion of indefinite pronominal adjectives (*kakoj-to, kakoj-nibud', kak-o*, etc. which are often untranslatable), the frequent use of *kazat'sja* (to seem), *kak budto, kak budto-by, pochti* (as if, almost). These combine to create the vagueness which is typical of Gogol's unreal world of phantoms and fantasy. To this catalogue one might add Gogol's constant use of euphemism and humorous periphrasis. For example, the important person does not have a mistress, he has a ''lady for friendly relations.''

But there is fact in fantasy, and we can feel sympathy even for caricatures. Even an unrealistic story full of comedy can be philanthropic. While Gogol shows us the ways in which Akaky Akakievich is ridiculous, he never scorns him; while he shows his ignorance, he puts him in positions so universal that the reader can feel pity. The plot itself is archetypically tragic: the painful quest for the desired object, acquisition, and then unjust loss and defeat. Defeat follows on the heels (or shoulders) of victory—for kings or Akakys. The plainly philanthropic comments (such as ''I am your brother''), the episode with the young clerk, and perhaps most important, the character change in the significant personage—to whom, incidentally, several significant pages of the story are devoted—cannot be explained away simply as ''contrast.'' Gogol wrote ''The Overcoat'' as he was finishing the first part of *Dead Souls*, and there are several parallels between the two works. For example, Akaky dies:

> Gone and disappeared was a being who was protected by no one, interesting to no one, who had not even attracted the attention of a naturalist who does not fail to impale an ordinary fly [earlier Akaky is compared to a fly] on a pin and examine it in his microscope.

In *Dead Souls* Gogol uses the same metaphor when declaring that his artistic principles include the portrayal of just such characters:

> For the judgment of the writer's own times does not recognize that equally marvelous are the lenses that are used for contemplating suns and those for revealing to us the motions of insects imperceptible to the naked eye; for the judgment of his times does not recognize that a great deal of spiritual depth is re-quired to throw light upon a picture taken from a despised stratum of life, and to exalt it into a pearl of creative art.

Akaky Akakievich is one of Gogol's dead souls, perhaps the most dehumanized of all; but it is clear from his works and correspondence that he felt deep sadness for his creatures. The lessons he hoped to teach by making the world look through his microscope were not those of art for art's sake.

We can also learn a lesson from the Freudian view of ''The Overcoat.'' There is an abundance of coprological [related to excrement] detail in the story: Akaky Akakievich's name itself suggests the child's word for excrement, the other names he was almost given suggest sucking and urination, his complexion is hemorrhoidal, and in one variant he even has a coat the color of a cow pie. Akaky's retarded sexual development is indicated by this imagery connected to other overt sexual imagery—the coat itself as a wife with a good thick lining, the woman that he inexplicably trots after, the picture of the Frenchwoman with her leg bared, the jokes about his landlady, the policeman's suggestion that he has been to a bordello, and the significant personage's inexplicable visits to Karolina Ivanovna. Freudian commentators have a tendency to fantasize about the implications of these remarks for *Gogol's* psychology. This, I think, is dangerous and mostly irrelevant; but their theory does focus our attention on facts (i.e., details) of the story which otherwise might be overlooked. One level of the story's humor remains closed to the reader if he does not notice the persistence of these scatological and sexual allusions.

Finally, I would warn that it is possible to exaggerate the importance of digressions in ''The Overcoat.'' The fact that digressions occur at the very beginning and at the very end tends to make us remember the story as more digressive than it really is. Actually, in the main body of the story, Gogol is quite business-like. For example, the central block of material is a single gigantic paragraph (unique in Gogol's fiction) almost nine pages long. This digressionless unit covers the entire period from Akaky Akakievich's decision to get a new coat until the moment when he steps onto the square where it will be stolen. Twelve pages precede this middle section and twelve pages come after it. There are two major dialogue scenes (one with Petrovich, one with the significant personage); the first begins seven and one-half pages from the beginning of the story, the second seven and one half pages from the end. Thus, these sections give the story an underlying symmetrical structure from which one is distracted by letter-writing captains, weak policemen, and ordinary full-grown young pigs.

Source: Carl R. Proffer, ''Practical Criticism for Students,'' in *From Karamzin to Bunin: An Anthology of Russian Short Stories*, edited by Elizabeth Trahan, Indiana University Press, 1969, pp. 12–17.

F. C. Driessen

In the following excerpt, Driessen provides a short summary of Gogol's ''The Overcoat,'' and alleges that the story is about ''an unhappy love, through which the hero discovers himself and comes to life.''

Although ''The Overcoat'' is amongst Gogol's best-known stories, a somewhat thorough analysis is not possible without a short summary of the course of the story, with at the same time a rough indication of its construction.

In a certain department a certain oldish, bald-headed, pock-marked little official used to sit, with a ''haemorrhoidal'' complexion, eternally bearing the rank of titular councillor and the name *Bashmachkin*. His Christian name, Akaky Akakyevich, is just as ridiculous, and Gogol relates in detail how the poor devil got it. How and when he appeared in the department no one knows any more. He is known there solely as a copyist. Since he is weak and defenseless, he is constantly exposed to being teased by his colleagues. He does not however let this disturb his work, namely copying, which dominates all his thoughts.

> It was only when the joke got too unbearable, when somebody jogged his arm and so interfered with his work, that he would say, ''Leave me alone, gentlemen. Why do you pester me?'' There was a strange note in the words and the voice in which they were uttered: there was something in it that touched one's heart with pity. Indeed, one young man who had only recently been appointed to the department and who, following the example of the others, tried to have some fun at his expense, stopped abruptly at Akaky's mild expostulation, as though stabbed through the heart; and since then everything seemed to have changed in him and he saw everything in a different light. A kind of unseen power made him keep away from his colleagues whom at first he had taken for decent, well-bred men. And for a long time afterwards, in his happiest moments, he would see the shortish Civil Servant with the bald patch on his head, uttering those pathetic words, ''Leave me alone! Why do you pester me?'' And in those pathetic words he seemed to hear others: ''I am your brother.'' And the poor young man used to bury his face in his hands, and many a time in his life he would shudder when

he perceived how much inhumanity there was in man, how much savage brutality there lurked beneath the most refined, cultured manners, and, dear Lord, even in the man the world regarded as upright and honourable. . . .

This serious intermezzo from the otherwise comic beginning has been quoted here in full, because it has acquired much notoriety and is usually indicated in Russia as the ''humane passage.''

After this passage there is a depiction of the happiness Akaky Akakyevich finds in writing. He takes documents home for sheer pleasure and knows no other amusement than copying.

He should consequently have been able to live from his salary of four hundred rubles, if he had not had an enemy, namely the St. Petersburg cold. This forces Akaky Akakyevich, who has never paid any attention to his external appearance, to the discovery that his coat is half worn away on the shoulders and in the back.

A visit to his tailor Petrovich is of no avail for the moment, for Petrovich refuses to mend the overcoat and says that only a new one would be any good. This means an enormous expense, eighty roubles to be sure.

By imposing on himself the greatest privations, drinking no more tea, walking on his toes to save his soles, yes even writing as little as possible at home (for that uses up candles), he succeeds in several months in scraping the money together. During that time something changes in him, his life acquires a purpose, namely the new overcoat. When the dream has finally been realised and the overcoat is ready and Akaky Akakyevich comes to the department unrecognisable, he is once again teased. His colleagues consider that he now has to treat them. A higher official saves him. He is giving a party that evening and invites the whole company. Akaky Akakyevich enjoys the evening only moderately. He leaves before the end and at a lonely spot he is robbed of his new treasure.

Attempts to trace it through the police lead to nothing, a charitable collection amongst his colleagues provides little, the only hopeful possibility is to turn to a certain ''important personality.'' He has only recently been important, is still practising his worthy role and considers he cuts a better figure the more he snaps at lower-placed persons. Akaky Akakyevich, who has not applied to him by the hierarchical path, gets the full brunt of him and when he stutters something in reply, the great man becomes so furious that Akaky Akakyevich totters out of the room horrified.

In the street he catches cold, and dies shortly after from pneumonia.

"And St. Petersburg carried on without Akaky Akakyevich." These words form the introduction to a second humane passage, which—although quoted less often than the first—is no less important.

The story is not yet finished however. Soon there are rumours about a corpse that haunts St. Petersburg at night and robs people of their overcoats without regard to person and even to rank. Finally the "important personality" also falls victim to such a robbery. He clearly recognises Akaky Akakyevich in his attacker. Since then he speaks more gently to his inferiors. After this last robbery, the ghost is no longer seen. . . .

If we wish to venture criticism . . . then we shall have to start from a seemingly slightly modified, but essentially completely different view of Gogol's main figure. This is, in my opinion, possible and necessary. Recognising that Gogol did not copy reality, in spite of the microscopic accuracy of his drawing, assenting that his heroes usually make a static impression and seem to be reduced to a few dominating features, even sharing the conviction that in Gogol death predominates over life, we may nevertheless doubt whether that domination is complete and ask ourselves whether Akaky Akakyevich is not, certainly to a minimum extent, after all a human being. The answer to this question must, in my opinion, without hesitation be in the affirmative, although he lacks almost everything which makes a person a human being and although the human element in him has been reduced to virtually nothing.

He nevertheless has one thing, even at the very beginning, namely a love. I do not mean that for the overcoat, but that for writing. As a result of this, he is vulnerable. The teasings of his colleagues are so cruel because they strike a living being in his purpose in life, in what gives him a right to recognition. It may be noted that this right likewise applies to an animal, and that we also call a child cruel if it disturbs an insect building its home. Yet Gogol says expressly that his hero is not only diligent, but works with love and forgets himself completely in the process, to such an extent that he has no thought for his external appearance, his food, his relaxation.

Is such a self-forgetfulness conceivable while being directed to such a trifling purpose? Of course

> ❝ Once Akaky is familiar with the thought of the overcoat, he changes in character, becomes more lively, surer, the undecided element even disappears from his facial expression."

it is in the case of a man who has been baptised Akaky Akakyevich, who has the family name Bashmachkin and is predestined to be a titular councillor, who feels his own personality as being so inferior that it is not worthy of the slightest attention, in whom natural love of self has to seek an object and can find it outside its own "ego," yet so closely connected with it that it enjoys its full satisfaction therein. The still infantile copyist finds himself in his writing and without being in the least aware of it, he retires into himself while writing and is at the same time "not himself."

Now the great shocks come in separate phases. Through the cold he is forced to devote attention to his old overcoat. The tailor Petrovich forces him to start thinking of a new one, this need in turn brings him to the discovery of himself. Gogol is very careful in depicting this development. When Petrovich speaks for the first time about a new overcoat, Akaky Akakyevich feels himself "as in a dream" (the expression is repeated), upon hearing the price he utters a cry, "probably for the first time in his life." Dreaming and muttering to himself he roams through the city. Then he recovers and there now begins a new monologue, but this time "not in broken sentences, but frankly and soberly, as though talking to a wise friend." Once he is familiar with the thought of the overcoat, he changes in character, becomes more lively, surer, the undecided element even disappears from his facial expression. He has an aim. This is all the result of the overcoat, his second love. He did not mind suffering from hunger,

> for spiritually he was nourished well enough, since his thoughts were full of the great idea of his future overcoat. His whole existence indeed seemed now somehow to have become fuller, as though he had got married, as though there were someone at his side, as though he was never alone, but some agreeable help-

mate had consented to share the joys and sorrows of his life.

Upon the approach of the fulfilment, "his heart, which was in general extremely calm, began to beat" and, how could it be otherwise, he becomes unfaithful to his first love, the static element disappears more and more. Thinking about the overcoat, he almost makes an error in copying. On the day on which the overcoat becomes his property, "the most glorious day in his whole life," for the first time he writes nothing at all in the evening.

He takes the following step when he begins in principle to discover the other world and with it the possibility of a sexual fulfillment. He who had never shown the slightest interest in any event in the street stops on the way to the soirée in front of a shop-window where a picture is hanging. The representation is that of a woman who is taking off her shoe, her *bashmak*, during which process she bares her well-shaped leg.

She is being stared at by a man out of the opening of a door. The reference to the erotic element was even clearer in an earlier version. There a second picture is mentioned, a sequel to the first; the same beautiful woman is represented in it, but she is now lying in bed naked. Akaky Akakyevich smiles. Is it "because he had come up against something that was completely unknown to him, of which a certain consciousness is nevertheless preserved in everyone?" Gogol answers that one cannot know what a person is thinking. It is however not here a question of "thoughts." What is it but a rising up of desire, as a result of which Akaky Akakyevich almost breaks into a trot behind a lady who shoots past him and who shows such an extraordinary mobility in all her limbs? Once again, Gogol finds it necessary to point out twice that his hero does not himself realise from where that wave has come. The fact that there was indeed a definite intention in Gogol's mind appears from the passage which functions as a counterpart to the one just mentioned. After being robbed Akaky Akakyevich in fact sees a half-naked woman who is wearing merely one *bashmak*: his terribly old landlady who "from modesty holds her chemise pulled together over a bosom." A sad contrast with what a few hours ago had been a vague enticement. If we become aware of this contrast, then we suddenly also surmise a hidden intention behind the seemingly arbitrarily chosen example of the teasings of the colleagues, who "told of his landlady, an old woman of seventy, that she struck him and asked when the wedding was to be."

It is, I think, undeniable that all these indications and references point to a process which is taking place in Akaky Akakyevich, the maturing and realisation of which are nevertheless prevented by the loss of the overcoat.

The growth of his personality also appears from quite different things. Before the robbery his increasing personal consciousness is expressed as an unmotivated anxiety; only afterwards does it properly appear how much has changed in him. The shy Akaky gaspingly shouts his reproaches to the night-watchman. His further reactions to the robbery are likewise completely normal. He does not allow himself to be fobbed off by the commissioner, "wants to show character once in his life," barks at clerks and even ventures to lie that he has come on departmental business. And when he is finally standing opposite the general, this person, the "important personality" is the one who has the most of a puppet about him. The acquired words and gestures of the powerful man are completely mechanical, but the unfortunate one who is shattered by them is a small, nervous man who, sweating from anxiety, defends his last human hope.

This development is not finished with his death. It is not difficult to see that the second part of the short story is, insofar as it concerns Akaky Akakyevich, a fantastic, but logical continuation of the first, in which he, if only in a feverish dream, had dared to express his anger while dying. . . .

As regards meaning, "The Overcoat" is the story of an unhappy love, through which the hero discovers himself and comes to life. He is a border-line case of what is human, the departmental world around him is mechanical and dead. The ending is the revenge of the living on the dead.

The humane passages are the places where the tragic side of the humour is accentuated. They do not contain the full meaning of the short story, but form the confrontation of the fantastic and "sub"-human element with reality. The comic element is through these passages alone raised to humour. If they are looked at away from the whole, then they can only partially be understood.

Gogol's work develops not from fantasy to reality, but it shows the development of a fantasy which absorbs more and more reality and which, having awakened from the dream, continues and illuminates the world of day into its farthest corners. It is a fantasy which can juggle in such a way with the attributes of reality and which knows the rules of the game of reality so accurately that it can in the end hazard comparison with reality which it seems to cover completely, and which is its opposite. Gogol has never lost an opportunity of reminding his reader of the change. This is also in part the meaning of the fantastic ending. In earlier work, what had begun as a dream is confronted with reality, here reality has to account for itself to the dream. . . .

Source: F. C. Driessen, ''Gogol as a Short-Story Writer: A Study of His Technique of Composition,'' in *Slavistic Printings and Reprintings*, edited by C. H. Van Schooneveld, translated by Ian F. Finlay, Mouton and Co., 1965, pp. 182–214.

Leon Stilman

In the following essay, Stilman gives a short overview of Gogol's ''The Overcoat'' and contends that the protagonist dies ''a death of his own making, defeated in a hopeless struggle against himself.''

In the parish register of one of Moscow's churches the entry was made of the death, on February 21, 1852 (March 4, new style), of retired collegiate assessor Nikolaj Vasiljevich Gogol, aged forty-three.

Collegiate assessor Gogol outranked the hero of ''The Overcoat,'' Akakij Akakievich Bashmachkin, a mere titular councilor. Titular councilor was a rank of the ninth class; collegiate assessors ranked one class above.

''The Overcoat'' is traditionally associated with a story which, according to the reminiscences of Gogol's friend Annenkov, [P.V. Annenkov, *Literaturnye vospominanija*, B. M. Eichenbaum, ed., 1928] was once told in his presence: the story of a poor government clerk who after months of privation and overtime work, saved enough money on his meager salary to buy a shotgun, which he lost, however, the very first time he went hunting with the weapon. Unlike ''The Overcoat,'' the story had a happy ending: a new gun was offered by his colleagues to the luckless Nimrod who lay in bed, sick with grief.

Annenkov states, perhaps somewhat too assertively, that the first thought of ''The Overcoat'' originated in Gogol's mind when he heard the anecdote, ''that very evening.'' Annenkov gives no date, but there is indirect evidence that Gogol heard the story sometime between August, 1833, and

> " The new overcoat, the thing of fabulous cost and overwhelming beauty which he has desired so ardently, is a precarious possession."

June, 1836, when he left Russia, probably during the earlier part of this period.

It may well be that the anecdote reported by Annenkov played a part in the inception of ''The Overcoat.'' But if it did, it was because it fitted into a pattern, because Gogol must have heard in the anecdote a tune, or a theme, already familiar to him: the theme of yearning and frustration, of fate's giving and taking away. . . .

Thus in desire frustrated at the very moment when it is about to be fulfilled Gogol saw a situation essentially grotesque: the hand that stretches out to grasp closes on nothing. Yearning, then short-lived possession (or a mere illusion of possession), and finally frustration is a thematic sequence which often recurs in Gogol's work. . . .

Akakij Akakievich Bachmachkin becomes for a short while the owner of the new and glorious overcoat; he is congratulated and admired. A garment changes the wearer's appearance; a garment is a disguise. But the new overcoat, the thing of fabulous cost and overwhelming beauty which he has desired so ardently, is a precarious possession. Akakij is soon robbed of it (of his ''royal mantle''), the illusion vanishes, reality is once more laid bare.

The ''real'' Akakij, stripped of his disguise, is characterized by coprological [relating to excrement] symbols, especially obvious in the earlier versions of the story. The borrowed identity of the magnificent overcoat is contrasted with the true identity symbolized by the name. In one of the early drafts, the episode of Akakij's baptism and of the choice of his Christian name included the following author's comment:

> Of course it might have been possible in some manner to avoid the frequent junction of the letter *k*, but the circumstances were of such a nature that there was no way at all of doing this. . . .

The name of the letter, in Russian, is pronounced *kab*, and its "junction" gives *kaka*, the Russian child-word for feces. In the earliest known version the "hero" (as yet anonymous) is said to wear a frock coat "the color of cow's pancake" (a popular Russian term for dry cow dung). "At that time," explains the author, "the ukase to the effect that all officials be buttoned up in uniform coats had not yet been issued." In the definitive version Akakij Akakievich wears a uniform, "not green, but some kind of a rusty-floury hue." On the other hand, Akakij's complexion, "reddish" in the first known version, becomes "hemorrhoidal" in the final text.

If Gogol expurgated the definitive text of the more direct coprological comments, he left the allusive name itself emphasizing the inevitability of the choice of the name, the predetermination in its choice. Akakij Akakievich's purchase—and short-lived possession—of the overcoat thus takes on the aspect of a revolt against pre-destination. . . .

In "The Overcoat," Akakij, with his poor man's treasure, is the victim of the robbers and of the General. The plot of "The Overcoat" is a triangular system of collisions, or aggressions: Akakij is attacked by the robbers; Akakij is attacked by the "person of consequence" (the General); the "person of consequence" is attacked by the robber (the reader may choose, according to his preferences and inclinations, between the "supernatural" explanation—that the author of the last aggression was "really" Akakij's ghost; or, if he prefers psychology—that the conscience-stricken General imagined his aggressor to be the clerk who died after his browbeating).

The last aggression is a retribution. It is Akakij's posthumous vengeance and posthumous triumph: he is identified with the robber, a man of great strength and daring; the "person of consequence" is humiliated, and the symmetrical structure of the story is completed.

The earliest known (unfinished) version of the story which Gogol dictated to Pogodin in 1839, in Marienbad, had the title "The story of the clerk who stole overcoats"; the motif of the clerk-aggressor (the poor man snatches the General's possession) was present, consequently, already in that early stage.

In the first version of the epilogue, the dying Akakij Akakievich sees himself, in his delirium, facing the "person of consequence"; at times he utters

> . . . profanity, expressing himself in the language of a cab driver, or in that language which is ordinarily used when order is being restored in the streets, something he was never known to do in all his born days. "I don't care that you are a general," he would cry in a loud voice. "I'll take your overcoat from you. I'll complain, . . ."

In the definitive text Akakij is less outspoken: on his deathbed he insults his offender, but does not state his intention to rob him of his coat; he utters

> . . . profanity, pronouncing the most dreadful words, so that his landlady, a little old woman, even crossed herself, for never in all her born days had she heard anything similar from him, those words, moreover, following immediately the words "your excellency."

Just as the coprological symbols were veiled in the final version, so the motif of Akakij's posthumous vengeance was made more subtly allusive. . . .

Gogol's Akakij Akakievich died of a fever he contracted when, deprived of his overcoat, he was exposed to the rigors of the Petersburg winter. The parish register already quoted is incorrect, however, in stating that the death of collegiate assessor Gogol was due to a cold. The learned physicians who treated him, and hastened his end, diagnosed *gastro-enteritis ex inanitione*. Inanition there certainly was, for Gogol had imposed upon himself rigorous fasting and, toward the end, refused all nourishment. He died a death of his own making, defeated in a hopeless struggle against himself. . . .

Source: Leon Stilman, "Gogol's 'Overcoat'—Thematic Pattern and Origins," in *The American Slavic and East European Review*, Vol. XI, No. 2, April, 1952, pp. 138–48.

Sources

Maguire, Robert, ed. *Gogol from the Twentieth Century: Eleven Essays*, Princeton, N.J.: Princeton University Press, 1974.

Nabokov, Vladimir. *Nikolai Gogol*, New York: New Directions, 1944.

O'Connor, Frank. *The Lonely Voice*, New York: World Publishing Company, 1962.

Stilman, Leon. Afterword to *The Diary of a Madman and Other Stories*, by Nikolai Gogol, New York: New American Library, 1960.

Stone, Wilfred, et al. *The Short Story: An Introduction*, New York: McGraw-Hill Book Company, 1983.

Further Reading

Ehrlich, Victor. *Gogol*, New Haven, Conn.: Yale University Press, 1969.

Excellent overview of Gogol's work and the development of the author's views throughout his life.

Fanger, Donald. *The Creation of Nikolai Gogol*, Cambridge, Mass.: Belknap Press of Harvard University, 1979.

Analyzes Gogol in the context of his times and cites interesting evidence from both published and unpublished writings by Gogol in discussing the author's creative genius.

Maguire, Robert, ed. *Gogol from the Twentieth Century: Eleven Essays*, Princeton, N.J.: Princeton University Press, 1974.

The essays in this book represent the most influential twentieth-century critical assessments of Gogol. Included in the volume are two essays by Russian scholars from the first half of the century which offer very close readings of "The Overcoat," emphasizing the formal aspects of Gogol's technique. The editor's introduction summarizes critical debate about Gogol from its beginnings in the nineteenth century through the 1960s.

Nabokov, Vladimir. *Nikolai Gogol*, New York: New Directions, 1944.

This mostly biographical study, written before Nabokov became an internationally famous and best-selling author. In addition to information about Gogol's life, the book offers several sections of critical analysis, including some on "The Overcoat." Nabokov describes Gogol as a strongly visual writer and emphasizes his stylistic excellence, concluding that Gogol's work "is a phenomenon of language and not one of ideas."

O'Connor, Frank. *The Lonely Voice*, New York: World Publishing Company, 1962.

A short story writer himself, O'Connor gives a fascinating critical analysis of the short story genre through history. He devotes considerable attention to Gogol and "The Overcoat," which he considers an early masterpiece of the short story form.

Stone, Wilfred, et al. *The Short Story: An Introduction*, New York: McGraw-Hill Book Co., 1983.

This textbook is an anthology of short stories arranged chronologically, beginning with ancient myths and ending with experimental short fiction from the 1960s. Its introduction and entries entitled "Nikolai Gogol" and "The Short Story Proper: The First Age" offer much insight into "The Overcoat" and its role in the development of the modern short story form.

Troyat, Henri. *Divided Soul*, translated by Nancy Amphoux, Garden City, N.Y.: Doubleday, 1973.

This authoritative study explores the connection between Gogol's life and his work, emphasizing the ways in which Gogol's works reflect the author's lifelong search for spiritual wholeness.

Raymond's Run

Toni Cade Bambara
1971

Toni Cade Bambara has long been admired for her short stories. ''Temperamentally, I move toward the short story,'' Bambara has said, defining herself, like her protagonist Hazel Parker, as ''a sprinter rather than a long distance runner.'' In ''Raymond's Run,'' the young Hazel Parker relates the events of two days in her life in which she prepares for and runs a race. The story first appeared in 1971 in an anthology edited by Bambara, *Tales and Short Stories for Black Folks*. A year later it appeared in her first collection of short stories, *Gorilla, My Love*.

Bambara's story of Hazel's race against the newcomer Gretchen, during which Hazel comes to a turning point in her relationship with her mentally challenged brother, Raymond, has been seen as a ground-breaking initiation story. Along with others in the collection *Gorilla, My Love*, it has been classed as among the first to place a young black female as a central character in the *bildungsroman* (a novel about the moral and psychological growth of the main character) tradition.

Critics have also praised Bambara's compassionate portrayal of the African-American community, a community in which Hazel Parker takes center stage and speaks with her own voice. The vibrant idiomatic language and upbeat tempo, which are compelling features of the story, are characteristic of Bambara's style. Her ability to capture, translate and play in and out of the voices and idioms of black communities has been widely admired.

Through the use of voice as well as theme, "Raymond's Run" emphasizes the importance of achieving selfhood for young black women within the context of community.

Author Biography

Born Miltona Mirkin Cade in 1939 in New York City, Bambara adopted the African name "Bambara" in 1970. Upon her death in 1995, the *New York Times* deemed her a "major contributor to the emerging genre of black women's literature, along with the writers Toni Morrison and Alice Walker." She grew up in Harlem, Queens, and Jersey City. In 1959 she received her B.A. in Theatre Arts and English from Queens College and won the John Golden award for short fiction. While enrolled as a graduate student of modern American fiction at the City College of New York, she worked in both civic and local neighborhood programs in education and drama and studied theater in Europe. After receiving her Masters degree, Bambara taught at City College from 1965 to 1969. Immersed in the social and political activism of the 1960s and early 1970s, Bambara sometimes saw her writing of fiction as "rather frivolous," yet this period of her life produced her most well-loved works.

Bambara is known as a member of the Black Arts Movement of the 1960s and 1970s. During this period in American history, civil rights, Black Power, anti-war and feminist movements were pressing issues, and Bambara joined in the political activism of the era. Along with other members of the black intelligentsia, Bambara sought to challenge traditional representations of blacks, celebrate African American history, and explore black vernacular English. Bambara's fiction and other writings also explore themes of women's lives and social and political activism.

In 1970 Bambara (writing as Toni Cade) was one of the first to explore feminism and race with her anthology *The Black Woman*. In her second anthology, *Tales and Short Stories for Black Folk* (1971), Bambara collected stories by writers such as Langston Hughes and Alice Walker as well as stories written by herself and her students. In 1972, Bambara's short stories, including "Blues Ain't No Mockin Bird" and "Raymond's Run," were collected in *Gorilla, My Love*. Celebrated for its focus

on the voice and experience of young black women and its compassionate view of African-American communities, this collection has remained her most widely read work.

Before publishing her second collection of stories, *The Sea Birds Are Still Alive* (1977), Bambara moved with her daughter to Atlanta, Georgia, where she took the post of writer-in-residence at Spelman College from 1974 to 1977 and helped found a number of black writers' and cultural associations. In 1980, Bambara published a novel, *The Salt Eaters*, which is set in Georgia and focuses on the mental and emotional crisis of a community organizer, Velma Jackson. The novel's experimental form received both praise and criticism. In form, and in its shift in perspective beyond the local neighborhood, the novel moves away from Bambara's early short stories; however, it remains linked to them through its emphasis on black women, community, and voice.

In the 1980s and 1990s Bambara concentrated on film, another medium for "the power of the voice," working as scriptwriter, filmmaker, critic, and teacher. She collaborated on several television documentaries, such as the award-winning *The Bombing of Osage Avenue* (1986). Her death at the age of fifty-six is seen by some as a profound loss to American culture not only because of her groundbreaking artistic contributions, but also because of her wide-reaching efficacy as teacher, critic and activist. A selection of her writings, *Deep Sightings and Rescue Missions,* was published posthumously in 1996.

Plot Summary

Setting the Scene

"Raymond's Run" plunges its readers immediately into the world of its narrator Hazel, known in her neighborhood as "Squeaky," a young black girl verging on adolescence. We meet Hazel walking down a street in Harlem with her older—but mentally younger— brother, Raymond. While she guards her mentally challenged brother from dashing into the traffic or soaking himself in the gutters, Hazel resolutely keeps up breathing exercises to train herself as a runner. Known in the neighborhood as "the fastest thing on two feet" she is determined to maintain her reputation by winning the fifty-yard

Toni Cade Bambara

dash at the school May Day track meet the following day. Unlike her schoolmate Cynthia, who pretends to be nonchalant about her abilities, Hazel works hard to be the best and does not care who knows it.

Suddenly Hazel and Raymond come face-to-face with Gretchen and her followers. Gretchen is a newcomer to the neighborhood and a potential rival of Hazel's for the fifty-yard dash. She is a rival in other ways as well: Gretchen's followers Mary Louise and Rosie were once friends of Hazel. Mary Louise attempts to tease Raymond, but is no match for Hazel's razor-sharp wit. Hazel and Gretchen size each other up, but decide against a confrontation. Hazel notes that Gretchen's smile at her is "really not a smile" because "girls never really smile at each other."

The May Day Race

Hazel walks slowly to the race the next day in order to miss the May Pole dancing that precedes the track meet. Even though her mother thinks she should participate, Hazel rejects the feminine role of dressing up and "trying to act like a fairy or a flower." Arriving at the park, she takes Raymond to the swings and finds her teacher Mr. Pearson approaching her, ready to sign up "Squeaky" as an

entrant in the fifty-yard race. Hazel insists he write down her full name, "Hazel Elizabeth Deborah Parker." When he suggests that she might consider letting someone else win this year, such as the new girl, Hazel stares him down and heads for the track.

Her race is called, and at the starting line Hazel sees Gretchen ready to run and Raymond, on the other side of the fence, bent over in starting position. Hazel feels herself enter a familiar dream world, where anger and rivalry is forgotten and she is "flying over a sandy beach in the early morning sun." As she runs, she sees Raymond on the other side of the fence, running the race with her "in his very own style," teeth bared, arms at his sides, "palms tucked up behind him." Astonished at this vision of her brother, Hazel is almost halted in amazement, but her body takes her tearing past the finish line. Seeing Gretchen cooling down like a professional, she feels the beginnings of admiration for her. The loudspeaker crackles and the girls look at each other, wondering who will be announced the winner.

> Then I hear Raymond yanking at the fence to call me and I wave to shush him, but he keeps rattling the fence like a gorilla in a cage like in them gorilla movies, but then like a dancer or something he starts climbing up nice and easy but very fast. And it occurs to me, watching how smoothly he climbs hand over hand and remembering how he looked running with his arms down to his side and with the wind pulling his mouth back and his teeth showing and all, it occurred to me that Raymond would make a very fine runner. Doesn't he always keep up with me on my trots? And he surely knows how to breathe in counts of seven cause he's always doing it at the dinner table, which drives my brother George up the wall. And I'm smiling to beat the band cause if I've lost this race, or if me and Gretchen tied, or even if I've won, I can always retire as a runner and begin a whole new career as a coach with Raymond as my champion. After all, with a little more study I can beat Cynthia and her phony self at the spelling bee. And if I bugged my mother, I could get piano lessons and become a star. And I have a big rep as the baddest thing around. And I've got a roomful of ribbons and medals and awards. But what has Raymond got to call his own? (Excerpt from "Raymond's Run")

Hazel laughs out loud as she sees both herself and Raymond in this new light, and Raymond runs over to her in his own inimitable style. The loudspeaker announces the winner, "Miss Hazel Elizabeth Deborah Parker," and "Miss Gretchen P. Lewis" in second place. The two girls smile at each other, but not as they had the day before. This time their smiles are real, "considering we don't practice smiling every day, you know, cause maybe we too busy being flowers or fairies . . . instead of something honest and worthy of respect . . . like being people.''

Characters

Gretchen P. Lewis

Gretchen is a newcomer to Hazel's neighborhood. She has attracted Mary Louise and Rosie, once friends of Hazel, to be her friends instead. Gretchen and Hazel meet and size each other up, but do not come to open conflict, although Mary Louise tries to make fun of Raymond and is put down by Hazel instead. The smile that Gretchen and Hazel give each other on this occasion is ''really not a smile'' because ''girls never really smile at each other.'' On the day of the race, Gretchen competes well with Hazel and comes in second. Gretchen's dedication to running and her abilities impress Hazel, and the two exchange real smiles of beginning friendship and respect.

Hazel Elizabeth Deborah Parker

The narrator and main character of the story, Hazel Parker describes herself as ''a little girl with skinny arms,'' whose voice had earned her the nickname ''Squeaky.'' She is known to be the fastest runner in her school. Contrasting her appearance, however, is the strength of her character. Hazel's narration conveys to the reader a spirited self-assurance. She takes care of her mentally challenged brother, Raymond, with both pride and compassion. She is ready to use her fists or her sharp tongue if anyone has ''anything to say about his big head.'' Moreover, her striving to be an athlete conveys to the reader her determination to make something of herself. By the end of the story, Hazel is able to recognize that same potential in her brother as well as in her rival, Gretchen.

Raymond Parker

Raymond is Hazel's brother; she feels she has to take care of him because he is mentally challenged. Under his sister's watchful and caring eye, Raymond is happy in his own world in which he imagines himself as a circus performer or stagecoach driver. He is vulnerable to teasing by others, but he can depend on Hazel to defend him, even with her fists if necessary. By the end of the story, Raymond is no longer a burden to Hazel and has become a catalyst. Raymond's ''run'' alongside

Media Adaptations

- ''Raymond's Run'' was adapted as a film for the American Short Story Series of the Public Broadcasting System (PBS) in 1985.

Hazel, ''with his arms down to his side and his palms tucked up behind him . . . in his very own style,'' reveals his individuality and potential. Hazel considers becoming her brother's coach so that he can become an accomplished runner.

Squeaky

See Hazel Elizabeth Deborah Parker

Themes

Identity

From the beginning, Hazel strongly voices her identity as an athlete—''Miss Quicksilver herself''—and establishes her outspoken assertiveness: ''no one can beat me and that's all there is to it.'' At the same time, the story shows that Hazel's identity has been and continues to be hard won. To become a good runner, she has had to persevere with her practicing, sometimes carving time for herself out of the hours she spends looking after her mentally challenged brother, Raymond. Caring for her brother is no easy task either, and in some ways sets her apart from others. Her confrontation with Gretchen's ''sidekicks'' demonstrates her loyalty to her brother and her readiness to challenge those who would tease or belittle him. Although she scorns girls who dress up in white organdy for the May Pole dancing, it is also true that Hazel ''can't afford to buy shoes and a new dress you wear only once in a lifetime.''

Nevertheless, Hazel's belief in herself and her refusal to accept less than the respect she deserves is

Topics for Further Study

- In an interview, Bambara has said that "An awful lot of my stories . . . were written, I suspect, with performance in mind." With a group of classmates, construct a staging and performance of Hazel's role and voice for your class. Ask the audience to write about what performing the story contributes to its meaning and impact.

- Consider "Raymond's Run" in light of social and economic conditions for African American women at the time. Research the historical attitudes toward black women and social conditions for women such as education, position in the family, employment, availability of community services, and average family incomes in the late 1960s and early 1970s.

- Consider the depiction of Raymond as a mental-ly challenged character by comparing him with other such characters in literature and film, such as those portrayed in John Steinbeck's *Of Mice and Men* and Daniel Keyes' *Flowers for Algernon*, or in movies such as *Rain Man* and *Forrest Gump*.

- Research attitudes toward mentally challenged people in the early 1970s and discuss how "Raymond's Run" reflects or challenges those attitudes. Have attitudes significantly changed today?

- Compare and contrast Bambara's portrayal of Hazel Parker with the portrayal of young black women in other works of literature such as in Toni Morrison's *The Bluest Eye* or in Alice Walker's short story "Everyday Use."

reflected throughout the story: in her willingness to strive to become an athlete despite the risk of failure or ridicule—"I'm serious about my running and I don't care who knows it"; in her refusal to let anyone "get smart" with Raymond; in her insistence that Mr. Pearson address her by her full name instead of the nickname "Squeaky"; and, ultimately, in her success. The story suggests that a self-respecting identity, like the ability to run, involves persistence and dedication.

Growth and Development

While the story dramatizes the importance of identity, it also reflects on a particular moment of growth and change for both Hazel and Raymond. As the title suggests, not only Hazel's but *Raymond's* run has implications for both characters. The title points not only to Raymond's own potential as an athlete, but also to Hazel's intuitive recognition of his possibilities, a recognition that redefines her. Up until that moment, which occurs, interestingly, while Hazel is in the process of fulfilling a goal, Hazel has led a somewhat lonely existence, despite her vivacious style and tone. Her closeness to her family is evident, both in her father's support for her running and in her mention of her mother, brother and grandfather.

Nevertheless, Raymond has been a burden as well as a companion, and a girl like Gretchen, with whom she shares a passion for running, is a rival rather than a friend. The distance Hazel feels between them is marked by their inability to smile sincerely at each other. According to Hazel, girls "never really smile at each other because they don't know how . . . and there's probably no one to teach us how." When Hazel, in that meditative state that running induces in her, looks over and sees Raymond running parallel to her, she is suddenly able to see him afresh, not just copying or following her, but "running in his very own style." Through him, her difficult and somewhat lonely struggle to define herself suddenly widens to include a connection that empowers them both. The realization of Raymond's potential, something that has always been there, enriches Hazel's sense of her own possibilities. What Raymond has taught her is marked by her new response to Gretchen: "And I look over at Gretchen. . . . And I smile. Cause she's good, no doubt about it. Maybe she'd like to help me coach Raymond.''

Style

Narration

The most prominent stylistic aspect of "Raymond's Run" is the narrator's voice. Hazel Parker, narrating in the first person ("I"), recounts her experiences on the city streets and at the May Day races with verve and flair. The immediacy of an oral voice is communicated by the use of colloquial expressions (the everyday language of a community), as in Hazel's declaration "I don't feature a whole lot of chit-chat, I much prefer to just knock you down from the jump and save everybody a lotta precious time."

Repetitive, rhythmic phrasing is another technique which contributes to the oral quality of the narration, such as when Hazel describes her mother's reaction to Hazel's "high-pranc[ing]" down 34th Street "like a rodeo pony" to strengthen her knees: "she walks ahead like she's not with me, don't know me, is all by herself on a shopping trip, and I am somebody else's crazy child." Hazel also makes asides to the reader ("Oh brother") and commands a range of tones from confident to defiant to lyric, as in her dream-like visions before the race: "I dream I'm flying over a sandy beach in the early morning sun, kissing the leaves of the trees as I fly by." Through these techniques, the narration of "Raymond's Run" engages the reader and reflects the exuberant vitality of a young girl and her particular community.

Point of View

Like the language, the point of view of "Raymond's Run" is that of Hazel Parker. The first-person point of view ("I") and the use of the present tense involve the reader in the pre-adolescent Hazel's perception of the world in the present moment. This point of view also limits the story's perspective; it does not allow the reader to enter the minds of other characters besides Hazel and does not allow Hazel the hindsight to consider the meaning of her experiences. The reader is invited to look beyond these limitations and evaluate Hazel's observations and declarations and consider what is left unsaid. For example, Hazel describes her own and Raymond's actions in the present, but it is up to the reader to assess and interpret the complexities of their relationship.

Epiphany

An epiphany is a sudden flash of insight, during which an ordinary object or person becomes illuminated with meaning. Hazel does not describe in any detail an experience of epiphany, but she implies that such a moment occurs during the race when she says "on the other side of the fence is Raymond . . . running in his very own style, and it's the first time I ever saw that and I almost stop to watch my brother Raymond on his first run." This important epiphanic moment in which Hazel's perception of her brother suddenly shifts is suggested in the title of story, "Raymond's Run."

Setting

Since we see the story through Hazel's eyes, there are few descriptive passages of setting. However, the story does contrast an urban and a pastoral setting. The most striking description of Hazel's urban environment occurs when she enters the "jam-packed" park to race. She describes "Parents in hats and corsages and breast-pocket handkerchiefs peeking up," "kids in white dresses and light-blue suits," "the parkees unfolding chairs and chasing rowdy kids from Lenox," and "big guys with their caps on backwards, swirling their basketballs on the tips of their fingers." Hazel comments that "even the grass in the city feels as hard as a sidewalk." This urban scene contrasts with Hazel's dreamy meditations just before running, when she imagines "the smell of apples, just like in the country when I was little and used to think I was a choo-choo train, running through the fields of corn and chugging up the hill to the orchard." The two settings indicate an earlier, more peaceful time in Hazel's life that she is able to invoke by running, yet both settings suggest the vitality associated with Hazel.

Historical Context

The Black Power Movement

When "Raymond's Run" was published in 1971, the Black Power Movement was having a significant impact among African-American artists and writers. While the Black Power movement, which extended through the decade from 1965 to 1975, grew out of the Civil Rights movement, the

Compare
&
Contrast

- **1970s:** With the backdrop of the sexual revolution as well as the feminist, civil rights, and Black Power movements, African-American women come to the forefront of American literature.

  1990s: The success of such African-American women authors such as Toni Morrison and Alice Walker signal the appreciation of the perspective of African American women in society.

- **1970s:** The Women's Movement (also known as the Feminist Movement) makes significant differences in the way women are treated and perceived in American society. Women avail themselves of a myriad of opportunities, including professionally and personally.

  1990s: Inequality and discrimination still persist, but women have more opportunities and legal support than ever before. Critics of the Women's Movement point to the breakdown of the family unit as an inevitable result. But women make significant contributions in every walk of life and continue to make progress.

- **1970s:** Viewed as a sign of progress, 4,000 black officials were elected to public office. This number represented a larger number than had ever held office, but were still only 0.5% of all American elected officials.

  1990s: African Americans constitute less than 2% of all elected officials.

Black Power movement opposed integration and demanded economic and political power as well as equality with whites. The movement was fueled by protest against such incidents as the shooting of Civil Rights leader James Meredith in 1966 while he led a protest march across Mississippi. Shortly after, Civil Rights leader Stokely Carmichael initiated the call for Black Power and the first National Conference on Black Power was held in Washington, D.C. in 1966. In the same year, the Black Panther Party was founded in Oakland, California by Bobby Seale and Huey P. Newton, taking a militant stand against police brutality and the appalling conditions of black urban ghettoes, which lacked adequate municipal services and suffered crime rates 35 times higher than white neighborhoods.

African-American communities were also seen as the source of a vibrant culture. By the early 1970s, Black Power had become a widespread demand for black people to control their own destinies through various means: political activism, community control and development, cultural awareness and the development of black studies and "Black Arts." Pride in both African heritage and in the cultural distinctiveness of black communities in the United States, often summed up in the word "soul," was reflected in a variety of forms, from "Afro" hairstyles to soul music and soul food. In the arena of sports, heavyweight champion Muhammed Ali embodied the self-confident attitude of black pride. In the arts, black writers saw themselves as both inheritors and creators of a black aesthetic tradition. African-American writers like Toni Cade Bambara played an important part in developing awareness of a distinct African-American culture and folk tradition which emphasized the collective and maintained oral forms of expression.

By the mid-1970s organizations like the Black Panthers, targets for police and FBI surveillance, were decimated—in part because of their insistence upon achieving their goals "by any means necessary," including armed violence. In 1976, the 4,000 black officials elected represented a larger number than had ever held office, but were still only 0.5% of all American elected officials. In the 1990s, African Americans constitute less than 2% of all elected officials. Economic conditions for African Americans suffered in the 1980s: the recessions in the early 1980s reduced black family income to only 56% of white family income, less than in 1952, and the gap remains the about same in the 1990s. Nevertheless, the cultural heritage of the Black Power movement, black self-awareness and the celebration of an African-American culture and identity has had a significant impact on American culture and politics.

Black Women and the Women's Movement

The Women's Movement developed in the late 1960s in North America partly in response to the radicalizing processes of the Civil Rights, Black Power, and antiwar movements. At the same time, many women were radicalized by their realization that they were treated as second-class citizens. Women analyzed their situation and advocated radical change, forming their own local organizations and national networks for women's equality and women's rights. Consciousness groups were formed and women's centers established, concerned about issues such as sexual discrimination and harassment, wife abuse, rape and the right to freedom of choice concerning abortion. In ''Raymond's Run'' Bambara challenges conventional female roles through Hazel's self-assertive and openly competitive behavior. Unlike her classmate Cynthia Proctor, Hazel doesn't hide her passion for running or her abilities with false modesty. She resists her mother's attempts to make her ''act like a girl'' and insists of defining herself: ''I do not dance on my toes. I run. That is what I am all about.''

Women in African-American communities, however, did not necessarily fight for the same issues as the mainly white, middle-class women who composed the majority of the women's movement. As Toni Cade Bambara did in her anthology, *The Black Woman*, black women tended to connect issues of race and class with sexual equality. The struggle for welfare rights and decent housing were also seen by women in the black community as women's issues.

Critical Overview

In her essay ''Salvation is the Issue,'' Bambara says ''Of all the writing forms, I've always been partial to the short story. It suits my temperament. It makes a modest appeal for attention, allowing me to slip up alongside the reader on his/her blind side and grab'm.'' When her first collection of stories, *Gorilla, My Love*, which included the story ''Raymond's Run,'' was published in 1972, it succeeded in

''grabbing'' the critics: the stories were lauded as ''among the best portraits of black life to have appeared in some time'' by the *Saturday Review*.

Bambara has been praised for her ability to capture the cultural richness of African-American communities, particularly as it is reflected in the voice of African-American people. Charles Johnson has noted Bambara's ear for language and dialogue in his study *Being and Race: Black Writing since 1970* (1988). He comments that ''Bambara's strength is snappy, hip dialogue and an ever-crackling narrative style that absorbs all forms of specialized dictions.''

The close connection between Bambara's characters and their communities has also been a recurring theme amongst her critics. In a 1983 article, Nancy Hargrove commented on ''Raymond's Run'' as a ''story of initiation,'' in which Hazel Parker, ''perhaps the most appealing and lovable of Bambara's young narrators'' in *Gorilla, My Love*, discovers ''the value of human solidarity, of love for family and friends.'' Martha M. Vertreace connects Hazel's development and growth to a more specifically tribal tradition within the community, in which children pass through different stages of ''identity formation.'' She suggests that in ''Raymond's Run'' Hazel is at the level of ''artisan'' when ''solutions to problems fall within one's personal control.'' By learning to trust and cooperate, Hazel and Gretchen together will benefit ''the community, represented by Raymond.''

Susan Willis also sees Hazel's and Gretchen's ''mutual appreciation'' as prefiguring ''the crucial role that all teachers will play in Bambara's later writing.'' Moreover, their connection, Willis asserts, is important in establishing a ''bonding between women'' which opposes the dehumanization of women in a society dominated by males. Willis also suggests that Hazel's recognition of Raymond's potential should be viewed not so much as ''altruism'' on Hazel's part, but as a representative of a ''black community'' that ''would embrace all its members, allowing each to fulfill a self-sustaining and group-supporting role.''

In his article on ''Raymond's Run'' (1990), Mick Gidley takes a slightly different approach by analyzing the narrative complexity of Bambara's ''exuberantly straightforward story.'' He considers the different levels of Hazel's narration that establish her own identity but also invite the reader to ''question the teller's version of things'' and tell the

The Apollo Theater on 125th Street in the Harlem section of New York City.

story not only of her own but of Raymond's life. He probes the complexity of Hazel's relationship with Raymond, suggesting that when she sees Raymond "rattling the fence like a gorilla in a cage," she "wants to bring him over the fence into the race of life." In her 1996 preface to Bambara's *Deep Sightings and Rescue Missions*, Toni Morrison sums up Bambara's abilities with this comment: "[A]lthough her insights are multiple, her textures layered and her narrative trajectory implacable, nothing distracts from the sheer satisfaction her story-telling provides."

Criticism

Lalage Grauer

Grauer is a professor of Canadian Literature at Okanagan University College, in Kelowna, British Columbia. In the following essay, she examines how the character of Hazel Parker in Bambara's "Raymond's Run" attempts to deny "false roles of femininity."

In her preface to the anthology in which "Raymond's Run" first appeared, *Tales and Stories for Black Folks*, Bambara notes that her stories are intended to present black young people with an opportunity "to learn how to listen, to be proud of our oral tradition, our elders who tell tales in the kitchen." Bambara suggests that both the form and the content of the stories, their language and their potential lessons, have something to reveal about the strengths of the African-American community. "Raymond's Run," and other stories published in Bambara's first collection *Gorilla, My Love*, have been admired for the construction of vibrant African-American voices and communities. Young Hazel Parker, in "Raymond's Run," self-confidently addresses the reader in her own particular colloquial voice. Her voice reflects her character. Moving through her community of Harlem, New York City, she appears, as Alice Deck has observed about many of Bambara's characters, "comfortably familiar with the people and each building, street lamp, and fire hydrant. . . ." In the course of the story, however, Hazel is faced with a source of discomfort. Interestingly, it turns out to be someone who is most like herself: a young, confident African-American girl.

From the beginning of "Raymond's Run," Hazel's voice and behavior reflect her strength. At the same time, her first words comment on her role as a female. Direct and outspoken, she tells the reader about herself: "I don't have much work to do around the house like some girls. My mother does that." She informs the reader of her responsibility for "mind[ing]" Raymond, her mentally-challenged brother who is "much bigger and older" but "not quite right." In defining herself this way, Hazel suggests that although she does not help her mother with the housework, she has taken on a caretaking role often associated with women. This idea is immediately negated by her declaration that "if anybody has anything to say to Raymond, anything about his big head, they have to come by me." She asserts that, though small and thin, she would rather

What Do I Read Next?

- *Gorilla, My Love* (1972), Toni Cade Bambara's first collection of short stories, contains "Raymond's Run" and places the story within a context of others in which Hazel Parker plays a part. In eight of the fifteen stories in the collection, young children and adolescents play central roles.

- Toni Cade's *The Black Woman: An Anthology* (1970) collects poems, short stories and essays discussing and reflecting a wide range of concerns of black women in the late 1960s and early 1970s.

- *Deep Sightings and Rescue Missions* (1996), an important posthumous selection of Toni Cade Bambara's writings, provides the most current context for Bambara's work, including a preface by Toni Morrison, and several important recent interviews, and Bambara's writings about film. The selection also includes previously unpublished short stories.

- *Daughters of the Dust: The Making of an African-American Woman's Film* (1992), by filmmaker Julie Dash, is prefaced by Toni Cade Bambara writing in her capacity as filmmaker, who sees the film as marking the coming of age of independent black cinema.

- Paula Giddings' *When and Where I Enter: The Impact of Black Women on Race and Sex in America* is a highly accessible narrative history of Black women and their concerns from the seventeenth century to the 1980s.

- The anthology *Black-Eyed Susans/Midnight Birds* (1990) combines two collections of stories by Black women writers originally published in 1975 and 1980, with an updated commentary on each author by the editor Mary Helen Washington. It contains stories by Toni Cade Bambara, Alice Walker, Toni Morrison and Paule Marshall, among others.

---

act against taunts from others than "[stand] around with somebody in my face doing a lot of talking. I much rather just knock you down and take my chances even if I am a little girl with skinny arms and legs." Although she is nicknamed "Squeaky," Hazel is no mouse. Rather than seeing her job of looking after Raymond as a self-sacrificing female role, Hazel undertakes it with responsibility and pride. Furthermore, she enters traditional male territory by adopting the role of warrior in defense of Raymond, and she implies that she does it better than her brother George who previously had the job of "minding" Raymond and had been unable to prevent the insults of "a lot of smart mouths."

Hazel also claims space in the traditional male territory of athlete with her dedication to running. As she simply states, "I run. That is what I'm all about." To become the champion runner she is, Hazel has taken every opportunity to practice. When she is out with her mother, she "high-prance[s]

down 34th Street like a rodeo pony to keep my knees strong," despite her mother's embarrassment. While looking after Raymond, she practices her breathing and pacing while he plays his own games of being a stagecoach driver. "I never walk when I can trot, and shame on Raymond if he can't keep up," she states. Feminine modesty is not characteristic of Hazel. She is proud of what she has accomplished and proclaims her skill to herself and to anyone else: "I'm the fastest thing on two feet," "I'm the swiftest thing in the neighborhood," "I am Miss Quicksilver herself."

In practicing as an athlete, Hazel differentiates her attitudes and behaviour from what she sees as two models of falseness or inauthenticity. One is the behaviour of her schoolmate Cynthia, who acts as if her hard-earned talents are spontaneous. Cynthia pretends to play the piano because she has accidentally landed on the piano stool, although Hazel has seen Cynthia "practicing the scales on the piano

"Hazel is no mouse. Rather than seeing her job of looking after Raymond as a self-sacrificing female role, Hazel undertakes it with responsibility and pride."

over and over and over and over." Unlike Cynthia, whose lacy blouses suggest the ideal of a refined, unperspiring femininity, Hazel is willing to show her sweat. She takes the risk of both failure and ridicule that openly striving for a goal and acknowledging its importance involves. The second model of inauthenticity is the participation of girls in the May Pole dancing on May Day, which involves dressing up in "a white organdy dress with a big satin sash" and "new white baby-doll shoes" and "trying to act like a fairy or flower or whatever you're supposed to be." What you're supposed to be, as far as Hazel is concerned is "a poor Black girl who really can't afford to buy shoes and a new dress you only wear once in a lifetime cause it won't fit next year." With these statements, Hazel states her belief in taking pride in what she is rather than pretending to be what she is not. She senses a false model of femininity that denies the varied potentials of African-American girls by reducing them to "baby-dolls." As she points out, the May Pole dancing, not the track meet, is seen as "the biggest thing on the program."

When Hazel confronts the newcomer Gretchen, however, she also comes face to face with her own inauthenticity. Gretchen "has put out the tale that she is going to win the first-place medal this year." Hazel is "strolling down Broadway" with Raymond at her side on the day before the May Day races, practicing her breathing, when she comes upon Gretchen and her "sidekicks." Gretchen's follower Mary Louise has abandoned Hazel for Gretchen, and her other cohort Rosie "has a big mouth where Raymond is concerned." Quelling her first instinct to duck into a store, Hazel decides to confront them in a "Dodge City"-style showdown. Gretchen and her friends do not draw sixguns,

however, but rather smiles. First of all Mary Louise hypocritically "smiles" her question to Hazel: "You signing up for the May Day races?" Hazel does not bother to respond to either Mary Louise or Rosie but says "straight at Gretchen": "I always win cause I'm the best." In answer, Gretchen smiles and Hazel observes "but it's not a smile, and I'm thinking that girls never really smile at each other because they don't know how and don't want to know...." She admits to herself that "there's probably no one to teach us how, cause grown-up girls don't know either." As it turns out, a physical confrontation is avoided and the rivals go their separate ways. Hazel is not bested by Gretchen either physically or verbally, but a personal defeat is implied. With the word "us," Hazel includes herself among the "girls" who can only exchange phony smiles.

Hazel's inability to be real with Gretchen seems of little import at the time; after the incident, Hazel strolls with Raymond towards 145th "with not a care in the world because I am Miss Quicksilver herself." The incident, however, allows the reader to glimpse Hazel's Achilles heel. In many ways, Hazel can overcome her society's stereotyping of women: she can talk with people, she can fight, she can become a champion runner. Her experience with Gretchen, however, suggests that the tendency to belittle and dehumanize women occurs not only externally but also internally. The phony smiles girls exchange mask real feelings of fear, contempt and hostility. In a society in which women are infantilized as "baby-dolls" and have little share of the power, they learn to devalue themselves and compete against each other for what advantage they can get. At the same time, open competition is often branded as unfeminine—do fairies or flowers compete?—and occurs indirectly, disguised by a smile. Distrust and rivalry between women become the norm. That these feelings exist among the women of Hazel's community and are passed on to the young girls is suggested by Hazel's insight that there is "no one to teach" girls how to smile with true feeling. However, someone from an unexpected quarter does teach Hazel. That someone is her brother Raymond, who has also been belittled and dehumanized.

The idea that girls should manipulate events and each other indirectly rather than compete openly and honestly is reinforced by Mr. Pearson's hint before the May Day race begins that Hazel should let Gretchen win. It is hard to imagine him asking this behaviour of a young boy. The incident suggests that Mr. Pearson does not consider "Squeaky," as he calls her, a real athlete who needs to test herself and deserves the recognition that comes from winning. That Hazel wants to test herself against a worthy rival is suggested by the way she looks for Gretchen as soon as she and Raymond enter the park and by the incipient admiration in her description of Gretchen at the starting line "kicking her legs out like a pro."

During the race, however, it is not Gretchen but Raymond who compels Hazel's attention. Although Raymond is on the other side of a fence from Hazel, he runs the race alongside her. Glancing out of the corner of her eye Hazel sees him running and "it's the first time I ever saw that and I almost stop to watch my brother Raymond on his very first run." The language here is ambiguous–it could be the first time Hazel has seen Raymond because it is the first time he has run in that way, or it could be the first time *Hazel* has ever been able to see Raymond's ability to run. In any case, Raymond has revealed himself to be a complex being, not reducible to a "pumpkin head" or someone who is "not quite right." In many ways, Raymond is like Hazel. Raymond runs well, and he runs despite society's labels. While she will "prance" like a pony for the sake of running, he runs "with his arms down to his side and the palms tucked up behind him." Furthermore, with no ulterior motives or attempts to manipulate, Raymond simply runs "in his very own style." For a moment, Raymond becomes a mirror for Hazel, and, more than that, a model. Raymond's run, in spite of all the forces that attempt to bind and reduce him, communicates to Hazel in a wordless fashion the diversity and possibility of human potential beyond social expectations, including that of girls like herself and Gretchen. Joyfully, Hazel welcomes Raymond over to her side of the fence.

When the winner and runner-up of the race are announced, "Miss Hazel Elizabeth Deborah Parker" and "Miss Gretchen P. Lewis," Hazel and Gretchen share "this great big smile of respect between us." The use of the girls' full names suggests not only that they have won respect as athletes but that Hazel is ready to accept and value her full self and therefore to be curious about rather than threatened by Gretchen's potential—"I look over at Gretchen wondering what the 'P' stands for." The reader has every reason to believe that the girls, at last able to exchange smiles of respect, will also learn how to exchange smiles of joy for and in each other, as Hazel and Raymond have done.

Source: Lalage Grauer, "Overview of 'Raymond's Run,'" for *Short Stories for Students*, The Gale Group, 2000.

Mick Gidley

In the following excerpt, Gidley provides a general overview of "Raymond's Run," and offers an interpretation of the characters Hazel and Raymond, particularly with regard to the themes of acceptance and identity.

Toni Cade Bambara's "Raymond's Run" (1971), reprinted in her first collection of tales, *Gorilla, My Love* (1972), seems an exuberantly straightforward story: the first person, present tense narration of specific events in the life of a particular Harlem child, "a little girl with skinny arms and a squeaky voice," Hazel Elizabeth Deborah Parker, usually called Squeaky. Squeaky is assertive, challenging, even combative, and concerned to display herself as she is—at one point stressing her unwillingness to act, even in a show, "like a fairy or a flower or whatever you're supposed to be when you should be trying to be yourself". Above all, she's a speedy runner, "the fastest thing on two feet", and proud of it. "I run, that is what I am all about," she says.

Squeaky's narrative records the movement towards a race she has won easily in previous years, the May Day fifty-yard dash. This year she is pitted against a new girl, Gretchen, and the organizing teacher, Mr. Pearson, comes close to suggesting that, as "a nice gesture" towards the new girl, she might consider losing the race. ("Grownups got a lot of nerve sometimes," Squeaky snorts.) Earlier, when out with and looking after her older brother Raymond—a boy with an enlarged head who is "not quite right" and often lost in his own world of mimicry, games and make believe—Squeaky has to confront Gretchen and her "sidekicks" in what she calls "one of those Dodge City scenes" of verbal barracking and incipient physical violence, a showdown in which, though outnumbered three to one, she bests the opposition without needing to resort to fisticuffs. Similarly, on May Day itself, though it is literally a close-run thing and there is marked suspense as she waits for the official announcement of the result, feisty Squeaky breaks the tape first. Even before the loudspeaker broadcasts her victory, honoring her with her full and proper name ("Dig that," she says), Squeaky grants Gretchen increased respect for such things as the way the new girl runs and then gets her breathing under control "like a real pro," so that at the actual announcement Squeaky

> " Squeaky has always accepted her duty to mind Raymond, she has monitored him and even fought for him, but at the end of the story she ventures a step further: rather than simply knowing him as her brother, she accepts and <u>acknowledges</u> him as such--a child, like her, of the same father."

can sincerely ''respect'' her rival and exchange ''real smiling'' with her. Thus one of the story's technical feats is the registration of Squeaky's enlarged awareness *despite* the use of the first person present tense, a perspective which does not permit the speaker—who, of necessity, is always limited to the here and now—any distance from which to reflect upon events.

Indeed, as several seminal discussions of narratological problems have insisted, this narrative perspective imposes much responsibility on the reader. All intimations must be disposed in and through the story, with the reader left to assess their import. Raymond, his nature and the burden he must represent to a young girl, forms one locus for such speculation. In the very first paragraph Squeaky tells the reader this: ''All I have to do in life is mind my brother Raymond, which is enough''. And it is. Minding him, coming to terms with the insults his condition provokes, gets her into scrapes and actual scraps—''I much rather just knock you down and take my chances,'' as she puts it—including the one with Gretchen and her two pals. And by the end of the story Squeaky is planning to quit running herself in order to concentrate on training Raymond—who, she has just realized, can also run. If she carries out such a decision Squeaky will not be just looking after Raymond but truly ''minding'' him: *he* will be considered, *in* her mind, no longer merely running alongside ''and shame on [him] if he can't keep up.'' That is, without making it the obvious center

of concern, indeed without even fully focusing on it, the story charts Squeaky's acceptance of Raymond.

This in itself constitutes a closer, more intimate and charged issue than might initially seem the case. In a detail which could be taken primarily as an admission of vulnerability on Squeaky's part, a rounding out, so to speak, of her character, she confides that her father is even faster than she is: ''He can beat me to Amsterdam Avenue with me having a two fire-hydrant headstart and him running with his hands in his pockets and whistling. But that's private information''. Later, in Squeaky's description of Raymond's running, *he* has ''his arms down to his side and the palms tucked up behind him'' in ''his very own style''; this is a style which contrasts with Squeaky's running, arms ''pumping up and down,'' and is very much Raymond's ''own,'' but it is also subtly reminiscent of the ''private'' image of Mr. Parker's relaxed-arm racing prowess. Squeaky has always accepted her duty to mind Raymond, she has monitored him and even fought for him, but at the end of the story she ventures a step further: rather than simply knowing him as her brother, she accepts and *acknowledges* him as such—a child, like her, of the same father. She renders this explicitly when she declares him ''my brother Raymond, a great runner in the family tradition''.

When Squeaky outlines her idea to make Raymond ''her champion'' she adds,

> After all, with a little more study I can beat Cynthia and her phony self at the spelling bee. And if I bugged my mother, I could get piano lessons and become a star. And I have a big rep as the baddest thing around. And I've got a roomful of ribbons and medals and awards. But what has Raymond got to call his own?

This constitutes both full consciousness of Raymond and a catalogue of the relativities of their relationship. There is a sense in which the whole tale works similarly: while in her own unmistakable voice it undoubtedly and overtly tells the reader much of Squeaky's life, including her insistence on her own identity and authenticity (especially in comparison, say, with Cynthia's ''phony self''), it is also, as its title indicates, the story of *Raymond's* run, Raymond's life.

Running, in fact, has an attested pedigree as a metaphor for life's passage, as in such semi-folk sayings as ''life's race well run, life's work well done.'' Interestingly, this usage often includes an injunction to live the good life; thus Isaiah's prophesy that "they that wait upon the Lord shall renew their strength: they shall mount up with wings as eagles; they shall run, and not be weary." [Isaiah, XL, 31] Saint Paul, as might be expected, was fiercer: "let us lay aside every weight, and the sin which doth so easily beset us, and let us run with patience the race that is set before us" [Epistle to the Hebrews, XII, I]—a sentiment that the famous Victorian hymn "Fight the good fight" rendered into cliche: "run the straight race through God's good grace."

The May Day fifty-yard dash signals the childrens' situations precisely: as Squeaky zooms towards the tape, "flying past the other runners," Raymond runs alongside, level with her, but literally "on the other side of the fence". Just before Squeaky resolves to "retire as a runner and begin a whole new career as a coach with Raymond as [her] champion", Raymond is imaged as "rattling the fence like a gorilla in a cage like in them gorilla movies", and the reader intuits that Squeaky's determination is complex: she wants to bring him over the fence and into the race of life; she hopes to lay aside his impediments and grant him the good life; she also seeks to free him from his anthropoid but King-Kong-like status and enter him into the *human* race. Hence, too, the subliminal logic in the deft inclusion of the detail of the means by which Raphael Perez "always wins" the thirty-yard dash. "He wins before he even begins by psyching the other runners," Squeaky discloses, "telling them they're going to trip on their shoelaces, etc.". Raymond merely imitates his sister's performance—before the race, for instance, he bends down "with his fingers on the ground just like he knew what he was doing"—because, until the hope at the very end of the story, *he* has been "psyched," psyched out of his own authentic identity and out of the race altogether. This narrative of Raymond's "first run" and his climbing of the fence "nice and easy but very fast" towards Squeaky is the story of a humanizing love; its double focus takes in both of its two protagonists.

Yet just as *The Adventures of Huckleberry Finn*—which, with its mischievous young narrator, is structured similarly—ends ambiguously, so Raymond's Run has its further ironies. When on the last page of the book Mark Twain's youthful protagonist tells the reader that he is going to "light out for the Territory ahead of the rest," the reader knows that Huck's perspective, however fresh and truthful, is limited: even if he gets there "ahead," civilization, with all that it entails, *will* catch up with him.

Bambara's young speaker's aspirations must be seen as likewise shot through with doubts—perhaps more so. It may be, for example, that "with a little more study" Squeaky could "beat Cynthia" at the spelling bee, but even after the hoped for piano lessons it would be a very chancy business for her to become, in line with her stated ambition, "a star." One of the most telling effects of present tense first person narratives is the creation of such ironies: the reader must always question the teller's version of things. Seen in this light, Squeaky's ambitions may *all* be wishful thinking. The reader knows, too, that Squeaky's blackness will also be made to militate against her in the world beyond Amsterdam Avenue. Thus, for her, this year's May Day fifty-yard dash could well prove not the initiation but the apex of her achievements, the climax of her life's run. And, of course, if this is so, Raymond will never be coached to become a champion. The present tense—which by definition precludes a known future—is relentless: the story tells of his "first run"—and it *is* his first and only run.

Then again, perhaps such a fraught perspective does not grant enough credence to Squeaky herself, especially to her voice. The first words of William Faulkner's *The Sound and the Fury*, given to Benjy, include repeated references to fences: "Through the fence, between the curling flower spaces, I could see them hitting. . . . I went along the fence. . . . They [the golfers] went on, and I went along the fence . . . and we went along the fence . . . and I looked through the fence. . . . 'Here, caddie.' He hit . . . I held to the fence and watched them going away." Benjy, the idiot Compson brother, clings to the fence, moaning and weeping for his lost sister, Caddy, whose image has been invoked by the golfer's call for his caddie. That sister had truly "minded" Benjy, had been his monitor, refuge and source of warmth. Caddy, indeed, was the representation of love for each of her three brothers. But, in that she was granted no narration of her own, she was also, as at least one critic has put it, the "absent center" of the novel [Carey Wall, *Midwest Quarterly*, 1970]. In "Raymond's Run" by contrast, Squeaky is not only very much present for her brother, but possesses a powerful voice of her own. Squeaky's voice—as is so often the case with Bambara's protagonists—is notable for its vibrancy and verve. The idiosyncrasy and sheer insistence of Squeaky's voice impinges on, even hustles, the reader in a triumphant exhibition of will. Interestingly, that will is expressed most explicitly in Squeaky's description of her usual pre-race "dream":

Every time, just before I take off in a race, I always feel like I'm in a dream, the kind of dream you have when you're sick with fever and feel all hot and weightless. I dream I'm flying over a sandy beach in the early morning sun, kissing the leaves of the trees as I fly by. And there's always the smell of apples, just like in the country when I was little and used to think I was a choochoo train, running through the fields of corn and chugging up the hill to the orchard. And all the time I'm dreaming this, I get lighter and lighter until I'm flying over the beach again, getting blown through the sky like a feather that weighs nothing at all. But once I spread my fingers in the dirt and crouch over the Get on Your Mark, the dream goes and I am solid again and am telling myself, Squeaky you must win, you must win, you are the fastest thing in the world, you can even beat your father up Amsterdam if you really try. And then I feel my weight coming back just behind my knees then down to my feet then into the earth and the pistol shot explodes in my blood and I am off and weightless again, flying past the other runners.

This fleeting vision takes in much. In terms of space, the evocation here of beach and country gently reminds the reader of Squeaky's actual situation, one in which she may lie on her back, "looking up at the sky," but can only try "to pretend" she is "in the country." Because, as she sees, "even grass in the city feels hard as sidewalk, as there's just no pretending you are anywhere but in a 'concrete jungle'." (The notion of the "concrete jungle," which she has heard her grandfather use, further energizes the image of Raymond's entrapment in terms of "them gorilla movies.") Also, young as Squeaky is, the dream is reminiscent of a more innocent time (perhaps primordially so, with its Edenic apples) of "choochoo" trains and cornfields—before, that is, she took over the particularly heavy responsibility for Raymond from an older brother and before, in general, she became conscious of the burdens of humanity. And here, as it is in the verse of Isaiah quoted earlier ("they shall mount up with wings as eagles"), flying is an exalted form of running in which, as Saint Paul phrased it, "every weight" is laid aside. Indeed, she can "kiss the leaves of the trees" as she soars by. But if flying constitutes a glorified version of running, running itself serves Squeaky, "a little girl with skinny arms and a squeaky voice"—and may well serve damaged Raymond—as the most practical form of exaltation. And, when celebrated, tongued—embodied—in that thrusting, vital voice of Squeaky's, running becomes its own exultation.

Source: Mick Gidley, "Reading Bambara's 'Raymond's Run,'" in *English Language Notes*, Vol. XXVIII, No. 1, September, 1990, pp. 67–72.

Nancy D. Hargrove

Hargrove is a professor of English at Mississippi State University and author of Language as Symbol in the Poetry of T. S. Eliot. *In the following excerpt, she offers her interpretation of the characters Hazel and Raymond in Bambara's "Raymond's Run," particularly with regard to the theme of childhood and initiation.*

In reading Toni Cade Bambara's collection of short stories, *Gorilla, My Love* (1972), one is immediately struck by her portrayal of black life and by her faithful reproduction of black dialect. Her first-person narrators speak conversationally and authentically: "So Hunca Bubba in the back with the pecans and Baby Jason, and he in love . . . there's a movie house . . . which I ax about. Cause I am a movie freak from way back, even though it do get me in trouble sometime". What Twain's narrator Huck Finn did for the dialect of middle America in the mid-nineteenth century, Bambara's narrators do for contemporary black dialect. Indeed, in the words of one reviewer, Caren Dybek, Bambara "possesses one of the finest ears for the nuances of black English" ("Black Literature"). In portraying black life, she presents a wide range of black characters, and she uses as settings Brooklyn, Harlem, or unnamed black sections of New York City, except for three stories which take place in rural areas. Finally, the situations are typical of black urban experience: two policemen confront a black man shooting basketball in a New York park at night; young black activists gather the community members at a Black Power rally; a group of black children from the slums visit F.A.O. Schwartz and are amazed at the prices of toys. Bambara's stories communicate with shattering force and directness both the grim reality of the black world—its violence, poverty, and harshness—and its strength and beauty—strong family ties, individual determination, and a sense of cultural traditions. Lucille Clifton has said of her work, "She has captured it all, how we really talk, how we really are" [quoted on the book jacket of *Gorilla, My Love*], and the *Saturday Review* has called *Gorilla, My Love* "among the best portraits of black life to have appeared in some time."

Although her work teems with the life and language of black people, what is equally striking about it, and about this collection particularly, is the universality of its themes. Her fiction reveals the pain and the joy of the human experience in general, of what it means to be human, and most often of what it means to be *young* and human. One of Bambara's special gifts as a writer of fiction is her ability to portray with sensitivity and compassion the experiences of children from their point of view. In the fifteen stories that compose *Gorilla, My Love*, all the main characters are female, thirteen of them are first-person narrators, and ten of them are young, either teenagers or children. They are wonderful creations, especially the young ones, many of whom show similar traits of character; they are intelligent, imaginative, sensitive, proud and arrogant, witty, tough, but also poignantly vulnerable. Through these young central characters, Bambara expresses the fragility, the pain, and occasionally the promise of the experience of growing up, of coming to terms with a world that is hostile, chaotic, violent. Disillusionment, loss, and loneliness, as well as unselfishness, love, and endurance, are elements of that process of maturation which her young protagonists undergo. . . .

"Raymond's Run," . . . [a] story of initiation, centers on Hazel Elizabeth Deborah Parker, perhaps the most appealing and lovable of Bambara's young narrators, and concerns two discoveries she makes on the way to growing up. One has to do with her retarded older brother, for whose care she is responsible, and the other with her rival in the May Day races. As in the two previous stories, both discoveries reveal the value of human solidarity, of love for family and friends.

Hazel is a totally engaging character. In a narrative style entirely free of the strong language used by most of the other young narrators, she reveals a refreshing honesty as well as a dedication to hard work and a dislike of phonies. She clearly knows who and what she is. Her life centers on two things: caring for Raymond and running. At the story's beginning she indicates that the former is a large and consuming task, but one which she accepts stoically and with love: "All I have to do in life is mind my brother Raymond, which is enough. . . . He needs looking after cause he's not quite right. And a lot of smart mouths got lots to say about that too. . . . But now, if anybody has anything to say to Raymond, anything to say about his big head, they have to come by me."

If Raymond has her heart, running has her soul. She tells us honestly, but not arrogantly, "I'm the fastest thing on two feet. There is no track meet that I don't win the first place medal." She works hard to improve her skill, and she illustrates her disgust with those who pretend they never practice by

> **Bambara's stories communicate with shattering force and directness both the grim reality of the black world--its violence, poverty, and harshness--and its strength and beauty--strong family ties, individual determination, and a sense of cultural traditions."**

describing Cynthia Procter, who always says, after winning the spelling bee, "'I completely forgot about [it].' And she'll clutch the lace on her blouse like it was a narrow escape. Oh, brother."

She is also determined to be herself, rather than what others want her to be. Rebelling against her mother's desire for her to "act like a girl for a change" and participate in the May Pole dance instead of the fifty-yard dash, she insists that "you should be trying to be yourself, whatever that is, which is, as far as I am concerned, a poor Black girl who really can't afford to buy shoes and a new dress you only wear once a lifetime cause it won't fit next year." Although when she was younger she had once been a "strawberry in a Hansel and Gretel pageant," she now asserts, "I am not a strawberry. I do not dance on my toes. I run. That is what I am all about."

The May Day race, the central episode of the story, is thus of tremendous importance to Hazel. She is determined to win again, especially because she has a new challenger in Gretchen, who has recently moved into the neighborhood. Her descriptions of her feelings before and during the race are superb in their realism, revealing her great intensity and concentration. Yet, as she is running, she notices that Raymond is running his own race outside the fence. Suddenly she realizes that she could teach Raymond to run and thereby make his life more meaningful; thus, whether or not she herself has won the race now becomes secondary: "And I'm smiling to beat the band cause if I've lost this race, or if me and Gretchen tied, or even if I've won, I can always retire as a runner and begin a whole new career as a coach with Raymond as my champion. . . . I've got a roomful of ribbons and medals and awards. But what has Raymond got to call his own?'' Her sincere love for her brother and her excitement at discovering something that he can learn to do well are so intense that ''by the time he comes over I'm jumping up and down so glad to see him—my brother Raymond, a great runner in the family tradition.'' Ironically, everyone assumes that she is elated because she has again won first place.

Almost simultaneously she realizes that, far from disliking her rival or feeling superior to her, she admires her for her obvious skill in and dedication to running: ''And I smile [at Gretchen]. Cause she's good, no doubt about it. Maybe she'd like to help me coach Raymond; she obviously is serious about running, as any fool can see.'' The story ends with the two girls smiling at each other with sincere appreciation for what the other is.

Hazel represents the best of youthful humanity in her unselfish desire to make her brother's life more significant, in her determination to be herself, and in her honest admiration of the abilities of a rival. But it is perhaps her wise understanding of what is most to be valued in ''being people'' that makes her such an appealing character. ''Raymond's Run'' is a story rare in this collection, and in modern literature, in that everyone wins in one way or another, and yet it is neither sentimental nor unrealistic, but sincere and believable.

Thus, with compassion, understanding, and a warm sense of humor, Bambara portrays in many of the stories in *Gorilla, My Love* an integral part of the human experience, the problems and joys of youth. Told from the viewpoint of young black girls, they capture how it feels as a child to undergo the various experiences of loneliness, disillusionment, and close relationships with others. Bambara's short fiction thus belongs to the ranks of other literary works portraying youth, such as Twain's *The Adventures of Huckleberry Finn*, Joyce's *A Portrait of the Artist as a Young Man*, and Salinger's *The Catcher in the Rye*. Furthermore, because her protagonists are female, black, and generally pre-adolescent, these stories, like the works of several other contemporary black female writers, contribute a new viewpoint to the genre.

Source: Nancy D. Hargrove, ''Youth in Toni Cade Bambara's *Gorilla, My Love*, '' in *Women Writers of the Contemporary South*, edited by Peggy Whitman Prenshaw, University Press of Mississippi, 1984, pp. 215–32.

Sources

Bambara, Toni Cade. ''Salvation is the Issue,'' in *Black Women Writers (1950-1980): A Critical Evaluation*, edited by Mari Evans, Garden City, N.Y.: Doubleday, 1984, pp. 13-38.

———. Interview: ''Toni Cade Bambara,'' in *Black Women Writers At Work*, edited by Claudia Tate, New York: Continuum, 1988, pp. 13-38.

Deck, Alice A. ''Toni Cade Bambara,'' in *Dictionary of Literary Biography*, Vol. 38: *Afro-American Writers after 1955, Dramatists and Prose Writers*, Detroit: Gale Research, 1985, pp. 12-22.

Johnson, Charles. *Being and Race: Black Writing since 1970*, Bloomington: Indiana University Press, 1988.

Morrison, Toni. Preface to *Deep Sightings and Rescue Missions*, by Toni Cade Bambara, edited by Toni Morrison, New York: Pantheon Books, 1996.

Vertreace, Martha M. ''The Dance of Character and Community,'' in *American Women Writing Fiction: Memory, Identity, Family, Space*, edited by Mickey Pearlman, Lexington: University of Kentucky Press, 1989, pp. 15-71.

Willis, Susan. ''Problematizing the Individual: Toni Cade Bambara's Stories for Revolution,'' in *Specifying: Black Women Writing the American Experience*, Madison: University of Wisconsin Press, 1987, pp. 129-58.

Further Reading

Bambara, Toni Cade. ''Salvation is the Issue,'' in *Black Women Writers (1950-1980): A Critical Evaluation*, edited by Mari Evans, Garden City, N.Y.: Doubleday, 1984, pp. 13-38.

    In this article, Bambara discusses the creative process and her political and artistic concerns with stimulating honesty and wit.

———. Interview: ''Toni Cade Bambara,'' in *Black Women Writers At Work*, edited by Claudia Tate, New York: Continuum, 1988, pp. 13-38.

    A wide-ranging interview in which Bambara discusses her life, her crafts (writing and filmmaking) and her views on art and politics from the 1960s to the 1980s.

———. *Deep Sightings and Rescue Missions*, edited by Toni Morrison, New York: Pantheon Books, 1996.

    Bambara's most recent work, published posthumously after her death in 1995, collects important interviews and short fiction never previously published.

Chevigny, Bell Gale. "Stories of Solidarity and Selfhood," in *The Village Voice*, April 12, 1973, pp. 39-40.

  This early review emphasizes the collection's insightful study of the black community and of adolescent girls, as well as its innovations in style.

Deck, Alice A. "Toni Cade Bambara," in *Dictionary of Literary Biography*, Vol. 38: *Afro-American Writers after 1955, Dramatists and Prose Writers*, Detroit: Gale Research, 1985, pp. 12-22.

  Overview of Bambara's life and literary career.

Hargrove, Nancy. "Toni Cade Bambara," in *Contemporary Fiction Writers of the South: A Bio-Bibliographical Sourcebook*, edited by Joseph M. Flora and Robert Bain, Westport, Conn.: Greenwood Press, 1993, pp. 32-45.

  A useful survey of major themes in Bambara's writings and literary criticism of her work. Includes a short biography and an excellent bibliography of writing by and about Bambara.

Johnson, Charles. *Being and Race: Black Writing since 1970*, Bloomington: Indiana University Press, 1988.

  Contains a short but illuminating discussion of Bambara as a humorist and writer of "highly energetic prose."

Polatnick, Rivka M. "Poor Black Sisters Decided for Themselves: A Case Study of 1960s Women's Liberation Activism," in *Black Women in America*, edited by Kim Mari Vaz, Thousand Oaks, California: Sage Publications, 1995, pp. 110-30.

  An interesting discussion regarding the participation of two key black women's groups in the women's movement which looks at the differences and similarities between their concerns and those of white women.

Van Deburg, William L. *New Day in Babylon: The Black Power Movement and American Culture, 1965-1975*, Chicago: University of Chicago Press, 1992.

  A comprehensive and accessible discussion of the Black Power movement, its precursors, leaders, ideologies, and cultural impact and legacy.

Vertreace, Martha M. "The Dance of Character and Community," in *American Women Writing Fiction: Memory, Identity, Family, Space*, edited by Mickey Pearlman, Lexington: University of Kentucky Press, 1989, pp. 155-71.

  Contains a brief but illuminating discussion of Hazel's relationship to the community. Includes a useful bibliography of Bambara's writings.

Willis, Susan. "Problematizing the Individual: Toni Cade Bambara's Stories for Revolution," in *Specifying: Black Women Writing the American Experience*, Madison: University of Wisconsin Press, 1987, pp. 129-58.

  An interesting analysis of political issues in Bambara's story is included in a longer analysis of stories from *Gorilla, My Love, The Seabirds Are Still Alive* and Bambara's novel *The Salt Eaters*.

Roman Fever

Edith Wharton

1936

"Roman Fever" is among Edith Wharton's last writings and caps off her noteworthy career. "Roman Fever" was first published in *Liberty* magazine in 1934, and it was included in Wharton's final collection of short stories, *The World Over* , in 1936. Several reviewers of this final collection from newspapers and magazines throughout the nation called special attention to "Roman Fever." Since then, however, the story has received little critical attention. The few critics who have written about the story describe it as artistic, complex, and reflective of Wharton's moral landscape.

"Roman Fever," however, is frequently included in anthologies, both of Wharton's work and of American literature, and this may be a better indicator of its value as worthwhile literature than its critical history is. The story, at first, seems to be little more than a tale about the nostalgic remembrances of two middle-aged women revisiting Rome. Yet the tone of both the outer and inner dialogue shows a deep-felt animosity between the two women. The more outgoing Mrs. Slade is envious of Mrs. Ansley's vivacious daughter and jealous of her past love for Mrs. Slade's husband. The final sentence of the story reveals that Mrs. Slade has a valid reason for her feelings of competition with Mrs. Ansley though she only learns of it after years of ill-feeling. Some readers may find this final sentence to be a trick ending, on par with those of Saki or O. Henry. But a close reading of "Roman Fever" shows that Wharton carefully crafted her story to lead up to that exact moment of truth. Wharton's fine construction indeed makes ''Roman Fever'' one of her greater works of short fiction.

Author Biography

Edith Wharton was born on January 24, 1862, to a wealthy New York family. She came from the most exclusive of old New York families, whose names had appeared in Washington Irving's accounts of Hudson River history. At the end of the Civil War, however, Wharton's parents were hard hit by inflation. To save money, the family lived and traveled throughout Europe until Wharton was about 10. By that time, she spoke five languages. After the family returned to the United States, Wharton embarked on a program of self-education, prompted mainly by her extensive reading. Just before her 15th birthday, Wharton finished her first creative work, a novella entitled *Fast and Loose*. It was not published until a century later, in 1977.

In her teens, Wharton again spent several years in Europe, accompanied at times by her fiance. Their engagement broke off in 1885, and Edith married the banker Edward Wharton, who came from the same high social circles as Edith's mother. Shortly afterwards, she began to write stories, which she sold to popular magazines. Her first short story appeared in 1891, when Wharton was 29 years old. Wharton was now independently wealthy, and therefore did not depend on writing for a living. She threw herself wholeheartedly into her work and recognized herself as a professional writer only after her first collection of stories, *The Greater Inclination*, was published in 1899. Around this time, Wharton also developed a lasting friendship with the writer Henry James. He became her mentor, and critics have often compared the two writers' works. Between 1900 and 1914, Wharton produced almost 50 short stories and some of her finest novels. These include *The House of Mirth* and *Ethan Frome*.

In 1910, Wharton returned to France, where she had spent several winters. The next year, she made France her permanent residence; and in 1913, she divorced her husband. Throughout the next two decades, with the exception of the war years, Wharton traveled extensively throughout Europe. In 1931, Wharton visited Rome for the first time in 17 years; she had spent part of her childhood there. Her personal writings from the period show a strong desire to visit old, familiar haunts, much as her characters do in ''Roman Fever.'' Scholars believe that her visits to Rome between 1931 and 1934 inspired the story; ''Roman Fever'' was one of her last writings about Italy.

Wharton continued to write until her death. In 1934, three years before her death, Wharton published her memoirs, *A Backward Glance*. These evoked old New York and the people who lived there. She was at work on *The Buccaneers* when she died. Her biographer R. W. B. Lewis believed it was her finest piece of work since the 1920s. It was published after her death.

Plot Summary

The story opens with two middle-aged American ladies enjoying the view of Rome from the terrace of a restaurant. Mrs. Slade and Mrs. Ansley have been lifelong friends, thrown into intimacy by circumstance rather than by true liking for each other. They first met as young ladies vacationing in Rome with their families, and they have lived for most of their adult lives across the street from each other in New York. Now, in the 1920s, they find themselves again in each other's company. Both are spending the spring in Rome, accompanied by their daughters, Jenny Slade and Barbara Ansley respectively, who are roughly the same age. Jenny is safe and staid, unlike her mother. Barbara is vivid and dramatic, apparently unlike either of her parents.

When Jenny and Barbara leave to spend the day with Italian aviators, Mrs. Slade and Mrs. Ansley wile away the afternoon on the terrace overlooking the ruins of the Forum and the Colosseum, chatting and remembering old times.

Mrs. Slade and Mrs. Ansley have in some ways led parallel lives. Besides living in the same New York neighborhood, they both became widows at approximately the same time. Mrs. Slade, the widow of a corporate lawyer, finds her new life dull, without the excitement of entertaining and going on business trips. She believes that Mrs. Ansley cannot find life as dull, because her life has never seemed interesting in the first palce. In Mrs. Slade's eyes, Mrs. Ansley and her husband represented ''museum specimens of old New York.'' However, Mrs. Ansley believes that Mrs. Slade must be disappointed with her life.

Edith Wharton

Toward the end of the afternoon, Mrs. Slade remembers how Mrs. Ansley became sick during the winter that they spent in Rome when they were young. Although at that time of year people no longer caught malaria, or Roman fever, the dampness and cold night temperatures could still make people quite sick. Mrs. Slade recalls how Mrs. Ansley became seriously ill after going to the Colosseum after sunset one evening. Mrs. Ansley seems to have a hard time remembering this event, but Mrs. Slade reminds her of the details.

Suddenly, Mrs. Slade, wanting to hurt her friend, bursts out that she must tell Mrs. Ansley that she knows why Mrs. Ansley went to the Colosseum that night. Mrs. Slade then recites the contents of a letter asking Grace [Mrs. Ansley] to meet Delphin Slade (then the fiancé of Alida [Mrs. Slade]) at the Colosseum. When Mrs. Ansley wonders how Mrs. Slade could know the contents of the letter, Mrs. Slade confesses that she had written it. She had been afraid that Grace [Mrs. Ansley], who was in love with her fiancé, would win Delphin away from her. She hoped that Grace would catch cold, and so be unable to be involved with Delphin for a few weeks until she (Alida/Mrs. Slade) could be more sure of Delphin's affections. But she never thought that Grace would get so sick.

Mrs. Ansley is upset by the revelation because it represents the loss of a cherished memory; as she says, "It was the only letter I had, and you say he didn't write it?" Mrs. Slade realizes that Mrs. Ansley still cares for Delphin, although Mrs. Ansley claims to cherish only the memory. Mrs. Slade says that she wishes she hadn't told her friend about the letter, but she defends her actions by saying that she didn't believe Grace (Mrs. Ansley) had taken Delphin so seriously, since, after all, Grace had married Mr. Ansley just two months later, as soon as she left her sick bed.

After a pause, Mrs. Slade says that she sent the letter as a joke; she remembers how she spent the evening laughing at her friend, waiting in the dark by the Colosseum. Mrs. Ansley surprises her companion by saying that she didn't wait, that Delphin had arranged everything and that they were let into the Colosseum immediately. Mrs. Slade accuses Mrs. Ansley of lying, wondering how Delphin would know that Mrs. Ansley was waiting for him. Mrs. Ansley says that she answered the letter, and that she is sorry for Mrs. Slade because Delphin came to her that night. Mrs. Slade responds by saying that she doesn't begrudge Mrs. Ansley one night; after all, she had Delphin for 25 years and Mrs. Ansley had only a letter that Delphin didn't write. Mrs. Ansley has the final word: "I had Barbara."

Characters

Barbara Ansley

Barbara Ansley is the brilliant and vivacious daughter of Mrs. Ansley. Barbara and her mother are vacationing in Rome with their neighbors, Mrs. Slade and her daughter Jenny Slade. Barabara and Jenny are away spending time with some Italian aviators during the story's conversation between Mrs. Slade and Mrs. Ansley. Mrs. Slade envies Mrs. Ansley for her brilliant daughter. During the course of this conversation, Mrs. Ansley reveals to Mrs. Slade that Barbara is the daughter of Mrs. Slade's late husband, Delphin.

Grace Ansley

Mrs. Grace Ansley, a middle-aged widow, is a wealthy New Yorker who is vacationing in Italy with her daughter Barbara, and her neighbor Mrs. Slade, and her daughter Jenny Slade. In Mrs. Slade's opinion, Mrs. Ansley has led a staid, uneventful life.

Although she presents the picture of the proper middle-aged widow, for instance, knitting and looking at the Roman view, her calm exterior hides a secret past.

As a young lady in Italy, Grace (Mrs. Ansley) fell in love with Alida's (Mrs. Slade's) fiance, Delphin. However, after meeting him one night at the ruins of the Colosseum, she had become quite ill. When she rose from her sickbed, she immediately married Mr. Ansley.

Despite her marriage to Mr. Ansley, she has always nursed the memory of her evening with Delphin, and the letter he had sent her. When Mrs. Slade reveals that she, in fact, sent the letter, not Delphin, Mrs. Ansley's fantasy is destroyed. She, in turn, reveals to her friend an even more devastating secret: that her dynamic daughter, who Mrs. Ansley has long noted is so different from either of her parents, is in fact Delphin's daughter.

Mrs. Ansley
See Grace Ansley

Alida Slade

Mrs. Alida Slade, a middle-aged, wealthy, New York widow, is vacationing in Italy with her daughter Jenny, her neighbor Mrs. Ansley, and her daughter Barbara Ansley. The wife of a famous corporate lawyer, Mrs. Slade found her married days filled with excitement and adventure. She prided herself on being a charming entertainer, a good hostess, and a vibrant woman in her own right. After the death of her husband Delphin, Mrs. Slade finds life dull, with only her daughter to divert her; however, Jenny is quiet and self-sufficient.

Mrs. Slade feels both superior to and envious of her lifelong friend, Mrs. Ansley. She also has been nursing a decades-long resentment against Mrs. Ansley, for falling in love with Delphin when Mrs. Ansley and Mrs. Slade were both young ladies on vacation in Italy. Afraid that Grace (Mrs. Ansley) would steal away her fiance, Alida (Mrs. Slade) sent Grace a note, signing Delphin's name. When Grace went to meet Delphin, she became quite ill.

During this trip to Italy, Mrs. Slade, wanting to hurt her friend even after all these years, confesses to Mrs. Ansley that she, not Delphin, sent the letter. Mrs. Slade immediately regrets her action, and she can't help but feel sorry for her friend, after she sees how Mrs. Ansley has cherished the memory of that letter. When Mrs. Slade expresses this feeling,

Media Adaptations

- "Roman Fever" is a one-act opera based on Wharton's short story; the music is composed by Robert Ward and the vocal score is written by Roger B. Brunyate. It was published by ECS Publishing in 1993.

however, Mrs. Ansley shocks her with the revelation that Barbara (the daughter of Mrs. Ansley) is Delphin's daughter.

Delphin Slade

Although Delphin Slade is dead at the time the story takes place, he remains a prominent figure in the minds of both his wife and his former lover, Grace (Mrs. Ansley). The story hinges on his past actions. As a young man, while engaged to Alida (Mrs. Slade), Delphin met Grace at the Colosseum one night and fathered Barbara. This secret has been concealed from his wife for the past 25 years.

Jenny Slade

Jenny Slade is the quiet, staid, self-sufficient daughter of Mrs. Slade. She is accompanying her mother to Rome along with Mrs. Ansley and her daughter Barbara Ansley. Jenny and Barbara are away spending time with some Italian aviators during the story's conversation between Mrs. Slade and Mrs. Ansley.

Mrs. Slade
See Alida Slade

Themes

Friendship

Mrs. Slade and Mrs. Ansley have been friends since they first met as young women in Rome, when

Topics for Further Study

- Investigate the effects of malaria in the early 20th century and how scientists have worked to combat this life-threatening disease.

- What can you determine about the role of wealthy Americans in the early 20th century? What social position did they occupy? How would you define their position abroad?

- Conduct research on the Roman ruins mentioned in the story. What role do you think their history and presence have in the unfolding drama?

- Read one of Edith Wharton's novels, such as *The House of Mirth* or *The Age of Innocence*. How do the characters and the social framework in the novel compare to those in ''Roman Fever''?

- Although ''Roman Fever'' was written in the 1930s, it is set in the mid-1920s. Which decade does the story more accurately reflect? What changes took place in society between these two periods?

- An opera was based on ''Roman Fever.'' Pick another art form, such as a play, a musical, or a mural. How would this art form depict the themes, actions, and characters of ''Roman Fever''?

- Imagine that you are a literary critic. How would you assess ''Roman Fever'' in terms of artistic composition and message? (Be sure to use the text to support your argument.) Create an outline for your essay.

Alida (Mrs. Slade) was engaged to Delphin Slade. This friendship forms the enduring tie between Mrs. Slade and Mrs. Ansley. However, their friendship is undercut by the deeper, hostile feelings they have for each other, feelings that they hardly dare to admit. Because each has something to hide about the early days of their friendship, they have not been honest with each other in their friendship.

In addition, their friendship has not been very intimate, despite their similar backgrounds and close proximity to each other on same street in New York. Mrs. Slade, in particular, strongly dislikes Mrs. Ansley, because of Mrs. Ansley's love for Delphin. She has made fun of Mrs. Ansley to their mutual friends, and she believes that Mrs. Ansley has led a much duller life than she and Delphin. At the same time, however, she cannot shake her envy of Mrs. Ansley. Mrs. Ansley, on the other hand, believes that ''Alida Slade's awfully brilliant; but not as brilliant as she thinks.'' She also believes that Mrs. Slade must be disappointed with her life, alluding to undisclosed failures and mistakes.

The competitive nature of their friendship reaches a climax one afternoon in Rome. As Mrs. Slade views the ruins of the Colosseum in Rome, she cannot help but remember the anger she felt at Grace's (Mrs. Ansley's) love at the time for her fiance. She confesses, after 25 years, that she had lured Grace to the Colosseum by forging a note from Delphin. Mrs. Ansley's repsonse to this confession that Barbara is Delphin's child completely alters the relationship between the women.

Rivalry

Mrs. Slade and Mrs. Ansley have been rivals throughout their long friendship. Sometimes this rivalry is expressed subtly, as when Mrs. Ansley says that the view upon the Palatine ruins will always be the most beautiful view in the world ''to me,'' as if she alone is privy to the glories of Rome. Sometimes the rivalry is expressed directly through the women's thoughts. For example, Mrs. Slade compares herself directly to Mrs. Ansley. She believes that her widowhood is more difficult than Mrs. Ansley's widowhood, for she had led a full, active life as the wife of an international corporate lawyer, while Mrs. Ansley and her husband were more of ''museum specimens of old New York,'' or in even less kind terms, ''nullities.'' Mrs. Slade also admits to envying her friend, a habit that she developed long ago.

The cause of this barely acknowledged rivalry becomes clear as the story develops. Mrs. Slade has never gotten over the fact that Grace (Mrs. Ansley) had fallen in love with her fiancé Delphin Slade, and had gone to the Colosseum to meet him.

The rivalry between these women runs very deep. At one point, Mrs. Slade implies a desire for her friend's death. When she brings up their past adventures in Rome, she refers to Mrs. Ansley's great aunt, a woman who sent her sister to the Forum because they were in love with the same man —the sister caught malaria that night and died.

Love and Passion

Mrs. Slade considers herself more dramatic and passionate than Mrs. Ansley. She believes that she had contributed as much as her husband to ''the making of the exceptional couple they were.'' She also values the quality of being dynamic, and admits that she has ''always wanted a brilliant daughter.'' However, neither Mrs. Slade's words nor her actions seem to reveal great depths of love or passion she felt for her husband or her daughter. Her greatest passion seems to have been for her late son, whose death made her feel ''agony.'' But she blocks out this feeling, because the ''thought of the boy had become unbearable.'' Finally, the life that Mrs. Slade now leads seems to be one of order, even if she does not embrace such order.

Ironically, Mrs. Ansley emerges as the more passionate of the two women. Although she seems to be involved in more mundane activities, such as knitting and playing bridge, her revelation of the night that she spent with Delphin at the Colosseum demonstrates that she is capable of hidden depths of passion. Living across the street from Delphin for twenty-five years and raising his child suggest that she is capable of enduring love as well.

Style

Setting

''Roman Fever'' is set in Rome, Italy, around the mid-1920s. On the one hand, the ruins of Rome become the focus of Wharton's skill at descriptive writing. On the other hand, the ruins of Rome remind both women of an earlier time spent in Rome together when their friendship and rivalry both began. More generally Wharton shows the kind of life a woman of independent means could lead in Rome at that time.

The setting of Rome is contrasted with the home neighborhood of the two women on Manhattan's East Side in NewYork. Mrs. Slade and Mrs. Ansley have lived across the street from each other so close that each woman knows all the mundane details of the other's everyday life. But this setting is too confining to allow them to communicate their true feelings. It is only in Rome that Mrs. Slade feels able to reveal the truth to Mrs. Ansley.

Point of View

The story is told from a third-person, omniscient point of view. This means that readers see and hear what the characters see and hear, and that readers are also privy to their thoughts. However, in this case, the interior life, motivations, and reactions of Mrs. Slade are revealed to a greater extent than those of Mrs. Ansley's. For example, readers know that Mrs. Slade decides to tell the truth about the letter Delphin was supposed to have written 25 years ago because she is envious of her rival and dislikes her, though at the same time she believes she is a good person. Readers also know that she regrets her words after she has said them. On the other hand, not much is revealed about Mrs. Ansley's motivation. Readers do not know, for instance, why Mrs. Ansley decides to reveal the truth about Barbara's parentage.

Structure

Although the story is relatively brief, it is divided into two sections. The first section provides the background and history of Mrs. Slade and Mrs. Ansley. The second section develops the theme of the rivalry between the two women, concluding with the truth about Barbara's parentage. The two parts also represent the past and the present.

In the first part of the story, Mrs. Slade notes Mrs. Ansley's odd emphasis on the personal pronoun *me* when she talks about the view of Rome from the terrace. She also notes Mrs. Ansley's emphasis on the personal pronoun *I* when she says ''I remember'' in response to Mrs. Slade's comment about the summer they spent in Rome as girls. Although Mrs. Slade attributes this emphasis to Mrs. Ansley's being old-fashioned, the emphasis really alludes to Mrs. Ansley's fond memories of the time she spent with Delphin.

In the second part of the story, Mrs. Slade's musings show that she is gearing up toward something more significant than a simple conversation about malaria. At one point, she watches Mrs.

Ansley knitting and thinks, ''She can knit—in the face of *this*!'' The reader wonders what *this* refers to, since up to this point the women are simply having a casual conversation about the past.

Symbolism and Imagery

Wharton makes use of a number of symbols and images to reinforce the emotions of the story. The ruins that the two women are gazing at of the Palatine, the Forum, and the Colosseum symbolize the ruins of these women's perceptions of themselves and each other. Mrs. Ansley calmly knits, which would seem to be the staid activity of a middle-aged woman, but what she is knitting is described as ''a twist of crimson silk.'' Her knitting can be said to represent the passionate and more frivolous side of her nature. Also, the women's actions can be viewed symbolically, to indicate their feelings toward the conversation and each other. As soon as Mrs. Slade starts to talk about their shared past, Mrs. Ansley lifts her knitting ''a little closer to her eyes,'' thus shielding herself and her reactions from Mrs. Slade. However, when Mrs. Slade learns that Mrs. Ansley did meet Delphin at the Colosseum, it is Mrs. Slade who must cover her face and hide her deepest emotions. In fact, by the end of the story, the power structure has changed, as shown by Mrs. Ansley's actions. After revealing the truth about Barbara's father, she ''began to move ahead of Mrs. Slade toward the stairway.''

Historical Context

Old New York

''Roman Fever'' was written in the 1930s and is set in the 1920s, but the story's characters and values reflect the attitudes of upper-class society in New York in the last half of the nineteenth century. Mrs. Slade and Mrs. Ansley are the product of that environment of affluence and relative ease. The author Wharton belonged to this circle and was able to make this society come alive in her story. In Wharton's world, families such as the Astors and the Vanderbilts could be found at the height of the social ladder. In addition to this aristocratic class of people who came from old names and old money were the *arrivistes*. These arrivistes had earned their fortunes more recently and were often richer than the aristocrats. These members of high society entertained themselves by attending the theater and opera, by paying and receiving social calls, by attending lunch and dinner parties and house parties, by traveling abroad, and by summering in such fashionable spots as Newport, Rhode Island.

In this society, women were seen as moral judges. But, despite this important role, most families did not believe that girls needed to be educated. Instead, they felt that education should be acquired only for womanly purposes, for instance, to fulfill her future husband's needs. A woman's role in life was to be a homemaker, and her single-minded purpose was to make a good marriage.

American Women in the 1920s and 1930s

The roles and accepted forms of behavior of American women in the 1920s and 1930s changed. After decades of struggling, women had won the right to vote when the 19th Amendment was ratified in 1920. Young women, known as ''flappers,'' exerted their greater independence by wearing shorter dresses, wearing makeup, and cutting off their long hair into bobs. They drove cars, played sports, and smoked cigarettes in public. Young women also increasingly worked outside the home, which brought them greater economic and social freedom. When a woman married, however, she was expected to quit her job and function solely as wife and mother. Thus, despite the achievements of women and changes in society, the homemaker still remained the ideal of American womanhood.

American Writers Abroad

Wharton was not the only American writer to spend a significant part of her life abroad, traveling and writing. Many of the writers known as the Lost Generation, such as Ernest Hemingway and F. Scott Fitzgerald, lived in Europe during the 1920s. Gertrude Stein, an American, even hosted a salon in Paris, where some of the greater artistic names of the day met and discussed ideas. Many of the writers of the 1920s were haunted by the death and destruction of World War I. They also scorned middle-class consumerism and the superficiality of the post-war years. Expatriate writers often chronicled the changes that were rapidly taking place in society and culture, emphasizing the new standards that were emerging.

Italy in the 1920s and 1930s

Italy was undergoing many political and social changes in the 1920s and1930s. Italians felt bitter about their experiences in World War I, particularly as the Versailles peace treaty failed to give Italy the

Compare
&
Contrast

- **1920s:** Malaria is a life-threatening, infectious disease. For instance, in 1914, around 600,000 Americans died after contracting malaria, primarily in the Mississippi River valley and along the East Coast. However, some of these fatal cases of malaria arose because doctors used the disease to treat another fatal disease, syphilis.

  1990s: The World Health Organization estimates that there are 300 to 500 million cases of malaria reported each year, resulting in 1.5 to 2.7 million deaths. In developing countries, malaria is one of the leading causes of sickness and disease. The occurrence of malaria has actually risen in many countries in the last half of the 20th century. However, malaria poses little threat to western countries, such as the United States and Italy. In 1992, the United States reported 910 cases of malaria, but only seven of these were acquired in the country. Many of these cases occur among immigrant populations.

- **1920s and 1930s:** Italy's government is based on totalitarianism, meaning the government controls all aspects of society, including the economy, politics, and culture. Benito Mussolini rules Italy with dictatorial power.

  1990s: Italy practices a parliamentary republic. The prime minister of Italy is the head of the ruling party, while the president functions largely as a ceremonial figure. Throughout the decade, Italy's government has been somewhat unstable, changing ruling parties numerous times.

- **1920s and 1930s:** Although figures are not available for the number of children conceived out of wedlock in the 1920s and 1930s, social stigma was attached to illegitimacy. In the early 1920s, Wharton wrote a story about a woman who conceived a child out of wedlock. This story was rejected by almost every magazine to which it was submitted, because the subject matter was too unpleasant. The number of births to unmarried women has steadily increased from 5.3 percent of the population since the mid-1900s, so perhaps the number of illegitimate births in the 1920s and 1930s was around or less than 5.3 percent of the U.S. population.

  1990s: Of U.S. women giving birth, 28 percent, or 1,165,384, are unmarried. The number of illegitimate births has grown by 60 percent since 1980. While some people still attach stigma to illegitimacy, illegitimacy has become an accepted part of American culture, as witnessed by the number of famous single women who have children and by the willingness of people to talk about such matters, for instance, on talk shows.

---

territory it wanted around the Adriatic Sea. In the years following the war, Italy entered a period of economic hardship, rising inflation, and workers' strikes. The government seemed incapable of resolving these problems. Under these conditions, Benito Mussolini emerged as a new and powerful leader. A strong nationalist, Mussolini founded Italy's Fascist Party, which rose to power in the early 1920s. Beginning in 1921, the Fascists and the Communists engaged in violent clashes. The situation in Italy quickly bordered on civil war.

Mussolini soon became the Italian premier. As early as 1925, he expressed his desire to create a complete dictatorship. He gained control of parliament and established a secret police. These measures allowed him to crush all dissenting members of society. Mussolini transformed Italy into a totalitarian state, meaning the government controlled all aspects of society, including politics, the economy, and culture.

Mussolini also expanded the Fascist Party's militia, and in the 1930s, he followed his plan for expanding Italy's territory and making the country an imperial power. In 1935, Italian forces invaded Ethiopia, and the African kingdom fell the following year. Italy also took control of Albania on the

Adriatic Sea, and controlled territory in Northern Africa. Italy's increased aggression was coupled with the rise of a totalitarian government in Germany and the rise of militarism in Japan. By 1939, Europe was in the grip of World War II.

Critical Overview

"Roman Fever" was first published in 1934 in *Liberty* magazine; two years later, Wharton included it in her final short story collection, *The World Over*. At the time, a few years before her death, Wharton was a literary star, both in the United States and abroad. As such, the story collection received reviews from newspapers and magazines ranging from the *The New York Times* to the *Saturday Review of Literature*. The majority of reviewers found the collection to be, on the whole, a pleasing and successful representation of Wharton's work. Fanny Butcher pointed out in the *Chicago Daily Tribune* that although many contemporary readers tended to think of Wharton primarily as a novelist, *The World Over* served as a "fresh reminder of her incomparable skill in the short story." Percy Hutchinson, writing for the *New York Times*, found that the collection proved that Wharton's reputation as a "master" of the short story art form could not be tarnished.

Many reviewers also singled out "Roman Fever" for special praise. *Punch* magazine found "Roman Fever" "worth re-reading, after an apparently unproductive first perusal, for the sake of the final sentence on which its every word converges." Butcher declared that of the stories in the collection, "there are three which any writer might envy and which few could equal" "Roman Fever" was one of these. Other publications, such as the *New Statesman and Nation* and *Catholic World*, also agreed that "Roman Fever" was the best story in the collection.

Over the decades, Wharton biographers and critics have made note of "Roman Fever", but have varied in their evaluation of the story. As early as 1959, Marilyn Jones Lyde claimed the story to be one of Wharton's best works. Almost 20 years later, Cynthia Griffin Wolfe, in *A Feast of Words: The Triumph of Edith Wharton*, agreed with this assessment. Neither of these authors explained why she felt the story was so successful. In 1970, Geoffrey Walton expressed a different opinion: "'Roman Fever' is a very light comedy that can be taken as a kind of farewell skit on the decorum of the great days." Yet Walton also found that the story presented a "glimpse of an unexpected kind of sophistication."

More recently, particularly as interest in the works of Wharton has increased, the body of contemporary criticism has grown. However, as Alice Hall Petry points out in her essay, "A Twist of Crimson Silk: Edith Wharton's Roman Fever," "[It] is curious that so widely-anthologized a work has generated such a paucity of critical interpretation." She categorized earlier criticism as "tepid." She then examines in her essay how a minor element of the story, the act of knitting, can be seen as a way of "appreciat[ing] the complex art of 'Roman Fever.'" Petry believed that Wharton used knitting in a particularly "provocative" manner, indicating Wharton's interest in developing a technique that, as stated by the critic E.K. Brown, shows that she cared "about the processes of art."

Another recent essay, Lawrence I. Berkove's "'Roman Fever': A Mortal Malady," explored the angle of the moral landscape represented by Wharton: "the story, besides being artistic, is a powerful exemplum about the dangerous susceptibility of human nature to the mortal diseases of the passions." Berkove discussed the moral standards evinced by Mrs. Slade and Mrs. Ansley, and concluded by declaring that "Roman Fever" "is a reminder that art as great as [Wharton's] is not only an aesthetic accomplishment but also a way to come to grips with the causes and cures of the maladies of the human soul."

Petry's calls for "serious critical attention" for "Roman Fever" have yet to be answered, but readers seem to view the story as a complex, refined work of art.

Criticism

Rena Korb

Korb has a master's degree in English literature and creative writing and has written for a wide

View of the ruins of the Colosseum in Rome.

variety of educational publishers. In the following essay, she discusses how the characters in "Roman Fever" reveal themselves to be not what they seem.

In 1934, the renowned author Edith Wharton, who had been writing for close to 50 years, published her memoirs, *A Backward Glance*. She had attained widespread critical and popular acclaim almost three decades earlier, with the publication of the novel *The House of Mirth*. The book quickly became a bestseller, earning Wharton $30,000 in 60 days and solidifying her reputation as a writer of merit. Wharton enjoyed a rich career, publishing 26

novels and novellas (including two after her death), 11 collections of short stories, nine works of nonfiction, and three volumes of poetry. Wharton's writings were enjoyed by readers in her own day, and in the 1980s and 1990s. Wharton's literary standing rose dramatically as new readers and critics rediscovered her writings.

In 1934, Wharton visited Rome. In many ways, this trip was not a success. Wharton had been hoping to visit parts of Italy she had not seen in 20 years, but when she arrived in Rome, she came down with the flu and had to spend the next two weeks in bed. The trip, however, did lead to what

What Do I Read Next?

- Wharton's *House of Mirth* (1905) brilliantly depicts the ruthless and destructive nature of New York society.

- *A Backward Glance* is Wharton's autobiography, published in 1934, three years before her death.

- *The Collected Short Stories of Edith Wharton* (1991), introduced and edited by Wharton's biographer R. W. B. Lewis, presents her finest works of short fiction.

- Ellen Glasgow's short story, "The Difference" (1923), shows one woman's reaction to finding out about her husband's unfaithfulness.

- *Daisy Miller* (1878) by Henry James tells of a young girl in Rome during the height of the malaria epidemic.

- *Lost New York* (1971) by Nathan Silver describes old New York society and surroundings.

- Nathalia Wright's *American Novelists in Italy* (1965) discusses a number of American writers and their relation to, and the influence of, Italy.

- *Edith Wharton and Henry James: The Story of Their Friendship* (1965), by Millicent Bell, uses the correspondence of the two writers to understand their relationship.

Wharton's biographer R.W.B. Lewis dubbed "another instance of backward glancing." After this trip, Wharton wrote what many critics and readers feel is one of her best short stories, "Roman Fever." The story centers on two middle-aged widows sitting on a hotel terrace overlooking the ruins of the Colosseum. Although they appear to be old friends, their intimacy masks a lifelong rivalry, caused by a love triangle. When they were young women, Grace (Mrs. Ansley) fell in love with Alida's (Mrs. Slade's) fiance, Delphin. Over the years, Mrs. Slade hid her resentment over Mrs. Ansley's love for her fiance, but she has never forgotten it, and her long-sup-

pressed anger finally emerges. She reveals her role in the conflict: she wrote a letter to Grace (Mrs. Ansley), asking her to come to the Colosseum one night, and signed Delphin's name. Mrs. Ansley appears to be broken-hearted by the news, but she reveals a surprise of her own. She wrote Delphin back, and the two young people met that night; their meeting resulted in the conception of Mrs. Ansley's daughter, Barbara.

"Roman Fever" shows that appearances are not what they seem; nearly every preconceived notion the women have of each other, as well as each of the reader's preconceptions, is overturned. At the same time, the story reveals a great deal about the expected roles of women in the early part of the century: that of passive onlookers, content to abide by society's rules and live out prescribed roles. As the story opens, Mrs. Ansley and Mrs. Slade appear to be little more than "two American ladies of ripe but well-cared-for middle age" sitting on a terrace in Rome. The conversation of their daughters, whose voices are overheard from the courtyard below, further emphasizes the role of the older women: "'[Let's] leave the young things to their knitting' and a voice as fresh laughed back: 'Oh, look here, Babs, not actually *knitting*!'" The daughters can conceive of no more engrossing activity that might interest their mothers. Indeed, Mrs. Ansley almost immediately and "half guiltily" drew her yarn and needles from her bag, thus fulfilling her daughter's prophecy.

Although the two women are seemingly content to wile away the afternoon peacefully on the terrace, their private thoughts are less tranquil. Mrs. Slade considers her friend a "nullit[y]" and a "museum specimen," while Mrs. Ansley believes Mrs. Slade to be "brilliant; but not as brilliant as she thinks." These private thoughts indicate both that the woman are not truly such good friends and that they are capable of keeping long-held secrets. The interior thoughts also show Mrs. Slade to be resentful of what the world has offered her. After her husband's death, she found life had become a "dullish business." Without the dynamic and successful Delphin, an international corporate lawyer, Mrs. Slade finds her role in the world to be greatly diminished. Instead, she now exists merely as "mother to her daughter." That daughter, Jenny, is yet another source of discomfort, for she is a quiet girl, one "who somehow made youth and prettiness as safe as their absence." Although she does not admit it, Mrs. Slade would prefer to have a daughter like Mrs. Ansley's Barbara, who is vivacious and vibrant.

This brief interlude, Part I of the story, shows how an older woman in the 1920s, who did not have the freedom allowed to younger girls, was defined primarily by her interactions with her husband and children. Although Mrs. Slade had compared herself to her husband "as equal in social gifts," without him, she is relegated to sitting on a terrace in Rome, or in New York, for that matter, watching others go on with the adventure of their lives. Barbara and Jenny, members of the younger generation, are embarking for an afternoon with eligible Italian aviators; and other travelers, who have also been lunching, demonstrate an interest in the Roman environment by "gathering up guide- books." For Mrs. Ansley and Mrs. Slade, however, the primary diversions are knitting, a potential bridge game, and conversation, all activities that could be carried out at home in New York City. Mrs. Ansley even verbalizes their feelings of doing nothing new. "'[S]ometimes I get tired just looking even at this.' Her gesture was now addressed to the stupendous scene at their feet." Mrs. Ansley, however, rejects her own challenge, merely returning to her thoughts.

In Part II of "Roman Fever," Mrs. Ansley's and Mrs. Slade's true feelings about each other are revealed. The two are not as good friends as they would appear. Mrs. Ansley (then single) was willing to destroy the bonds of friendship by developing, and following up on, romantic feelings for the fiance of Mrs. Slade (also then single). Mrs. Slade recognizes the enormity of this transgression when she prods Mrs. Ansley, "'But I was the girl he was engaged to. Did you happen to remember that?'" When Mrs. Ansley admits to remembering this, Mrs. Slade reiterates her point with the words, "'And still you went?'" Clearly, Mrs. Slade cannot understand why Mrs. Ansley made such a choice. What is more surprising is their pretense for all these years, when both of them know how Mrs. Ansley broke the rules of friendship in pursuing a relationship with Delphin.

Mrs. Slade shows that her hatred toward Mrs. Ansley took on murderous proportions that summer long ago when she brings up Mrs. Ansley's great-aunt Harriet, who sent her younger sister to the Colosseum because they were both in love with the same man. The younger sister caught malaria, more romantically known as Roman fever, and died, and the tale became family folklore used to frighten children. "'And you frightened *me* with it, that winter when you and I were here as girls. The winter I was engaged to Delphin.'" The *obvious* reason that Mrs. Slade would be frightened would be of

> "Although Mrs. Slade had compared herself to her husband, 'as equal in social gifts,' without him, she is relegated to sitting on a terrace in Rome, or in New York, for that matter, watching others go on with the adventure of their lives."

getting sick. But if she did not go out at night, when the cold air could dangerously chill the body, she would have no cause to fear for her health. Thus, the *implied* reason for her fear is that she would use this knowledge against someone else. This is exactly what she does, when she lures Mrs. Ansley to the Colosseum one night with a note falsely signed by Delphin.

Mrs. Slade's actions indicate that holding on to her man was more important than holding on to her friend. While she could be justified in making such a decision, particularly because Mrs. Ansley held no scruples in pursuing a relationship with Delphin, she takes risks with Mrs. Ansley's health and life. Although she claims that she had no idea Mrs. Ansley would get so sick, Mrs. Slade, in her own words, acted out of a "blind fury." Reasoning knew no bonds when it came to protecting her engagement from the "quiet ways," "the sweetness," of Grace (now Mrs.) Ansley. In so doing, Alida (now Mrs. Slade) also protected her future prosperity, for Delphin proved himself to be an extremely capable provider.

Mrs. Ansley's response to Mrs. Slade's provocation is more astonishing. She reveals that she had an affair with Delphin that night. Although she married soon afterwards apparently taking to her bed not because of illness but because of her precarious and embarrassing condition: the child she gave birth to, Barbara, was Delphin's. In revealing this information, Mrs. Ansley shows that since that moment she has lived out her life as a lie. It can be fairly assumed that Mrs. Ansley did not share this news with anyone; Mrs. Ansley's mother's rush to get her daughter married demonstrates the importance of keeping the pregnancy secret. Wharton had also previously dealt with the issue of illegitimacy in stories in which the true parentage of the child was covered up. As R.W.B. Lewis put it, ''The situation of Grace Ansley's whole lifetime is revealed in a single phrase.''

Mrs. Ansley's confession, presented in an assertive manner and accompanied by the assertive action of ''mov[ing] ahead of Mrs. Slade toward the staircase,'' profoundly alters Mrs. Slade's perception of her. Not only has Mrs. Ansley betrayed a friendship (though Mrs. Slade had already done so), she has acted in a manner that completely defies societal codes. Mrs. Ansley's confession also gives Mrs. Slade more pause for thought. For there is also the implication that Jenny's lack of brilliance comes not from Delphin, who produced Barbara, but from Mrs. Slade.

In her book *Edith Wharton's Women*, Susan Goodman maintains that the rivalry between Mrs. Slade and Mrs. Ansley feeds their sense of intimacy. Because both women define themselves through their relationship with the other and through their competition for Delphin, their identities are ''collaborative'' and ''interdependent.'' For the complex relationship between Mrs. Slade and Mrs. Ansley alone, ''Roman Fever'' could well merit the appreciation of decades of readers. As Margaret B. McDowell points out, ''Those who have re-read the story many times are still startled by the force and power of its compressed narrative as the women suddenly see beyond their familiar assumptions.''

Source: Rena Korb, for *Short Stories for Students*, The Gale Group, 2000.

Lawrence I. Berkove

In the following essay, Berkove asserts that ''Roman Fever'' is much more than a ''satire on the manners of the American upper class,'' claiming that the various ''violations'' of decency and social custom are far more important.

''Roman Fever,'' judging from the frequency with which it is included in anthologies of short stories and American literature, is undoubtedly one of Edith Wharton's most respected stories. Edith Wharton, too, has been the subject of a recent revival of interest. It is therefore surprising that the story has received so little critical attention. First published in *Liberty* magazine in 1934 and subsequently collected in her anthology, *The World Over*

(1936), it is generally considered one of the finest achievements of her ''remarkable final creative period''. In one of the most recent articles on it, Alice Hall Petry demonstrates evidence of the story's artistic composition, but surprisingly little was done before her article and nothing has been done since to suggest what ''Roman Fever'' is artistic *about*. Wharton's genius, it turns out, is moral as well as aesthetic; the story, besides being artistic, is a powerful exemplum about the dangerous susceptibility of human nature to the mortal diseases of the passions.

To think of ''Roman Fever'' as a satire on the manners of the American upper class—more particularly as an expose of the bitter rivalry that cankered the lives of two society matrons beneath their veneers of supposed gentility—is to see Edith Wharton as a critic of manners, but there are even greater depths in both the story and the author. Far more central to the story than who comes out on top in the viciously catty final encounter of the two women are the moral issues at stake. The offenses committed are serious. Not only do the women violate standards of decency and social custom, but in the course of their lifetime of silent combat against each other, they also negate their marriage vows, poison their lives with hatred and deception, and—even more importantly—verge upon murder.

One clue to the ominous level of immorality in the story is implicit in its title. ''Roman Fever'' refers, in part, to a local term for malaria. Before the disease was scientifically understood, it was believed that malaria was caused by exposure to ''bad air'' such as was thought to gather around marshes at night when the wind died down. Rome encompassed some marshland, including the ground on which the Forum and the Colosseum were built, and such places were regarded as dangerous, even deadly, after sunset during malarial seasons.

Another, related clue is quietly presented with seeming irrelevance in the story when Alida Slade reminds Grace Ansley of her great-aunt Harriet—a ''dreadfully wicked'' woman ''who was supposed to have sent her young sister out to the Forum after sunset to gather a night-blooming flower''—with the result that the girl caught ''Roman fever'' and died. Aunt Harriet's real motive, confessed years later, was murder. Both she and her sister were in love with the same man, and Harriet maliciously deceived her sister/rival into going to the Forum, hoping to get her out of the way with malaria. Although the incident was a familiar part of Grace's family history, Alida knew of it when both women were young and single and living in Rome, and both remembered it on the fateful night recalled in the story.

The clues add up to attempted murder on Alida's part when several apparently independent incidents are linked in their proper chronological sequence and the reader is able to reconstruct the true picture. First, immediately after reminding Grace of Aunt Harriet, Alida admits that her own passionate love for Delphin Slade—then her fiance and later her husband—"was why the story of your wicked aunt made such an impression on me. And I thought: 'There's no more Roman fever, but the Forum is deathly cold after sunset. . . . And the Colosseum's even colder and damper.'" Alida, it turns out, was aware that Delphin and Grace were attracted to each other, so to get her rival out of the way, she forged a note from Delphin to Grace asking her to meet him alone at the Colosseum after dark. More than twenty-five years afterward, Alida is able to repeat every word of the letter, but there is no need because Grace has also memorized it. For Alida, the memory of the letter is sweet because it accomplished its purpose: "People always said that expedition was what caused your illness." Alida feels no guilt, however, because "you got well again—so it didn't matter."

This statement is grimly ironic. "[S]o it didn't matter" blurs the fact that Alida, having sent Grace to a place more than "deathly cold," directly purposed murder. Later, Alida confesses her awareness of what she was doing, although she couches it in a defensive protest: "Of course, I never thought you'd die," but this is contradicted by her active and longstanding hatred of Grace as well as by her action. Alida consciously and deliberately repea ed the act of Aunt Harriet and hoped at the time for the same consequence to result. That Grace did not die does not exculpate Alida; the malicious intention was there. It mattered a lot.

The statement is also ironic in light of the outcome of Grace's "illness." Until the story's climactic moment of mutual confession, both women have kept secret certain parts of the episode that, when put together, reveal and explain essential aspects of their lives since. Grace does not know until Alida tells her that it was Alida and not Delphin who wrote the letter appointing a meeting place. Alida does not know until Grace tells her that Grace's "illness" was not malaria but pregnancy. Grace, assuming that Delphin had written the letter,

> "The clues add up to attempted murder on Alida's part when several apparently independent incidents are linked in their proper chronological sequence and the reader is able to reconstruct the true picture."

had sent him a note in reply. The next-to-last thing Grace tells Alida in the story is that she "didn't have to wait that night"—Delphin came.

With this, Alida recognizes that her victory over Grace was not quite as full as she had supposed, but she still believes that she came out ahead: "After all, I had everything; I had him for twenty-five years. And you had nothing but that one letter that he didn't write." This provides the opening for Grace's final retort: "I had Barbara."

In the context of the story, this admission has to be devastating to Alida on multiple levels. Alida feels that her daughter, Jenny, has an excess of virtue. She is too nice, too boringly straight-laced, too angelic. All her married life, Alida has envied the two "nullities," Horace and Grace Ansley, their attractive and vivacious daughter. But now she knows that Grace's daughter is also Delphin's daughter. That has to be a terrible shock. She also must realize that inasmuch as Jenny and Barbara have the same father, the genetic difference has to have come from her. If Jenny is less "brilliant" than Barbara, this reflects—negatively—on her own contribution to Jenny. Finally, and perhaps worst of all, it means that her victory over Grace was hollow.

Thus far, Alida Slade appears the villain of the story and Grace Ansley the innocent victim, but Grace, despite her name, is not entirely virtuous, either. Alida "fears" Grace for her quiet ways and "sweetness," but Grace's final retort to Alida is vengeful, and Grace has to have known how deadly it would be. That she might have been, in a measure, driven to the remark by Alida's pressure does not alter the fact that it reveals a capacity and even a talent for malice. It also reveals the fact that her ladylike appearance is only a veneer; at heart, she is proud of having been attractive to Delphin and having had his child, even out of wedlock.

This in turn reveals what kind of lie Grace has lived for a quarter of a century. She was two months pregnant when she married Horace Ansley under pressure from her mother. There is no mention of love for Horace. On the contrary, it is obvious that Grace has never stopped loving Delphin. Were she and Horace married under false pretenses? Indeed, one wonders what sort of man he was either not to have been aware somewhere along the line that a seven months' pregnancy was suspicious, or not to have minded being drafted to marry Grace for appearance's sake. Grace has also kept from her own daughter the secret of her true father—another lie to match the cover-up of her own illicit romance with another woman's fiance. One must also wonder what sort of man Delphin Slade was to have agreed to a tryst with his fiancee's friend, to have succumbed so quickly to her charms, and to have kept this a secret from his wife. How much had he really loved Alida? Finally, one must wonder again at Grace's character, not just for having been infatuated with Delphin but also for having kept from him the truth about his relation to Barbara, for having lived as a wife with a man she does not love, and for having cherished for twenty-five years her dirty little secret about why her daughter outshines Alida's.

"Roman Fever" opens with two "American ladies of ripe but well-cared-for middle age" looking down upon the "outspread glories of the Palatine and the Forum." Several pages later, the same scene is described as a "great accumulated wreckage of passion and splendour." In light of the later description, the earlier one must be regarded ironically. Only sentimental minds would deny the wreckage and think only of the glories of ancient Rome. The central action of the story takes place in the Colosseum, a place where gladiators fought. Unbeknown to themselves, Alida and Grace continue the gladiatorial tradition. They have been relentless and unscrupulous, using their bodies, their husbands, their daughters, and their lives of lies as weapons to score on each other. In the name of love, they have been rivals for twenty-five years and sought to kill each other, one literally and the other figuratively.

Edith Wharton not only reveals these women to be little better than savages at heart but also reveals what makes them so: the primitive motives and crude pride that serve them for morality. At this

point, "Roman fever" acquires another, ironic, and dark connotation: the moral disease of pagan Rome. Rome was the center of a pagan as well as a Christian culture; it remains in the story a place where a choice is made between the two extremes of pagan self-indulgence and fevered passion, on the one hand, and Christian submission to God's laws and institutions, on the other. Nominal Christianity, Wharton shows, is no Christianity at all. In not governing their passions, the two women merely revert to becoming gladiators—sophisticated, perhaps, but pagan. Attempted murder is the ultimate step in their moral degradation, but it does not occur out of the blue; the way Alida and Grace have conducted their entire lives prepares the way. In selecting two such women to be the protagonists of "Roman Fever" Wharton demonstrates her distance from the position that women are by nature morally superior to men. She also conveys her seriousness about the moral standards that women as well as men must obey to rise above the natural human tendency to savagery.

There are moral depths in Edith Wharton's fictions that have yet to be examined. Beneath her social criticisms lies another level of values, a surprisingly traditional Christian one. "Roman Fever" is not at all an isolated instance of how Wharton's sense of morality may surface in her stories; rather, it is a reminder that art as great as hers is not only an aesthetic accomplishment but also a way to come to grips with the causes and cures of the maladies of the human soul.

Source: Lawrence I. Berkove, "'Roman Fever': A Mortal Malady," in *The CEA Critic,* Vol. 56, No. 2, Winter, 1994, pp. 56–60.

Alice Hall Petry

In the following essay, Petry explores the significance of knitting in "Roman Fever."

Probably Edith Wharton's best-known short story is "Roman Fever," the product of a 1934 trip to Rome, and the most enduring tale from her uneven late collection entitled *The World Over* (1936). It is curious that so widely-anthologized a work has generated such a paucity of critical interest, and even more curious that the few appraisals which it has received have been so tepid: Geoffrey Walton, for example, simply dismisses it as "a very light little comedy that can be taken as a kind of farewell skit on the decorum of the great days." More appreciative are Cynthia Griffin Wolff and Marilyn Jones Lyde, both of whom — without explaining the bases of their appraisals — find the story to be one of Wharton's best works. But ''Roman Fever'' is considerably more substantial than Walton's remark would suggest, and Wolff's and Lyde's appraisals can — and should — be explored at length. One way that we can begin to appreciate the complex art of ''Roman Fever'' is to examine Wharton's handling of what might at first appear to be a minor element in the story: the act of knitting.

That knitting will occupy a special position in ''Roman Fever'' is signified at the outset by the simple fact that it is the first matter to receive attention in the story. Grace Ansley and Alida Slade overhear their young daughters discussing them:

> ''. . . let's leave the young things to their knitting''; and a voice as fresh laughed back: ''Oh, look here, Babs, not actually *knitting* —'' ''Well, I mean figuratively,'' rejoined the first. ''After all, we haven't left our poor parents much else to do. . . .''

Since Wharton had asserted in the brief introductory paragraph that Grace and Alida were ''two American ladies of ripe but well-cared-for middle age'', it is apparent that their daughters' appraisal of them as ''young things'' is mocking. The implication clearly is that the ladies are physically, emotionally, and intellectually capable of nothing more than the traditionally passive, repetitive, and undemanding task of knitting. By having the daughters patronize their mothers in this fashion, Wharton is predisposing the reader to perceive the ladies as stereotypical matrons; and the rest of the story will be devoted to obliterating this stereotype, to exposing the intense passions which have been seething in both women for more than twenty-five years.

A major rupture in the stereotype is the simple fact that (the daughters' remarks notwithstanding) Alida Slade does not knit at all. This unexpected situation focuses the reader's attention more intensely on Grace Ansley, whose apparently passionate devotion to knitting ultimately will enable us to probe the psyches of both women and to reconstruct the remarkable events of a generation before. The complex relationship between Grace and knitting is evident in her first action in the story: ''Half-guiltily she drew from her handsomely mounted black handbag a twist of crimson silk run through by two fine knitting needles''. The sentence presents two distinct aspects of Grace's character. The phrase ''half-guiltily'' is in keeping with the persona she has presented to the world throughout her

> **&& . . . the knitting offers Grace an ideal excuse for responding neither immediately nor extensively to Alida's painful interrogation.''**

adult life. ''Smaller and paler'' than the assertive Alida, Grace is ''evidently far less sure than her companion of herself and of her rights in the world''. The ''evidently'' is eloquent, for although Grace may seem embarrassed by her hobby, the physical objects themselves tell a far different story about her: she has chosen ''crimson'' silk, an insistently passionate color; and the skein has been ''run through'' by needles, a startlingly assertive image. The sensuality and forcefulness suggested by her knitting materials will help to render plausible her passionate moonlight tryst with Delphin Slade twenty-five years earlier, as well as her capacity to stand up to the vicious taunts of Alida, the ''dark lady'' of the piece.

Quite early in the story, then, knitting has ceased to be a general symbol of complacent middle-age: it is rapidly becoming a complex personal emblem for Grace, and in fact one may gauge Grace's mental state according to how she manipulates her knitting materials. This element first becomes obvious in the second portion of the story, wherein Grace recognizes instinctively that she and Alida have reached, ''after so many years, a new stage in their intimacy, and one with which she did not yet know how to deal''. That intimacy is far from positive: both women recognize that Alida is very much in control of the situation, steadily steering the conversation to the matter of the love triangle in which they had been involved so many years before. Grace's response to Alida's catty remark that Rome is '''so full of old memories''' is to begin knitting: ''She settled herself in her chair, and almost furtively drew forth her knitting. Mrs. Slade took sideway note of this activity, but her own beautifully cared-for hands remained motionless on her knee''. The aggressive Alida needs nothing to occupy her hands, but the guilt-ridden Grace —

predisposed to ''fidget''—uses her knitting as a physical means of containing her growing stress, of maintaining some semblance of order in a situation not in her control. As Alida continues to press her advantage, ironically lamenting how much modern girls were ''missing'' out on in disease-free, twentieth-century Rome, Grace ''lifted her knitting a little closer to her eyes''— not simply because ''the long golden light was beginning to pale'', but also because it serves as a physical barrier behind which to protect herself from Alida's probing. Closely aligned with this, the knitting offers Grace an ideal excuse for responding neither immediately nor extensively to Alida's painful interrogation. Further, it enables her to avoid making eye contact with her tormentor:

> ''When Roman fever stalked the streets it must have been comparatively easy to gather in the girls at the danger hour; but when you and I were young, with such beauty calling us, and the spice of disobedience thrown in, and no worse risk than catching cold during the cool hour after sunset, the mothers used to be put to it to keep us in — didn't they?''

> She turned again toward Mrs. Ansley, but the latter had reached a delicate point in her knitting. ''One, two, three — slip two; yes, they must have been,'' she assented, without looking up.

Alida Slade's reaction to this is noteworthy:

> Mrs. Slade's eyes rested on [Grace] with a deepened attention. ''She can knit — in the face of *this*!''

Alida's palpable annoyance suggests that Grace's knitting is more than just an evasion tactic: those needles are effective psychological weapons against a woman who is deliberately tormenting her for having once loved Delphin Slade. In fine, the fact that Grace knits under duress indicates that she is vastly different from the pale, cringing matron of the story's opening paragraphs.

As the strength of character of which the knitting is an emblem becomes more insistent, Grace gradually begins to rely less upon it. Alida's ''hardly audible laugh'' over Grace's imagined use of drab Jenny as a foil for lovely Barbara causes Grace, for the first time, literally to drop her knitting. Her '''Yes —?''' is virtually an offer of an open confrontation, and Alida seems to back down: '''I — oh, nothing'''; but Alida's painful questioning of how the ''exemplary'' Ansleys could have produced the exquisite Barbara is momentarily too much for Grace: ''Mrs. Ansley's hands lay inert across her needles. She looked straight out at the great accumulated wreckage of passion and splendor at her feet''. Instinctively, Grace then attempts

to regain her composure by knitting — an act which Alida ironically misinterprets:

> Mrs. Ansley had resumed her knitting. One might almost have imagined (if one had known her less well, Mrs. Slade reflected) that, for her also, too many memories rose from the lengthening shadows of those august ruins. But no; she was simply absorbed in her work.

The temporarily thwarted Alida accelerates the process of steering the conversation to the winter evening twenty-five years earlier when the letter brought Grace to the Coliseum; and it is the fact that Alida can '''repeat every word of the letter''' which causes Grace to stand up: ''Her bag, her knitting and gloves, slid in a panic-stricken heap to the ground''. To a certain extent, Grace's mental state (panic) is being projected onto the physical objects with which she has been associated throughout the story; but more importantly, her anxiety — like her knitting — is falling away. Alida Slade is frankly stunned by Grace's emotional strength: ''Mrs. Ansley met the challenge with an unexpected composure''; ''' I shouldn't have thought she had herself so well in hand,' Mrs. Slade reflected, almost resentfully''. For the first time in the story, Alida is at the disadvantage, waiting ''nervously for another word or movement,'' and Grace's revelation that she had indeed met Delphin at the Coliseum causes Alida to cover her face with her hands — just as Grace had once hid behind her knitting. As the story closes, Grace realizes she has the upper hand, having not only slept with Delphin, but also given birth to the daughter whom Alida so covets. Grace's newly dominant status is signified by changed body language (previously, Alida always stood above — and looked down upon — Grace; now, Grace ''began to move ahead of Mrs. Slade'' toward the stairway; but more importantly, Grace is no longer associated with knitting. She departs the restaurant terrace apparently without bothering to pick up her dropped knitting materials. Further, she wraps her throat in a scarf — not a knitted scarf, but one of sensuous fur. And as a subtle underscoring of the reversal of the two women's roles, it is the defeated Alida who picks up her hand-bag — presumably to do some knitting (of the usual, mundane sort) of her own.

In its way, the act of knitting is as vital to ''Roman Fever'' as is, say, the pickle dish to *Ethan Frome*. That so seemingly benign an activity can be utilized in so provocative a fashion is indicative of Wharton's particular interest in technique — ''an interest which makes ... her shorter pieces of fiction suggestive to the reader who cares, as she did, about the processes of art.'' Far from being ''a very light little comedy,'' ''Roman Fever'' is a complex work of art, richly deserving serious critical attention.

Source: Alice Hall Petry, ''A Twist of Crimson Silk: Edith Wharton's 'Roman Fever,''' in *Studies in Short Fiction*, Vol. 24, No. 2, Spring, 1987, pp. 163–6.

Sources

Butcher, Fanny. A review of *The World Over,* in the *Chicago Daily Tribune*, April 25, 1936, p. 10.

Goodman, Susan. *Edith Wharton's Women*, Hanover, N.H.: University Press of New England, 1990.

Hutchinson, Percy. A review of *The World Over*, in the *New York Times*, April 26, 1936, p. 6.

Lewis, R. W. B. *Edith Wharton, A Biography,* New York: Harper & Row, 1975.

McDowell, Margaret B. *Edith Wharton,* Boston: Twayne Publishers, 1991.

Petry, Alice Hall. ''A Twist of Crimson Silk: Edith Wharton's 'Roman Fever,''' in *Studies in Short Fiction*, Vol. 24, No. 2, 1987, pp. 163-166.

Review of *The World Over*, in *Punch*, May 6, 1936, p. 130.

Wharton, Edith. *The Collected Short Stories of Edith Wharton*, edited and introduced by R. W. B. Lewis, New York: Charles Scribner's Sons, 1968.

Further Reading

Bloom, Harold, ed. *Edith Wharton*, New York: Chelsea House, 1986.
    A collection of critical essays on the works of Wharton.

Dwight, Eleanor. *Edith Wharton, An Extraordinary Life*, New York: Harry N. Abrams, 1994.
    An overview of the life and times of Wharton. Includes personal correspondence and photographs.

Lewis, R. W. B. *Edith Wharton, A Biography*, New York: Harper & Row, 1975.
    A comprehensive work about the life and literature of Wharton.

McDowell, Margaret B. *Edith Wharton*, Boston: Twayne Publishers, 1991.
    A critical overview of Wharton's writing.

Nevius, Blake. *Edith Wharton: A Study of Her Fiction*, Berkeley: University of California Press, 1953.
    Discounts prevailing critical thought and presents insightful criticism of Wharton's work.

Wharton, Edith. *Collected Letters of Edith Wharton*, edited by R. W. B. Lewis and Nancy Lewis, New York: Scribner's, 1989.
    Collection of 400 annotated Wharton's letters.

Wolff, Cynthia Griffin. *A Feast of Words: The Triumph of Edith Wharton*, New York: Oxford University Press, 1977.
    Presents a psychological biography of Wharton, as well as criticism.

The Stone Boy

Gina Berriault

1957

First published in *Mademoiselle* in 1957, Gina Berriault's "The Stone Boy" catapulted its author to national fame after it was made into a movie in 1984. Even before this widespread recognition, "The Stone Boy"—which was included in the author's first collection of short stories, *The Mistress, and Other Stories* (1965)—had helped to solidify Berriault's reputation as a writer concerned with the serious issues of the human condition. Despite acclaim from prominent reviewers as well as other American writers such as Andre Dubus, who called Berriault "a splendid and unheralded writer," Berriault has not won the attention of a wide body of readers. Molly McQuade expressed regret in the *Chicago Tribune Book World* that Berriault's work "has not met with a splashy success or even with the sustained and sustaining respect that it deserves."

Readers who do take note of "The Stone Boy," however, are rewarded with an accomplished yet compact story filled with complex human emotions and relationships. Set on a small family farm, "The Stone Boy" tells the story of nine-year-old Arnold who accidentally and fatally shoots his older brother. When Arnold does not respond to this event emotionally, his family assumes that he must be some sort of "monster." As the story unfolds, Arnold, thus isolated from those who are closest to him, turns himself into the image that his family now holds of him. The story demonstrates the immeasurable, almost insurmountable, effect that

other people's opinions have on the self-perception of people, especially younger people. It also raises socially important questions about how and why children develop into the adults they become.

Author Biography

Berriault was born on New Year's Day in 1926 in Long Beach, California, to a Russian Jewish immigrant couple. Berriault's father worked as a marble cutter and later as a writer, but he was not able to find steady work, and the family lived under precarious financial circumstances. Berriault's mother lost her sight while Berriault was a teenager, which Berriault later said influenced her writing. Berriault has spent much of her life in California, the setting for many of her works of fiction.

As a child, Berriault was an avid reader, a self-described "restless spirit" who felt "confined in a classroom and yearning to be out and roaming, either in the landscape or in her own imagination." Reading satisfied this restlessness, and she began to write original stories on her father's old typewriter when she was in elementary school. She also found herself drawn to drama and art. Although one of her high school teachers offered her the opportunity to attend drama school for free, after her father's death, Berriault made the decision to forgo her schooling to help support her family, working as a clerk, waitress, and reporter.

Berriault continued to write in her spare time, and she first came to the notice of critics in 1958, when seven of her stories were collected in a volume called *Short Story*. Berriault then won a writer's fellowship from the Centro Mexicano de Escritos in Mexico City, Mexico, and she moved there in 1963. Three years later, she received an appointment as a scholar at the Radcliffe Institute for Independent Study. Throughout the 1960s, Berriault supported herself through these academic appointments as well as by writing articles for *Esquire* magazine. Berriault has also taught creative writing at San Francisco State University and Ohio University.

Throughout her career, Berriault has produced three collections of short stories, four novels, and a screenplay adapted from "The Stone Boy." Despite her lengthy and successful career, Berriault

has led a very private life. She claims to make the acquaintance of no critics, is not a member of any writing societies, and refuses to share any anecdotes about her life. Her work, however, has drawn her into public view, particularly after *Women in Their Beds*, published in 1996, won the Book Critics Circle Award for fiction and the PEN/Faulkner Award the following year.

Plot Summary

One morning nine-year-old Arnold wakes up early in order to go pick peas in the garden with his older brother Eugie. Despite the ring of the alarm clock, Eugie continues to sleep, and Arnold feels uncomfortable, as if he—fully awake and dressed—is placed unexpectedly in the superior position. Arnold wakes his brother and goes downstairs. He takes his rifle from the rack with the expectation of going duck shooting. Eugie comes downstairs, too, reminds Arnold that it isn't duck season. Then the two boys leave the house.

They come to the wire fence that divides the fields from the lake. Eugie passes through the fence first. As Arnold goes between the wires, his gun catches. He jerks at it to free it, and it fires. Arnold feels foolish, expecting his brother to make fun of him for this mistake. Instead, he finds his brother lying on the ground. Arnold sees a spot of blood at the back of his neck. After trying unsuccessfully to rouse Eugie, Arnold sets to work picking peas.

When the sun has fully risen, Arnold returns to the house, where his mother, father, and sister are all up and going about their day. He tells them that Eugie is dead. At first they don't believe him, but they go down to the lake and find the body. While family and the undertaker gather at the house, Arnold retreats to the barn.

Later that day, Arnold goes with his father and his Uncle Andy into town, to the sheriff's office. The sheriff questions the boy. He wants to know if the two brothers got along well, and Arnold's father says he believe they did. Then he wants to know why Arnold did not report the shooting immediately, but Arnold has no answer. Finally, the sheriff concludes that Arnold is either stupid or a boy with no feelings, but he believes in the latter. The sheriff sends the family home. Arnold realizes that his

Gina Berriault

uncle concurs with the sheriff's assessment of him: he is a cruel boy who cared nothing for his brother.

After a silent supper, the family's neighbors come to visit. In order to not attract attention to himself, Arnold remains in the room with the men, listening to them tell stories about Eugie. Uncle Andy shares the sheriff's words with the men, and they talk about Arnold as if he wasn not even there. After all the men have left, Arnold goes to bed, feeling nothing, not even grief.

Arnold wakens later that night. He goes to his parents' room, wanting his mother to hold him while he tells her about the terror he felt as he knelt alongside Eugie. When he knocks on the door, however, his mother turns him away. She asks, "Is night when you get afraid?" Arnold is shocked. He also suddenly realizes he is naked and feels ashamed.

The next morning at breakfast, Arnold's sister attempts to ignore him, but their father makes clear that such behavior will not be tolerated. Arnold understands that his parents are acknowledging his existence. But he has already taken the sheriff's words to heart. When his mother asks why he knocked on the door last night, he merely answers, "I didn't want nothing." He goes out of the house to get a lost calf, scared at his own words.

Characters

Andy

Uncle Andy is the mother's brother. He has a special fondness for Eugie because the boy resembled him. After Eugie's death, Andy immediately embraces the sheriff's interpretation of Arnold: that he is essentially a cold, cruel boy who cares nothing for his brother. It is also Andy who brings up this interpretation in front of the neighbor men who come to visit the family in the evening. He explains the sheriff's idea as if it is an irrefutable fact, helping to cement its validity in Arnold's mind.

Uncle Andy

See Andy

Arnold

Nine-year-old Arnold is the protagonist of the story. Arnold is the youngest child of the family and feels that he is in a subordinate position to his older brother Eugie. Because of this power imbalance, Arnold both looks up to and dislikes Eugie. Arnold's role within the family is not made clear in the story, but clearly he defines himself, his growth, and his actions in terms of Eugie.

After Arnold kills Eugie, he has no one against whom to measure himself any longer. He does not know how to react to his family, and he allows other people—particularly the sheriff and his Uncle Andy—to impose their view of him and his actions on his self-perception. By the end of the story, Arnold has tacitly accepted their judgment and has determined to turn himself into what they see him as. To them, he is a "reasonable" killer, one who is detached from his feelings and the hurt he inflicts on others, and certainly a boy who will only become more detached and more dangerous as time progresses.

Eugene

See Eugie

Eugie

In his brother Arnold's eyes, 15-year-old Eugie is almost a godlike creature, one who possesses beauty, strength, and also the knowledge of his superiority. Part of Arnold's perception of Eugie stems from Eugie being the oldest child and an obvious help on the family farm. Eugie, however, appears to be a normal teenager, self-absorbed and sure of his power over those who are younger. His last words show that he treats Arnold as many older brothers would treat their younger siblings. For example, Eugie will fetch any ducks they shoot from the lake because, as he tells Arnold, "You'd drown 'fore you got to it, them legs of yours are so puny." At the same time as he degrades Arnold, Eugie also looks out for him and spends time with him.

Father

The boys' father is a taciturn man who shows little reaction to Eugie's death or to the sheriff's assessment of Arnold's character. He does not defend Arnold to the sheriff or to Uncle Andy and even allows his brother-in-law to share the sheriff's beliefs with all their neighbors. The morning after the shooting he attempts to acknowledge Arnold as the boy he is, not the monster he has been dubbed, but by this time Arnold has already accepted the earlier judgment.

Mother

The boys' mother displays an immediate emotional reaction on learning of Eugie's death, but then retreats into her own grief. The day that Eugie dies she ignores Arnold, even "curving her fingers over her eyes so as not to see him." That evening she repels Arnold when he attempts to find solace and share his great terror and sadness about what he has done. This action helps Arnold to accept his new role as a heartless monster, despite his mother's attempts to reach out to him the following morning.

Nora

Nora is the middle child in the family. The morning following Eugie's death, she is the only one who continues to ignore Arnold. Nora's parents, however, clearly demonstrate that such behavior is not to be tolerated.

Sheriff

The sheriff questions Arnold to find out the details of the shooting and to determine if it was an accident or deliberate. He gives only two possible explanations for Arnold's immediate reaction, or lack thereof, to Eugie's death. To the sheriff, Arnold is either stupid or simply feels nothing. He also prophesies a grim future for Arnold, expecting that this "heartless" boy will be involved in, and most likely be the catalyst for, further violence.

Media Adaptations

- "The Stone Boy" was adapted into a movie by 20th-Century Fox in 1984. Berriault wrote the screenplay.

Themes

Death

Death is one of the foremost themes in "The Stone Boy." It is expressed literally in Eugie's death, but this accident brings about a series of metaphoric deaths. For Arnold, Eugie's death represents not only the physical loss of his brother but also of his male ideal. Eugie's loss means that Arnold no longer has a role model upon which to base his own life. The death of Eugie means the death of the young man that Arnold would have become.

By the end of the story, Arnold undergoes a metaphoric death of his own. As he realizes that his family has no faith in him and seems only to want to shut him out, he withdraws, not simply from his family, but from humanity in general. In essence, by the end of the story, Arnold has lost his very soul. The theme also can be found in examination of the family itself; by the time the story concludes, the family truly no longer exists. Instead, each member functions apart from the others.

Failure

As a number of critics have pointed out, much of Berriault's fiction centers on how humans fail one another. As Molly McQuade wrote in *Chicago Tribune Book World*, "Every so-called fault deforming a character seems to link up with another fault in someone else, complicating and completing the moral neighborhood they share." In Arnold's eyes, his family has failed him by refusing to forgive his reaction to Eugie's death, however out of place they may feel it to have been. This failure is

Topics for Further Study

- The sheriff suggested only two possible explanations for Arnold's behavior following the death of his brother. Do you think there are other possible explanations? What are they? Do you think Arnold's actions demonstrate a psychological disability on Arnold's part?

- In the 1990s, the rise of teen violence has alarmed many Americans. Investigate how teen violence has affected American society over the decades since the 1950s. Do you think teen violence has worsened? If so, what factors have attributed to this rise?

- The sheriff's description of Arnold, as a person who "don't feel nothing," describes sociopaths. Investigate sociopathic behavior and then determine whether or not you believe Arnold to be a sociopath.

- The 1950s, when this story was written, is generally regarded as a period epitomized by happy families, economic prosperity, and strong moral values. How do you think typical readers of the 1950s and 1960s might have reacted to the story?

- Family farms in the United States have been on a decline for most of the 20th century. Conduct research on reasons for this decline and the effect it has had on farming families.

---

seen nowhere so clearly as when Arnold's mother turns him away in his moment of need. In refusing to take on crucial parental roles—those of nurturer and teacher—she demonstrates a serious maternal failure. Conversely, in his family's eyes, Arnold has failed in not reacting to Eugie's death in a manner they find appropriate. This failure of the family to experience their grief and pain together will only perpetuate further miscommunication and alienation. Nor is the community guiltless in the tragedy. In accepting Andy's analysis of Arnold's action, which derive from the sheriff—an authority figure who stands outside of the community—the neighboring farmers who form the backbone of the community solidify Arnold's isolation and reinforce the inability of the family members to help one another.

Identity

The theme of identity plays a crucial role in "The Stone Boy." Arnold undergoes a drastic transformation in self-perception and identity based on the opinions of the people around him. At the beginning of the story, Arnold demonstrates his unease at being in any way superior to Eugie, even if this only manifests itself through his ability to wake up earlier than his brother. As the story unfolds, the reason for Arnold's discomfort becomes clear; he sees and defines himself in comparison to Eugie. Arnold believes Eugie to be the ideal young man—tall, attractive, and fit; in contrast, Arnold is small for his age and has straight hair. He wonders if he will ever become like Eugie. Such a stunted self-image makes it impossible for Arnold to process these new feelings of superiority.

By the end of the story, Arnold has transformed himself into the "stone boy" referred to in the title. Yet, he does not do so because he feels himself unable to experience emotions and share feelings; he does so because he realizes that this is how his family now views him. Thus Arnold's new identity is not self-imposed but placed upon him by the perceptions of others. Although Arnold accepts this identity, he does not embrace it; in fact, he even fears it. Yet, he is so accustomed to seeing himself through the eyes of others that he makes no effort to negate this identity and carve out a new one, an identity that feels comfortable to him and aptly reflects his interior self. Instead, Arnold will only become what others see in him.

Violence

In "The Stone Boy," Berriault takes a brutal action and renders it, in her writing, in fairly mild

---

terms. She likens Eugie in his death throes to a man climbing, and the only truly discomfiting detail in the scene is Arnold's comparison of Eugie's blood dripping from the bullet hole to a parasite. Despite this depiction, the hint of violence prevails throughout the story, even to the extent that some reviewers believed that Arnold willfully killed his brother; in essence, they have sided with the sheriff, not Arnold.

The theme of violence, however, is far more disquieting in its mere threat. As the sheriff pronounces judgment on Arnold, defining him as a cold-blooded, merciless monster, everyone present feels the chill of his words. The sheriff's next words prophesize a grim future for Arnold. When Uncle Andy wonders that the sheriff does not want to keep Arnold in custody, the sheriff answers, ''Not now. . . . Maybe in a few years.'' With these sentences, the sheriff foresees for Arnold a continuing future of violent actions against others.

Style

Point of View

''The Stone Boy'' is told from a third-person, limited point of view; everything is filtered through Arnold's eyes and senses, and only his thoughts are shared. Readers can understand other characters' feelings only through their words and actions, but are privy to Arnold's innermost feelings. Early in the story, such use of point of view makes clear Arnold's love/hate relationship with his brother. Although Arnold is in awe of his brother, the author uses such terms as *stupidly* and *mocking* to describe Eugie, all of which explain Arnold's complex feelings toward Eugie. After Eugie's death, however, Arnold is so distant from his own emotions that in actuality, the reader learns very little about what Arnold thinks about Eugie's death and his role in it. Arnold does reveal, toward the end of the story, that he felt terror as he knelt beside his brother and that his newly self-imposed separation from his parents scares him deeply.

Setting

Although Berriault's never designates the exact location of ''The Stone Boy,'' the farm setting has a strong bearing on the drama that unfolds. Arnold's family functions within an agricultural community,

one that is both isolated and dependent on the other members. Arnold's isolation from his family is reinforced through the farm's physical isolation from neighboring farms. The distance that Arnold and Eugie travel to the lake—down the slope, through the wheat field, and into the marshy pasture—reflects the distance that Arnold will have traveled away from his family by the end of the story. The county seat, Corinth, which is located nine miles from the farm, serves as a central meetingplace for the community and for the action of the story. Corinth is the place where Arnold receives judgement on his actions and where he first comes to accept this pronouncement.

Imagery and Metaphor

The most arresting image in ''The Stone Boy'' is that of Arnold creeping naked through the house. The story opens with Arnold pulling overalls and a sweater over his unclothed body. At this time, he feels no particular emotion attached to this natural state of undress. On the night of Eugie's death, however, Arnold ventures downstairs to his parents' bedroom, again naked. After he is turned away by his mother, Arnold suddenly becomes aware of his naked body. He feels shame at being in such a state, representing his shame both at wanting his mother and at being rejected by her. He internalizes this shame, realizing the need to protect himself from his parents. Thus he metaphorically clothes himself. He will no longer allow anyone to view him naked, that is, as a person in need of comfort, a person willing to let his guard down and let others see what he is really like.

The most important metaphor of the story is the one implied by the title itself. By the end of the story, Arnold has metaphorically turned into stone. He has become an inhuman creature; no trace of feelings nor any betrayal of emotions will escape from him.

Style

The style of writing employed in ''The Stone Boy'' is direct and realistic. There is little extraneous description or verbiage for scenes or actions. In addition, all the characters in the story act matter-of-factly. Arnold acts straightforwardly in completing the job he set out to accomplish—picking the peas. The family has accepts without question the sheriff's judgment that there is something fundamentally wrong with Arnold. Similarly, Arnold accepts without question the judgment of the sheriff and of his family about his character.

Historical Context

The Decline of the American Farm Family

In the early years of the United States, farming was the main economic activity of Americans. Most farms were self-sufficient and owned by single families who lived on and ran the farm. In 1900 the average family farm was located half a mile away from its nearest neighbor, which served to isolate farm families. However, farm families formed communities by exchanging labor, attending church, and sending their children to schools.

Beginning in the 1920s, however, the number of farms in the United States began to dwindle. In 1930 a little over 30 million Americans lived on farms. In 1950 the farm population had shrunk to around 23 million, and by 1960, only a few years after Berriault wrote ''The Stone Boy,'' only about 15.6 million Americans still lived on farms. The decade also brought many changes to the way farms were run. In 1953 President Dwight Eisenhower cut government subsidies to farms. As well, throughout the decade, automation began to be introduced on farms. While the use of new machinery boosted production, it effectively reduced the labor force, which partially accounts for the drop in farm population. Overall, the number of farm jobs decreased.

The farm population also decreased throughout the 1950s and 1960s as increasing numbers of Americans around the country decided to move to suburbs and planned communities. By 1960, 100 million Americans—one third of the total population—lived in the suburbs. This flight affected many rural farm areas. For instance, in the 1950s, the Midwest, where many of the nation's farms have traditionally been located, experienced lower population gains than many other parts of the country. Life in rural areas often lagged behind urban or suburban life. In 1957 about half of the nation's poor lived in rural areas; these residents suffered from poor nutrition and health care. By 1960 the American farm family's way of life was on the decline and anomalous to most members of society.

Social Conformity and Rebellion

The 1950s saw the rise of the value placed on social conformity. Americans, particularly those who lived in the suburbs, had similar houses, cars, activities, and even life goals. Teenagers were not immune from this conformity, and many observers dubbed middle-class youth the silent generation because they did not protest against societal demands. Some teenagers, however, did question society and even rebel. Rock 'n' roll music became the anthem of teenagers in the 1950s. Many parents disliked rock 'n' roll, believing that it contributed to juvenile delinquency and immorality. Movies of the decade, such as *Rebel Without a Cause* and *The Wild One*, portrayed young men who felt frustrated with life in general. They were not angry at any one person or thing but were angry at society. In these movies, the heroes often acted out their antisocial behavior by skipping school or committing misdemeanors. Skirting on the edge of violence and danger, such movies raised the possibility of bad things happening in what many adults viewed as an orderly world.

The Beatniks

In the mid-1950s, a new artistic movement emerged. The Beatniks, or Beats, were a small group of writers who challenged the social conformity that ran rampant. They cared little for material goods, but instead searched for a higher consciousness. In their work, Beatnik writers raged against middle-class conventions. They created their work free from the impositions of formal structure, plot conventions, and planning—much in the same way they lived their lives. One of the best-known Beat works was Jack Kerouac's *On the Road*, which was published in 1957, the same year as ''The Stone Boy.'' This novel follows its heroes as they travel around the country, searching for real experiences and values. It celebrates the search for individual identity.

Critical Overview

Although Berriault's career had spanned almost four decades and led to the creation of short stories

Compare & Contrast

- **1960:** The United States had close to 4 million farms, which totaled around 990 million acres. The average farm had assets worth almost $53,000 and earned just under $10,000 per year. Around 15.5 million Americans lived on farms.

  1990: There were only a little over 2 million farms in operation in the United States, also totaling around 990 million acres. The average farm had assets worth around $460,000 and earned a little over $91,000 per year. Just under 5 million Americans lived on farms.

- **1960:** 1,200 accidental shooting deaths occurred in American homes. Just over 51 percent of polled Americans said they had a gun in the house.

  1990s: 800 accidental shooting deaths occurred in American homes in 1995. In 1991, 46 percent of polled Americans had a gun in the house. Of the American households with guns, 40 percent also had children in the house.

- **1950:** There are an estimated 54 million rifles, shotguns, and handguns in the United States. Around 2,399,000 firearms are available for sale.

  1990: There are an estimated 201 million firearms in the United States. Around 5,122,000 are available for sale.

- **1965:** Less than five 15 year olds per 100,000 commit murder.

  1992: Ten 15 year olds per 100,000 commit murder. Studies show that most high school students either carry or have carried illegal guns or can get them easily. As many as 1 in 20 students had brought their guns to school.

---

as well as novels, Berriault's work has never received a great deal of critical attention. Nonetheless, her fiction is generally recognized as powerful, realistic, and unsentimental, often focusing on a crisis situation in which characters are unable to break free from their loneliness and despair. Julia B. Boken, writing in the *Dictionary of Literary Biography*, compares Berriault's fiction to that of Russian writers Leo Tolstoy, Fyodyor Dostoyevsky, and Anton Chekov because of her "probing [of] the human psyche."

"The Stone Boy" is one of Berriault's better known and frequently anthologized pieces of short fiction. It first appeared in *Mademoiselle* in 1957, and eight years later it was included in Berriault's first collection of short stories, *The Mistress, and Other Stories*. It was also included in Berriault's next published collection, *The Infinite Passion of Expectations: Twenty-Five Stories*, which appeared in 1982. Andre Dubus, himself a noted American short story writer, called this collection "the best book of short stories by a living American author."

Berriault chose to preface *The Mistress, and Other Stories* with a quote from the writer Jose Ortega y Gasset: "Every life is more or less a ruin among whose debris we have to discover what the person ought to have been." The stories in the book echo this sense of desolation. As Dorrie Pagones described Berriault's characters in the *Saturday Review*: "No one behaves as he should, and even supposing anyone did, it is quite clear, as the title of one story puts it, that 'All Attempts Will End in Failure.'"

In discussing young Arnold, his killing of his brother, and his family's reaction to these unfortunate events, many reviewers have evaluated the culpability of the characters, that is, whose life has been ruined and who has failed whom. Pagones saw the parents as having failed their child, and she compares this story to Berriault's "The Bystander," in which the child instead fails the parents. *New York Times* writer Charles Poore, however, saw Arnold's actions as akin to homicide. In his words, "Murder, Miss Berriault shows us, has many forms

Two young boys with a rifle, a scene perhaps typical of rural America earlier in the twentieth century.

and devices. It is seemingly explicit in ''The Stone Boy,'' where a life ends in a shooting accident. How much of an accident was it? we are left to ask. At that point, the explicit and the implicit merge in shadows.''

Other reviewers did not see the incident as so ambiguous and chose instead to focus on other aspects of the story. For instance, Richard Kostelanetz, in the *New York Times Book Review*, remarked that Arnold expressed no feelings of remorse about the death of his brother but feels ''considerable embarrassment at being caught na-

ked.'' Several years after this first round of reviews and criticism, Edith Milton revisited ''The Stone Boy'' when she discussed *The Infinite Passion of Expectation* for the *New York Times Book Review*. She followed up on Kostelanetz's theme, noting that many of Berriault's characters experience such emotional ambiguity that they find themselves paralyzed, as does Arnold, who becomes numbed.

Overall discussion of Berriault's stories tends to focus on her evaluation and understanding of the human psyche, particularly on the psychological and emotional pain and distance that her characters experience. Some critics, however, have asserted that while Berriault is adept at presenting complex feelings, her writing style sometimes disappoints. They charge that her writing can be too pessimistic, precise, and intellectual. Kostelanetz believed that her ''prosaic'' and ''clumsy'' style detracted from her impressive knowledge of human emotions and motivations. For the majority of critics, however, her range of characters, convincing characterization, and understanding of humanity outweighs any stylistic difficulties with her writing. As Boken noted, Berriault's ''themes usually focus on the pain that comes from inevitable loss, . . . Through her keen insight, imaginative art, and finely honed craft, Berriault creates a world of flawed people.''

Berriault's most recent book of short stories, *Women in Their Beds*, won the 1997 Book Critics Circle Award for fiction and the PEN/Faulkner Award that same year. These awards as well as genuine admiration for Berriault's work have led some contemporary critics to believe that Berriault's short fiction will become increasingly appreciated and influential. As Gary Amdahl stated, Berriault, ''having written so beautifully and so consistently for nearly forty years, ought to be as familiar to us as Toni Morrison and John Updike.''

Criticism

Cynthia Bily

Bily teaches English at Adrian College in Adrian, Michigan. In the following essay, she discusses experiences of grief in ''The Stone Boy.''

When nine-year-old Arnold realizes that he has accidentally shot his brother Eugene to death in ''The Stone Boy,'' his response seems strange: rather than running back home for help, he continues on to the garden as the brothers had intended to do together, and picks half a tub of peas—his share of the job. Only when he has finished the picking does he return home, and only when his father speaks to him does he tell his parents the awful truth: ''Eugie's dead.'' For the rest of the story, as the people around Arnold try to come to terms with what has happened, the fact of Eugie's death seems less troublesome to them than Arnold's first re-

What Do I Read Next?

- *The Butcher Boy* (1992) by Irish writer Patrick McCabe chronicles the descent of a neglected boy as he plunges deeper into madness and violence.

- The short story ''Walking Out'' (1980) by David Quammen tells the gripping story of a father-son hunting trip that goes awry.

- Gina Berriault's second novel, *Conference of Victims* (1962, 1985), describes the effects a man's suicide has on his closest family members.

- Fyodor Dostoevsky's classic novel *Crime and Punishment* (1911) explores the psychological effects of murder.

- Andre Dubus' short story ''The Fat Girl'' (1988) tells of a girl who withdraws from the world through food.

- *Women in Their Beds* by Gina Berriault (1996) includes some of the author's finest works from her 40-year career as well as new short stories.

- Flannery O'Connor's short story ''Good Country People'' (1955) tells about how the actions of a merciless man affects a farm family.

sponse. They might come to forgive him for killing his brother—after all, it was an accident—but they cannot forgive him for not appearing sorrier about it.

Arnold realizes, when his father and Uncle Andy ask him about the accident, that it is his own response that is so troubling to the adults. ''When they had asked him why he hadn't run back to the house to tell his parents, he had had no answer—all he could say was that he had gone down into the garden to pick the peas. His father had stared at him in a pale, puzzled way, and it was then he had felt his father and the others set their cold, turbulent silence against him.'' That night, when the neighbors come to comfort the family and share memories of Eugie, Arnold sits silently among them, and the men notice and taunt him. ''Not a tear in his eye.'' ''He don't

> As child psychologists
> and pediatricians have
> pointed out in recent decades,
> children manage grief in
> their own predictable ways."

give a hoot, is that how it goes?'' ''If your brother is shot dead, he's shot dead. What's the use of gettin' emotional about it? The thing to do is go down to the garden and pick peas. Am I right?''

Their reaction to Arnold's reaction causes him to question it himself. When he tells the story to the sheriff, this time ''it seemed odd now that he had not run back to the house and wakened his father, but he could not remember why he had not.'' With a child's trust in the adults around him, he accepts their judgment about him. ''Andy and his father and the sheriff had discovered what made him go down into the garden. It was because he was cruel, the sheriff said, and didn't care about his brother.''

But surely the adults, confused by their grief, are wrong about Arnold. Arnold, after all, is only a young boy. The narrator emphasizes his youth in the story's beginning, revealing in the third sentence that ''he was nine, six years younger than Eugie,'' and presenting a striking, peculiar image soon thereafter: as Arnold tries to wake Eugie and the boys wrestle, ''all in an instant, he was lying on his back under the covers with only his face showing, like a baby.'' The age comparisons and the baby image serve to reinforce the boys comparative positions. Arnold is younger, ''it was he who was subordinate,'' and Eugie is older, in command, and literally ''on top.''

As child psychologists and pediatricians have pointed out in recent decades, children manage grief in their own predictable ways. Penelope Leach, for example, in *Your Growing Child*, explains that ''children's grief does not always show itself in ways adults approve or can even recognize. Tears, loss of appetite, and disturbed sleep, almost universal in mourning adults, may be almost or completely absent in a grief-stricken child whose distress may show up in . . . a stalwart refusal to admit to feeling anything at all.'' Arnold demonstrates this clearly,

particularly when he goes to bed that first night in the room he previously shared with his brother. ''He felt nothing, not any grief. There was only the same immense silence and crawling inside of him, the way the house and fields must feel under a merciless sun.''

The mistake the adults make is in forgetting that Arnold is a child. Uncle Andy, who doted on Eugie, taunts Arnold by pointing out to the other men, ''If we d've shot our brother, we d've come runnin' back to the house, cryin' like a baby.'' But as Leach points out, that kind of response to grief is more typical of adults than of children. Andy is a grown man, and what he would have done does not help explain what a child should have done. The sheriff points out to Arnold's father, ''It's come to my notice that the most reasonable guys are mean ones. They don't feel nothing.'' But Arnold is not one of the ''guys'' the sheriff has come across in his duties. He is not a hardened criminal, but a little boy.

Arnold's behavior rings true to anyone who spends time observing children, or who can remember what it was like to be a child. When Arnold realizes what he has done, his first action is to pick the half a tub of peas he was sent for. Isn't it typical for a child to try to make up for a bad deed by making a display of doing his chores? After he has told his parents that Eugie is dead, he runs out to the barn to hide in the loft—again, very typical behavior. (In the often-told family legend about the time I kicked in the screen door, I hide out in the attic until my parents come home and find me.) Andy may be right about how he would respond to a terrible accident, but he shows no understanding of Arnold's predictable behavior.

The neighbors seem to want Arnold to feel guilty, and to see him punished. Orion, who is older than Eugie and married, almost brags when he claims, ''If I'd of done what he done, Pa would've hung my pelt by the side of that big coyote's in the barn.'' The question of Arnold's guilt and feelings of guilt has drawn the attention of reviewers, some of whom believe that Arnold—consciously or subconsciously—killed Eugie on purpose because he was jealous of his older brother's power and status. The sheriff raises the issue when he asks whether Arnold and Eugie were ''good friends,'' and whether they ever quarreled. I cannot find any hint of Arnold intending to cause harm in the description of the accident, but Leach explains that guilt feelings are to be expected in Arnold whether he intended harm or not: ''Most children will feel guilt over any death which is significant to them . . . . Most children find it difficult to sort out feelings from actions and may believe, or half-believe, that the anger they felt on the morning of the death actually caused or contributed to it. Brothers and sisters often wish each other dead—and then find themselves apparently monstrously all-powerful.''

Through all of the neighbors' and relatives' sly accusing, Arnold's parents remain silent. They do not say anything against Arnold, but neither do they speak up for him. Most importantly, they do not speak to him. On the ride to the sheriff's office, Arnold sits between his father and his uncle. ''No one spoke.'' Arnold avoids his family for the rest of the day, but joins them again at dinner time. Again, ''no one spoke at supper, and his mother, who sat next to him, leaned her head in her hand all through the meal, curving her fingers over her eyes so as not to see him.'' In the story's most heartbreaking scene, when Arnold goes downstairs to see his mother, ''hoping to dig his head into her blankets and tell her about the terror he had felt when he had knelt beside his brother,'' she will not even let him enter her room. She rejects him, sends him back to bed, and he is left only with an insistent silence: ''silently, he left the door and for a stricken moment stood by the rocker. Outside everything was still. The fences, the shocks of wheat seen through the window before him were so still it was as if they moved and breathed in the daytime and had fallen silent with the lateness of the hour.''

The image of the nine-year-old boy standing in the dark, utterly alone and ''unpardonable,'' is painful. Arnold's reaching for his mother, his wish to ''clasp her in his arms and pommel her breasts with his head. grieving with her for Eugene,'' is instinctive, and her rejection seems cruel. But psychology points out that her response, too, is natural and predictable. Leach cautions parents that ''it is easy to be so lost in personal grief that the child's is underestimated. This is especially liable to happen when it is a brother or sister who dies. Parents feel themselves the principal mourners and those around them do too. The grief of brothers and sisters is often underestimated; sometimes they are openly pushed out of the way.'' Arnold's mother fails him, but she is not cruel—at least not intentionally. Like Arnold, she is doing her best to bear an unbearable grief.

Although ''The Stone Boy'' depicts characters who have failed themselves and each other, Berriault does not condemn them for their failures. She

presents a clear and unfaltering narration of painful events, and challenges the reader to confront the images directly, but she does not judge. This is a story, she seems to say, of a terrible grief and the damage is does to a family. There are no villains, and no heroes—just ordinary people struggling with an extraordinary circumstance. As she explains in a *Literary Review* interview with Bonnie Lyons and Bill Oliver, ''If there is a recurring theme'' in her work, ''it's an attempt at compassionate understanding. Judgment is the prevalent theme in our society, but it's from fiction we learn compassion and comprehension.''

Source: Cynthia Bily, for *Short Stories for Students*, The Gale Group, 2000.

Liz Brent

Brent has a Ph.D. in American Culture, with a specialization in cinema studies, from the University of Michigan. She is a freelance writer and teaches courses in American cinema. In the following essay, she discusses the imagery of light and darkness in terms of judgment and redemption in ''The Stone Boy.''

The main character in Gina Berriault's ''The Stone Boy'' is a nine-year old boy who, having accidentally shot and killed his older brother with a .22 caliber rifle, suffers from such extreme shock that he is unable to express even the slightest signs of grief. However, although Arnold shows no outward signs of sadness or remorse, his fear of judgment and his yearning for forgiveness are expressed through the story's imagery. Arnold's feelings of guilt and fear of judgment are expressed through references to light, which are suggestive of a godlike presence, both accusatory and redemptive. The stares and looks of the members of his family and community also indicate themes of judgment and guilt, as associated with vision and light. Finally, imagery suggestive of the mother-child relationship implies the possibility of redemption and mercy through the spiritual properties of maternal love and forgiveness.

Arnold's awareness of the properties of light, after he accidentally shoots his brother Eugie, evoke a Christian iconography suggestive of a godlike presence. After accidentally shooting Eugie in the face and killing him in the early hours of the morning, Arnold goes to the garden to pick peas, as he and his brother had originally planned. In a state of shock at this horrible event, Arnold automatically behaves as he normally would. Yet, while Arnold at

> **"**Getting ready for bed that night, Arnold fears both the darkness and the light. Fear of darkness is sometimes associated with fear of one's own conscience, or fear of death.**"**

this point seems to have no consciousness that his brother has been killed, his awareness that the sun has risen is described in language which implies the hand of God upon his back: "It was a warmth on his back, like a large hand laid firmly there, that made him raise his head." At this point, the large warm hand evokes imagery of a forgiving God, who has placed a "warm," comforting or guiding hand on the back of the boy.

Later in the story, however, Arnold, associating vision with light, comes to associate light through the gaze of others with the negative judgment of those around him. Arnold's perception of condemnation in people's gaze is reinforced by his perception of the condemnation implied by silence. When Arnold can only tell the sheriff that his reason for not immediately informing the family of his brother's death was that he had gone to pick peas, Arnold perceives that he has been deemed a guilty man: "it was then he had felt his father and the others set their cold, turbulent silence against him." And it is his father's eyes in particular which seem to condemn him: "Arnold shifted on the bench, his only feeling a small one of compunction imposed by his father's eyes." The sheriff's judgment of Arnold takes on religious implications when he sends Arnold and his father home after questioning: "Then the sheriff lifted his hand like a man taking an oath." From Arnold's perspective, the sheriff's judgment upon him comes in the form of a "oath" before God, proclaiming him guilty. The judgment represented by the sheriff's hand contrasts markedly with the judgment represented by the warmth of the sun as the hand of God.

After leaving the sheriff's office, Arnold, his father and his uncle return to their car. It is at this point that Arnold becomes increasingly aware of the eyes of others bearing down upon him: "Arnold saw that his uncle's eyes had absorbed the knowingness from the sheriff's eyes. Andy and his father and the sheriff had discovered what made him go down into the garden. It was because he was cruel, the sheriff had said, and didn't care about his brother." Because Arnold experiences the gaze of others as a judgment upon him, an affirmation of his guilt, he responds by deferentially avoiding their eyes: "Arnold lowered his eyelids meekly against his uncle's stare." In the light of the accusatory stares of those around him, Arnold attempts to make himself as inconspicuous as possible. When relatives and neighbors stop by his family's house that evening, Arnold is almost paralyzed by the fear of calling attention to himself, "He knew that although they were talking only about Eugie they were thinking of him, and if he got up, if he moved even his foot, they would all be alerted."

Getting ready for bed that night, Arnold fears both the darkness and the light. Fear of darkness is sometimes associated with fear of one's own conscience, or fear of death. Contrary to his usual habits, Arnold waits until the last minute to blow out the light after going to bed that night: "In his room he undressed by lamp light, although he and Eugie had always undressed in the dark, and not until he was lying in his bed did he blow out the flame." But, once in bed, Arnold again associates light with the godlike judgment of a "merciless sun": "He felt nothing, not any grief. There was only the same immense silence and crawling inside of him, the way the house and fields must feel under a merciless sun." When he awakens in the middle of the night and approaches his parents bedroom, in hopes of expressing to his mother his grief over his brother's death, Arnold is met with an implied condemnation by his mother; she responds to his knock by replying: "Go back! Is night when you get afraid?" His mother's reply harshly implies that Arnold is afraid of the night because he is afraid of his own guilty conscience. With this condemnation, she turns him away from the possibility of redemption he seeks in her arms.

Upon being condemned and turned away by his mother, Arnold again fears the light, which is associated with his father's judgment upon him. He sees his father outside in the yard, "his lantern casting a circle of light by his feet." In association with his father's arrival back in the house, "the lantern still lighting his way," Arnold suddenly becomes aware that he is naked. This sudden awareness of his nakedness is associated with the light which his father's lantern is soon to cast upon him. Arnold's nakedness is symbolic of the nakedness of his soul, as if his father's judgment, upon seeing Arnold, would be utterly unforgiving, since: "his nakedness had become unpardonable." Arnold thus wishes to escape the light of his father's judgment: "At once he went back upstairs, fleeing from his father's lantern."

While Arnold fears the light of judgment in the eyes of his father, he conceptualizes forgiveness and redemption in association with that which is maternal: his mother's breast, the pitcher of milk at the breakfast table, the cow with the newborn calf. In knocking at his mother's door at night, Arnold had imagined a scene of confession or begging of forgiveness at his mother's breast, in hopes of a kind of redemption through maternal love: "He had expected her to realize that he wanted to go down on his knees by her bed and tell her that Eugie was dead. She did not know it yet, nobody knew it, and yet she was sitting up in bed, waiting to be told. He had expected her to tell him to come in and allow him to dig his head into her blankets and tell her about the terror he had felt when he had knelt beside his brother. He had come to clasp her in his arms and pommel her breasts with his head, grieving with her for Eugene."

Turned away from this possibility of forgiveness at his mother's breast in the night, Arnold the next morning vows never to ask his parents for anything again. He lowers his eyes deferentially, fearing their accusatory stares: "At breakfast, he kept his eyelids lowered to deny the night." But when his father reminds his sister to pass him the pitcher of milk at breakfast, Arnold is given some hope that he may be welcomed back into the bosom of his family: "Relief rained over his shoulders at the thought that his parents recognized him again." The pitcher of milk is suggestive of the nurturing powers of maternal love and forgiveness, for which Arnold longs. This maternal imagery as a sign of redemption is echoed in Arnold's father's mention of the cow which has gone up the mountain to have its calf. Arnold immediately sets out to retrieve the cow and newborn calf, to "switch the cow down the mountain slowly, and the calf would run at its mother's side." The image of the calf running at its mother's side is evocative of Arnold's desire to be back in his mother's good graces, to regain her maternal affection and nurturing love.

But, while the image of the cow and calf express a sense of hope that Arnold may be granted his mother's forgiveness, the closing lines of the story leave the reader in doubt as to whether or not Arnold will be capable of asking this of his mother, and whether or not his mother will be capable of granting it. At the point when his mother asks what he had wanted from her the night before, Arnold is incapable of telling her: "'I don't want nothing,' he said flatly." The final line of the story leaves the reader with a chilling doubt as to whether or not Arnold and his mother will ever be able to restore the mother-child bond represented by the cow and calf: "Then he went out the door and down the back steps, frightened by his answer."

Source: Liz Brent, for *Short Stories for Students*, The Gale Group, 2000.

Rena Korb

Korb has a master's degree in English literature and creative writing and has written for a wide variety of educational publications. In the following essay, Korb discusses several of the questions raised by "The Stone Boy" and poses possible answers.

In 1975, in one of her rare public statements, Gina Berriault commented on the weltanschauung, or "world view," of her writing. She told *World Authors:* "My work is an investigation of reality which is, simply, so full of ambiguity and of answers that beget further questions that to pursue it is an impossible task and a completely absorbing necessity. It appears to me that all the terrors are countered by a perceptible degree by the attempts of some writers to make us known to one another and thus to impart or revive a reverence for life." Berriault's statement certainly applies to her well-known short story which invites analysis and inquiry but provides no absolute answers.

The Stone Boy first appeared in *Mademoiselle* magazine in 1957, but it drew the attention of reviewers when it was included in Berriault's collection, *The Mistress, and Other Stories,* eight years later. *The Stone Boy* is immediately riveting in its subject matter. Nine-year-old Arnold, while passing through a wire fence, catches his gun. It discharges, and a bullet lodges in the neck of his older brother, Eugie. Eugie dies. However, this tragic incident is only the departure point for Berriault's story of alienation and failed relationships. For Arnold does not immediately return to his family and tell them what happened; instead, he continues with the task he set out to do that morning: picking peas. His

> Indeed, the story provides substantiation for both a reading of Arnold as murderer and Arnold as accidental killer."

family is horror stricken, both by the news of Eugie's death and by Arnold's reaction to it. They do not know how to view Arnold so they cling to the sheriff's assessment of Arnold. According to the sheriff, Arnold is such a cold person that he didn't bother to change his schedule because there was nothing that could alter the fact of Eugie's death. The sheriff labels Arnold a "monster," but in essence, he defines Arnold as a sociopath. By the next day, Arnold, too, comes to accept this opinion of himself, and in one heartfelt moment, transforms himself into such a being.

While *The Stone Boy* does not employ intricate narrative devices, it nevertheless presents a full, compelling story. This story invites even the casual reader to speculate as to its whys and wherefores. Ambiguity, a central theme in much of Berriault's work and to her perception of her writing, emerges foremost in the story, almost from the opening lines. Although the casual reader may be tempted to think this story will be a coming-of-age or a rite-of-passage story, Berriault dispels that notion quickly and efficiently, with Eugie's sudden death. At this point, the story truly begins to invite the readers' careful analysis, as Berriault would want it to.

Although Charles Poore wrote in *The New York Times* that Arnold's "murder" of Eugie is "explicit," whether Eugie's death was an accident emerges as just one of Berriault's many ambiguities. A solid determination of any intention to kill Eugie cannot be found in Arnold's reaction to this horrible event. Later in the story it is revealed that Arnold felt "terror" at what had occurred; at the moment it happens, however, Arnold only feels "discomfort." In the immediate seconds following Eugie's death, Arnold views his dead brother as an object causing displeasure bordering on disgust. He notes that Eugie's blood "had an obnoxious movement, like that of a parasite." Arnold is loath to approach or

touch his brother; to determine whether or not Eugie is able to get up, Arnold only nudges him with a foot. When Eugie does not get up, Arnold commences picking peas.

The description of this task seems straightforward, with Arnold's physical reaction mirroring his mental reaction: "Arnold set his rifle on the ground and stood up. He picked up the tub and, dragging it behind him, walked along by the willows to the garden fence and climbed through. He went down on his knees among the tangled vines." However, Arnold is metaphorically repeating the actions that led to Eugie's death; climbing through the garden fence is like climbing through the wire fence into the pasture; even the tangled vines echo the enmeshment of the barbed wire. Note is also made that Arnold's "hands were strange to him." While Arnold determines that this is caused by the cold weather, which numbs his hands, in reality, they have turned into something foreign—the hands of a killer. The numbing of Arnold's hands foreshadows the numbing of his very soul.

Indeed, the story provides substantiation for both a reading of Arnold as murderer and Arnold as accidental killer. The opening scene clearly sets up Arnold's animosity toward his brother, as he laughs "derisively" when Eugie is having trouble getting out of bed. In the kitchen, Arnold recognizes Eugie's vanity—his older brother "offer[s] silent praise unto himself. "Also in the kitchen, Arnold notes that Eugie's "brown curls grew thick and matted, close around his ears and down his neck, tapering there to a small whorl." To Arnold's perceptive eye, Eugie's hair forms the very bullseye that Arnold's bullet will strike just a short time later. At the same time, however, Arnold cares for and idealizes his brother. Arnold's father, too, has noted the affection that Arnold seems to have for his older brother. Indeed, Arnold's conflicted feelings for Eugie are best expressed by one sentence: "Eugie had had a way of looking at him, slyly and mockingly and yet confidentially, that had summed up how they both felt about being brothers." Based on this evidence, answering the question as to whether or not Arnold intended or even wanted to kill his brother is not possible.

Another question posed by the story is why Arnold and his family so readily accept the sheriff's judgment that the boy's actions demonstrate that he has no feelings. For some undisclosed reason, the sheriff offers no other explanation. With little thought as to why Arnold would continue to pick peas, and with no explanation forthcoming from Arnold himself, the family's authority figures—Arnold's father and Uncle Andy—decide to accept the sheriff's point of view; they willfully believe Arnold to be that merciless, unfeeling person. Arnold internalizes these opinions, particularly because the criticism comes from Uncle Andy, whose power over Arnold derives from his close resemblance to Eugie. Uncle Andy's disapproval is further reinforced by the neighbors' reactions. While Arnold hopes for their understanding, remaining in the parlor despite his discomfort so "they would see that he was only Arnold and not the person the sheriff thought he was," Andy's vocal assessment of the situation prevails.

By the end of the evening, Arnold is almost completely undone. Lying alone in bed that night, "[H]e felt nothing, not any grief." However, Arnold still retains a spark of humanity. When he wakes suddenly in the night he only wants his mother to comfort him while he "tell[s] her about the terror he had felt when he knelt beside Eugie." This is the first time the reader has heard about Arnold's true reaction to Eugie's death, but the reader hears little else about it, for Arnold's mother not only rejects him but reminds him of how his community now views him. Her words, "Is night when you get afraid?" tell him that she believes that her son is indeed the kind of monster who can commit any sort of atrocity in the light of day. While returning to his room, Arnold realizes that he is naked, viewing it as an "unpardonable" offense. His state of undress symbolizes his feeling that his family and his community have seen through his skin, into the hidden recesses of his heart. Ironically, that terror actually resided in his heart at Eugie's death, not malice, has no bearing anymore. Without anyone willing to see the "real" boy, Arnold becomes what they choose to see.

The next morning, however, Arnold almost grasps a chance at rehabilitation. His father forces his sister to acknowledge Arnold's presence at the breakfast table. Although "relief rained over his shoulders at the thought that his parents recognized him again," Arnold almost immediately "called upon his pride to protect him from them." This final scene begs the question of why Arnold refuses to accept their peace offerings. Many possible answers can be posed, but as with other questions the story raises, perhaps no answer seems satisfactory. Arnold may have come to accept his new role in the

course of one night, or he may be so angry at his parents for allowing him to be unfairly cast that he wants to punish them by withholding himself.

Perhaps the most likely answer stems from Eugie's and Arnold's relationship. Arnold has always modeled himself after Eugie, "enthralled" by his older brother. Because Eugie valued his place as the eldest child, so did Arnold. Now Arnold has become the eldest boy, and he feels he must fulfill the tasks that thus befall him. This explanation may help clarify why Arnold picked peas while Eugie lay dead—because that was the task he and Eugie had set out to fulfill. Now, at the breakfast table, as Arnold seems ready to accept his parents' tacit apology, his father announces that a cow and her calf are up in the mountains. "That had been Eugie's job, Arnold thought." This short exchange reminds Arnold of what Eugie's loss will mean to the family, that he is to blame for it, and that his family had excluded him in his time of need. When Arnold volunteers to get the calf himself, his is attempting to step into Eugie's shoes, but he knows that he will never be able to truly do so.

Although so much of *The Stone Boy* is ambiguous and cannot be fully understood, what is clear is that by the end of the story, Arnold has undergone a complete transformation. When he tells his mother that he doesn't want anything, his legs are "trembling from the fright his answer gave him." Arnold does not embrace his new identity but feels he has little choice but to take it on. The reader is left with little doubt that the sheriff's dreadful prophecy of seeing Arnold again in the future is likely to come true.

Source: Rena Korb, for *Short Stories for Students*, The Gale Group, 2000.

Sarah Madsen Hardy

Madsen Hardy has a doctorate in English literature and is a freelance writer and editor. In the following essay, she discusses how Berriault uses figurative language to illuminate the protagonist's emotional state in

"The Stone Boy" is named for its protagonist, nine-year-old Arnold, who symbolically turns to stone after he accidentally kills his older brother in a hunting accident. In a story composed mostly of realistic exposition, this title stands out as a striking metaphor. Stone is cold and inert. It is associated with cruelty and also with death, both of which are states of unfeeling. A ''stone boy'' is simultaneously living and inert, warm and cold, sentient and insentient. While many stories offer readers the chance to vicariously experience a range of different emotions, ''The Stone Boy'' brilliantly represents emotion's absence. Berriault uses both precise, unadorned description and lyrical similes to represent almost paradoxically—what it feels like to be unable to feel.

There is a contrast between the matter of fact exposition that makes up most of the story which reflects the way the literal minded farm community thinks and speaks—and the figurative language associated with Arnold's moments of heightened trauma. Among the latter, particularly significant are the similes that Berriault uses to invest the inanimate land and atmosphere of the farm with sentience. Personification is a form of metaphor in which an inanimate object is endowed with the qualities of a living being. Berriault uses similes to the same effect. For example, when Berriault writes that the shocks of wheat outside of Arnold's window were ''so still it was as if they moved and breathed in the daytime and had fallen silent with the lateness of the hour'' she attributes an almost human animation to the wheat by light of day, then remarks on its death-like absence. In the same passage, she also endows the quiet of the nighttime atmosphere with sight and consciousness: ''It was a silence that seemed to observe his father.'' Such personifying similes are interesting not only because they stand in contrast to the style of the majority of the story's narration, but because they relate to the larger themes of life and death, emotion and coldness. Through the title, Berriault compares Arnold to an inanimate object, but through her similes, she gives inanimate objects human qualities, drawing a connection between feeling and its absence.

The opening scene of ''The Stone Boy,'' taking place before Arnold's humanity has been called into question, describes the events of an ordinary morning as Arnold perceives them. Arnold experiences a range of typical emotions in regard to his older brother Eugie, from resentment and envy to admiration. The boys get up early to fulfill their responsibility to pick peas in the cool of the morning. Arnold takes his rifle with him to shoot for ducks, despite Eugie's teasing and the fact that it is not hunting season. While crawling through a fence, the hammer of Arnold's rifle gets caught on a piece of wire.

When he tries to free it, it fires in the direction of his brother, who has just gone through the fence ahead of him. Berriault narrates the terrible events in direct, realistic language. ''His rifle caught on the wire and he jerked at it. The air was rocked by the sound of the shot. Feeling foolish, he lifted his face, baring it to an expected shower of derision from his brother. But Eugie did not turn around. Instead, from his crouching position, he fell to his knees and then pitched forward onto his face.'' Arnold thinks first about being teased for his clumsiness with the gun. When he sees that Eugie has been hit, he is completely surprised. As Arnold watches Eugie die, he undergoes a kind of death himself, for these feelings of foolishness and surprise are the last ordinary 'human' emotions that Arnold experiences. The impact of Eugie's death stands in contrast to the complete normalcy of Arnold's thoughts and feelings over the course of the morning, up through his last defensive feeling of embarrassment.

Then Arnold makes a choice that defines him as a ''stone boy''—he continues with his morning chore of picking peas as if nothing remarkable had happened at all. Only when he returns home with the harvest and realizes that the family will wonder where Eugie is does he tell them flatly, ''Eugie's dead.'' Based on the fact that Arnold has expressed no outward sign of grief or remorse as evidenced in his direct and emotionless report of the tragedy, his family and community judge him. They agree with the county sheriff's assessment that Arnold is ''too reasonable'' to feel anything and they condemn him, leaving him outside of the circle of their human society at a time when his unarticulated need for warmth and empathy is most intense. They treat him as if he were an object rather than a subject, a rock rather than a person. Undeniably, Arnold is emotionally numb. The third-person limited narrator has access to Arnold's inner thoughts and feelings, and these do not directly refute the grounds for his condemnation. Indeed, Arnold regards himself as no longer human, acting only in order to maintain the family routine and reduce his conspicuousness, and making no attempt at contact with the people around him. Because Arnold becomes so detached from the innermost parts of himself, the narrational position may seem to offer readers little more than an objective account of events over the course of twenty-four hours following the shooting. So then, is it correct to conclude, along with the sheriff and Arnold's Uncle Andy, that Arnold is simply cruel?

Berriault delicately offsets the flat, reasonable narration of the events of the day with striking figurative descriptions of the natural world. She uses lyrical language to define a view of the inanimate realm of nature as conscious and perceptive. This view, which is implicitly Arnold's, stands in stark contrast to the spoken language the boy uses to communicate within the hostile human community. While the story's exposition—like Arnold's own explanations of his actions—is almost cruelly reasonable, Berriault's figurative language is both gentle and illogical. The best writers employ figurative language such as metaphors and similes not just to make their writing sound beautiful or interesting, but to emphasize their ideas and add dimension to their characters. Berriault uses personification and simile to create a sense of empathy between Arnold and the farmland around him. By using figurative language to endow natural objects with feelings, Berriault suggests that Arnold's very "stoniness" is a testament to the profundity of his experience of loss.

In death Eugie becomes part of the inanimate natural world, separate from human forms of communication. After Arnold watches his brother die, he calls out to him, "Hey, Eugie," and is answered with silence. As Arnold looks at the inert body, Berriault uses a simile to connect Eugie, in death, to the non-human realm of the farm setting: "Eugie was as still as the morning around them." From this point forward, Arnold too enters a non-human realm. Hereafter, he is detached from his family, his community, and what he had always taken for granted as himself, a boy defined against the towering figure of his older brother. As he leaves the scene of the accident and goes to pick peas, doing the task assigned to him, he cannot feel himself, "his hands were strange to him, and not until some time had passed did he realize that the pods were numbing his fingers." Hereafter as well, nature is endowed with human characteristics. Berriault uses a simile that personifies the morning sun: "It was a warmth on his back, like a large hand laid firmly there, that made him raise his head." The morning sun—an authoritative figure that is potentially both intimidating and comforting—calls him back to his role in the distant farmhouse, even as it reminds him of the irrevocable loss of that role. The sun reaches out and touches him, something that no one else does over the course of the harrowing day.

At the end of the day, in a scene that is contrasted to the normalcy of the story's opening, Arnold goes to bed by himself in the room he had always shared with Eugie. At this moment when Arnold's

> " In death Eugie becomes part of the inanimate natural world, separate from human forms of communication.... From this point forward, Arnold too enters a non-human realm."

loss is so tangible, Berriault writes, "He felt nothing, not any grief." This description is consistent with the conclusion the neighbors have just reached, discussing Arnold's cold "reasonableness" as if he were not there, as if he were as imperceptive as stone. Lacking any other way to understand his state of shock, Arnold has accepted the literal-minded explanation offered by the sheriff and repeated by the others. "Andy and his father and the sheriff had discovered what had made him go down into the garden. It was because he was cruel, the sheriff had said, and didn't care about his brother." However, Berriault subtly modifies this assessment of Arnold's emotional state with an unusual comparison. "There was only the same immense silence and crawling inside of him, the way the house and fields must feel under a merciless sun." Arnold has no reasonable explanation for his numbness, so he draws a strange analogy between his feelings and those of the inanimate world with which he is most intimate. He imagines that the house and the fields have feeling—not a feeling that is comparable to the range of emotions he and those close to him have ever experienced, but feeling nonetheless. They feel "immense silence" and "crawling." They feel the dreadful absence of emotion, connection, and communication. They are passive and helpless before the "merciless sun," but they are not cruel. By all appearances Arnold does not feel sorry, his own loss or the loss that he has inflicted on his family, but he does feel for the world of objects of which he and Eugie, each in his way, are both now a part.

As the story ends, Arnold still feels like stone. His mother has rejected his bid for comfort, and he has in turn denied this bid. Verbal communication remains on both sides reasonable and cruel. But the careful reader sees the difference between what

Arnold says and who he is, between his flat demeanor and the vast depth of his loss.

Source: Sarah Madsen Hardy, ''The Sentient Stone: Simile and Empathy,'' for *Short Stories for Students*, The Gale Group, 2000.

Sources

Amdahl, Gary. A review of *Women in Their Beds*, in *The Nation*, June 24, 1996, pp. 31-32.

Berriault, Gina. Preface to *The Mistress and Other Stories,* by Gina Berriault, New York: Dutton, 1965.

Berriault, Gina. with Bonnie Lyons and Bill Oliver. An interview with Berriault, in *The Literary Review*, Summer, 1994, pp. 714-723.

Boken, Julia B. A discussion of Berriault's career, in *Dictionary of Literary Biography*, Vol. 130, Gale Research, Detroit, MI, 1993.

Dubus, Andre. A discussion of Berriault's work, in *America*, September 8, 1984.

Kostelanetz, Richard. A review of *The Mistress, and Other Stories*, in the *New York Times Book Review*, November 13, 1965, pp. 104-105.

Leach, Penelope. *Your Growing Child: From Babyhood through Adolescence*, New York: Knopf, 1986, p. 182.

Lyons, Bonnie, and Bill Oliver. '' Don't I Know You? : An Interview with Gina Berriault,'' in *The Literary Review*, Vol. 37, No. 4, Summer 1994, pp. 714-22.

McQuade, Molly. A discussion of Berriault's work, in *Chicago Tribune Book World*, February 6, 1983.

Milton, Edith. Review of *Infinite Passions of Expectation*, by Gina Berriault, in *New York Times Book Review,* Vol. 88, January 9, 1983, p. 8.

Pagones, Dorrie. A review of *The Mistress, and Other Stories*, in *Saturday Review*, September 11, 1965, p. 25.

Poore, Charles. A review of *The Mistress, and Other Stories*, in *The New York Times*, September 11, 1965, p. 25.

Review of *Women in Their Beds*, in *Kirkus Reviews*, June 15, 1965.

Wakeman, John, ed. ''Gina Berriault,'' in *World Authors, 1950-1970,* New York: H. W. Wilson Company, 1975.

Further Reading

Berriault, Gina. ''Almost Impossible,'' in *The Confidence Woman: Twenty-six Women Writers at Work*, Atlanta: Longstreet Press, 1991, pp. 127-32.
    Discusses the nature of writing, focusing on students' reactions to Berriault's short stories.

Berriault, Gina, with Bonnie Lyons and Bill Oliver. An interview with Berriault, in *The Literary Review*, Summer, 1994, pp. 714-723.
    Berriault discusses how she became a writer, her writing style and major themes, and contemporary American fiction.

To Build a Fire

Jack London
1908

Jack London had already established himself as a popular writer when his story "To Build a Fire" appeared in the *Century Magazine* in 1908. This tale of an unnamed man's disastrous trek across the Yukon Territory near Alaska was well received at the time by readers and literary critics alike. While other works by London have since been faulted as overly sensational or hastily written, "To Build a Fire" is still regarded by many as an American classic. London based the story on his own travels across the harsh, frozen terrain of Alaska and Canada in 1897-98 during the Klondike gold rush; he is also said to have relied on information from a book by Jeremiah Lynch entitled *Three Years in the Klondike*. Critics have praised London's story for its vivid evocation of the Klondike territory. In particular, they focus on the way in which London uses repetition and precise description to emphasize the brutal coldness and unforgiving landscape of the Northland, against which the inexperienced protagonist, accompanied only by a dog, struggles unsuccessfully to save himself from freezing to death after a series of mishaps. Involving such themes as fear, death, and the individual versus nature, "To Build a Fire" has been categorized as a naturalistic work of fiction in which London depicts human beings as subject to the laws of nature and controlled by their environment and their physical makeup. With its short, matter-of-fact sentences, "To Build a Fire" is representative of London's best work, which influenced such later writers as Ernest Hemingway.

Author Biography

Jack London was born in 1876 in San Francisco, California, to Flora Wellman, whose common-law husband left her upon learning that she was pregnant. London took his surname from his stepfather, John London, whom his mother married shortly after her son's birth. The family settled in Oakland, California, in 1886. London quit school at age fourteen and took a series of jobs along the Oakland waterfront, working in a cannery and as a longshoreman, making money by stealing from the oyster beds in San Francisco Bay, and, later, serving as a seaman on a ship bound for Japan. London traveled across the United States while still in his teens. Throughout his early experiences, he read intensively in both literature and philosophy. London enrolled in Oakland High School at age nineteen and completed his course study within a year. The following year he joined the Socialist Labor Party and later briefly attended the University of California, until lack of money forced him to withdraw.

In 1897 London took part in the Klondike Gold Rush in northwestern Canada. Although he proved unsuccessful as a miner, his experiences in the grim and frozen North land provided him with a wealth of ideas for fiction. When he returned to Oakland, he began his career as an author, selling his first Klondike story, "To the Man on Trail," in 1898. In 1900 London published *The Son of the Wolf*. This collection of short stories quickly brought him fame. London's readers were captivated by his vivid tales of life in the wilds of Alaska and northwestern Canada, where men and dogs worked with, as well as battled against, each other to survive the harsh and brutally cold environment. London received international fame in 1903 with the publication of *The Call of the Wild*, a novel which is also set in the Klondike territory. Its companion novel, *White Fang*, was published in 1906. In 1908 London published "To Build a Fire," a story which is now considered a classic. In it, a *chechaquo* (cheechako), or newcomer, ignores the advice of an old-timer and travels in the Klondike with only a dog to accompany him even though the temperature is a lethal seventy-five degrees below zero. London's straightforward account of the man's death earned "To Build a Fire" critical acclaim.

During his lifetime, London also wrote novels and stories about his political beliefs and his journeys in the South Seas. In addition, he worked as a journalist and published his autobiography. London became a millionaire as a result of his popularity and his prodigious literary output, which includes more than two hundred short stories, twenty novels, three plays, and numerous nonfiction works. He was married twice and had two daughters by his first wife. London died in 1916 at the age of forty from uremia and an overdose of morphine.

Plot Summary

Part I

"To Build a Fire" begins at nine o'clock on a winter morning as an unnamed man travels across the Yukon Territory in Northwestern Canada. The man is a *chechaquo* (cheechako), a Chinook jargon word meaning "newcomer." This is the man's first winter in the Yukon, but because he is "without imagination" and thus unaccustomed to thinking about life and death, he is not afraid of the cold, which he estimates at fifty degrees below zero. He is on his way to join the rest of his companions at an old mining camp on a distant fork of Henderson Creek, and he estimates his arrival time will be six o'clock in the evening. The man is traveling on foot; all he has by way of supplies is his lunch. It is not long before he realizes that the temperature is colder than fifty below, but this fact does not yet worry him.

Part II

The man is accompanied only by a dog—"a big native husky," wilder than other breeds. Despite its heavy fur, the dog dislikes traveling in brutally cold weather. It knows instinctively that the temperature is actually seventy-five below zero and that no one should be out in such "tremendous cold." The man reaches Henderson Creek, which has frozen and can be used as a trail but is also riddled with dangerous winter springs that never freeze and are hidden beneath a thin layer of river ice. Although he is short on imagination, the man uses human judgment and alertness to avoid these traps. At one suspicious-looking spot on the trail, he forces the dog to go ahead of him. The dog breaks through into the water but scrambles out, saving itself from freezing to death by instinctively biting away the ice that clings to its feet. The man removes a glove to help the dog, and to his surprise, his bare fingers are numbed instantly by the bitter cold.

Part III

When the man stops for lunch he is startled at the speed with which his fingers and toes go numb, and for the first time he becomes frightened at the intensity of the freezing weather, knowing that numbness precedes hypothermia. Suddenly he remembers that he must build a fire ''and thaw out'' before trying to eat; he does so methodically, carefully building the fire with twigs as kindling before piling on larger pieces of wood. He also remembers that he once laughed at a man from Sulphur Creek who had warned him how cold the weather could get in the Yukon. Warmed and reassured after eating lunch by the fire, the man continues his journey—much to the dog's disappointment, as it longs to remain by the fire.

Part IV

After resuming his trek, the man breaks through the ice himself, getting soaked ''half-way to the knees.'' Heeding the advice he'd been given by the ''old-timer'' from Sulphur Creek, the man builds another fire to save his frozen feet. He is angered yet unfrightened by this unexpected delay. He feels confident in his ability to save himself and smiles when he remembers the old-timers ''womanish'' injunction against traveling alone in temperatures colder than minus fifty. Nevertheless, he is disconcerted by the speed at which his extremities are freezing and realizes that his face and toes are frostbitten.

Part V

As the man starts to remove his frozen moccasins to dry them by the fire, disaster strikes:

> It was his own fault, or, rather, his mistake. He should not have built the fire under the spruce-tree. He should have built it in the open. But it had been easier to pull the twigs from the brush and drop them directly on the fire. Now the tree under which he had done this carried a weight of snow on its boughs. No wind had blown for weeks, and each bough was fully freighted. Each time he had pulled a twig he had communicated a slight agitation to the tree—an imperceptible agitation, so far as he was concerned, but an agitation sufficient to bring about the disaster. High up in the tree one bough capsized its load of snow. This fell on the boughs beneath, capsizing them. This process continued, spreading out and involving the whole tree. It grew like an avalanche, and it descended without warning upon the man and the fire, and the fire was blotted out! Where it had burned was a mantle of fresh and disordered snow.

> The man was shocked. It was as though he had just heard his own sentence of death. (Excerpt from ''To Build a Fire'')

Jack London

Afterwards, the man calmly acknowledges to himself that the old-timer had been right about traveling with someone else who could help him out of danger. Just as calmly, he decides to rebuild the fire. Unfortunately, his hands are now so numb that he cannot make his fingers strike the matches and he drops them in the snow. He retrieves and lights the matches after several tries, burning himself badly in the process, but his damaged hands are too clumsy to prepare a fire that will last. The man thinks of killing the dog and thawing his hands in its carcass, but when he approaches the dog, it instinctively recoils at the fear in his voice and backs away. When the man at last catches the dog, he is unable to kill it; his hands have grown so numb that they are useless.

Part VI

Once the man fully realizes that he will die rather than simply lose his feet or hands to frostbite, he panics. He runs frantically, hoping to regain the feeling in his feet and to reach camp. Then he drops in exhaustion. Realizing that the numbness is creeping up his body, he starts off again in wild terror. The dog remains with him throughout his panic, and the man feels jealous anger at the animal's warm and healthy condition. Finally the man accepts his fate, letting the warmth and sleepiness of death-by-freezing overtake him. As he is dying, he has an out-of-body experience: first he sees himself walking with his companions and discovering his frozen body; then he hears himself telling the old-timer from Sulphur Creek that he was right about not traveling alone in the brutal cold. Once the dog senses that the man is dead, it leaves him and heads for camp, where it knows it will find ''other food-providers and . . . fire-providers.''

Characters

Dog

The dog is a ''big native husky'' and the man's only companion on the trail. While it depends upon the man for food and for warmth from campfires, the dog is ''not concerned in the welfare of the man'' and obeys him only to avoid being whipped. The dog is motivated by instinct. Critics Earle Labor and Jeanne Campbell Reesman describe the dog as a ''foil'' to the man. A foil is a character who sets off, or emphasizes, by way of contrast the traits of another character. In this case, the dog's reliable instincts contrast with the man's faulty human judgment. Unlike the man, the dog can sense that the temperature is below minus fifty degrees Fahrenheit, and despite the natural insulation provided by its fur coat, the dog does not travel willingly in such weather. After it falls into the water on the river trail, the dog instinctively knows how to save itself by cleaning the ice from its legs and feet. Later, while the man freezes to death as a result of his unreliable powers of reason, the dog instinctively knows how to survive by curling up in the snow; ultimately, it senses the man's death and saves itself by leaving for camp on its own.

Man

The protagonist in ''To Build a Fire'' is known simply as ''the man.'' He is a *chechaquo*, or new-comer, who undertakes a nine-hour walk in brutally cold weather to meet his companions at an old mining camp during his first winter in the Klondike. Accompanied by a dog but lacking both its instincts and its physical adaptation to the cold, the man freezes to death before reaching camp. At the beginning of the story, the man is described as being ''without imagination . . . quick and alert in the things of life, but only in the things, and not in the significances.'' Thus, when he first sets out, the man notices that it is uncomfortably cold, but he cannot imagine that he is risking death by hypothermia. As critic James I. McClintock points out, the man does not at first think in terms of life versus death, or of the weakness of human beings versus the power of nature, but rather in terms of his own ability to solve any difficulties through the power of reason. He believes that all he has to do to survive is to ''keep his head,'' and he laughs when he remembers the ''womanish'' warnings spoken by an old-timer. Critics Earle Labor and Jeanne Campbell Reesman observe that it is in fact the man's pride in his ''own rational faculties'' that finally results in his demise.

Old-timer

The old-timer from Sulphur Creek is the man's major source of advice in the story. Although he never actually appears in the story, the old-timer and his words of wisdom are frequently remembered by the man. For example, the old-timer once told the man how cold the temperatures could get in the Klondike. He also advised the man about the absolute necessity of building fires and—most importantly—warned him never to travel alone when the temperature drops below minus fifty degrees Fahrenheit. The old-timer's advice is at first remembered with mild derision by the man, who considers his warnings ''womanish'' and overcautious. But as the man's condition becomes increasingly perilous, he admits that the old-timer was right about never traveling without a companion ''after fifty below.'' Critic James I. McClintock describes the old-timer as someone whose ''experience has given him the imagination to continue living'' in extremely cold temperatures but who nevertheless stays indoors rather than risk death on the trail during winter.

Themes

''To Build a Fire'' is about an unnamed man who embarks on a nine-hour trek across the Klondike's harsh winter landscape to meet his companions at a mining camp. Against the advice of an old-timer, the man makes the journey alone, except for a dog, and as a result of a series of disasters, he freezes to death before reaching camp. The man's behavior and his ultimate fate highlight the story's themes of survival in the wilderness, the individual versus nature, and death.

Survival in the Wilderness

Early in the story, it becomes clear that the odds are against the man's chances of surviving in the Klondike wilderness. He is a *chechaquo*, or newcomer to the region, and has never before experienced its extreme winters. Further, he is "traveling light"—on foot rather than by sled and carrying only a bacon sandwich, tobacco, matches, and some birch-bark kindling. What is more, he is outdoors in temperatures well below minus fifty degrees Fahrenheit. Although he has been warned never to travel "after fifty below" without a partner who can help him in emergencies, the man's only companion on this trek is a half-wild husky—a "toil-slave" who has no affection for him. At the best of times the Klondike wilderness would seem alien to the newcomer because of its vast stretches of snow ("as far as his eye could see it was unbroken white" except for the trail). As it is, the man travels with few supplies and without a partner in extreme cold. Under such conditions, it doesn't matter that he is both "quick and alert" to his surroundings, for without someone to help him, his "bad luck" (which is how the man refers to his fall into the icy river) and "mistake" (which is how he describes the blotting out of his second fire by snow falling from a tree) become full-fledged catastrophes and destroy the man's chances of survival.

The Individual versus Nature

Closely related to the issue of survival in the wilderness is "To Build a Fire"'s theme of the individual versus nature. According to the story, the "trouble" with the man is that he is "without imagination" and therefore never speculates about "man's place in the universe," his "frailty in general," or the fact that people are "able only to live within certain narrow limits of temperature." Yet during his trek the man is confronted again and again by his weakness as a lone individual against the formidable power of nature in the form of the brutal cold. Each time he removes his gloves, the man is surprised at how quickly his fingers are numbed. He is also startled at how fast his nose and cheeks freeze, and he is amazed when his spittle freezes in midair before it ever hits the snow. When the man stops for lunch, his feet go numb almost as soon as he sits still, a fact that finally begins to frighten him. Even the dog—who is half-wild and thus closer to nature—feels "depressed" by the cold. Thanks to its natural instincts and its dense winter coat, the dog survives the extreme temperature long enough to head for camp, where it knows it will find food and warmth. Without fur or instinct,

Media Adaptations

- "To Build a Fire" was adapted as a 56-minute film with actor-director Orson Welles providing the story's narration. The film is in VHS format and is distributed by Educational Video Network.

- The story was also adapted as a recording, read by Robert Donly and distributed by Miller-Brody.

the man is too frail on his own to withstand nature— or "the cold of space"—as it presents itself in the Klondike: "The cold of space smote the unprotected tip of the planet, and he, being on that unprotected tip, received the full force of the blow."

Death

Once his fire is blotted out by snow and his body is threatened by hypothermia, the man must come to terms with death. His first reaction is to acknowledge calmly that the advice given to him by the old-timer was accurate: "If he had only had a trail-mate he would have been in no danger now." This thought occurs to him again as he fails in his effort to rebuild the fire. From there he moves to "controlled despair"; next, to apathy; and then to panic as he makes a last, futile effort to save his life by frantically running on his frozen feet in hopes of making it to camp. The man's ultimate response to death is to try "meeting [it] with dignity." His final words—"You were right, old hoss; you were right"—are part of a conversation that he imagines having with the old-timer who had warned him not to travel alone. They are also an acknowledgment of nature's power over the individual.

Style

"To Build a Fire" is the story of an unnamed man traveling across the Klondike territory in winter to

Topics for Further Study

- Research the symptoms of and treatments for frostbite and hypothermia. Use your findings to discuss the deterioration of the man's condition in "To Build a Fire."

- Investigate the Klondike Gold Rush of 1897: the types of people who participated in it; the "sourdoughs" versus the "cheechakos"; the routes they took and the supplies they carried with them; and the dangers they encountered. Compare what you learn about these people with what you know about the man in "To Build a Fire."

- As mentioned in "To Build a Fire," the Yukon River formed the main route for prospectors on their way to Dawson to search for gold. Research the indigenous people living near the Yukon River and the effects of the Klondike Gold Rush upon their way of life.

meet his partners at a mining camp. Ignoring the advice of an old-timer, the man makes the journey alone except for a dog, despite the intense cold. As the result of a series of mishaps, the man freezes to death without reaching camp.

Point of View

Point of view means the perspective from which the story, or narrative, is told. The point of view in "To Build a Fire" is third-person omniscient. In other words, the narrator stands outside of the story and refers to the characters in the third person ("he," "the man," "the dog," "it") and sometimes comments on their behavior and personalities. The omniscient narrator is by definition all-knowing—able to present not only what the characters are doing and saying but also what they are thinking. Thus the narrator in "To Build a Fire" shows us that the man in the story is observant and careful enough to look for dangerous cracks in the river trail, but he also remarks that the "trouble" with the man is that he is unreflective and "without imagina-

tion," so that he never thinks about his own mortality and cannot imagine that the intense cold could be anything worse than uncomfortable. Similarly, the narrator comments on the dog's thoughts, telling us that the animal can sense that the temperature is dangerously below minus fifty degrees Fahrenheit and asserting that the dog feels no affection for the man.

Setting

The setting denotes the time and place of a story as well as the social circumstances of the characters. Although the exact date and country are never given in "To Build a Fire," references to the Klondike, to such rivers as the Yukon, and to such cities as Dawson, as well as the mention of an "old claim" on Henderson Creek, indicate that the story takes place in the Klondike region of Canada near Alaska during the "gold rush" which began in 1897. Of greatest significance is that the story takes place during the winter in the far north, where temperatures can fall to minus seventy-five degrees Fahrenheit and the sun does not rise for days. Into this setting walks the man, who is a *chechaquo*, or newcomer, to the region. His inexperience and lack of imagination do not allow him to prepare for the brutal cold.

Style

The style of a story means the way in which its ideas are expressed—what words have been chosen and how the sentences have been structured to tell the story. One element of style which characterizes "To Build a Fire" is repetition. Certain words and actions are repeated in the story to emphasize the intense coldness of the weather and the seriousness of the man's plight. The word "cold" itself recurs frequently, beginning with the opening sentence: "Day had broken cold and gray, exceedingly cold and gray . . . ," and ending with a mention of the "cold sky" in the story's final paragraph. Elsewhere the man continually expresses his surprise at the coldness of the weather. The repetition of other words and actions also contributes to the sense of bitter coldness: for example, each time that the man removes his mittens, his fingers instantly go numb, and he has to struggle to warm them up, "threshing his arms back and forth" to regain feeling.

The old-timer's advice against traveling alone is frequently repeated, adding a sense of foreboding to the story. Even more ominous is the use of the phrase ''it happened'' to introduce the two disasters—first when the man breaks through the ice, and next when his fire is extinguished. Literary critics have noted that the cumulative effect of such repetition is to make the man's death by freezing seem inevitable.

Naturalism

''To Build a Fire'' has been called a naturalistic story. Naturalism is a literary movement which developed during the late nineteenth century. Influenced by scientific determinism as well as by Darwin's theory of evolution, naturalism contends that human beings are determined by their heredity and the laws of nature and are thus controlled by their environment and their physical makeup rather than by spirituality or reason. As a naturalistic creature, the man in ''To Build a Fire'' lacks imagination, and although he tries to survive by using reason, he is overwhelmed by the forces of nature.

Historical Context

Late Nineteenth- Early Twentieth-Century America

Although Jack London's ''To Build a Fire'' was first published in 1908, the story was inspired by the Klondike Gold Rush, which began in 1897. America's focus during the early years of the twentieth century was much the same as it had been during the closing years of the nineteenth century. The country had recently undergone significant expansion across the western plains and along the Pacific coast. In 1898 America expanded offshore as well, with the annexation of Hawaii and—as a result of the Spanish-American War—Guam, the Philippines, and Puerto Rico.

The late nineteenth century also saw an influx of immigrants into the United States and, with it, the opening of Ellis Island in 1891 as a processing station for the new Immigration Bureau. Immigrants became an important part of the country's industrialized economy, which produced not only the textiles of earlier years but also focused on mining as well as on the production of steel and heavy machinery. Whole families became involved in the work force. Labor laws were passed and labor unions were formed in response to unsafe working conditions and to the economic depressions which occurred in 1893-97.

The late nineteenth and early twentieth centuries brought about an increase in the number of public schools and libraries. By 1900 most states had compulsory education laws, and an increasing number of women were graduating from college. During the early 1900s, when London published ''To Build a Fire,'' the short story as a genre was experiencing enormous popularity.

The Klondike Gold Rush—beginning in 1897 and lasting until 1910—contributed to the late nineteenth- and early twentieth-century atmosphere of territorial expansion and industrial growth, with their attendant economic cycles of boom and bust. The Klondike also proved to be a rich source of inspiration for much of London's most successful fiction.

The Klondike Gold Rush

A rich vein of gold was discovered in August 1896 by George Cormack at Rabbit Creek, off the Klondike and Yukon rivers in northwestern Canada. The rush to Canada's Klondike region began a year later, after steamships loaded with prospectors and their gold docked in San Francisco. Reports of the prospectors' success set off a mania for gold. By then the richest claims had already been staked out, but this did not prevent many people, including Jack London, from heading North. This ''stampede'' of goldseekers had a profound effect on northwestern Canada. In Dawson, a city created as a result of the rush, Americans outnumbered Canadians by a ratio of five to one. The influx also affected Canada's western neighbor, the American territory of Alaska, through which many of the would-be prospectors traveled on their way to the Klondike. In 1890, there were approximately 4,000 white settlers in Alaska; by 1910, thanks to the Klondike stampede and to later discoveries of gold in Alaska itself, that number had increased to 36,400.

Jack London spent time in both Alaska and Canada. In ''To Build a Fire'' he writes about the Yukon trail that winds in and out of Alaska and Canada: ''[The] main trail—that led south five hundred miles to the Chilcoot Pass, Dyea, and salt water; and that led north seventy miles to Dawson, and still on to the north a thousand miles to Nulato, and finally to St. Michael on Bering Sea. . . .'' Thousands of goldseekers traveled this and other

Compare & Contrast

- **1890s:** In 1895, Guglielmo Marconi transmits a message using radio waves recently discovered by Heinrich Rudolph Hertz in 1887. This is the beginning of the "wireless telegraph." News of the gold discoveries, made in the Klondike region of Canada's Yukon Territory since August of 1896, reach the U.S. in January, 1897, and start another gold rush.

   1990s: The network of telecommunication lines, radio and television transmitters, cellular phones, and orbiting satellites makes it possible to transmit news even from remote locations to most urban places in the world in a matter of minutes.

- **1897:** English physicist J.J. Thomson formulates the idea of an atomic nucleus orbited by one or more electrons. This number of electrons characterizes the atom, giving it its atomic number.

   1905: Swiss theoretical physicist Albert Einstein introduces the concept of the equivalence of matter and energy with his equation $E=mc^2$, and raises the possibility of new sources of power and heat.

   1911: Ernest Rutherford at the University of Manchester in England proposes that an atom is composed of a positively charged nucleus with electrons orbiting this nucleus.

   1938: German chemist Otto Hahn and his assistants Fritz Strassman and Lise Meitner produce the first recorded fission of uranium atoms with the consequent release of a large quantity of energy and heat.

   1952: The U.S. Atomic energy commission explodes a nuclear fusion bomb on their testing grounds in the Pacific.

   1979: An accident at the nuclear power plant on Three Mile Island near Harrisburg, Pennsylvania, results in the shutting down of the plant and in lack of confidence in nuclear power plants by the public in the U.S.

   1985: An accident at the nuclear power plant at Chernobyl near Kiev in the Ukraine renders a vast amount of land uninhabitable for thousands of years. Public opinion becomes very pessimistic in regard to the safety and value of nuclear power.

---

land and water routes to the Klondike, hoping to strike it rich. They ignored warnings about the harsh winters they would encounter in the Northland, just as the man in "To Build a Fire" ignores the warnings of the experienced old-timer at the Klondike mining camp of Sulphur Creek.

Critical Overview

Since its first publication in 1908, Jack London's short story "To Build a Fire" has been well-received. Today, it is regarded as a classic of American literature. In his literary biography, *Jack London: The Man, The Writer, the Rebel* (1976),

Robert Barltrop asserts that "To Build a Fire" is one of a group of "outstanding stories" which distinguish London "as one of the masters of that form." Similarly, James Lundquist (*Jack London: Adventures, Ideas, and Fiction*, 1987) describes the story as "starkly elegant, a masterpiece of quiet tone and subdued color . . ." and points out that it is the most frequently anthologized of all of London's works. Earle Labor and Jeanne Campbell Reesman (*Jack London*, 1994) likewise praise "To Build a Fire" as a "masterpiece," while in *Jack London: An American Myth* (1981), John Perry credits the story with being "fine-textured."

Indeed, stories like "To Build a Fire" helped establish Jack London's reputation as a gifted author, inspiring some critics who were London's contemporaries to applaud him as the "successor to Poe" and the "equal of Kipling" (see Charles Child Walcutt's discussion of early criticism in his *Jack London*, 1966). However, not all of the Klondike stories were considered at the time to be of the same high quality as "To Build a Fire." London freely admitted that his principal aim in writing was to make money; thus many of his stories of men and dogs at odds with each other in the frozen north were published in adventure magazines and were written to satisfy a reading public that was fascinated by tales of daring exploits. The result was that many of the Klondike stories were criticized as lurid and hastily written potboilers. It has been pointed out that when London published collections of these magazine stories, he did not distinguish between those of good and bad quality. Hence his 1910 collection, *Lost Face*, contains a mixture of both good and bad stories, including "To Build a Fire." In consequence, a 1910 review in the *Nation* acknowledged London's talent but condemned the blood and violence in his stories, declaring that London "seems to us the victim of a disease of the fancy from which, and from the effects of which, it is impossible not to shrink" (as quoted by John Perry in his *Jack London: An American Myth*).

The variable quality of London's writing causes difficulties for critics today as well. In a 1967 article for *Studies in Short Fiction*, for example, Earle Labor and King Hendricks reprint a 1902 version of "To Build a Fire" which London wrote for a boy's magazine and compare it with the author's later, more famous 1908 version in order to prove that "Jack London was not merely a prolific hack, but, contrary to modern critical opinion, an astute craftsman who understood the difference between juvenile fiction and serious literary art." In his 1986 article for the *Journal of Modern Literature*, Lee Clark Mitchell observes that London's "flat prose," "childish plots," and reputation for hasty writing has caused "embarrassment" for some critics, but argues that in the case of "To Build a Fire," London wrote carefully rather than sloppily, trying to achieve a particular effect in the story. Finally, Robert Barltrop has asserted that because his books continue to be popular, London "cannot be dismissed" by critics but should instead be ranked as an important writer (in Barltrop's *Jack London: The Man, the Writer, the Rebel*).

A sinister aspect of London's work is his championing of white supremacy. Although this attitude does not appear in "To Build a Fire," it

Travellers along Alaska's Yukon Trail, c. 1897.

does manifest itself in a number of his Klondike stories, where Anglo-Saxons are represented as superior to the indigenous people they encounter in Alaska and Canada. In *Jack London: An American Myth*, John Perry notes that London's belief in Anglo-Saxon superiority was "a reflection of the time," and was thus overlooked in the late nineteenth and early twentieth centuries by the magazines who published his stories as well as by people who read them. Perry also remarks that "London's faith in Anglo-Saxon superiority seems at odds with itself, considering his best-drawn and most convincing characters are half-breed Indians, who live simple lives of honor and respect in the wilds, while his brutal whites, the chosen race, are limned as savage elementals."

Criticism

Jill Widdicombe

Widdicombe is a freelance editor of college textbooks who lives in Alaska. In the essay below, she examines the mysterious effect of the merci-

What Do I Read Next?

- *The Call of the Wild* (1903) is one of Jack London's most famous Klondike novels. The novel's hero is a dog named Buck, a family pet that is stolen and sold as a sled-dog for use in the Klondike Gold Rush. The novel depicts Buck's experiences as he is brutalized by his captors, grows increasingly wild, and fights to become lead dog.

- Published in 1906, Jack London's novel *White Fang* is often considered the counterpart to *The Call of the Wild*. It recounts the adventures of White Fang, a dog that is also part wolf, living half-wild in the Klondike and subject to both the savagery and kindness of humans. The novel portrays White Fang's eventual domestication.

- The Library of America edition of Jack London's *Novels and Stories* (1982) contains not only the texts of *The Call of the Wild* and *White Fang* but also includes maps of the areas featured in London's Klondike fiction as well as a "Historical and Geographical Note" by the volume's editor, Donald Pizer.

- Pierre Berton's *Klondike: The Last Great Gold Rush, 1896-1899* (rev. ed., 1987) examines the rush for gold in Canada's Klondike territory from the Canadian point of view, discussing the clash of cultures that occurred between order-loving Canadians and libertarian Americans as they hunted for gold.

- *Alaska: Reflections on Land and Spirit* (1989) is a collection of essays written over the last hundred years edited by Robert Hedin and Gary Holthaus. The editors describe their collection as a gathering of "travelogues, diaries, meditations, and narratives by homesteaders, missionaries, anthropologists, psychologists, ornithologists, poets, teachers, and conservationists, all of whom go beyond the typical cliches and advertising slogans about Alaska to provide an authentic record of a given time and place." Included is a report by Jack London about housekeeping in the Klondike.

- *Always Getting Ready/Upterrlainarluta: Yup'ik Eskimo Subsistence in Southwest Alaska* (1993) by James H. Barker contains interviews and photographs of Yup'ik Eskimos who still make their living on the delta of the Yukon and Kuskokwim rivers. (The Yukon River was well-known to Jack London and is featured in "To Build a Fire.") One interview is from a man who got his arm caught in his snow machine while traveling alone in winter. To survive, he had to amputate his own arm after allowing it to freeze.

---

less cold in "To Build a Fire" and in everyday Alaskan life.

The third paragraph of Jack London's "To Build a Fire" offers a concise assessment of the personality and motivation of the story's unnamed central character as he embarks across the vast and snowy winter landscape of the Klondike:

> But all this—the mysterious, far-reaching hair-line trail, the absence of sun from the sky, the tremendous cold, and the strangeness and weirdness of it all—made no impression on the man. It was not because he was long used to it. He was a new-comer in the land, a chechaquo, and this was his first winter. The trouble with him was that he was without imagination. He was quick and alert in the things of life, but only in the things, and not in the significances. Fifty degrees below zero meant eighty-odd degrees of frost. Such a fact impressed him as being cold and uncomfortable, and that was all. It did not lead him to meditate upon his frailty as a creature of temperature, and upon man's frailty in general, able only to live within certain narrow limits of temperature; and from there on it did not lead him to the conjectural field of immortality and man's place in the universe. Fifty degrees below zero stood for a bite of frost that hurt and that must be guarded against by the use of mittens, ear-flaps, warm moccasins, and thick socks. Fifty

degrees below zero was to him just precisely fifty degrees below zero. That there should be anything more to it than that was a thought that never entered his head. (Excerpt from ''To Build a Fire'')

Referring to the above passage, James I. McClintock asserts that this ''quick and alert'' man tries to use reason instead of imagination to get him past his difficulties and safely to camp but that human rationality proves to be helpless against the Klondike's ''killing landscape.'' In the same vein, Earle Labor and Jeanne Campbell Reesman refer to the frozen landscape as a powerful enemy or ''antagonist,'' asserting that the man ''falls into misfortune because of . . . an overweening confidence in the efficacy of his own rational faculties and a corresponding blindness to the dark, nonrational powers of nature, chance, and fate.''

In the context of ''To Build a Fire,'' then, ''imagination'' is the ability to recognize one's limitations. As it happens, the man does not possess this ability until it is too late. From the beginning, he is aware of and responds to the intensity of the cold. At first, he greets this ruthless cold matter-of-factly and with relatively mild surprise: ''It certainly was cold, he concluded, as he rubbed his numb nose and cheek-bones with his mittened hand.'' This reaction seems especially low-key when compared with the dog's response in the paragraph immediately afterward: ''The animal was depressed by the tremendous cold. It knew it was no time for traveling.''

As the story progresses, the man becomes more keenly aware of the magnitude of the cold. Nevertheless, this awareness does not fundamentally alter his mundane response to the unearthly ''cold of space'': he feels only a ''pang of regret'' after realizing that he should have covered his nose and cheeks against frostbite; he is only ''a bit frightened'' at the speed with which his fingers go numb when he removes his mittens; he is merely ''angry'' at his bad luck when he plunges knee-deep through the ice on the river-trail. It is not until snow falls from a tree and extinguishes his poorly placed fire that the man becomes ''shocked'' rather than merely surprised and at last acknowledges ''his own sentence of death'' as a result of this calamity.

Readers of ''To Build a Fire'' have judged the man's casual response to the cold to be at best naively reckless and at worst downright stupid. They have argued that the man was not being reasonable by relying on his own ability ''to keep his head'' and arrogantly ignoring the old-timer's

> **" In the context of 'To Build a Fire,' then, 'imagination' is the ability to recognize one's limitations. As it happens, the man does not possess this ability until it is too late."**

advice to travel with a partner. Some have pointed out that at the very least, he should have dispensed with ''traveling light'' and instead used his dog as a pack animal for hauling extra supplies—a practice that was not only customary in the Klondike but logical as well. Most obviously, the man never should have been so foolish as to build his second fire underneath a snow-laden tree.

Rational or not, the man's behavior is what makes ''To Build a Fire'' such a powerful story. His inability to imagine himself in danger from the cold and his fruitless attempts at ''keeping his head'' once he recognizes that death is near constitute behavior most of us can understand. Such disasters as fires, earthquakes, tornadoes, and floods bring with them enough eye-popping or ear-splitting devastation to make them clearly life-threatening. However, the extreme cold of frosty landscapes or ''the White Silence,'' as London describes it, is so quiet and abstract that it does not immediately appear to be lethal. Besides for most people, cold is easily rendered harmless by well-insulated houses and central heating, so that like the man in ''To Build a Fire'' (who has come from and is going to a warm cabin) we tend to forget that human beings are ''able only to live within certain narrow limits of temperature.''

Critic James I. McClintock emphasizes this point when he remarks that, even had the man been capable of imagining his own mortality before he set out on his journey—that is, even if he had traveled with a partner—there is no guarantee that he would have survived nature at its most extreme during a Klondike winter. Ultimately, McClintock argues, imagination is proof against unimaginably cold temperatures only if it keeps us indoors when they occur.

Indeed, the cold itself functions as an invisible antagonist in "To Build a Fire." It meets the man as soon as he goes outside into the brutal Klondike winter, stays close by him throughout the story, and finally kills him through the effects of hypothermia—the lowering of body temperature to subnormal levels at which frostbite and eventually death occur. Hypothermia does not happen exclusively to newcomers or *chechaquos*, however. James H. Barker's book *Always Getting Ready/Upterrlainarluta* consists of photographs and interviews with Yup'ik Eskimos living on the Yukon-Kuskokwim Delta in Alaska. The Yup'ik word *upterrlainarluta* means "being ever prepared," and for the Yup'ik culture on the Delta this means "that one must be wise in knowing what to prepare for and equally wise in being prepared for the unknowable." This concept is similar to the "imagination" in "To Build a Fire." One interview in particular in the book provides a grim example of the importance of *upterrlainarluta*:

> Morrie told us how he lost his arm. During the winter of 1974 he was traveling downriver by himself on a snowmachine. The track became caked with ice. Attempting to clear it, he reached into the track and accidentally hit the throttle. His arm was caught. He couldn't reach his tools to release the tension on the track so he sat there for some time trying to work his arm loose. Knowing he would die without help, he lay there long enough for his arm to freeze, cut it off and walked the couple of miles downriver to a nearby cabin for help. (Excerpt from *Always Getting Ready/Upterrlainarluta*)

Some may think that in "To Build a Fire" London exaggerates the dangers of extreme cold in order to tell a good story, but this is not the case. In January 1996, a Yup'ik couple and their grandchild were traveling by car in Interior Alaska when they got stuck in a snowbank far from the main highway. Unable to free their car, they stamped out the word "HELP" in the snow and set off on foot for the nearest dwelling—a roadhouse about ten miles away. Although not traveling alone, they suffered a fate similar to London's character in "To Build a Fire." With the temperature dropping below minus sixty degrees Fahrenheit, they tried unsuccessfully to build a fire. As hypothermia set in, they became disoriented. In a classic response to the last stages of hypothermia, they began to hallucinate and overheat. They wandered around in circles and threw off their parkas and mittens. Then all three died from the "tremendous cold."

In "To Build a Fire," London's *chechaquo* is confident that to survive the harsh Klondike winter "all a man had to do was to keep his head." That confidence is, however, misplaced. As Peter Stark puts it in his article on hypothermia, "The cold remains a mystery, more prone to fell men than women, more lethal to the thin and well-muscled than to those with avoirdupois, and least forgiving to the arrogant and unaware."

Source: Jill Widdicombe, "Overview of 'To Build a Fire,'" in *Short Stories for Students*, The Gale Group, 2000.

Lee Clark Mitchell

Lee Clark Mitchell is affiliated with Princeton University. In the following excerpt, she discusses how London's repetitious writing style in "To Build a Fire" ultimately undermines the meaning of his language.

Even enthusiasts cringe at naturalism's style. Given excesses so plain and a motion so plodding, sensible critics have simply dropped the subject. And perhaps the greatest embarrassment has been caused by Jack London, whose flat prose seems especially open to criticism. His very methods of composition prompt a certain skepticism; the speed with which he wrote, his suspiciously childish plots, perhaps even his self-advertising pronouncements have all convinced readers to ignore the technical aspects of his fiction.

Yet good manners seem misplaced once we grant that literature need not appear a certain way, since it is difficult to see then what it might mean to reject a work's style as inappropriate. Indeed, the very strangeness of naturalism's vision emerges so vividly in its prose that wrenched stylistic maneuvers soon seem to the point. As we have come to acknowledge with cubist perspectives, metaphysics shapes style, not maladroitness. Once admit certain large claims about time and character, and naturalism appears less inadequate to conventional criteria than at last merely inaccessible to them. Or viceversa, allow the contorted styles of naturalism to achieve their effect, and customary assumptions about time and character all of a sudden begin to erode. Such writing clearly testifies to what is for most an alien vision of experience and, therefore, almost by definition veers from realist standards. But it is far from inept.

Still, all of this risks too much too soon by linking the varied styles of naturalism to individual author's control. What we need to do here is merely to loosen our critical categories and to agree that while metaphysics may not disprove maladroitness, at least maladroitness can be approached as a kind of after-the-fact metaphysic. Postponing for the moment, that is, the question of London's ultimate purpose, we can simply describe what happens in one seemingly rough-hewn work—his short story, "To Build a Fire" (1906).

I

As good a place as any to begin is with the story's concluding paragraph, where the style's very strengths appear most dramatically to be little more than flaws. The unnamed man who has repeatedly failed to ward off the Arctic cold at last slips into frozen sleep, watched over by a gradually bewildered dog:

> Later the dog whined loudly. And still later it crept close to the man and caught the scent of death. This made the animal bristle and back away. A little longer it delayed, howling under the stars that leaped and danced and shone brightly in the cold sky. Then it turned and trotted up the trail in the direction of the camp it knew, where were the other food providers and fire providers.

These lines seem a bit abrupt and lend a halting rhythm to the story's "sense of an ending," but we cannot merely ascribe their oddity to London's personal quirkiness. For whatever his intentions, there is no denying that this is a self-consciously structured prose, evident specifically in the paragraph's minor transgressions. London refuses to subordinate clauses, for instance, though the more natural form of description invites such a pattern. And as if even greater formality were desired, phrases are self-consciously inverted ("a little longer it delayed," for example, and "the camp it knew, where were the other food providers").

Yet the more convincing evidence of stylistic control appears in the paragraph's most striking feature: its multiple repetitions. Just as alliteration echoes a series of "l"s, "c"s, "b"s, and "t"s through to the final clause's "f-p"s, so syntax compounds that phonic stutter by trusting almost exclusively to the copulative—seven times in five relatively short sentences. Prepositional phrases emerge additively instead of in the usual subordinated pattern (as when the dog trots " *up* the trail *in* the direction *of* the camp"); one phrase merely rewords, that is, rather than extends another. Even the shifters repeat, crosshatching the whole through identical words and sounds ("Later" "later"; "still" "little later"). And although it may first seem that this gives events a certain progressive sequence, that effect is countered by the passage's reliance on the simple past tense, as if it were

> ❝Repetition establishes a compelling pattern in London's Arctic for reasons that are neither simple nor straightforward. Most obviously, however, its effect is entropic, reducing the man to the purely physical by depriving him initially of a will, then of desires, and at last of life itself."

avoiding the very temporal elaborations that might otherwise reflect a controlling narrative consciousness. Throughout, each sentence and sometimes each clause offers itself autonomously—as units only loosely interconnected. Phonemic and syntactic repetitions, in other words, reveal not an interdependent world larger than the sum of its grammatical parts, but the very absence of an organizing grammar to the text.

The paragraph's verbal echoes remind us that the plot itself reiterates a few basic events. On a single day, an unnamed man walks in seventy-five-below-zero temperature, stops to build a fire and eat lunch, resumes walking, falls into an icy spring, builds another fire that is obliterated by snow from a tree, then fails to build a third fire before finally freezing to death. Banal as these events are one by one, they repeat themselves into an eerie significance, as the man attempts over and over to enact the story's titular infinitive. In turn, everything that somehow contributes to those attempts is doubled and redoubled, iterated and reiterated, leaving nothing to occur only once. Just as verbal repetition disrupts a normal grammatical progression by breaking phrases into autonomous units, so the recurrence of things themselves has a curiously disruptive narrative effect. By disconnecting things from each other, repetition instills a certain static quality to the story's motion. Moreover, the reiterated concentration on the material lends a paralyzing quality to the story's events, which gradually draws into question the very notion of plot as onward narrative progress.

Its unsettling effect in "To Build a Fire" is nicely illustrated in the repetitions of this passage:

> Once, coming around a bend, he shied abruptly, like a startled horse. . . . The creek he knew was frozen clear to the bottom—no creek could contain water in that arctic winter—but he knew also that there were springs that bubbled out from the hillsides and ran along under the snow and on top the ice of the creek. He knew that the coldest snaps never froze these springs, and he knew likewise their danger. They were traps. They hid pools of water under the snow that might be three inches deep, or three feet. Sometimes a skin of ice half an inch thick covered them, and in turn was covered by the snow. Sometimes there were alternate layers of water and ice skin, so that when one broke through he kept on breaking through for a while, sometimes wetting himself to the waist.
>
> That was why he had shied in such a panic. . . .

Whatever it lacks as exposition, the passage clearly shows that what might have seemed one paragraph's idiosyncrasies actually integrates the story. The subject—some form of H_2O—is repeated over and over, whether "creek," "water," "snow," and "ice" three times apiece, or "springs" and "skin" twice, or the implied referent of "froze," "frozen," "bubbled," and "wetting." For both man and dog, that alternating substance forms a series of fatal "traps" that are themselves phonemically reiterated in the cold "snaps" which never quite freeze the springs. Other internal sentence rhymes reverberate through the text, as does an alliteration that extends from the hard "c"'s in the second sentence. Sentence structures themselves repeat, whether resuming from similar subjects and adverbs ("They were . . ." "They hid . . ."; "Sometimes . . ." "Sometimes . . ."); or dividing in the middle ("Three inches deep, or three feet"; "he knew . . . but he knew"; "He knew . . . and he knew"); or turning on chiasmus ("Sometimes a skin of ice half an inch thick covered them, and in turn was covered by the snow"). Finally, the grammatical whole binds together with the repeated claim that the man "shied" away.

As in the earlier paragraph, multiple repetitions return us back to where we began and tend in the process to drain whatever suspense we might otherwise have felt in the action. Narrative progression seems denied through the very stylistic recurrences that integrate the passage. Or rather, to be more precise, the text's very doubleness belies the singularity asserted at the opening—"Once, coming around a bend. . . ." Through multiform repetitions

of phoneme and syntax, the implied danger of the scene is rendered commonplace. And that effect is compounded by the passage's overarching shift in preterite, from the simple opening tense of "he shied abruptly" to the closing perfect of "he had shied," all of which is subtly divided by a series of past participial constructions. Instead of spurring expectation onward, repetition and tense forestall action in a tableau of ever-recurring, never-changing elements.

II

Repetition establishes a compelling pattern in London's Arctic for reasons that are neither simple nor straightforward. Most obviously, however, its effect is entropic, reducing the man to the purely physical by depriving him initially of a will, then of desires, and at last of life itself. The process of repetition, moreover, again first appears at a verbal level—and notably with the word most often repeated. "Cold" occurs in the first half of this short story more than twenty-five times, with an effect that is altogether predictable. For as the narrative's focus on the physically immediate contributes to a paralyzing "tyranny of things," so the repetition of a thermal absence gradually seems to lower the textual temperature. Or rather, it is the emphasis on intense cold—no more, after all, than molecular inactivity—that exposes an irreducible corporeality to the very air itself.

The "tyranny of things" that develops from a repetitive concentration on the material world tends, as we have seen, to break down characteristic connections between both objects and events. Yet repetition itself implies a more ontological stasis in terms of the story's hero, exercising its power most fully by isolating not event from event, but event from actor. The repetition of things and events creates an environment that seems to resist human intention—one in which desires fail over and over to be able to shape results. Consequence ever falls short of anticipation, and the narrative gradually separates the man from his world by exposing the ineffectiveness of his will—not merely to reach camp by six o'clock, but to avoid various "traps," then to build a fire, and finally to forestall the Arctic's numbing effects. The "tyranny of things" prevails over the man first by depleting his physical resources, and then more importantly by separating him as agent from an environment in which deliberate actions might have determinate consequences.

As repetition of things makes the conditions they form seem somehow fixed and determined, its effect on ephemeral states of being similarly drops them to lower levels of possibility. And as plot recurrences seem to diminish the capacity for personal control, so verbal reiterations more generally foreclose the prospects we normally assume in experience. When the man carefully builds a second fire, for instance, the warning implied by the repetitions offsets the description's calm understatement.

> This served *for* a *foundation* and prevented the young *flame* from drowning itself in the snow it otherwise would melt. The *flame* he got by touching a match to a small shred of birch bark that he took *from* his pocket. This burned more readily than paper. Placing it on the *foundation*, he *fed* the young *flame* with wisps of dry grass and with the tiniest dry twigs.
>
> He worked slowly and carefully, keenly aware of his danger. Gradually, as the *flame* grew stronger, he increased the size of the twigs with which he *fed* it. He squatted in the snow, pulling the twigs out *from* their entanglement in the brush and *feeding* directly to the *flame* . He knew there must be no *failure*. (emphases added)

The very invocation of ''flame'' five times in seven sentences ensures not the prospect of fiery success, but rather ephemeral hope—an effect that seems even more fully confirmed by the fricatives that proliferate through the passage. Likewise, the reiteration shortly thereafter of the confident claim that ''he was safe'' establishes instead a mood of imminent peril. By translating the singular into a set, doubled language subverts linguistic authority, in the process replacing routine assurance with a series of lingering doubts.

This verbal effect is especially clear with words that unlike ''flame'' refer to capacities, not conditions. And it is hardly surprising in a story devoted to the consequences of low temperature that the privileged capacity should be a knowledge of how to forestall them—or that the word ''know'' should occur nearly as often as does ''cold.'' Keep in mind that ''know'' is a special kind of word, invoking possibilities of certainty as well as consciousness, and thereby suggesting capacities for deliberation and choice. By extension, it implies control of contingency, since knowledge of the past can help mediate the present and in turn directly shape the future. Huck and Jim ''knowed'' all sorts of signs, just as Lord Mark knows why Kate Croy rejects him, and the terms of knowledge in both cases dictate how consequent action is to be understood. That possibility is jeopardized in ''To Build a Fire'' and finally precluded by repetition, as the man's alleged knowledge, increasingly invoked, comes to seem first inadequate, then simply irrelevant. Hav-

ing thoroughly subverted the effectiveness of knowledge, repetition at last lapses into silence.

Compounding the effect of these verbal echoes is the repetitive syntactic pattern of the story. Indeed, its paratactic flatness creates a world where everything appears somehow already ordered, constraining a single fixed character in a narratively static, seemingly timeless world. The implications of London's simple, disconnected sentences can be appreciated only through illustrative contrast, and perhaps no more obvious one could be found than Henry James's late style. That style, it hardly needs stating, reflects a wholly different conception of character, since James valued individuals less for adapting to the unalterable than for imaginatively altering experience itself. The way clauses tumble out of grammatical thickets, or characters complete (only to distort) each other's claims, or shifting perspectives illumine prospects for action: these narrative patterns seem to confirm James's philosophical pragmatism. Instead of perspectives *on* the world, his late novels elaborate perspectives that *create* the different worlds in which his characters as well as his readers live.

The pattern of London's prose itself suggests a vision radically at odds with this epistemological model. Avoiding narrative contingency, his syntax denies what James everywhere celebrates: the authority of individual perspective. Clauses rest on an equal footing instead of linking in dependent structures, with the effect that experience seems already fixed and thoroughly unalterable. James's flexible grammar and tentative tone reveal experience as ever open-ended, ever to be reshaped by the power of language. London's regular, flat sentences have the contrary effect of denying any shaping power: ''everything must happen as it does happen, it could not be otherwise, and there is no need for explanatory connectives.'' Erich Auerbach does not mean in this famous definition that parataxis defies rules of causation or consequence; rather, it is the absence of clausal subordination that encourages us to read plots as if they lacked alternatives. While James's hypotactic texts seem to encourage characters to order life idiosyncratically, London's prose instead enforces a single causal order and instills a sense of certitude by returning again and again to the same stylistic place.

Yet the syntactic repetitions of parataxis have a further effect worthy of attention—one much like that of repeated words, but best illustrated in spatial terms. Just as the close doubling of physical objects blurs distinctions between this and that, here and there (or rather, this and this, here and here), so the repetition of something in time dissolves the edges between then and now. Something that happens once—a jar placed in Tennessee, say—not only enables, but seems to encourage a mapping of fixed coordinates. By contrast, something exactly repeated tends to confuse a single determinate order. Seeing double, like hearing exact echoes, disorients precisely by not allowing a fixed priority, and until sequence can be asserted, that unsettling effect remains. One of the results of the momentary disorientation produced by this kind of repetition is that time itself seems suspended. In the same way, paratactical repetitions structure a narrative that more generally denies its own temporality and, in the process, creates an aura of timelessness. Such an effect seems unlikely in a story that opens at 9 o'clock, pauses at 10, stops for lunch at 12:30, and ends at dusk, and in which a variety of shifters abound (such as "when," "before," "after," "at last," and "once in a while"). But this very specificity, when coupled with an absence of singular events, effectively elides the passage of time that it pretends to demarcate.

In the central sequence, for example, the man starts a fire to thaw his freezing legs and is just about to cut free his moccasin lacings:

> But before he could cut the strings, it happened. It was his own fault or, rather, his mistake. He should not have built the fire under the spruce tree. He should have built it in the open. But it had been easier to pull the twigs from the bush and drop them directly on the fire. Now the tree under which he had done this carried a weight of snow on its boughs. No wind had blown for weeks, and each bough was fully freighted. Each time he had pulled a twig he had communicated a slight agitation to the tree—an imperceptible agitation, so far as he was concerned, but an agitation sufficient to bring about the disaster. High up in the tree one bough capsized its load of snow. This fell on the boughs beneath, capsizing them. This process continued, spreading out and involving the whole tree. It grew like an avalanche, and it descended without warning upon the man and the fire, and the fire was blotted out! Where it had burned was a mantle of fresh and disordered snow. . . .

Without plotting multiple repetitions once again, we should not fail to notice that "it happened" echoes the earlier disaster when the man fell into the spring water ("And then it happened"). As there, the two words contain the experience. Yet more to the point, we never confuse the versatile "it" that floats through the passage and that bobs up so variously in each of the first four and last two sentences. The very shifting of referents under the

pronoun paradoxically clarifies the scene, as one completed, timeless event unfolds from a basic paratactic structure.

The real clincher, however, is the curiously immediate "Now": "Now the tree under which he had done this carried a weight of snow. . . ." While the word seems at first to recover us to time by breaking the text's completed pattern, the "Now" serves here not as adverb but expletive. Indeed, by merely marking time, it reinforces the narrative's pervasive timelessness. As well, the overly simple syntax, the pronounced lack of subordinate clauses, the subject references and verbs that each atomize the scene—all work as do repetition and tense. The whole resists normal sequence from the initial "it" onwards and simply elaborates an experience that seems already completed. Here as elsewhere, the text links sections by stylistic rather than narrative causality—by a pattern of grammatical signifieds, not narrative signifiers. Actions prompt not other actions, sentences contingent sentences, so much as each turns back on itself, in the process fostering the impression of temporal collapse.

Perhaps the best way to understand this effect is by turning to London's earlier, one-page version of the story. There the man has a name, builds a fire, and survives, toeless but with the hard-learned moral, " *Never travel alone* !" Clearly, the stories define different experiences, a difference nowhere better exemplified than in their central paragraphs:

> But at the moment he was adding the first thick twigs to the fire a grievous thing happened. The pine boughs above his head were burdened with a four months' snowfall, and so finely adjusted were the burdens that his slight movements in collecting the twigs had been sufficient to disturb the balance.
>
> The snow from the topmost bough was the first to fall, striking and dislodging the snow on the boughs beneath. And all this snow, accumulating as it fell, smote Tom Vincent's head and shoulders and blotted out his fire.

Exactly half as many words (92 vs. 183) appear in only a third as many sentences (4 vs. 13). Though brief, in other words, the passage links compound sentences with a leisured ease that assumes narrative contingency. Events can be anticipated and intentionally avoided, and therefore responsibility can be affirmed. By contrast, the later version avoids participial constructions. Simple repeated sentences only serve to confirm the response presaged by the ominous "it happened": all has been already enacted, and the human will can have no effect. As explanatory connectives help to authorize the didactic force of the early version, so the repetitive, tableau-like style of the latter shapes a narrative world free of contingency—as free in the future as in the past, and therefore as inevitable as determinism requires.

Source: Lee Clark Mitchell, "'Keeping His Head': Repetition and Responsibility in London's 'To Build a Fire,'" in *Journal of Modern Literature*, Vol. 13, No. 1, March, 1986, pp. 76–96.

Joan D. Hedrick

In the following excerpt, Hedrick discusses London's depictions of "aloneness," comradeship, and death in "The White Silence," "In a Far Country," and "To Build a Fire."

His purse exhausted after a year at the University of California, in 1897 London joined the second wave of fortune-hunters in the Klondike. He returned with little more than a case of scurvy to show for his efforts, but the stories he wrote from his Alaskan experience established his literary career. In them we can see the lineaments of a hero who would never appear in London's "civilized" fictions. He represents the most fully mature and human character London was to imagine. The aloneness of this Alaskan hero is different from the aloneness of London's romantic heroes. Martin Eden's aloneness grows out of a syndrome of self-abasement and self-exaltation like that which was operating in London's consciousness as he entered the middle class. The Alaskan hero's aloneness is based on a more realistic assessment of his strengths and weaknesses. He understands that there is something stronger than he—Death. Death is the ultimate equalizer, and in this awareness London wrote a handful of stories that imply the need for human solidarity.

In *Jack London and the Klondike,* Franklin Walker provides a carefully researched account of London's day-by-day adventures, against which he parallels his use of similar experiences in his fictions. Walker contributes significantly to our knowledge of London's sources and artistic techniques, but he does not analyze the more subtle movements that occurred in London's inner life, as he internalized the white landscapes of Alaska. For this, one must turn to James McClintock's *White Logic*. McClintock traces the movement of London's consciousness from the affirmation, in the early Malemute Kid stories, of the individual's ability to master the universe, to an awareness of "a more complex view of reality" in which "limited protagonists . . . [reach] an accommodation with a hostile, chaotic cosmos

by living by an imposed code," to a loss of faith in the ability of the code to order the universe. Then the cycle begins over again, as London "turns to race identification" to provide the illusion of mastery that the individual hero could not sustain. McClintock's ground-breaking analysis of London's Northland stories [*White Logic*, 1975] is the starting point for this chapter, and his work makes it unnecessary to dwell in detail on London's Alaskan fictions. It is sufficient to point out the pattern that emerges from a comparison of three stories: "The White Silence," "In a Far Country," and "To Build a Fire."

The first story is about three people (plus one unborn) traveling in mutual comradeship; the second is about two men who are together but who are not bound by comradely ties; in the third story "the man," as he is designated, insists on defying sourdough wisdom and traveling alone. Death enters each story. "In a Far Country" and "To Build a Fire" deal with unnecessary death—death that could have been avoided had the protagonists the imagination to perceive their finitude and their need to rely on others for mutual support and protection. The relationship between Cuthfert and Weatherbee in "In a Far Country" hinges on mutual fear and suspicion. Together in a cabin for the duration of the Alaskan winter, their distrust of each other encourages waste of food and fuel rather than the economy that is necessary for mutual survival. In the end they kill each other over a cache of sugar. The man in "To Build a Fire" believes that "a man who is a man" travels alone. He reads no message in the vast Alaskan landscape, nor does he understand, in human, mortal terms, the significance of sixty-five degrees below zero. When he breaks through the ice and wets himself to his knees, his limbs begin to freeze before he can get a fire started to dry himself out. Only when death is upon him does he realize his own mortality.

These deaths were avoidable, and the way to avoid them is clearly through human solidarity. But if solidarity can prevent some unnecessary deaths, it cannot, of course, undo the inevitability of death. That is the reality London faces in "The White Silence." The Malemute Kid is traveling with Mason, his close companion of five years, and Mason's Indian wife, Ruth. London establishes the odds early in the story. They have two hundred miles to travel and only enough food for six days. The reader may expect a tale of struggle and sacrifice in which—perhaps—the trio united can cope with nature's odds against them. But this is not, London hints in

Marshall and Louis Bond with their dog, Jack, the inspiration for Buck in Jack London's "The Call of the Wild," sitting in front of a log cabin in the Yukon.

the following passage, simply a tale of heroic struggle. It is a tale of human finitude:

> The afternoon wore on, and with the awe, born of the White Silence, the voiceless travellers bent to their work. Nature has many tricks wherewith she convinces man of his finity,—the ceaseless flow of the tides, the fury of the storm, the shock of the earthquake, the long roll of heaven's artillery,—but the most tremendous, the most stupefying of all, is the passive phase of the White Silence. All movement ceases, the sky clears, the heavens are as brass; the slightest whisper seems sacrilege, and man becomes timid, affrighted at the sound of his own voice. Sole speck of life journeying across the ghostly wastes of a dead world, he trembles at his audacity, realizes that his is a maggot's life, nothing more. Strange thoughts arise unsummoned, and the mystery of all things strives for utterance. And the fear of death, of God, of the universe, comes over him,—the hope of the Resurrection and the Life, the yearning for immortality, the vain striving of the imprisoned essence,—it is then, if ever, man walks alone with God.

Death comes unexpectedly, from an unexpected quarter. There is still food, and in the three travelers, warmth and energy. But an old pine, "burdened with its weight of years and of snow," falls and crushes Mason. He is half-paralyzed but not dead. He urges the Malemute Kid to go on with his wife and the unborn child she carries—urges him to save his family and leave him to his inevitable death. He only asks that he not have to face death alone. "'Just a shot, one pull on the trigger,'" he asks of the Kid before they leave. The Kid is reluctant to part with his traveling companion of five years with whom, "shoulder to shoulder, on the rivers and trails, in the camps and mines, facing death by field and flood and famine," he had "knitted the bonds of . . . comradeship." He asks that they wait with Mason for three days, hoping for a change of luck. Mason agrees to a one-day wait. The Kid's request for a delay turns out to be costly. He is unable to kill a moose, and, when he returns to camp, he finds the dogs have broken into their food cache. They now have "perhaps five pounds of flour to tide them over two hundred miles of wilderness." But fear of death is not, in this story, as great as the fear of aloneness.

The Kid sends Ruth on ahead, and then sits by Mason's side, hoping that he will die so that he will not be obliged to shoot him. Mason is in pain and knows he is dying, but his torment is not as acute as the Kid's. Mason places his hopes in the continuation of life through his wife and the child ("flesh of my flesh") she will bear. During his last day his mind wanders euphorically back to scenes of his early manhood in Tennessee. Although Mason bears some resemblance to London's description of his ideal Man-Comrade, who, he wrote, should be both "delicate and tender, brave and game," and "who, knowing the frailties and weaknesses of life, could look with frank and fearless eyes upon them," he also has traces of the "smallness or meanness" that was explicitly not a part of London's conception. For, earlier in the story, Mason—over the Kid's gentle protest—brutally whipped a dog who was unfortunate enough to fall in the traces. The weakened dog is subsequently devoured by her teammates. Mason is very much an ordinary man, loving his wife, loving life, having no grand philosophy but only a realistic practicality that says life must go on. He does not appear an idealized Man-Comrade but only a garrulous traveling companion, full of stories and gab. Indeed, the extent to which his rambling monologues fill up the story makes all the more awesome his death—marked by a sharp report, followed by silence.

In this story London portrays death as an event with a human character that quickly yields to a nonhuman force—the White Silence, which "seem[s] to sneer" in the moment before the Kid performs his last act of comradeship. Death is clearly harder for the survivor than for the dying. It is easier for Mason to die than for the Kid to live with the knowledge of death. He has been forced to participate in a ritual confirmation of death's power and man's finitude. Worse, he has had, in the name of comradeship, to break the bond that makes death human, that made death bearable for Mason. He is now alone. In terror, he lashes the dogs across the waste of land.

Unlike the man in "To Build a Fire," the Malemute Kid has the imagination to perceive in the vast silences of the Northland the message of his finitude. He knows the value of comradeship. But neither his imagination nor his sensitivity can protect him from the pain of loss, the pain of experiencing death before death through the death of another to whom he is bound. Written within months after London learned of John London's death (he died while Jack was in Alaska), this story probably draws on the emotions of that loss. In one stroke London lost a father, a comrade, and a model of male working-class identity. In "The White Silence" the Kid is almost in the role of a redeemer: he takes the suffering of Mason on himself; by acquiescing in Mason's request that he not be left to die alone, the Kid takes that aloneness on himself. He redeems Mason's death and renders it human. But the unspoken question hanging in the silence,

> "The Alaskan hero's aloneness is based on a more realistic assessment of his strengths and weaknesses. He understands that there is something stronger than he—Death. Death is the ultimate equalizer, and in this awareness London wrote a handful of stories that imply the need for human solidarity."

the question that fills the Kid with fear, is this: Who will redeem his own death?

As McClintock writes, this story ends in an ambiguous balance between human significance and human futility. The Kid has shown himself to be a true comrade. It remains to be seen whether or not someone will yet be a true comrade to him. This future, which is beyond the scope of the story, depends on whether or not the Kid can be open and trusting of others, whether or not he can be passively receptive to the significance that others might invest in his life; whether or not, in religious terms, he can leave his salvation up to others. If he cannot, then it is hard to escape the conclusion that, by severing the bond between himself and Mason, he has condemned himself to a living death.

"In a Far Country," written probably a few months after "The White Silence," suggests that death may also come in nonredemptive ways. Cuthfert and Weatherbee are bound together by their situations, but, not being bound emotionally, they engage in a ghastly inversion of comradely rituals. They are united not in life-giving rituals like washing and eating, but in their mutual disregard for cleanliness, order, and economy. London suggests that the reasons for their mutual suspicion are their class differences. Weatherbee is a lower-class clerk, Cuthfert a Master of Arts who writes and paints. Both think of themselves as gentlemen but, London pointedly remarks, ''a man can be a gentleman without possessing the first instinct of true comradeship.'' Master of Arts Cuthfert ''deemed the clerk a filthy, uncultured brute, whose place was in the muck with the swine, and told him so.'' The sensuous, adventure-loving clerk calls the Master of Arts ''a milk-and-water sissy and a cad.'' They perceive each other through class stereotypes, and the mechanical nature of their togetherness is like the articulation of classes and occupations in a capitalist society in which a physical interdependence of parts is accompanied by emotional anomie. Having killed each other, they die in each other's arms. Like the ''devil dog'' and his cruel master, LeClerc, in London's story ''Batard,'' like Hawthorne's Dimmesdale and Chillingworth, they are bound not by love but by a dark necessity.

The stories in which London writes of such false comradeship tend to dwell on a materialistic, positivistic view of man. The inevitable degeneration of the characters in these stories is rendered in laboratory detail as if all that were at stake were a piece of flesh. Thus in ''Love of Life,'' which looks at the struggle of a man who has been abandoned by his traveling mate, although the protagonist survives, he is described as an ''it,'' a squirming mass of cells. This is the positivistic view of man that Wolf Larsen propounds to Van Weyden in *The Sea-Wolf*. The loss of human significance in these stories of comradeship betrayed make survival a sorry boon.

In ''To Build a Fire,'' written after that period of disillusionment he called the ''long sickness,'' London takes the next logical step. If comradeship inevitably will be betrayed, one might as well travel alone. When the man in this story finally realizes that he is going to die, he ''entertained in his mind the conception of meeting death with dignity.'' But what sort of dignity is available to him? It was possible for Mason in ''The White Silence'' to meet death with dignity without cutting his emotional ties to life—because of his comradeship with the Kid and his biological link through Ruth to the next generation. But when one travels alone, death holds all the cards. The only way to meet it with dignity is to surrender oneself totally to it. The man in ''To Build a Fire'' gives himself drowsily to these thoughts. ''Well, he was bound to freeze anyway, and he might as well take it decently. With this new-found peace of mind came the first glimmerings of drowsiness. A good idea, he thought, to sleep off to death. It was like taking an anaesthetic. Freezing was not so bad as people thought. There were lots

worse ways to die.'' Several years later London described Martin Eden's attempt to drown himself: ''He breathed in the water deeply, deliberately, after the manner of a man taking an anaesthetic''. Unable to take charge of the life-forces, the characters who travel alone maintain a modicum of dignity by giving themselves willingly to their deaths.

''To Build a Fire'' and ''In a Far Country'' plot a retreat from the comradeship of ''The White Silence.'' The solace of comradeship is supplanted in ''To Build a Fire'' by the whispers of a dreamless sleep. The fire has gone out, and along with it, all hope of campfire fellowship. If we are to judge from ''The White Silence,'' London's reason for retreating from the bonds of comradeship is not simply that his comrade failed him. Mason may have differed with the Kid, but as he lay dying he apologized for his mistreatment of the dog. The only way in which Mason betrayed his comradeship was in the very act of death itself, when of mortal necessity he left the Kid behind. Perhaps this ''betrayal'' was more than the Kid could bear. It brought him up against the irrefragable aloneness of each human being. He was afraid. The delicate ecological balance London achieves in ''The White Silence'' between the forces of life and the forces of death is perhaps all that human beings should hope for in their living and dying. For London, it was not enough.

Like so many American writers, Jack London early in his career realized a vision that he could not sustain. The decline of artistry in his later fictions paralleled his retreat from the knowledge apprehended in ''The White Silence.'' It was a retreat from death, from limitation, from aloneness. In his search for a way out of the human condition, London did, in a measure, deny himself humanity. By retreating from all that life has to offer in the way of human solidarity, London exiled himself. Like Hawthorne's Wakefield, he was an ''outcast of the universe.'' Just as Wakefield, by leaving his marriage partner, lost his ''place'' in human society, so London, by leaving the lower class, found himself with no niche, no place to rest himself. The decline of London's writing career in many ways parallels that of Nathaniel Hawthorne's. Both men began their careers with short stories of superior quality, followed by a novel that became a classic. For London this was not his first novel, *A Daughter of the Snows*, but his second, *The Call of the Wild*. London followed with novels of mixed quality, like *The Sea-Wolf*, just as Hawthorne followed *The Scarlet Letter* with the less forceful *The House of the Seven Gables*, and then succumbed to the repressed sexuality of *The Blithedale Romance* and the tortured symbolism of *The Marble Faun*. But the real similarities are in their choices of theme and in their modes of retreat from the primary truth of their earlier work. Both write about characters who suffer from their aloneness. Hawthorne was able to distinguish between an aloneness that is human and necessary, indeed, inescapable, and an aloneness that is inflicted on oneself out of overweening pride, that is to say, between the aloneness of the modern hero, Hester Prynne, and that of the romantic hero, Arthur Dimmesdale. Both London and Hawthorne attempted to retreat from aloneness through the sentimental Victorian strategy of love and marriage. What neither of them fully understood was that, in using a platitudinous domesticity to shield them from the terror of aloneness, what they were seeking was not a comrade, a mate, a wife, but something altogether different: a mother.

The fire of the Victorian hearth did not burn as brightly as the Alaskan campfire. It replaced intimacy with sentiment and comradeship with courtship. For a relationship between equals, struggling against mutual dangers, it substituted a relationship between a boy-man and a girl-woman who played at being grown-ups. This ploy enabled London to come out of the long sickness and to resume life, but it vitiated his art and provided only a stay of execution for his life.

Source: Joan D. Hedrick, "Journeying across the Ghostly Wastes of a Dead World," in *Solitary Comrade: Jack London and His Work*, The University of North Carolina Press, 1982, pp. 48–55.

James I. McClintock

In the following excerpt, McClintock attempts to illustrate his assertion that "To Build a Fire" is London's "most mature expression of his pessimism."

"To Build a Fire" is London's most mature expression of his pessimism. The nameless "chechaquo" or tenderfoot who confronts the white silence in this short story possesses neither the imagination that gives man an intuitive grasp of the laws of nature and allows him to exercise his reason to accommodate himself to them, nor the "thrice cursed" imagination that convinces man of the absurdity of confronting the unknown with ridiculously finite human powers:

> The trouble with him was that he was without imagination. He was quick and alert in the things of life, but

only in the things, and not in the significances. Fifty degrees below zero meant eighty-odd degrees of frost. Such fact impressed him as being cold and uncomfortable, and that was all. It did not lead him to meditate upon his frailty as a creature of temperature, and upon man's frailty in general, able only to live within certain narrow limits of heat and cold; and from there on it did not lead him to the conjectural field of immortality and man's place in the universe.

He does not recognize that man is so finite that the bitterly cold Alaskan landscape inevitably destroys the individual. The rest of the story suggests that man is totally unequipped to face the unknown and inherently too limited to explore life's mysteries and live. If the individual is to survive, he must avoid truth-seeking and "spirit-groping."

Only two other living beings are mentioned in "To Build a Fire": the "old timer" and the dog who accompanies the tender-foot along the "hairline trail" into the "unbroken white" of the mysterious land. The old timer offers one way to survive, and as it turns out, the only way. In the autumn before the young man takes his fatal journey, "the old timer had been very serious in laying down the law that no man must travel alone in the Klondike after fifty below." His experience has given him the imagination to continue living; but, significantly, he adjusts to the unknown by refusing to venture into it. He remains with other men, away from the trail during the heart of winter. The lesson he attempts to teach the young wanderer is that if one hopes to survive, he must retreat from a solitary confrontation with cosmic power, "the full force of the blow" delivered by "the cold of space" at the "unprotected tip of the planet." The kind of accommodation the Kid makes, practicing the code in order to adjust, is impossible. The dog, however, accompanies the reckless young man into the cold and does survive. Instinct protects him. Nevertheless, instinct gives no comfort to man, since it is unavailable to him. The dog has "inherited the knowledge" from his savage ancestors who, like he, had never been separated from the brutal landscape by civilization. In fact, the dog is part of the inhuman Alaskan wilderness and, like it, "was not concerned in the welfare of the man." The old timer's imagination, then, warns that man cannot confront the depths of experience and live; the dog's instinct for survival is unavailable to man. Having been divorced from nature by civilization, no man is fit to undertake the most arduous journey.

In addition to imagination, the quality that permitted the Malemute kid and other protagonists

> Now that London's everyman has become merely a helpless victim of the killing landscape, the mystical light goes out of the Alaskan sky. Rather than, as some would have it, portraying man's insignificance but unsystematically depicting affirmations of the American Dream, the reverse had happened: London tried to dramatize a new version of human dignity but unintentionally drifted towards the pessimism which undeniably informs these Northland stories."

to survive in the Northland had been their knowledge of the concrete and their mastery of facts. Suspicious of abstractions, London had given his characters control over the factual. For example, Sitka Charlie may not understand the reasons for the bizarre occurrences in "The Sun-Dog Trail," but he sees the details in the "picture" and knows how to respond to them effectively. The Kid, too, is able to master situations because he knows Northland lore, knows facts and can order them rationally. But by the time London had written "To Build a Fire" he had lost his faith in the potency of reason.

The chechaquo in this story has a command of facts and is "quick and alert in the things of life." Clell Peterson argues perceptively and convincingly [in "The Theme of Jack London's 'To Build a Fire,'" *American Book Collector*, *XVII*, November, 1966] that the young man is not, as many readers assume, merely "a fool who dies for his folly"; he

is "not a fool" but the "modern, sensual, rational man." Rather than a deficient character, he is another of London's limited protagonists; and his death denies the efficacy of reason. The plot presents the mythic journey of the limited man into the unknown where his reason, his only support, no longer can sustain him:

> The "dark hairline" of the main trail in the "pure snow" on the broad frozen Yukon suggests the narrow limits of man's rational world compared with the universe beyond his comprehension . . . The events of the story take place in a world devoid of sunlight, of day-light, which is also the light of reason and common sense. Thus the absent sun, "that cheerful orb," represents the dominant qualities of the man which are useless in a sunless world where reason fails and common sense proves unavailing.

The power of reason has collapsed. London has even lost his faith in "facts": symbolically, the man falls through the snow into the water, the accident which begins his desperate struggle to live, because there are "no signs" indicating where the snow is soft. The man's tragic flaw has been his masculine pride in his rationality.

Neither the abstract nor the concrete, imagination nor reason, sustain life. The romantic and the realistic impulses both lead nowhere. Without their protection, the unknown becomes a destructive agent whose white logic is the "antithesis of life, cruel and bleak as interstellar space, pulseless and frozen as absolute zero." The landscape in "To Build a Fire" has become killer. What remains for London to do in this story, which everyone agrees he does masterfully, is to record the grotesque details which describe the nightmare of impaired physical activity that is the prelude to the modern man's death. In "To Build a Fire" London has employed a controlled artistry to present the theme that was struggling to life in "In a Far Country."

Now that London's everyman has become merely a helpless victim of the killing landscape, the mystical light goes out of the Alaskan sky. Rather than, as some would have it, portraying man's insignificance but unsystematically depicting affirmations of the American Dream, the reverse had happened: London tried to dramatize a new version of human dignity but unintentionally drifted towards the pessimism which undeniably informs these Northland stories. Throughout the best of his Alaskan stories, London had made a series of adjustments in order to stave off a darkening vision and to preserve some reason for "spirit-groping."

Although his temperament and reading called upon him to affirm life, he exhausted the positive as he found himself forced to move from themes of mastery, to themes of accommodation, to themes of failure. His honesty compelled him to deny affirmations. Even the archetypal quest motif and the evocative imagery of the wasteland, artistic elements which distinguish his stories from those of lesser writers, disappear from his fiction as he discovered that it is not undertaking the dangerous and desperate quest that determines the quality of life but, instead, inexorable, external forces of nature and man's irrationality, his link with that nature. The Alaskan nightmare had reached its conclusion, and London retreated from the "Unknown."

Source: James I. McClintock, "Alaskan Nightmare and Artistic Success: 1898–1908," in *White Logic: Jack London's Short Stories*, Wolf House Books, 1975, pp. 79–119.

Sources

Barker, James H. *Always Getting Ready/Upterrlainarluta: Yup'ik Eskimo Subsistence in Southwest Alaska*, Seattle: University of Washington Press, 1993, pp. 13, 118.

Barltrop, Robert. "The Materials of Fame," in his *Jack London: The Man, the Writer, the Rebel*, Pluto Press, 1976, pp. 179-91.

Komarnitsky, S. J. "Grandparents, Child Freeze to Death." *Anchorage Daily News*, Vol. 51, January 19, 1996, A1, A12.

Labor, Earle, and King Hendricks. "Jack London's Twice-Told Tale," in *Studies in Short Fiction*, Vol. 4, Summer, 1967, pp. 334-41.

Labor, Earle, and Jeanne Campbell Reesman. "The Literary Frontiersman," in *Jack London*, edited by Nancy A. Walker, rev. ed., New York: Twayne, 1994, pp. 18-48.

Lundquist, James. "Meditations on Man and Beast," in his *Jack London: Adventures, Ideas, and Fiction*, The Ungar Publishing Company, 1987, pp. 77-113.

Perry, John. *Jack London: An American Myth*, Nelson-Hall, 1981.

Sinclair, Andrew. "The Beauty Ranch," in his *Jack: A Biography of Jack London*, Harper and Row, 1977, pp. 159-69.

Stark, Peter. "Death by Degree," *We Alaskans: The Anchorage Daily News Magazine*, February 2, 1997, G4-G11.

Walcutt, Charles Child. *Jack London*, University of Minnesota Press, 1966.

Further Reading

Barker, James H. *Always Getting Ready/Upterrlainarluta: Yup'ik Eskimo Subsistence in Southwest Alaska,* University of Washington Press, 1993.

A collection of contemporary interviews and photographs of Yup'ik Eskimos who make their living on the delta of the Yukon and Kuskokwim rivers. According to Jack London, the Yukon River was part of the main route for prospectors during the Klondike Gold Rush of 1897.

Barltrop, Robert. "The Materials of Fame," in his *Jack London: The Man, the Writer, the Rebel*, Pluto Press, 1976, pp. 179-91.

Acknowledging that London has produced many badly written "pot-boilers," Barltrop asserts that "To Build a Fire" is one of London's "outstanding" stories. On the basis of such excellent stories and considering his popularity with readers, Barltrop concludes that London's reputation as a writer cannot be dismissed by literary critics.

Berton, Pierre. *Klondike: The Last Great Gold Rush, 1896-1899*, McClelland and Stewart Inc., rev. ed., 1987.

Writing from a Canadian point of view, Berton traces the history of the Klondike Gold Rush, distinguishing between the behaviors of Canadian and American prospectors and their reactions to Canadian law enforcement in the territory.

Elliott, Emory, Linda K. Kerber, A. Walton Litz, and Terence Martin. "Expansion and National Redefinition: The Late 19th Century," and "Jack London," in their *American Literature*, Vol. 2, Prentice-Hall, 1990, pp. 1-9, 894.

The authors place the literature of the nineteenth century in the context of land acquisition and the boom and bust cycle of the period. They also provide a short biography of London.

Hedin, Robert, and Gary Holthaus. *Alaska: Reflections on the Land and Spirit*, The University of Arizona Press, 1989.

A collection of essays on Alaska, including one by Pierre Berton about the Alaskan connection to the Klondike Gold Rush and another by Jack London about housekeeping in the Klondike.

Johnston, Carolyn. "Boy Socialist," in her *Jack London—An American Radical?*, Greenwood Press, 1984, pp. 27-61.

Johnston examines London's brand of socialism and discusses how his experiences in the Klondike brought out his racism, especially when he encountered Alaska's indigenous people.

Kingman, Russ. *A Pictorial Life of Jack London*, Crown Publishers, Inc., 1979.

Kingman presents photographs of London and of his family and friends, maps of his travels, relevant cartoons and newspaper clippings of the period, and a textual biography of London's life.

Komarnitsky, S. J. "Grandparents, Child Freeze to Death," in *Anchorage Daily News*, Vol. 51, January 19, 1996, A1, A12.

Newspaper account of death by hypothermia of a Yup'ik Eskimo couple and their grandchild after their car became stuck in the snow on a rural road in Alaska.

Labor, Earle, and King Hendricks. ''Jack London's Twice-Told Tale,'' in *Studies in Short Fiction*, Vol. 4, Summer, 1967, pp. 334-41.
    Labor and Hendricks reprint London's 1902 version of ''To Build a Fire'' that was directed towards an adolescent audience and compare it with his 1908 version of the story to prove that the later, adult version demonstrates London's genuine ability to write serious fiction.

Labor, Earle, and Jeanne Campbell Reesman. ''The Literary Frontiersman,'' in *Jack London*, edited by Nancy A. Walker, rev. ed., New York: Twayne, 1994, pp. 18-48.
    Labor and Reesman examine the tragic imagery and symbolism in ''To Build a Fire'' and argue that London's harsh winter setting functions as an antagonistic and mythical character in the story.

London, Joan. ''Introduction,'' in her *Jack London and His Times: An Unconventional Biography*, University of Washington Press, 1968, pp. xi-xvii.
    In this new introduction to her 1939 biography of her father, Joan London assesses the changing critical attitudes to Jack London's writings.

Lundquist, James. ''Meditations on Man and Beast,'' in his *Jack London: Adventures, Ideas, and Fiction*, The Ungar Publishing Company, 1987, pp. 77-113.
    In this chapter, Lundquist focuses on the mood and setting of ''To Build a Fire,'' calling the story ''starkly elegant.''

O'Connor, Richard. ''Self-Discovery in the Klondike,'' in his *Jack London: A Biography*, Little, Brown, and Company, 1964, pp. 80-103.

O'Connor discusses ''Klondicitis,'' or America's mad rush for gold in 1897, and describes London's own trek into the Klondike territory and his attitudes towards the people he met there.

Perry, John. *Jack London: An American Myth*, Nelson-Hall, 1981.
    In this biography, Perry devotes several chapters to London's Klondike fiction and observes that ''To Build a Fire'' elicits ''moods of impotence and loneliness through images of cold.''

Pizer, Donald. ''Historical and Geographical Note,'' in *Jack London: Novels and Stories*, The Library of America, 1982, pp. 1001-04.
    In this selection of London's novels and stories, Pizer provides maps and a history of the ''Klondike stampede'' to Canada's principal mining town of Dawson.

Sinclair, Andrew. ''The Beauty Ranch,'' in his *Jack: A Biography of Jack London*, Harper and Row, 1977, pp. 159-69.
    In this chapter, Sinclair observes that London was unable to distinguish between his good stories, among them ''To Build a Fire,'' and his poorly written stories, and thus included both types in his collections *Lost Face* and *When God Laughs*.

Stark, Peter. ''Death by Degree,'' in *We Alaskans: The Anchorage Daily News Magazine*, February 2, 1997, G4-G11.
    Stark uses scientific data and anecdotal accounts to define hypothermia.

Walcutt, Charles Child. *Jack London*, University of Minnesota Press, 1966.
    In this overview of London's work, Walcutt remarks that the early critical reception to London's stories was positive.

Waldo

Robert A. Heinlein
1942

Originally published in 1942 in the magazine *Astounding*, ''Waldo'' is one of the few stories in which Heinlein tackles magic rather than concentrating on hard science. In this story, humanity's refusal to sufficiently test new technologies leads to a debilitating exhaustion in humans which in turn causes a series of power failures in a ''fail-safe'' system. Waldo, a crippled genius who lives in a house that orbits the earth, discovers that the only way to cure the power failures is to treat the affected power receptors with magic. Waldo reaches into the ''Other World'' and grasps power from that other dimension. Accordingly, the broken parts work again, but in an unexpected way: they no longer use radiant energy and, even though they are made of a rigid metal alloy, they begin waving like the tentacles of a sea anemone.

While Heinlein utilizes his favorite themes in this piece (self-reliance and independence), his warning about hidden dangers in new technology seems somewhat unusual. Heinlein, and the other authors of the ''Golden Age'' of science fiction (notably Arthur C. Clarke and Isaac Asimov), generally glorify technology as a kind of savior of the human race. However, in several of the main characters, Heinlein reiterates his insistence on the independence of the individual. Waldo tries to live his own life without any reliance on others; Dr. Grimes and Gramps Schneider live in their own ways and are not concerned with how other people see them. The

ultimate concentration of the story, then, continues Heinlein's theme of self-reliance.

The mechanical "hands" or series of mechanical joints used today in engineering and mechanical puppetry are now called "waldoes" after this Heinlein story, demonstrating the significant impact that Heinlein's works have enjoyed over the years.

Author Biography

Born on July 7, 1907, in Butler, Missouri, Robert Anson Heinlein was one of seven children. He finished high school in 1924, spent a year at the University of Missouri and then entered the Naval Academy at Annapolis, majoring in naval science. He graduated in the top ten percent of his class in 1929, moving to active duty in the Navy on destroyers and experimental aircraft carriers. However, he contracted tuberculosis in 1934 while serving as a gunnery officer on the *U.S.S. Lexington* and was forced to retire from the military.

For the next five years, Heinlein attended graduate school (which he was forced to abandon due to further health problems), architecture, real estate, silver mining, and politics before discovering an ad in *Thrilling Wonder Stories* which offered a fifty dollar prize for the best piece of amateur fiction. Heinlein wrote the short story "Life-Line" in four days. He considered the story too good for the "pulp" magazine (literally, a magazine printed on pulp, or poor quality, paper) that had placed the ad and sent the story to John W. Campbell at *Astounding Science-Fiction* where it was ultimately published. For the rest of his life, Heinlein maintained that he did not write for art, but for cash.

Over the course of his career, however, the quality of his writing garnered him four Hugo awards. In 1975, the Science Fiction Writers of America presented him with a special Grand Master Nebula Award for lifetime achievement. Heinlein's works are usually divided into three categories: short fiction, juvenile novels, and adult novels. The juvenile novels, however, should not be dismissed merely as children's literature—the theme of self-reliance and independence that he uses in the juvenile fiction appears in his other fiction as well.

Considered one of the "Big Three" authors of science fiction (alongside Arthur C. Clarke and Isaac Asimov), Heinlein wrote more than thirty novels and story collections. He was influential in the development of NASA's space suits and was a guest commentator during the Apollo 11 lunar landing.

Perhaps his best-known work is *Stranger in a Strange Land*, which has enjoyed immense popularity since its publication in 1961. By the end of his career he was interested in bringing most, if not all, of his fictional characters together into one "multiverse" by developing a theory that strong fiction writers did not just create believable stories but actually created alternate universes or realities. Heinlein includes characters from his own works in this multiverse. Many critics praise his vivid and engaging depiction of this world, his ability to create characters that live and breathe on the page.

Plot Summary

Problem One

James Stevens, the Chief Traffic Engineer of North American Power Air (NAPA), is summoned to his superior's office because NAPA, the company that supplies power to air vehicles as well as the cities, suffers several unexplainable power breakdowns. "DeKalb receptors," components that receive the radiant power, utilize the power for the aircars. Scientists proclaim the deKalbs infallible, and yet they have been failing in commercial freighters for some time. NAPA cannot figure out what causes the problem. The head physicist of NAPA, Dr. Rambeau, insists that the deKalbs cannot fail and that the engineers have somehow "operated them incorrectly" yet the engineering department cannot figure out just what they're doing wrong.

NAPA is completely puzzled, so Dr. Stevens suggests that they contact Waldo, a bitter genius who is particularly hateful toward NAPA, to solve the problem for them. The suggestion is met with some dismay, but Gleason, Dr. Stevens's superior, admits that he's already contacted Waldo, but that Waldo is "still sore over the Hathaway patents" and doesn't wish to help NAPA. The people at NAPA are worried about the failure of the deKalbs in the air vehicles because the same technology is used to power cities, and NAPA is afraid that while the power to the cities hasn't yet failed, it's only a matter of time until it does. Because of these worries, Gleason tells Stevens to use his connections to contact Waldo.

Problem Two

Stevens meets with Doc Grimes, an eccentric doctor who dresses in anti-radiation suits and is Waldo's only friend. Grimes berates Stevens for his out- of-shape condition and speculates that the reason for Stevens's out-of-shape condition is not solely overwork, as Stevens maintains, but that humanity cannot "pour every sort of radiant energy through the human system year after year and not pay for it." Grimes's thesis is that the radiant energy that NAPA uses for power is dangerous to humans. Grimes maintains that even though it was tested before being put into widespread use, the power source was not tested long enough to determine whether it would be dangerous to humans who were exposed to it every day, day in and day out. Grimes hypothesizes that this radiant energy is running down the human race—people act tired and thus don't exercise enough. He has kept records for years, noting that in athletic events, the all-time records are no longer getting broken and the top athletes of the present day could not compete with athletes from previous times—humankind is getting weaker physically instead of continuing to strengthen and improve.

Stevens finally asks Grimes to introduce him to Waldo. Grimes considers Waldo's disorder, *myasthenia gravis*, which affects the muscles. Essentially, Waldo is as relatively weak as a newborn baby—he cannot move in Earth's gravity and so he has moved to his own space station and moves with relative ease in an anti-gravity environment. Grimes agrees to take Stevens up to Freehold, Waldo's space station, to meet Waldo and attempt to convince him to take on the problem of the failing deKalb receptors. Once at Freehold, Grimes convinces Waldo not only to take on the NAPA problem, but also to devise a way to fix the problem that will do away with the radiant power that Grimes believes is causing the tired and rundown feeling in the human race.

Finding a Solution

Stevens returns to NAPA only to discover that one set of deKalbs has been miraculously fixed.

Robert A. Heinlein

Stevens's assistant, Mac, had a failed set of deKalbs in his air-car. Since he was near his hometown, he went walking and came to the house of Gramps Schneider, who fixed the deKalbs by "thinking" them fixed. If that weren't unscientific enough, the rigid metal "fingers" of the deKalbs now wiggle like fingers reaching for the power they need to operate.

The story then shifts back to Waldo's attempt to discover the cause for the failing deKalbs. He tries to determine if the manufacturing or the operation of the deKalbs is at fault, but so far, Waldo has discovered no reason for the deKalbs to be faulty. He also has discovered that Doc Grimes's theory on humankind becoming weaker is true, and is discovering that radiant energy is in fact the prime reason—humankind is slowly poisoning itself on the radiant energy technology. Meanwhile, Stevens has sent the deKalbs that Gramps Schneider fixed to Waldo. Dr. Rambeau, the physicist, calls Waldo to explain that he, too, can make the deKalbs work. He tells Waldo: "You are here and I am there. Or maybe not. Nothing is certain. Nothing, *nothing*, NOTHING is certain! Around and around the little ball goes, and where it stops nobody knows. Only I've learned how to do it." He goes on to tell Waldo that "nothing is certain any more. . . . Chaos is King and Magic is loose in the world!'' Rambeau disappears soon after his conversation with Waldo (before he is locked up as a lunatic) and Waldo must study the wiggling deKalbs (Rambeau has made a second set behave in the same way) and discover an answer to the problems on his own.

Learning

Waldo finally comes down to Earth in order to meet Gramps Schneider and hopefully learn how Gramps Schneider made the deKalbs work—and wiggle. Essentially, Gramps tells Waldo that he told the deKalbs to reach into the ''Other World'' for energy and implies that Waldo could do the same in order to be cured of his *myasthenia gravis*. Gramps Schneider also tells Waldo that the deKalbs seem to be failing not because of any mechanical problem— but because the operators of the deKalbs are ''tired and fretting,'' and essentially think their deKalbs into not working.

Waldo returns to Freehold interested, but puzzled by Gramps Schneider's ideas about how the deKalbs and other machinery work. After Stevens calls Waldo and warns him that time is growing short and they need an answer quickly, Waldo reconsiders the ''Other World'' and begins researching magic and begins to accept that the ''Other World'' is a reality. Eventually, Waldo also makes a set of broken deKalbs wiggle and work. However, while visiting with Doc Grimes, they notice that the ''fixed'' deKalbs aren't using the radiant energy. They are taking energy from somewhere else, and Waldo hypothesizes that they are taking energy from the ''Other World.'' Hence, by ''hexing'' all of the deKalbs (or simply building ''Schneider-deKalbs''), he has solved both problems: There will be no more need for the radiant energy that was causing humankind's muscles to deteriorate, and he can create functioning deKalbs.

Waldo considers the nature of the ''Other World'' and its relation to our own:

Suppose*Chaos were* king and the order we thought we detected in the world about us a mere phantasm of the imagination; where would that lead us? In that case, Waldo decided, it was entirely possible that a ten-pound weight *did* fall ten times as fast as a one-pound weight until the day the audacious Galileo decided in his mind that it was not so. Perhaps the whole meticulous science of ballistics derived from the convictions of a few firm-minded individuals who had sold the notion to the world. Perhaps the very stars were held firm in their courses by the unvarying faith of the astronomers. Orderly Cosmos, created out of Chaos—by Mind!. . .

More recently it had been different. A prevalent convention of materialistic and invariable causation had ruled the world; on it was based the whole involved technology of a machine-served civilization. The machines *worked*, the way they were designed to work, because everybody believed in them.

Until a few pilots, somewhat debilitated by overmuch exposure to radiation, had lost their confidence and infected their machines with uncertainty—and thereby let magic loose in the world. (Excerpt from ''Waldo'')

Waldo continues to study the phenomenon of the ''Other World'' and begins to apply what he has learned to his own condition, *myasthenia gravis*, until he can finally walk and endure in gravity again. He returns to Earth as a whole man—a brilliant mind and a vibrant body.

Characters

Waldo Farthingwaite-Jones
See Waldo F. Jones

Mr. Gleason
See Stanley F. Gleason

Stanley F. Gleason
Gleason is Dr. Stevens's boss at North American Power-Air. He is the first to contact Waldo in regard to the problems with the ''infallible'' deKalb receptors which are causing air-cars to crash.

Grandfather
See Gramps Schneider

Doc Grimes
Doc Grimes is a somewhat eccentric doctor who delivered Waldo despite his concerns that something was wrong with the infant. Only Grimes has the audacity to speak plainly to the adult Waldo. He treats Waldo like the bright, but spoiled man that Waldo has become. He believes that humankind is gradually becoming weaker as they are continually exposed to low levels of radiation. He thus convinces Waldo to not only take on the problem of the failing deKalb receptors, but to find a solution that would also solve the problem of radiation exposure.

Dr. Augustus Grimes
See Doc Grimes

Dr. Gus Grimes
See Doc Grimes

Uncle Gus
See Doc Grimes

Waldo F. Jones

Waldo F. Jones is an eccentric genius who has a serious muscle disorder that renders him physically weak. To compensate for this physical handicap, Waldo has developed his mental capabilities. Moreover, Waldo invented a device to act as a strong hand for him. Though this device requires little strength to properly function, it demands the user's complete control. Waldo lives in an isolated space station of his own design, orbiting Earth. With his muscle disorder, Waldo is convinced that he is intellectually superior to the "smooth apes" that inhabit the Earth and perform physical labor for him.

Mac
See Hugh Donald MacLeod

Hugh Donald MacLeod

Dr. Stevens's assistant, Hugh introduces the hex doctor, Gramps Schneider.

Gramps Schneider

A "hex doctor" who ultimately shows Waldo how to fix the balky deKalb receptors and his own body by reaching into the "Other World" for energy, Gramps Schneider is a childhood acquaintance of Hugh MacLeod. Gramps Schneider dislikes machines and technology, yet agrees to fix the broken deKalbs that Hugh brings him because he likes to help "boys."

James Stevens

As the Chief Traffic Engineer for North American Power-Air, Dr. James Stevens must find a solution for the failing power in the "infallible" deKalb receptors. Dr. Stevens is a practical man looking for a practical solution where none exists. He decides to consult Waldo to help him solve the problem. He solicits his friend, Doc Grimes, to help

him convince Waldo to solve the problem of the failing deKalbs.

Jim Stevens
See Dr. James Stevens

Jimmie Stevens
See Dr. James Stevens

Themes

Science and Technology

Ultimately, most works of science fiction deal with the theme of science and technology, and especially with how humanity deals with the technology it has created. In "Waldo," Heinlein seems to express some concern that humanity is creating technology too quickly and not testing it thoroughly enough. Because of human carelessness, then, technology becomes harmful, causing a physical deterioration of the human race. He compounds this theme with a warning against becoming too intellectual and not balancing both the physical and intellectual aspects of human life. By equating the overly intellectual Waldo with technology (Waldo's creation of the waldo and his home, Freehold) and then having Waldo become independent of that technology (both his waldoes and Freehold), Heinlein warns against relying too heavily on technology and instead reminds readers to live life without being dependent upon it.

Individual vs. Machine

Heinlein modifies this theme somewhat in "Waldo," as Waldo really is part machine in the beginning of the story. Since he cannot move easily on his own, Waldo creates machines (which bear his name, further emphasizing his connection and dependence on machines) that will help him manipulate the world around him. He also builds Freehold, nicknamed "Wheelchair," the space station in which he lives. Freehold has earned its nickname because it is the machine that allows Waldo some semblance of a mobile life; without it, he would be at the mercy of others and essentially motionless. By the end of the story, however, Waldo has freed himself from the waldoes he created, and from his "wheelchair" in order to become his own complete person.

Topics for Further Study

- Why do you think Heinlein framed this story with Waldo as a ballet-tap dancer/brain surgeon? Why does he have Waldo repeat that "they were all such grand guys?"

- Research the use of waldoes. What is a waldo, and in what discipline is it most commonly used today?

- Do some research on the differences between fantasy and science fiction literature. Is "Waldo" a science fiction story or a fantasy story? Why do you think so?

- Research the levels of radiation that we receive from everyday appliances such as computers, televisions, and microwaves. How could these levels of radiation affect our bodies? Could Heinlein have been serving a warning to us against using such technologies? Use examples from the story to support your view.

Search for Identity

As in some of his juvenile novels, Heinlein explores humanity's search for a sense of individuality, a sense of self. Waldo, at the beginning of the story, is hardly distinguishable from his own machines, his waldoes. He is completely dependent on technology to keep him functioning, and so in a sense, his identity is lost in the machines around him. Forced from childhood into a life of physical inactivity, Waldo threw himself into the only activity remaining to him: that of intellectual exercise. However, Waldo the intellectual is only half of a man, and despite his constant posturing to the contrary, he realizes that he is incomplete.

Within the framework of the story, Waldo is both a dancer and a brain surgeon, melding both the physical with the intellectual. By Waldo's choice of professions, Heinlein emphasizes the importance of this balance between the physical and the intellectual and implies that both are necessary for a person to be complete. Waldo's search for an answer to the

problem of why the infallible fails, mirrors his search for his complete self; he must reach beyond the machines and technology for his own identity, and for solutions to his immediate problem.

Style

Point of View

As in many science fiction and fantasy stories, the point of view in "Waldo" constantly shifts from one character to another. The point of view of "Waldo" initially can be identified as Waldo's, but in the space of a few paragraphs changes to that of Dr. Stevens. By attaching the point of view to a character, an author can place the reader in the story and learn what a specific character thinks and feels.

Many science fiction and fantasy pieces strive to make their characters familiar to the reader since the technology or the land itself might be very unfamiliar (i.e., Mars or Jupiter). By pairing the reader with a particular character for the point of view of the story, the author limits what the reader can know to what that particular character might know. However, if the author wants the reader to know something that the character does not know, he has to become creative in telling the reader that information. In many cases the author will simply imply the information, but this is an unreliable technique. Perhaps the reader will miss a vital piece of data.

In science fiction and fantasy stories, the writer will often change the point of view from character to character in order to reveal necessary material. This method also allows the author to develop characters not only by their actions, but also by how other characters perceive those actions. In "Waldo," Heinlein shifts his point of view between Waldo, Dr. Stevens, and Doc Grimes in order to give the reader a clearer picture of each man. Waldo seems quite reasonable in his own sections, but when seen through the eyes of Dr. Stevens, he is revealed more as a spoiled child than a slightly eccentric genius. When seen through the eyes of Doc Grimes, Waldo is even more of a spoiled child. Doc Grimes has to remind Waldo of his own selfishness in order to manipulate him into agreeing to help Dr. Stevens find a cause for the failing power receptors.

Structure and the Framing Device

Heinlein begins and ends "Waldo" with a glimpse of an older, more mature Waldo than is seen in the rest of the story. This is a Waldo who is both physically and intellectually fit, he is both a body and a brain (a dancer and a brain surgeon). When a reporter asks Waldo how he got started in dance, the story flashes back to Dr. Stevens and the problems at North American Power-Air with the non-functioning deKalb receptors. The rest of the story unfolds in a straightforward chronological pattern explaining how Waldo solves both the problems of the balky deKalbs and the radiant power that is weakening humankind. At the end of the story, Heinlein closes his frame by returning to the older, physically fit Waldo in order to emphasize the fitness (and politeness) of Waldo now that he has become a whole person in mind and body.

Historical Context

Heinlein wrote "Waldo" prior to 1942, the date of its publication in *Astounding*. He actually did not write new material during World War II, but did publish some material that he had previously written. By the late 1930s and the early 1940s, the Industrial Age was becoming the Technological Age. Progress equaled technology, and Americans wanted to be the most progressive country in the world. As a result, the United States in particular enjoyed a boom period from the development of electricity, up through the development of the microcomputer.

While various technologies were tested for short-term effects on the environment and on human health, little was done to test whether or not there might be any long-term effects from the technologies discovered. For example, X-ray machines were placed in shoe stores in the 1950s because merchants wanted to use the new technology to show their customers how well their shoes fit. It was discovered later that too much radiation was harmful to the human body. Consequently, the X-ray machines were quickly removed from the stores. It is this lack of foresight to consider possible consequences of technologies that Heinlein highlights in "Waldo." How do we really know what the effects of those technologies will be unless we test them over a period of time? Since Heinlein writes science fiction, he sets the story somewhat in the future, which seems to divorce it from a distinct historical perspective, but the concerns of his own time period show through the text itself.

Critical Overview

While Heinlein has long been considered the "dean of science fiction," some critics debate whether or not "Waldo" is really a work of science fiction. For example, Charles N. Brown, in his introduction to the 1979 edition of *Waldo and Magic, Inc.*, maintained that "Waldo" is obviously a work of fantasy by the inclusion of details like the following: "aircars that look like broomsticks. When Waldo shouts, 'Magic is loose in the world!' he is not being facetious. The power failures turn out to be caused by people worrying; the solution is to believe and be able to tap the power of the 'other world.'"

While Brown is certain that "Waldo" is a work of fantasy, Alexei Panshin in *Heinlein in Dimension*, claimed that "I am certain that 'Waldo' is a science fiction story rather than a fantasy story." Panshin suggests that the very scientific way that Waldo goes about solving his technological problems, and even their magical solution, make the story more science fiction than fantasy. Bruce Franklin, in his *Robert A. Heinlein: America as Science Fiction*, claims that Heinlein is preoccupied by "two quite contradictory conceptions of the relations between mind and matter. On one side he has faith in science and technology. . . . On the other side, he rejects science and embraces wishful thinking, the direct, unfettered immediate control of matter by mind."

Nor is "Waldo" the only story that critics have derided this tension between the rational world of science and the more irrational world of fantasy. Heinlein's entire canon, particularly *Assignment in Eternity*, demonstrates this science fiction versus fantasy tension.

Other critics have commented on Heinlein's ability to draw a complete world in his fiction, not simply a single technological difference to distinguish the fictional world from the actual, but a well-fleshed-out new world that is still somehow familiar. Brown comments on this when he states that "broadcast power is the invention that makes the world of "Waldo" possible. Instead of just replacing automobiles with radiant power vehicles, Heinlein mentions some of the changes which have happened. . . . There is enough background texture."

While Heinlein's worlds are often praised, his characterizations have more often drawn fire from the critics, especially his characterizations of wom-

Compare & Contrast

- **1940s:** Workers during the Great Depression are faced with unemployment rates as high as 25% and relief comes through socialistic government programs. The U.S. also increases defense spending as the nation enters World War II in 1941.

  1990s: Unemployment stands around 6%, but corporate downsizing has many workers concerned about their future. The government must reduce a multi-billion dollar deficit, yet the stock market continues its strong performance.

- **1940s:** Blacks are excluded from the suburban housing boom of the era. The Federal Housing Authority practices "redlining": on city maps it draws red lines around predominantly black inner-city areas and refuses to insure loans for houses in those areas. This practice contributes to the demise of the inner city.

  1990s: Though many upper- and middle-class blacks live and work in the suburbs, poor blacks are often confined to substandard housing in decaying urban areas, or ghettos.

- **1940s:** Technological advances increase dramatically during the war years. In the later part of the decade, as wartime economy is replaced by peacetime economy, America is still in the forefront of technical exploration and knowledge.

  1990s: Technology has a ever-increasing role in American life. Nearly all business transactions are done via computer; databases hold vital information to every aspect of human life. Critics warn that privacy is impossible in such a society. Meanwhile, the Internet makes it possible to communicate quickly and efficiently, and its possible uses are still being explored. Critics charge that it further alienates people from each other and disseminates subversive information to young children and adults.

---

en. Despite lip service given to the idea of the equality of women and men by creating competent and intelligent female characters, Heinlein's actual characterizations of female characters are almost invariably sexist. For example, in E. F. Bleiler's *Science Fiction Writers*, Peter Nicholls writes that the main character from *Podkayne of Mars* "is the least bearable of all of Heinlein's heroines. Although her competence is high, her language is arch, whimsical, and frankly sticky throughout. Heinlein's usual inability to create women who can communicate directly with other people in any terms other than coy banter is one of his most obvious flaws."

Over the course of a long career in writing, Heinlein's writing gained commercial popularity. However, he also suffered disapproval from critics who often considered his novels to be somewhat symptomatic of what was wrong with science fiction as a genre. Some commentators maintained his work featured too much science and too little skill in the art of creating fully believable worlds *and* characters, as well as stories that engaged the reader in terms of craft, not just sensationalism.

Criticism

Robin MacRorie

MacRorie has taught literature and composition at the University of Notre Dame. In the following essay, she examines the techniques Heinlein uses to illustrate the necessity of self-reliance in "Waldo."

Science fiction stories are often characterized as stories about technology and gadgetry. We often expect science fiction to laud the merits of technology, especially the "golden age" of science fiction, such as Heinlein's early works, which have earned a reputation for painting a rosy picture of a future filled with time-saving gadgets and robots. "Waldo,"

United States International Space Station, a product of engineering and of the new technologies developed since the Second World War.

however, is an early example of one of Heinlein's most prominent themes—that man should rely on himself and his own intelligence, not solely on technology.

First of all, Heinlein has created a central character who, by all rights, should be dependent on other people. Waldo has *myasthenia gravis*, a muscle disorder which renders Waldo quite incapable physically. He must use two hands in order to feed himself with a spoon, and even at that, the process is quite tiring and laborious. If Waldo were to remain on Earth at our normal gravity, he would have to

have caretakers to pander to his every need, from feeding him, to turning the pages of a book if he wished to read.

However, Waldo is not content to remain so reliant on those around him. By the age of ten he has invented a machine which will hold a book for him as well as both light the pages and turn them with a simple control panel sensitive to Waldo's touch. While Waldo must have someone else build his invention for him at that age, by the time Waldo becomes an adult, he is capable of building his own inventions. Waldo, trying to become more indepen-

What Do I Read Next?

- Orson Scott Card's *Ender's Game* won both the Hugo and Nebula awards for 1985. Ender Wiggin, a brilliant young child, must learn to excel at military games and make his subordinates love him, all while trying to understand how the Buggers think before the Buggers attack Earth a third time. Ender must use not only his physical prowess to survive his training, but he needs all of his wits about him to survive the games and the Buggers.

- In *Assignment in Eternity* (1953), Robert A. Heinlein again tackles the ability of the mind to perform a kind of magic, or extra-sensory perception. A series of four short stories, each deals in some way with humanity's reaching into the "Other World" or another dimension.

- Heinlein's 1965 novel, *The Moon Is a Harsh Mistress*, deals with Manny, Wyoh, and Professor de la Paz trying to free their land from the tyranny of Earth with the help of a sentient computer named Mike. While the revolution is deadly serious to the humans involved, it begins solely as an elaborate practical joke for the bodiless Mike until he realizes his own mortality.

- Mercedes Lackey's The Last Herald-Mage trilogy—*Magic's Pawn* (1989), *Magic's Promise* (1990), and *Magic's Price* (1990)—deals with the "science" of magic and how it works in the land of Valdemar. Young Vanyel must learn the laws of magic as well as use that magic to protect his family and friends.

---

dent, realizes that he must escape Earth's gravity if he is ever to be able to take care of himself. Without gravity to hold him down, his muscular weakness will not matter, he will not need to exert a great amount of force to accomplish simple tasks. Heinlein, however, very specifically tells his readers that Waldo's home, Freehold, is nothing more than a fancy crutch rather than a cure when he has Dr. Stevens refer to Waldo's home as Wheelchair.

Nor is Freehold/Wheelchair the only crutch on which Waldo relies. Waldo has also invented a mechanical "hand" of sorts, a series of joints that he can control by making small movements in a glove which acts as a remote control for the mechanical hand. This invention gives Waldo the strength he needs to be able to do anything. For example, he uses one of these mechanical hands to catch his dog, Baldur, when the dog rushes a visitor. Other people call this invention a waldo, after their creator. In a sense, they are very right to name the invention after the inventor, for Waldo cannot exist on his own without the aid of his waldoes. He has, to a certain extent, become machine himself since he is reliant on both his space station and the mechanical hands which bear his name in order to exist "on his own."

Despite Waldo's seeming independence from others, Heinlein emphasizes just how dependent Waldo really is on technology. In fact, Heinlein goes on to have Doc Grimes underline Waldo's dependence, not just on technology, but on other people as well, in the very beginning of the novella. When Waldo first learns of the failing deKalb receptors and North American Power-Air asks Waldo for help, he brushes NAPA off, claiming that the problem is interesting, but that he will not help them discover the answer. Doc Grimes reminds him just how dependent on other people Waldo still is. Waldo imports all of his food, an obvious necessity and a surprising dependence on others. Once reminded of this dependence, Waldo agrees to tackle both the problem of the failing deKalb receptors as well as the problem that Grimes reveals to him: the use of radiant, broadcast energy (such as the deKalbs) is causing humans to become weaker and weaker. His decision to solve these two problems eventually leads to Waldo solving his own personal problem as well: his own physical weakness.

Waldo has two types of dependency, then. First, he is reliant on his technological gadgetry to lead the life of a normal person. Second, he relies on other people to make sure that he has all of the necessities of life. A smaller third dependence is his reliance on Doc Grimes, Uncle Gus to Waldo, to keep him acting somewhat civilized. Despite Heinlein's insistence on self-reliance in the first two categories, though, he makes it quite clear in this novella that self-reliance does not equal a complete isolation from others.

With the types of dependency established, we can now examine exactly how Heinlein goes about convincing the reader that self-reliance is the answer, not technology. First, of course, we see Waldo's determination to be independent of others, to not have to rely on them to do everything for him. Since Waldo is the title character, we can assume that we are to learn something from him. In most ways, however, Waldo seems to be a character hard to like or to learn from. His personality is overbearing and arrogant. His only redeeming quality seems to be his fierce independence. But, as previously stated, Waldo is not quite as independent as he first seems. He is entirely dependent on technology, from the very house in which he lives to the mechanical waldoes which allow him to lead some semblance of a normal life. He is also dependent on others to make sure that he is provided with the necessities of life. What at first seemed to be Waldo's saving grace is a bit more complicated than it appeared. However, by looking closely at the frame (a device which both begins and ends the story) of the novella, Heinlein's insistence on self-reliance is, in fact, one of the main tropes of the story.

In the framing device of the novella, Heinlein gives a small episode with Waldo. In the beginning, Heinlein spends several paragraphs explaining that this character has it all—a lucrative performing career (in ballet-tap, indicating great physical grace, strength and endurance) as well as being a brain surgeon (indicating a great physical dexterity, but more importantly, this profession indicates intelligence). Heinlein does not reveal to the reader just who this paragon of the physical and the intellectual is, but instead he jumps back in time by having a reporter ask the great performer/surgeon how he came to take up dancing. Heinlein then begins narrating "Waldo" in a more-or-less chronological order beginning with a description of the immediate problems to be solved and ending with the solution of those problems. He then concludes the novella with Waldo telling the reporter that the reason he

> **Waldo's joining of the human race is the result of his leaving behind the technology that he had relied upon to make him independent."**

went into dance is quite a long story and implies that it is one that he does not have time to go into at the moment.

But Heinlein's characterization of Waldo in this framing device is dramatically different than that of Waldo in the central story. Waldo in the frame is a polite and genuinely nice individual. Rather than dismiss the reporters and photographers, he thanks them for their attention and offers them drinks in his dressing room. He thinks of them as "grand guys" repeatedly. When the former head of NAPA, Gleason, approaches Waldo with a batch of legal papers to sign, Waldo does so without reading them, telling Gleason that if the papers are to Gleason's satisfaction, then they are to Waldo's satisfaction as well. Heinlein ends the story with Waldo's thought, "They were all such grand guys."

However, in the course of the main story, Heinlein portrays Waldo as a man nearly incapable of behaving politely. When Waldo first meets Stevens, for example, Waldo acts as if he will help solve the problem of the balky deKalb receptors but finally tells Stevens that he will do nothing to help NAPA out of its troubles. He goes so far as to tell Stevens that he is no "roller-skate mechanic for apes," implying that the men on Earth mean as little to him as apes do to humans; he is contemptuous of them. Even when Gramps Schneider reveals the answer to the deKalbs as well as eliminating the need for radiant power, he thinks of Gramps Schneider as that "hex doctor," as if it is an accident that this man was able to discover the answer when Waldo had been unable to do so himself.

What changes from the main text of the story to the framing device? The answer is simple. Waldo is no longer reliant on his Wheelchair or on his waldoes. Waldo's joining of the human race is the result of his leaving behind the technology that he had relied upon to make him independent. Once he thought of himself as free of that dependence, he became free of it in reality as well. It is in the frame, which seems at first as only a superficial reason for the telling of the story, that Heinlein's main focus becomes readily apparent: by relying on our own selves instead of technology we can find the strength we need to do whatever it is we need to do.

Source: Robin MacRorie, "Overview of 'Waldo,'" for *Short Stories for Students*, The Gale Group, 2000.

Alice Carol Gaar

In the following excerpt, Gaar maintains that Heinlein's failure to depict characters reacting emotionally to intense experience results in shallow characterization.

... "Waldo" develops Heinlein's cosmic personality by focusing on an individual who is transformed from a physically inferior person (although mechanically brilliant) into someone who is superior in the sense that the new Waldo begins successfully to create the world of men in his own image. The story moves from the self-isolation of the physically inferior, compensating individual to a totally new spatial and temporal orientation on the part of that genius who, as a result of his newly positive attitude toward the rest of humanity, shares his discovery with others. As in "Universe" weightlessness symbolizes the freedom of outer space where one is closer to one's own true nature as a dweller in space. Waldo's genius has lifted him above the physical confines of gravity. Out there he becomes aware of another world which is a source as well as a depository of energy. The Other World is the place where Waldo searches for speed, where he compares electricity to nerve impulses. Waldo proceeds on the assumption that the energy from the Other World is also subject to laws which can be discovered and used if the formulas are known.

Heinlein's shallowness in character portrayal reveals itself here in these machinations. His characters avoid traumatic shock by refusing to confront something unpredictable within a system. Waldo calls Gramps Schneider a hex doctor and then proceeds to work out basic rules for tapping the power source of the unpredictable. Like Heinlein, Waldo is the mechanical genius who avoids the confrontation with the all-encompassing theoretical implications of this new energy. Rambeau really seems more consistent when he loses his sanity because of the traumatic shock to his rigid scientific outlook. Waldo remains, however, a very clever child intrigued by the possibilities and blind to the real import.

But there are some interesting insights in Waldo's attempts to develop a terminal for the power source. When he mentally reduces the Other World to the size of an ostrich egg, he shows his own mastery of a comprehensive structure—a process which in itself becomes the new source of his strength. In this way Waldo has gone beyond the mere sense of another world, as in "Magic, Inc.," and as an individual, beyond the helpless exposure to other dimensions, as in *Methuselah's Children*. Energy from the Other World makes him into a complete human being who wants nothing more than to be surrounded by other people who like him.

Here again Heinlein's conceptual weakness becomes obvious. The Other World is actually other people, and learning how to manipulate energy corresponds to learning how to interact with the other people, and at the same time, learning how to be a man. But the real interaction with the Other World has to admit its basic mystery, as the theoretician would even while he speculated about it. The author allows the energy exchange between Waldo and his counterpart in the Other World to degenerate into "nerve surgery"—a mechanical and most inadequate description of the process that Waldo thinks he has discovered. The emotional complexity of the exchange is missing, therefore the intimation of the Other World is flat.

Waldo's transformation from an embittered, weak genius into a physical superman is an obvious spin-off from Faust and Nietzschean motifs. The greatness of Goethe's masterpiece is due, among other things, to a consistent following through in the bargain that Faust makes with Mephistopheles. Faust's reign of glory is always in the shadow of the final payment. Every ounce of energy that he receives demands its physical and emotional price. His return to youth at the beginning is balanced by the mistakes of youth and the blindness of old age. The wisdom, wealth, and power that he gains bring with them an emotional winnowing. In the science fiction novel it is the lack of an accompanying developmental trauma that suggests Waldo's powers are spurious. Only in Rambeau's madness and a short description of Waldo's bitter hatred of the "smooth apes" are there the rudiments of an emotional interaction to intense experiences, but these lines are never developed. Though Waldo decides that mental concentration can prevent the myasthenia gravis which is weakening the people below and is the source of his own crippled state, he does not analyze the nature of mental control over the body. His mechanics lead nowhere, and nothing important is really demonstrated. But the positive point made is that Waldo becomes a ''real'' man, even wants to impress girls (echoing Faust's pathetic wish to fall in love), when he can draw off the energy of the Other World not only to heal himself, but to give himself physical capabilities that others do not possess.

Source: Alice Carol Gaar, ''The Human as Machine Analog: The Big Daddy of Interchangeable Parts in the Fiction of Robert A. Heinlein,'' in *Robert A. Heinlein*, edited by Joseph D. Olander and Martin Harry Greenberg, Taplinger Publishing Company, 1978, pp. 64–82.

Alexei Panshin

In the following excerpt, Panshin provides an overview of the plot of ''Waldo,'' and discusses his reasons for considering the story a work of science fiction rather than fantasy.

Beyond the fact that it was originally published in a science fiction magazine, I am certain that [''Waldo''] is a science fiction story rather than a fantasy story, but I am very far from certain that I can satisfactorily explain why.

The basic elements of ''Waldo'' are four: a Pennsylvania hex doctor who may be well over a hundred years old and whose magic actually works; ''deKalb power receptors'' that have suddenly ceased to operate properly though nothing seems to be wrong with them; a rising incidence of general myasthenia—abnormal muscular weakness and fatigue—in the population; and Waldo, an engineering genius and paranoid misanthrope afflicted by myasthenia gravis who lives in a satellite home popularly known as ''Wheelchair.'' Heinlein has managed to tie this all together into a fascinating whole.

The deKalbs are failing, and their proprietors, North American Power-Air Co., are worried. They can't lick the problem and are convinced that the only man who might is Waldo. However, the company once cut Waldo out of some patents that he is convinced should have been his and they are far from sure that he will do any further business with them.

Dr. Gus Grimes, Waldo's personal physician since childhood and his only friend, is worried by the rise of myasthenia in the population and is convinced that background radiation has something

> The Other World is actually other people, and learning how to manipulate energy corresponds to learning how to interact with the other people, and at the same time, learning how to be a man."

to do with it. He wants Waldo to take on the problem of the failing deKalbs and not only work out a solution, but find one that will necessitate cutting down the amount of general radiation.

Waldo's own problem is his sickness and his misanthropy, the misanthropy being a direct result of his sickness. His success is a matter of over-compensation, and the more successful he is the more alienated he becomes, thus leaving him with that much more to compensate for.

Gramps Schneider, the Pennsylvania hex doctor, has no problems except that he has no particular love for machines and complicated living. He is, however, the key to the whole situation. Waldo takes on NAPA's problem, but then is unable to solve it, let alone in the manner Dr. Grimes would prefer. For all that he can tell, the machines *ought* to be working properly. Gramps Schneider, however, can fix the machines, and he is able to give Waldo the insights by which he solves the problem of the failing deKalbs, the problem of radiation and general myasthenia, and the problem of his own sickness.

Completely aside from the main problem, Heinlein has included some truly lovely conceits. The best-known of these are the machines known as ''waldoes,'' devices for remote control manipulation. Similar machines are in commercial use today, first developed for handling radioactive material, and are generally known as waldoes after those described in the story. But this is not the only ingenious idea given. Waldo's satellite home and the behavior of Waldo's pets, a canary and a mastiff, raised from birth in free fall, are particularly well-imagined. None of this is necessary to the story, but it does add richness to it.

> Waldo's own problem is his sickness and his misanthropy, the misanthropy being a direct result of his sickness."

The reason for my original puzzlement as to how "Waldo" should be categorized—science fiction or fantasy—is the nature of the solution to the various given problems. It turns out that the deKalbs are failing because their operators are thinking negative thoughts. Gramps Schneider fixes the deKalbs by reaching for power into the "Other World." And Waldo fixes both himself and the failing deKalbs by learning to reach for power into the Other World, too.

More than this, Waldo becomes convinced that the various magical arts are all aborted sciences, abandoned before they had been made clear; that the world has been made what it is by minds thinking it so (the world *was* flat until geographers decided it was round, and the deKalbs worked because their operators thought they would); that the Other World does exist; and that he, Waldo, can make the Other World what he wants it to be, for all time, by deciding its nature and convincing everybody else of his ideas.

Throughout much of his fiction, Heinlein has injected bits of mysticism, just as he did here in "Waldo." What keeps "Waldo" and most of the others from being fantasies, it seems to me, is his approach to the mysticism. "Magic, Inc." is a fantasy because the answers are cut-and-dried. Magic does work, period. Do thus-and-such and thus-and-thus will result. In "Waldo" we only know one thing for certain: there *is* something out there, call it the "Other World" for convenience, from which power can be siphoned. All the rest is Waldo's tentative construction of the state of affairs—he may be right or he may be wrong, but we have no certain way of knowing. In part, this is Heinlein's way of saying, "There are more things in heaven and earth than are dreamt of in your philosophy," and that is a far from illegitimate thing for a science fiction story to say. In part, too, I think this derives from Heinlein's background and training. As a

writer, he remains very much an engineer. His interest has always been not so much in why things work as in how they work, and as long as he exposits the "how" clearly, he is willing to leave the "why" as a tentative answer.

If the answers Heinlein were to give were not tentative, if the story said, "And this is exactly what those things in heaven and earth you haven't dreamt of are," and these answers fall outside what we think the world to be like, the story would be a fantasy. As long as the answers remain tentative, as in "Waldo," the story remains one that I can point to when I say "science fiction," even though the answers may again be ones that fall outside the bounds of what we think the world to be like.

Source: Alexei Panshin, "The Period of Influence," in *Heinlein in Dimension: A Critical Analysis*, Advent Publishers, Inc., 1968, pp. 9–40.

Sources

Brown, Charles N. Introduction to *Waldo and Magic, Inc.*, by Robert A. Heinlein, Gregg Press, 1979, pp. v-ix.

Franklin, H. Bruce. "From Depression into World War II: The Early Fiction," in *Robert Heinlein: America as Science Fiction,* Oxford University Press, 1980, pp. 17-63.

Nicholls, Peter. Quoted in *Science Fiction Writers,* edited by E. F. Bleiler, New York: Scribner, 1982.

Further Reading

Brown, Charles N. Introduction to *Waldo and Magic, Inc.*, by Robert A. Heinlein, Gregg Press, 1979, pp. v-ix.
    Examines the plot of "Waldo," as well as some of the story's imagery, and argues that the story is a work of fantasy.

Franklin, H. Bruce. "From Depression into World War II: The Early Fiction," in *Robert A. Heinlein: America as Science Fiction*, Oxford University Press, 1980, pp. 17-63.
    Contends that "Waldo" is characterized by the contradictory points of scientific faith and power of the mind.

Glossary of Literary Terms

A

Aestheticism: A literary and artistic movement of the nineteenth century. Followers of the movement believed that art should not be mixed with social, political, or moral teaching. The statement ''art for art's sake'' is a good summary of aestheticism. The movement had its roots in France, but it gained widespread importance in England in the last half of the nineteenth century, where it helped change the Victorian practice of including moral lessons in literature. Edgar Allan Poe is one of the best-known American ''aesthetes.''

Allegory: A narrative technique in which characters representing things or abstract ideas are used to convey a message or teach a lesson. Allegory is typically used to teach moral, ethical, or religious lessons but is sometimes used for satiric or political purposes. Many fairy tales are allegories.

Allusion: A reference to a familiar literary or historical person or event, used to make an idea more easily understood. Joyce Carol Oates's story ''Where Are You Going, Where Have You Been?'' exhibits several allusions to popular music.

Analogy: A comparison of two things made to explain something unfamiliar through its similarities to something familiar, or to prove one point based on the acceptance of another. Similes and metaphors are types of analogies.

Antagonist: The major character in a narrative or drama who works against the hero or protagonist. The Misfit in Flannery O'Connor's story ''A Good Man Is Hard to Find'' serves as the antagonist for the Grandmother.

Anthology: A collection of similar works of literature, art, or music. Zora Neale Hurston's ''The Eatonville Anthology'' is a collection of stories that take place in the same town.

Anthropomorphism: The presentation of animals or objects in human shape or with human characteristics. The term is derived from the Greek word for ''human form.'' The fur necklet in Katherine Mansfield's story ''Miss Brill'' has anthropomorphic characteristics.

Anti-hero: A central character in a work of literature who lacks traditional heroic qualities such as courage, physical prowess, and fortitude. Anti-heroes typically distrust conventional values and are unable to commit themselves to any ideals. They generally feel helpless in a world over which they have no control. Anti-heroes usually accept, and often celebrate, their positions as social outcasts. A well-known anti-hero is Walter Mitty in James Thurber's story ''The Secret Life of Walter Mitty.''

Archetype: The word archetype is commonly used to describe an original pattern or model from which all other things of the same kind are made. Archetypes are the literary images that grow out of the ''collective unconscious,'' a theory proposed by psychologist Carl Jung. They appear in literature as incidents and plots that repeat basic patterns of life. They may also appear as stereotyped characters. The ''schlemiel'' of Yiddish literature is an archetype.

Autobiography: A narrative in which an individual tells his or her life story. Examples include Benjamin Franklin's *Autobiography* and Amy Hempel's story ''In the Cemetery Where Al Jolson Is Buried,'' which has autobiographical characteristics even though it is a work of fiction.

Avant-garde: A literary term that describes new writing that rejects traditional approaches to literature in favor of innovations in style or content. Twentieth-century examples of the literary *avant-garde* include the modernists and the minimalists.

B

Belles-lettres: A French term meaning ''fine letters'' or ''beautiful writing.'' It is often used as a synonym for literature, typically referring to imaginative and artistic rather than scientific or expository writing. Current usage sometimes restricts the meaning to light or humorous writing and appreciative essays about literature. Lewis Carroll's *Alice in Wonderland* epitomizes the realm of belles-lettres.

Bildungsroman: A German word meaning ''novel of development.'' The *bildungsroman* is a study of the maturation of a youthful character, typically brought about through a series of social or sexual encounters that lead to self-awareness. J. D. Salinger's *Catcher in the Rye* is a *bildungsroman*, and Doris Lessing's story ''Through the Tunnel'' exhibits characteristics of a *bildungsroman* as well.

Black Aesthetic Movement: A period of artistic and literary development among African Americans in the 1960s and early 1970s. This was the first major African-American artistic movement since the Harlem Renaissance and was closely paralleled by the civil rights and black power movements. The black aesthetic writers attempted to produce works of art that would be meaningful to the black masses. Key figures in black aesthetics included one of its founders, poet and playwright Amiri Baraka, formerly known as LeRoi Jones; poet and essayist Haki R. Madhubuti, formerly Don L. Lee; poet and playwright Sonia Sanchez; and dramatist Ed Bullins. Works representative of the Black Aesthetic Movement include Amiri Baraka's play *Dutchman,* a 1964 Obie award-winner.

Black Humor: Writing that places grotesque elements side by side with humorous ones in an attempt to shock the reader, forcing him or her to laugh at the horrifying reality of a disordered world. ''Lamb to the Slaughter,'' by Roald Dahl, in which a placid housewife murders her husband and serves the murder weapon to the investigating policemen, is an example of black humor.

C

Catharsis: The release or purging of unwanted emotions—specifically fear and pity—brought about by exposure to art. The term was first used by the Greek philosopher Aristotle in his *Poetics* to refer to the desired effect of tragedy on spectators.

Character: Broadly speaking, a person in a literary work. The actions of characters are what constitute the plot of a story, novel, or poem. There are numerous types of characters, ranging from simple, stereotypical figures to intricate, multifaceted ones. ''Characterization'' is the process by which an author creates vivid, believable characters in a work of art. This may be done in a variety of ways, including (1) direct description of the character by the narrator; (2) the direct presentation of the speech, thoughts, or actions of the character; and (3) the responses of other characters to the character. The term ''character'' also refers to a form originated by the ancient Greek writer Theophrastus that later became popular in the seventeenth and eighteenth centuries. It is a short essay or sketch of a person who prominently displays a specific attribute or quality, such as miserliness or ambition. ''Miss Brill,'' a story by Katherine Mansfield, is an example of a character sketch.

Classical: In its strictest definition in literary criticism, classicism refers to works of ancient Greek or Roman literature. The term may also be used to describe a literary work of recognized importance (a ''classic'') from any time period or literature that exhibits the traits of classicism. Examples of later works and authors now described as classical include French literature of the seventeenth century, Western novels of the nineteenth century, and American fiction of the mid-nineteenth century such as that written by James Fenimore Cooper and Mark Twain.

Climax: The turning point in a narrative, the moment when the conflict is at its most intense. Typically, the structure of stories, novels, and plays is one of rising action, in which tension builds to the climax, followed by falling action, in which tension lessens as the story moves to its conclusion.

Comedy: One of two major types of drama, the other being tragedy. Its aim is to amuse, and it typically ends happily. Comedy assumes many forms, such as farce and burlesque, and uses a variety of techniques, from parody to satire. In a restricted sense the term comedy refers only to dramatic presentations, but in general usage it is commonly applied to nondramatic works as well.

Comic Relief: The use of humor to lighten the mood of a serious or tragic story, especially in plays. The technique is very common in Elizabethan works, and can be an integral part of the plot or simply a brief event designed to break the tension of the scene.

Conflict: The conflict in a work of fiction is the issue to be resolved in the story. It usually occurs between two characters, the protagonist and the antagonist, or between the protagonist and society or the protagonist and himself or herself. The conflict in Washington Irving's story "The Devil and Tom Walker" is that the Devil wants Tom Walker's soul but Tom does not want to go to hell.

Criticism: The systematic study and evaluation of literary works, usually based on a specific method or set of principles. An important part of literary studies since ancient times, the practice of criticism has given rise to numerous theories, methods, and "schools," sometimes producing conflicting, even contradictory, interpretations of literature in general as well as of individual works. Even such basic issues as what constitutes a poem or a novel have been the subject of much criticism over the centuries. Seminal texts of literary criticism include Plato's *Republic,* Aristotle's *Poetics,* Sir Philip Sidney's *The Defence of Poesie,* and John Dryden's *Of Dramatic Poesie.* Contemporary schools of criticism include deconstruction, feminist, psychoanalytic, poststructuralist, new historicist, postcolonialist, and reader-response.

D

Deconstruction: A method of literary criticism characterized by multiple conflicting interpretations of a given work. Deconstructionists consider the impact of the language of a work and suggest that the true meaning of the work is not necessarily the meaning that the author intended.

Deduction: The process of reaching a conclusion through reasoning from general premises to a specific premise. Arthur Conan Doyle's character Sherlock Holmes often used deductive reasoning to solve mysteries.

Denotation: The definition of a word, apart from the impressions or feelings it creates in the reader. The word "apartheid" denotes a political and economic policy of segregation by race, but its connotations—oppression, slavery, inequality—are numerous.

Denouement: A French word meaning "the unknotting." In literature, it denotes the resolution of conflict in fiction or drama. The *denouement* follows the climax and provides an outcome to the primary plot situation as well as an explanation of secondary plot complications. A well-known example of *denouement* is the last scene of the play *As You Like It* by William Shakespeare, in which couples are married, an evildoer repents, the identities of two disguised characters are revealed, and a ruler is restored to power. Also known as "falling action."

Detective Story: A narrative about the solution of a mystery or the identification of a criminal. The conventions of the detective story include the detective's scrupulous use of logic in solving the mystery; incompetent or ineffectual police; a suspect who appears guilty at first but is later proved innocent; and the detective's friend or confidant—often the narrator—whose slowness in interpreting clues emphasizes by contrast the detective's brilliance. Edgar Allan Poe's "Murders in the Rue Morgue" is commonly regarded as the earliest example of this type of story. Other practitioners are Arthur Conan Doyle, Dashiell Hammett, and Agatha Christie.

Dialogue: Dialogue is conversation between people in a literary work. In its most restricted sense, it refers specifically to the speech of characters in a drama. As a specific literary genre, a "dialogue" is a composition in which characters debate an issue or idea.

Didactic: A term used to describe works of literature that aim to teach a moral, religious, political, or practical lesson. Although didactic elements are often found in artistically pleasing works, the term "didactic" usually refers to literature in which the message is more important than the form. The term may also be used to criticize a work that the critic finds "overly didactic," that is, heavy-handed in its delivery of a lesson. An example of didactic literature is John Bunyan's *Pilgrim's Progress*.

Dramatic Irony: Occurs when the reader of a work of literature knows something that a character in the work itself does not know. The irony is in the contrast between the intended meaning of the statements or actions of a character and the additional information understood by the audience.

Dystopia: An imaginary place in a work of fiction where the characters lead dehumanized, fearful lives. **George Orwell's** *Nineteen Eighty-four*, and Margaret Atwood's *Handmaid's Tale* portray versions of dystopia.

E

Edwardian: Describes cultural conventions identified with the period of the reign of Edward VII of England (1901-1910). Writers of the Edwardian Age typically displayed a strong reaction against the propriety and conservatism of the Victorian Age. Their work often exhibits distrust of authority in religion, politics, and art and expresses strong doubts about the soundness of conventional values. Writers of this era include E. M. Forster, H. G. Wells, and Joseph Conrad.

Empathy: A sense of shared experience, including emotional and physical feelings, with someone or something other than oneself. Empathy is often used to describe the response of a reader to a literary character.

Epilogue: A concluding statement or section of a literary work. In dramas, particularly those of the seventeenth and eighteenth centuries, the epilogue is a closing speech, often in verse, delivered by an actor at the end of a play and spoken directly to the audience.

Epiphany: A sudden revelation of truth inspired by a seemingly trivial incident. The term was widely used by James Joyce in his critical writings, and the stories in Joyce's *Dubliners* are commonly called "epiphanies."

Epistolary Novel: A novel in the form of letters. The form was particularly popular in the eighteenth century. The form can also be applied to short stories, as in Edwidge Danticat's "Children of the Sea."

Epithet: A word or phrase, often disparaging or abusive, that expresses a character trait of someone or something. "The Napoleon of crime" is an epithet applied to Professor Moriarty, arch-rival of Sherlock Holmes in Arthur Conan Doyle's series of detective stories.

Existentialism: A predominantly twentieth-century philosophy concerned with the nature and perception of human existence. There are two major strains of existentialist thought: atheistic and Christian. Followers of atheistic existentialism believe that the individual is alone in a godless universe and that the basic human condition is one of suffering and loneliness. Nevertheless, because there are no fixed values, individuals can create their own characters—indeed, they can shape themselves—through the exercise of free will. The atheistic strain culminates in and is popularly associated with the works of Jean-Paul Sartre. The Christian existentialists, on the other hand, believe that only in God may people find freedom from life's anguish. The two strains hold certain beliefs in common: that existence cannot be fully understood or described through empirical effort; that anguish is a universal element of life; that individuals must bear responsibility for their actions; and that there is no common standard of behavior or perception for religious and ethical matters. Existentialist thought figures prominently in the works of such authors as Franz Kafka, Fyodor Dostoyevsky, and Albert Camus.

Expatriatism: The practice of leaving one's country to live for an extended period in another country. Literary expatriates include Irish author James Joyce who moved to Italy and France, American writers James Baldwin, Ernest Hemingway, Gertrude Stein, and F. Scott Fitzgerald who lived and wrote in Paris, and Polish novelist Joseph Conrad in England.

Exposition: Writing intended to explain the nature of an idea, thing, or theme. Expository writing is often combined with description, narration, or argument.

Expressionism: An indistinct literary term, originally used to describe an early twentieth-century school of German painting. The term applies to almost any mode of unconventional, highly subjective writing that distorts reality in some way. Advocates of Expressionism include Federico Garcia Lorca, Eugene O'Neill, Franz Kafka, and James Joyce.

F

Fable: A prose or verse narrative intended to convey a moral. Animals or inanimate objects with human characteristics often serve as characters in fables. A famous fable is Aesop's "The Tortoise and the Hare."

Fantasy: A literary form related to mythology and folklore. Fantasy literature is typically set in non-existent realms and features supernatural beings. Notable examples of literature with elements of fantasy are Gabriel Garcia Marquez's story "The Handsomest Drowned Man in the World" and Ursula K. LeGuin's "The Ones Who Walk Away from Omelas."

Farce: A type of comedy characterized by broad humor, outlandish incidents, and often vulgar subject matter. Much of the comedy in film and television could more accurately be described as farce.

Fiction: Any story that is the product of imagination rather than a documentation of fact. Characters and events in such narratives may be based in real life but their ultimate form and configuration is a creation of the author.

Figurative Language: A technique in which an author uses figures of speech such as hyperbole, irony, metaphor, or simile for a particular effect. Figurative language is the opposite of literal language, in which every word is truthful, accurate, and free of exaggeration or embellishment.

Flashback: A device used in literature to present action that occurred before the beginning of the story. Flashbacks are often introduced as the dreams or recollections of one or more characters.

Foil: A character in a work of literature whose physical or psychological qualities contrast strongly with, and therefore highlight, the corresponding qualities of another character. In his Sherlock Holmes stories, Arthur Conan Doyle portrayed Dr. Watson as a man of normal habits and intelligence, making him a foil for the eccentric and unusually perceptive Sherlock Holmes.

Folklore: Traditions and myths preserved in a culture or group of people. Typically, these are passed on by word of mouth in various forms—such as legends, songs, and proverbs—or preserved in customs and ceremonies. Washington Irving, in "The Devil and Tom Walker" and many of his other stories, incorporates many elements of the folklore of New England and Germany.

Folktale: A story originating in oral tradition. Folktales fall into a variety of categories, including legends, ghost stories, fairy tales, fables, and anecdotes based on historical figures and events.

Foreshadowing: A device used in literature to create expectation or to set up an explanation of later developments. Edgar Allan Poe uses foreshadowing to create suspense in "The Fall of the House of Usher" when the narrator comments on the crumbling state of disrepair in which he finds the house.

G

Genre: A category of literary work. Genre may refer to both the content of a given work—tragedy, comedy, horror, science fiction—and to its form, such as poetry, novel, or drama.

Gilded Age: A period in American history during the 1870s and after characterized by political corruption and materialism. A number of important novels of social and political criticism were written during this time. Henry James and Kate Chopin are two writers who were prominent during the Gilded Age.

Gothicism: In literature, works characterized by a taste for medieval or morbid characters and situations. A gothic novel prominently features elements of horror, the supernatural, gloom, and violence: clanking chains, terror, ghosts, medieval castles, and unexplained phenomena. The term "gothic novel" is also applied to novels that lack elements of the traditional Gothic setting but that create a similar atmosphere of terror or dread. The term can also be applied to stories, plays, and poems. Mary Shelley's *Frankenstein* and Joyce Carol Oates's *Bellefleur* are both gothic novels.

Grotesque: In literature, a work that is characterized by exaggeration, deformity, freakishness, and disorder. The grotesque often includes an element of comic absurdity. Examples of the grotesque can be found in the works of Edgar Allan Poe, Flannery O'Connor, Joseph Heller, and Shirley Jackson.

H

Harlem Renaissance: The Harlem Renaissance of the 1920s is generally considered the first significant movement of black writers and artists in the United States. During this period, new and established black writers, many of whom lived in the region of New York City known as Harlem, published more fiction and poetry than ever before, the first influential black literary journals were established, and black authors and artists received their first widespread recognition and serious critical appraisal. Among the major writers associated with this period are Countee Cullen, Langston Hughes, Arna Bontemps, and Zora Neale Hurston.

Hero/Heroine: The principal sympathetic character in a literary work. Heroes and heroines typically exhibit admirable traits: idealism, courage, and integrity, for example. Famous heroes and heroines of literature include Charles Dickens's Oliver Twist, Margaret Mitchell's Scarlett O'Hara, and the anonymous narrator in Ralph Ellison's *Invisible Man*.

Hyperbole: Deliberate exaggeration used to achieve an effect. In William Shakespeare's *Macbeth,* Lady Macbeth hyperbolizes when she says, ''All the perfumes of Arabia could not sweeten this little hand.''

I

Image: A concrete representation of an object or sensory experience. Typically, such a representation helps evoke the feelings associated with the object or experience itself. Images are either ''literal'' or ''figurative.'' Literal images are especially concrete and involve little or no extension of the obvious meaning of the words used to express them. Figurative images do not follow the literal meaning of the words exactly. Images in literature are usually visual, but the term ''image'' can also refer to the representation of any sensory experience.

Imagery: The array of images in a literary work. Also used to convey the author's overall use of figurative language in a work.

In medias res: A Latin term meaning ''in the middle of things.'' It refers to the technique of beginning a story at its midpoint and then using various flashback devices to reveal previous action. This technique originated in such epics as Virgil's *Aeneid.*

Interior Monologue: A narrative technique in which characters' thoughts are revealed in a way that appears to be uncontrolled by the author. The interior monologue typically aims to reveal the inner self of a character. It portrays emotional experiences as they occur at both a conscious and unconscious level. One of the best-known interior monologues in English is the Molly Bloom section at the close of James Joyce's *Ulysses.* Katherine Anne Porter's ''The Jilting of Granny Weatherall'' is also told in the form of an interior monologue.

Irony: In literary criticism, the effect of language in which the intended meaning is the opposite of what is stated. The title of Jonathan Swift's ''A Modest Proposal'' is ironic because what Swift proposes in this essay is cannibalism—hardly ''modest.''

J

Jargon: Language that is used or understood only by a select group of people. Jargon may refer to terminology used in a certain profession, such as computer jargon, or it may refer to any nonsensical language that is not understood by most people. Anthony Burgess's *A Clockwork Orange* and James Thurber's ''The Secret Life of Walter Mitty'' both use jargon.

K

Knickerbocker Group: An indistinct group of New York writers of the first half of the nineteenth century. Members of the group were linked only by location and a common theme: New York life. Two famous members of the Knickerbocker Group were Washington Irving and William Cullen Bryant. The group's name derives from Irving's *Knickerbocker's History of New York.*

L

Literal Language: An author uses literal language when he or she writes without exaggerating or embellishing the subject matter and without any tools of figurative language. To say ''He ran very quickly down the street'' is to use literal language, whereas to say ''He ran like a hare down the street'' would be using figurative language.

Literature: Literature is broadly defined as any written or spoken material, but the term most often refers to creative works. Literature includes poetry, drama, fiction, and many kinds of nonfiction writing, as well as oral, dramatic, and broadcast compositions not necessarily preserved in a written format, such as films and television programs.

Lost Generation: A term first used by Gertrude Stein to describe the post-World War I generation of American writers: men and women haunted by a sense of betrayal and emptiness brought about by the destructiveness of the war. The term is commonly applied to Hart Crane, Ernest Hemingway, F. Scott Fitzgerald, and others.

M

Magic Realism: A form of literature that incorporates fantasy elements or supernatural occurrences into the narrative and accepts them as truth. Gabriel Garcia Marquez and Laura Esquivel are two writers known for their works of magic realism.

Metaphor: A figure of speech that expresses an idea through the image of another object. Metaphors suggest the essence of the first object by identifying it with certain qualities of the second object. An example is "But soft, what light through yonder window breaks?/ It is the east, and Juliet is the sun" in William Shakespeare's *Romeo and Juliet.* Here, Juliet, the first object, is identified with qualities of the second object, the sun.

Minimalism: A literary style characterized by spare, simple prose with few elaborations. In minimalism, the main theme of the work is often never discussed directly. Amy Hempel and Ernest Hemingway are two writers known for their works of minimalism.

Modernism: Modern literary practices. Also, the principles of a literary school that lasted from roughly the beginning of the twentieth century until the end of World War II. Modernism is defined by its rejection of the literary conventions of the nineteenth century and by its opposition to conventional morality, taste, traditions, and economic values. Many writers are associated with the concepts of modernism, including Albert Camus, D. H. Lawrence, Ernest Hemingway, William Faulkner, Eugene O'Neill, and James Joyce.

Monologue: A composition, written or oral, by a single individual. More specifically, a speech given by a single individual in a drama or other public entertainment. It has no set length, although it is usually several or more lines long. "I Stand Here Ironing" by Tillie Olsen is an example of a story written in the form of a monologue.

Mood: The prevailing emotions of a work or of the author in his or her creation of the work. The mood of a work is not always what might be expected based on its subject matter.

Motif: A theme, character type, image, metaphor, or other verbal element that recurs throughout a single work of literature or occurs in a number of different works over a period of time. For example, the color white in Herman Melville's *Moby Dick* is a "specific" *motif,* while the trials of star-crossed lovers is a "conventional" *motif* from the literature of all periods.

N

Narration: The telling of a series of events, real or invented. A narration may be either a simple narrative, in which the events are recounted chronologically, or a narrative with a plot, in which the account is given in a style reflecting the author's artistic concept of the story. Narration is sometimes used as a synonym for "storyline."

Narrative: A verse or prose accounting of an event or sequence of events, real or invented. The term is also used as an adjective in the sense "method of narration." For example, in literary criticism, the expression "narrative technique" usually refers to the way the author structures and presents his or her story. Different narrative forms include diaries, travelogues, novels, ballads, epics, short stories, and other fictional forms.

Narrator: The teller of a story. The narrator may be the author or a character in the story through whom the author speaks. Huckleberry Finn is the narrator of Mark Twain's *The Adventures of Huckleberry Finn.*

Novella: An Italian term meaning "story." This term has been especially used to describe fourteenth-century Italian tales, but it also refers to modern short novels. Modern novellas include Leo Tolstoy's *The Death of Ivan Ilich,* Fyodor Dostoyevsky's *Notes from the Underground,* and Joseph Conrad's *Heart of Darkness.*

O

Oedipus Complex: A son's romantic obsession with his mother. The phrase is derived from the story of the ancient Theban hero Oedipus, who unknowingly killed his father and married his mother, and was popularized by Sigmund Freud's theory of psychoanalysis. Literary occurrences of the Oedipus complex include Sophocles' *Oedipus Rex* and D. H. Lawrence's "The Rocking-Horse Winner."

Onomatopoeia: The use of words whose sounds express or suggest their meaning. In its simplest sense, onomatopoeia may be represented by words that mimic the sounds they denote such as "hiss" or "meow." At a more subtle level, the pattern and rhythm of sounds and rhymes of a line or poem may be onomatopoeic.

Oral Tradition: A process by which songs, ballads, folklore, and other material are transmitted by word of mouth. The tradition of oral transmission predates the written record systems of literate society.

Oral transmission preserves material sometimes over generations, although often with variations. Memory plays a large part in the recitation and preservation of orally transmitted material. Native American myths and legends, and African folktales told by plantation slaves are examples of orally transmitted literature.

P

Parable: A story intended to teach a moral lesson or answer an ethical question. Examples of parables are the stories told by Jesus Christ in the New Testament, notably ''The Prodigal Son,'' but parables also are used in Sufism, rabbinic literature, Hasidism, and Zen Buddhism. Isaac Bashevis Singer's story ''Gimpel the Fool'' exhibits characteristics of a parable.

Paradox: A statement that appears illogical or contradictory at first, but may actually point to an underlying truth. A literary example of a paradox is George Orwell's statement ''All animals are equal, but some animals are more equal than others'' in *Animal Farm.*

Parody: In literature, this term refers to an imitation of a serious literary work or the signature style of a particular author in a ridiculous manner. A typical parody adopts the style of the original and applies it to an inappropriate subject for humorous effect. Parody is a form of satire and could be considered the literary equivalent of a caricature or cartoon. Henry Fielding's *Shamela* is a parody of Samuel Richardson's *Pamela.*

Persona: A Latin term meaning ''mask.'' Personae are the characters in a fictional work of literature. The persona generally functions as a mask through which the author tells a story in a voice other than his or her own. A persona is usually either a character in a story who acts as a narrator or an ''implied author,'' a voice created by the author to act as the narrator for himself or herself. The persona in Charlotte Perkins Gilman's story ''The Yellow Wallpaper'' is the unnamed young mother experiencing a mental breakdown.

Personification: A figure of speech that gives human qualities to abstract ideas, animals, and inanimate objects. To say that ''the sun is smiling'' is to personify the sun.

Plot: The pattern of events in a narrative or drama. In its simplest sense, the plot guides the author in composing the work and helps the reader follow the work. Typically, plots exhibit causality and unity and have a beginning, a middle, and an end. Sometimes, however, a plot may consist of a series of disconnected events, in which case it is known as an ''episodic plot.''

Poetic Justice: An outcome in a literary work, not necessarily a poem, in which the good are rewarded and the evil are punished, especially in ways that particularly fit their virtues or crimes. For example, a murderer may himself be murdered, or a thief will find himself penniless.

Poetic License: Distortions of fact and literary convention made by a writer—not always a poet—for the sake of the effect gained. Poetic license is closely related to the concept of ''artistic freedom.'' An author exercises poetic license by saying that a pile of money ''reaches as high as a mountain'' when the pile is actually only a foot or two high.

Point of View: The narrative perspective from which a literary work is presented to the reader. There are four traditional points of view. The ''third person omniscient'' gives the reader a ''godlike'' perspective, unrestricted by time or place, from which to see actions and look into the minds of characters. This allows the author to comment openly on characters and events in the work. The ''third person'' point of view presents the events of the story from outside of any single character's perception, much like the omniscient point of view, but the reader must understand the action as it takes place and without any special insight into characters' minds or motivations. The ''first person'' or ''personal'' point of view relates events as they are perceived by a single character. The main character ''tells'' the story and may offer opinions about the action and characters which differ from those of the author. Much less common than omniscient, third person, and first person is the ''second person'' point of view, wherein the author tells the story as if it is happening to the reader. James Thurber employs the omniscient point of view in his short story ''The Secret Life of Walter Mitty.'' Ernest Hemingway's ''A Clean, Well-Lighted Place'' is a short story told from the third person point of view. Mark Twain's novel *Huckleberry Finn* is presented from the first person viewpoint. Jay McInerney's *Bright Lights, Big City* is an example of a novel which uses the second person point of view.

Pornography: Writing intended to provoke feelings of lust in the reader. Such works are often condemned by critics and teachers, but those which can be shown to have literary value are viewed less harshly. Literary works that have been described as pornographic include D. H. Lawrence's *Lady Chatterley's Lover* and James Joyce's *Ulysses.*

Post-Aesthetic Movement: An artistic response made by African Americans to the black aesthetic movement of the 1960s and early 1970s. Writers since that time have adopted a somewhat different tone in their work, with less emphasis placed on the disparity between black and white in the United States. In the words of post-aesthetic authors such as Toni Morrison, John Edgar Wideman, and Kristin Hunter, African Americans are portrayed as looking inward for answers to their own questions, rather than always looking to the outside world. Two well-known examples of works produced as part of the post-aesthetic movement are the Pulitzer Prize-winning novels *The Color Purple* by Alice Walker and *Beloved* by Toni Morrison.

Postmodernism: Writing from the 1960s forward characterized by experimentation and application of modernist elements, which include existentialism and alienation. Postmodernists have gone a step further in the rejection of tradition begun with the modernists by also rejecting traditional forms, preferring the anti-novel over the novel and the anti-hero over the hero. Postmodern writers include Thomas Pynchon, Margaret Drabble, and Gabriel Garcia Marquez.

Prologue: An introductory section of a literary work. It often contains information establishing the situation of the characters or presents information about the setting, time period, or action. In drama, the prologue is spoken by a chorus or by one of the principal characters.

Prose: A literary medium that attempts to mirror the language of everyday speech. It is distinguished from poetry by its use of unmetered, unrhymed language consisting of logically related sentences. Prose is usually grouped into paragraphs that form a cohesive whole such as an essay or a novel. The term is sometimes used to mean an author's general writing.

Protagonist: The central character of a story who serves as a focus for its themes and incidents and as the principal rationale for its development. The protagonist is sometimes referred to in discussions of modern literature as the hero or anti-hero. Well-known protagonists are Hamlet in William Shakespeare's *Hamlet* and Jay Gatsby in F. Scott Fitzgerald's *The Great Gatsby.*

R

Realism: A nineteenth-century European literary movement that sought to portray familiar characters, situations, and settings in a realistic manner. This was done primarily by using an objective narrative point of view and through the buildup of accurate detail. The standard for success of any realistic work depends on how faithfully it transfers common experience into fictional forms. The realistic method may be altered or extended, as in stream of consciousness writing, to record highly subjective experience. Contemporary authors who often write in a realistic way include Nadine Gordimer and Grace Paley.

Resolution: The portion of a story following the climax, in which the conflict is resolved. The resolution of Jane Austen's *Northanger Abbey* is neatly summed up in the following sentence: "Henry and Catherine were married, the bells rang and every body smiled."

Rising Action: The part of a drama where the plot becomes increasingly complicated. Rising action leads up to the climax, or turning point, of a drama. The final "chase scene" of an action film is generally the rising action which culminates in the film's climax.

Roman a clef: A French phrase meaning "novel with a key." It refers to a narrative in which real persons are portrayed under fictitious names. Jack Kerouac, for example, portrayed various his friends under fictitious names in the novel *On the Road.* D. H. Lawrence based "The Rocking-Horse Winner" on a family he knew.

Romanticism: This term has two widely accepted meanings. In historical criticism, it refers to a European intellectual and artistic movement of the late eighteenth and early nineteenth centuries that sought greater freedom of personal expression than that allowed by the strict rules of literary form and logic of the eighteenth-century neoclassicists. The Romantics preferred emotional and imaginative expression to rational analysis. They considered the individual to be at the center of all experience and so placed him or her at the center of their art. The Romantics believed that the creative imagination reveals nobler truths—unique feelings and attitudes—than those that could be discovered by logic or by scientific examination. "Romanticism" is also used as a general term to refer to a type of sensibility found in all periods of literary history and usually considered to be in opposition to the principles of classicism. In this sense, Romanticism signifies any work or philosophy in which the exotic or dreamlike figure strongly, or that is devoted to individualistic expression, self-analysis, or a pursuit of a higher realm of knowledge than can be discovered by human reason. Prominent Romantics include Jean-Jacques Rousseau, William Wordsworth, John Keats, Lord Byron, and Johann Wolfgang von Goethe.

S

Satire: A work that uses ridicule, humor, and wit to criticize and provoke change in human nature and institutions. Voltaire's novella *Candide* and Jonathan Swift's essay ''A Modest Proposal'' are both satires. Flannery O'Connor's portrayal of the family in ''A Good Man Is Hard to Find'' is a satire of a modern, Southern, American family.

Science Fiction: A type of narrative based upon real or imagined scientific theories and technology. Science fiction is often peopled with alien creatures and set on other planets or in different dimensions. Popular writers of science fiction are Isaac Asimov, Karel Capek, Ray Bradbury, and Ursula K. Le Guin.

Setting: The time, place, and culture in which the action of a narrative takes place. The elements of setting may include geographic location, characters's physical and mental environments, prevailing cultural attitudes, or the historical time in which the action takes place.

Short Story: A fictional prose narrative shorter and more focused than a novella. The short story usually deals with a single episode and often a single character. The ''tone,'' the author's attitude toward his or her subject and audience, is uniform throughout. The short story frequently also lacks *denouement*, ending instead at its climax.

Signifying Monkey: A popular trickster figure in black folklore, with hundreds of tales about this character documented since the 19th century. Henry Louis Gates Jr. examines the history of the signifying monkey in *The Signifying Monkey: Towards a Theory of Afro-American Literary Criticism,* published in 1988.

Simile: A comparison, usually using ''like'' or ''as,''of two essentially dissimilar things, as in ''coffee as cold as ice'' or ''He sounded like a broken record.'' The title of Ernest Hemingway's ''Hills Like White Elephants'' contains a simile.

Social Realism: The Socialist Realism school of literary theory was proposed by Maxim Gorky and established as a dogma by the first Soviet Congress of Writers. It demanded adherence to a communist worldview in works of literature. Its doctrines required an objective viewpoint comprehensible to the working classes and themes of social struggle featuring strong proletarian heroes. Gabriel Garcia Marquez's stories exhibit some characteristics of Socialist Realism.

Stereotype: A stereotype was originally the name for a duplication made during the printing process; this led to its modern definition as a person or thing that is (or is assumed to be) the same as all others of its type. Common stereotypical characters include the absent-minded professor, the nagging wife, the troublemaking teenager, and the kindhearted grandmother.

Stream of Consciousness: A narrative technique for rendering the inward experience of a character. This technique is designed to give the impression of an ever-changing series of thoughts, emotions, images, and memories in the spontaneous and seemingly illogical order that they occur in life. The textbook example of stream of consciousness is the last section of James Joyce's *Ulysses.*

Structure: The form taken by a piece of literature. The structure may be made obvious for ease of understanding, as in nonfiction works, or may obscured for artistic purposes, as in some poetry or seemingly ''unstructured'' prose.

Style: A writer's distinctive manner of arranging words to suit his or her ideas and purpose in writing. The unique imprint of the author's personality upon his or her writing, style is the product of an author's way of arranging ideas and his or her use of diction, different sentence structures, rhythm, figures of speech, rhetorical principles, and other elements of composition.

Suspense: A literary device in which the author maintains the audience's attention through the build-up of events, the outcome of which will soon be revealed. Suspense in William Shakespeare's *Hamlet* is sustained throughout by the question of whether or not the Prince will achieve what he has been instructed to do and of what he intends to do.

Symbol: Something that suggests or stands for something else without losing its original identity. In literature, symbols combine their literal meaning with the suggestion of an abstract concept. Literary symbols are of two types: those that carry complex associations of meaning no matter what their contexts, and those that derive their suggestive meaning from their functions in specific literary works. Examples of symbols are sunshine suggesting happiness, rain suggesting sorrow, and storm clouds suggesting despair.

T

Tale: A story told by a narrator with a simple plot and little character development. Tales are usually relatively short and often carry a simple message. Examples of tales can be found in the works of Saki, Anton Chekhov, Guy de Maupassant, and O. Henry.

Tall Tale: A humorous tale told in a straightforward, credible tone but relating absolutely impossible events or feats of the characters. Such tales were commonly told of frontier adventures during the settlement of the west in the United States. Literary use of tall tales can be found in Washington Irving's *History of New York,* Mark Twain's *Life on the Mississippi,* and in the German R. F. Raspe's *Baron Munchausen's Narratives of His Marvellous Travels and Campaigns in Russia.*

Theme: The main point of a work of literature. The term is used interchangeably with thesis. Many works have multiple themes. One of the themes of Nathaniel Hawthorne's "Young Goodman Brown" is loss of faith.

Tone: The author's attitude toward his or her audience may be deduced from the tone of the work. A formal tone may create distance or convey politeness, while an informal tone may encourage a friendly, intimate, or intrusive feeling in the reader. The author's attitude toward his or her subject matter may also be deduced from the tone of the words he or she uses in discussing it. The tone of John F. Kennedy's speech which included the appeal to "ask not what your country can do for you" was intended to instill feelings of camaraderie and national pride in listeners.

Tragedy: A drama in prose or poetry about a noble, courageous hero of excellent character who, because of some tragic character flaw, brings ruin upon him- or herself. Tragedy treats its subjects in a dignified and serious manner, using poetic language to help evoke pity and fear and bring about catharsis, a purging of these emotions. The tragic form was practiced extensively by the ancient Greeks. The classical form of tragedy was revived in the sixteenth century; it flourished especially on the Elizabethan stage. In modern times, dramatists have attempted to adapt the form to the needs of modern society by drawing their heroes from the ranks of ordinary men and women and defining the nobility of these heroes in terms of spirit rather than exalted social standing. Some contemporary works that are thought of as tragedies include *The Great Gatsby* by F. Scott Fitzgerald, and *The Sound and the Fury* by William Faulkner.

Tragic Flaw: In a tragedy, the quality within the hero or heroine which leads to his or her downfall. Examples of the tragic flaw include Othello's jealousy and Hamlet's indecisiveness, although most great tragedies defy such simple interpretation.

U

Utopia: A fictional perfect place, such as "paradise" or "heaven." An early literary utopia was described in Plato's *Republic,* and in modern literature, Ursula K. Le Guin depicts a utopia in "The Ones Who Walk Away from Omelas."

V

Victorian: Refers broadly to the reign of Queen Victoria of England (1837-1901) and to anything with qualities typical of that era. For example, the qualities of smug narrow-mindedness, bourgeois materialism, faith in social progress, and priggish morality are often considered Victorian. In literature, the Victorian Period was the great age of the English novel, and the latter part of the era saw the rise of movements such as decadence and symbolism.

Cumulative Author/Title Index

Nationality/Ethnicity Index

Subject/Theme Index